SPIRITUAL HUSBANDS-
SPIRITUAL FATHERS

PRIESTLY FORMATION FOR THE 21ST CENTURY

BISHOP FELIPE J. ESTÉVEZ, S.T.D.
BISHOP ANDREW H. COZZENS, S.T.D.

En Route Books and Media, LLC

St. Louis, MO

D1091898

En Route Books and Media, LLC
5705 Rhodes Avenue
St. Louis, MO 63109

Cover credit: TJ Burdick

Library of Congress Control Number: 2020936765

ISBN-13: 978-1-950108-90-9

DEDICATION

To St. Joseph, who radiates the Father's Heart as husband for Mary and the Church, and who served as the living icon of the Father's tenderness for Jesus.

TABLE OF CONTENTS

INTRODUCTION

The deep significance of the celibacy of Jesus is revealed and fulfilled on the Cross where through his priestly self-gift for our salvation he becomes both bridegroom of the Church and Father of all her spiritual children. The Fathers of the Church often spoke of the Cross as the consummation of the spiritual marriage between Christ and the Church because it was the place of the fruitful self-gift of Christ for his Bride the Church. This reality of Christ's self-gift which establishes the spiritual marriage of the New Covenant in his blood, reveals why Jesus lived his whole life as a "eunuch" for the sake of the Kingdom of Heaven (Mt. 19:12). As St. John Paul II wrote in *Pastores Dabo Vobis*, "Christ's gift of himself to his Church, the fruit of his love, is described in terms of the unique gift of self-made by the bridegroom to the bride." Through his spousal self-gift Christ fulfills his mission to give life to the spiritual family of the Church.

Priestly celibacy, in order to be properly understood, must be rooted in this same mission. Celibacy is much more than a practical reality which leaves a man more time for mission, rather it is a deeply spiritual reality that is central to his self-gift in imitation of Christ's gift as husband and father. Through his configuration to Christ's priesthood, the ordained priest is called to celibacy because he shares in the spousal vocation of Jesus Christ to become a husband to the Church and a father of souls. As the 2016 *Ratio Fundamentalis Institutionis Sacerdotalis*, "The Gift of the Priestly Vocation," states, "Priestly ordination requires, in the one who receives it, a complete giving of himself for the service of the People of God, as an image of Christ the Spouse.... The priest is called to have within himself the same feelings and attitudes that Christ has towards the Church, loved tenderly through the exercise of the ministry" (*Ratio*, para. 39). Celibacy is a way to live in communion with God, so the priest can serve Christ in pastoral charity with an undivided heart. Again as the *Ratio Fundamentalis* states: "Rooted in Christ the Spouse, and totally consecrated to the People of God in celibacy, priests 'adhere to [Christ] more easily with an undivided heart, they dedicate themselves more freely in him and through him in the service of God and men. [...] and thus they are apt to accept, in a broad sense, fatherhood in Christ'" (*Ratio*, para. 110, quoting also *Presbyterorum Ordinis*, n. 16).

In this book many resources are offered that assist in an integral formation that takes into account the human and spiritual needs of each candidate. First to help determine if they are capable of living the fullness of self-gift required by celibacy and second to form them deeply in that self-gift. This requires both an understanding of the deeper spiritual meaning of celibacy in its spousal dimension as well as a deeper understanding of how to form the affective maturity required for living this self-gift. This book provides resources for both of these.

The authors were chosen because of their dedicated and extensive experience in diocesan seminary formation. One author stands alone as a former Lutheran Evangelical Pastor whose essay entitled "Unilateral Forgiveness" has been especially fruitful for those seeking the interior freedom necessary for self-gift. This article was partly inspired by Dietrich Bonhoeffer's reflections on discipleship and forgiveness during the World War II era. We believe that this teaching deserves special attention because of its fruitfulness. Otherwise each author is either currently serving in diocesan seminary formation or has in the past. We are indebted to each of them for their creative generosity as contributors to this publication. Their love for the Church as Christ's bride motivated each of them.

The book is split into three sections. The first part of the book provides theological and spiritual meditations to help the priest and seminarian understand the spousal self-gift of his celibacy. These meditations, based on deep theological reflection of Jesus own celibacy, seek to serve the priests call "to live in an intimate and unceasing union with the Father through His Son Jesus Christ in the Holy Spirit" (*Optatam Totius*, 8), as Vatican II called for. Perhaps unique to this book, although not unknown in the tradition as our authors show, is the collection of reflections on the spiritual role of the Blessed Virgin Mary in the priest's spousal and paternal love. These reflections attempt to show how a relationship with the Blessed Virgin Mary may help to draw the priest into this spiritual intimacy with the Trinity. Additionally there are two articles on spiritual fatherhood, one exploring this philosophically and the other exploring it in the Fathers of the Church. Together the spiritual vision of these first eight chapters seek to paint a picture of the priest who has integrated the masculine self-gift of his celibacy into the sacrificial life of his priesthood.

A note about the end of each chapter. A template that consists of supplying a "Prayer," "Practicum Reflection Questions" and "Suggested Resources" is attached at the conclusion of each article or essay. The "Practicum Reflection Questions" are supplied for use in human formation advising/mentoring, spiritual direction, vocational discernment, etc. These are intended for the formator to help him to enter deeper into prayer and reflection on the article.

The second part of this volume provides a collection of psychological resources for forming affective maturity. Affective maturity is the key human foundation for the spousal self-gift of celibacy. Articles explore both how to form and to measure affective maturity in order to help the seminarian come to the interior freedom by which he will be able to make a gift of himself.

In this section special attention is given to the problem of same sex attraction. We seek to provide tools to help seminary formators be faithful to the vision of the Church expressed in the *Ratio Fundamentalis*: "the Church, while profoundly respecting the persons in question, cannot admit to the seminary or to holy orders those who practise homosexuality, present deep-seated homosexual tendencies or support the so-called 'gay culture'" (*Ratio*, 199). We also attempt to offer some aids in how to discern what the *Ratio Fundamentalis* means when it says, "Different, however, would be the case in which one were dealing with homosexual tendencies that were only the expression of a transitory problem - for example, that of an adolescence not yet superseded" (*Ratio*, 200) and what it means to overcome these tendencies three years before ordination. With humility we want to mention that these articles are introductory in terms of expressing our understanding of what is necessary for overcoming transitory homosexual tendencies. In dealing with these issues, we desire to give not only some psychological depth around the formation of masculine identity, but also testimony from someone who did overcome transitory same sex attraction to become a natural husband and father. As the Church documents makes clear (cf. *Ratio*, para. 199), this is the real issue. If a man cannot be a natural husband and father because of the struggle with same sex attraction, then he cannot be a spiritual husband and father who makes a gift of himself for the Church. We also have an article here that looks at the problem of pornography and how this affects seminary formation. The depth of practical experience in formation that the authors of this section bring, make it a special help to seminary formators. Also, just as in the previous section, reflection question at the end of each article and further resources are intended to help deepen its understanding and application.

The third section of this work provides spiritual tools for deepening affective maturity. In this section the psychological and spiritual come together, as every good formator knows, to paint a picture of the spiritual freedom of the affectively mature man. Here we give important tools for the spiritual healing of the wounds in a person's life which can prevent affective maturity. Also, we give special attention to the spiritual tools of St. Ignatius of Loyola, since many have found they are especially useful in the interior awareness and healing necessary for affective maturity. Articles explore the healing that can come through imaginative prayer, the importance of the examine prayer and the role of forgiveness in interior healing.

The book closes with two short reflections on Nazareth. The life of the Holy Family in Nazareth becomes the icon of the environment of love necessary for true formation. Since this is the place where the first priest was formed we propose that this relational reality might serve as a model for seminary formation.

We wish to especially thank Deacon Thomas Pulickal and Fr. John Horn, S.J. as managing co-editors for orchestrating much of this work, and also Fr. Llane Briese for his editing assistance which was a great help.

What is the goal of this book? To provide an in-depth spiritual and psychological resource that engenders affective maturity and fruitful chaste celibacy for a renewal of priestly formation. This is the desire of the Church expressed in the 2016 *Ratio Fundamentalis* and the *Program for Priestly Formation* 6th edition. We hope seminary formators, seminarians and many others will find here a resource helpful to this mission.

SEGMENT 1

Affective Maturity:
The Self-Gift of Spousal and Paternal Celibate Love

Chapter One

REAL CELIBACY IS AN INVITATION FROM DIVINE BEAUTY

Deacon James Keating, Ph.D.

Deacon James Keating, PhD is Director of Theological Formation in The Institute for Priestly Formation at Creighton University, Omaha, NE. Previous to his appointment at IPF he was Professor of Moral and Spiritual Theology at the Pontifical College Josephinum, Columbus, Ohio. Deacon Keating serves as well as the Director for Deacon Formation in the Archdiocese of Omaha. He also serves in the ministry of spiritual direction and has been a presenter on topics related to seminary formation at a wide variety of national and international conferences. He has published numerous books and articles in Spiritual and Moral Theology. These include: "Resting On The Heart Of Christ - The Vocation and Spirituality of the Seminary Theologian," "Listening for Truth - Praying Our Way To Virtue," "The Priest As Beloved Son" (editor), and his latest book, "Remain in Me: Holy Orders, Prayer and Ministry" (Paulist Press, 2019).

The personal call of Christ to follow him in a life of chaste celibacy brings a seminarian into a suffering that involves his whole person. Seminary formation serves such a man by assisting him to integrate chastity within his body. Such integration is the work of grace and the acceptance of personal suffering. This grace and suffering works in sync with a man's prayer life and his capacity for self-knowledge and self-revelation, all within the formative relationships which define seminary. Such formation prepares a man to be a priest who labors disinterestedly to serve the spiritual needs of his people. A priest's own needs are to be satisfied in the deepest of contemplative prayer, in substantive friendships with other clergy and laity, and within a sustained love for his own parents and biological family.

If a man receives *a true call* to sacrifice marriage and fatherhood *in light of the* overwhelming *beauty of God's own love* and enter priesthood, then this gift of God will deepen within the formative relationships that constitute a seminary's mission. Reducing celibacy to *a way of life that is practical and useful* to parish ministry threatens the very masculinity of seminarians. Few, if any, men *voluntarily sacrifice the beauty of woman for a lifetime* so an institution might more easily serve others. If such were the case, there would be many more celibate soldiers, physicians, firemen, and police. To enter such a sacrifice one needs to rightly be seized *by Divine beauty* and then *accidentally*, because this beauty has defined one's whole body, become more available to serve. The whole purpose of the seminary is to deepen the aspirant's interior life so he can internalize his being seized by Divine beauty. The seminary exists to enfold a man into Christ the Good Shepherd's love for him as intimate knowledge, forming the seminarian to share in Christ's own pastoral charity. This knowledge is not separate from academic study, but is larger and deeper than discursive knowledge alone. A seminarian should live within a more generous definition of study born of a sustained engagement with the beauty of God in prayer. He ought to long for a prayer-soaked study.

As a seminarian's prayer life grows, certainty about the call to celibacy becomes clear and internalized. In other words, as he prays, the living God communicates this call to the seminarian in a definitive way, thus securing within the man a deep peace about sharing in the spousal identity of Christ the priest. This very personal call is corroborated publicly by his formators through evidence of the seminarian's behavior and disposition. These two foci of discernment — the prayer-soaked conscience of the seminarian and the expertise of the formation staff — must be in sync. If the call is true, the man will be happy and the virtue of chastity will develop apace. If the call is not both personal and ratified within the ecclesial context (i.e., as a vocation, not simply an idiosyncratic desire), inevitable "sadness" will occur with all the attending compensations in behavior. Integrity is sustained by a man appropriating an authentic call to priestly celibacy. Formators are to turn aside pressure from those who may not know the seminarian as well, but advocate for his advancement based upon the urgent need of the Church for priests. Seminaries must be places of free discernment: the staff ought not to be "cheerleaders" for any one particular man, encouraging him to "stick it out" or "keep trying." Like a future father-in-law scrutinizing the potential of a suitor for his daughter, the heart of a formator is keen to protect the Church from someone whose self-involvement determines his primary interest. No father would let a man "use" his daughter to achieve a private and self-serving end, while this man tries to hide such under the cover of being "needed." No woman or Church is ever *that* desperate.

Seminary is a time that allows Christ to come alongside a man, deepen his discipleship, configure him in a mystical way to Christ's own priesthood, and support him in developing an "undivided heart." It is not a time for a man to accept a divided heart as his normal interior state. True relationships for helping a man discern celibacy should be set up before seminary even begins by the diocesan vocation office. This simpler set of relationships, either informally established between a man and his vocation director, or more formally rooted within a house of discernment, should focus only on deepening prayer and clarifying priestly celibacy as a vocation. Seminaries do feel pressured to keep enrollment up, satisfy bishops who need future priests, and calm seminarians' anxiety (and perhaps distraction) as they strive for academic and pastoral-formation success. If the celibacy issue could be answered prior to seminary (perhaps college seminary can help here, but I am thinking of a simpler accompaniment by the vocation office where there is no institutional expectation to have the man "advance" in any way), the weight of this momentous decision would be lifted and the man could participate more freely in his formation. Of course, discernment by the Church even after seminary begins is still in play, as a man's individual acceptance of celibacy is not coextensive with the Church's discernment regarding his fitness in competencies, personality, and virtue.

God doesn't call men to be sad. He calls them to His side so that they can espouse either a woman in Him or the mission of the Church in Him. Vocation gives a man great joy. It is a consolation and joy to be with Christ in the proper vocation that sustains him in fidelity when crosses appear. And the Cross will appear whenever love invites self-renunciation. One's vocation is not a cross; crosses come within one's vocation as love bids us to die to self.

Whether a man discerns celibacy before entering the seminary or during formation, it is vital to bring the seminarian into intimate knowledge of God by contemplating the mysteries of Christ. Living in intimate knowledge of God by contemplation simply means that *one wants to be affected* by the mysteries of Christ's own life. Contemplation invites a man to behold the beauty of these mysteries through Scripture, and is eucharistically engaged, and its fruit is expressed publicly as ministry. This prayer, along with human formation, psychological counseling, the study of philosophy and theology, and good, mature friendships, assists the seminarian to internalize the truth about himself in the light of Truth itself, Christ. This formation readies him to sacrifice one form of spousal love (marriage) and take up another form so he can "lay down his life for the sheep." All husbands, either priest or spouse, lay down their lives.

> The priest, who welcomes the call to ministry, is in a position to make this a loving choice, as a result of which the Church and souls become his first interest, and with this concrete spirituality he becomes capable of loving the universal Church and that part of it entrusted to him with the deep love of a husband for his wife. The gift of self has no

limits, marked as it is by the same apostolic and missionary zeal of Christ, the good shepherd. (JPII, *Guardian of the Redeemer*, 1989)

This is what it means to be engulfed by a spousal imagination: the woman or the Church becomes a man's "first interest." Because of this disposition, a seminarian's self-donative commitment yields life, produces fruit, has an effect. The Church seeks celibates who have the other as their first interest. This can only happen, however, if a man has first received love and is capable of continuing to receive love; otherwise, he may "use" others in his quest to be "known," to be loved. One doesn't enter priestly formation to find love. One seeks formation as a response to already being loved by God. This love continues to be received so that *compassion* for those who have yet to do so can be born within him. Pope Emeritus Benedict XVI articulated this clearly, "Anyone who wishes to give love must also receive love as a gift. Certainly, as the Lord tells us, one can become a source from which rivers of living water flow (cf. Jn 7:37–38). Yet to become such a source, one must constantly drink anew from the original source, which is Jesus Christ, from whose pierced heart flows the love of God (cf. Jn 19:34)" (*Deus Caritas Est*, 2005). The truth expressed here by Benedict XVI is an articulation of the very origin of celibacy and an expression of how one can be sustained in such a vocation.

His First Interest

A seminarian or priest can only have the Church as his first interest if he is fundamentally fascinated with the Holy, with God. With this fascination a man can "constantly drink anew from the original source, which is Jesus Christ." It is *mysticism which moors ministry*. Mysticism is a life penetrated by the mysteries of Christ through prayer and sacramental worship. Unless the celibate cleric is securely fascinated with God, ministry can become a search for communion rather than a fruit of it.

The genius of the seminary system is its mission to form integrated men. Integrated seminarians possess a holy affective maturation. They suffer this maturation within their own bodies as they develop psychological and affective health; a deep, rich prayer life; charitable service to those in need; and conversion through a love for doctrinal and theological truth. This integration happens in the messy, sometimes annoying, and always grace-filled environment of peers, formation mentors, spiritual directors, and teachers. These seminary relationships should also expand to include more women, lay people, permanent deacons, and families.

Sexual integration is completed in seminary by one suffering a deeper reception of

Divine Love in prayer, yielding a new heart that wants to serve, not be served (Mt 20:28). Seminaries must build a very strong gate into priestly formation. The Church is not desperate for priests; she is desperate for holy, mature priests who think of the needs of others because their own affective needs are being met in sacramental and personal prayer, familial relations, and sound peer friendships. A man ought not to become a priest if he simply "wants to help people." A man becomes a priest because he wants to yield his whole body to God, and in the service of pastoral charity, through a life of celibate love. "Helping" people flows from his receiving Divine Love at a level that satisfies a priest's need for love. When it comes to a celibate priesthood, its *supernatural* origins can never be muted. Seminaries need to accept men who are established in love by family, capable of entering holy friendships, sustained in deep prayer, and desirous of spending their lives in pastoral charity.

Bishops ought not to retain inadequate candidates out of fear. Instead they ought to concentrate on filling seminaries with candidates who are vulnerable to being formed into men like this seminarian:

> Seminary formation offered me a grace-filled time of contemplation and meditation on the gift of the priesthood and God's call to celibacy as a way of spousal living. My most profound awareness of this was shortly after my pastoral internship, while in prayer before the Blessed Sacrament, when I identified my deepest need, not coming from my ego or from the comfort that any other person could provide, but from communion in Jesus Christ. In that moment I felt my whole identity found its purpose, joy, and fulfillment in the self-gift of priesthood.

> This article was originally published in *Homiletic & Pastoral Review* (http://www.hprweb.com, 2019). It is republished here with the permission of HPR and the author, who has additionally provided the following prayer, practicum reflection questions, and suggested resources.

Prayer

Father, thank you for revealing your true beauty to me in the actions and virtues of Christ's own spousal love. I praise you for in such revelation I heard your call for me to offer my own body in complete self-giving to you in service to Christ's Church. This way of life satisfies my masculine desire to give all for love. To sacrifice the beauty of woman is only possible because of the Beauty you revealed in prayer, a beauty only glimpsed in this life but fulfilled in the Kingdom (Mt 19:29). May you sustain me in this sacrifice and help me to notice the consolations you offer in response to this gift of my life to you. Amen.

Practicum Reflection Questions for Formators

1. Why is chaste celibacy such a point of anger and dramatic opposition in the age we live in? Why is such sacrifice troubling to popular and political Western Culture?
2. Who is teaching you contemplative prayer, a prayer deep enough to sustain a man's heart in the sacrifice of the woman?
3. How can chaste celibates help one another to maintain confidence and joy? How can Catholic husbands also assist chaste celibates with true friendship?

Suggested Resources

1. Philippe, Jacques. *Time For God* (NY: Scepter, 1992).
2. Selin, Gary. *Priestly Celibacy* (DC: Catholic Univ. Press, 2016).
3. Keating, James. *Remain in Me: Holy Orders, Prayer and Ministry* (NJ: Paulist, 2019).

Chapter Two

THE BLESSED VIRGIN MARY'S ROLE
IN THE CELIBATE PRIEST'S SPOUSAL AND PATERNAL LOVE

Msgr. John R. Cihak, S.T.D.

Msgr. John Cihak is the Pastor of Christ the King Parish and School and the Director of Continuing Education for Clergy in the Archdiocese of Portland in Oregon. He has a B.A. in Philosophy from the University of Notre Dame, a Licentiate in Fundamental Theology and Doctorate in Dogmatic Theology from the Pontifical Gregorian University, Rome. He has served as Director of Human Formation and Professor of Theology at Mount Angel Seminary in Oregon and taught Theology at the Pontifical Gregorian University. For several years he served as an Official in the Congregation for Bishops and as a Papal Master of Ceremonies for Pope Benedict XVI and Pope Francis. He is the author of *Balthasar and Anxiety* (T&T Clark, 2009), the co-author of *The Catholic Guide to Depression* (Sophia Institute, 2013), the editor of *Charles Borromeo: Selected Orations, Homilies and Other Writings* (Bloomsbury, 2017), and several articles in theology and priestly formation.

Introduction [1]

I wrote this article more on my knees than at my desk. It began with jottings from mental prayer over the past year. When I finally sat down to assemble them into a coherent whole, I had a pile of Post-It notes and scribblings on the last pages of *Magnificat* issues – a collection of my own pensées. This article is entitled, "The Blessed Virgin Mary's Role in the

---

[1] This article originated as a presentation at the *Marian Symposium* for the Bicentennial Celebration of Mount Saint Mary Seminary, Emmitsburg, Maryland (USA), 9 October 2008. I am grateful to Dr. Aaron Kheriaty, MD, Deacon Theodore Lange, and Fr. Jerome Young, OSB, for their helpful comments on earlier drafts.

Celibate Priest's Spousal and Paternal Love."[2] I will argue in the following pages that Our Lady plays an essential and indispensable role in the development of the priest's masculinity, especially its spousal and paternal dimensions, and the manner that masculinity is lived out in celibate love.[3] In other words, I want to show how Our Lady helps the priest become a husband and father as a celibate and thus come to fulfillment as a man.

The Recent Challenges and the Perennial Condition

I offer this reflection in the here and now of the 21st century Catholic Church in America, institutionally still reeling, I suspect, from the revelations of clerical misconduct that have shamed us, exposed us to ridicule and derision, and have also called us to accountability. However, one easily overlooked dimension of the recent challenge we have faced is the departure from active ministry of those who are called "JPII priests" (John Paul II priests). After we thought the 60s, 70s and 80s were over, we have had a discouraging repeat of attrition of priests from active ministry. I have known several of them who have subsequently attempted marriage, or suffered alcohol and drug problems. These are not dissenting priests. These "JPII priests" are committed to the Church and the priesthood and espouse the orthodox faith and the Church's disciplines, including clerical celibacy.

Why is this happening? One obvious answer is that intellectual orthodoxy, while necessary, is not sufficient for perseverance in the priesthood in these times. Another obvious answer is to place much blame on the culture and the state of family life. Many of these men who have come unmoored in their vocations have suffered from the effects of our culture of divorce, abuse, materialism and sexual license. A third answer is the deplorable example for many men given by their own fathers, who teach through their own behavior that to be a man means sexual conquest. A man, in this view, does not need to take responsibility for his actions, and is responsible to no one. Young men come to prepare for the priesthood with much more relational brokenness than in previous generations. I believe these answers are true, but do not go deep enough.

---

[2] I began an exploration of this topic of the spousal and paternal dimensions of priestly identity in an earlier article, cf. John Cihak, "The Priest as Man, Husband and Father," *Sacrum Ministerium* 12:2 (2006): 75-85.

[3] Attention is focused on the area of human and spiritual formation since they figure most prominently in *Pastores dabo vobis* (John Paul II, Post Synodal Apostolic Exhortation *Pastores dabo vobis*, 25 March 1992, nn. 43-50), and where the greatest need in seminary formation still exists.

Perhaps more subtly considered the "JPII priest" attrition is simply a recent example of the perennial struggle for the celibate priest in his affectivity and relationships, in his heart and most especially in his spousal and paternal love. To put it simply, how are all those natural desires—including erotic desires—to be a husband and father supposed to function in the priest's free promise of celibacy? The answer that some ex-priests in the 1970s offered was that those desires have no place in celibacy and therefore the discipline of celibacy should change. The argument was that the discipline of celibacy prevented a man from fully developing as a man. When it was perceived that the Church would not change the discipline, they left. But this answer is too superficial for the deep mystery that is the celibate priesthood. Nevertheless the clash is felt deeply in the heart of a man called to celibacy in the priesthood. The gap appears not in the alignment of one's intellect to the truth of priestly celibacy, but how this truth of priestly celibacy becomes enfleshed in the priest's heart and in his relationships as a man.

Pope Benedict has given us an initial stab at the challenge in *Deus caritas est* in his treatment of the relationship between *eros* and *agape* and the transformation of disordered *eros* into an ordered *eros* that provides the vitality for *agape* love.[4] In the case of the celibate priest, it is the transformation of his disordered *eros* into a truly spousal and paternal love that is expressed in his celibate *agape*.

Can this happen? I think we would all say, Yes. But *how* does this happen? There is nothing automatic about it, and there are many potential pitfalls. Careerism, illicit relationships, alcoholism, drug abuse, exotic vacations, collections of various kinds, pornography and the flight into television and the Internet are simply inadequate ways of grappling with a mystery that lies, I would argue, at the very heart of the priesthood, and which we will explore in a moment. Because of our fallen nature, there is need for a deep healing of *eros* in the heart of every man. I suggest that we are still coming to terms with this challenge in our human and spiritual formation programs, and are only beginning to come literally to the heart of the matter. I propose that Our Lady plays an indispensable role in the transformation of the priest's masculinity, and the foundation for all that is said in this article lies in the important work of John Paul II in his Theology of the Body and Benedict XVI in *Deus caritas est.*

---

[4] Benedict XVI, Encyclical Letter *Deus caritas est*, 25 December 2005, especially nn. 3-18.

The Four Major Dimensions of Priestly Masculinity and Feminine Complementarity

Being a man involves a set of four basic relationships, which comprise the four basic dimensions of his masculinity. Through these four basic relationships a man develops, matures and attains to male fulfillment. Each dimension is important for his development in becoming an integral man and thus being able to become a holy and effective priest. As Pope John Paul II taught, the priest's human personality is at the very heart of a fruitful priesthood; it is the human bridge that connects others with Jesus Christ.[5]

These four relational dimensions of manhood are son, brother, husband and father. The first two dimensions (son and brother) are necessary preparations for manhood and the last two (husband and father) bring about the fulfillment of manhood. In other words, a man must be a good son, then a good brother, then a good husband and then a good father to become a good man and attain his fulfillment as man. All four together are necessary to attain mature manhood, and never is any dimension left behind. To be a good father a man still needs to be a good son, if possible to his earthly father, and surely to his heavenly Father, with Whom he should live in a relationship of divine filiation. Each relationship, nevertheless, brings its own peculiarity and focus. We know as well that in this broken world, not every man has healthy relationships with parents and siblings. Nevertheless, we can talk about these dimensions even if they do not always function well in this life. Much could be said about each dimension; for the purposes of our discussion we will focus on the final two dimensions as lived out in the celibate priesthood.

According to the theological anthropology revealed in Holy Scripture (primarily Gen. 1-3, Mt. 19:3-12, Eph. 5:21-33) especially as interpreted and developed by John Paul II, man is in an essential, indispensable relationship with *woman*. They are equal in dignity, both made in the image and likeness of God, and complementary in mission. Being made in the divine image, both were made for self-giving love. God alone fulfills a man, yet the Lord has willed that this fulfillment happen through a man's relationship with woman.[6] This is to say, man cannot attain mature manhood without the help of woman and vice versa. Adam's solitude (Gen 2:20) taught him that he cannot attain fulfillment by himself; we could also say that he cannot do it in relationship only with other men. In the same way woman cannot attain her fulfillment alone or only with other women, but only through the complementary relationship with man.

A corollary to this truth of male-female complementarity is that we must reject false

---

[5] Perhaps the most well known passage from *Pastores dabo vobis*, n. 43.

[6] Cf. *Catechism of the Catholic Church*, nn. 371-372.

philosophical anthropologies often implicit in the psychological sciences (and that sometimes surface in our human formation programs), most especially Freud's idea that every human person is bi-sexual, a hermaphrodite, containing both male and female within himself. This idea, which Freud never substantiates but considers part of his "meta-psychology" (a mythic presupposition), is perpetuated today by the gay and transgender movements in this country. Biblical revelation and even DNA say otherwise. A man is man from his image of God all the way down to his very chromosomes; a woman is woman from her image of God all the way down to her very chromosomes. The truth is that human beings were made for relationship, made to come out of themselves and develop as a man or woman through a complementarity that lies outside of themselves. Man and woman were made for each other so that each would help the other to attain fulfillment in his or her nature. Thus the ideal in any psychological healing is not to try to recover some primal monadic, hermaphroditic existence, but to cast oneself forward, outside of oneself in love, and this can only happen in relationships – for man and woman with God and man and woman with each other.

Through this essential and complementary relationship with woman, a man in the natural order can grow in his four dimensions as son, brother, husband and father in order to attain full maturity. A son has a mother, a brother hopefully has sisters and brothers, a husband has a wife and together they become father and mother. In the order of nature, we can begin to see the importance of women in the development of the priest as a man: his mother and his sisters help to lead him into maturity as a good son and brother. A man's relationship with his mother begins *in utero* where as son he begins to become attuned to his mother, her heartbeat, her bodily processes, her movements, her emotions; we could say even her soul. In infancy, it is hoped, at some point the mother's smile awakens him to self-consciousness. Her smile gives him his awareness in the midst of her feminine love that he is a unique person. The beauty, goodness, and truth evinced in the mother's smile awakens in the child an awareness of the beauty, goodness, and truth of the world, and, by analogy, of God.[7]

Psychiatry and neurobiology describe this as a process of "secure (healthy) attachment,"

---

[7] These are insights especially developed by Hans Urs von Balthasar in his theological anthropology, for example in his *Wenn ihr nicht werdet wie dieses Kind* (repr. 2, Einsiedeln-Freiburg: Johannes Verlag, 1998); *Unless you become like this Child*, trans. Erasmo Leiva-Merikakis (San Francisco: Ignatius Press, 1991); and his essay "Bewegung zu Gott," *Spiritus Creator: Skizzen zur Theologie*, vol. III (Einsiedeln: Johannes Verlag, 1967); "Movement Toward God," *Explorations in Theology*, vol. III: *Creator Spirit*, trans. Brian McNeil, CRV (San Francisco: Ignatius Press, 1993), 15-55.

a subtle attunement between mother and child which is essential for normal brain and psychological development, as well as normal spiritual development, especially in those crucial first five years of life. This relationship continues in childhood where a boy continues to learn how to be a son and eventually a brother. In all of this development the mother's (and sisters') role is neither as an object to be used, nor as being overprotective or cultivating a "womanish" affect in her son – all of which would be a collapsing of the masculine-feminine complementarity. The healthy son or brother does not identify with the mother or sister in such a way that he imitates her femininity (e.g., in imitating effeminate characteristics himself); rather, he relates to her as truly an "other" with whom he, in his masculinity, can relate through a process of complementary, self-giving love.

A man's mother is his primal relationship to the feminine out of which he grows in all his relationships with women. Of course his father and brothers, if he has them, have essential roles as well, especially in how his father treats his mother. In his father, a man finds the primary masculine response to feminine complementarity; the father hopefully confirms it: cherishing his wife, loving her, and giving himself over to her. A mother also prepares her son for his wife.

In marriage, a man's wife changes him. He practices giving himself in love to her. He allows himself to be determined by her. He must attune himself to her, and she engages his heart and helps to develop his *eros* into *agape* love. As a man, he desires to protect her, to provide for her, to give her children, to do mighty deeds for her, to cherish her and shower his affection upon her. Of course this describes something ideal, and does not automatically happen in marriage. But the reader can see what I mean.

The Blessed Virgin Mary's Role
in the Celibate Priest's Attainment as Husband and Father

In the life of grace, we immediately grasp Our Lady's role in helping a man be a good son. As the archetype of Mother Church she gives birth to him and nurtures him through grace. She plays an essential feminine role in leading him to relate to the Father, her Incarnate Son and the Holy Spirit. She teaches her sons about trust, surrender, and the acceptance of weakness and poverty without self-hatred. She cultivates in her sons the spirit of childhood. But what about the last two dimensions for the celibate priest? In the natural order, a man's wife helps him develop into a husband and father. I suggest that in the order of grace, the Blessed Virgin Mary assumes this role in a very real, though nuanced way.

When it comes to developing the spousal and fatherly dimensions of his masculinity, we cannot help but see the Freudian in the audience raise his hand in objection that the idea that the Blessed Virgin Mary helps bring about the celibate priest's fulfillment as husband and father is simply rife with Oedipal "stuff". I think our response to such an objection begins with the distinction between the Blessed Virgin Mary and the Church; she is a type of the Church, in fact, she is the *archetype* of the Church. Mary is not the spouse of the celibate priest as the Church is. Our Lady is the spouse of the Holy Spirit, not her Incarnate Son. There is nothing Oedipal going on here if we understand the relationships correctly, and understand them in symbolic and spiritual terms and not in a crude, literal way. Moreover, we cannot forget that the concrete form of the priest' spousal love is a *celibate* love.

With this distinction, allow me to be a bit provocative. Our Lady herself, in a very concrete way, brings a celibate priest into his spiritual marriage with the Church and his spiritual paternity as he participates in Christ's spousal relationship to the Church. She engages him deeply in his masculine heart, even in his *eros*, with her feminine love to bring about this transformation in her priest from a disordered *eros* to an ordered *eros* and celibate *agape*.

The Central Mystery: The Cross

This complementary engagement of the Blessed Virgin Mary's feminine love with the priest's masculine love happens within the central mystery of the priesthood: the Cross, and specifically in the scene of Our Lady and St. John at the foot of the Cross. Call to your imagination the scene: there is Our Lord nailed to the Cross, bloodied and broken in His passion. At the foot of the Cross, we find Our Lady and the only priest who stood with Our Lord *eis telos* (Jn. 13:1), St. John. The Blessed Virgin Mary is in utter agony; both she and His priest are being interiorly drawn into His crucifixion.

There is so much silence around this mystery. We are basically only told the geographical facts of the scene. Jesus is the one who sets it all in motion with His *gaze*: "When Jesus saw his mother, and the disciple whom he loved standing near, he said..." (Jn. 19:26). It begins with a gaze from our Lord seeing His Mother and His priest. None of the Lord's words in the Gospels are superfluous, especially those he uttered while upon the Cross. Therefore, these words from the Cross are some of the most important words uttered to Our Lady and one of His first priests.

She hears, "Woman, behold your son" (Jn. 19:26). He calls her "Woman", not "Mom". Feel the distancing. These words must have been especially painful for her. As mother all she wants is to be close to Him and even to die with Him so that she can be close to Him.

"Woman" isolates her from Him. He pushes her away, not in cruelty, but so that she can become the New Eve, the mother of all those who would live eternally. Her agony is the labor pains giving birth to the Church. Here the distinction between Our Lady and the Church, which should never be a separation, is perhaps a little more pronounced. Here she is giving birth to the Church, acting as Mother of the Church, through her interior agony.

St. John is at her side. It is no coincidence that a priest of the new covenant stands at the Cross with Jesus. St. John also is undergoing his own interior crucifixion, being conformed as priest to the Cross of the eternal High Priest. Perhaps we can sense St. John's helplessness. There is no worse feeling for a man than that of helplessness. What words could he utter seeing her in such agony? The sword piercing her Immaculate Heart is going through his priestly heart as well. This is not some heroic charge to victory. It is blackness, loneliness, a dark night; it is the whole messed-up incongruity of the collision between love and sin. It feels like and is death.

"Then Jesus says to the disciple, 'Behold your mother!'" (Jn. 19:27). At this moment, Jesus asks the Apostle in the depth of his own pain to attune himself to her. As priest, he must decide to put her first, attune himself to her heart. He must put her suffering ahead of his own. I imagine St. John turning toward Our Lady, and looking at her with such tenderness and reverence. Jesus sends His command deep into the heart of his priest, "Look at her...receive her...take care of her." As a man, he must feel helpless and inadequate, but now he has been given a manly task. St. John is commanded to care for her, to comfort her, to hold her, to protect her because she is so alone and vulnerable at that moment. Such a command would resonate deeply in the heart of such a man: he must look beyond his pain and accommodate himself to her, and have all that is best about being a man rise up within him in a great act of celibate *agape*. The choice to be attentive to her pain brings him to the threshold of entering into his spousal love and paternity as a celibate, as the Church is coming to birth.

I like to meditate on that scene, pondering the eyes of Our Lady and St. John as they meet in their mutual agony. Neither of them seems to have Jesus anymore. At that moment she needs St. John; she also allows him to help her. She is so alone at that moment. She who is sinless allows her great poverty of spirit to need this man and priest beside her. Her feminine complementarity draws out the best in St. John's masculine heart. The need for his support and protection must have connected to something deep within him as a man. How does he help her? St. John says that he then took her "into his own" (in Greek, *eis ta idia*). What does this mean? "His house," as many translations read? "His things"? What about "everything that he is"? Perhaps it indicates that he takes her into his life as a priest.

She also is supporting him. He is depending on her in that moment for he too is so alone. I wonder if he felt abandoned by the other apostles. She leads the way in sacrificing herself, for her feminine heart is more receptive and more attuned to Jesus'. She is not only present but leads the way for him, helping the priest to have his own heart pierced as well. There is much here to ponder as she engages his masculine love. He gives himself over to her, to cherish her and console her. At this moment she needs him and needs him to be strong, even if she is the one really supporting him.

The Blessed Virgin Mary's role is to call out of the priest this celibate *agape* to help him become a husband to the Church and a spiritual father—a strong father, even in his weakness. She does this at the Cross by drawing the priest out of his own pain to offer pure masculine love in the midst of her own pure feminine love. This scene becomes an icon of the relationship between the priest and the Church. The priest hands himself over to the Church in her suffering and need – to have his life shaped by hers. At the foot of the Cross the Church agonizes in labor to give birth to the members of the mystical body. I am struck by the next verse in this passage from the Gospel of St. John: "After *this* Jesus, knowing that all was now finished, said... 'I thirst'" (Jn. 19:28). It was after this exchange of love at the foot of the Cross that "all was now finished".

St. Charles Borromeo often gave conferences to his priests when he was Archbishop of Milan. In the opening lines of the conference he addressed to his diocesan synod on April 20, 1584, he draws the connection between the woman of the Apocalypse in Revelation and Rachel in Genesis to the Church:

"She was with child and she cried out in her pangs of birth, in anguish for delivery." (Rev 12:2).... O what pain, O what wailing of Holy Church! She cries out with prayers in the presence of God, and in your presence through my mouth, pronounces divine words to you. It seems that I am hearing her saying to her betrothed, the Lord Jesus Christ, what Rachel had formerly said to her husband Jacob, "Give me children or I shall die" (Gen30:1). I am truly desirous of the one to be born. Indeed I dread this sterility; so unless you [priests!] come to Christ and give to me many sons, I am precisely at this very moment about to die.[8]

The implication of St. Charles' words is that Holy Mother Church cries out to her Divine Bridegroom, and to the one who participates in Christ's spousal relationship – the priest, for children. It is at the Cross where the priest in the sting of his celibacy becomes a

---

[8] *Acta Ecclesiae Mediolanensis*, Pars II, 20 April 1584, 347. [Trans. Gerard O'Connor]

husband to the Church and a spiritual father. For the celibate priest, the Cross is his marriage bed, just as it was for Our Lord.

It is through the love exchanged between Our Lady and St. John at the foot of the Cross that the priest's own fallen *eros* begins to be healed and transformed to image the celibate priestly love that Jesus is revealing on the Cross. We priests get into trouble when we try to run away from this mystery or refuse to enter into it. The only fruitful love is the love that flows from the Cross. For this reason the celibate priest's spousal and paternal love must be more, not less, and it has the potential to become superabundant because it is so sacrificial. No offense to my brother priests of the eastern churches who are married, but I think they would agree that there is an eschatological, and even ontological, primacy of celibacy in the priesthood. This is not to claim a moral primacy since promising celibacy is no guarantee that a celibate priest will live it well or fully. Only to the degree that he allows himself to be taken into the mystery of Calvary with the Blessed Virgin Mary can the celibate priest attain the lofty call that is celibate spousal love and spiritual paternity.

When I was newly ordained and I heard older priests complain about loneliness in the priesthood, I must confess I thought that it was due to a lack of good relationships or prayer life. And of course for some this was true. We are often lonely because we do not have good, deep friendships with others, especially with other priests, or quite simply we do not pray. However, after ten years as a priest I have come to a more realistic conclusion. There is an *essential felt loneliness* in the priesthood because there is an essential loneliness in the Cross, the Cross that stands at the very center of the priesthood. We priests feel the sting especially in celibacy, and understandably we struggle to come to terms with it. We know the terrifying loneliness that comes crashing in, the coldness of walking back into the rectory – certainly exhausted and tired of people – but lonely because there does not seem to be anyone to share it with or who understands our hearts. A pious thought would be to pray, but prayer in those moments may well seem dry and distasteful.

This is not giving way to self-love. It is simply being a man. There is something deep inside us that longs for a woman's understanding and comfort, and a longing to comfort and understand a unique woman and to generate life with her. Some try to numb this longing through careerism in the Church, food, drugs, alcohol, illicit relationships, pornography; probably the most common forms of numbing are through the television or Internet. Nor is this to suggest that "life is tough, so get over it." Rather, it is an invitation for the celibate priest to enter more deeply into precisely this mystery of caring for the Church at the foot of the Cross and becoming united to her. The priest must struggle in accepting being co-crucified with Jesus and entering the compassion of Our Lady. She for her part comes to the aid of the priest by engaging his masculinity as a husband and father to help bring about his union with the Church—not in sexual union but through *crucifixion*, by dying for her. The priest, in his loneliness, becomes attuned to the Church's loneliness in this world.

Our line of thinking brings us to consider the joy of the Cross. The transformation of the priest through consoling the Mother of God at the Cross not only brings him into his spousal and paternal love, but also transforms his whole notion of joy. From its revaluing by the Cross, Christian joy is less a passing emotional state and more of a spiritual condition. Joy is not found in the lack of suffering or on the other side of suffering but in self-giving love. Thus joy can flow clearly and directly from suffering. This is joy as a fruit of the Holy Spirit and thus something indestructible, something the world cannot give.

Helping the Seminarian or Priest to embrace the Mystery

How do we help our seminarians and priests enter into this profound mystery of the development of their masculinity as celibate priests?

I think we need to continue freeing our human and spiritual formation programs from the narrowness of an overly psychological perspective. The psychological sciences are important and necessary. But human and spiritual formation is wider than psychology can measure. We must keep in mind that psychological approaches, when they depart from the physiology of the human body, cross over into philosophical and theological realms. As Dr. Paul Vitz observes, every psychological theory, whether it is recognized or not, is an applied *philosophy* of life.[9] Human formation should be founded on a sound philosophical and theological anthropology.

I have yet to find a more solid anthropology than that from St. Thomas, especially as interpreted by John Paul II. I would add further insights from scholars following a more Augustinian line of thinking, such as Pope Benedict XVI and Hans Urs von Balthasar. I think a human formation program for priests needs also to draw from the best of our spiritual theology, especially the ascetical theology of St. John Climacus, Don Lorenzo Scupoli, and St. Francis de Sales.[10] These treasures of the tradition resonate well with all the

---

[9] Cf. Paul Vitz, "Psychology in Recovery," *First Things* 151 (2005), pp. 17-21.

[10] Cf. St. John Climacus, *The Ladder of Divine Ascent* in *The Classics of Western Spirituality* (Mahwah: Paulist, 1982); St. Francis de Sales, *Introduction to the Devout Life,* trans. John Ryan (New York: Doubleday, 1989); Lorenzo Scupoli. *The Spiritual Combat,* trans. William Lester (Rockford: TAN, 1990).

excellent research emerging in neurobiology, social biology and brain development.[11] Perhaps the four-fold dimensions of relational masculinity could provide an initial framework.

From this wider perspective, the important work of the psychological sciences comes into play. As formators seek to help men become better sons, brothers, husbands and fathers, sometimes the need for therapeutic intervention arises to heal broken relationships with father and mother and to develop secure attachments, so that one becomes capable of *agape* love. Such intervention should be done by therapists who fully appreciate and understand sound philosophical and theological anthropology, and grasp the priest's unique ecclesial mission and vocation.

It is also important to integrate into our human formation programs, and insist upon, a masculine affectivity in both formators and seminarians. I think anyone who grew up in a semi-normal family has some idea about what a masculine affect looks like. No matter what one's home life was like, much good material can be gleaned from the holy men of Scripture including David, Jeremiah, Ezekiel, St. John the Baptist, St. Joseph, St. Peter, St. John, St. Paul, and the holy men who are saints, especially the priest saints. I think there is still much from the lives of St. Francis de Sales and St. John Vianney that can show seminarians and priests what priestly masculinity looks like and how it is lived out concretely in diocesan life.

It is not politically correct, even within some ecclesial circles, to follow the mind of the Church with regard to same-sex attraction as clarified by the Congregation for Education in 2005.[12] The difficulty surfaces precisely when we begin to talk about the priest's spousal and paternal love. Everyone seems fine with the concept of the priest as a son or a brother. But begin to speak of the priest as a husband and father, and in some circles resistance begins to emerge. Nevertheless, in *Pastores dabo vobis* masculine affectivity is repeatedly coupled with

---

[11] Cf. Mary Ainsworth, *Patterns of Attachment: A Psychological Study of the Strange Situation* (Mahwah: Erlbaum, 1978); John Bowlby, *A Secure Base: Parent-Child Attachment and Healthy Human Development* (New York: Basic Books, 1990); Stanley Greenspan, *Building Healthy Minds: The Six Experiences That Create Intelligence and Emotional Growth in Babies and Young Children* (Cambridge: Da Capo Press, 2000); *The Growth of the Mind: And the Endangered Origins of Intelligence* (Cambridge: Da Capo Press, 1998); Daniel Siegel, *The Developing Mind: Toward a Neurobiology of Interpersonal Experience* (New York: Guilford, 1999); Daniel Stern, *The Interpersonal World of the Infant: A View from Psychoanalysis and Developmental Psychology* (New York: Basic Books, 2000).

[12] Cf. Congregation for Education. *Instruction Concerning the Criteria for the Discernment of Vocations with regard to Persons with Homosexual Tendencies in view of their Admission to Seminary and Holy Orders*, 2005.

"pastoral charity". The love that the seminarian or priest shows Our Lady at the foot of the Cross is exactly that – charity, the highest form of love, but it must be a masculine incarnation of it. Pastoral charity is where a man's disordered *eros* becomes ordered into celibate *agape*, in his care for the Church in the concreteness of a single soul.

Seminarians and priests should be helped to pray from the heart. One initial suggestion is to encourage praying the Rosary using Ignatius' application of the senses that help engage the heart of the one praying. Sr. Mary Timothea Elliot, RSM offers insight into how to pray like Mary: to hold the word of God tenaciously, to ponder it with other words, to apply it to the life situation, and to mature in the word.[13] A helpful way to pray from the heart is taught by the Institute for Priestly Formation through the memorable phrase, "Pray like a Pirate!"[14] A pirate says, "ARRR!", which stands for a helpful acronym: Acknowledge, Relate, Receive, Respond. Acknowledge means to be real and honest in prayer. Relate means to be in relationship and to grapple with whatever is there, to engage the Lord, to be present to Him. Receive means to allow Him the freedom to do what He wishes. Respond means that having received from Him, one is able to respond to Him in love. Praying in this manner helps to cultivate honesty in prayer, and help one practice giving oneself in sincerity.

Part of praying from the heart is praying with the Blessed Virgin Mary, not as an idea but as a woman. As men and priests we need to develop an affective relationship with her, and let her help us become attuned to her heart. As I read St. Louis De Montfort, I think this is what he was really seeking to accomplish. His spirituality is not simply emotive sentimentalism, but learning to model one's heart on hers. His spirituality is a spirituality of attunement. This important spiritual work in learning how to love with the heart and to truly give oneself in prayer will help build the habit of giving oneself in the offering of Holy Mass, to enter into the fire of Calvary with arms wide open.

As human and spiritual formators, we must strive to enter deeply into this mystery ourselves, and then lovingly cast forth these wonderful priests and priests-to-be into this mystery, to help them grapple and wrestle with it, to allow the fire of Calvary to penetrate the depths of their hearts and finally to incarnate this mystery. Then a priest can enter into the spousal and paternal reality with all the *eros* of his masculine heart taken up into celibate *agape*.

---

[13] Mary Timothea Elliott. "Mary – Pure Response to the Word of God," presentation at the Marian Symposium for the Bicentennial Celebration of Mount Saint Mary Seminary, 8 October 2008.

[14] In my view, the Institute for Priestly Formation, under the direction of Fr. Richard Gabuzda and Fr. John Horn, SJ, is currently doing some of the best work in the United States on the spiritual and human development of seminarians and diocesan priests.

The Mystery Transposed: Holy Mass at Ephesus

I cannot leave this scene at the foot of the Cross, which reveals Our Lady's role in the celibate priest's spousal and paternal love, without describing another scene. This scene came to me on one of those days when it was not thrilling to be a priest and I was praying, reluctantly. It began with the scene at the Cross, but the scene was transposed at some point to a later event. It was Ephesus and St. John was preparing to offer the Mass. Mary was there with him. Bear with me if some anachronisms crept into the meditation. She was helping him vest, first with the amice, alb, cincture, etc. Her fingers working to make sure everything was fitting correctly. I can imagine their eyes meeting. Nothing need be said, especially when she lifts up the stole to put it on him. They both know from where the generative power symbolized in the stole comes. I can see the delight in her eyes to see him as a priest, a man who is truly and totally her son. The joy and love in her eyes makes him strong, and confident to go and offer this sacrifice whereby his spousal and paternal love is once again confirmed and made fruitful. I think these can be fruitful scenes for any priest to ponder every time he goes to offer the Mass: the feminine presence of Our Lady at the foot of the Cross and before Mass at Ephesus.

Conclusion

My intention is not to offer a deductive investigation and proof that answer the contemporary challenge and perennial condition of the celibate priest's spousal and paternal love. What I do offer is an emerging interior conviction that the answer to the perennial condition of the celibate priest's masculinity lies in the depth of this mystery—the apostle's pure embrace of the Mother of God at Calvary.

This is no saccharine or sugar-coated Marian piety. This is a Marian piety that is so real it will give you splinters, will make you shed tears and will even drive a lance right through the heart of a priest. This is a real Marian piety for real men.

I suggest that this mystery lies at the center of every priest's life whether he can recognize it as such or not. Priests leave, misuse their sexual powers, or turn to other things because they cannot seem to surrender to and embrace this mystery. It is the mystery of his masculinity and the Cross. The Blessed Virgin Mary is there to draw it out of him and help him bring it to a new level of realization as husband and father.

The only way the priest will make it through the Cross is by allowing her to help him and for him to unite himself mystically to her in her suffering. Through her feminine love the celibate priest becomes a husband to the Church and spiritual father to all. And from the depths of his masculinity the priest can say, "It is no longer I who live, but Christ who lives in me" (Gal. 2:20).

This article was originally published in *Sacrum Ministerium* 15:1 (2009): 149-164. It is published here with the permission of the author, who has additionally provided the following prayer, practicum reflection questions, and suggested resources.

Prayer

Loving and merciful Father, I humbly beg you to irradiate my heart with your grace, penetrating every fear and healing every unchastity and selfishness. Set me on fire with a husband's love, pure and brave, for the Bride of your Son, so that she may be made fruitful through my love for her and I may become a true spiritual father. May the free offering of my heart and body on the altar of holy celibacy conform me into the likeness of Jesus Christ our High Priest. Through our Lord Jesus Christ, your Son, who lives and reigns with you in the unity of the Holy Spirit, one God for ever and ever. Amen.

Practicum Reflection Questions for Formators

1. What image, phrase or moment stirred your heart while pondering this article? Describe the stirrings.
2. Describe your internal reaction to the overall point of the article, which is that you are being invited to develop your love as a husband and a father through celibacy.
3. What resistance, conflict, joy or relief do you sense when you consider your life as a priest or future priest in terms of being a husband to the Church and a spiritual father? How are you being invited to grow in these two areas?
4. What role has Our Lady played in your heart as a man thus far in your life? Have you invited her into your fears and the emotional and moral "messiness" of celibacy? How would you like that relationship to grow?

Suggested Resources

1. Cihak, John. "The Priest as Man, Husband and Father," *Sacrum Ministerium* 12:2 (2006): 75-85.

2. [http://www.ignatiusinsight.com/features2007/jcihak_priesthood2_mar07.asp]

3. _____. "More than just Friends: Reflections on the Priest as Friend of the Bridegroom," *Homiletic and Pastoral Review*(August/September 2011): 22-28.

4. Griffin, Carter. *Why Celibacy?: Reclaiming the Fatherhood of the Priest.* Steubenville: Emmaus Road Publishing, 2019.

5. Keating, James. "Chaste Celibacy and Spiritual Fatherhood," *The Priest* (April 2008).

6. _____. "Falling in Love and Staying in Love: the Gift and Labor of Prayer in the Priesthood," *Sacrum Ministerium* 1-2 (2012).

7. _____. "Real Celibacy is an Invitation from Divine Beauty." *Homiletic and Pastoral Review* (February 2019). [https://www.hprweb.com/2019/02/real-celibacy-is-an-invitation-from-divine-beauty/]

8. Nerbun, David. *The Original Icons of Faithful Discipleship Within the Eschatological Family of Jesus: John and Mary Standing By the Crucified (Jn 19:26-27).* Dissertation John Paul II Institute, Washington D.C., 2017.

9. Selin, Gary. *Priestly Celibacy: Theological Foundations.* Washington D.C.: CUA Press, 2018.

Chapter Three

MORE THAN JUST FRIENDS

Reflections on the Priest as Friend of the Bridegroom in
John the Baptist, Joseph and John the Beloved

Msgr. John R. Cihak, S.T.D.

Msgr. John Cihak is the Pastor of Christ the King Parish and School and the Director of Continuing Education for Clergy in the Archdiocese of Portland in Oregon. He has a B.A. in Philosophy from the University of Notre Dame, a Licentiate in Fundamental Theology and Doctorate in Dogmatic Theology from the Pontifical Gregorian University, Rome. He has served as Director of Human Formation and Professor of Theology at Mount Angel Seminary in Oregon and taught Theology at the Pontifical Gregorian University. For several years he served as an Official in the Congregation for Bishops and as a Papal Master of Ceremonies for Pope Benedict XVI and Pope Francis. He is the author of *Balthasar and Anxiety* (T&T Clark, 2009), the co-author of *The Catholic Guide to Depression* (Sophia Institute, 2013), the editor of *Charles Borromeo: Selected Orations, Homilies and Other Writings* (Bloomsbury, 2017), and several articles in theology and priestly formation.

The priest's free promise of celibacy is a beautiful mystery and a daunting prospect. Beautiful in the way it mirrors Jesus' own priesthood and ushers into the Church and the world an otherwise unattainable spiritual fecundity; challenging because the priest is also both a man, with all the good and natural desires for marriage and family, and a sinner whose desires are disordered. From the beginning of the New Covenant, celibacy has had a strong and positive connection to the priesthood, and has always been a sign of contradiction to this fallen world whether in first century Palestine, eleventh century Europe or today.

The effective integration of the priest's free promise of celibacy in his good, manly, yet weak and sinful heart occurs primarily through prayer. This article offers some brief reflections on the priest as friend of the Bridegroom to aid the encounter in prayer so that the priest may assimilate this promise more deeply and to help others better appreciate what is going on in the hearts of their priests.[1]

The Priest as Friend of the Bridegroom

The identity and mystery of the priest as both the Bridegroom and the Friend of the Bridegroom is rooted in Scripture and developed in the writings of the Church Fathers. Recently it seems these biblical and patristic themes have been taken up anew, developed in light of Pope John Paul II's theology of the body and Pope Benedict XVI's writings on love, and put into a spiritual and mystical key through St. Ignatius' spiritual doctrine of praying with the imagination to facilitate the integration of these truths in the heart.[2]

What is meant by the priest as the "Friend of the Bridegroom"? While it is true that the priest participates with Jesus in a spousal relationship with the Church, the priest is not the Bridegroom in the fullest sense. There is only one Christ. Jesus Christ alone could and did pay the price on the cross to be husband to the Church. But the two mysteries of Bridegroom and friend of the Bridegroom are related, namely, because the priest is not the Bridegroom in the fullest sense as Jesus is, the Lord generously invites his priest to participate in the spousal dimension of his priesthood. By keeping together these two dimensions of priestly identity like a diptych, one can contemplate more completely the mystery of the priest. The two sides of the diptych express the mystery of the celibate priest as a virgin-spouse.[3]

These reflections are not intended to be a theological discourse on the topic, yet it seems helpful to offer the following analogy to free up the mind for the encounter in prayer.[4] The

---

[1] This article originated from three conferences to the seminarians and faculty of the Pontifical North American College, Rome, 20-21 February 2010. I am grateful to Fr. Derek Lappe, Msgr. Thomas Powers, Fr. Andrew Cozzens and Deacon James Keating for their helpful comments on earlier drafts. I intend in these reflections to fill out more completely the ideas on priestly identity sketched in two previous articles: Cihak, John. "The Blessed Virgin Mary's Role in the Celibate Priest's Spousal and Paternal Love," *Sacrum Ministerium* 15:1 (2009) 149-164, and "The Priest as Man, Husband and Father," *Sacrum Ministerium* 12:2 (2006) 75-85.

[2] One recent example: Keating, James. "Surrendering to the Healing Power of Christ's own Chastity" (http://www.ignatiusinsight.com/features2009/keaing_chastity1_aug09.asp).

[3] Cf. the development of this concept in the article by Deacon James Keating, Ph.D. in this issue.

[4] This brief article presupposes much theological reflection, and so the interested reader is invited to pursue some of the underlying theology in Cozzens, Andrew. *Imago Vivens Iesu Christi*

Church is both the Body and Bride of Christ. The Church as the Body of Christ is the principle of union and identity with Christ. The Church as the Bride of Christ is the principle of distinction and non-identity with Christ. Yet precisely because the Church is not Christ (but his Bride), she can be united with him in a communion of love to be his Body. In other words, the distinction between Christ and the Church is acknowledged not to separate but to relate and establish a communion of love. In a similar way, the priest as the Bridegroom is the principle of identity and participation in Christ's own identity as husband to the Church; the priest as the friend of the Bridegroom is the principle of distinction and non-identity. But precisely because the priest is the friend of the Bridegroom, he can be admitted by Christ to participate in his identity as the Bridegroom to the Church.

"Just" Friends?

It is in the mystery of being the friend of the Bridegroom that the priest often feels the sting of celibacy. One of the deepest longings in a man's heart is for that natural spousal relationship for which he was created, the natural and holy consummation of love with one's wife for the unification of spouses and the procreation and education of children. It can be enthralling for the priest to know that he is given a share in Christ's spousal relationship with the Church (the spousal dimension). Yet how does it strike him to hear that he is not the Bridegroom in the full sense but "just" his friend (the virginal dimension)? If he is especially attentive to his heart, it might make him squirm a bit, feel uncomfortable and perhaps even agitated or angry. That deep down longing to be a bridegroom can be converted into a rage that fuels all sorts of unspoken anxiety, sadness, short temper and sins of the flesh. He may sometimes fume: "How dare God ask me to surrender to him what he gave to me by nature?" When a young man is dating, what is the worst thing he could hear from the girl he loves? "I want to be *just* friends." In this type of relationship being called a "friend" comes across as rejection, being pushed away from intimacy, perhaps a felt rejection of his masculinity. "I want to be just friends," was the signal that he was just dumped.

It seems that the distinction of being the friend of the Bridegroom can feel like a separation from both the Bridegroom and the Bride, and seems to frustrate that natural

---

Sponsi Ecclesiæ: The Priest as a Living Image of Jesus Christ the Bridegroom of the Church through the Evangelical Counsels, Dissertatio ad doctoratam (Rome: Angelicum, 2008); Griffin, Carter. *Why Celibacy?: Reclaiming the Fatherhood of the Priest* (Steubenville: Emmaus Road Publishing, 2019).

longing for spousal communion. And if the priest has decided to be honest in his prayer, he may notice an unpleasant movement of jealousy of the Bridegroom which if not dealt with can become resentment, depression, bitterness and spiritual sterility. He may accept, praise and defend celibacy for the sake of his priestly vocation, but there is no guarantee he will not resent the Lord for asking it of him.

The problem he may sense in the heart is that if he does not get to take the Bride for himself, he misses out on the uniqueness of her love, and of offering his own unique love to her. There is both a truth and a deception operating here. The truth is that living the mystery of friend of the Bridegroom, involves moments and even periods of feeling separated from both Bridegroom and Bride. The deception is if he decides to embrace this identity and place the desires of his heart for spousal consummation in the Lord's hands, Jesus somehow thwarts the possibility for his happiness: "He may be good to other people, but is not good to me. I may see his goodness toward others and he may even work that goodness through me as a priest. But I do not get to be the recipient of his goodness. I will be a witness but not a real participant." In the train of that deception a discouraging thought may arise: "Look at yourself, you are a real sucker, you have been left out in the cold and the joke is on you!" This understandable masculine response to being the friend of the Bridegroom perhaps can reveal a place of rebellion against the Lord in one's heart.

The free choice for celibacy lived out in a fallen human nature, therefore, often will involve wrestling with this identity. The promise of celibacy has a way of stretching the priest's desires, which in one sense enlarges them and makes them more worthy of Heaven, and in another sense just really hurts. It is important for the priest and the seminarian to be aware of and to sense the apparent dissonance within himself of these two dimensions of priestly identity. These are not simply two ideas to consider intellectually. They are a mysterious convergence of two realities that he is.

Having briefly indicated the difficulty of embracing the identity as friend of the Bridegroom, I would like to chart a course by not turning away from these painful movements in the heart but rather to bring them into imaginative prayer with these three great saints, so that these convergent mysteries can become more enfleshed in the heart. As will become apparent, this course cannot be charted without the Blessed Virgin Mary who plays an essential role not only in developing the priest's spousal and paternal love, but also in helping him embrace and live his identity as the friend of the Bridegroom.

These three men had moments when they were reminded that they were not the Bridegroom; one can even observe a physical distance from him. St. John the Baptist is told, "'Rabbi, he who was with you beyond the Jordan, to whom you bore witness, here he is, baptizing, and all are going to him'" (Jn. 3:26).[5] St. Joseph spent his entire married life under the same roof with his wife whom he must have loved deeply and who was perpetually a virgin. St. John the Apostle gazed upon the crucified Bridegroom at Calvary, and the Bridegroom gazed upon him. Yet this prophet, carpenter and fisherman are anything but impotent, frustrated men. By praying with these great men, the priest and seminarian can discover a way of addressing the sting felt in being the friend of the Bridegroom, and to embrace deeply and even joyfully of this crucial dimension of the priesthood.

St. John the Baptist: the Friend is the Best Man

The first and most explicit scriptural reference of our theme comes from the very lips of John the Baptist: "He who has the bride is the bridegroom; the friend of the bridegroom, who stands and hears him, rejoices greatly at the bridegroom's voice; therefore this joy of mine is now full" (Jn. 3:29). Immediately noticeable is the friend's lack of jealousy or resentment. In fact, he indicates that far from jealousy or resentment, being the friend of the Bridegroom is a wellspring of joy. It is utter joy for him to stand near to the Bridegroom and to hear his voice. John the Baptist declares his joy, moreover, precisely at the time when he would be tempted to be most jealous: when everyone is going over to Jesus.

John the Baptist's embrace of his identity as the Bridegroom's friend likely originated in his familiarity with Jesus and was joyful from the beginning (Lk. 1:44). The first meeting of the Bridegroom and his friend happen in the womb through the mediation of their mothers. The words from the mouth of the Blessed Virgin Mary carrying the future Bridegroom, stir the tiny heart of John the Baptist to leap for joy. Even before he was born, John the Baptist began to be attuned to the presence of the Bridegroom.

Presumably the relationship between the two cousins continued as they grew up. During this time the Lord perhaps taught his friend something that they both would share: being a son of the heavenly Father. Thus the Bridegroom's friend would be also his brother. Embracing one's identity with joy as the friend depends upon drinking deeply of the divine sonship which the Son has by nature and his friend has by adoption. The Bridegroom initiates his friend into the love of the Father so that the Father becomes his Father and calls him "son". The Bridegroom wants his friend to hear in the depth of his heart the voice of his Father, "You are my beloved son." In other words, the friend of the Bridegroom is made a son through the generosity of the Bridegroom. There is no rivalry on his part. Jesus is not threatened or resentful in opening up his sonship to others. In fact, he is so eager to share

---

[5] All Scripture quotations are taken from the *RSV*.

his sonship that he will suffer and die on the cross so that his friend might have a share in it. Rivalry can find no foothold where everything is bestowed in abundance.

As he grew in his familiarity with Jesus, this friend, fellow son and brother began to resemble him. When the friend begins his mission of preparing the way for the Bridegroom, the people initially think that the friend is the Bridegroom himself. He was so much like him that people were going to confuse them. In this moment, the friend of the Bridegroom, who was incredibly virtuous yet also lived with a fallen human nature, is given the possibility to usurp the place of the Bridegroom and to grasp the power for himself. When they ask, "Who are you?", how does John the Baptist respond? He states simply and emphatically, "I am not the Christ" (Jn. 1:20). Ponder the humility of the friend. He goes even further, "He must increase, but I must decrease" (Jn. 3:30)! In our weakness and sinfulness, does it not bother us to say, "I am not the Christ. He must increase; I must decrease"?

Nevertheless, by distinguishing himself from the Bridegroom, John the Baptist can do something remarkable. He can testify to him. He, the Apostle John writes, "came to testify to the light" (Jn. 1:7-8). A fellow son and brother, who resembles the Bridegroom yet refuses to usurp the Bridegroom for his own purposes, instead testifies to the Bridegroom: "Behold the Lamb of God!" (Jn. 1:29), and sends his followers after Jesus.

Here a new quality emerges regarding the friend of the Bridegroom. John the Baptist reveals the friend of the Bridegroom as the Bridegroom's *best man*.[6] The celibate priest, as the friend of the Bridegroom, is to be Jesus' best man for the wedding feast of the Lamb. What place does the best man have? He stands at the Bridegroom's side. He is the intimate friend of the Bridegroom. The best man is entrusted with the deepest and most intimate secrets of the Bridegroom's heart, especially his love for his Bride. When the Bridegroom wants to talk about his love, he tells his best man. He entrusts his best man with everything. Jesus loves John the Baptist so much that he says about him, "Truly, I say to you, among those born of women there has risen no one greater than John the Baptist" (Mt. 11:11).

As the best man, the friend helps to bring the Bridegroom and Bride together. One priest shared with me that one of the reasons he loves being a priest is that he helps to bring a soul and Jesus together. He facilitates the encounter. He gets to set them up so that they fall in love, and he gets to do it again and again, soul after soul. John the Baptist reveals this dimension clearly. He sees the Lord Jesus walking and exclaims to his disciples: "Behold, the Lamb of God!" He brought Andrew and John into the relationship with Jesus. The choice, therefore, to surrender certain deep desires in celibacy is an invitation to embrace his

---

[6] This insight was shared with me by Fr. David Nicgorski, O.M.V.

identity as the best man. "He who has the bride is the bridegroom; the friend of the bridegroom, who stands and hears him, rejoices greatly at the bridegroom's voice; therefore this joy of mine is now full."

However, what if the priest is struggling to accept this identity? He may still experience frustration or sadness to be "just" the best man. If he is honest, letting go of the jealousy and rivalry and embracing this special offer of friendship within celibacy will involve struggle in the gap between the intimacy surrendered and the intimacy yet to be gained. For most men, growth in maturity does not occur without fighting it out. Brothers and best friends, especially while growing up, often settle their differences by physically fighting. Here there is much exertion and perhaps anger, but both are a function of the love between the two friends. When we wrestle our friend we are exerting our power to best him, but not to really hurt him, let alone to kill him. So there are unspoken rules like no punching in the face (so Dad and Mom will not find out) and no dirty tricks. I think this is also true in some way on the level of the soul. Sometimes the best spiritual progress is made when we follow the example of our father Jacob (Gen. 32:22-31).[7] He inherited the divine promise in a sneaky way. The Lord wants Jacob to bear the promise but also intends that Jacob be a *good* bearer of the promise. So he ambushes Jacob in a real vulnerable moment and they wrestle. To become that man who will be Israel, Jacob had to fight it out with the Lord and even limp a bit afterward. In seeking to embrace this sometimes painful identity of being friend of the Bridegroom in his celibacy, the priest may find himself wrestling with God. Interior wrestling in imaginative prayer can open a man to new intimacy. How does one wrestle with the Lord? By continuing to show up to prayer and to engage the pain with Jesus, by being vulnerable and exerting himself in the depths of his heart. Then gradually the Lord creates something new and beautiful in the priest's celibacy – a stronger love, a greater freedom and a deepened joy. By wrestling with Jesus through the rebellion, the priest grows in the likeness of the Bridegroom and becomes a better friend.

One final thought on John the Baptist as the friend of the Bridegroom. The Bridegroom is so generous with his friend, that he even invites him to share his destiny in giving himself unto death for the Bride. Not only does he get to be familiar with the Bridegroom and the sound of his voice, to testify to him, to help bring the Bridegroom and Bride together, he also gets to shed his blood for him (Mk. 6:27-28). Such is the communion between the Bridegroom and his friend.

---

[7] This insight was shared with me by Fr. Casey Bailey, O.S.C.O.

St. Joseph: The Friend conquers temptation with Our Lady

John the Baptist's final testimony to the Bridegroom as his true friend in shedding his blood points to the cosmic battle that rages in this world and within one's own heart. When the Lord Jesus was tempted in the desert, he revealed this war in a clear light by exposing the real enemy and defeating him. Jesus said this enemy is "murderer from the beginning" and a "liar and the father of lies" (Jn. 8:44). It is not difficult to see lies, deception and violence swirling out there in the world, but one also may find lies, deception and violence swirling around in his own heart. We discover that we have yielded more territory to this enemy than we initially thought. We do not enter this battle on neutral turf but begin behind enemy lines as it were due to original sin and concupiscence. Even more territory is yielded through subsequent personal sin. Because the enemy is a liar and murder from the beginning, he never compromises and never stops. He will continue taking until he is opposed. In other words, the lost ground in our hearts must be re-conquered – inch by inch. In the priest's free choice of celibacy, the battle is over the purity of his heart.

Throughout the hidden life of Nazareth, there is much room to consider the influence Joseph had on our Lord and vice versa. The Father deliberately chose this man, who as a virgin-spouse lives the mystery of the friend of the Bridegroom, to be the example of manhood to the Incarnate Son. While being the Divine Son and therefore not inclined toward sin, Jesus had no need to learn from anyone how to defeat the evil one. Yet according to the logic of the Incarnation, Jesus not only learned in his human soul directly from his Divine Person but also from the ordinary process of human life.[8] Scripture, summing up the thirty plus years of the hidden life in Nazareth, says that Jesus "increased in wisdom and in stature" (Lk. 2:51-52).

In the home in Nazareth, Jesus in his human nature learned from Joseph how to be a man: how to treat the poor, how to work hard for a living, how to relate to women and how to confront evil. The Lord was so alike to his foster father that the townsfolk thought that he was Joseph's son by nature. Besides taking up his profession, Jesus would likely have also picked up his mannerisms, sayings, particular turns of phrases, maybe even the tone and cadence of voice. With regard to overcoming temptation, it is reasonable to believe, given Joseph's deep goodness, that he gave our Lord an example of how to confront evil as man, even a man who suffered from concupiscence and so who knew what it was like to have to have the territory of his heart re-conquered.

For the sake of our theme, let us just consider the first temptation of our Lord, the

---

[8] Cf. S.Th., III, q. 11.

temptation of the flesh. It is worth pondering how the Lord's temptations came to be recorded in Scripture. No disciple was there to witness the event. Jesus thought it so important for his followers to know that he defeated satan's temptations as a man that he must have told his apostles about it, and that is a very comforting thought. A striking aspect of this confrontation is the Lord's serenity. He is neither anxious nor upset by the fact that he is being tempted. It seems as if he is expecting it. Is not that serene attitude reminiscent of the impression given by Joseph? Yet in the face of evil this serenity is also ruthless. When surrounded by the temptation of the flesh, the Lord responds: "Man does not live on bread alone!" It is possible that the words he used were the same ones that Joseph used to conquer such temptations. After all, the Lord commanded his people in the Old Covenant: "And these words which I command you this day shall be upon your heart; and you shall teach them diligently to your children, and shall talk of them when you sit in your house, and when you walk by the way, and when you lie down, and when you rise" (Dt. 6:6-7).

Joseph, as friend of the Bridegroom, gave Jesus an example that man cannot live simply by trying to satisfy the drive for pleasure. Rather, a man lives from every word that comes from the mouth of God, the Word that comes forth from the virginal womb of his *wife*. He, as a virgin-spouse, shows us that a man can live on the love that comes to him through *her*. If a man can receive the Word, the Divine love that comes from the mouth of God through her, he can not only live, but flourish and conquer armies, climb mountains, journey to the ends of the earth, endure suffering, even be a faithful priest.

Joseph and Mary had a special relationship of living out marriage in virginity. As a true friend of the Bridegroom, he lived in perfect continence with her. He loves her knowing that she belongs totally to God. Yet he shows that being the friend of the bridegroom, far from being separated from Bridegroom and Bride, has everything to do with being *close to her*. His virginal-spousal love was shaped by her. It is reasonable to think that she, being totally given over to the Father, could tutor her husband in this special calling and be a formative, even essential, force in his ability to conquer any temptation, especially those of the flesh. In fact, her total consecration to God means that she could be more freely given over to Joseph in love within their special vocation.

Like John the Baptist, one finds in Joseph no jealousy, resentment or rebellion as the friend of the Bridegroom. Also, nothing indicates that he was anything but a real man. This dimension of his vocation, furthermore, was not lived in stoic isolation or immature bachelorhood, but in a deep, intimate and pure relationship with the Blessed Virgin Mary. She is a flesh and blood woman and a fierce lover of God, completely given over to deep, intimate and complete relationship with the Father, Son and Holy Spirit. I would doubt that she would be in love with and marry anyone but a real man who was striving to be holy.

One can only imagine how attractive she was to Joseph that they were already betrothed before St. Gabriel's arrival. In prayer, one might ask Joseph how he fell in love with her and how he loved her. One may consider how she told him about the Annunciation, and about his choice of taking her as his wife nonetheless, to risk everything and to set out into the unknown with great vulnerability and trust. He was not there for Jesus' conception, not even to witness the Holy Spirit overshadow her. Yet he loved her with all his heart knowing all the time that she belonged totally to God, which is the essence of celibate love.

It is important to meditate on the way he looked at her, the way she looked at him, the particular love she had for him and how she taught him by her purity, by the way she prayed and by her total dedication to the Father. Perhaps he dealt with temptations against chastity by simply looking to her. She, knowing him so well, perhaps could sense the agitation of his heart, and maybe draw near to him and place a reassuring hand in his shoulder to lift that good, natural yet fallen eros up into agape love of her. One only needs to gaze for a moment upon her and to be gazed upon by her. She has a particular gift in her presence and gaze to quiet a man's restless heart. That love serenely and ruthlessly eviscerates the temptation to lust.

From the example of Joseph, the friend of the Bridegroom can draw some conclusions for his own spiritual life. He need not be surprised, anxious or upset when temptations of the flesh come, but defeat them with the same serenity and ruthlessness of our Lord and his foster father springing from a love of Mary. Because of his fallen nature, the priest can expect that the battle will not be some quick, heroic charge to victory but rather more like a street fight – gritty, messy, appearing hopeless at times – and he may end up limping a bit like Jacob. Just as the Lord, as both God and man, did not rise from the dead and ascend to Heaven without his scars, the friend of the Bridegroom will have his as well. Moreover, he is expected neither to fight alone nor succeed on his own. Conquering sin as the friend of the Bridegroom means being close to our Lady, and allowing his manly heart to be loved intensely by her. When she puts her foot down in the friend of the Bridegroom's heart, the enemy is inevitably crushed.

St. John the Beloved: The Friend is at home with Our Lady

John the Baptist reveals how the friend of the Bridegroom is a son with the Bridegroom, his brother, his most trusted friend and even his best man. Joseph shows that the friend of the Bridegroom, as a virgin-spouse, lives in an intimate and pure relationship with the

Blessed Virgin Mary. It seems that these two lines of thought converge in John the Beloved and this convergence reveals something new regarding our theme.

I have nothing against renaissance artists except that often their depictions of John the Apostle remind me of a sissy. While he was young when called by Jesus to be an apostle, he most definitely was not a sissy. He was a fisherman. He ran with the likes of Peter, Andrew and his brother James. He was not afraid of conflict (Lk. 9:49). The Lord, perhaps tongue-in-cheek, named him a "son of thunder" (Mk. 3:17) because the zealous disciple thought those ignorant, hard-hearted Samaritans who refused Jesus ought to be taught a firm lesson (Lk. 9:54). He had the guts, at Peter's beckoning, to ask the Lord at the Last Supper who would betray him (Jn. 13:25). Most of all, when all the other apostles ran away, he stood near and watched his Lord be crucified, even meeting his gaze with his own eyes (Jn. 19:26). He saw the Lord Jesus breathe his last. He did not avert his eyes in horror as the spear went through the Lord's heart and witnessed the blood and water flow (Jn. 19:34-35). It is difficult to assess what kind of physical shape Peter was in, but John the Beloved out ran him to the tomb (Jn. 20:4). As with the other two, this friend of the Bridegroom is all man.

As we look at the life of the Beloved disciple, we can see that he was being formed as the friend of the Bridegroom all along. He was a follower of the Bridegroom's best man who directed him to Jesus. He must have also been familiar with Joseph through what Mary told him in what must have been their many conversations. He also knows that he is loved by the Bridegroom, referring to himself as "the disciple whom Jesus loved", and was able to lay on the Master's chest at the Last Supper (Jn. 13:13). This all bespeaks a deep familiarity between the Bridegroom and his best man.

Out of this familiarity and through the mystery of the cross, something new is revealed in this friend of the Bridegroom and for all future priests. At Calvary, John and Mary are standing near (Jn. 19:25). Our Lady, archetype of the Church, is in the midst of her agony. Present with her is the friend of the Bridegroom, one of his first priests, who at this moment is also participating in the suffering of the Bridegroom. Here we can speak of the relationship, even communion, between the two sides of the diptych, both Bridegroom and friend of the Bridegroom. Because he is the friend of the Bridegroom, he can be led into a participation of being the Bridegroom.

The Bridegroom's hand is transfixed to the wood of the Cross. As the sword of sorrow is being plunged into his mother's heart, he is unable to reach her. She is suffering profoundly yet his hand is nailed to the wood. What does he do? He *gazes* upon each of them. The priest, as a friend of the Bridegroom, is called to be the recipient of this gaze as John the Beloved. Are we man enough to stand near and meet the gaze of the crucified

Lord? At this most vulnerable moment for the Bridegroom, Jesus calls upon his friend, his best man, who is always at his side, whom he knows he can trust: "When Jesus saw his mother, and the disciple whom he loved standing near, he said to his mother, 'Woman, behold, your son!' Then he said to the disciple, 'Behold, your mother!' And from that hour the disciple took her to his own home" (Jn. 19:26-27).

The words comprise a mere two verses of Scripture, but contained within them is a mystery so powerful that can mean the difference between being a priest or not, between being a priest who is faithful to his promises or one who is not, between being a repentant priest who remains and seeks new fidelity or one who abandons his vocation, between being a priest who can connect with people or one who is superficial, cold or distant, between being a priest who uses the Bride for his own position and power and one who serves her as a loving husband, between being a joyful priest or a jaded, bitter one.

The Bridegroom's hand is nailed to the wood, so he asks his trusted friend to offer his hand to receive Mary. The friend of the Bridegroom is given the crucial task of receiving the Blessed Virgin Mary into his own, that is, as Pope Benedict XVI has interpreted the passage, receiving her "into the depths of his being".[9] The priest cannot hope to be a true friend of the Bridegroom or to be led into our participation into the reality of the Bridegroom without her. The Master commanded it from the cross.

His first word of command is to behold. After meeting his gaze, Jesus commands his beloved disciple to turn that gaze of love toward another. The Bridegroom's friend is told not simply to observe, but to behold, to gaze, to pay attention to, to be attuned to her. Behold her. Behold her eyes, her tears and her pierced heart. What does she need right now? She is sharing in his abandonment, and likely feels isolated in this dark night engulfed in the throes of a crushing grief. She needs his gaze and to feel his hand. Jesus tells her to look at his friend as she looks upon him, to love John as she loves her own Son. What is it like to gaze into her eyes in her deepest moment of need and vulnerability? What is it like to be gazed upon by her? What is it like for the priest to feel the squeeze of her hand as she is overtaken by these mystical labor pains? In an act of pure, celibate, agape love, this friend of the Bridegroom receives her. Within his life as a priest, she is to occupy the deepest center of his priestly and manly heart, and they are to remain inseparable companions for the rest of their days on earth and for all eternity.[10]

---

[9] Pope Benedict XVI, General Audience, 12 August 2009.

[10] The RSV translation offers an illuminating explanatory note about this verse: "Joseph must now have been dead," implying a close connection between these two friends of the Bridegroom through their relationship with Mary (*Revised Standard Version*, Catholic Edition [San Francisco:

Imagine what kind of relationship Calvary forged between John and Mary, and how this beautiful, deep relationship unfolded in the wake of the Resurrection and Ascension. Like Joseph, John could be tutored by her in this new life and learned to be attuned to her, her heart, her thoughts, her feelings, her desires. Her complete obedience to her Son meant that, for her part, she loved John fiercely and received him into her life. One could only imagine what it meant for John in his celibacy to be so thoroughly understood and loved by such a woman. Her pure feminine love fills his celibate masculine heart so much and he is to be so attuned to her that there is no longer any room at the center of this priest's heart for another feminine heart.

Implicit to receiving her into his own meant for John learning to be "at home" with her. Up until her Assumption, we assume that she lived with him, that she traveled, ate, conversed and prayed with him. Scripture says that our Lady knew how to ponder the mysteries of faith in her heart (Lk. 2:19). I would imagine she taught John how to ponder and meditate, and perhaps as a fruit of those lessons inspired his own Gospel. John as friend of the Bridegroom had to learn to be comfortable with her around and receive the pure and reassuring touches of affection and the looks of confidence and love.

Such a relationship indicates that the friend of the Bridegroom is no bachelor. Bachelorhood is completely inimical to the priesthood because it is completely inimical to the relationship that was created at Calvary. The priest in his rectory is asked to receive her into his own and attune himself to her presence. In receiving her, the priest finds a beautiful and powerful feminine response to the pain and restlessness of his manly heart. She wants to kiss that heart and draw it into her own. The restless heart of a celibate priest can find tranquility in hers. The frustration from being "just" a friend yields to a privileged relationship with her. Precisely because the priest is celibate and is the friend of the Bridegroom, Jesus establishes him in this special relationship with the Blessed Virgin Mary. He is invited to live the inner life of John, to give his love to her and be the recipient of hers. Moreover, he need not worry about opening himself up to her intense love because she is utterly pure.

As with Joseph, her love shapes his heart. All grace is Trinitarian and originates within the Trinity, but the Lord can bestow his grace however he wishes. He knows that perhaps certain parts of a man's heart are not open to, or cognizant of, grace coming in a masculine way in prayer. So he gives the graces to Mary who gives them a feminine shape, perfectly formed to fit a man's heart.[11] When the friend of the Bridegroom receives those feminine

---

Ignatius, 1966] 239).

[11] This insight was shared with me by Fr. Robert Geisinger, S.J.

graces, when she begins to walk the corridors, even the innermost sanctum, of a his heart his heart is soothed, calmed and becomes strong, confident and joyful.

The celibate priest is given this privileged relationship with her. He always comes home to her; he always has the complete attention of her heart; he always has a relationship to deepen. By cultivating an awareness of her presence and learning to be at home with her, celibacy can be transformed into something joyful and very powerful. Sin becomes more distasteful because she is shaping his desires. In a moment of loneliness or boredom, he would be less likely, for example, to go on a bad Internet site knowing she is at his side asking him to pay attention to her and to receive the love of her heart. The friend of the Bridegroom discovers in her a unique love from the greatest of women. Because her love is so pure and utterly chaste, he need not worry if she has intimate relationships with other priests. The power and beauty of celibate love is that it is universal and inclusive while never ceasing to be unique.

Conclusion

The identity of the priest as the friend of the Bridegroom points to an intimate communion with Christ, his dwelling in the priest and the priest in him. As he told his first priests on that first Holy Thursday: "If a man loves me, he will keep my word, and my Father will love him, and we will come to him and make our home with him" (Jn. 14:23), and in that intimate conversation with the Father, "I in them and you in me" (Jn. 17:23). By acknowledging the distinction between himself and Jesus, the priest is reminded ever so clearly that the power within him is never to be confused with his own self, but rather flows from the Divine Persons who dwell within his soul. Because he is not Jesus, Jesus can abide in him. The distinction indicated by friend of the Bridegroom opens up a space in the heart for this special indwelling of Christ in the priest, a place where the voice of the Bridegroom can resound and speak intimately to the priest's own heart and to others through him.

Furthermore, this dimension of the priest's identity finds its most complete meaning in the Blessed Virgin Mary. In this special place of a man's heart is where she is, where she walks, where she loves him and where a priest's restless heart finds a home because as the friend of the Bridegroom he is at home with her. The moments of felt loneliness and pain, which can and do happen, occur within the context of intimacy both with the Bridegroom and with the Blessed Virgin Mary. She helps priests become true friends of the Bridegroom, and by becoming a true friend, the priest is led to participate in the reality of the Bridegroom and grow into the very likeness of the Bridegroom.

Nevertheless the appropriation of this mystery will often involve struggle. Grace, time and perseverance are needed to embrace and be defined by this mystery. The graces received by the interior senses in prayer have the power to heal the exterior senses.[12] Perhaps we have been raised on too many movies where we see a couple heroic acts by the protagonist which brings the drama to a swift resolution. Real life is so different. It is more like a street fight or a marathon. The daunting prospect of celibacy, to use a scriptural image, often feels like having to walk on water. John the Baptist, Joseph and John the Beloved invite the priest to strike out where the world and our own fallen nature says "Impossible! There is nothing there but cold, lonely darkness." Over such cold, dark waters, Jesus beckons, "Come!" Our Lady also says, "Come! I want to know you, to love you, to live with you all your days as a priest in this world and forever." She asks the celibate priest to receive her into his own, and do what he never thought would be possible or even desirable. He also need not be surprised if, as his priesthood unfolds with her, he is led into the very likeness of Christ, even to the point of sharing the same destiny and shedding his blood. The Church's history is full of many such friends who left this life having taken on the likeness of the Bridegroom.

A version of this article was published in *Homiletic & Pastoral Review* (Vol. 111, Issue 10, 2011) under the title "The Priest as Friend of the Bridegroom." It is published here with the permission of the publisher and author.

Prayer

Holy Spirit, please strengthen your gift of courage with me so that I might receive the penetrating gaze of Mary. Help me not be bound by shame and fear. Set me free. Let my heart be set ablaze in love by courageously receiving Mary's presence into my home, Amen.

Practicum Reflection Questions for Formators

1. Have I wrestled with Jesus through rebellion in imaginative prayer, opening my heart to new intimacy and deeper friendship with Him?

---

[12] Cf. Arminjon, Blaise. *The Cantata of Love*, trans. Nelly Marans (San Francisco: Ignatius, 1988) 147.

2. Have I experienced being the intimate friend and best man of Jesus as Bridegroom in the joy of introducing others to Him? Please describe. Am I willing to ask for the desire to taste this type of intimacy and joy?

3. Am I in a stoic relationship with the Blessed Virgin Mary? Am I willing to ask for an on-going tasting in faith of her intimate love for me, similar to the love she poured into the hearts of Joseph and John the Beloved? If this is already being enjoyed please describe and how best you can give witness to this gift.

4. What is it like to gaze into Mary's eyes (like John the Beloved) in her deepest moment of need at the cross with Jesus? What is it like to be gazed upon by her? Have I received Mary into my home to live with me? Please describe.

Suggested Resources

1. Pope Benedict XVI, *Deus Caritas Est*.
2. Deacon James Keating, "Surrendering to the Healing Power Of Christ's Own Chastity."
3. Carol Houselander, *The Reed Of God*.

Chapter Four

MARY AS THE BRIDAL COMPANION OF THE PRIEST

Fr. Evan Koop, STL, S.T.D. (candidate)

Rev. Evan S. Koop, S.T.L., is a priest of the Archdiocese of Saint Paul and Minneapolis, MN, and a member of the faculty of the Saint Paul Seminary School of Divinity. He is currently pursuing doctoral studies in Rome at the Pontifical Gregorian University, writing on the Mariology of Matthias Joseph Scheeben. Prior to his time in Rome, he served as spiritual director at Saint John Vianney College Seminary in Saint Paul, MN. Fr. Koop is a member of the diocesan priestly fraternity of The Companions of Christ.

Not long ago the members of a community of diocesan priests from the archdiocese of Saint Paul and Minneapolis, the Companions of Christ, held a series of meetings to discern more clearly the essence of the charism of priestly fraternity that God had given them. As they prayed, crowded together into the small chapel of a Marian shrine surrounded by the heavy winter snows, the brothers became increasingly aware of the gentle but insistent presence of Mary in their midst.

Gradually, they began to grasp more clearly a deep truth that until then had been dimly perceived but unexpressed among them: that Mary wished to accompany them no less intimately than she had accompanied the first apostles at Pentecost; that it was she who, better than any other, could teach them how to be conformed to the image of their Master; that she was the Woman who stood ready to receive their sacrificial gift of self; that she offered herself to them as the indispensable helpmate and companion of their priestly life; in short, that she who was their mother in the order of grace was also, by virtue of their ordination, the human face of their bride, the Church.

It was thus a joyful discovery when, in the course of writing their *Rule*, the Companions of Christ found that the name they had given themselves was also a title that the Church's tradition had lovingly bestowed upon Mary: she is truly the *socia Christi*, the first and most perfect Companion of Christ. What the brothers had first sensed in prayer was now confirmed by theological study: all that Mary was for Jesus—mother and queen, sister and bride—she desires to be for those who are called to share in the priesthood of her Son.

The essential insights gained by the Companions of Christ into the intimate relationship that Mary desires to have with all priests are contained in the sixth and final chapter of their *Rule*, "The Blessed Virgin Mary: Companion of Christ and Our Companion". By way of introduction to that chapter, reproduced below, we begin by offering an extended theological reflection upon Mary's role as the companion both of Christ and of every priest—giving special attention to its bridal dimension—in the hope that it will contribute to a renewed understanding of priestly celibacy as a privileged expression of the priest's identity as a chaste bridegroom and spiritual father.

a.   Some Theological Preliminaries

With roots that stretch back to the patristic era, the Marian title *socia* was used increasingly in the Christian West from the Middle Ages onwards, and was ultimately enshrined in the Marian teaching of the Second Vatican Council.[1] Meaning a feminine "companion", "associate", "partner", *socia* serves to denote Mary's intimate association with the person of Christ and her free cooperation in his work, most often with clear spousal overtones.[2] As it is often understood as an allusion to woman's role in the original creation as man's *adiutorium simile sibi* ("It is not good that the man should be alone; I will make a helper fit for him," Gen. 2:18), *socia Christi*, when applied to Mary, is evocative of her identity as the New Eve and the type of the Church, the bride of Christ. Mary's status as the companion of Christ, in turn, becomes a fruitful image for her relationship to all priests, who may look to her as the most perfect icon of their bride, the Church, and thus as the woman most personally and intimately associated with them in their life and ministry.

The use of spousal language to describe Mary's relationship both to Christ and to his priests can sometimes elicit a certain discomfort and even resistance among those not accustomed to it—not least among priests themselves! After all, how can one woman be understood, in any sense at all, as standing in *both* a maternal and bridal relation toward the

---

[1] SECOND VATICAN COUNCIL, Dogmatic Constitution on the Church *Lumen gentium*, §61: "The Blessed Virgin was on this earth the virgin Mother of the Redeemer, and above all others and in a singular way the generous associate [*generosa socia*] and humble handmaid of the Lord."

[2] See M. O'CARROLL, "Socia: The Word and the Idea in Regard to Mary", *Ephemerides Mariologicae* 25 (1975), 337-357.

same person? Isn't this all rather strange, not to say Freudian? In answer to these legitimate questions, it must be pointed out that the conceptual tension one senses in the use of such terms is a necessary result of the inadequacy of human language to exhaustively describe the intellectual content of divine mysteries. While analogies can help to disclose certain truths about the mysteries of faith, they will always fall short of the full reality they seek to express.[3] In the present case, the bridal analogy—so dear to both Scripture and Tradition—is being employed to illuminate Mary's relationship to the mystery of Christ in his Incarnation, on the one hand, and to the mystery of the priest in his sacramental character, on the other.

Is not Mary, above all, a mother—the physical mother of Christ and the spiritual mother of the priest? It is undoubtedly in her maternal aspect that Mary is first presented to the Christian consciousness. In the Gospels she is referred to simply as the "mother" of Jesus far more frequently than she is called by her own name (cf. Matt. 1:18, 2:13, 12:16; Mark 3:31; Luke 1:43, 8:19; John 2:1-3, 6:42, 19:25-27), such that her maternity may almost be said to constitute her personal identity. Through his humanity Christ is indeed the true Son of Mary, and she is his true and natural mother—in the most literal sense of the word. In order to come nearer to grasping the profound mystery of Mary's relationship to Christ, however, it must be remembered that she is not the mother of a mere man, but of the *God-man*. For this reason, the concept of maternity can in no way exhaustively describe Mary's relationship to Christ, since in this case, unlike every other instance of human motherhood, the Son is already a pre-existent divine Person. It is he who takes the initiative to enter into a most intimate spiritual and physical union with Mary, and who chooses to elicit her free consent in order to be clothed with her flesh[4]. Seen from the perspective of Christ's divinity, therefore, Mary's relationship with her Son is best understood in spousal terms, and she is

---

[3] As the Fourth Lateran Council (1215) declared, "For between Creator and creature no similitude can be expressed without implying a greater dissimilitude" (DH 806).

[4] Cf. M.J. SCHEEBEN, *Mariology*, vol. I, trans. T.L.M.J. GEUKERS (St. Louis, MO: B. Herder Book Co., 1946), 189: "This supernatural, spiritual union with the divine person cannot be set forth more simply or clearly or with more regard to reality than through the expression *matrimonium divinum* or *connubium Verbi* in the strictest sense of the words. It is a relation which, with regard to God, forms the highest and most complete association conceivable between a created person with Himself […]. Thus understood, this union includes, in accordance with the nature of marriage, a solidarity of both persons in an organic whole, in which they have grown together, and also a mutual belonging to and clothing of both persons. Mary, as united with the Logos, is taken complete possession of by Him; the Logos, as infused and implanted in her, gives Himself to her and takes her to Himself as partner and helper, in the closest, strictest, and most lasting community of life."

thereby revealed as the "bride of God" in person, the one woman in whom humanity's bridal consent to the divine covenant is most fully realized (cf. Hos. 2:16-25; Jer. 2:1-2; Is. 62:4-5; Eph. 5:22-33; Rev. 21-22, etc.).[5] Thus, far from being the result of a confused religious psychology, Mary's maternal-spousal relationship to Jesus is a direct consequence of his human-divine constitution: the irreducible duality of *natures* in the person of Christ inexorably produces a duality of *relations* in the person of Mary. An acknowledgment of Mary's simultaneous role as both mother and bride of Christ is therefore at the service of an acknowledgement of the full reality of the union of humanity and divinity in Christ.

Priests, by analogy with Christ, likewise experience a certain irreducible duality in their relationship to Mary, though obviously for very different reasons. With respect to their personal constitution, of course, priests remain—as is only too apparent to all who know them!—purely, even distressingly human. Yet, in the realm of their sacramental identity, priests are placed in a uniquely multi-valent relationship with respect to Christ and his Church, a reality which in turn finds an echo in their relationship with Mary. By virtue of his baptism the priest becomes a member of the Body of the Christ, inhabiting a kind of *immanent* space within the Church; by virtue of his priestly ordination, however, the priest becomes an icon and agent of Christ the Head, called to take up a kind of *transcendental* position toward the Church as an *alter Christus*.[6]

With regard to the first and most fundamental aspect of his sacramental identity, therefore, the priest is (and will always remain) a baptized member of the bride of Christ, and in this respect Mary relates to him above all as his spiritual *mother*, the one who teaches

---

[5] Cf. I. DE LA POTTERIE, *Mary in the Mystery of the Covenant*, trans. B. Buby (New York: St Pauls, 1992), 265: "From a biblical point of view, the fundamental meaning of the mystery of Mary resides in her spousal and maternal roles: she is mother of Jesus and mother of the disciples; but to her relationship with Christ is added another dimension, her role as Spouse: she, "the Woman", the Daughter of Zion, is the Spouse of Christ, as we have already seen above [*ibid.*, 23-39, 193-242, etc.]. Yet, how surprising the number of theologians [and, we might add, priests] still hesitating to acknowledge this! They question how Mary can be, at one and the same time, mother of Jesus and his Spouse? Obviously, this reality is only possible on two different planes. As an individual person, she is the mother of Jesus; in her symbolic and representative role (as Daughter of Zion) she becomes his Spouse and his collaborator in the work of salvation. There should be no hesitation before this truth, for it is clearly found in the Scriptures."

[6] In this sense, if we may be permitted to borrow the more technical vocabulary that first arose in the field of Mariology, we may speak of the priest as bearing an "ecclesiotypical" and "christotypical" aspect, respectively. Cf. M. O'CARROLL, *Theotokos: A Theological Encyclopedia of the Blessed Virgin Mary* (Eugene, OR: Wipf and Stock Publishers, 2000), 100-101.

him how to associate himself personally and intimately with Christ and his redemptive work. With regard to his sacramental ordination to the priesthood, on the other hand, the priest becomes a "living image of Jesus Christ, the Spouse of the Church,"[7] and thus glimpses in Mary the person of his spiritual *bride*, the feminine companion and helpmate who responds with a bridal *fiat* to his spousal self-gift to the Church. We may identify a scriptural icon of Mary's twofold relationship to the priest as both mother and bride in the mysterious exchanges between Christ, Mary, and John on Calvary (cf. John 19:25-27). Like the beloved disciple, the priest beholds Mary as a spiritual "mother" who introduces him into the mystery of Christ's sacrificial self-offering on the cross and teaches him how to receive this saving gift into his heart. But inasmuch as the priest, by virtue of his ordination, has been sacramentally conformed to the Victim of Calvary, he also finds himself with Christ on the cross, and from this perspective he is enabled to behold Mary as the "Woman" who represents the bride to whom he gives himself in spousal love.

Neither dimension of the priest's sacramental identity can ever simply be collapsed into the other, for even as he acts *in persona Christi capitis* he must also recognize himself as a member of the *corpus Christi mysticum*. Given this fact, it is not surprising to note that many priests experience a certain indefinable ambivalence—even, at the limit, an intolerable tension—in their vocation, with the resulting temptation to forget or deny one aspect of their sacramental identity so as to seek refuge in the easy intelligibility of an exclusive focus on the other. To succumb to such a temptation always constitutes a spiritual disaster, for the priest himself no less than the Church as a whole. The priest who so identifies with Christ the Head that he no longer retains a sense of himself as a member of the bridal Church, whose most fruitful activity consists in *receiving* the gift of redemption, will inevitably fall into a sterile activism in his life and ministry, embracing that faith in self-redemption that is "the specifically masculine madness of our secularized age".[8] Rather than representing the person of Christ the Bridegroom, such a priest ends up usurping his place (cf. John 3:29). Of course, it is equally possible for the priest to resist at all costs his configuration to Christ the Priest and Victim, a resistance often cloaked with a self-effacing insistence on his solidarity with the other members of the Church. His sterility is that of the bachelor or the hireling (cf. John 10:12-13), the man who has become so accustomed to passivity and self-seeking that he has effectively deadened in himself both the desire and the ability to lay down his life for the bride.

---

[7] JOHN PAUL II, Apostolic Exhortation *Pastores dabo vobis* (March 25, 1992), §22.

[8] G. VON LE FORT, *The Eternal Woman: The Timeless Meaning of the Feminine* (San Francisco: Ignatius Press, 2010), 18.

A mature and healthy priestly identity, therefore, requires that *both* the priest's distinction from and union with Christ the Head be held together in an inseparable harmony. Mary, in her dual role as spiritual mother and bride of the priest, offers him an irreplaceable point of personal crystallization in this ongoing work of integration. To refuse to acknowledge either facet of her unique relationship with the priest is to attempt to dissolve the tension that defines his sacramental identity as such. While a one-sided emphasis on the bridal dimension of Mary's relationship to the priest would threaten to obscure his baptismal identity as a member of the Church, the bride of Christ, an exclusive attention to the maternal dimension of Mary's relationship to the priest tends to inhibit the full development of his priestly configuration to Christ the Head and Bridegroom of the Church. Both excesses—the over-identification of the priest solely with Christ or solely with the members of the Church—have been operative in the life of priests at various moments in the Church's history, and if the former was perhaps the predominant tendency in an earlier age, the latter is arguably the greater temptation for many priests today. If, therefore, it is desired that priests rediscover their sacramental identity as bridegrooms of the Church and fathers of souls, especially in the gift of their chaste celibacy, then it is likewise necessary to recover a sound understanding of Mary's identity as *bride*—the bride of Christ, and the bride of the priest.

b.   Mary's Bridal Relationship to Christ

Since the priest's relationship with Mary is modeled on that of Christ, we must briefly sketch the outlines of the latter, with special attention to its spousal aspect. The Fathers of the Church, inspired by the frequent use of the spousal analogy in Scripture, were fond of speaking of the mystery of the Incarnation as a marriage between humanity and divinity. According to this image, at least in its earlier expressions, it is the human nature of Christ himself that plays the bridal role, while Mary, or her womb, is understood as the *thalamus*, the "bridal chamber" (cf. Ps. 19:5), in which Christ's humanity is intimately wedded to its Bridegroom, the divine person of the Son.[9] But, as the Fathers knew well, Mary is clearly presented in the Scriptures at the Annunciation not as a mere passive instrument or inert substrate, but as a free, responsible agent: this is a "bridal chamber" who is herself a member of the bride to be wed, and who is asked to give her consent on behalf of all humanity to its

---

[9] See J.M. BOVER, "Tanquam sponsus procedens de thalamo suo," *Estudios Eclesiásticos* 4 (1925), 59-73.

espousal with God.[10] In the moment of the Incarnation, therefore, Mary not only *represents* the Church as bride, but *is* the bridal Church in person, "the Church at the source".[11] Thus it was natural that Mary, too, should begin to emerge in the developing Christian imagination as the personal bride of God—and even of Christ himself.[12]

Modern studies of Mary's biblical profile as the fulfillment of Israel, the covenantal spouse of the Lord, only serve to strengthen this intuition.[13] At the Annunciation, Mary is invited by the angel to "rejoice" (*chaïré*, Luke 1:28) and is assured of God's presence with her, just as the "Daughter of Zion" was told by the prophets to rejoice because "the Lord is in your midst" (Zeph. 3:14-15). At Cana, Mary takes the role of the bride at the side of Christ, the messianic Bridegroom, and her command to the servants, "Do whatever he tells you," (John 2:5)—her final words as recorded in the Gospels—serves as an eloquent summation of Israel's spousal adherence to God in the covenant enacted at Mt. Sinai: "All that the LORD has spoken, we will do!" (Ex. 19:7). Seen in this light, Christ's mysterious words to Mary at Cana (cf. John 2:4) take on a new significance: while the "hour" of consummation is "not yet," nevertheless he recognizes her as the "Woman" whom the Father has willed to share in it with him.[14] The cross, therefore, reveals itself as Mary's

---

[10] Cf. THOMAS AQUINAS, *Summa Theologiae* III, q. 30, art. 1: "In order to show that there is a certain spiritual wedlock between the Son of God and human nature [...] in the Annunciation the Virgin's consent was besought in lieu of that of the entire human nature [*loco totius humanae naturae*]."

[11] Cf. J. RATZINGER – H.U. VON BALTHASAR, *Mary—The Church at the Source*, trans. A. Walker (San Francisco: Ignatius Press, 2005).

[12] See D. FLANAGAN, "The Image of the Bride in the Earlier Marian Tradition", *Irish Theological Quarterly* 27 (1960), 111-124.

[13] For the following, see I. DE LA POTTERIE, *Mary in the Mystery of the Covenant*, 54-58, 223-225, 253-255. Cf. J. RATZINGER, *Daughter Zion*, esp. 9-29.

[14] Thus Bl. John Henry Newman insightfully observes, "In saying the hour was not yet come, [Christ] implied that the hour would come, when He would have 'to do with her,' and she might ask and obtain from Him miracles. Accordingly, [...] that hour had come, when He said upon the Cross, '*Consummatum est*,' and, after this ceremonial estrangement of years, He recognized His Mother and committed her to the beloved disciple," (*A Letter Addressed to the Rev. E.B. Pusey, D.D., on Occasion of His Recent Eirenicon of 1864*, in ID., *Certain Difficulties Felt by Anglicans in Catholic Teaching*, vol. II [London: Longmans, Green and Co., 1865], 149-150). Likewise, St. Irenaeus of Lyon interprets Mary's request at Cana as the expression of her desire to share in his messianic cup: "With Him is nothing incomplete or out of due season, just as with the Father there is nothing incongruous. For all these things were foreknown by the Father; but the Son works them out at the proper time in perfect

"hour", too, the hour of her sorrow when she labors with Christ to give birth to the Church (cf. John 16:21; Rev. 12:2).

It is first of all as a mother that Mary presents herself to our gaze on Calvary, where we find her "standing by the cross of Jesus" (John 19:25), "uniting herself with a maternal heart with His sacrifice, and lovingly consenting to the immolation of this Victim which she herself had brought forth."[15] But, as the parallels with the Cana scene make clear, at the crucifixion Mary also exercises a bridal cooperation in Christ's redemptive work. In fact, there can be no higher instance of spousal love than that which united the hearts of Jesus and Mary on Calvary.[16] This is the "hour" of the messianic nuptials, when the Bridegroom lays down his life for his bride, the Church (cf. Eph. 5:25). In the person of Mary, the "Woman" associated with him in his victory over the evil one (cf. Gen. 3:15), this bride opens her heart to receive the grace of redemption through his gift of self. Thus conceived, we begin to see why it was *only* a woman, such as Mary, who could so intimately participate in Christ's sacrifice on the cross, for precisely in her feminine receptivity she is able to complement his redemptive activity in the most fitting way imaginable.[17] As a bride, Mary is

---

order and sequence. This was the reason why, when Mary was urging (Him) on to (perform) the wonderful miracle of the wine, and was desirous before the time to partake of the cup of emblematic significance, the Lord, checking her untimely haste, said, 'Woman, what have I to do with you? My hour is not yet come.' — waiting for that hour which was foreknown by the Father," (*Adversus haereses* III, 16, 7, in A. ROBERTS – *al.* (eds.), *Ante-Nicene Fathers*, vol. I [Grand Rapids, MI: Eerdmans, 1973], 443).

[15] SECOND VATICAN COUNCIL, Dogmatic Constitution on the Church *Lumen gentium*, §58.

[16] The perfection of marriage consists, as Thomas teaches, in "the inseparable union of souls, by which husband and wife are pledged by a bond of mutual affection that cannot be sundered" (*ST* III, q. 29, art. 2). The essence of spousal love, therefore, consists in an intimate spiritual communion that is expressed through mutual self-donation (cf. K. WOYJTŁA, *Love and Responsibility*, trans. H.T. WILLETTS [San Francisco: Ignatius Press, 1993], 96).

[17] On the basis of a prophecy of Isaiah ("I have trodden the wine press alone, and of the peoples there was not a man [*vir*] with me," Is. 63:3), St. Ambrose famously declared, "Jesus, for the redemption of all, had no need of assistance" (*Expositio Evangelii secundum Lucam* 10, 132, cited in L. GAMBERO, *Mary and the Fathers of the Church: The Blessed Virgin Mary in Patristic Thought* [San Francisco: Ignatius Press, 1999], 203). But it is nevertheless important to point out that the scriptural text does not say, "there was not a *woman* with me". While, therefore, the completion of Christ's sacrificial death through a second bloody death on the part of a fellow combatant is indeed to be excluded, Mary cooperates with Christ not by the shedding of her own blood but by her compassionate union with his sufferings. As such her redemptive activity at the cross offers the

not present on Calvary in order to supplement or duplicate Christ's redemptive work, but to be intimately joined with *his* priestly offering through her compassion and intercession, such that "the activity of the Bridegroom and bride appear, not as next to each other, but in each other."[18] In the spousal union of Jesus and Mary at the cross the mystery of redemption reveals itself in its full beauty: the shedding of the blood of the Lamb draws forth the mourning of the dove, the activity of the Priest and Bridegroom is met by the receptivity of the bride, and the authority of the Head is echoed in the affection of the heart.[19]

c.   Mary's Bridal Relationship to the Priest

If Mary plays such an integral role in Christ's mission as his spiritual bride, it should not surprise us that the priest, too, will find it salutary and even necessary to look upon her as the woman whom God has willed to place at his side as helpmate and companion in every aspect of his life and ministry. The priest's bride is indeed the Church in the totality of her mystery; but a man can love a collectivity only with difficulty, since spousal love, to be truly real and personal, longs to be given not to an object but to a subject. Understanding himself as given to *everyone in the abstract*, the priest can easily feel and act as if he were given to *no one in particular*, thus failing to faithfully represent the love of Christ the Bridegroom in the world. Mary, as the personal fulfillment of bridal Israel and the type of the Church, is able unlike any other to represent for the priest that feminine "thou" to whom he can and must entrust his human and Christian "I", thus bringing to completion his masculine gift of self in chaste celibacy. For God has created man in such a way that he "cannot fully find himself except through a sincere gift of himself,"[20] a fact which is nowhere

---

perfect icon of the essentially feminine receptivity of the human creature toward the grace of God.

[18] M.J. SCHEEBEN, *Mariology*, vol. II, trans. T.L.M.J. GEUKERS (St. Louis, MO: B. Herder Book Co., 1947), 219.

[19] Cf. M.J. SCHEEBEN, *Mariology*, vol. II, 216: "This form of Mary's cooperation can be described, clearly and unequivocally, by consistently using the characteristic language of the Sacred Scriptures and the Fathers. It is thus expressed: the redemption of the world is effected, or the grace of salvation was obtained, by the blood of the Lamb as the ransom or purchase price, and by the murmur of the Dove as a prayer which is sanctified by the Holy Ghost, and offered in the name of the redeemed for the acceptance of the ransom; or also, on the one hand, it is the activity of the head and the authority of the priest, on the other, the disposition of the heart and the supplication of the bride."

[20] SECOND VATICAN COUNCIL, Pastoral Constitution on the Church in the Modern World *Gaudium et spes*, §24.

more evident than in the realm of human sexuality. In his humanity the priest, too, will experience this Law of the Gift as an ineluctable fact of his embodied existence, and like Adam in the garden this exigency of his nature will remain frustrated and incomprehensible until he glimpses ("at last!") the feminine face, the answering word, that returns his searching gaze with understanding and love (cf. Gen. 2:19-24).[21]

The priest's vocation to sacrificial self-offering in union with Christ the Bridegroom, therefore, must first of all be understood within this anthropological perspective. Precisely in his masculinity the priest already discovers within himself a desire for self-gift, a longing to be received. This longing, moreover, is such that it will inevitably find expression in one way or another: either he will entrust his heart to his bride, finding in her an "unfailing prize" (Prov. 31:11), or, like Samson, he will give himself away to a paramour, suffering the loss of his spiritual strength (cf. Jgs. 16:4-21). In order to find fulfillment, both as a priest and as a man, the priest must thus be able to say, in and through his chaste celibacy, "This is my body which is given for you" (Luke 22:19). But he must say this concretely to *someone*—to Mary—if he can ever hope to say it, intelligibly and credibly, to *everyone*. To her alone can the priest truly say, in the words of the bridegroom, "There are sixty queens and eighty concubines, and maidens without number. My dove, my perfect one, *is only one*" (Sgs. 6:8-9).

Many priests may find themselves blushing at the thought of taking Mary as their spiritual bride. Even once they have been assured that such a relationship is not to be understood in a crassly physical or excessively sentimental sense, still the thought of their own unworthiness may prompt them to cry out to her in shame, "Depart from me, for I am a sinful man!" (cf. Lk. 5:8). If so, they are in good company. Joseph, too, knew what it was to be called to a task for which he must have judged himself wholly inadequate: to love and honor this immaculate bride, Mary, whose dignity far surpassed his own, and to protect and care for the divine child growing within her. Even to have been invited to be a part of this

---

[21] Cf. H.U. VON BALTHASAR, *Theo-Drama: Theological Dramatic Theory*, III. *The Dramatis Personae: The Person in Christ*, trans. G. HARRISON (San Francisco: Ignatius Press, 1992), 284-285: "The first Adam calls nature's animals by name, and as he names them, so they are called. But no adequate response comes to him from them. [...] If man is the word [*Wort*] that calls out, woman is the answer [*Ant-Wort*] that comes to him at last (in the *end*). The two are related and ordered to each other. [...] Man and woman are face to face. Here their equal rank is given even more emphasis: man looks around him and meets with an answering gaze that turns the one-who-sees into the one-who-is-seen. [...] Thus the woman, who is both 'answer' and 'face', is not only man's delight: she is the help, the security, the home man needs; she is the vessel of fulfillment specially designed for him."

Holy Family, to say nothing of being asked to *lead* it—this was surely enough to fill Joseph's heart with fear and a desire to flee, to send Mary away quietly rather than presume to "unveil" her great mystery. Yet the Lord, seeing his weakness and yet still choosing him, reassured him, "Do not be afraid to take Mary as your wife" (Matt. 1:20). In that moment Joseph's fear gave way to awe, to wonder and gratitude, and to a joyful surrender to his own vocation to be wholly consecrated to God.[22]

Joseph's humble obedience to God's will that he take Mary into his home, even in the face of his urge to remove himself from the discomfiting glare of the divine mystery at work in her, offers an example to every priest who, out of an exaggerated sense of shame, is tempted to draw back from relating to Mary as his spiritual bride. He need have no fear that such a relationship could possibly compromise his celibate chastity; to the contrary, he will only find it strengthened. Do not faithful spouses inevitably come to resemble one another, sharing the same interests, the same pastimes, the same loves? So also with the priest and Mary. As he lovingly gazes upon her, he will always find her gazing on the Lord, and slowly but surely her desire to live in total dedication to God, in body and soul, will become his own. The priest who thus refuses to flee from Mary, and who chooses to allow her to see and love him in his unworthiness each day, will learn from her the invaluable lesson of how to resist yielding to fear and shame in his daily ministry, where he is constantly called to come into intimate contact with a bride, the Church, of whom he must feel himself profoundly unworthy. Conversely, the priest who, through a false humility, shrinks from intimacy with Mary, will find himself—*for the very same reasons*—refusing to respond to God's choice of him, in spite of his unworthiness, to love and serve the Church as her bridegroom.

---

[22] This interpretation of the "annunciation" to Joseph follows that of St. Bernard of Clairvaux: "Why did he wish to leave her? Listen, now, no longer to my opinion, but to that of the Fathers. The reason why Joseph wished to leave Mary is the same for which Peter distances himself from the Lord by saying, *depart from me, Lord, for I am a sinner;* this is also the reason why the centurion left his home while saying: *Lord, I am not worthy that you should come under my roof.* And so, Joseph, considering himself unworthy and a sinner, said to himself that such a great person, whose marvelous and superior dignity he admired, could not deign to live together with him. He saw, with sacred astonishment, that she bore a special quality of the divine presence, and while not being able to understand this mystery, he wished to leave her" (*Hom. "Super missus est"*, 2, 14, cited in I. DE LA POTTERIE, *Mary in the Mystery of the Covenant*, 103-104). In his extensive exegesis of this Gospel scene, de la Potterie concludes that Joseph's reasoning for wishing to send Mary away could be summarized thus: "God is here at work. I must let him act; I must take myself away from this" (*ibid.*, 80).

What did Mary offer Joseph in turn, and what does she offer the priest who receives her as his spiritual bride and allows her entry into the most intimate details of his personal life? It is well known how necessary for a man is the trust and confidence of his bride to inspire him to a magnanimity of spirit—a gift that only a woman can give him. How precious it must have been for Joseph, finding himself entrusted with the monumental task of providing for the welfare of Mary and Jesus, to glimpse the look of support in his wife's eyes. As he took those first steps to lead them into an uncertain future, her look of belief and encouragement carried the promise, "Where you go I will go, and where you lodge I will lodge; your people shall be my people" (cf. Ruth 1:16). In moments of anxiety and terror, through years of strenuous labor and humble fidelity to his duties, Joseph found in Mary a refreshing oasis of love and support.

The priest, no less than Joseph, has need of the encouragement and counsel of his bride in difficult moments, of her comfort in his sorrows and her companionship in his joys. While he will certainly find these to some extent in the affection of the people he serves and in the support of his brother priests, no one can offer this to him as perfectly as Mary. Only of her can the priest say, as Solomon did of wisdom, "I determined to take her to live with me, knowing that she would give me good counsel and encouragement in cares and grief. […] When I enter my house, I shall find rest with her, for companionship with her has no bitterness, and life with her has no pain, but gladness and joy" (Wis. 8:9,16).

But it is above all when the priest encounters the cross in his life that he will feel most keenly the need of Mary's bridal companionship. As he experiences the pain of being misunderstood and suspected by the world around him; as he feels himself failing under the weight of his own sins and weaknesses; as he suffers the wounds of rejection and even persecution at the hands of those he has come to serve; as he calls out to the Lord in anguish, "I am not able to carry all this people alone, the burden is too heavy for me" (Num. 11:14)—it is then that Mary will draw near to him. Just as Jesus' eyes found rest in the loving countenance of Mary as he scanned the angry crowd from the cross, so the priest can be sure of discovering in his darkest hours that Mary desires to "be the one" to offer him comfort and consolation when he finds none (cf. Ps. 69:20),[23] and to stand by him faithfully in his trials (cf. Luke 22:28). It is this experience of Mary's bridal companionship that serves to free the priest from the fear of suffering in isolation. For, as he offers himself to be

---

[23] In reference to the words of the psalmist, "I looked for compassion, but there was none, for comforters, but found no one" (Ps. 69:20), Mother Teresa often urged her sisters to imitate Mary by "being the one" to console Jesus on the cross. Cf. MOTHER TERESA, Come, Be My Light: The Private Writings of the "Saint of Calcutta", ed. B. KOLODIEJCHUK (New York: Image, 2007), 260-1.

crucified for the salvation of others, he will find Mary clinging so closely to him that it is impossible that the sword of sorrow should pierce his heart unless it first passes through her soul, too (cf. Lk. 2:35).[24] In this way, the image of the *pietà* can become for the priest a personal icon of his relationship with Mary: it is in her arms, upon the altar of her heart, that the priest, like Jesus, can lay the sacrifice of his life. As a seed only bears fruit if it falls to the earth and dies (cf. Jn. 12:24), so, as the priest consents to die to himself, it is Mary, the fertile ground, who receives his self-offering, takes it up into her heart and makes it her own, producing an abundant harvest of new life for souls.[25]

Our exploration of Mary's bridal relationship to the priest has thus yielded one last insight of crucial significance for helping him to experience his celibate chastity as a truly spousal and paternal love: Mary, as the Mother of the Church, presents herself to every priest as the mother of his spiritual children. This is a fact which is too often ignored by most priests, with the result that they carry out their ministry with the unacknowledged belief that they are single fathers. In seeking to provide for the spiritual welfare of their people, they believe they can consult no other counsel but their own, rely on no one's efforts but their own, and share the joys and sorrows of fatherhood with no one but God. Such an attitude cannot help but impoverish both the priest and the spiritual family that is the parish, the diocese, and the Church at large. Having been configured to Christ the Head and Bridegroom, the priest is indeed called to lead and govern the mystical body—yet surely in this body the most necessary and most noble member of all, the heart, cannot be lacking![26]

---

[24] Cf. BERNARD OF CLAIRVAUX, *Sermo in dom. infra oct. Assumptionis*, 14-15: "Truly, O blessed Mother, a sword has pierced your heart. For only by passing through your heart could the sword enter the flesh of your Son" (cited in *The Liturgy of the Hours*, vol. IV [New York: Catholic Book Publishing Corp., 1975], 1401).

[25] Cf. M.J. SCHEEBEN, *Mariology*, vol. II, 242: "By His sufferings Christ, as the father, produces the new mankind, the Church. By His sacrificial death He makes Himself its fertile seed [cf. Jn. 12:24], and from His side He pours into it the efficacy of His sufferings as the sap of the new life. Likewise, by her compassion, Mary, as mother, brought forth the new mankind. By the closest bodily and spiritual union with Christ's sacrifice, she takes up this sacrifice in herself as the seed of the new mankind and helps the rest of men to appropriate its vivifying power."

[26] It is no accident that it was a bride of Christ, hidden in the heart of Mother Church, who first grasped this mystery: "Charity gave me the key to my vocation. I understood that if the Church had a body composed of different members, the most necessary and most noble of all could not be lacking to it, and so I understood that the Church had a Heart and that this Heart was BURNING WITH LOVE. I understood it was Love alone that made the Church's members act, that if Love ever became extinct, apostles would not preach the Gospel and martyrs would not shed their blood." (THÉRÈSE OF

For if the priest, in his capacity as an official and authoritative representative of Christ, is the *head* of the ecclesial family in its visible aspect, Mary is the *heart*, the hidden center of its spiritual dynamism, silently pumping the divine life to the other members of the body.[27] If the priest, like the father of every human family, is called to occupy the chief place in ruling, then Mary, the mother, occupies the chief place in love.[28]

It is immediately apparent that, once a priest allows himself to recognize Mary as the mother of his spiritual children, new spiritual horizons open up before him, both in his experience of his own celibacy and in the way in which he ministers to the souls under his care. As Fr. Joseph Langford reports, "Mother Teresa always held a rosary in her hand, even when doing something else. People would ask her why she held a rosary when she was obviously not praying it. She answered that this was her way of reminding herself that she was holding Our Lady's hand."[29] How much difference it would make in the life of the Church if every priest likewise understood himself to be holding Mary's hand as he ministered to his people! No longer would he walk through life as though he were a single father—or worse, a religious bureaucrat—feeling that the burden of responsibility for the

---

LISIEUX, *Story of a Soul: The Autobiography of St. Thérèse of Lisieux*, third ed., trans. J. CLARKE [Washington: ICS Publications, 1996], 195). If St. Thérèse could rightly understand her vocation as a consecrated woman—a spiritual bride and mother—in terms of distributing the love of God to the members of the Church, as a heart silently pumps the life of the head through the body, all the more can Mary.

[27] Cf. M.J. SCHEEBEN, *Mariology*, vol. I, 233-234: "However, so far as mankind, built up on Christ as an organic body, is connected with Him as with its Head, Mary's position in this body may be considered that of the heart. This is true of the mother in the natural community of the family. [...] As there exists between Mary and Christ the same organically mutual relation as there is between heart and Head, there also takes place in Mary an organic mediation between the Head and the other members, as the heart does in physical bodies. In particular, Mary, as the heart of the mystical body, appears as the privileged seat of the Holy Ghost, who proceeds from the Head to animate the entire body. [...] Moreover, in Mary this representation strikingly characterizes her personal position, full of life, in the internal organism of the body of Christ, as contrasted with that place which belongs to the official representatives of Christ in the external organism of the Church." Cf. *ibid.*, vol. II, 192.

[28] Cf. PIUS XI, Encyclical letter *Casti Connubii* (December 31, 1930), §27: "In this body which is the family, the heart [must not] be separated from the head to the great detriment of the whole body and the proximate danger of ruin. For if the man is the head, the woman is the heart, and as he occupies the chief place in ruling, so she may and ought to claim for herself the chief place in love."

[29] J. LANGFORD, *Mother Teresa: In the Shadow of Our Lady* (Huntington, IN: Our Sunday Visitor, 2007), 29-30.

Family of God falls solely upon his shoulders. Walking hand-in-hand at every moment with Mary, his bride, the priest will gradually find her face reflected in his spiritual children, and their faces in hers. Her constant presence at his side will impart to his spiritual fatherhood the mutuality and complementarity that will preserve his ministry from becoming sterile and heartless. As only a mother can, she will never fail to point out to him the needs of their common children ("They have no wine!", John 2:3), ensuring that all the members of their household are clothed in the fine garments of virtue and holiness (cf. Prov. 31:21). When the priest finds it difficult to love and honor the Church because of the coldness and indifference of her members, he can always turn to Mary and say from his heart, "You are all fair, my love; there is no flaw in you" (Sgs. 4:7). In this way Mary, like the mother at the heart of every human family, serves as the bond of love, the organic binding member between the father and his children—the more ardently a priest loves her, the more faithfully he will love "the rest of her offspring" (cf. Rev. 12:17).

This is the essential gift that Mary offers to each priest through her identity as his bridal companion: by relating to her as his spiritual bride and the mother of his spiritual children, he is thereby enabled to relate to the Church as a chaste bridegroom and spiritual father through his gift of self in celibacy. Admittedly, for the vast majority of priests today, learning to enter into such a relationship with Mary would constitute a kind of spiritual revolution. But, if the recent experience of the Church has shown us anything, it is that such a revolution of priestly spirituality is long overdue.

Practicum Reflection Questions for Formators

1. How have I experienced the need and the desire for bridal companionship in my life, both as a man and as a priest? How might Mary's understanding and acceptance of me serve to fulfill that desire?

2. In what ways have I experienced an ambivalence in my vocation as both a baptized member of the Church and an ordained priest called to act in the person of Christ the Head? How have I been tempted to deny or flee from either of these dimensions of my sacramental identity?

3. What do I sense in prayer is new or unique about the way Mary desires to accompany me as my spiritual bride, as compared to her role as my spiritual mother? What resistance do I find in my heart towards exploring this aspect of my relationship with Mary?

4. How have I experienced myself acting as a single father in my ministry as a priest? What are some concrete ways in which I could allow Mary to act as the spiritual mother of those I am called to serve?

Suggested Resources

1. Philippe, Pierre-Paul, O.P., *The Virgin Mary and the Priesthood*, trans. Laurence J. Spiteri (New York: Alba House, 1993).
2. de La Potterie, Ignace, *Mary in the Mystery of the Covenant*, trans. Bertrand Buby, S.M. (New York: St Pauls, 1992).
3. Miravalle, Mark, ed., *Mariology: A Guide for Priests, Deacons, Seminarians and Consecrated Persons* (Goleta, CA: Queenship Publishing, 2007).

~ Fr. Evan Koop

As mentioned above, the foregoing theological reflection on Mary's identity as the bridal companion of the priest is intended to serve as an introduction to the insights contained in the sixth and final chapter of the Rule *of the Companions of Christ.*

Taking as its point of departure the priest's identification with both John and Jesus on Calvary, the chapter is composed of two parts, which—as is immediately apparent—roughly correspond to the two inseparable dimensions of the priest's sacramental identity outlined above. In the first part the priest is considered under the aspect of his membership in the bridal Church, in which case Mary, as his spiritual mother, teaches him how to become a companion of Christ by intimately associating himself with Christ and his work. In the second part the priest is considered under the aspect of his sacramental configuration to Christ the Head and Bridegroom through his ordination, in which case Mary presents herself to him as his spiritual bride and intimate companion in his priestly life and ministry.

Although the conception of Mary's intimate relationship to the priest, as outlined here, emerged from the context of a particular community of diocesan priests, the Companions of Christ, this by no means limits its significance or applicability for all other priests. Not all, of course, will choose to embrace the language of Mary's "companionship" of Christ and the priest. Nevertheless, since all priests share a solidarity in their sacramental identity through their common baptism and ordination, it remains true that they all can and indeed must relate to Mary as both their spiritual mother and their spiritual bride.

VI. The Blessed Virgin Mary: Companion of Christ and Our Companion[30]

A. Our Devotion to Mary

77. The Blessed Virgin Mary was the original companion of Christ, the one true *socia Christi*. As Mary was the constant companion of her Son and the one most closely associated with him in his life, death, and resurrection, we find in her the greatest model and highest inspiration of our own vocation to be the Companions of Christ. Yet also, since we have been sacramentally configured to Christ the High Priest through our ordination, we sense the Blessed Virgin's mysterious desire to be our companion, the indispensable helpmate and associate of our priestly life. Thus, even as we seek to imitate Our Lady as the perfect companion of Christ, we also humbly receive her as our own companion.

78. Our unique relationship with Mary finds its clearest expression on Calvary. There, where Our Lord offered himself to the Father "once for all" (Heb 10:10) as both Priest and Victim, we first of all stand beside Our Lady in the person of the beloved disciple, contemplating with her and in her the Cross of her Son, and learning from her how to associate ourselves with Jesus in his act of perfect self-giving for the salvation of the world. Yet it is also in the mystery of the Cross that Mary draws near to us in our priestly identity as *alter Christi*, desiring to be our companion by sharing with us her compassionate love for her Son. In this way, our intimate union with Our Blessed Lady is realized through both our personal and sacramental union with her Son in his priesthood.

B. Mary as the Companion of Christ the Priest

"And Mary said: Behold, the handmaid of the Lord: let it be done to me according to your word." (Lk 1:38)

79. Our Blessed Lady's companionship with her divine Son in his priestly identity and mission began already at the first moment of his Incarnation in her immaculate womb. For it was from her that the Eternal Word took his flesh, and so was consecrated a priest *in aeternum*, the one mediator between God and man.[31] In conceiving Christ the Priest, Mary

---

[30] Excerpt from *The Rule of the Companions of Christ* (Saint Paul, MN: self-published, 2015), 95-119. Used with permission.

[31] Pierre Paul Philippe, O.P., *The Virgin Mary and the Priesthood*, trans. Laurence J. Spiteri (New York: Alba House, 1993), 13.

was not merely a passive instrument of God; instead, he willed from all eternity that she should freely cooperate in the work of salvation through faith and obedience.[32] Therefore, at the moment Our Lady received Gabriel's joyful greeting, all of heaven and earth held its breath, as it were, prostrate at her feet to hear her reply; even the Lord of the universe chose to wait upon her word. Moved by a fullness of his grace, Mary opened her heart to him in the obscurity of faith, opened her lips in loving consent, and opened her womb to conceive her Creator in the flesh.[33]

"Blessed is she who believed that there would be a fulfillment of what was spoken to her from the Lord!" (Lk 1:45)

80. In surrendering herself completely to the Lord's invitation, this humble handmaid became "the faithful spouse of the Holy Spirit,"[34] and thus ensured that already at the first moment of its existence the priesthood of Jesus Christ should become incarnate through a free and unconditional gift of self on the part of a human creature. Indeed, it was Mary's heroic act of faith—even more than the marvelous fact of her virginal conception—that inspired the praise of her kinswoman Elizabeth. "Mary is more blessed in receiving the faith of Christ than in conceiving the flesh of Christ," and so "it was for her a greater thing to have been Christ's disciple than to have been his mother."[35]

81. At the Annunciation Mary thus becomes a model for our imitation, for although we cannot share in her divine maternity, we are indeed called to imitate her faith. In his loving Providence, the Father does not desire that we who have been ordained to share in the priesthood of his Son should merely be passive instruments of his grace. Rather, we must allow his priesthood to take flesh in us—as it did in Mary—through our free and unconditional "yes" in faith to the divine plan for our life and ministry. As Christ takes flesh in our hands each day when we speak the words of institution, we are invited with Mary to renew our act of self-surrender: "Let it be done to me according to your word!" In this way, the personal *fiat* of each Companion of Christ will serve to echo throughout the ages that

---

[32] Cf. LG §56: "Rightly therefore the holy Fathers see her as used by God not merely in a passive way, but as freely cooperating in the work of human salvation through faith and obedience."

[33] Cf. St. Bernard of Clairvaux, *Sermons on the Blessed Virgin Mary*, trans. a priest of New Melleray Abbey (Devon: Augustine Publishing Co., 1984), 70-72.

[34] Cf. John Paul II, Encyclical Letter *Redemptoris Mater* [RMat] (1987), 26.

[35] Augustine, *De Virginitate*, 3 (PL 40:397-398); *Sermo* 25, 7-8 (PL 46:937-938).

"first *fiat* of the New Covenant"[36] spoken by Our Lady, which was itself but the herald of the full and definitive "*fiat*" offered by her Son to the Father's perfect will (cf. Lk 22:42).[37]

"Mary kept all these things, pondering them in her heart." (Lk 2:19, 51)

82. The mystery of Mary's identity as the *Socia Christi* only deepened as she accompanied him throughout his life. "From the house of Nazareth to the place of Calvary," Jesus, the Suffering Servant, made Mary "his constant companion," and granted her the privilege of "always sharing his lot."[38] She knew the poverty of his birth in a humble stable, the harsh necessity of his flight into Egypt, and the anxious days of searching for him in Jerusalem—until at length the Lord revealed her at Cana to be the "Woman" whom he would ask to share his messianic "hour" on the Cross (cf. Jn 2:4; Gen 3:15).

83. With Mary, we too desire to walk with Jesus as his companions in our daily ministry, intimately associating ourselves with him in his proclamation of the Kingdom and his salvific work in souls. We do not hesitate to exhaust ourselves with Christ when he is tired (cf. Jn 4:6, Mk 4:38), to suffer dishonor with him when he is dishonored (cf. Mk 3:21-22, Jn 8:48)—in short, to experience whatever he experienced on earth.[39] We long to hear him speak to us those words that fittingly apply to his mother also: "It is you who have stood by me in my trials" (Lk 22:28).

"Standing near the cross of Jesus were his mother...and the disciple whom he loved." (Jn 19:25-26)

84. Most of all it was at Golgotha that Mary, like her Son, passed through "her hour *par excellence.*"[40] Just as Jesus mounted the wood of the Cross as the innocent victim for our redemption, so also Mary "suffered in the very depths of her soul with his most bitter sufferings...and in her heart died with him, stabbed by the sword of sorrow," as Simeon had

---

[36] RMat 1.

[37] Cf. John Paul II, Letter to Priests (25 March 1998): "The priest is called to match the *fiat* of Mary at all times, allowing himself to be led by the Spirit as she was...Accompanied by Mary, the priest will be able to renew his consecration day after day."

[38] Cf. Pope St. Pius X, Encyclical Letter *Ad Diem Illum* [ADI] (1904), 15; Ven. Pope Pius XII, Apostolic Constitution *Munificentissimus Deus* [MD] (1950), 38.

[39] Cf. Ignatius of Loyola, *Spiritual Exercises*, n. 167.

[40] Bl. Columba Marmion, *Christ the Ideal of the Priest*, trans. Matthew Dillon (San Francisco: Ignatius Press, 2005), 345.

foretold (cf. Lk 2:35).[41] For "only by passing through her heart could the sword enter the flesh of her Son," so that while "he died in body through a love greater than anyone had known, she died in spirit through a love unlike any other since his."[42]

85. The mystery of Mary's companionship with Christ on the Cross surpassed even the bonds of her maternal affection for him and took on a certain spousal character. Though at Calvary Mary was indeed always a mother, watching and praying close to the Cross of her Son, yet she was also revealed there precisely as "'*Socia*,' that is, as collaborator in his salvific work, 'under him and with him, by the grace of almighty God, serving the mystery of redemption'."[43] Mary's association with Jesus in his salvific work did not consist principally in offering with him his redemptive sacrifice, but above all in her complementary role as the New Eve at the side of the New Adam, "as a witness to [his] passion by her presence, and as a sharer in it by her compassion."[44] For "the Blessed Virgin Mary was not chosen by the Lord to be a 'minister,' but as 'spouse' and 'help'," in accord with the words of Genesis: "It is not good that the man should be alone; let us make a helpmate fit for him" (Gen 2:18).[45] By espousing all the sentiments of her Son's priestly heart, Mary's heart became for him, like the bride in the Song of Songs, "a spring of living waters," "a closed garden," "a sealed

---

[41] Pope Leo XIII, Encyclical letter *Jucunda Semper* (1894).

[42] Bernard of Clairvaux, *Sermo in dom. infra oct. Assumptionis*, 14-15: *Opera Omnia*, Edit. Cisterc. 5 (1968), 273-274; from the Office of Readings for the Feast of Our Lady of Sorrows (September 15).

[43] John Paul II, Wednesday General Audience (23 March 1983); cf. LG 56.

[44] SD 25. On the patristic origins of Mary's title as the "New Eve," cf. LG 56; CCC 411, 489, 726, 2618, 2853; Reginald Garrigou-Lagrange, O.P., *The Mother of the Saviour and Our Interior Life* (Rockford, IL: TAN Books and Publishers, 1993), 159-62; and Mark Miravalle (ed.), *Mariology: A Guide for Priests, Deacons, Seminarians and Consecrated Persons* (Goleta, CA: Queenship Publishing, 2007), 350ff.

[45] Pseudo-Albert the Great, *Mariale, sive quaestiones super Evangelium, 'Missus est Angelus Gabriel'*, q. 42, art. 5. Hence, he continues, "the Blessed Virgin is not a 'vicar', but a 'helpmate' [*coadjutrix*] and 'companion' [*socia*], participating in the Kingdom as she had participated in the Passion, when all the disciples and 'ministers' had fled and she alone remained beneath the Cross: the wounds which Christ received in His body, Mary felt in her heart." This is one of the earliest references in the Catholic theological tradition to Mary specifically as "*socia*," or companion of Christ. Magisterial uses of this little-known Marian title became more frequent in the twentieth century: cf. ADI 15; MD 14, 40; LG 61; John Paul II, Wednesday General Audience (23 March 1983), and Homily for the Feast of Our Lady of Sorrows (15 September 1984). A balanced exploration of the theological import and limits of this term can be found in Philippe, *Virgin Mary*, 54, 57, 98, 100-1.

fountain" (Sgs 4:12-15), offering to Jesus the consoling presence of at least one creature who understood him perfectly during his agony on the Cross. Thus, Our Lord could say of Mary that during the Crucifixion, "her heart was in my heart," as a bride's heart is in that of her bridegroom.[46]

86. Our priestly vocation does not consist merely in being the instruments through which the redemptive sacrifice of Jesus is ceaselessly offered to the Father; rather, as Companions of Christ we feel the deeper need of becoming personally conformed to him in mind and heart, just as Mary was.[47] As we stand beside Our Lady at the foot of the Cross and contemplate her loving union with Jesus in his Passion, we find in her the perfect icon of our particular charism. Under Mary's tutelage we begin to make all our Master's dispositions and priestly activity our own, sharing with him the same thoughts and plans, the same sentiments he has for his Father and for all of humanity. In the crosses of our priesthood, at every moment in which we find ourselves with Our Lord on Golgotha, we look to Our Lady and cry out:

Iuxta crucem tecum stare	To stand beside the Cross with you
te libenter sociare	and gladly be your companion
in planctu desidero	in weeping, this I desire![48]

"When Jesus saw his mother, and the disciple whom he loved standing near, he said to his mother, 'Woman, behold, your son!' Then he said to the disciple, 'Behold, your mother!' And from that hour the disciple took her to his own home." (Jn 19:26-27)

87. The spousal love that united the hearts of Jesus and Mary on Calvary bore immense fruit for the redemption of the world. In his words to her, "Woman, behold your son" (Jn. 19:26), we can hear the invitation, "Woman, who suffer with me, be fruitful with me, be the mother of my children."[49] Like the beloved disciple, we as priests marvel that Our Lord and

---

[46] St. Bridget of Sweden, *Revelations*, 3, quoted in Philippe, *Virgin Mary*, 99. Cf. ST, I-II, q. 28, art. 2: "In the love of friendship, the lover is in the beloved...so that it seems as though he felt the good or suffered the evil in the person of his friend."

[47] Cf. Philippe, *Virgin Mary*, 75.

[48] Sequence for the Feast of Our Lady of Sorrows, *Stabat Mater Dolorosa*, attr. to Jacopone da Todi (1228-1306).

[49] Jacques-Bénigne Bossuet, "Sermon on the Compassion of Our Lady," quoted in Garrigou-Lagrange, *Mother of the Saviour*, 190.

Master should have entrusted his mother particularly to us as her sons, and that among the first fruits she merited through her union with Jesus as he died on the Cross was our own priestly vocation.[50] In humble gratitude for so precious a bequest, we too choose to take her "into our own," granting her a place of honor in every one of our fraternities and chapels, introducing her into every aspect of our interior life, and welcoming her into the midst of our human brokenness.[51]

88. As we "behold our mother," who so tenderly "cares for the brethren of her Son,"[52] our common status as sons of Mary serves to strengthen our fraternal bonds as Companions of Christ and moves us to care for one another. Our mother Mary teaches us how to discover one another constantly anew, receiving each brother generously into our lives with the same unconditional love with which she welcomed John into her heart.

C. Mary as our Companion

"And behold, you will conceive in your womb and bear a son, and you shall call his name Jesus." (Lk 1:31)

89. Because of our resemblance to Christ in the sacramental character we share as priests, Our Lady "sees her divine Son in us and cannot reject us; it would be to reject Jesus himself."[53] Therefore, we humbly recognize that just as Mary teaches us how to become

---

[50] Cf. Philippe, *Virgin Mary*, 18-20: "Mary became the mother of every one of us while she stood at the foot of the Cross…At that moment the Virgin Mary, with Christ and in Christ, merited all the graces of our vocation and our life as priests…This is due to the fact that she stood united with her son on Calvary…She loves all priests and looks after every one of us as if we were the only person in the world…It is she who, along with Christ, has petitioned that we be priests."

[51] Cf. RMat 45: "Entrusting himself as a son to Mary, the Christian, like the apostle John, welcomes 'into his own [home]' the mother of Christ and introduces her to every aspect of his interior life, that is to say into his human and Christian 'I': 'he took her into his own home'." Cf. Marmion, *Ideal*, 336: "He pronounces these words: 'Woman, behold thy son' (Jn 19:26). These last words of Jesus are for Mary a testament of incomprehensible value. We may see in St. John all the faithful souls to whom Mary became a mother, but we must not forget the fact that he had been ordained priest the evening before. On this account, he represents especially all priests. We like to think that at the hour of His death, at that moment of supreme solemnity, Jesus turned to us; in the person of the apostle whom He love, He entrusted us to His mother."

[52] LG 62.

[53] Marmion, *Ideal*, 331.

companions of Christ, so also she earnestly desires to become our own companion, to see and love in us what she sees and loves in her Son.

90. Mary's intimate association with us begins already from our time in seminary, that "seedbed" in which we are mysteriously formed by the Holy Spirit into the image of her Son within her womb, close to her maternal heart.[54] As our priestly vocation is brought to birth at ordination, it is Our Lady's look of love, her graceful smile, that awakens us to the knowledge that we are "sons in the Son," beloved of the Father.[55] Throughout our priestly lives we seek to abide with Christ in the warmth of our Blessed Mother's loving gaze, setting our souls in silence and peace, "as a child has rest in its mother's arms" (Ps 131:2).

"Behold, an angel of the Lord appeared to him in a dream, saying, 'Joseph, Son of David, do not fear to take Mary your wife.'" (Mt 1:20)

91. Having been sacramentally configured to the person of Jesus Christ the Bridegroom of the Church, we as priests, with a prudent reserve, sense that Our Lady's desire to be our companion reaches even to the spousal dimension.[56] Recognizing our own unworthiness to enter into such an intimate relationship with one so exalted and holy as Mary, we may at times, like Joseph, be hesitant to "unveil" this mystery, seeking to "send her away quietly" (Mt 1:19).[57] Yet, by remaining faithful to the message of the angel, Joseph took Mary into

---

[54] Cf. LG 63: "The Son whom she brought forth is He whom God placed as the first-born among many brethren, (Rom. 8:29) namely the faithful, in whose birth and formation she cooperates with a maternal love."

[55] Cf. John Cihak, "The Blessed Virgin Mary's Role in the Celibate Priest's Spousal and Paternal Love," *Ignatius Insight* (July, 2009).

[56] To speak of our spousal relationship with Mary as priests is to employ metaphorical rather than literal language, and naturally requires a certain prudent reserve. Nevertheless, "we must not be so nervous in approaching [these realities] to the point that we begin to fear them...We recognize in Mary herself the most beloved spouse of the Lord...Such terms, borrowed from the language of marriage and friendship, are chosen solely to help us sense, through human analogies, the divine transcendence of that love which unites us to God and neighbor" (Philippe, *Virgin Mary*, 78-80). Throughout the centuries many saints have not shied away from referring to Our Lady in spousal terms, including most notably St. John Eudes in his *Contrat d'Alliance*.

[57] Cf. Bernard of Clairvaux, *Sermons*, 30. It was the nearly unanimous consent of the Fathers that Joseph's attitude to his betrothed was one of reverential fear rather than suspicion, as amply demonstrated by Thomas Aquinas (*Commentary on Matthew*, I, no. 117). Cf. Marie-Dominique Philippe, O.P., *The Mystery of Joseph* (Bethesda, MD: Zaccheus Press, 2010), 169, n. 117.

his home and made her consecration his own, receiving from her his identity as chaste husband and defender of the Holy Family. So too, as spiritual fathers we cleave to Mary—rejoicing in what she rejoices in, and willing what she wills[58]—and so receive from her a deepening of our own identity as chaste spouse and defender of God's family. Our spousal devotion to Our Lady is thus not an emotional escape from our celibate consecration but rather a strengthening of it, for in choosing to give ourselves to Mary we are, by that very fact, given all the more completely to God with her and in her.[59] By entrusting our hearts to her we find an unfailing prize, since she brings us good all the days of our life (cf. Prv 31:11-12). In turn, her tender gaze of trust and affirmation brings out the best in us as spiritual leaders, just as it did in Joseph.

"When the wine failed, the mother of Jesus said to him, 'They have no wine.' And Jesus said to her, 'O woman, what have you to do with me? My hour has not yet come.' His mother said to the servants, 'Do whatever he tells you.'" (Jn 2:3-5)

92. As we enter into the priestly ministry of Jesus, proclaiming to the world the Good News of the Kingdom, we rejoice to have Mary at our side as our constant companion. Not only do we experience the consolation of her presence with us in our apostolic labors, but we also rely on her feminine heart to point out to us the needs of our spiritual children. By trusting her guidance at every moment in our ministry and yielding obediently to her word, the Lord once more changes water into wine, marvelously transforming our poor human resources into a divine abundance of pastoral fruits, whether they be visible to us or not.

"So they took Jesus, and he went out, bearing his own cross, to the place called the place of a skull, which is called in Hebrew 'Golgotha'. There they crucified him...He said, 'It is finished'; and he bowed his head and gave up his spirit." (Jn 19:17-18, 30)

93. Our priestly offering, like that of our Lord, is fully consummated only on the wood of the Cross.[60] As we enter into the sufferings of Calvary each day of our life and ministry,

---

[58] Cf. ST, II-II, q. 25, art. 6, obj. 4.

[59] Cf. Philippe, *Mystery of Joseph*, 60.

[60] In the words of St. Cyril of Alexandria, commenting on Sgs 3:11: "The day of the marriage he calls the day of the passion, in which he betroths the Church in his blood." (*In Cantica Canticorum Commentarii Reliquiae*, in J.P. Migne (ed.), *Patrologiae Cursus Completus: Series Graeca*, Vol. 69 [Paris: Petit-Montrouge, 1864], 1288.)

always carrying about in our bodies the death of Jesus (2 Cor 4:10), it is precisely then that Mary draws nearest to us to be our companion. There, at the Tree of Life, we are given in Mary a New Eve in place of the old, since "it is not good for man to be alone" (Gen 2:18). That which Adam once made a reproach against God we now proclaim with joy and gratitude: "The woman whom you gave me to be my companion, she gave me of the tree and I ate" (Gen 3:12). For Mary offers us at the Cross not the poisoned fruit that leads to death, but the very flesh of her Son, the Bread that endures to eternal life (cf. Jn 6:27).[61]

94. We experience this truth most forcefully each day when we offer the holy sacrifice of the Mass. Going up to the altar of God (cf. Ps 43:4), as beloved sons of Mary we beseech her motherly love: "As you stood by your most dear Son while he hung on the Cross, so in your kindness may you be pleased to stand by me, a poor sinner, and all priests who today are offering the sacrifice here and throughout the entire holy Church, so that with your gracious help we may offer a worthy and acceptable oblation in the sight of the most high and undivided Trinity."[62] In order to unite ourselves more intimately to the Victim of Calvary, to imitate what we celebrate, "we need to have near us the one who through heroic faith carried to its zenith her union with her Son, precisely then on Golgotha."[63] Indeed, "every Mass puts us into an intimate communion with [Mary], the mother whose sacrifice 'is made present once again'," in the sacrifice of her Son.[64]

"When he makes himself an offering for sin, he shall see his offspring...he shall see the fruit of the travail of his soul and be satisfied." (Is 53:10-11)

95. As Our Lord expired on the Cross, the blood and water that flowed from his pierced side became fountains of new life for his Bride, the Church (cf. Jn 19:34). Mary, too, suffered at his side as the New Eve, laboring with and in him to bring forth spiritual children, and so become the "mother of all the living" (Gen 3:20). In her, Jesus' words to his apostles were fulfilled in a special way: "You will be sorrowful, but your sorrow will turn into joy. When a woman is in travail she has sorrow, because her hour has come; but when she is delivered of the child, she no longer remembers the anguish, for joy that a child is born into the world" (Jn 16:20-21).

96. We do not endure the Cross of Christ in vain as priests, but for the precious gifts of

---

[61] Bernard of Clairvaux, *Sermons*, 16-17.

[62] Cf. Preparation for Mass, "Prayer to the Blessed Virgin Mary," in *The Roman Missal*, 1439.

[63] John Paul II, Letter to Priests (25 March 1988).

[64] John Paul II, Wednesday General Audience (5 June 1983).

apostolic fruitfulness and spiritual fatherhood. We gladly accept the challenges and sufferings of priestly ministry so as to beget spiritual children who will be our joy and crown (cf. Phil 4:1). In this labor we know that we have the help of the Blessed Virgin. In her face we look to glimpse the beauty of our Bride, the Church, when it has become obscured for us in the griefs of our daily ministry. So also, we delight to see her face in the persons of the poor, the suffering, and the troublesome, "as a mother is seen in her children."[65]

"All these with one accord devoted themselves to prayer, together with the women and Mary the mother of Jesus, and with his brethren…When the day of Pentecost had come, they were all together in one place." (Acts 1:14, 2:1)

97. Our Blessed Mother, who stands with us on Calvary as our companion and help, always carries us through the darkness of the Cross to the dawn of the resurrection. Even as the first apostles gathered in expectation around Mary in the Upper Room, we feel her maternal presence among us whenever we come together for prayer. She who first received the Holy Spirit in an "eminent fullness" at the Annunciation now prays with us and for us— like a mother praying for her son on the eve of his ordination—so that we may share in her "fullness of prayer" by the outpouring of the Holy Spirit.[66] It is Mary who teaches us how to be open to the Spirit and docile to his movements. Through her hands pass the spiritual gifts that are given to each of us for the benefit of all.[67] In her company we feel ourselves brothers all the more as the Spirit of her Son rushes upon us.

"A great sign appeared in heaven, a woman clothed with the sun, with the moon under her feet, and on her head a crown of twelve stars; she was with child and she cried out in her pangs of birth, in anguish for delivery…And the dragon stood before the woman who was about to

---

[65] St. John Eudes, *Contrat d'Alliance*, in Philippe, *Virgin Mary*, 79.

[66] John Paul II, Wednesday General Audience (2 October 1983): "Mary, who on the day of the Annunciation had received 'the Holy Spirit in an eminent fullness,' prayed with them [the apostles]. This special fullness of the Holy Spirit also determined in her a particular 'fullness of prayer.' Through the means of this singular fullness Mary prays 'for us'—and prays 'with us.'" In Philippe, *Virgin Mary*, 20.

[67] Cf. St. Bernardine of Siena (*Sermo in Nativitate*, 8): "The Mother of God obtained the right to be called Queen of Mercy. And because such is the mother of the Son of God from Whom proceeds the Holy Spirit, all the gifts, virtues and graces of the same Spirit are distributed through her hands to whom she wishes, as she wishes, and as much as she wishes." (In Philippe, *Virgin Mary*, 105)

bear a child, that he might devour her child when she brought it forth." (Rev 12:1-2, 4)

98. At the close of her earthly life, Mary, who had been the faithful companion of Christ from the Annunciation to the Ascension, at last accompanied her Son into heaven, in fulfillment of his promise: "Where I am, there shall my servant be also" (Jn 12:26). Having received from the Most Holy Trinity the "crown of righteousness" (2 Tim 4:8), she now reigns as Queen of heaven and earth. Sensing her maternal longing to see Christ formed in the world, our hearts are set on fire with apostolic zeal. In the anguish of the Woman of the Apocalypse we as priests hear the plea of our Bride, the Church, "Give me children or I shall die!" (Gen. 30:1).[68] Thus, with the help of Our Lady, Star of the New Evangelization,[69] we seek to spread the Gospel tirelessly in our ministry, raising up spiritual children in our day for Our Lord and Master.

99. This apostolic work always provokes a spiritual battle, "for we are not contending against flesh and blood, but against the principalities, against the powers, against the world rulers of this present darkness, against the spiritual hosts of wickedness in the heavenly places" (Eph 6:12). Yet, even as the evil one pursues the Woman and seeks to make war on her children and ours (cf. Rev 12:3), Our Lady herself leads us into battle, "fair as the moon, bright as the sun, terrible as an army in battle array" (Sgs 6:10). With her help we endeavor to crush the serpent's head—in our own hearts no less than in the world—even as he strikes at our heel (cf. Gen 3:15).

100. When we have become exhausted in our daily ministry and our hearts seek some rest and consolation, we choose to seek it in the heart of Mary, in the "cool breath of the Immaculate and the fragrance of the Rose of Sharon" (cf. Sgs 2:1).[70] When we are wearied

---

[68] Such was the insight that St. Charles Borromeo once shared with his priests: "O what pain, O what wailing of Holy Church! She cries out with prayers in the presence of God, and in your presence through my mouth, pronounces divine words to you. It seems that I am hearing her saying to her betrothed, the Lord Jesus Christ, what Rachel had formerly said to her husband Jacob, 'Give me children or I shall die' (Gen. 30:1). I am truly desirous of the one to be born. Indeed I dread this sterility; so unless you come to Christ and give to me many sons, I am precisely at this very moment about to die." (Address to Diocesan Synod, April 20, 1584; *Acta Ecclesiae Mediolanensis*, trans. Gerard O'Connor, Pars II, 347.)

[69] Cf. NMI 58.

[70] John Henry Newman, *Discourses to Mixed Congregations* (Boston: Patrick Donahoe), 281-2: "O my dear children, young men and young women, what need have you of the intercession of the Virgin-mother, of her help, of her pattern, in this respect! What shall bring you forward in the narrow way, if you live in the world, but the thought and the patronage of Mary! What shall seal your

by the conflict with evil, discouraged by failures, assailed by temptations, and burdened by the knowledge of our own sin and weakness—it is then that we "look to the star, and call upon Mary."[71] For we know that it is she who will grant us patience and endurance in the heat of battle, peace and tranquility in the face of opposition, and comfort in our discouragements. When we fall, it is she who desires nothing more than to lift us up by her prayers and restore us to friendship with her Son. Therefore, we place the whole of our priestly consecration as Companions of Christ under her care, freely consecrating ourselves to her, utterly and without reserve, as we pray:

> *O Most Blessed Virgin Mary,*
> *Companion of Christ and my Companion,*
> *At the Tree of Life you showed yourself*
> *A helpmate fit for Jesus, sharing completely*
> *In his obedient immolation to the Father*

---

senses, what shall tranquillize your heart, when sights and sounds of danger are around you, but Mary? What shall give you patience and endurance, when you are wearied out with the length of the conflict with evil, with the unceasing necessity of precautions, with the irksomeness of observing them, with the tediousness of their repetition, with the strain upon your mind, with your forlorn and cheerless condition, but a loving communion with her?—She will comfort you in your discouragements, solace you in your fatigue, raise you after your falls, reward you for your successes. She will show you her Son, your God and your all.—When your spirit within you is excited, or relaxed, or depressed, when it loses its balance, when it is restless and wayward, when it is sick of what it has, and hankers after what it has not, when your eye is solicited with evil, and your mortal frame trembles under the shadow of the Tempter, what will bring you to yourselves, to peace and to health, but the cool breath of the Immaculate and the fragrance of the Rose of Sharon?"

[71] Bernard of Clairvaux, *Sermons*, 37-38: "When the storms of temptation burst upon thee, when thou seest thyself driven upon the rocks of tribulation, look up at the star, call upon Mary. When buffeted by the billows of pride, or ambition, or hatred, or jealousy, look up at the star, call upon Mary. Should anger, or avarice, or carnal desires violently assail the little vessel of thy soul, look up at the star, call upon Mary…In dangers, in doubts, in difficulties, think of Mary, call upon Mary. Let not her name depart from thy lips, never suffer it to leave thy heart. And that thou mayest more surely obtain the assistance of her prayer, neglect not to walk in her footsteps. With her for guide, thou shalt never go astray; whilst invoking her, thou shalt never lose heart; so long as she is in thy mind, thou art safe from deception; whilst she holds thy hand, thou canst not fall; under her protection, thou hast nothing to fear; if she walks before thee, thou shalt not grow weary; if she shows thee favor, thou shalt reach the goal."

For the salvation of the world.

Called as I am to be with him,
And to be conformed to the mystery
Of his perfect self-giving,
I humbly accept your desire to be for me
All that you are for your Son:
Mother and Queen, Sister and Spouse.

Trusting in your care for me,
I commit to you all my desires and plans,
Knowing that only through your virginal faith
Will they bear fruit that will last.

As I am brought to share in the Cross of my Lord,
To participate in his priesthood and victimhood,
Stripped of all I possess,
May I receive as my only wealth the infinite riches
Of your sorrowful and immaculate heart.

With you at my side,
I am confident that no suffering can pierce my heart
Unless it first pierce your compassionate soul.

Therefore, in union with Christ,
And together with my brothers,
I lay the sacrifice of my life on the altar of your heart,
There to be consumed by the fire of the Holy Spirit,
That it may rise as a fragrant offering to my God and Father,
To whom be glory and praise forever and ever.
Amen.

Chapter Five

IMAGINATION, PRAYER, AND THE SPOUSAL GIFT

In and through Christ's Spirit, St. Joseph stands ready to assist any priest in going to Mary, thus concretizing the priest's own spousal identity.

Deacon James Keating, Ph.D.

Deacon James Keating, PhD is Director of Theological Formation in The Institute for Priestly Formation at Creighton University, Omaha, NE. Previous to his appointment at IPF he was Professor of Moral and Spiritual Theology at the Pontifical College Josephinum, Columbus, Ohio. Deacon Keating serves as well as the Director for Deacon Formation in the Archdiocese of Omaha. He also serves in the ministry of spiritual direction and has been a presenter on topics related to seminary formation at a wide variety of national and international conferences. He has published numerous books and articles in Spiritual and Moral Theology. These include: "Resting On The Heart Of Christ - The Vocation and Spirituality of the Seminary Theologian," "Listening for Truth - Praying Our Way To Virtue," "The Priest As Beloved Son" (editor), and his latest book, "Remain in Me: Holy Orders, Prayer and Ministry" (Paulist Press, 2019).

In this essay, I will explore the identity of the Blessed Virgin Mary in her powerful role as a priest's spiritual spouse. While her role as spiritual mother is well-known within the clergy, her mission as spiritual spouse is less recognized. This mission, however, carries significant truths for the spiritual and human formation of priests; thus, seminaries ought to affirm this mission of Mary in both the external and internal fora of seminary culture. This mission is mediated to the priest through the love and prayers of St. Joseph, husband of Mary. He stands with the priest as one who gives himself completely in chaste love to Mary—the primordial image of the Church, Bride and Mother.

St. Joseph, Husband of Mary, Brother to Priests

St. Joseph assists the priest to receive his spousal identity because Joseph himself knew the surprise of being called into the same paradoxical vocation: the virgin-spouse (cf. Mt 1:20). Joseph desired to be married to Mary, and committed himself to such. Mary, however, may have deeply desired a life of consecrated virginity, while possessing no clarity as to how this desire would be fulfilled since she was betrothed to Joseph. After the Annunciation, it fell to her to tutor Joseph in the mystery that God prepared for them: to be married, yet called to virginity in the company of the Son of God. In his prayer life, the priest is rightly called to entrust to Mary, as did St. Joseph, the processes and struggles of becoming a man of complete self-donation. In so doing, the priest experiences Mary's heart as a place of emotional and spiritual formation. As the priest's companion, Joseph intercedes and inspires the priest to share his entire heart with Mary, to receive healing wisdom about such a vocation from her, who is full of grace. In this kind of praying, it is the imagination, in concert with Scripture, which mediates insight, communion, and healing.

In and through Christ's Spirit, St. Joseph stands ready to assist any priest in going to Mary, thus concretizing the priest's own spousal identity. In a real sense, there is a conspiracy of the Holy Family to affect the priest in his own development as chaste spouse and spiritual father. Mary's love is affectively and spiritually formative because she lives only to do what the Father wills (cf. Lk 1:38), thus participating in the grace of Christ's own sacrificial love, which was given to her before her birth. Christ himself desires that each priest share in his own spousal disposition, his own virtue of self-donation. As Jean Jacques Olier wrote, "Now, by coming into man, this Spirit of our Lord spreads there the virtues, inclinations, and feelings *of our Lord*; he paints in us, so to speak, the same qualities that are in our Lord."[1] Like Bl. Dom Marmion, seminary formation affirms that Christ wants to live his Mysteries over again in the priest. As a gift for all bishops and priests of the Latin rite, Christ wants to share his mystery of virginal, spousal love. What he lived by nature, the

---

[1] Quoted in John O. Barres, *Jean Jacques Olier's Priestly Spirituality: Mental Prayer and Virtue as the Foundation for the Direction of Souls* (Roma: *Pontificia Universitas Sanctae Crucis*, 1999) 105.

priest will live by grace.[2]

Beyond Christ and St. Joseph, a third figure emerges who is related to Mary's spousal character: St. John the evangelist at the cross of Christ. Joseph Ratzinger noted that the apostle John allowed the fullness of Mary's feminine identity to be received into his heart at the cross (Jn 19:27: "He took her into everything that was his own"). This taking "implies a … personal relation between the disciple … and Mary; a letting of Mary into the inmost core of {his} own mental and spiritual life; a handing {of himself} over into her feminine and maternal existence; a reciprocal self-commitment that becomes the ever-new way to Christ's birth and brings about Christ's taking form in man."[3] If Christ wanted such a spiritually intimate relationship between Mary and one of his first priests, St. John, it is reasonable to conclude that he wills such a relationship for all those who share in his sacred priesthood, even in our present day. Pope Benedict XVI commented: "The Gospel tells us that from that hour, St. John, the beloved son, took his mother Mary 'to his own home.' This is what it says in the {English} translation; but the Greek text is far deeper, far richer. We could translate it: *he took Mary into his inner life, his inner being, 'eis tà idia,' into the depths of his being.* To take Mary with one means to introduce her into the dynamism of one's own entire existence, it is not something external, and into all that constitutes the horizon of one's own apostolate."[4]

Here we have the "taking" of Mary by John into "his inner life," but in St. Joseph, we have another form. This related "taking" by Joseph is less utilized in the imagination of priests at prayer, but in our age is appearing more and more. Unlike the bond between St. John and Mary under the cross, where he is given by Christ specifically as mother, Joseph is given to Mary in an explicit nuptial bond. No woman can have her spousal-maternal bond separated, and in the case of Mary, she is my mother as she forms me, through her prayers, into her "son." Here, she is also my spiritual spouse, as she tutors me in how to donate the self out of love for the Bride. God, through a dream, told Joseph, "Do not be afraid to take Mary as your wife" (Mt 1:20). Another way of phrasing what God said to Joseph might be, "Even though you are right to reverence Mary as Mine, I give her to you, so that you, too, might be led into the intimacy we have, while at the same time protecting and defending her from external danger." These words are also addressed to the priest in his own prayer.

Going to Mary as *spiritual spouse and, with her, to Christ* is a new image for many

---

[2] Dom Marmion, OSB, *Christ in His Mysteries* (St. Louis: Herder, 1939) 248ff.

[3] Hans urs von Balthasar and Joseph Ratzinger, *Mary Church at the Source* (San Francisco: Ignatius, 2005) 58.

[4] Benedict XVI, General Audience, August 12, 2009.

priests in the depths of their prayer. And, yet, Christ himself is related to Mary as spouse in that she represents the Church, his Bride. Christ, as noted above, wants to share *all of his mysteries* with the priest; now he wishes to invite men, as was St. Joseph, into this spiritual espousal. It is an espousal that essentially calls forth complete trust and complete self-giving. Christ gave his entire being in sacrifice for the salvation of the Church, his Bride.

St. Joseph's humility operates very powerfully here. He, more than any other, understands the struggle of the priest to offer his spousal-paternal identity to the Church in a commitment to lifelong chaste celibacy. It was Joseph who had to learn from *Mary herself* what new kind of marriage[5] was being given to them from God. Each priest also needs to be tutored by Mary, along with the intercessory prayer of Joseph, to receive in joy this new kind of marriage that is offered to him by God.

Even though Mary is given wholly to God, Joseph is still her spouse because he loves her within the parameters of God's claim upon her. His love is still real, his desire to cherish her is still reverenced, his reception of her love is still spousal at its roots, his paternal character still binds him to her in their mutual love for Jesus, and his protection of her as mystery still envelops him in God's grace as it does for all husbands. For her part, Mary teaches Joseph how to be with her, how to be with, and for, her who has been taken up into the prevenient grace that is her Immaculate Conception and perpetual virginity. She reaches Joseph and leads him into the depths of loving her from within the truth that *she has already been reached by Love itself in an exceptional fashion.*

She is the New Eve[6] and will form the priest, as she did Joseph, in what it means to be spousal in this new way of celibate, chaste giving. Despite any initial disquieting feelings around imagining Mary as spiritual spouse, the priest should entrust his own desire for spousal love and paternity to Mary, just as Joseph did. This kind of entrusting was established by Christ himself when Mary (Church) was given to the *priesthood* under the cross, and the priesthood was given to Mary.[7]

---

[5] John Paul II, *Redemptoris Custos* (1989) n. 7.

[6] St. Irenaeus says that Eve "by disobeying became the cause of death for herself and the whole human race, so also Mary . . . was obedient and became the cause of salvation for herself and the whole human race" (*Against Heresies* 3.22.4). Later he says of Eve and Mary, "Just as the human race was subject to death by a virgin, it was freed by a virgin, with the virginal disobedience balanced by virginal obedience" (ibid. 5.19.1).

[7] There is a helpful summary of the relationship between Mary as Mother and Mary as spouse in John O'Donnell, SJ, *Hans Urs von Balthasar* (London, Continuum, 1991) 117-119 ; see also, St Thomas Aquinas, Commentary on the Sentences, III, Dist. 3, q.1, a.2, q.1, ad 4

Joseph as Model Spouse

What Joseph wants to share with the chaste, celibate priest is this: Mary is your helpmate (cf. Gn 2:18).[8] Mary is the spiritual spouse of the "priest," particularly in her embodying Christ's one Church as Bride.[9] It is to her that the priest must go in prayer to receive the grace of giving himself completely to Christ's spouse, the Church. Or, as then Cardinal Ratzinger said about St. Joseph's own "priesthood" in relation to Joseph's spousal love: "Joseph is … the prototype of the Christian bishop. For her part, Mary is the living church. … Mary is the bride. {Joseph} thus becomes the icon of the Bishop, to whom the bride is betrothed; she is not at his disposal but under his protection."[10] The Church's welfare is entrusted to priests. Their Bride, Christ's own Church, has a "Marian countenance."[11] Beholding this face in prayer becomes a way for the priest to receive, not only the grace he needs to be sustained in his spousal identity, but Mary's face becomes the real object of his masculine commitment to the woman. The priest is called to protect, serve, provide for, and sacrifice for, Mary. To invite the seminarian to desire such a depth of contemplative beholding ought to be the true compass of all spiritual formation in the seminary.

Joseph's prayerful aid is particularly lodged around issues of chastity, self-donation, and the release of courage needed by each priest to share his own interior life with Christ and the saints. Just imagine the essential, intimate conversations Joseph needed to have with Mary. Conversations about who she was, about their own unique marriage. These conversations must have been ongoing as befits the mystery that Mary and Joseph were to one another, conversations that led to their deepest communion, and conversations that became prayer. Joseph wants to introduce the priest to this level of intimacy in his prayer with Mary as well.

St. Joseph brings the priest to Mary so that the priest can know the same love that Joseph did; he desires to bring the priest into the loving conspiracy that is Nazareth, the love within the Holy Family. Such love will satisfy the priest as man, as spouse. We see this love's

---

[8] See below commentary from note 23.

[9] *Lumen Gentium* §63-65. See also Ignace de la Potterie, SJ, *Mary in the Mystery of the Covenant* (NY: Alba House, 1992) where he says, "In Revelation 12 the relationship of who Mary personifies is inverse. Here in the foreground is the ecclesiological aspect: the Woman Zion, the Church, will become the Spouse of the Lamb in the definitive conclusion of the Covenant (cf. Rev 21:1-9).

[10] Hans urs von Balthasar and Joseph Ratzinger, *Mary: Church at the Source*, footnote 5, 88.

[11] Ignace de la Potterie, SJ, *Mary in the Mystery of the Covenant*, 263.

power in what Pope John Paul II said about Joseph's love life with Mary in Nazareth: "The deep spiritual closeness arising from marital union and the interpersonal contact between man and woman have their definitive origin in the Spirit, the Giver of Life (cf. Jn 6:63). Joseph, in obedience to the Spirit, *found in the Spirit the source of love, the conjugal love which he experienced as a man.* And this love proved to be greater than this 'just man' could ever have expected within the limits of his human heart."[12]

These are stunning sentences about an even more powerful grace that is given to Joseph. Due to the nature of the communion of saints, Joseph wants to intercede, that this grace be given to all those who bind themselves in love to the Bride, the Church: "Joseph, in obedience to the Spirit, found in the Spirit the source of love, the conjugal love which he experienced as a man." For the celibate priest, his spousal identity is satisfied in having spiritual communion with the Bride, Mary, in the Spirit, who loves his priesthood more than he does himself. His erotic desires, if need be, are purified and ordered toward *the source of love* and not toward any one woman exclusively. Mary will order the priest toward the Source and ask this Spirit to come to him and bring to him "the conjugal love" he wants to experience as a man.

This spousal mystery carries with it the fullness of Christ's own identity as being fully human and fully God. By way of the flesh he received from Mary, the Second Person of the Blessed Trinity was placed in communion with humanity in a new way, in a way that would eventually lead to the total self-donation of his body and blood for the salvation of his Bride, the Church. From, and *in*, Mary, his mother, came his communion with his chosen Bride, humanity. Above, I pointed to this arresting sentence in the Catechism: she now knows the humanity which, in her, *the Son of God espouses.* I did so because its truth is being experienced in the prayer lives of some priests for whom I serve as spiritual director: Mary comes to them in prayer as spouse.[13] Some might argue it is "better" to relate to Mary as

---

[12] John Paul II, *Redemptoris Custos* (1989) n. 19.

[13] "… Although Mary remains the Mother of Jesus at the foot of the Cross, it is necessary to have another term to delineate precisely the particular bond which unites her to Christ. Tradition and Liturgy have found this term in the Song of Songs: "spouse". Mary is truly the spouse [in the Song for she espouses all the sentiments that Christ crucified has for His Father and for humanity. (…) Mary is transformed into Jesus without ceasing to be herself." –Fr. Antonio Carvalho, *A Pessoa E A Missão Da Bem-Aventurada Virgem Maria No Livro AOS Sacerdotes Filhos Prediletos De Nossa Senhora De PE. Stefano Gobbi* ,(Dayton Ohio: STD dissertation, International Marian Research Institute, 2008) 113. The author is quoting from: Philippe, Card. Pierre Paul. *The Virgin Mary and the Priesthood,* Translated by Rev. Laurence J. Spiteri, Society of St. Paul, Staten Island, NY, 1993, pp.52-53.

mother because she "forms" one into Christ. It is also, however, a powerful role of the woman to "form" the man she marries into her "spouse." There is in the woman a formative power ordered toward the complete man, son and spouse.]

The Spiritual Aid of Mary

Since Mary is the New Eve, the Woman (Jn 2:4; 19:26), she desires to order men correctly toward their spousal-masculine identity. In the case of the priest particularly, she wants to see her Son's Church secured in salvation through his grace given to priests in their commitment as chaste spouses. Hence, in prayer, many priests turn to Mary to assist them with their commitment to chaste celibacy. She knows the spousal nature of man is under attack within western culture (androgyny, homosexual "unions," high divorce and remarriage rates, addiction to pornography, etc.). It appears that the movement of the Holy Spirit in, and through, the Holy Family, endeavors to counteract this attack by securing the spousal nature of the priesthood. Mary's love for the priesthood, a priesthood which embodies her own Son's sacrificial gift of himself, draws her to be the strongest of "helpmates" (Gn 2: 18) for the priest.

The erotic energy of the chaste celibate reaches its rest only in, and through, the truth of his vocation itself. The man called to priesthood must live in reality. He will never have a spouse to hold, and yet, as a man, he desires with all his heart to give himself to woman. If such good and natural desires are not acknowledged directly, truthfully, and in the context of one's vocation, they have the potential to break out in underground ways, ways filled with distortion and lies (e.g., the viewing of pornography as a habit, or other acts of infidelity).[14] Those seminarians or priests who have become alienated from their masculine and spousal identity by repression can be invited to open their hearts to Joseph and Mary so that their fears or shame can be healed. Alternately, those men who have courageously suffered the coming of sexual integration, chastity, and desire to deepen their intimacy with God can count on Mary and Joseph to intercede for them. In prayer, the celibate approaches Mary in the Spirit and asks for St. Joseph's intercession to overcome any fear he might have in sharing with Mary his deepest longings for a bride. Since in faith, hope, and love, imagination connects the priest to the Paschal Mystery, he can be assured that his communication with the saints about his deepest affective movements, and his need to love and be loved, will be received in all truth. They will also be received by the saints in accord with any affective and spiritual healing needed by the priest as well. Here, of course, is

---

[14] See William Lynch, SJ, *Images of Hope* (Ind.:Univ.of Notre Dame, 1987) 244-245.

where the skilled spiritual director can be most helpful as he encourages the priest to hide nothing from Christ and the saints *in his prayer*. The spiritual intimacy carried by *deep contemplative prayer* in the Spirit, and in the company of the saints, carries with it a healing that purifies the sinfully disordered,[15] erotic drive, leaving a man free to give himself in mature love. If such contemplative prayer becomes a way of life, the purified *eros* becomes characteristic of a man, established as a virtue, a virtue longing to be completed in holiness. As Benedict began his pontificate, he states: "An intoxicated and undisciplined *eros*, then, is not an ascent in 'ecstasy' towards the Divine, but a fall, a degradation of man. Evidently, *eros* needs to be disciplined and purified if it is to provide, not just fleeting pleasure, but a certain foretaste of the pinnacle of our existence, of that beatitude for which our whole being yearns."[16]

Conclusion

Since marriage does not exist solely for the reproduction of another member of the species, but for the creation of a communion of persons, those who live consecrated to priesthood are sustained, too, in a communion of persons, in intimacy with their friends, saints, and God. Issuing forth from a life of such communion is much spiritual fruit for the sake of the Church. To enter such intimate prayer with the Mary, Joseph, and Jesus is to have the very rationale for a celibate clergy born anew in the priest's heart, obliterating all doubt that such a call exists simply for pragmatic reasons. The priest, sacramentally sharing in Christ's own self-donative love, continues the love that Christ had for his Church: a singular, pure, and satisfying love for both Spouse and Bride. Such a love calls out to society that this passing age (cf. Rm 12:1-2) does not exhaust the meaning of life. There is more. There is the hope of complete rest in divine love. Mary's earnest hope is to bring all priests to love like her Son did … a Bridegroom giving all, even unto death itself.

This article was originally published in *Homiletic & Pastoral Review* (http://www.hprweb.com, 2013). It is republished here with the permission of HPR and the author, after having been revised by the author, who has additionally provided the following prayer, practicum reflection questions, and suggested resources.

---

[15] Here, we are arguing that for the affectively normal and maturing male prayer can assist with the integration of his sexual identity moving him from vice to virtue. Obviously, sexual deviancy as a mental or emotional illness needs psychological treatment outside of priestly formation.

[16] Benedict XVI, *Deus Caritas Est* (2005) n. 4.

Prayer

Lord, give me the courage to share all my desires with you and the saints. May this commitment to self-revelation in the presence of Love itself sustain my chaste celibacy and render it fruitful in ministry and mission. Amen.

Practicum Reflection Questions for Formators

1. In what ways in prayer and devotion have you invited Mary into your heart, allowing her presence to draw you into believing that you are a spousal gift? How are you tasting the desire to give yourself to the Church in spousal self-donation?

2. Have you invited St Joseph teach you how to provide for and protect the Church's teachings (doctrinal, moral, spiritual) in the way he provided for and protected Mary as spouse? What transpires in your heart as you allow St. Joseph to mentor you?

3. Like St Joseph are you allowing yourself to enter into daily prayer, abiding with Mary's love, sharing your burdens and joys in the gift of chaste celibacy? What transpires when you allow yourself to abide with Mary in daily events?

4. Have you asked St John Paul II to intercede for you so that you may receive what St. Joseph knew in his marriage to Mary, a spousal tasting of virginal-conjugal-love in the Holy Spirit? St. John Paul II wrote about this in "Guardian of the Redeemer." Are you ready, willing and able to ask for this grace in the gift of chaste celibacy? How would this be spiritually and morally related to your own call to chaste celibacy as one married to Mary as the face of the Church? Where must your prayer life go to more fully understand this mystery?

Suggested Resources

1. Donald Haggerty, *The Contemplative Hunger* (Ignatius, 2016).
2. Jacques Philippe, *In the School of the Holy Spirit* (Scepter, 2007).
3. Dietrich von Hildebrand, *In Defense of Purity* (Hildebrand Project, 2017).

Chapter Six

EXIGENT RELATIONS: PHILOSOPHICAL REFLECTIONS ON THE CENTRALITY OF FATHERHOOD AND SONSHIP

Dr. Timothy Fortin, M.S., Ph.D.

Timothy Fortin is an Assistant Professor in Philosophical Theology at Immaculate Conception Seminary School of Theology at Seton Hall University in South Orange, New Jersey where he has engaged in the intellectual formation of seminarians since 2009. He holds a Ph.D. in philosophy from the Pontifical University of the Holy Cross in Rome, an M.S. in clinical psychology from the Institute for the Psychological Sciences, and an M.A. in philosophy from the Catholic University of America. His doctoral dissertation, *Fatherhood and the Perfection of Masculine Identity: A Thomistic Account in Light of Contemporary Science* was published by EDUSC, Rome, 2008. More recently, he has published the following articles on the nature of human sexual difference: "Finding Form: Defining Human Sexual Difference", *Nova et Vetera,* English Edition, Vol. 15, No. 2 (2017), and "To Be from Another: Nature, Sexual Difference, and the Gift of Existence", *Forum: Supplement to Acta Philosophica,* Volume 3 (2017).

Must all men be fathers? The draw of women towards motherhood seems evident, but men do not seem so strongly disposed towards fatherhood. What, then, is the nature of man's inclination towards fatherhood? Is such a desire — insofar as it exists at all — something that can be set aside for the sake something else? And, how do priests and seminarians stand in the face of man's natural inclination towards fatherhood? If a man is called by nature to be a father, does the fatherhood of the priest answer this call? "Father" is the name the priest will bear perhaps more than any other. But, what does it mean when said of him? Is it, perhaps, at best a sign of respect, but, too often, a title emptily said? In this short work, I will argue that it is for good reason that a priest is called father. And further, that, if he is to lead a fulfilled and flourishing life, he must, in fact, embrace the internal call to fatherhood and render his life an expression of that call. Without such generativity, freely, generously, and authentically embraced, bitterness — perhaps secret bitterness — is likely to begin to seep through his life. Thus, a great imperative falls to the formator: he must kindle the fire of fatherhood in the souls of seminarians so that seminarian-become-priest may embody his name of "father" as something he really is rather than bear it as an empty title.

The work will unfold as follows: It will have two main parts: the first will be mindful of the supernatural, but will focus on the natural. The second part is the inverse: it will focus on the supernatural but with a continual backward glance to our prior philosophical work. Part I has three subparts: First, I will establish a sufficiently robust definition of fatherhood that is able to accommodate all the modalities that necessarily enter into a discussion of the fatherhood of the priest: natural, spiritual, and divine. Next, I will argue that fatherhood is an imperative for *all* men: married, priest, religious, single. Regardless of one's state in life, fatherhood stands as a kind of invitation that importunes all. Having established the universal call to fatherhood, next, I will show how the call to fatherhood implies the necessity of both sonship and espousal. Part II turns expressly to the fatherhood of the priest. It begins with a brief argument solidifying the priestly call to fatherhood and espousal. Next, there follows a brief theological reflection on the nature of priestly fatherhood, espousal, and sonship.

Part I: *What is fatherhood?*

What defines fatherhood? The question seems simple enough. In fact, we utilize the word every day with little trouble. But, upon reflection, many questions open before us — especially in a work with a theological trajectory. Our most immediate experience of fatherhood, and hence the genealogical origin the word, lies in human fatherhood. And so, the definition seems quite simple: a father is a human male who has successfully actualized his power of generation: he has performed his essential role in the act of reproduction and so, along with the mother, produced a son or daughter. This is a relatively simple definition that explains our facile use of the term. But, from this frame of reference, we must look around; in fact, we must look down, look up, and look around.

As we look down, we see other living things that reproduce sexually. There are male cannabis plants and female cannabis plants. When the two have successfully reproduced, should we call the male a father? And, if we do, is that predication univocal with its application to a human father? The same question could be asked about the papa bear — or any animal that has reproduced by means of spermatozoa. And if we look up, we are confronted by the fatherhood of God. Does not the Vulgate tell us that it is from God's paternity that all paternity is named? "For this cause I bow my knees to the Father of our Lord Jesus Christ, of whom all paternity in heaven and earth is named (Eph. 3: 14-15, Douay-Rheims)."[1] But, we must also look sideways to our usages of the word within the realm of our human experience: there are adoptive fathers, father-figures, fathers of nations, and, finally, that which interests us most here, spiritual fathers. How do all these predications relate? What do all these fathers have in common? How do they differ?

Engaging all such question is, of course, impossible here. But, if philosophy is to help theology in understanding the fatherhood of the priest and hence its importance for the seminarian, we must at the very least establish a working definition that will accommodate the analogy of human and divine paternity. To that end, perhaps it will be helpful to consider an elegant solution that allowed St. Thomas Aquinas to relatively easily unravel many of the above questions. For St. Thomas, in humans, the essential distinction between male and female was quite clear: males possess the *active* power of generation, while females possess the *passive* power of generation.[2] What this meant was that, while females provided *that which could be formed* into a new human person — the matter (from the *mater*) — the male provided the seed which contained the *forming power*, i.e., that which could dispose the special matter provided by the mother such that it was able to receive the human soul and thereby bring about the coming to be a new human being.[3] Roughly speaking, the male provides that which gives form to the matter, and the mother provides the special matter. Thus, male and female possess the power of generation differently. Fatherhood, indicates the completion of the power of generation according to the male mode of possessing that power.[4] A man becomes a father when he has generated another like in kind to himself according to his mode of possessing the power of generation. So, putting the two together, a father is one who has generated according to the active power of generation.

This formulation of human fatherhood gives Thomas a clear thoroughfare forward for linking human and divine fatherhood. God's fatherhood most properly names the origin of

---

[1] "...*huius rei gratia flecto genua mea ad Patrem Domini nostri Iesu Christi ex quo omnis paternitas in caelis et in terra nominatur* (Eph. 3: 14-15)."

[2] See, for example, ST.I.92.1.

[3] Thomas argues that, because the human soul has an immaterial operation and hence is immaterial, it must be created directly by God. Hence, the direct agency of God is necessary in the generation of a new human person. See ST.I.118.2. Hence, the agency of man is limited to the disposition of the matter to make it suitable to receive the divine agency.

[4] ST.I.33.2 ad 2. In fact, this definition will prove to be a good definition. We will just have to refine what is meant by the male mode of possessing the power.

Christianity's central mystery, the Trinity: The Father eternally begets the Son. Though the term is used analogically, there is generation here. There is no question but that the Father's generation is active, not passive. Hence, God the Father is rightly called "Father." So, when we look back to human generativity in light of the revelation of Divine generativity, we see the analogy between the terms; in spite of the unfathomable difference that exists between them, each is called father because each has generated according to an active power of generation. And so, the Latin rendering of Ephesians 3:15 likewise makes sense. For, while human paternity is first in our *knowledge*, divine paternity is first in the order of being; while our *knowledge* of paternity begins with human fathers, *fatherhood itself*, begins in God.

Thomas's understanding is clear and relatively simple. The problem is that advancements in biology rendered the understanding of the distinction between human fatherhood and motherhood no longer tenable in the way he understood it. It can no longer be reasonably held that the human male possesses the active power of generation while the female possesses the passive power. It is simply not the case that the female provides matter while the male provides that which can give form to the matter. In fact, each show an equal activity in shaping their proper gametes, sperm and egg. With this in mind, we might think to return to the biological definition of a father hinted at above: a father is one who has reproduced by means of spermatozoa, while the mother has reproduced by means of ova. This is clear. But it certainly could only be applied to the Trinity by a metaphor stretched well beyond the breaking point. Thus, if we wish to try to maintain a rendering of fatherhood that pertains analogically to God and man we must look beyond spermatozoa.

It is here that we must look to the nature of the human body and to St. John Paul II's understanding of what the body signifies. Biologically, sexual difference regards the asymmetrical division of the power of generation. Some plants and almost all animals have taken the radical step of dividing their power of generation between two members of the species. As surprising as nature's move to divide the power of generation was her opting to do so non-identically. The power of generation is divided into two distinct mating types that both equally possess the nature of the species in its fullness, but possess the power of generation in distinct ways. Again, biologically, that which distinguishes one from the other is production of distinct reproductive cells — sperm vs. ova. However, in addition to this distinction, we can also see a kind of modal distinction in masculine and feminine generativity that perhaps returns the predication of "father" to analogy from metaphor when applied to God and man.

St. John Paul II identifies what he calls a hermeneutic of gift when observing the dynamic of male and female.[5] In that dance — as is the case of any instance of gift giving — there is an order; there is one who must first give the gift in an outward procession of being and another who must receive the gift in an inward acceptance of that which is given. These modes of participating in the dynamic of gift are constitutive of the essential difference between the masculine and feminine. Fatherhood, then, regards generativity in the masculine mode, which is to say to have generated by an outpouring of self, a kind of procession of being that ultimately terminates in another like in kind. In human generation, the masculine must be met by a feminine, co-generative principle who receives the gift from the father and, in so doing, simultaneously gives the gift of fatherhood to the father in return. Thus, there is a reciprocal dynamic of giving established that differs only in priority of order: the masculine gives and receives in the giving; the feminine actively receives and gives in the receiving.[6] In this dynamic, the father and mother share a common gift, the child, which is the fruit of their reciprocal giving and receiving. The father then is the one who initiates the gift in the outward proceeding of his being.[7]

Fatherhood in Time

Up to this point, I have been speaking about fatherhood in its proper sense, which is when one generates another *like in kind* unto himself. Thus, fatherhood is said most properly of God and His relation within the Blessed Trinity. It is also said in a proper, but secondary way of human fathers in relation to their children. However, we must now, briefly say more about human fatherhood; for it does not — and cannot — end simply with the act of the generation of a new human person. Divine fatherhood is eternal and perfect: the Son, as the creed says, is eternally begotten of the Father; there is no becoming. He possesses all that the Father possesses and possesses this perfection eternally. Such is not the case with human fathers and human sons and daughters. All of us begin our substantial being — that first moment when we become a new human being, i.e., the moment of

---

[5] John Paul II, *Man and Woman He Created Them: A Theology of the Body*, Michael Waldstein [trans.], Pauline Books and Media, Boston, 2006, 13:3.

[6] For a discussion of the reciprocal dynamic between male and female see David L. Schindler, "Catholic Theology, Gender, and the Future of Western Civilization," *Communio* Volume XX, Number 2 (Summer 1993): 200-239.

[7] Here we have a rendering of maleness and femaleness that is like that of St. Thomas's in that it associates a certain initiation and outward procession with the father, but unlike it in that it does not define maleness and femaleness in terms of presence or absence of the active power of generation.

conception — in a state of profound imperfection: while we are fully human in that we possess that which defines us as the kind of thing we are, we are profoundly lacking in that which pertains to the perfections that are due to us.[8] Thus, in a way, a man can be called "father" once his seed has fertilized an egg. But, this is only the beginning of human fatherhood. St. Thomas is clear on this point:

> But man's generative process would be frustrated [*Frustra autem esset hominis generatio*] unless it were followed by proper nutrition, because the offspring would not survive if proper nutrition were withheld. Therefore, the emission of semen ought to be so ordered that it will result in both the production of the proper offspring and in the upbringing of this offspring.[9]

Man's fatherhood would be empty if the new human being in whose coming to be he essentially participated were to cease to be shortly after being generated. The father, if he is truly to be a generator, must continue his generative activity regarding his offspring; he must bring his fatherhood to completion.[10] As such, we can begin to look at different ways in which human fatherhood unfolds in time.

First, if, as Thomas noted, that which began in the emission of the seed is not to be in vain, a human father must be a *protector*. Beginning with the new life in the womb of his spouse, he must anticipate and obviate that which threatens the life he has begotten. Next, he must be a *provider*; as is possible for him, he must provide that which is necessary for the growth of his new child. Human development is famously slow in comparison with other higher animals. During that prolonged development, father and mother must provide everything necessary so that the child's developmental path is not frustrated; the child is

---

[8] Thomas holds that all the perfections of our powers flow from the essence of the soul; hence, once the soul is present, i.e. once we are human, all the perfection are *in a way* present as there in potency, but much actualization of potential lies in front of a newly conceived human life, beginning with the radical development of all his or her parts and organs within the womb. See ST.I.77.

[9] "Frustra autem esset hominis generatio nisi et debita nutritio sequeretur: quia genitum non permaneret, debita nutritione subtracta. Sic igitur ordinata esse seminis debet emissio ut sequi possit et generatio conveniens, et geniti educatio (*Summa Contra Gentiles*, 3.122)."

[10] It is worth noting that in almost all other primates and mammals the father plays almost no role in care for young beyond the act of insemination. Evolutionists speculate that it was only paternal investment that allowed the human brain to develop to the size and complexity that permit human thought. See David C. Geary, *Male, Female: The Evolution of Human Sex Differences* (Washington, DC: American Psychological Association, 1998), 118.

simply unable to do so. Finally, the father must act as *teacher and guide*. He must share from his being and give of that which he possesses in wisdom and virtue, as is possible, to his children. In short, he must not only provide external things the absence of which would harm his child — the most basic things such shelter, water, fire, and food — he must give his children all he has; he must share the full wealth of himself as a being that is both matter and spirit.[11]

Recently, a good friend of mine told me about his week: five of his six children had a stomach virus. In the three nights prior to our conversation, he had had close to no sleep. He had counted seventeen instances of vomiting that he had to clean-up, some of which were directs hits upon him. He was being a father. He was protecting his children and providing for them. More importantly, he was teaching them and guiding them: he was modeling wisdom and virtue both in his sacrifice for his wife, whom he knew needed sleep after spending the day with the sick children, and in the love he showed towards his kids in patiently attending to them in their suffering. Human fatherhood is a many faceted reality that centers upon the gift of self in a generative outpouring that bears the fruit of new being.

A Universal Call

But, are *all* men called to fatherhood? Or, are some men, perhaps, exempted from the exigence of generativity? It might be argued that human genetics testifies against the claim that all men are called to fatherhood: variance in DNA in the Y chromosome (inherited from the father) versus mitochondrial DNA (inherited from the mother) indicates that we have all had many more female ancestors than male ancestors. This means that there were many more women who were mothers than males who were fathers, and so many men who were never biological fathers. Thus, perhaps evolution would argue that fatherhood pertains to the stronger and more genetically fit, not to all men. St. Thomas himself notes that not *all* men *must* be fathers in the order of natural generation. It is true, that men *considered generally* are bound by natural law to continue the existence of human race through procreation, but not all men *individually* must do so. In fact, the spiritual advancement of the human race is also necessary; so, some men may set themselves aside for this and forego natural generation.[12] Thus, might we say that not *all* men are called to fatherhood?

---

[11] For a brief summary of sociological and psychological effects of father absence, see Warren Farrell and John Gray, *The Boy Crisis: Why Our Boys Are Struggling and What We Can Do About It* (Dallas, TX: BenBella Books, Inc., 2018)

[12] See ST.II-II.152.2 ad 1.

Perhaps a bit of a peculiar philosophical exercise suggested by French philosopher Fabrice Hadjadj will shed light upon this question. However, before following Hadjadj in his reflections, it will be helpful first to consider briefly an anthropological point that underpins his thought; it is the same fundamental anthropological point that underlies St. John Paul II's Theology of the Body. The human being is a substantial unity composed of two constituent principles: form *and matter*. Matter and form *together* constitute the essence of the human person. The human body comes into being through its form, that is, through its soul. The body is thus, in a sense, the manifestation of the soul. And, in the case of the human being, the soul is spiritual.[13] The body is not, as the dualists would have it, a kind of cloak we wear in this mortal life and then shed in death, nor is it *only* a *manifestation* of who we *truly* are; it is an *essential* aspect of who we truly are. We are our bodies; for our bodies are the *result* of the union of form and matter that is us. Our bodies are not mere matter; they are the *formed* matter that is a human being. It just so happens that the bodily beings that we are also have a faculty that transcends the matter that man's form holds in existence. With this mind, let us then follow Hadjadj in his meditation.

In a work provocatively titled *"La Transcendance en Culottes"* — "Transcendence in Underpants" — he begins by asking his readers to contemplate their underbellies.[14] As one glances at the belly and below, one first notices the navel. As Hadjadj observes, it is a sign that we have come *from another*. Most immediately, it is a permanent carnal monument to our connection with our mothers. Brief reflection however further implies the presence of our fathers without whom we would have neither come to be simply, nor come to be connected with our mothers. Thus, the navel speaks eloquently of generational difference — of the fact that we were generated not just by one, but by two others, one of whom begot us, the other of whom bore us.

As our eyes move lower, we see the organs of generation. As the navel implied relation, so too do the organs of generation. The navel is a monument to the fact that we are *from* another. The genitals are a sign that we are *for* another, and this in at least two ways. At the beginning of his *Politics*, Aristotle famously wrote: "In the first place there must be a union of those who cannot exist without each other; namely, of male and female, that the race may

---

[13] For an explication of these points see ST.I.75-76.

[14] Fabrice Hadjadj, *Qu'est-ce qu'une famille? Suivi de La Transcendance en culottes* (Paris: Edition Salvador, 2014), 54-57. For a shortened version of this essay presented in English in New York City on January 18, 2014, see: https://youtu.be/yWO0PLsHYdM [Accessed March 9, 2019], from 29:40 to 59:50.

continue."[15] Hadjadj underscores the strength of this statement: male and female cannot exist without each other. The reproductive organs reveal this mutual dependence. As we have already discussed, the human power of generation is held jointly. We do not grow buds that become new humans. Male and female must join their partial powers of generation together. The genital organs testify to this ordering to the other. They imply that we cannot become whole in and through ourselves alone. We are for another — the spouse, through whom our generativity can be realized.

But, this generativity implies that we are also for another other; for the power that spousal union completes (the power of generation) precisely leads to the becoming of another, the child, who is the fruit of the union. Thus, a glance down his body reveals a man's destiny in fatherhood and espousal. It is written in every cell of his body; for every cell contains the genetic principle of the sexual difference that resolves in fatherhood. Thus, we could say that man's call to fatherhood is written in his flesh. And it's written in the flesh of every man. Hence, every man's body testifies to his destiny as father and spouse.

And God Saw That It Was Good

We have just noted how the human body indicates a kind of imperative written within man towards fatherhood and espousal. But, I have chosen to use strong language in this section; I have spoken of these two relations in terms of a "call". Certainly, human morphology points towards coupling and parenthood, but could this not simply be explained in the most rudimentary evolutionary terms? Human appetites would have to evolve to direct man towards fatherhood, otherwise, he would remove himself from the gene pool. But, does such a blunt reality constitute a call? And further, why does the mere presence of organs of generation constitute a *call* to their use?

Hadjadj notes that it is just such questions that bind human sexual difference with the power of reason: human beings are persons; they have dominion over their actions. They must *decide* to give new life. This means they must have a *reason* to do so. Generation cannot be a merely instinctive act if it is to be a truly *human* act. It is the outcome of a conscious decision. And the implications of that decision are momentous. Hadjadj eloquently frames the issue: "What good is it to keep filling-up cemeteries? What good is it

---

[15] Aristotle, Politics, B. Jowett [trans.] in, The Basic Works of Aristotle, Richard McKeon [ed.], Random House, New York, 1941, 1252a 26-28. For an insightful discussion of this text see F. Hadjadj, *Qu'est-ce qu'une famille?*, 65-68.

to have children, if it is only delay the triumph of the dust?"[16] The decision to have a child is a testament to the ultimate victory of life over the dust. It is a witness to a transcendent hope.

The teaching of St. Thomas on the Natural Law expresses the same radical implications of fatherhood. The Natural Law is man's participation in the Eternal Law.[17] Through the Eternal Law, God governs all things and directs them to Himself as to their end.[18] As a rational being, capable of understanding his own ends and able to govern himself regarding the attainment of those ends, man participates in the Eternal Law in a unique way. Man is inclined towards his good by inclinations written in his heart.[19] These inclinations are in the form of the most fundamental goods recognized by the intellect and sought by the will.[20] They are at the heart of man's deepest desires. Ultimately, they order him, according to the Eternal Law, to God. In a way, the deepest inclinations, the deepest desires that man has are those he shares with all other beings, all other substances. Fr. Lawrence Dewan is illustrative here:

> I have long maintained that the first level of inclination spoken of by Thomas should rather be considered in terms of the great universality it has. It pertains to all substances as such. Thus, it has not to do merely with the individual as an individual. It rather has to do with the being and well-being of being as such. It is the inclination of the creature as a creature. This is the inclination that is present in each thing, but present in that thing according to the proper mode of being of the thing.… This should not be read, for example, as though it did not include the tendency to reproduction, by which the

---

[16] F. Hadjadj, *Qu'est-ce qu'une famille?*, 71. English translation taken from Hadjadj's presentation at the New York Encounter, January 18, 2014.

[17] ST.I-II.91.2.

[18] ST.I-II.91.1.

[19] See ST.I-II.94.2. The concept of "heart" is not a simple one. I use the term roughly in the sense as used by Dutch psychiatrist, Conrad Baars. In this sense, heart has reference to both man's intellectual and emotional life. For Baars, heart encompasses both that which is intuitive in the intellect and the emotions of the concupiscible appetite. See Conrad Baars, "Psychic Causes and Consequences of the Abortion Mentality" in David Mall and Walter F. Watts eds., *The Psychological Aspects of Abortion* (Washington, DC: University Publications of America, 1979) 116-117.

[20] In ST.I-II.94.2, St. Thomas famously divides the precepts of the Natural Law according to man's "natural inclinations." I follow Fr. Stephen Brock in holding that these inclinations are inclinations of *reason* rather than sensory appetites. See: Stephen L. Brock, "Natural inclination and the intelligibility of the good in Thomistic natural law," *New Series*, Volume 6 (2005): 57-61.

species is preserved.[21]

All things are inclined towards the goodness of their own being. All things seek to maintain their own being, thus implying the goodness of their own being and the goodness of "being as such." Each being participates in this inclination in its own way. The human does so rationally. Hence man understands the goodness of being and longs for that being. (It is thus that the words are Christ are so compelling: "I have come that you might have life and have it abundantly." This speaks to our very desire for being.) Fr. Dewan holds that a man's inclination towards fatherhood is contained within that deepest recognition of the goodness of being.

But, it does not end there. he continues:

We see that the inclination common to all substances is a natural love for itself as an individual, and even more for its species, and still more again for the author of being, God Himself. In this respect, one should notice that in ST.I-II.94.2, the third inclination does not speak of love of God, but of knowledge concerning God.... Love of God, on the other hand, is presented everywhere in Thomas's writings as present in every substance as such, and indeed such that *every being loves God naturally more than it loves itself.* It is this domain of what might be called "transcendental inclination" that is being referred to in the first place in ST.I-II.94.2. The other two sorts of inclination are clearly relative to the genus and the species.[22]

Man shares a love for God with all that exists. For St. Thomas, all things love God. All things are ordered to Him by the Eternal Law. Fr. Dewan calls this a transcendental inclination. Hence, we touch upon a profound truth here: the call to fatherhood flows from the deepest longings implanted in man — a love that he shares with all beings. A love that ultimately longs for union with God. As Hadjadj noted, it is for this reason that the call to fatherhood is bound with our most fundamental judgement regarding being itself: it is better to be than not to be.

So, why, as Hadjadj so jarringly questions, keep filling cemeteries? For the human being, it is not enough even to see that being is good. He must see that God is good and that man's destiny is ultimately in His hands. Otherwise, we merely "delay the triumph of the

---

[21] Lawrence Dewan, "Natural Law and the First Act of Freedom: Maritain Revisited," in *Wisdom, Law, and Virtue* (New York: Fordham University Press, 2007), 238.

[22] Ibid. Emphasis added.

dust". Thus, Hadjadj astutely observes that, "… from the dawn of time human sexuality is surrounded less by rats than by rites."[23] The decision to bring a new human being into the world implies hope that even death can be transcended. It is thus surrounded by religious rites; for it is matter's highest expression of the love-song of all being for God.

Thus, all men are called to fatherhood. All men are called to espousal. And further this call comes in the form of the most fundamental desires of the heart of man. But, have we not gone too far? Is the implication then that all men, if they are to answer the desire to affirm the goodness of being, must then answer the call to natural fatherhood? Were this so, then certainly the Church's discipline regarding priestly celibacy would make little sense. To answer this, let us look in some detail to a text from St. Thomas to which we alluded earlier.

In replying to an objector who states that embracing virginity would be contrary to the natural law, Thomas replies:

A precept implies a duty, as stated above. Now there are two kinds of duty. There is the duty that has to be fulfilled by one person; and a duty of this kind cannot be set aside without sin. The other duty has to be fulfilled by the multitude, and the fulfillment of this kind of duty is not binding on each one of the multitude. For the multitude has many obligations which cannot be discharged by the individual, but are fulfilled by one person doing this, and another doing that. Accordingly the precept of natural law which binds man to eat must needs be fulfilled by each individual, otherwise the individual cannot be sustained. On the other hand, the precept of procreation regards the whole multitude of men, which needs not only to multiply in body, but also to advance spiritually. Wherefore sufficient provision is made for the human multitude, if some betake themselves to carnal procreation, while others abstaining from this betake themselves to the contemplation of Divine things, for the beauty and welfare of the whole human race.[24]

It is important to note in Thomas's reply what he is saying and what he isn't. Human being is a good that must be preserved. However, to achieve that good, not every individual must procreate. It is at least not necessary that every man be called to natural fatherhood. However, for what does man forego this natural generativity? For any reason? We see from the text that it is only for another mode of generativity that man foregoes natural fatherhood. He may forego the enriching of being in one way for the sake of dedicating

---

[23] Hadjadh, *Qu'est-ce qu'une famille?*, 71.

[24]ST.II-II.152.2 ad 1

himself to enriching being in another. Put otherwise, he may forego one mode of fatherhood for the sake of another kind of fatherhood. Thus, the embracing of virginity is not about the negation of those inclinations proper to the most fundamental stratum of the Natural Law; it is rather about directing those desires to a different mode of generativity. Another text from St. Thomas is helpful here. In considering the relative merits of active versus contemplative orders he explains that that life is highest which not only gathers the rare fruits of contemplation but also shares that fruit with others:

> Accordingly we must say that the work of the active life is twofold. One proceeds from the fullness of contemplation, such as teaching and preaching. Wherefore Gregory says (Hom. v in Ezech.) that the words of Psalm 144:7, "they shall publish the memory of . . . Thy sweetness," refer "to perfect men returning from their contemplation." And this work is more excellent than simple contemplation. For even as it is better to enlighten than merely to shine, so is it better to give to others the fruits of one's contemplation than merely to contemplate. [25]

It is a greater sign of the fullness of one's own being not only that he possesses such being, but also that he shares that being with others. But, we are now speaking of a kind of spiritual fatherhood, and, hence, the final section of this essay. However, before entering into our final discussion, we must quickly return to the navel.

Sons and Spouses

We began this section on the universal call to fatherhood following Hadjadj in a reflection on man's underbelly. Up to this point, we have focused upon the implications of the genital organs — in man's being *for* another, viz., for his spouse and for his daughters and sons. Our focus has been upon fatherhood. So, before concluding this section, we should say a little more about man as son and expand upon the understanding of man as spouse.

Before a man can become a spouse and father, he must first be a son. It is clear that no man is his own cause. Our navels proclaim to us that we have come from another. All that we have has been given to us. As such, there is nothing that we can give to another that we have not first received. If a man is to be a father, he must first be a son; he must first have received from the fullness of the being of another. If man is ever to reach a state in which he

---

[25] ST.II-II.188.6.

will be able not only to possess a certain fullness, but also to be able to share that being, he must begin as a beggar. He must begin realizing that, in the order of contingent being, sonship precedes fatherhood. His fatherhood must be received fatherhood.

But, we are now confronted with another mystery. For, as we have observed before, man cannot be generative of new being — at least not substantial being — on his own. To produce another like himself, he needs another unlike himself: he needs woman. And so, this mystery opens up before us: It is only in giving himself to another (his spouse) that he may give himself to another (his child). In order to become a father, he must first become a spouse. He must offer himself and his own partial, imperfect power of generativity to the other who can complete him. He must engage in the dance of giving and receiving discerned by St. John Paul II. Thus, it is only in giving himself to his spouse that he may, to use the potent language of Aristotle, fully exists. For only in losing his being in another, may he then give his being to another.

Part II: *Priest and Father*

So, what are we to say then of the priest and the seminarian? We have seen that the call to fatherhood is implanted in depths of each man's heart. And, if to be father, a man must first be spouse, then so too does the desire for this mysterious other echo deeply in a man's being. Must a man negate these desires if he wishes to become a priest? Is it the role of formators to learn to identify these inclinations and at best wipe them clean out of a young man's heart, or at least drive them deep into hiding, into a place so hidden and remote that they are not likely to cause any harm? Or, by sharp contrast, must the formators find and rouse the desire for fatherhood, rouse the desire for to be a spouse and fan the embers into a flame of love that, by God's grace, will enlighten and give warmth to all whom he is called to serve? We have already indicated the key to answering these questions: The issue is not whether or not a man is called to be a father. All men are called to be fathers; all men are called to profoundly share their being in and through first giving themselves to another. I have tried to make the case, up to this point, that all being, in its love for God, proclaims the goodness of that-which-is, and hence seeks out the goodness of that being in a way proper to its own mode of existing. For the human male, this is done in and through fatherhood. Priest and natural father must each pour out their being so as to generate those like in kind unto themselves[26] — to share the gift they've been given. The gift must be as total as possible

---

[26] For the priest, this means others like him in the order of grace, that is, in the order of divine adoption.

in each case. But, they will do so in different ways and in different orders. Hence, our discussion now turns to spiritual fatherhood. But, in so turning, we now step into waters far deeper than the philosopher as such can traverse.

We have spoken of modes of fatherhood, of how a biological father's fatherhood does not cease but rather only begins in the conception of his child. From that point on, he must protect, provide, and, even more closely resembling the initial act of fatherhood itself, teach and guide. In these ways, he continues to give of himself to his children. In the original act of fatherhood, he is an essential part in generating another human person. In his teaching and guiding, he adds to the perfection of these children. Certainly, the priest will be teacher and guide — and protector and provider as well. However, understanding the priest's role in the radiance of fatherhood from the Eternal Father, to the Eternal Son, and then, through the Holy Spirit, to the priest, is clearly the work of the theologian, which I, precisely, am not. My task has been primarily to show the need for such a theological resolution precisely to the inclinations that necessarily inhabit the heart of the priest in in his masculinity. However, though wandering outside the philosopher's realm, I will offer a few thoughts on such a theological vision. To do so, I will turn to the work of Christopher West.[27]

At the Foot of the Cross

Reflecting upon the thought of Archbishop Fulton Sheen,[28] West draws out attention to what he calls the Nuptial Cross. The image is of Mary the mother of Jesus at the foot of the Cross. She carries a chalice in which she gathers the blood and water that flows from the side of Christ. Were John the Apostle pictured in this image, we would have all we needed to begin our understanding of the sonship, espousal, and fatherhood of the priest. On the Cross, the High Priest, Jesus, in an act of fatherhood received from the Father, pours Himself out completely for His Bride, for those who will now become "sons in the Son". Through Him, with Him, and in Him, we are able to become sons of God. Hence, by grace, Jesus is generating those "like in kind" unto Himself. He is "becoming"[29] a father. St Augustine underscores the paternal quality of this sacrifice by noting that the blood and

---

[27] Christopher West, *At the Heart of the Gospel: Reclaiming the Body for the New Evangelization* (New York: Image Books, 2012), 119-123.

[28] Fulton Sheen, *Through the Year with Fulton Sheen*, compiler Henry Dieterich (San Francisco: Ignatius Press, 1985), 60.

[29] I do not intend to imply change in the Godhead.

water that flows from His side are His seed[30] — the seed that will bear the fruit of new creations in His image. Mary catches the blood and water flowing from Christ's side. As we have now entered into Divine realities penetrating the human realities, we see that, as in human marriage, there is a co-generative principle. Mary is the image of the Church. And she will nurture the seed given by the Bridegroom now Father — just as happened in the Incarnation itself when Mary's "yes" resulted in contemporaneous acts of fatherhood and motherhood. Not by necessity, but by Divine Wisdom, Mary as paradigmatic member of the Church now becomes the co-generative principle in the fatherhood of the High Priest. Mary is the new Eve. And so, those who have been begotten in the Lord so as to become new creations in Him — the Church, the Body of Christ, the Bride of Christ — become co-generators with him in begetting yet newer life.

Also, at the foot of the Cross is the young priest, John. Just the night before, he had been ordained by the High Priest to do as the High Priest had done: "Do this in memory of Me". Now, at the foot of the Cross, he is pronounced as a kind of first fruit of the co-generative principles of the High Priest/Bridegroom, and His bride, the Church as paradigmatically present in Mary: "Woman, behold your son. Son, behold your mother." The New Adam and the New Eve stand as father and mother of a new order of creation. But, what are we to say of the new, young priest, John and his priesthood? It is only now, at the foot of the Cross, that the meaning of his priesthood has come into focus. The One, True Priest has just offered His Eternal Sacrifice in love to the Father, and, in so doing, became the father of a nation whose members are, at least in call and potency, as numerous as the stars of the sky and the sands of the sea shore. This is the priesthood to which John has been ordained. It is likewise thus the fatherhood in which he is thereby called to participate in a special way. But, if he is to allow the fullness of this fatherhood to come to be, there is an order which must be followed — the order established on Calvary.

Beggars, Sons, and Spouses Revisited

Before John can enter into the fullness of priesthood, he must first become a son — "Woman, behold your son." John must begin with his poverty, with his nakedness, with his need to receive all. Thus, we first see the act of God's pure mercy, His looking with compassion upon the lowliness of His servant and offering, not His castigation, but the greatest possible participation in His very life: He offers John sonship in the blood and

---

[30] Archbishop Sheen quotes St. Augustine on this point in the above-mentioned reference. As of yet, I have not been able to find the original text in the work of Augustine.

water flowing from the side of the Son, nourished by the Virgin Mother and fructifying in the soul and body of the Beloved Disciple. Having received sonship and thus becoming part of the Bride of Christ, the Church, he can now receive from the Bridegroom the gifts He wishes to lavish upon His bride, the Church. Simply as a member of the body of Christ, John is now called, as is every baptized member, to be a co-generator of new life with and through the Bridegroom, Jesus Christ. In John's case, however, among the gifts latent in the seed of the blood and the water, was the gift of sacramental priesthood. He thus now has a unique relationship with the Church; he will now stand in the Person of the High Priest and thus engage the Church as her bridegroom. He is called to lay down his life for the bride. His side must now also be pierced so that blood and water may flow out, so that he may participate in the priesthood of Christ and thereby participate in His fatherhood. Each day, at Mass, he will gather anew from Jesus, through the Church, the blood and water from the side of Christ and offer it anew for the sake of Jesus' Bride, who is now likewise the bride of the priest, in the hope that the seed will find receptive soil.

An Existential Call

Before concluding, one important point remains to be made: Perhaps it could seem that, because of the ontological change that the sacrament of Holy Orders effects, and the instrumental channels of grace that it opens through the priest, that it is enough for the priest to merely exercise his sacramental role in his post or parish in order to find the fulfillment of fatherhood in his life. Experience, however, belies this proposal. The priest who becomes a mere dispenser of the sacraments does participate in the fatherly and spousal acts of Christ, but, he does so as a mere instrument. He becomes a functionary. He is like the sperm-donor father whose only involvement in the life of his children is the fleeting moments necessary to plant the seed and then walk away. Such a living (or rather avoidance) of priestly fatherhood will not fulfill the desires of the priest's heart for fatherhood and espousal, for it is precisely his heart that is missing, that has not entered into the essence of his priestly life. A priest in mortal sin can draw the Real Presence down to the altar over which he stands, and speak those momentous words in the person of Christ that every penitent longs to hear: I absolve you from your sin in the name of the Father and the Son, and the Holy Spirit. But is such a priest, in merely fulfilling his functions, really a father in the same way that Padre Pio or John Paul II was a father? What is the difference? Both exercises the instrumental causality proper to the Holy Orders, but, how differently the word "father" rings upon our lips and tastes upon our tongues when said of a man like John

Paul II or Padre Pio in contrast to a priest who has forsaken his fatherhood.

Perhaps the difference is that men such as these great saints have truly lived all the relationships of which we have spoken: in their poverty they have accepted the adoption as sons in the Son and heard the words of the Father spoken of them: "Behold my beloved son, in whom I am well pleased." They have accepted their role in the Church as bride to the eternal Bridegroom and so become co-generators with Him. And finally, they have not run from their own *personal* call to fatherhood. They have, of course, accepted their role as instruments of God's grace in confecting the sacraments, but to this inestimable gift, they have added the total gifts of themselves from the depths of their being — a being which is ever more conformed to the being of Christ. Thus, in pouring out the gifts of the sacraments they simultaneously pour out the gifts of themselves. It is only in this way, in the true, impassioned, and loving outpouring of themselves that they will fulfill the rumbling longings in the depths of their soul to be spouse and father. Teaching, managing a parish and balancing a budget are tasks that a father and spouse need to attend to doing. These necessary things may give the priest a certain level of fulfillment. But only freely and willingly entering into the nuptial and paternal activity of being with Christ on the Cross will make his heart burn. Functions must be rooted in an intimate foundational love affair with Christ crucified. For only then will all the relational identities of his destiny come to fruition: He is son. He is spouse. And he is father with Christ.

A Brief Summary

Perhaps what we have said in this short work may seem simple, almost self-evident. Fatherhood refers to one who has generated another according to the masculine mode of generation; he has generated another according to the initiation of an outward-flowing gift of self. In human fatherhood, this outward procession implies a co-generative principle that receives the gift, adds her gift to it and thereby returns two gifts to the father: the child and his fatherhood. What exists perfectly and eternally present in God, in human fatherhood, stretches out throughout the lifetime of a man: man's gift of self begins with the substantial being of his children, but is ordered to the ultimate fullness of their being — which lies ultimately in the Eternal Father. Hence, that which exists simply in God, exists in many facets in man. However, we also noted that, if a man is to be a father, he must first be a son. He must first be a beggar. He must first receive all that subsequently he might give. And yet further, if he is to give, he cannot give alone. If he is to give himself to another (his child), he must first give himself to another (his spouse). Next, we saw how the desire for this generativity is implanted deeply in the heart of man. It is a desire that flows from the recognition of the goodness of being itself. It rests on the fulcrum upon which pivot man's most fundamental judgments: the choice of hope or despair; life or death; being or non-being. As such, the desire for fatherhood and the allied desire for espousal cannot be eradicated from the heart of man except at the cost of a negation of being itself. With this in mind, we noted the imperative that the seminarian neither run nor hide from these desires, but rather embrace them in the modality that is proper to the life to which he is called. Hence, we offered some reflections on the sonship, espousal, and fatherhood of the priest.

Epilogue: Reflections and Challenges for Formators

To close, I would like to offer a few thoughts about the role of formators in awakening and developing the sense of all three of these relations within the seminarian. (Though not a priest myself, but as one involved in seminary formation, these are thoughts with which I continually challenge myself.) Seminarians must begin as sons; they must begin in poverty, recognizing first that they stand in need of being filled and formed by another. This sonship stands most profoundly in reference to their relationship to the Eternal Father, whose sons they are in Jesus Christ. However, their sonship is mediated, to a certain extent, through the fatherhood of the formators. Hence, the formator stands as father to the seminarian; he stands as one already given a gift which he now must, in turn, share with another. But, this means that the formator first must intensify his own position as son, as beggar, as one who stands, in his poverty, in need in receiving all always from the Father. Fatherhood radiates. It can never be severed from its ultimate source, the Father. The radiance, however, is not automatic. At every step it involves free agents who must first embrace their poverty and then freely, maturely embrace the gift received. This demands honesty as regards what one has truly and freely received; it demands honesty regarding that which one truly believes and has verified in his own experience, in contrast to what he merely pronounces with his lips. This need for a free, mature embracing of what is received is needed as much for formator as for seminarian. Fatherhood is given first in sonship. Only in continually embracing their sonship can formators answer the imperative to be fathers, to pour out their lives for those whom they hope to help to make into true fathers. You cannot give what you don't have. Thus, the seminarian cannot give being that he has not received. And, from where will he learn to be a father as a priest? Again, the ultimate answer to this question is always the Eternal Father, but he will learn proximately from his formators. They must model fatherhood. This is, obviously, a challenge to all formators. For true fatherhood is a challenging reality. Because by its essence, it involves a gift of being, it can only arise from a gift of being that has first been received; thus, it cannot be faked. It can be mimicked. Ultimately, you cannot get blood from a stone. The first step, then, is for the formator to beg the Lord that He turn any stony portions of his heart into a heart of flesh. Then, like Jesus on the Cross, he must allow blood and water to flow from that new heart of flesh. It is this heart poured out for the seminarian that will bear the fruit of fatherhood in the future priest. Let us seek to receive from the Eternal Father in our poverty and may we trust in the promise: "I will give you a new heart and put a new spirit within you; and I will remove the heart of stone from your flesh, and I will give you a heart of flesh" (Ezek. 36: 26).

A Prayer to the Trinity

Heavenly Father, teach us to be fathers after your own heart. Teach us to pour ourselves out completely. Teach us to make a perfect gift of ourselves, counting no cost, holding nothing back in fear of loss. Let Your grace open the clenched hands with which we grasp and hoard the gifts that You have freely given, and allow us instead to enter into the floods of living waters flowing generously from Your fatherly heart.

Lord Jesus, Eternal Son of the Father. Teach us to be sons even as you are always a Son. Teach us to always receive all from the Father. Break through the arrogance and pride that prefers the illusion of our independence and self-authoring to the preeminence of the Father's Love. Lord Jesus, give us the eyes to see that all we have is the gift of a loving Father. Let us see that He wishes to transform us in Your image, to make us each a new Incarnation. Give us the ears to hear and to believe that the Father speaks to us the same words that He spoke to You: "Behold my beloved son, in whom I am well pleased."

Holy Spirit, love of Father for Son, and Son for Father, You through Whose power the Word was made flesh in the womb of the virgin Mary, come and dwell in our souls. Come that the Eternal Word may be conceived in our souls and bodies, so that we too may become sons. Come in Your power that, as members of the Church, the bride to the Eternal Bridegroom, that we may cooperate with the Bridegroom in begetting new life. Come as flame in the hearts of priests and seminarians that they might enter into the blood and water flowing from the side Jesus and, in so pouring themselves out for the sake of the Bride, the Church, that they might find fulfillment of their deepest longings to be a true father in the Father, a true son in the Son, and a true spouse in the Holy Spirit.

Practicum Reflection Questions for Formators

1. What is fatherhood?

2. Have you found within yourself the deep longing for fatherhood and for espousal?

3. Have you found in Christ an answer to these longings for fatherhood and espousal? How is living daily life changing in practical ways as you continue to discover Christ as the answer to these longings?

4. Do you find the source of your fatherhood in your poverty? And, are you discovering the free gift of sonship offered to you by the Father in that poverty?

Suggested Resources

1. Camisasca, Massimo. *The Challenge of Fatherhood: Thoughts on the Priesthood.* Edited by Jonah Lynch. Translated by Adrian Walker. Milano: Edizione San Paolo, 2003.

2. Giussani, Luigi. *The Risk of Education: Discovering Our Ultimate Destiny.* Translated by Rosanna M. Giammanco Fongia. New York: The Crossroad Publishing Company, 2001.

3. Griffin, Carter. *Supernatural Fatherhood through Priestly Celibacy: Fulfillment in Masculinity: A Thomistic Study.* Washington, DC: *Self-published*, 2011.

4. West, Christopher. *At the Heart of the Gospel: Reclaiming the Body for the New Evangelization.* New York: Image Books, 2012.

Chapter Seven

"Some Procreate by the Body, Others by the Soul":
Spiritual Paternity in the Fathers of the Church

Sr. Agnes Cunningham, S.S.C.M., S.T.D.

Patristic Scholar, theologian and educator. Sr. Agnes Cunningham, was born in Yorkshire, England in 1923. She is a member of the Congregation of the Servants of the Holy Heart of Mary since 1940. After teaching in Elementary and Secondary Education she became the first woman to obtain a doctorate in sacred theology from the Facultes Catholiques in Lyon, France. She also became the first woman to join the theological faculty at the University of St. Mary of the Lake/Mundelein Seminary in 1967. For over twenty five years she served at Mundelein Seminary as Professor for Patristic Theology and Early Church History. From 1982 to 2001 she conducted the Annual Seminar in Ecumenical Spirituality at the Northside Chicago Theological Institute. She became the first woman president of the American Association of Theological Schools. Sr. Agnes served as a consultant to the NCCB Committees on Doctrine, the Permanent Diaconate, Women and Society, and Priestly Formation. A prolific author, she has written six books and co-authored fifteen on patristics, ecumenism, prayer and the role of women in the Church. One focus of her research has been the French School of Spirituality. She has written more than 80 articles and has published in English, French, and Spanish journals. Sr. Agnes has lectured extensively across the United States and has given courses in theology and spirituality in Argentina, Cuba, Cameroon, Canada and France. Loyola University (Chicago), St. John Fisher College (Rochester, NY) and North Park University (Chicago) awarded her honorary doctorates. In the year 2000, the Catholic Theological Society of America gave her the highest honor , the John Courtney Murray Medal for her "distinguished and enduring contributions to theology."

The title of this presentation is taken from a text by Clement of Alexandria (C. AD 150 c. AD 215) in his work, *The Stromata.*[1] Faithful to his conviction that there was a real

---

[1] *Stromata* ("Carpets") is a work in eight books that treats, primarily, of the relation of the Christian religion to secular learning. The literary form of the *Stromata* was a popular genre of the

relationship between Christian faith and Greek philosophy, Clement brings together in this text both Plato and St. Paul:

> As [Socrates] says in the *Theaetetus,* "[The virtuous man] will beget and train men; for some procreate by the body, others by the soul." For among the barbarian philosophers to teach and to enlighten is also called begetting, just as the Apostle says, "I have begotten you in Jesus Christ." [2]

Thus, the concept of spiritual fatherhood according to the Church Fathers developed from ideas that had preceded them. What then can we learn from the Fathers of the Church about spiritual fatherhood, especially as it pertains to the life and ministry of the priest today?

Fathers like Clement of Alexandria, himself a philosopher, knew well the writings of pagan thinkers who were models for a life of virtue, asceticism, self-mastery, and inner peace.[3] Their influence on their disciples was, indeed, a type of spiritual fatherhood, as that came to be known. Later ages looked on them as having prepared, in a certain way, for the call to holiness that came with the Christian revelation.

In their writings we find, as it were, foreshadowings of true divine wisdom and clear intuitions of the human longing for the one who would call himself the way of truth and Truth, itself: Christ.[4]

All the early Fathers were influenced by St. Paul's teaching that spiritual fatherhood was sacramental and prophetic. The sacramental dimension referred, primarily, to the role of one who became a spiritual father through administration of the sacraments of initiation. The prophetic character of spiritual paternity was found in the ministry of the word, that is, in handing on the teaching that had come from the Apostles. It is not surprising to find spiritual fatherhood attributed by writers as early as the Apostolic Fathers to the *episkopos,* the primary minister of sacrament and word in the age of Christian Antiquity.

Here, St. Ignatius of Antioch is our principal witness to the sacramental character of the bishop's spiritual fatherhood. Ignatius considered the bishop to be the "representative of the

---

day, used by philosophers to discuss various questions free from any imposed format. The topics were "woven together like colors in a carpet;" cf. J. Quasten, *Patrology* II, 12. We might say they were like a patchwork quilt.

[2] *Stromata V.2.2-3,* citing Plato, *Theaetetus,* 150 b-c, and 1 Cor 4:15.

[3] Some of these thinkers were Socrates, Plutarch, Epictetus, Seneca, and Marcus Aurelius.

[4] Cf. A. Mercatali, "Père spirituel," 872; my translation.

Father in all things."[5] The bishop, a "type of the Father," is the visible representative of God the Father and is to be followed "as Jesus Christ follows the Father."[6] One who would deceive the bishop wrongs the Father of Jesus, for the Father is the bishop of all."[7] Indeed, the bishop participates in a unique way in the Fatherhood of God. Ignatius taught that the sacramental ministry of the bishop reached beyond his own person:

It is not permitted without the authorization from the bishop either to baptize or to hold an *agapê*.[8]

Let no one do anything touching the Church apart from the bishop. Let that celebration of the Eucharist be considered valid which is held under the bishop or anyone to whom he has committed it. [9]

For those of both sexes who contemplate marriage, it is proper to enter the union with the sanction of the bishop.[10]

The prophetic character of the bishop's spiritual fatherhood was also highlighted by Ignatius: "Where the bishop appears there let the people be, just as where Jesus Christ is, there is the Catholic Church."[11] Once the assembly has gathered, the "bishop is to preside in the place of God."[12] Ignatius affirms that it is right and proper for the people "to act in agreement with the mind of the bishop."[13] Communion with the bishop as a teacher responsible for the faithful is a safeguard against error and heresy.[14]

The role of the bishop as presider and teacher is also affirmed by St. Justin Martyr, the second-century Greek Apologist, in his description of the celebration of the Eucharist.

---

[5] St. Ignatius of Antioch, *Epistle to the Trallians,* 3.15.

[6] St. Ignatius of Antioch, *Epistle to the Smyrneans,* 8.1.

[7] St. Ignatius of Antioch, *Epistle to the Magnesians,* 3.1-2.

[8] St. Ignatius of Antioch, *Epistle to the Smyrneans,* 8.2.

[9] St. Ignatius of Antioch, *Epistle to the Smyrneans,* 8.1.

[10] St. Ignatius of Antioch, *Epistle to Polycarp,* 5.2.

[11] St. Ignatius of Antioch, *Epistle to the Smyrneans,* 8.2.

[12] St. Ignatius of Antioch, *Epistle to the Magnesians,* 6.1.

[13] St. Ignatius of Antioch, *Epistle to the Ephesians,* 4.

[14] Cf. J. Quasten, *Patrology* I, 67, citing his epistles *To the Trallians,* 6 and *To the Philadelphians,* 3.

Justin states that, following the reading of the *memoires* of the Apostles and the writings of the prophets, the president verbally instructs and exhorts us to the imitation of these excellent things."[15] In the same century, St. Irenaeus, bishop of Lugdunum (Lyons) in Gaul, clearly teaches this same idea:

> Son has a twofold meaning ... one is a son in the natural order because he was born a son; ... the second is made so ... by the teaching of doctrine. For when any person has been taught from the mouth of another, he is called the son of the one who instructs him, and the latter is called his father.[16]

So strongly was this principle rooted in the thought of Irenaeus that he appealed to it in his efforts to recall to the true faith the Roman presbyter, Florinus, who had chosen to become a disciple of the Gnostic, Valentinus:

> For, when I was still a boy, I knew you (Florinus) in lower Asia, in Polycarp's house, when you were a man of rank in the royal hall, and endeavoring to stand well with him. I remember the events of those days more clearly than those which happened recently, for what we learn as children grows up with the soul and is united to it. ... I listened eagerly even then to these things through the mercy of God which was given me, and made notes of them, not on paper, but in my heart, and ever by the grace of God do I truly ruminate on them.[17]

What a challenge to spiritual fathers to teach truths that can be so treasured by their spiritual children! One further quotation from Clement of Alexandria confirms the teaching of Irenaeus from another point of view:

> It is a good thing to leave good children to posterity: such is the case with children of our bodies. But words are the progeny of the soul; thus we call those who have taught us "fathers." ... The word that is sown is hidden in the soul of the learner, as in the earth, and this is spiritual planting. ... I believe that soul united to soul and spirit to spirit in the sowing of the word will make what is sown germinate and grow. And everyone who

---

[15] St. Justin Martyr, *I Apology*, 67.

[16] St. Irenaeus of Lyons, *Against Heresies* IV, 41-42.

[17] Cf. J. Quasten, *Patrology* I, 282.

is instructed is, from the viewpoint of dependence, the son of his teacher.[18]

By the end of the Ante-Nicene era, the spiritual fatherhood of the bishop was unquestionably acknowledged by the writers of the early Church. The *Didascalia Apostolorum (or Teaching of the Apostles)*, an anonymous early third-century document, states:

> Let the bishop love the laity as his children. … He is the teacher of piety and, next after God, he is your father, who has begotten you again to the adoption of sons by water and the Spirit.[19]

The author of this document affirms that the Old Testament command to honor our natural parents reminds us of another responsibility that is ours:

> How much more should the word exhort you to honor your spiritual parents, and to love them as your benefactors and ambassadors with God, who have regenerated you with water, and endued you with the fullness of the Holy Spirit, who have fed you with the word as with milk, who have nourished you with doctrine, who have confirmed you by their admonitions.[20]

This early idea of the spiritual father as the bishop or, as Clement of Alexandria would later say, the *Paidagogos*, was expanded by a new development in the East following the Council of Nicaea (AD 325) and, especially, after the adoption of Christianity as a state religion. Many Christians, eager to escape the worldliness that accompanied a new found freedom, were caught up in the *fuga mundi* phenomenon. Their search for holiness and perfection led to the "desert experience" as a significant component of Christian spirituality. One aspect of this entire movement was reflected in the concept of spiritual fatherhood as it emerged in Eastern Christianity in a movement parallel to the role of the bishop.

A new form of asceticism developed among "desert" Christians who became either anchorites or hermits seeking isolation and solitude. The search for necessary guidelines to understand a penitential life, discernment of spirits, and spiritual warfare in the pursuit of inner peace and, ultimately, union with God, led to the need for a spiritual father. This gave

---

[18] Clement of Alexandria, *Stromata* 1.1, III.15.

[19] *Didascalia Apostolorum*, II.20-26.

[20] *Didascalia Apostolorum*, II.33.

rise to relationships that developed between a "master" experienced in the ways of the Spirit and a "disciple" eager to learn from this experience.

The spiritual father in the desert was recognized by his charity, discretion, patience, and meekness. He led an austere life and was known to possess the gift of wisdom. The disciple who would be a spiritual son to such a father was expected to show faithfulness, obedience, love, and respect to the master and to follow the counsels he gave. The "elder," as the father came to be known, especially with the development of the cenobitic or monastic life, was usually but not necessarily, a man advanced in years. What was important was his own experience of the spiritual life and the holiness he had achieved in his personal struggles against his passions and the attacks of the demons.

The figure who most fully exemplifies the spiritual desert father is, of course the hermit whom we know through the *Life of St. Antony* by St. Athanasius. St. Antony, Athanasius tells us, was a man of "divine wisdom," of "grace and urbanity." Although sought out by many disciples and surrounded by "great colonies of monks," he and his closest followers lived alone, faithful to their vocation as hermits. But "to all," Athanasius tells us, "he was a father and a guide."[21]

The history of St. Antony leads us to ask if the spiritual father, in this new development, was always a bishop or a presbyter. It would seem that Antony was not. Indeed, the literature that has come to us from this period indicates that the role of these fathers was ordinarily exercised by monks who were not priests, by religious, and even by the laity. The presence of the *amma,* the "spiritual mother," among women hermits also bears witness to this.[22]

As monasticism grew and spread throughout the Christian world, the idea of spiritual fatherhood was influenced by the relationship that developed in the cenobitic life, as disciples gathered around a recognized *abba.* In early forms of the cenobitic life, the spiritual fatherhood of the abbot was the "constitutive basis" of the coenobium. "Fatherhood" and "sonship" were terms not unfamiliar to the monks. One example of this is found in a text in which the author claims that the words of Jesus against calling any man "father" (Mt 23:9) do not apply here. Quoting Pachomius, the author writes: "[Y]ou may

---

[21] St. Athanasius, *Life of Antony, passim;* see also discussion in J. Quasten, *Patrology* III, 148-150.

[22] It is interesting to note that, in the Orthodox Church, today, the priest is called by the Greeks *presbyteros or pappas,* and his wife *presbytera or pappadia*; the Russians use the term *batushka,* "little father," and his wife is *matuschka,* "little mother". "Just as the priest is father not to his own children alone but to the entire community, so the priest's wife is called to be mother alike in her own family and in the parochial family as a whole," K. Ware, "Man, Woman and the Priesthood of Christ," 32.

know for certain that a man who begets another in the work of God is his father after God, both in this age and in the other." Paul, the author continues, begot some by the gospel but also "by good and admirable deeds. … All who resemble the Apostle in their actions deserve to be called fathers because of the Holy Spirit who dwells in them."[23] However, it did happen that in Eastern monasticism the *apa* was, at times, simply the "organizer" required for life where an increasing number of monks shared "common ownership of property, common table and sometimes other common exercises."[24]

The most significant contribution to the understanding of the abbot of a monastery as the spiritual father was made by St. Benedict. Two entire chapters of the *Rule of St. Benedict* are devoted to this topic. The abbot is the one who takes Christ's place, who is responsible for a teaching that conforms to divine precepts, and who must account at the Judgement for his disciples' - his sons' - souls.[25] The abbot is to teach by word and deed, adapting his instructions to the needs and differences of individuals. The very name of the abbot – *abba* – means father and identifies his essential role as the father of his monks. In the monastic world, the idea of spiritual fatherhood was always attributed to the abbot who was, even into the sixth century, most frequently a layman. Because the monastery was seen as analogous to a local church with the abbot as its bishop, it was understood that he belonged to the charismatic rather than the sacramental hierarchy.

As we move into the Golden Age of the patristic era, the attraction of the fathers of that age to the monastic way of life cannot escape our attention. This is particularly true of the Cappadocians: Sts. Basil the Great, his friend Gregory of Nazianzus, and Basil's brother, Gregory of Nyssa. Following his baptism, Basil traveled widely to visit the most honored ascetics and to devote himself to a life of solitude. Before long, he was joined by others with whom he established a cenobitic life, becoming himself a spiritual father. Together with Gregory of Nazianzus, he composed two monastic rules. Called from his life of solitude to serve the Church in another capacity, he was ordained a priest and became bishop of Caesarea. His interest in the solitary way of life remained significant in his pastoral ministry as a bishop. He was, in truth, a spiritual father to those in monasteries under his care.

Gregory of Nazianzus, drawn by the kind of life he found Basil pursuing, sought to stay with his friend in Pontus so as to lead a life of solitude, reflection, and prayer. Against his will, he was summoned insistently by his aged father to accept ordination to priesthood and, eventually, to the episcopacy. The story of his flight back to Pontus and solitude after

---

[23] T. Fry, *Rule of St. Benedict*, 340, quoting from an anonymous Coptic *Life of Pachomius*.

[24] T. Fry, *Rule of St. Benedict*, 337.

[25] Cf. T. Fry, *Rule of St. Benedict*, 347.

ordination is well known. He did return to assume a ministry for which he never felt suited. One of the fruits of this experience was his discourse on the priesthood in the second of his collected *Orations*, an important source for both St. John Chrysostom and St. Gregory the Great in their reflections on the presbyterate and episcopacy.

In his considerations on the priesthood, Gregory Nazianzen refers to the priest as "one who is to instruct others in virtue," but who is not to suppose that all things are suitable to all persons.[26] Inspired by St. Gregory, St. John Chrysostom produced what has been called the great "classic on the priesthood and one of the finest treasures of Patristic literature."[27] Chrysostom clearly attributes spiritual fatherhood to the priest:

> These verily are they who are entrusted with the pangs of spiritual travail and the birth which comes through baptism: by their means we put on Christ and are buried with the Son of God and become members of that blessed Head. Wherefore they might not only be more justly feared by us than rulers and kings, but also be more honored than parents; since these begot us of blood and the will of the flesh, but the others are the authors of our birth from God, even that blessed regeneration which is the true freedom and the sonship according to grace.[28]

Chrysostom also attributes the qualities he assigns to priests to those who minister in priesthood's "highest grade," episcopacy.

The witness of Eastern Christianity attests to the grace of spiritual fatherhood found in the bishop or in those with whom this grace was shared, either one perceived as exercising an episcopal ministry – an abbot in the monastic life – , or one mandated to participation in episcopal ministry as a priest. How was Western Christianity in the Golden Age influenced by the earlier patristic tradition and by the eremetical and monastic experiences?

Men like Sts. Ambrose of Milan, Jerome, Augustine of Hippo, and even Pelagius, were among those drawn to the ideal of a life of solitude, asceticism, prayer, and contemplation. They founded monasteries or joined already existing communities. They exercised spiritual fatherhood by writing rules of life for both women and men. As some of them were called – or obliged – to accept ordination to priesthood and episcopacy, they continued their care of monks and nuns through instructions, visits, and other ways of pastoral charity. Their own experience of having known a spiritual father marked them as they sought to understand

---

[26] St. Gregory of Nazianzus, *Oration 2: In Defense of his Flight to Pontus*, 14-15.

[27] J. Quasten, *Patrology* III, 459; cf. also F. Cayré, *Patrologie et Histoire de la Théologie* I, 543.

[28] St. John Chrysostom, *On the Priesthood*, III, 6.

this ministry to which they too were summoned by the Church,

The witness of St. Ambrose as a spiritual father is especially striking. Called, then impelled, into baptism, ordination, and episcopacy, before he had even completed the catechumenate, Ambrose understood clearly that he had received the grace of spiritual fatherhood. While insisting that the instructions he gave in homilies and sermons were intended as much for himself as for his hearers, he did not hesitate to call them his children. In a work dedicated in the first place to his clergy, but perhaps, as Quasten notes, to all the faithful of his church, he states: "[I] deliver to you as to children those things which the Spirit of Wisdom has imparted to Christ and through him, to us."[29] He reminds those whom he is addressing that, just as Cicero had written instructions for his son, so too he is to instruct those he calls "my children ... whom I have begotten in the gospel."[30] "[N]ature," Ambrose continues, "does not make us love more ardently than grace. ... [You] are loved on the ground of our deliberate choice." Book Two of this document ends with his final commendation to those he calls, "my sons."[31]

Like Ambrose, St. Augustine found himself, as a bishop, engaged in a ministry that corresponded in every way to the longstanding idea of spiritual fatherhood: a ministry of sacrament and word, of guidance and encouragement for others who sought Christian perfection in a life of asceticism, solitude, and contemplation.

There are, especially, two examples of Augustine's exercise of spiritual fatherhood worthy of mention. Both are recorded in *The Confessions.* The first is his reference to Ambrose to whom he presented himself prior to baptism. "That man of God," he tells us, "received me like a father."[32] This simple affirmation reflects a richer, deeper experience that Augustine had known, one he recalled as his began writing *The Confessions,* shortly after the death of Ambrose.

The second reference reveals Augustine's awareness of his own spiritual fatherhood. As he recounts the event of his baptism and that of his friend and companion, Alypius, he tells us that his son, Adeodatus, – the one "given by God" – was baptized at the same time. This was the youth in whom Augustine acknowledged that there was nothing of himself except his sin. And yet, the boy was blessed with qualities that his father knew could have been given only by God. Augustine recognized that, through grace, he had been an instrument in the spiritual formation of his son. "We fostered him in Thy discipline," he says, and refers to

---

[29] St. Ambrose, *On the Duties of the Clergy,* I.i.1; cf. J. Quasten, *Patrology* IV, 166.

[30] St. Ambrose, *On the Duties of the Clergy,* I.vii.21.

[31] St. Ambrose, *On the Duties of the Clergy,* II.xxx.

[32] St. Augustine, *Confessions,* V.xiii.

one of his own earlier writings, *On the Teacher,* a dialogue between him and his son that shows that one learns wisdom only from the interior teacher, the Father of all, God.[33] This insight confirmed the years of searching for God with others who shared his quest. It revealed Augustine's own role in bringing them, in one way or another, to "regeneration" and a new way of life.

In Augustine's letters to other bishops, he addresses them as "my brothers and partners" in the presbyterate. An older bishop, Xantippus, is his "father and colleague in the priestly office."[34] Jerome, in writing to Augustine, salutes him as "my son in years, my father in ecclesiastical dignity."[35]

We have seen that the concept of spiritual fatherhood as it emerged in Christian Antiquity was attributed, first, to the bishop, then to the desert *abba or apa,*[36] to the abbot in monastic life, and then to the bishop or to one mandated by him to share the ministry of *episcopê.* This development points to two theological principles underlying the spiritual elements that apply to the life and ministry of the priest.

The understanding of spiritual fatherhood through a ministry of sacrament and word is based on a rich ecclesiology. The importance of Baptism and Eucharist, of fidelity to the Apostolic *traditio,* and of *communio* as found, for example, in the writings of Ignatius of Antioch, Justin, and Irenaeus witnesses to this. It is in the Church, in her mission and ministry, her mystery, her members, her hierarchy, and her call to be "a people brought into unity from the unity of the Father, the Son and the Holy Spirit"[37] that spiritual fatherhood is preserved and transmitted.

Spiritual fatherhood especially as it was influenced by the desert and the monastery is rooted, in a theology that is trinitarian and incarnational. That is, it is christological. Through Christ, we enter into the *Abba*-mystery of divine adoption. Through Christ, with Christ, and in Christ, we are configured to the beloved Son, through the power of the Spirit, for the glory of the Father. Spiritual fatherhood effects participation in the mystery of the God "who has bestowed on us in Christ every spiritual blessing in the heavens" (Eph 1:3) strengthening us through the presence and action of the Spirit (cf. Eph 3:16). The trinitarian aspect of spiritual fatherhood, already indicated in the theological principle of ecclesiology,

---

[33] St. Augustine, *Confessions,* IX.vi.

[34] St. Augustine, *Epistles,* 65, address.

[35] St. Augustine, *Epistles,* 72.3.5.

[36] The two terms are the same word, both derive from the Aramaic word for 'father'. In general, *abba* was used by writers outside of Egypt, and *apa* by native Egyptian writers [ed. note].

[37] Cf. *Lumen gentium,* 4.

is readily recognized and celebrated.

The incarnational dimension of spiritual fatherhood as it flowed out of the "desert" experience, either eremetical or cenobitic, recalls a lesser known patristic tradition of the fatherhood of Christ. Neither specifically Pauline nor Johannine, this theme appears in documents as early as the second century.[38] Representative texts can be found, for example, in the *Acts of Justin Martyr*, Irenaeus *Against Heresies*, and Origen's *On First Principles*. St. Ambrose and St. Augustine were among those who accepted this concept. The incarnational dimension of spiritual fatherhood was also characterized by a christocentric piety that looked to a "master" or "elder" as one whom the Spirit had fashioned, as Christ Jesus had been, in wisdom, humility, simplicity, and holiness of life.

The message that comes from the patristic age is clear. One who shares in the priesthood of Jesus Christ through sacramental ordination is called, by that very fact, to exercise a ministry of spiritual fatherhood. Through dispensation of word and sacrament; through the teaching of true doctrine; through instructions for a life of faith and virtue; through dedicated, all-embracing love, the spiritual father is to procreate in the soul as others do in the body. The only appropriate response to this call is a single, simple word, a word of surrender. It is the word of a woman whose motherhood made it possible, we might say, for Christ to reveal the Fatherhood of God to us: *fiat*! (Lk 1:38)

This article was originally published in *Spiritual Fatherhood: Living Christ's Own Revelation of the Father* (proceedings from the Symposium on the Spirituality and Identity of the Diocesan Priest, ed. by Edward G. Mathews. Omaha: Institute for Priestly Formation, 2003) and is published here with the permission of the author and publisher.

Prayer of Self Abandonment, by Blessed Charles de Foucauld

Father, I abandon myself into your hands; do with me what you will. Whatever you may do I thank you; I am ready for all, I accept all. Let only your will be done to me, and in all your creatures. I wish no more than this, O Lord.

Into your hands I commend my soul; I offer it to you with all the love of my heart, for I love you, Lord, and so need to give myself to surrender myself into your hands, without reserve, and with boundless confidence, for you are my Father.

---

[38] For a discussion of the fatherhood of Christ, cf. T. Fry, *Rule of St. Benedict*, 356-361.

Practicum Reflection Questions for Formators

1. How do I desire to cultivate spiritual fatherhood through the practice of charity, discretion, patience, and meekness as I imitate the desert fathers. Where are these virtues already at work in my daily life of discipleship with Christ?

2. Who are the spiritual fathers who, as St. John Chrysostom says, "authored my birth from God....even that blessed regeneration which is true freedom and the sonship according to grace?" How did this birthing transpire in your faith journey?

3. What are the activities of priesthood which I do where I experience being a true spiritual father?

4. Jean Vanier the Catholic founder of the worldwide L'Arche faith communities says, "For a human being, the awareness of his or her fecundity allows him or her in part to overcome the fear of death." Have I experienced the gift of spiritual fatherhood in a manner that is fruitful/fecund? How is this addressing my human fear of death, helping me to overcome this fear?

5. Jean Vanier teaches us; "The awareness of one's fecundity is to know that one day someone will look at me and say… 'If I am alive and happy it is because of you'!" Have I seen and tasted this reality in Christian faith? Please describe this with a brief story.

Suggested Resources

1. Benedict. *The Rule of St. Benedict in Latin and English with Notes*. Compiled by Timothy Fry. Collegeville: Liturgical, 1980.

2. Richardson, Cyril Charles, ed. *Early Christian Fathers*. New York: MacMillan, 1970.

3. Pitre, Brant James. *Jesus the Bridegroom: Seeing Christ and the Cross Through Ancient Jewish Eyes*. New York: Image, 2014.

Bibliography

Cayré, Fulbert. *Patrologie et Histoire de la Théologie*. Paris-Tournai-Rome: Desclée & Cie, 1953.

Flannery, Austin, ed. *Vatican Council II: The Conciliar and Post Conciliar Documents*. New Revised Edition. Northport: Costello, 1992.

Fry, Timothy, ed. *RB80: The Rule of St. Benedict in Latin and English with Notes*.

Collegeville: Liturgical, 1980.

Mercatali, Andrea. "Père spirituel," in *Dictionnaire de la Vie Spirituelle*. Eds. S. De Fiores, T. Goffi. French adaptation, F. Vial. Paris: Cerf, 1987. Pp. 871-883.

Quasten, Johannes. *Patrology*. 4 vols. Westminster: Christian Classics, 1986.

Ware, Kallistos. "Man, Woman and the Priesthood of Christ." In *Women and the Priesthood*. Ed. T. Hopko. Crestwood: St. Vladimir's Seminary, 1983. Pp. 9 37.

Unless otherwise indicated, patristic citations are from the Collegeville Logos Library System CD: "Early Church Fathers, Special Catholic Edition," 1997.

Chapter Eight

ABIDING IN MARY'S WOMB WITH THE HOLY SPIRIT

Fr. John Horn, S.J., D. Min.

Fr. John Horn, S.J., D. Min. is a priest of the Maryland Province of the Society of Jesus and was ordained in 1985. He is a Co-Founder of The Institute for Priestly Formation at Creighton University in Omaha, Nebraska and is currently serving as a spiritual director and professor in Spiritual Theology at St. Vincent de Paul Regional Seminary in Florida. In his early years of priesthood, he served in the Jesuit Refugee Service and Jesuit Secondary Education. For over twenty-five years a call within a call to serve diocesan seminarians and priests has been his apostolic mission in the ministry of The Spiritual Exercises of St. Ignatius Loyola. He is Co-Founder of the Seminary Formation Council and previously served as President-Rector of Kenrick-Glennon Seminary St. Louis. He also serves in prison ministry. Fr. Horn has written several books including "Heart Speaks to Heart – A Review of Life And Healing Prayer," Editor for "Eyewitnesses – Biblical Foundations in Christian Spirituality," and authored "Healing Prayer –Practical Mysticism and St. Ignatius Loyola's Spiritual Exercises." In Priest Magazine (1994) he published an article, "Spiritual Fecundity and Virginal Love - A Christian Anthropology of the Heart."

The Baptism of the Spirit, the release of the Holy Spirit in our hearts, is meant to be an on-going reality in the ordinary events of everyday faith. This transpires through participation in the Trinity's laboring love. We believe that the reality of the Holy Spirit's coming at Pentecost is active and present in everyday events .

St. Francis of Assisi spoke about Mary's presence as Spouse of the Holy Spirit, and this title carries a special significance. It is by abiding in her womb at prayer that the Holy Spirit is able to be received new each morning. By participating in this ongoing Pentecost the Holy Spirit is also released in our hearts for ministry and brings us to fuller maturity in Christ Jesus (Eph. 4: 11-13).

The Father's desire is that Jesus' own life be conceived of in our hearts each day in the power of the Spirit. As his disciples you and I learn to actively wait in trust and rest in

Mary's womb as did Jesus. It is there that we receive the Holy Spirit anew (Lk. 1: 30-35). It is in Mary's womb that we are born again and again from above (John 3:3-5). In the ordinariness of life's events, in our Nazareth's, we learn the Father's desires to give affection and delight. We learn that his providential care is real (Is. 62: 1-5). This is what Mary and Joseph taught the Child Jesus, as they taught him how to pray the Psalms.

Praying the Psalms as Jesus did to the Father places us in a faith-filled disposition. We can imagine and receive the presence and the ongoing release of the Holy Spirit in the Church as Mary's womb. With Jesus we can return, to Nazareth to receive refreshment as the wind of the Spirit winnows away any doubt or anxiety acquired during trials. Returning to Nazareth with the Child Jesus we learn the truth and glory of Psalm 23. Here Jesus entrusts all of his human sorrow and fear to the Father:

> The Lord is my shepherd there is nothing that I lack. In green pastures you let me graze; to safe waters you lead me; you restore my strength. You guide me along the right path for the sake of your name. Even when I walk through a dark valley, I fear no harm for you are at my side; your rod and your staff give me courage. You set a table before me as my enemies watch; you anoint my head with oil; my cup overflows. Only goodness and love pursue me all the days of my life; I will dwell in the house of the Lord for years to come.

As we pray other Psalms to the Father we begin to understand part of the mystery of how Jesus "grew and became strong, filled with wisdom" (Lk. 2:40). Mary and Joseph taught the Child Jesus how to walk forward in his identity as Son of the Father by praying these Psalms with him. They transmitted what they experienced in faith as the Holy Spirit rested upon them, and lead them to always 'look up' to receive all of their blessings from above (Jn. 3: 3-5). The laboring love of the Holy Spirit was always uniting them to the Father's providential care. Through their instruction, and the gaze of love that radiated from them, the Child Jesus came to know that the "favor of God was upon him" (Lk. 2:40). The same is true for us.

The image of Jesus indwells in our hearts through the Sacrament of Baptism. We each come to understand that we have been called from birth, from our mother's womb, and it is there that we are strengthened, concealed, polished, given our names and become a glorious light to the nations, proclaiming Jesus' salvation to the ends of the earth (Is. 49: 1-6). It is in Mary's womb that the Holy Spirit refashions us. We become who we are as saintly images of Jesus. St. Louis Marie de Montfort in his book, "True Devotion to the Blessed Virgin," promoted this truth when he wrote: "Saint Augustine, surpassing himself as well as all that I have said so far, affirms that in order to be conformed to the image of the Son of God all the predestinate, while in the world, are hidden in the womb of the Blessed Virgin where they are protected, nourished, cared for and developed by this good Mother, until the day she brings them forth to a life of glory after death, which the Church calls the birthday of the just."[1]

While visiting Nazareth on pilgrimage the beauty of this living mystery was tasted by St. Paul VI. He exclaimed; "Nazareth is the kind of school where we begin to discover what Christ's life was like and even to understand the Gospel......Here we can learn who Christ really is."

St. John Paul II has designated Our Lady of Guadalupe," Star of the New Evangelization" and Pope Francis relies on her to guide the new evangelization in "The Joy of the Gospel." Mary's womb is pregnant with images of Jesus. And, she comes to us in ordinariness, as one like us. Let us place ourselves in her gaze and allow her to draw us to abide in her womb where Pentecost is ever present. There, through an active waiting in faith, the Holy Spirit will continually re-conceive each of us and the entire Church to be born again and again in and for mission (Jn. 3:3).

Prayer

Dear Holy Spirit, draw me this day by your all-powerful gentleness to rest in Mary's gaze as Our Lady of Guadalupe. I choose to actively wait in patient trust, as Mary carries me and all the nations, making all things new. I give you my heart. Fashion within me the image of Jesus, who is the center of my personality, to the glory of the Father. May all the nations know you and come to worship and adore you! Amen!

Practicum Reflection Questions for Formators

1. Am I ready, willing and able to identify the interior movements of the Holy Spirit that makes all things new? What do I need to learn so that I can identify the interior movements of the Holy Spirit?
2. Am I ready, willing and able to courageously surrender each day to the interior movements of the Holy Spirit that are active in my heart? What is my experience in faith when I choose to surrender to these interior movements?

---

[1] St Louis Marie de Montfort, "True Devotion to the Blessed Virgin," Montfort Missionaries, http://www.montfort.org/content/uploads/pdf/PDF_EN_26_1.pdf (accessed August 24, 2019), #33.

3. Am I ready, willing and able to exercise the gift of faith by courageously standing against the voices of interior fear and shame, to behold Mary's tender and penetrating gaze as Our Lady of Guadalupe? What transpires when I allow myself to behold Mary's eyes? What transpires when I exercise the gift of faith and allow Mary to behold me?

4. Am I ready willing and able to ask Mary and the Holy Spirit to reveal to me how I often live life on my own terms by pulling away from remaining with the power of their love and mercy? What transpires in faith when I ask them this question and listen for their answer(s)?

Suggested Resources

1. Anderson, Carl A., and Eduardo Chávez. *Our Lady of Guadalupe: Mother of the Civilization of Love.* New York: Doubleday, 2009.

2. Houselander, Caryll. *Reed of God.* Notre Dame, IN: Ave Maria, 2006.

3. Cantalamessa, Raniero. *Sober Intoxication of the Spirit: Filled with the Fullness of God.* Translated by Marsha Daigle-Williamson. Cincinnati, OH: Servant Books, 2005.

4. Doctrinal Commission of International Catholic Charismatic Renewal Services. *Baptism In The Holy Spirit.* Locust Grove, VA: National Service Committee Of the Catholic Charismatic Renewal in the U.S. Inc., 2012.

SEGMENT 2

Affective Maturity: Markers of Human Development, Psychological Insights and Resources

Chapter Nine

MARKERS OF HUMAN MATURATION IN SEMINARY FORMATION: BECOMING A GIFT FOR OTHERS[1]

Sr. Marysia Weber, R.S.M., M.A., D.O.

Sister Marysia Weber, R.S.M., M.A., D.O., is a physician, board certified in psychiatry with a fellowship in consultation-liaison psychiatry, who trained at the Mayo Clinic in Rochester, MN. She also holds a Master's degree in Theology from Notre Dame, South Bend, Indiana. She practiced psychiatry at her religious institute's multidisciplinary medical clinic, Sacred Heart Mercy Health Care Center in Alma, MI from 1988-2014. She became the Director of the Office of Consecrated Life for the Archdiocese of Saint Louis in 2014. She currently serves as a member of the Saint Louis Archdiocesan Review Board, the Child Safety Committee, is a facilitator for Project Rachel, is chair of the board of directors of MyCatholicDoctor, an executive board member of the Saint Louis Guild Catholic Medical Association and the Institute for Theological Encounter with Science and Technology. She also serves as Adjunct Clinical Instructor in the Department of Psychiatry at Washington University School of Medicine in Saint Louis, Missouri.

Sister Marysia offers workshops on a variety of topics including human attachment, boundaries and character development, depression and anxiety, dialogue and conflict resolution, as well as on social media and its effects on the brain for clergy, seminarians, women's and men's religious communities, parents, teachers and students. She is a formator within her own religious community. She presents on Internet pornography addiction—a Catholic approach to treatment to bishops, clergy, seminarians, religious communities, and laity throughout the United States and Europe She presented to the U.S. Bishops in Dallas TX in 1992 on "Pedophilia and Other Addictions." She was a member of the U.S.C.C.B. Ad Hoc Committee on Sexual Abuse in 1994-1995. Sister Marysia has presented to the Curia, Vatican City State on "Sexual Abuse of Minors by Clergy in North America"

---

[1] Cf. Template for Markers of Human Maturation in Seminary Formation: Becoming a Gift for Others on pp. 140-146.

in 2002. She has served as a psychological expert consultant for the Secretariat of Clergy, Consecrated Life and Vocations, U.S.C.C.B.

Sister Marysia's publications include "Medical Aspects of Addiction"; "The Roman Catholic Church and the Sexual Abuse of Minors by Priests and Religious in the United States and Canada: What Have We Learned? Where Are We Going?"; "Pornography, Electronic Media and Priestly Formation"; Her publications in *Seminary Journal* include: "Significant Markers of Human Maturation Applied to the Selection and Formation of Seminarians"; "The Discernment of a Priestly Vocation and the Expertise of Psychiatry and Psychology"; and "Internet Pornography and Priestly Formation: Medium and Content Collide With the Human Brain". She has published two books: *The Art of Accompaniment: Practical Steps for the Seminary Formator* (En Route Books and Media, 2018) and *Screen Addiction: Why You Can't Put that Phone Down* (En Route Books and Media, 2019). Her chapter "Guideposts for the Seminary Formator in Understanding and Assessing Levels of Preoccupation with Use of Internet Pornography and a Formative Process for Moving from Vice to Virtue" in Spiritual Husband-Spiritual Fathers: Priestly Formation for the 21st Century is pending publication. She also has a short video on "Screen Addiction" located at www.cathmed.org/videos.

The 2008 document from the Congregation for Catholic Education, *Guidelines for the Use of Psychology in the Admission and Formation of Seminarians for the Priesthood* and the recent document from the Congregation for Clergy the *Ratio Fundamentalis Institutionis Sacerdotalis* highlight the duty of bishops and formators to discern the suitability of seminarians for ordained priestly ministry.[2] Formators must know how to evaluate a man in his totality.[3] Cited among the virtues and abilities required in a priest are a positive and stable sense of his masculine identity, the capacity to form mature relationships, a solid sense of belonging, self-knowledge, the capacity for self-correction, the ability for trust and loyalty, and the courage to stay faithful to decisions made before God.[4]

A seminarian does not automatically possess these virtues and abilities upon acceptance to the seminary. Maturation gradually occurs through the integration of human, spiritual, intellectual, and pastoral dimensions of formation joined with the seminarian's continued cooperation with the work of divine grace.[5] The *Program for Priestly Formation*

---

[2] Congregation for Catholic Education, *Guidelines for the Use of Psychology in the Admission and Formation of Seminarians for the Priesthood* (October, 2008), no.2. Congregation for the Clergy, *Ratio Fundamentalis Institutionis Sacerdotalis* (December 8, 2016), no. 44, 46.

[3] *Guidelines*, no.4.

[4] *Guidelines*, no.2. *Ratio* no. 41.

[5] Committee on Priestly Formation of the United States Conference of Catholic Bishops, *Program of Priestly Formation*, 5th edition. (Washington, D.C.: United States Conference of Catholic

states: "Since formation assumes that a seminarian will be growing both in God's grace and in his free human response to that grace it is important that there be a process to note the markers of that growth."[6]

This chapter is intended to assist formators in that responsibility. Determining the level of affective maturity of a seminarian and his potential for human development requires that formators ask suitable questions and make prudential observations. A seminarian may be more developed in one area than another. A composite view is necessary to determine the level of maturation of each seminarian and to discern the seminarian's suitability for priestly formation and for diaconal and priestly ordination when that time comes.

Markers of human maturation reflect characteristics that indicate increasing personal and interpersonal affective development. Major theories of psychiatry and psychology depict a sequential process in human personality development. There are theoretical differences in the human maturational models of Freud, Jung, Erikson, and Maslow, for example, but all models contain similar characteristics that indicate increasing personal and interpersonal integration.[7] A similar sequential process of human becoming is expressed by Saint John Paul II in *The Acting Person*.[8]

There are six interrelated markers that are common to all major theories of human development. The following terms will be used to characterize them: self-knowledge, self-direction, self-control, self-discipline, self-governance, and spiritual fatherhood. They are listed in ascending order of affective maturity. Since personal growth and development does not take place in discretely delineated stages, you will note overlap in the markers. Each marker has a sampling of questions to guide bishops, vocation directors, and seminary formators in their evaluation of a seminarian's level of affective maturity. Placing check marks beside the questions within each marker of affective maturity or immaturity will offer formators a focus for a written narrative of a seminarian's level of affective functioning as well as specific examples of where the seminarian has room to grow. Most seminaries recommend an annual assessment of each seminarian.

Bishops, September, 2006), no. 272.

[6] *Ibid,* no. 272.

[7] Benjamin James Sadock, M.D. and Virginia Alcott Sadock, M.D., *Kaplan and Sadock's Synopsis of Psychiatry*, ninth edition (Philadelphia: Lippincott Williams and Wilkins, 2003), p. 18-21, 199-216.

[8] John Paul II, *The Acting Person* (Boston: D. Reidel Publishing Company, 1979).

Self-Awareness to Self-Knowledge

The first maturational marker is self-knowledge. This entails the capacity to understand one's thoughts and feelings and how these relate to behavior. This provides the basis for capacities to give and receive from others without excessive dependence or defensiveness.[9] Self-knowledge allows one to rely on other people with a sense of trust as well as a sense of self-reliance and self-trust.

A seminarian who understands his thoughts and feelings and how they relate to behavior is self-reliant yet at the same time able to rely on and entrust himself to others.

Questions to assess whether a seminarian is exhibiting this maturational marker:

☐ Does he exhibit:

- The ability to acknowledge his feelings?
- Emotional stability?
- A desire to gain a more complete and accurate knowledge of his motivations?
- Appropriate self-disclosure?

☐ Does he manifest a willingness to admit to mistakes?

☐ Is he appropriately self-reliant with a capacity to trust himself yet at the same time able to rely on and entrust himself to others?

A seminarian who is limited in his ability to reflect upon his emotions and thoughts and how they relate to his behaviors demonstrates tendencies toward emotional turmoil and anxiety. He may be a "people-pleaser" who can feel alienated from others due to his anxiety or anger about "not measuring up." He may try to "make up" for what is lacking in his sense of self by excessive ingratiating behaviors. He may also blame others for his relational difficulties without insight or desire to grow in self-knowledge.

---

[9] Sadock and Sadock, p. 212.

Questions to assess whether a seminarian exhibits limited self-knowledge:

☐ Are the seminarian's relationships needy and emotionally charged?

☐ Do his relationships terminate in frustration because of his neediness or emotional outbursts?

☐ Does he withdraw when emotionally conflicted?

☐ Does he exhibit excessive ingratiating behaviors?

☐ Does he give evidence of feeling undervalued?

☐ Does he give evidence of being self-focused?

For example:

● Is he mostly about me, my, and mine?

● Is he unaware of what is going on around him?

☐ Does he frequently avoid acknowledging personal faults?

☐ Does he prefer to have others make decisions for him so as to avoid responsibility?

Self-Direction

Self-direction is the basis for evolving personal autonomy without undo self-doubt or ambivalence. Self-direction is necessary for cooperation in which there is neither excessive submissiveness nor will-fulness.[10]

A seminarian who is mature in his interactions is motivated to prevent the buildup of frustration from emotionally conflicted situations. He does not require that he get his own way in order to be successful. He has the capacity to engage in interdependent activities with peers and persons in authority. His interactive style often elicits co-operation from others. People who exude a strong personal presence do not intimidate the mature seminarian. He is able to differ with other people without dismissing those with whom he disagrees. He is empathic but does not assume others' feelings and behaviors.

---

[10] Ibid. p. 213.

Questions to assess whether a seminarian exhibits appropriate self-direction:

☐ Is he able to receive criticism with docility and address it?

☐ Does he exhibit appropriate initiative?

☐ Can he accept a difficult situation and function within it?

☐ Has he achieved the capacity to differ with others' opinions without dismissing those with whom he disagrees?

☐ Is he comfortable in the presence of authority persons without antagonism or withdrawal from relationship?

A seminarian struggling with limited self-direction can be impulsive or rigid. He has difficulty making everyday decisions. As a consequence of his self-doubt, he assumes an ambivalent posture of suspicious vigilance to guard against being hurt by others. He may be excessively compliant, exhibiting a lack of personal autonomy and initiative. He may conform, yet internally he is filled with rebellion and critical judgment.

Questions to assess whether a seminarian exhibits limited self-direction:

☐ Does he prefer to have others make decisions for him?

☐ Does he demonstrate excessive compliance?

☐ Is he rigid and lacking a capacity for flexibility in interactions?

☐ Does he seek the attention of authority persons to build up his self-worth?

☐ Does he use others for what they can do for him?

☐ Does he exhibit a lack of personal autonomy and initiative?

☐ Does he exhibit ambivalence and self-doubt?

☐ Does he lack a capacity to cooperate with others?

☐ Is he frequently in conflict with authority persons?

Self-Control

Self-control entails establishing the motivation for necessary change, setting clear goals, and monitoring behaviors toward that goal. This capacity underlies all kinds of achievements. Self-control provides a healthy sense of pride and self-competence derived from performance.[11]

A seminarian with self-control is able to delay gratification for a future good. He has the capacity to realistically anticipate and plan for future potential difficulties. He derives a healthy sense of pride and self-competence from his work. A seminarian who exhibits appropriate self-control prefers to work with others and is viewed by his peers as a "team player." He is open to others' ideas and seeks harmony while appreciating diversity.

Questions to assess whether a seminarian exhibits self-control:

- ☐ Does the seminarian exercise responsible stewardship in his use of time and resources?

- ☐ Does he exhibit a healthy sense of pride and self-competence from his work?

- ☐ Is he able to delay gratification for a future or greater good?

- ☐ Does he have a capacity for balancing harmony and diversity?

- ☐ Does he experience a heightened sense of fulfillment through collaboration with others in ministry?

- ☐ Does he encourage those with whom he is working to search for the good in others' ideas?

Inferiority and inadequacy are common experiences for a seminarian who struggles with self-control. He does not feel competent or valued in his efforts and is critical of others and himself. He lacks joy in authentic self-giving. Such a seminarian needs to "prove" his adequacy. This can lead to "burn out," as he realizes increased labor does not substitute for his impaired self-esteem. A seminarian who experiences these limitations demands frequent affirmation.

---

[11] Ibid. p. 213.

Questions to assess whether a seminarian exhibits limited self-control:

- ☐ Does he exhibit strong emotional reactions when someone "crosses" him?
- ☐ Does he feel incompetent or undervalued?
- ☐ Is he excessively critical of others or himself?
- ☐ Does he lack a sense of joy in authentic self-giving?
- ☐ Is he bothered by feelings of inferiority and inadequacy?
- ☐ Does he exhibit frequent negative murmuring or sarcasm?
- ☐ Does he exhibit apathy or "burnout" when his work performance does not compensate for his low self-esteem?
- ☐ Does he lack the capacity for appropriate delayed gratification?

Self-Discipline

Self-discipline requires motivation to achieve core values or habits. This necessitates effectively aligning thoughts and behaviors toward achieving those core values or habits. This process requires change and adaptation, gradually transforming how one sees oneself and how one interacts with others in various circumstances. Focused effort at living one's life also enhances self-confidence through the experience of greater self-control in executing tasks directed toward specific goals.[12]

A seminarian who exhibits balanced self-discipline has a sufficiently developed self-concept, is able to acknowledge his strengths and weaknesses, and demonstrates realistic problem solving skills. He has the capacity to form relationships in a mature manner; he is not preoccupied with his own needs.

Questions to assess whether a seminarian exhibits self-discipline:

- ☐ Does he exhibit appropriate interpersonal boundaries?
- ☐ Does he relate respectfully to women and men?

---

[12] Ibid. p. 214.

☐ Does he exercise discretion in his use of technology and choices of entertainment?

☐ Does he make choices that enable him to refrain from addictive behaviors? (For example, regarding his use of alcohol and use of the Internet)

☐ Does he demonstrate realistic problem solving skills?

A seminarian who exhibits limited self-discipline may seek self-gratifying behaviors, such as overeating, alcohol abuse, or sexual activity, as a means to address or avoid stress, loneliness, or frustration. He is unsure of himself and relies on the role he plays to define his value and sense of personal security. Struggling to "find" himself, he may also be envious of others. His envy can flare into aggressive impulses or patterns of isolation.

Questions to assess whether a seminarian exhibits limited self-discipline:

☐ Does he have enmeshed relationships with poor interpersonal boundaries?

☐ Does he have more acquaintances than friendships?

☐ Does the seminarian rely heavily on the role he plays to define his sense of personal adequacy and security?

☐ Does he have to "prove" his adequacy by his performance?

☐ Does he engage in pleasurable excesses?

Self-Governance

A person who exhibits self-governance has integrated and consolidated previous attainments and is establishing decisive patterns for future adaptive functioning.[13] That is, he not only takes responsibility for his actions but has taken responsibility for the quality of his actions.[14] He is able to form relationships that are responsible, respectful, and marked by integrity. He does not focus on his emotional turmoil but instead invests his energy in problem-solving or bringing a situation to a positive conclusion. In stressful situations, he reflects on his own thoughts, feelings, and behaviors in order to better understand himself and other people's reactions to him. He has the ability to sustain loyalties freely pledged in

---

[13] Ibid. p. 214.

[14] John Paul II, *The Acting Person* (Boston: D. Reidel Publishing Company, 1979), p. 107.

spite of inevitable contradictions. The capacity for fidelity is the cornerstone for overall human stability.

A seminarian who exhibits self-governance takes responsibility for the quality of his actions. A seminarian who demonstrates a capacity for healthy friendship is able to respond to the challenges of relationship as a normal part of human bonding. At the same time, he is comfortable with solitude.

Self-governance is the quality that directs our free acts to the existential ends that God places in our nature, so that we can live a truly human life as *imago Dei*.[15] With such personal integration, the acting person manifests fidelity to transcendental truths. He embraces suffering in his own life and is empathic with people who are suffering. He demonstrates a capacity for fidelity to his faith and the courage to make decisions according to his faith.

Questions to assess whether a seminarian exhibits self-governance:

☐ Does he demonstrate sound prudential judgment in his choices?

☐ Is he able to form relationships that are responsible, respectful, and marked by integrity?

☐ Does he manifest an ability to forgive others and seek forgiveness for personal shortcomings?

☐ Does he understand suffering in his own life and respond accordingly?

☐ Does he show compassion to those who are suffering?

☐ Does he exhibit faithful perseverance in fulfilling commitments?

☐ Is he faithful to the vocation with which he is identifying?

☐ Does he address self-denial, loneliness, and celibacy in a mature manner that also serve to enrich his life?

A seminarian who is limited in self-governance has difficulty controlling his own actions and responses. The choices he makes are not linked to any particular hierarchy of ends. He allows his emotions, his mere likes and dislikes, to control the actions he takes. He excuses himself from responsibilities when in situations that make him uncomfortable. He

---

[15] Ibid. p. 106-108.

has a poor self-image. He tends to have difficulty setting aside his own needs. He consequently has a limited sense of the needs of others. He is more focused on being viewed as "good" rather than striving to grow in virtue. He alternates between idolizing certain individuals when they satisfy his needs and disliking persons who do not meet his needs. When contradictions in values or morals present themselves, he lacks fidelity and the courage necessary to make decisions in accord with the Catholic Church to which he is called to bear witness.

Questions to assess whether a seminarian exhibits limited self-governance:

☐ Does he function poorly in a stressful or delicate situation?

☐ Does he fail to fulfill commitments he has made?

☐ Are his interpersonal relationships characterized by superficiality?

☐ Does he demonstrate a limited sensitivity to the sufferings of others?

☐ Is he ambivalent about his sexual orientation, moral values, or commitments?

☐ Is celibacy a burden for him?

☐ Does he lack a capacity for fidelity to the teachings of the Catholic Church?

Spiritual Fatherhood

Saint John Paul II in *Pastores Dabo Vobis* speaks of the priest as one called to make a gift-of-self in likeness to Christ:

> The gift of self has no limits, marked as it is by the same apostolic and missionary zeal of Christ, the good shepherd, who said: "And I have other sheep that are not of this fold; I must bring them also, and they will heed my voice. So there shall be one flock, one shepherd" (Jn. 10:16).[16]

A seminarian who demonstrates a capacity for spiritual fatherhood has a disposition to minister to the needs of others. He is personally enriched by his self-gift. He has primary

---

[16] John Paul II, Post Synodal Apostolic Exhortation, *Pastores Dabo Vobis* (March 25, 1992), no. 23.

concern for the welfare and enrichment of others. He does not shrink from self-sacrifice.

Questions to assess a seminarian's disposition for spiritual fatherhood:

☐ Does he manifest a "strong, lively, personal love" of Jesus Christ?

☐ Does he exhibit the capacity to mentor?

☐ Is he an instrument directing others to God?

☐ Does he exhibit a disposition for service?

☐ Is he enriched by his service?

☐ Is he striving for conversion from attitudes contrary to pastoral charity?

☐ Does he consistently exhibit a capacity for self-sacrifice trusting in God?

☐ Does he display the capacity to renounce the goods of marriage for spiritual fatherhood?

A seminarian who has a limited disposition for spiritual fatherhood struggles with generosity. He seeks self-aggrandizement, undue recognition, and relationships that provide him with status or human respect. In short, a seminarian who does not demonstrate qualities of spiritual fatherhood will be limited in a capacity for self-sacrifice and altruism.

Questions to assess a seminarian who has a limited disposition for spiritual fatherhood:

☐ Does his love for himself surpass his love for others?

☐ Does he prefer "privileged" work?

☐ Does he manifest a need to be "successful" in ministry?

☐ Does he use relationships with others for self-aggrandizement?

☐ Does he manifest inappropriate possessive-ness of his gifts?

☐ Is he insensitive to what is going on around him?

☐ Does he lack a capacity to be self-sacrificing and altruistic?

Narrative Assessment

After placing a check mark beside each question where a seminarian exhibits observable behaviors related to a marker of maturation, the next task is to write a narrative assessment. The formator is to write specific examples of the traits observed in a particular seminarian. These include the seminarian's presently noted strengths and specific examples of where he has room to grow. It is also important to make practical recommendations regarding ways a seminarian can address areas where affective growth is necessary. An example is provided below.

Seminarian:
Year in Formation:
Formator:
Date:

- What are the seminarian's strengths presently in his formation process? Give specific examples as reflected in significant markers of human maturation.

- Where does he have room to grow? Give specific examples as reflected in significant markers of human maturation.

- List practical recommendations to address vocational growth and development.

Conclusion

By assessing the level of affective maturity, the Church provides seminarians encouragement to continue their formation and wisdom to identify ways in which their formation may take deeper root.[17] It is through receptivity to God's grace, joined to the exercise of human freedom, whereby one grows to become most fully oneself. It will be important to ascertain if the seminarian is growing both in God's grace and in his free human response to that grace.

Saint John Paul II, in addressing the formation of seminarians for the priesthood, describes that it is only when one becomes a gift for others that one most fully becomes oneself:

---

[17] *PPF,* no. 272.

Human maturity, and in particular affective maturity, requires a clear and strong training in freedom which expresses itself in convinced and heartfelt obedience to the "truth" of one's own being, to the "meaning" of one's own existence, that is to the "sincere gift of self" as the way and fundamental content of the authentic realization of the self.[18]

The *Ratio* re-echoes this necessary pastoral sentiment:

Thus, by growing in charity, the future priest must seek to develop a balanced and mature capacity to enter into relationship with his neighbor. Indeed, he is called above all to a basic human and spiritual serenity that, by overcoming every form of self-promotion or emotional dependency, allows him to be a man of communion, of mission and of dialogue. In contemplating the Lord, who offered His life for others, he will be able to give himself generously and with self-sacrifice for God's people.[19]

May the vineyard of the Lord be rich with such self-sacrificing priests.

MARKERS OF HUMAN MATURATION IN SEMINARY FORMATION: BECOMING A GIFT FOR OTHERS[20]

There are six interrelated markers of human maturation significant to the formation of seminarians:

self-knowledge,
self-direction,
self-control,
self-discipline,
self-governance, and
spiritual fatherhood.[21]

---

[18] *PDV,* no. 44.

[19] *Ratio,* no.41.

[20] Cf. pp. 33-56. The template may also be downloaded as a PDF from En Route Books and Media http://enroutebooksandmedia.com/artofaccompaniment/

[21] These markers were first described and presented in the article "Significant Markers of Human Maturation Applied to the Selection and Formation of Seminarians" (Sister Marysia Weber, *Seminary Journal,* 15(1): 35-41 (2009). The specific names of the markers have evolved and changes

They are listed in ascending order of affective maturity.

Self-Awareness to Self-Knowledge

Questions to assess whether a seminarian is exhibiting this maturational marker:

☐ Does he exhibit:

- The ability to acknowledge his feelings?
- Emotional stability?
- A desire to gain a more complete and accurate knowledge of his motivations?
- Appropriate self-disclosure?

☐ Does he manifest a willingness to admit to mistakes?

☐ Is he appropriately self-reliant with a capacity to trust himself yet, at the same time, able to rely on and entrust himself to others?

Questions to assess whether a seminarian exhibits limited self-knowledge:

☐ Are the seminarian's relationships needy and emotionally-charged?

☐ Do his relationships terminate in frustration because of his neediness or emotional outbursts?

☐ Does he withdraw when emotionally conflicted?

☐ Does he exhibit excessively ingratiating behaviors?

☐ Does he give evidence of feeling undervalued?

☐ Does he give evidence of being self-focused?

For example:

- Is he mostly about me, my, and mine?

---

will be noted.

- Is he unaware of what is going on around him?

☐ Does he frequently avoid acknowledging personal faults?

☐ Does he prefer to have others make decisions for him so as to avoid responsibility?

Self-Direction

Questions to assess whether a seminarian exhibits appropriate self-direction:

☐ Is he able to receive criticism with docility and address it?

☐ Does he exhibit appropriate initiative?

☐ Can he accept a difficult situation and function within it?

☐ Has he achieved the capacity to differ with others' opinions without dismissing those with whom he disagrees?

☐ Is he comfortable in the presence of authority persons without antagonism or withdrawal from relationship?

Questions to assess whether a seminarian exhibits limited self-direction:

☐ Does he prefer to have others make decisions for him?

☐ Does he demonstrate excessive compliance?

☐ Is he rigid and lacking a capacity for flexibility in interactions?

☐ Does he seek the attention of authority persons to build up his self-worth?

☐ Does he use others for what they can do for him?

☐ Does he exhibit a lack of personal autonomy and initiative?

☐ Does he exhibit ambivalence and self-doubt?

☐ Does he lack a capacity to cooperate with others?

☐ Is he frequently in conflict with authority persons?

Self-Control

Questions to assess whether a seminarian exhibits self-control:

☐ Does the seminarian exercise responsible stewardship in his use of time and resources?

☐ Does he exhibit a healthy sense of pride and self-competence from his work?

☐ Is he able to delay gratification for a future or greater good?

☐ Does he have a capacity for balancing harmony and diversity?

☐ Does he experience a heightened sense of fulfillment through collaboration with others in ministry?

☐ Does he encourage those with whom he is working to search for the good in others' ideas?

Questions to assess whether a seminarian exhibits limited self-control:

☐ Does he exhibit strong emotional reactions when someone "crosses" him?

☐ Does he feel incompetent or undervalued?

☐ Is he excessively critical of others or himself?

☐ Does he lack a sense of joy in authentic self-giving?

☐ Is he bothered by feelings of inferiority and inadequacy?

☐ Does he exhibit frequent negative murmuring or sarcasm?

☐ Does he exhibit apathy or "burnout" when his work performance does not compensate for his low self-esteem?

☐ Does he lack the capacity for appropriate delayed gratification?

Self-Discipline

Questions to assess whether a seminarian exhibits self-discipline:

- ☐ Does he exhibit appropriate interpersonal boundaries?

- ☐ Does he relate respectfully to women and men?

- ☐ Does he exercise discretion in his use of technology and choices of entertainment?

- ☐ Does he make choices that enable him to refrain from addictive behaviors? (For example, regarding his use of alcohol and use of the Internet)

- ☐ Does he demonstrate realistic problem solving skills?

Questions to assess whether a seminarian exhibits limited self-discipline:

- ☐ Does he have enmeshed relationships with poor interpersonal boundaries?

- ☐ Does he have more acquaintances than friendships?

- ☐ Does the seminarian rely heavily on the role he plays to define his sense of personal adequacy and security?

- ☐ Does he have to "prove" his adequacy by his performance?

- ☐ Does he engage in pleasurable excesses?

Self-Governance

Questions to assess whether a seminarian exhibits self-governance:

- ☐ Does he demonstrate sound prudential judgment in his choices?

- ☐ Is he able to form relationships that are responsible, respectful, and marked by integrity?

- ☐ Does he manifest an ability to forgive others and seek forgiveness for personal shortcomings?

- ☐ Does he understand suffering in his own life and respond accordingly?

☐ Does he show compassion to those who are suffering?

☐ Does he exhibit faithful perseverance in fulfilling commitments?

☐ Is he faithful to the vocation to which he is identifying?

☐ Does he address self-denial, loneliness, and celibacy in a mature manner that also serve to enrich his life?

Questions to assess whether a seminarian exhibits limited self-governance:

☐ Does he function poorly in a stressful or delicate situation?

☐ Does he fail to fulfill commitments he has made?

☐ Are his interpersonal relationships characterized by superficiality?

☐ Does he demonstrate a limited sensitivity to the sufferings of others?

☐ Is he ambivalent about his sexual orientation, moral values, or commitments?

☐ Is celibacy a burden for him?

☐ Does he lack a capacity for fidelity to the teachings of the Catholic Church?

Spiritual Fatherhood

Questions to assess a seminarian's disposition for spiritual fatherhood:

☐ Does he manifest a "strong, lively, personal love" of Jesus Christ?

☐ Does he exhibit the capacity to mentor?

☐ Is he an instrument directing others to God?

☐ Does he exhibit a disposition for service?

☐ Is he enriched by his service?

☐ Is he striving for conversion from attitudes contrary to pastoral charity?

☐ Does he consistently exhibit a capacity for self-sacrifice trusting in God?

☐ Does he display the capacity to renounce the goods of marriage for spiritual fatherhood?

Questions to assess a seminarian who has a limited disposition for spiritual fatherhood:

☐ Does his love for himself surpass his love for others?

☐ Does he prefer "privileged" work?

☐ Does he manifest a need to be "successful" in ministry?

☐ Does he use relationships with others for self-aggrandizement?

☐ Does he manifest inappropriate possessive-ness of his gifts?

☐ Is he insensitive to what is going on around him?

☐ Does he lack a capacity to be self-sacrificing and altruistic?

Narrative Assessment[22]

Seminarian:
Year in Formation:
Formator:
Date:

- What are the seminarian's strengths presently in his formation process? Give specific examples as reflected in significant markers of human maturation:

- Where does he have room to grow? Give specific examples as reflected in significant markers of human maturation:

- List practical recommendations to address vocational growth and development:

---

[22] The template may also be downloaded as a PDF from En Route Books and Media http://enroutebooksandmedia.com/artofaccompaniment/

This article was originally published in *The Art of Accompaniment: Practical Steps for the Seminary Formator* (St. Louis, MO: En Route Books and Media, 2018). It is published here with the permission of the publisher and the author, who has additionally provided the following prayer and suggested resources to accompany it.

Prayer from Pastores Dabo Vobis

> *O Mother of Jesus Christ,*
> *you were with him at the beginning*
> *of his life and mission,*
> *you sought the Master among the crowd,*
> *you stood beside him when he was lifted*
> *up from the earth*
> *consumed as the one eternal sacrifice,*
> *and you had John, your son, near at hand;*
> *accept from the beginning those*
> *who have been called,*
> *protect their growth,*
> *in their life ministry accompany*
> *your sons,*
> *O Mother of Priests.*
> *Amen.*

Suggested Resources

1. Weber, Sr. Marysia, "The Discernment of a Priestly Vocation and the Expertise of Psychiatry and Psychology," *Seminary Journal,* Winter 2009, Vol. 15, no. 3, pp. 23-31.

2. Cencini, Amedio, "The Formator", Spiritual and Emotional Maturity: Guiding Young People in Religious and Priestly Formation, pp. 35-43 (Paulines Publications Africa, 2004).

3. Caserta, Thomas G. "Ananias and the Elephants: Formation Ministry Examines Its Conscious," *Seminary Journal,* Fall 1998 , Vol. 4 no. 2, pp. 37-42.

Chapter Ten

THE ESSENTIAL ROLE OF THE MENTOR-FORMATION ADVISOR

Most Reverend Andrew Cozzens, S.T.D., D.D.
Auxiliary Bishop of the Archdiocese of St. Paul and Minneapolis

I want to begin by expressing my gratitude to the Institute for Priestly Formation (IPF) which has truly had a profound impact on my life as a priest. I know I have been greatly assisted in my own work of integrating my spiritual life with my pastoral and human life by learning to find God in all things through what I have been taught by IPF.

I'm also aware that I'm speaking to a unique group: a group of priests who are spending their lives in seminary formation. Seminary work is beautiful work but it is a very different kind of priestly work. If you are like me then it took some time for you to embrace it fully.

I spent the first 5 years of my priesthood working in two very different parishes. I loved parish work because of the incredible sense of belonging to a family and the wide variety of things a parish priest does.

I have to admit that there was a certain death that happened when I had to leave parish work and enter seminary work full time. A priest in a parish easily feels like the Father of a whole family, and the work of the seminary can feel like much more institutional and administrative work.

The analogy I use is that of soldiers. Soldiers love the front lines of the battle. This is why we became priests to be on the front lines. But, someone has to work in supply or we have no more soldiers and we lose the war.

It is easy to think that the most important work is that of the front lines... this is not necessarily the mind of the Church:

"The formation of future priests, both diocesan and religious, ... is considered by the Church one of the most demanding and important tasks for the future of the evangelization of humanity" (*Pastores Dabo Vobis*, 2).

Here we have a room of priests doing demanding and important work for the future of the evangelization of humanity.

Gradually in my work as a seminary formator, I began to find it very rewarding. It is very different than parish work, but one develops deep relationships with the men. I remember very well watching a man come to the altar on the day of his ordination, and thinking to myself of all the things he had gone through and all the struggle and growth that I had witnessed. What a beautiful thing it was to see him lay down his life, and how much I felt like a true father.

I have been asked to speak about the essential role of the Formation Advisor or Mentor, but I wanted to start with this internal experience, because I really believe that the role of the Formator must be a priestly role – that is a fatherly role. Here is where we will be able to do formation the way Jesus did formation.

As has already been said, this presumes the priest doing formation is working on his own integration. He is in spiritual direction. He is relating his own struggles to Christ and working through them as he seeks to serve the men.

My talk this evening presumes that you all are familiar with the two main documents that guide seminary work *Pastores Dabo Vobis* and the Program for Priestly Formation. These are very helpful documents to review regularly. I don't intend to summarize them, but rather to give you my own formulation of those truths based on my experience in formation.

But first let us start with the definition of what I'm talking about. PPF 80 refers to the "Formation advisors/mentors and directors." It says this:

"Although the titles may differ, on every seminary faculty, certain members function as formators in the external forum. These formation advisors/mentors and directors should be priests. They observe seminarians and assist them to grow humanly by offering them feedback about their general demeanor, their relational capacities and styles, their maturity, their capacity to assume the role of a public person and leader in a community, and their appropriation of the human virtues that make them 'men of communion.' These same formators may, on occasion, teach the ways of human development and even offer some personal mentoring or, at times, coaching. More generally, they offer encouragement, support, and challenge along the formational path. These formators function exclusively in the external forum and are not to engage in matters that are reserved for the internal forum and the spiritual director."

I served as one of these formators at St. Paul Seminary for seven and a half years. In our model the formators were priests who were also teachers. Each of us had about 15 men in formation and we met with them 5 times each semester (about once every 3 weeks).

The formator plays an essential role in the evaluation of the seminarian according to the PPF. They are the ones who walk with the man in his time of seminary and oversee formation in all four dimensions – human, spiritual, intellectual and pastoral. They make a recommendation to the rector about his continuance and ordination.

The key is that the Formator is the one who is appointed to oversee the formation of this individual man – to see that he integrates all the areas of his formation. He makes sure the man is fulfilling all the areas of formation he needs, and tailors the formation to fit this man. This means he often has to challenge the seminarian in those areas where he needs more formation. He often has the difficult job of giving feedback to the seminarian that the seminarian may or may not want to receive. He reveals the truth about the seminarian to himself. As Msgr. Trapp added earlier in our conference, he sees the man truly and helps the man come to see himself truly.

In fact, this is one way I have thought about the distinction between the formator and the spiritual director. In formation, Jesus reveals the truth about the man to himself. In spiritual direction, Jesus reveals himself to the man. The formator has to learn to love the priest out of the man. Just as a sculptor looks at a stone and sees the statue. The formator looks at the seminarian and tries to see the priest. He affirms what in the man is priestly and helps him to let go of what is not priestly.

You can see that the task for the formation director is not an easy one., especially because he often has to challenge the man. He can begin to see himself as the bad cop – the spiritual director is the good cop.

The formator must see a deeper understanding of his role so he doesn't simply become a disciplinarian or a judge. Here is where I believe the model that St. John Paul II gives us for seminary formation is so important. When St. John Paul II wanted to describe the seminary, he gave it a scriptural model, the relationship that Jesus had with his Apostles. He wrote:

"The Church's work of formation is a continuation in time of Christ's own work, which the evangelist Mark illustrates in these words: "And he went up on the mountain, and called to him those whom he desired; and they came to him. And he appointed twelve, to be with him, and to be sent out to preach and have authority to cast out demons" (*Mk.* 3:13-15)" (*Pastores Dabo Vobis*, 2).

Notice it is a relational model, not an institutional model. Notice it is more like a family than a classroom. Jesus called to himself those whom he wanted. Jesus does formation by inviting them into a relationship with him, not inviting them into an institution. It is a kind of school, but it is a living, relational, school, a relationship the scriptures call discipleship.

What are the hallmarks of this relationship? The main hallmark is "Being with." They are called to "be with" Jesus. The disciples are with Jesus all the time. They learn from his example. They grow to trust him and the way he does things. They become his friends.

Listen to John Paul II. He begins the section on Formation in PDV by quoting from Mark: "And he went up on the mountain, and called to him those whom he desired; and they came to him. And he appointed twelve, to be with him, and to be sent out to preach and have authority to cast out demons" (Mk. 3:13-15). Then he says:

> "'To be with him': It is not difficult to find in these words a reference to Jesus' 'accompanying' the apostles for the sake of their vocation. After calling them and before he sends them out, indeed in order to be able to send them out to preach, Jesus asks them to set aside a "period of time" for formation. The aim of this time is to develop a relationship of deep communion and friendship with himself. In this time they receive the benefit of a catechesis that is deeper than the teaching he gives to the people (cf. Mt. 13:11); also he wishes them to be witnesses of his silent prayer to the Father (cf. Jn. 17:1-26; Lk. 22:39-45)." (*Pastores Dabo Vobis*, 42, emphasis added)

St. John Paul II is proposing the model of formation as discipleship. Through Jesus living with his disciples day in and day out he was able to form them.

Think for a moment how often Jesus did actual formation with the disciples. They are walking along talking about who is the greatest and when they get to where they are going he asks them: "What were you talking about?" (Mark 9:33). He uses the opportunity to teach about humility by taking a child and putting it in their midst.

Or, they are out doing a mission and preaching and they run out of food. Jesus teaches them how to trust him by inviting them to give some food themselves.

Or, another day as they are walking along he asks them – who do people say that I am? He uses opportunities when he is alone with them to explain his teaching more deeply. He explains to them how he must suffer, and die.

So much of Jesus' life with the disciples is formation. He is sharing with them his heart and teaching them. He is letting them observe him. He is dealing with issues directly when they come up.

This is the model the Church gives us for formation: disciple-ing, which is different than other types of formation. Different than the classroom, different than the sports team, it is a sharing of life. It requires being with them and walking with them on the way. It means getting into their lives and inviting them into your life. It is a kind of mentoring. This is the way Jesus did formation. It came through inviting the disciples into a relationship with him.

Formative Model vs. an Evaluative Model

I acknowledge that this is different than much of how seminary formation is done today. Often times the formator meets with the seminarian in his office about once a month. They discuss two types of issues: 1. Issues the seminarian brings from his own experiences. 2. Issues that the formator must bring which come from the seminary faculty, or field supervision, or the formators own experience.

Of course, these types of formation meetings have to happen, but I am submitting that this is not the primary model for the relationship of the seminarian and the formation advisor. That model is based more on evaluation than formation. I think this is one of the major issues that our seminaries must face. Have we become cultures of evaluation and not cultures of formation. Evaluation is measuring the seminarian by a set of objective standards, and asking him to incorporate those standards.

Seminaries have to do evaluation and we need objective standards. But if the seminary is experienced primarily as an environment of evaluation, it does not encourage the kind of growth we need to happen in seminarians. Rather, it encourages a kind of external performance, not integrated growth. It's much more akin to the professional world that teaches skills, even relational skills, but doesn't actually allow the integrated growth needed for priesthood.

An overly evaluative environment can even encourage hiding instead of integration. A formation environment creates a relationship of trust which allows true growth, whereas an evaluation environment creates a set of standards that encourage performance.

The foundational virtue for this formational environment is **trust**. Real formation only happens in an environment of trust. To be able to help men grow, you have to be able to speak into their lives. They have to give you permission, or real change will not happen. Remember the Thomistic idiom – "whatever is received is received according to the mode of the receiver." Unless they are open to receive from you, you cannot form them. Thus, in order to form them they have to trust you.

How does the formator get them to trust him? He doesn't have to be their buddy, but he does have to spend time with them. They have to see that their formator wills their good – that he loves them. When they realize he truly cares for them, they will begin to open up. <u>The formator has to be Father to them</u>. When they accept my Fatherhood they will reveal themselves to me, and I can form them. This happens over time – cannot be immediately forced.

I believe this is why the PPF strongly recommends that the Formators live with the seminarians. This again is one of the great deaths of seminary formation. Parish priests don't live with their parishioners. But if I'm going to do formation the way Jesus did, I need to have real access to their lives and they need to have access to mine.

This doesn't mean that there are no boundaries, but it does mean the sharing of life beyond office hours. The formator needs to be around them, to spend quality time with them. They will learn to gain the virtues of the heart of the priest by watching a priest live those virtues even towards them. They will learn courage by the patient love of the formator – who is not afraid to bring up difficult things but still loves them. They will learn friendship by the way the formator chooses to love them in the truth of their own weaknesses.

By living with the seminarian the Formator creates an environment that encourages real growth. In some ways, it is like a family environment. The environment is built on trust and allows appropriate vulnerability amongst brothers. This vulnerability allows real growth and conversion, not just external conformation. This requires relationships of trust where the seminarians feel accepted but also challenged to grow. This is the kind of environment Jesus gave his disciples when he was forming them.

I often wondered what it would look like if each formator in a seminary actually lived on the same floor with his formatees. What if he had men across the years of formation who formed a small but not exclusive community within the seminary. Maybe once a year he took them on a weekend trip or retreat somewhere, so he could get extra time with them. He worked with the older guys on his floor to help him to form the younger guys and reach out to them. Perhaps once or twice a week he had dinner with some of them.

Suppose there began to be a smaller community that was led by this formator where different types of interactions could happen - one where he could be with the seminarians in more informal times to actually get to know them and develop that trust. This would also allow him to see the seminarians in their day to day environment, and like Jesus, take the opportunity when he sees it to do formation.

One way I tried to create a more relational model for formation is that I used to avoid doing every formation meeting in my office. I also would not simply go through a checklist each time of formation topics. Sometimes I would go on a walk with a seminarian or go to a coffee shop. I'd spend time letting him talk and getting to know their lives, when appropriate sharing my life. We could exchange in spiritual conversations. I would notice what excites him.

I learn a lot about a man in these times and can begin to see the real man in formation. He learns that I care for him and I am out for his good – this allows him to trust me and allows real growth.

Two other practical suggestions about ways to spend time together:

1. Let the seminarians see you do ministry outside sometimes. Jesus did this. He brought them along when he preached. This can help them to develop and grow through real ministry experiences.
2. Consider doing actual pilgrimages. Trips or times away from the seminary are great formation opportunities. Jesus did a lot of his forming "on the way," walking from one place to the next. A lot can happen when you have time travelling together. We have a few trips in our seminary and those are always very powerful formation times, because you are with the guys all the time and in those down times, as you're walking along, they bring things up and you can build trusting relationships.

External vs. Internal Forum

When you see the formation relationship the way Jesus does it, it automatically brings us into one of the tensions of the formation relationship: What things in formation belong to the external forum verses internal forum?

I could spend a whole talk on this and I don't want to, but I need to say a few things. If you do formation well, you will find yourself close to things which are often considered part of the internal forum – but they are not. This is because to do formation well you have to see the real man – and real persons are not split up into external and internal forums. What is the purpose of these forums? The needs of both must be held in tension.

Internal forum exists to provide the central role of protecting the conscience of the person. A seminarian needs that place of absolute freedom of conscience to speak in depth about the things which are most intimate to him. Without this freedom the person might not be able to grow and get the advice necessary.

However, as we all know the call to priesthood is not only subjective and interior but must be confirmed by the Church. <u>The Church has the obligation to know the man</u> she is going to ordain, which requires a real transparency before the formators. Msgr. Jim Shea has said it well in his little book on ecclesial discernment:

> "Because the ecclesial call to prepare one's life for priesthood originates in the external forum, that is also where the question of priesthood is properly brought to resolution…. Spiritual direction…guides the man when he needs to say in the external forum anything he does not want to say. Because catholic vocational discernment is ecclesial, <u>a condition for peace in discernment is deep mutual trust and total transparency in the external forum</u>." (Jim Shea, *Discernment Within The Heart Of The Church*)

I would often tell the men in formation, that if they are honest in formation and I still recommend them for ordination, then they can have peace in their discernment.

Things to note in your formation relationship about the external forum: First, there is a danger of hiding in the internal forum. If a man never talks about prayer, chastity, sinful habits, disordered emotions in the external forum, how can I know if he is really growing? He must be willing to talk about what is really going on in him. He does not have to share in the same depth for sure, but he must give his formator a real picture of his life. He must not approach the external forum as "anything you say can and will be used against you"; rather, he has to learn to trust that his formator wants to help him and open up to his formator.

Second, the formator must be able to see that the man has a living relationship with God and is able to talk about it. You have to be able to see that he is internalizing the formation. This means he must at times talk about what happens in his prayer. Life happens in prayer and we have to be able to discuss this in the external forum, not with the same detail or intimacy as spiritual direction, but really. This is what it means to become a spiritual man – people can see I am a man of prayer.

When one of my seminarians came back from retreat I always asked him – how was your retreat? How did it impact or change your life? If it never did impact his life, then I had concerns. If he could not talk about his relationship with God, this is a concern.

There is a danger of creating a bifurcated man – one who thinks that human things and spiritual things are separate – they are all part of my growth into the image of Christ.

The external forum is the place where that growth into the image of Christ is being witnessed. When there is authentic growth that is being experienced in spiritual formation, it is a joy for the man to share that appropriately with his formator. When there is real struggle that affects the man's vocation – this too must enter some way into the external forum relationship.

If the relationship is working well and he trusts you as his formator, when he brings up something especially intimate that needs some particular attention in terms of exploring interior affective movements and motivations, it is easy to encourage the man to take these intimate matters up in spiritual direction, and to explore them over time in prayer and discernment. At the same time the formator can count on a unified vision of formation for the seminarian so that the spiritual director would   encourage the man to talk with his formator about areas of intimate growth that have transpired in spiritual direction and can be further integrated through more transparent conversations with his formator.

Here are some practical helps for the formator as he seeks to walk with the man in this relationship. First, he needs to take the long view with a man. I need to get to know the man well. I may see plenty of things in him that need to change, but I can really help him if I get to know him and help him see where these things come from. This means getting to know his family of origin, his life experience. It means getting to know his gifts and weaknesses as he knows them and helping him to see others. I should expect that the relationship will deepen over time. I wouldn't expect him to trust me from the beginning and I wouldn't ask him difficult questions in the beginning.

To give an example – it is always difficult to talk about the area of chastity – yet I have to do it! I have to give a witness that this man is able to live chastity; at some point this area must come up in formation for frank discussion. But I often don't bring it up the first year – I wait until there is trust and more knowledge there to begin to have real discussions about this.

The formator needs to learn some of the skills of a spiritual director – formation needs to be Spirit-directed. I must understand that Jesus Christ is the primary formator. I am cooperating in the formation that Jesus does. Listen to how St. John Paul II describes this Spirit-directed formation:

"It is the Spirit of Jesus that throws light on and gives strength to vocational discernment and the journey to the priesthood. So we can say that there cannot exist any genuine formational work for the priesthood without the influence of the Spirit of Christ. Everyone involved in the work of formation should be fully aware of this. How can we fail to appreciate this utterly gratuitous and completely effective 'resource,' which has its own decisive 'weight' in the effort to train people for the priesthood? How can we not rejoice when we consider the dignity of every human being involved in formation, who for the candidate to the priesthood becomes, as it were, the visible representative of Christ? If training for the priesthood is, as it should be, essentially the preparation of future 'shepherds' in the likeness of Jesus Christ the good shepherd, who better than Jesus himself, through the outpouring of his Spirit, can give them and fully develop in them that pastoral charity which he himself lived to the point of total self - giving (cf. Jn. 15:13; 10:11) and which he wishes all priests to live in their turn?" (*Pastores Dabo Vobis*, 65)

What does this mean practically? It means that just as a spiritual director learns to watch for and see Christ's work in their directee and then encourage and compliment that work – so also the formator must watch for Christ's work and encourage and compliment it.

Let me give you a couple of examples: I remember a seminarian who had a stutter who really struggled with self-confidence. He went out and gave a reflection at Masses on a weekend to raise money for the seminary. He had to speak at all the Masses in a large parish. It went really well – he came back filled with confidence and joy! What an important formative moment. My job is to highlight: "that is Jesus working in you."

I remember another seminarian who was the victim of a practical joke that got out of hand. He got really angry and when the seminarian who did the joke came up – he took a swing at him! Then he was convicted and went to the chapel and poured out his heart to God. Then he came to see me preparing to get kicked out of the seminary. Rather, it turned out to be a great opportunity for him to face his anger issues and get some counseling – and real growth ensued. Christ was working here – my role is to help that. Christ is the primary formator, I must be attentive to what he is doing.

What I have found is that when I could help the man see where Christ was working to help him grow – growth happened so much faster and easier. I'm helping him cooperate with grace – which as St. John Paul II said is "utterly gratuitous and completely effective 'resource,'" of seminary formation.

This also applies to the listening skills of a spiritual director. The formator is listening for where God is working in the experience of the seminarian. He is also listening for where the enemy is working or where lies from the man's past are still affecting him. He is listening with the Spirit to help the man be formed into the priest God wants him to be.

You can see some of what the formator is supposed to be by studying the qualities that *Pastores Dabo Vobis* says a formator should have (66). First, John Paul II simply highlights the importance of the formator:

"It is evident that much of the effectiveness of the training offered depends on the maturity and strength of personality of those entrusted with formation, both from the human and from the Gospel points of view. And so it is especially important both to select them carefully and to encourage them to become ever more suitable for carrying out the task entrusted to them."

Then he points out the qualities which the Synod Fathers said formators should have:

"The task of formation of candidates for the priesthood requires not only a certain special preparation of those to whom this work is entrusted, one that is professional, pedagogical, spiritual, human and theological, but also a spirit of communion and of cooperating together to carry out the program, so that the unity of the pastoral action of the seminary is always maintained under the leadership of the rector."

He speaks about the way that the formators witness to a true community amongst themselves and with the seminarians:

"The body of formation personnel should witness to a truly evangelical lifestyle and total dedication to the Lord. It should enjoy a certain stability, and its members as a rule should live in the seminary community. They should be intimately joined to the bishop, who is the first one responsible for the formation of the priests."

He continues by giving advice about who should be chosen:

"For this ministry, priests of exemplary life should be chosen, men with a number of qualities: "human and spiritual maturity, pastoral experience, professional competence, stability in their own vocation, a capacity to work with others, serious preparation in those human sciences (psychology especially) which relate to their office, a knowledge of how to work in groups."

All this is required to allow the formator to create this formative environment where true growth can happen.

A final practical piece of advice: Learning to catch formative moments

As formators, we need to be attentive to formative moments and be there to help the seminarian go through this well. How the seminarian goes through these moments teaches us a lot about their affective maturity.

The first point is the moment of difficult obedience. Many men who are affectively immature have abnormally strong reactions to difficult obedience. By difficult obedience, I mean a situation where obedience to their superiors requires them to do something they really don't like, don't agree with, or are afraid of. This obedience that is asked touches an area of lack of freedom in them and they get angry, or try to get out of it, or complain.

The truth is that sometimes obedience is difficult. Even Christ struggled under difficult obedience of the Cross as we see in the Agony in the Garden! But this is the picture of affective maturity. In difficult obedience, I am able to acknowledge the truth of the pain I feel, yet still trust in God's goodness and providence, and through surrender go forward in peace.

If I don't have affective maturity, the process will be short-circuited at some point. Either I will deny my anger, hurt or frustration and just do it – bringing all kinds of hidden anger and bitterness or fear, that often leads to self-seeking behaviors to medicate the pain. Or, I will not be able to trust in my pain that God is going to bring about good.

Here is the question: Can the man learn to relate his own suffering to that of Christ and find joy?

Sometimes the only way to help these men experience and come to know their affective immaturity is to provoke the reaction. I almost never do this on purpose, but I do let it happen. Asking them to do something that they are afraid of or which provokes their feelings can help them see how they lack affective maturity. It can help them come to self-knowledge and self-acceptance. So, we should not be afraid of using this tool with prudence.

The second formational moment is the moment of failure. This can often be one of the most graced moments in formation - when a man fails in something, and I get to see how he reacts.

Does his failure lead to discouragement, sadness, or a desire to give up? Can he accept himself in his failure? You learn a lot about his affective maturity. Can he allow himself to be loved in failure? Can he love himself?

Most often, more important than almost any particular failure is the way a man deals with it. The failure can usually be dealt with, if the man is willing to grow and learn through it. You learn a lot about how a man reacts when he fails. If he hides in his failure and cannot admit it or if he gives up in his failure, than you know he has a false identity. He may not be open to receiving the truth about himself.

On the other hand, if he allows himself to be humbled and acknowledges his failure, then often times this is the moment when you can speak truth about who he is to him. You can speak to him about how his identity is deeper than this failure. This is the moment when he can begin to come to freedom because you can show him the false ways he has built his identity.

By way of example, consider St. Peter. Peter is a man who hated weakness and failure and had to learn the depth of his own weakness. See how the Lord formed him? He let him fail, while still showing him love (Luke 22). Then he invited him to begin anew in love – accepting the truth of himself in love. Jesus invites him to self-gift (John 21). Peter is much more sober after his failure. Before the passion he does not know his weakness. Now he knows it and he is able to be dependent. Now he is ready for pastoral authority. This is true strength!

I hope you can see from these reflections that in some way the formator is the most essential man in the seminarian's formation. He is the one who actually brings to bear the integration of spiritual and human formation which we have been talking about. He is the one who sees that the spiritual formation is integrated into all the other areas of formation. He has the difficult task of helping form the priest in this man. He brings the insights of the whole community to this man in a way that the man can receive them and grow from them. He walks with him as the Lord works on him and finds ways to assist the Lord's formation.

For these reasons he must see himself truly as a father and be a spiritual man himself who is capable of entering into relationship that allows true growth.

This article was originally published in *Christ as the Foundation of Seminary Formation* (Omaha: Institute for Priestly Formation, 2016) and is published here with the permission of the publisher and the author, who has also added the following prayer, reflection questions, and suggested resources.

Prayer adapted from St. John Henry Newman

> *Dear Jesus, help me to spread Your fragrance wherever I go.*
> *Flood my soul with Your spirit and life.*
> *Penetrate and possess my whole being so utterly, that my life may only be a radiance of Yours.*

Shine through me, and be so in me that every soul I come in contact with may feel
Your presence in my soul.
Let them look up and see no longer me, but only Jesus!
Stay with me and then I shall begin to shine as You shine, so to shine as to be a light
to others.
The light, O Jesus, will be all from You; none of it will be mine.
It will be you, shining on others through me.
Let me thus praise You the way You love best, by shining on those around me.
Let me preach You without preaching, not by words but by my example, by the
catching force of the sympathetic influence of what I do,
the evident fullness of the love my heart bears to You.
Amen.

Practicum Reflection Questions for Formators

1. What can you learn from Jesus' method of doing formation that will allow you to make the institutional environment of the seminary a place where a formative relationship can flourish and not only evaluative?

2. What have you learned by sharing life with other seminarians? With priest formators? How can you invest in sharing life together for more formation? What would this community look like?

3. What is my reaction to Msgr. Jim Shea's comment: "Because catholic vocational discernment is ecclesial, a condition for peace in discernment is deep mutual trust and total transparency in the external forum." How do we help overcome fear in formation? What are the obstacles to trust that make me afraid to share my real struggles with my formator? What would it feel like or look like if I could share openly?

4. Have the seminarian explain a moment when they found obedience difficult. How did you feel? How did you react? How did you pray through this? Can you see how Jesus is working in this?

Suggested Resources

1. Archbishop Jorge Patron Wong, "Foundations of Priestly Formation" http://www.clerus.va/content/dam/clerus/Dox/Conference%20-%20Foundations%20of%20Priestly%20Formation.pdf

2. Msgr. James Shea, *Discernment Within the Heart of the Church*, NCDVD Resources.

3. Caserta, T.(1998). *Ananias and the elephants: Formation ministry examines its consciousness.* Seminary Journal, 4, 37-42.

Chapter Eleven

The Importance of Human Formation and Affective Maturity in the Man of Communion

Dr. Suzanne Baars, Ph.D.

Dr. Sue Baars is a marriage and family therapist in Irving, Texas, where she teams with other Catholic therapists and a psychiatric nurse practitioner as the clinical director of In His Image Counseling Center. Dr. Baars has worked extensively in the field of counseling since 1986 in both hospital and outpatient settings. She bases her work on the integration of the Christian anthropology of St. Thomas Aquinas with the treatment of a variety of emotional & spiritual problems, among them Emotional Deprivation Disorder, obsessive-compulsive disorder and scrupulosity. She is frequent presenter at Catholic conferences around the country, and has been interviewed on EWTN's *Women of Grace* as well as *Coffin Nation.* She often presents the psychological contributions of her late father, psychiatrist and author Conrad Baars, a pioneer in the field of Catholic psychology.

Dr. Baars has been privileged to have been on the faculty of the Institute for Priestly Formation (IPF) from 2008 until 2015, where she taught diocesan seminarians. She was a contributor to two IPF publications that focused on developing affective maturity in priestly formation. The importance of human formation in seminary is of great interest to Dr. Baars, as she believes that the health of the Church depends largely on mature, happy clergy. Her lecture, *St. Thomas Aquinas and Affective Maturity,* reflects this belief.

Dr. Baars is Past President of the Catholic Psychotherapy Association. She also operates the Baars Institute, which is dedicated to offering hope to those affected by emotional deprivation, as well as educating the public on the concept of affirmation and the healing of emotional disorders.

Dr. Baars' lecture series entitled, *The Abode of Love: Developing the Heart*, introduces listeners to the importance of the emotional life for all persons, but especially Christians, both clergy and religious and lay people, who have suffered from misperceptions about their emotions. Along with a colleague,

Dr. Baars edited a collection of her late father's articles and monographs related to the priesthood entitled, *"I Will Give Them a New Heart: Reflections on the Priesthood and the Renewal of the Church."*

More information may be found at www.BaarsInstitute.com

Affective maturity is crucial for the formation of seminarians, for priests and for the priesthood itself. Without it, a man may on the one hand have difficulty in forming relationships and self-confidence, and on the other may be driven to prove himself through accomplishments or find inauthentic ways to feel loved and worthwhile. The mean between these two extremes can be somewhat elusive, leaving formators and others at a loss as to how to aid a man's development towards, or to assess a man's level of, affective maturity.

In speaking about affective maturity, we necessarily turn to the subject of human formation, for it is upon the foundation of an authentic human anthropology that maturity may develop. As the priest will always be ministering to human beings, he himself needs to be able to care, teach and preach with compassion, following the example of Jesus Christ, the Good Shepherd. He must take care that he 'becomes a bridge and not an obstacle for others in their meeting with Jesus Christ the redeemer of humanity" (PDV 43). Therefore, "the priest should be able to know the depths of the human heart, to perceive difficulties and problems, to make meeting and dialogue easy, to create trust and cooperation, to express serene and objective judgements" (PDV, 43). Furthermore, the priest must have the capacity to relate to others personally. He should be "affable, hospitable, sincere in his words and heart, prudent and discreet, generous and ready to serve, capable of opening himself to clear and brotherly relationships and of encouraging the same in others, and quick to understand, forgive and console" (PDV 43). All these qualities refer to affective maturity in the man who is called to the priesthood, to be a man of communion with and for others.

"The priest who is affectively mature and who therefore is aware of the emotional wounds of his parishioners will be better able to preach, teach and hear confessions with compassion. His ministry will touch their hearts more readily if he understands how these emotional disorders weaken their moral life and their capacity for spiritual joy. His call will be to give *spiritual and intellectual affirmation* through conveying the truth & sound moral guidance rather than *emotional affirmation*. However, for this to be fruitful, his parishioners will need to feel beforehand that he is their loving spiritual father. This means that the man has already successfully integrated his emotions and sexuality under the guidance of reason and will. This in turn demands that the man not only know intellectual and spiritual truths, but that he has received the gift of himself through the affirming presence of others in his life, and so is free to give himself to others."[1]

Affective maturity means that the man is free to give himself as a gift, which depends on interior freedom.[2] As St John Paul II says in Pastores Dabo Vobis, 'Freedom, therefore, is essential to vocation - a freedom which, when it gives a positive response, appears as a deep personal adherence, as a loving gift - or rather as a gift given back to the giver who is God who calls, an oblation' (PDV 36). An oblation is a self- offering - a gift of self. Without interior freedom I cannot make that gift of self."[3] "This interior freedom that is so essential is often defined as affective maturity. The freedom for sacrifice is the remote goal, but affective maturity is the proximate goal. Affective maturity is the necessary foundation for this freedom to exist" (Cozzens, n.d.).

St. Thomas Aquinas and Affective Maturity

What denotes the capacity for affective maturity in a person? Bishop Andrew Cozzens says, "the key benchmark of human formation which summarizes all the others is the ability to live a sacrificial life, a life of self-gift."[4] Evidence of it lies in the man's ability to restrain his own wants and desires when necessary or appropriate, as well as to experience the joy of their fulfillment. Even more importantly is the ability to freely give himself to others. This might manifest itself for example in the capacity for deep friendships, where the man not only is present for others, but is willing to reveal himself. The man who is able, not only to be supportive but also vulnerable himself, demonstrates a capacity for deeper relationships, which in turn indicates that he has the capacity to sacrifice himself and his own desires for the good of others.

The anthropology of St. Thomas Aquinas offers an understanding of the human person that helps to refine these ideas and bring clarity to the subject of affective maturity. Aquinas states that it is the nature of the sensitive appetite to obey reason.[5] He also says that the passions can contribute positively to the development of virtue. Both of these statements demonstrate that the virtuous man has brought his passions under the control of his

---

[1] Baars, S. M. 2013. Paraphrase, YouTube Lecture, *St. Thomas Aquinas and Affective Maturity.*

[2] Cozzens, Andrew. (n.d.) Human Formation Benchmarks for the Diocesan Seminarian.

[3] Quoted in Cozzens, Andrew. (n.d.) Human Formation Benchmarks for the Diocesan Seminarian.

[4] Cozzens, A. (n.d.). Human Formation Benchmarks for the Diocesan Seminarian.

[5] Summa Theologica Ia IIae, q. 74, a. 3 ad 1 um.

intellect by cultivating them towards what is good. He has neither extinguished them nor allowed them to dominate him. This integration of the emotions with reason is necessary for the mature development of the person, as well as for his personal happiness.[6] This is particularly important for the priest who in addition to his teaching, preaching and sacramental duties will become a spiritual father to many persons. However, in order to be a spiritual father, the man must *possess the capacity* to give his *entire* self – intellect, will, body, personality, temperament, - that is, *everything about him* – to his Bride, the Church, at ordination. This depends on the man's affective maturity, or the development and integration of the emotional life under the direction of reason.

However, besides the question of how to assess the presence of affective maturity in a man, there is the more fundamental question of where and how it develops. Although affective maturity is evidenced most clearly in the capacity for relationship, it also develops *within* relationships – for the most part those of the man's family of origin.

Affirmation and Relationships

Affective maturity indicates that the man, through his human formation, has received his identity by having been sufficiently affirmed. The concept of affirmation was introduced in the 20th century by two Catholic psychiatrists who revived and further developed St. Thomas Aquinas' anthropology, Drs. Anna Terruwe and Conrad Baars. Affirming love[7] refers to someone *revealing* to another person his goodness, lovableness and unique, innate identity. These authors defined affirmation is a *way of being* which manifests itself in a three step process, whereby one is 1) present, open, and receptive to another, without wanting to change or possess them, 2) allows himself to be moved by the other person, and 3) when he is so moved, he *reveals* his inner feelings to the other person through his countenance, tone of voice and choice of words. Over time, the person is strengthened to be himself, and he comes to experience himself as good and worthwhile. Through being affirmed, he grows in self-confidence and is able to be present to others and strengthen them in turn.

Affirmation in this sense is not something that is done to or for the other person, no matter how well-intentioned. It is a way of *being* rather than *doing*, allowing the other to be just as he is, thus strengthening the other to be himself. In effect, affirmation or affirming presence is the 'ingredient' necessary for attachment in relationships to occur. This brings

---

[6] Baars, C. W. 1974. *The Priest,* The Christian Anthropology of Thomas Aquinas, p. 32.

[7] Terruwe, A., & Baars. C. 2002. *Healing the unaffirmed.* Staten Island, NY: Society of St. Paul.

about a growing sense of identity, security and interior freedom that enable the person to know who he is and thus feel confident in himself, able to face difficulties and obstacles, and to make decisions without effort. The boy and later the man develops the capacity to be spontaneous and joyful, because he has been accepted for who he is. It is in this primary way that affective maturity is fostered and grows.

Because affirming love endows the recipient with a sense of identity as being lovable just as he is, he does not need to search for an identity, or prove to himself or others that he is worthwhile. Affirming love is the integral factor that bestows the peace of interior freedom, which enables the man to possess the capacity to confront the world around him, whether evil or good. This man has access to all his emotions and can allow them to arise spontaneously, to help him love the good and be moved by it emotionally and in a similar way be moved with hate and aversion for what is evil and so fight or avoid it. This man possesses an ordered emotional life; the emotions support his will for doing good in life and are under the guidance of reason informed by faith.

Our best example of affective maturity, of course, is Jesus Christ, fully human and fully divine. Here are just a few examples of Our Lord's display of emotion: "when he drew near and saw the city, he wept over it" (Luke 19:41); His anger was evident in the temple: "And making a whip of cords, he drove them all out of the temple" (John 2:15); He was afraid: "And being in agony he prayed more earnestly; and his sweat became like great drops of blood falling down to the ground" (Luke 22:44). Like Jesus Christ, Who loved, hated, grieved, felt sad, rejoiced and was angry, grace can more readily perfect the man who lives a fully human life.

The Role of the Emotions

St. Thomas' anthropology identifies two types of passions or emotions: one that Aquinas called the concupiscible passions, which have to do with whether one experiences a thing as pleasant and good or unpleasant and bad. These passions are love or liking, desire, joy, and their opposites, hate or dislike, aversion and sadness. Terruwe and Baars call these passions the *pleasure emotions*.[8] The other passions are the irascible passions or the *assertive drive*, which move one to act, to fight or flee, to face and overcome difficulties (to do 'the arduous good') or to feel that they cannot be surmounted. The emotions of the assertive drive are hope, despair, courage, fear, and anger. Moreover, Aquinas notes that the

---

[8] Terruwe, A., and Baars, C. 2016. *Psychic wholeness and healing: Using all the powers of the human psyche.*. Eugene, Oregon: Wipf and Stock Publishers.

relationship between the two sensitive appetites is important: "the irascible appetite [assertive drive] operates to enable the concupiscible appetite [pleasure emotions] to reach its goal,"[9] not the other way around. That is, when one loves something, he desires it (e.g. the pleasure appetite is moved), but it is only the stimulation of the assertive drive that enables him to *attain* that which he desires, and so experience joy, happiness, satisfaction, etc. An example of this is when a man wants to pass a difficult course and thus be able to graduate, but has difficulty studying for it. He is moved with the desire to attain his diploma, but needs the emotions of hope and courage to be able to surmount, with tutoring and extra studying, the difficulties he faces. His courage enables him to continue to do what his reason tells him is necessary, despite the fact that his pleasure emotions deem it unpleasant, and thus he is able to pass the course, and finally feel relieved and happy.

Furthermore, Terruwe and Baars state,

Our claim that the pleasure appetite of human beings is more spiritual and intuitive – as compared with the more 'rational' and mechanistic character of the assertive drive – can be understood only in the realization that we are not restricting sense pleasure to the meaning which is often given it: namely, to indicate simply and solely the gratification of the sense of touch and taste. In humans the intellectual pervades and elevates the entire sensory life, including the pleasure appetite. The most perfect and beautiful human emotions belong to this level of life and can be the source of the purest human happiness. What ultimately matters is *what* people strive for, not the striving itself. When persons choose that which is most proper to them as human beings, from all the possible objects which can stimulate their pleasure appetite, it will only be through the subordination of the assertive drive to the pleasure appetite that they can do full justice to their human nature.[10]

When the relationship between these two sensory appetites is reversed, a man strives for everything, but does not come to rest and enjoy the fruits of his labors. "The main accent in the emotional life must naturally rest on the pleasure appetite [concupiscible] and not on the assertive drive [irascible]. When the emphasis is shifted to the assertive drive, there is a

---

[9] Terruwe, A., and Baars, C. 2016. *Psychic wholeness and healing: Using all the powers of the human psyche..* Eugene, Oregon: Wipf and Stock Publishers. See Summa Theol., Ia IIae, q. 25, a.1: "The irascible passions both arise from and terminate in the passions of the concupiscible faculty."

[10] Terruwe, A. A., & Baars, C. W. 2016. *Psychic wholeness and healing: Using all the powers of the human psyche.* Eugene, OR: Wipf and Stock Publishers, pp. 16-17.

disharmony of the emotional life, with potentially disastrous consequences to the psychological life."[11] This leaves the person in a state of constant striving without a means to access the enjoyable experience of attaining a good. In fact, Baars and Terruwe note that,

> "the predominance of the assertive drive...leads to an extreme materialist and mundane spirit and stifles emotional life. This is a frequent occurrence in modern times and is caused to a great extent by a premature development of the reasoning intellect before the emotional life has matured sufficiently. Since the assertive drive participates more in the functioning of the reasoning intellect, it will overstep its limits whenever the intellect exercises undue influence over a person's actions. This disturbance of the proper order of the psychological powers is the cause of emotional illness."[12]

When the assertive drive takes precedence, the man's affective life is stamped by the emotions of fear, courage or anger -- all of which keep him in motion and enable him to accomplish things but do not in themselves permit him to find rest or enjoyment in the attainment of the good. An improper understanding of authentic leisure may be lacking in such a person: he may believe that hard work makes things more meritorious than if something good comes easily. However, Aquinas says, "the essence of virtue consists in the good rather than in the difficult."[13] An attitude of workaholism may be the source of this way of living. There may even repression of the pleasure emotions because they are viewed as useless or to be feared. This focus on striving while stifling rest or enjoyment will naturally permeate and affect the man and his relationships negatively. Such a man has lost or perhaps has never developed the capacity for simple enjoyment by being present to things, nature, the fine arts, or persons in an attentive, receptive, affirming way. A man who renders himself unable to enjoy the fruits of his labors will also not be able to enjoy friendship for its own sake. This will hinder his ability to relate to the experiences of others.

A utilitarian, energetic attitude may easily leave the impression on others that the man is simply interested in results, not in people and their concerns. The priest who has this attitude will not be perceived as a warm spiritual father by his flock, which may prevent some from being able to encounter God the Father's love. Such a man may become an obstacle for others rather than a bridge to Jesus Christ.

---

[11] Ibid, p. 16.

[12] Terruwe, A. A., & Baars, C. W. 2016. *Psychic wholeness and healing: Using all the powers of the human psyche*. Eugene, OR: Wipf and Stock Publishers, p. 16.

[13] Summa Theologica, II, II, 123, 12 ad 2.

This man should be introduced to the concepts of leisure, the goodness of all the emotions, the idea that repression is against his nature, and affirming living, in which one encounters and is moved by the things that touch the heart and do not just serve the mind. It is mind and heart *together* that provide an openness to the possibility of a joyful and effortless life, rather than living by simply moving from one task to another.

Affectivity and Effectivity

Baars further discusses the importance of this development of the affective, intuitive heart before that of the working mind. He discusses the anthropology of St. Thomas, which teaches

> reason and will are not the only principles of the human act. The emotions are positive principles which add moral value to the human act. Having a feeling, a liking for the good, definitely adds something to the moral value of the will-act. It is not only psychologically important to strive after the good with heart and soul, but also morally better.[14]

Baars notes that Aquinas taught that the will is not meant to be the sole principle of human acts. In fact, the will not only moves, but it is itself moved.[15]

> The will must first be moved *affectively*... [as in being] 'moved to tears'. If at all possible, the good must please the will emotionally, and at the same time appeal to it via reason. To will, in the broader Thomistic concept, is first of all *affectivity*. Only secondarily, and dependent on this affectivity, is the will an active mover – *effective*. Virtue, therefore, is not only in the will and reason, but also in the emotions.[16]

Baars defined these terms more specifically: affectivity is

---

[14] Baars, C. W. 2008. *I will give them a new heart: Reflections on the priesthood and the renewal of the Church.*. New York: Society of St. Paul/Alba House, p. 43-44.

[15] Baars, S. M. 2013. *The role of affectivity in forming the man of communion: Receiving the priestly identities,* in *Seminary Theology III: Seminary Formation and Psychology.* Omaha, Nebraska: IPF Publications, p. 17.

[16] Ibid, p. 44.

the habitual disposition of the heart to be moved by the good of the other (and other things and beings) and to act on his behalf. Affectivity consists of the fully or adequately developed emotions of the [concupiscible] appetite in their close interaction with the intuitive intellect...Effectivity (is) the habitual disposition of the mind to see and grasp the other (and other things and beings) for his own utilitarian purposes...[17]

While effectivity is necessary for human life inasmuch as it assists one in the accomplishment of tasks, developing affectivity is crucial for the man to experience the joy of the happiness for which he is created.[18]

Based on these complementary concepts, Terruwe and Baars introduced the concept of affirming living as a way of being which has the effect of bringing peace and resolving difficulties.[19] This concept includes the theory of affirming presence already outlined, but refers more broadly to a way of living in which the person remains open to everything around him affectively, that is with his entire self. When affectivity is appreciated more than effectivity there is an attitude of receptivity and openness that characterizes the man.

The Importance of Affectivity in the Family of Origin

What, then, does the man who grew up in a family characterized by healthy affectivity learn? How has he been affected by this experience? He knows the happiness of being with others, of being considered important and cherished, what it means to be a part of a family, of having fun and interacting with others. He knows what it is like to be vulnerable, to be loved and supported when he experienced failure, to be celebrated when he succeeded. He knows the look of acceptance in his parents' eyes; he knows he is special to someone. He has likely experienced discipline that has affirmed the goodness of his being while any behaviors that were immature or morally wrong were met with firm encouragement and forgiveness. He has experienced the difficulty of relationships, of misunderstandings and reconciliation, and lack thereof. He has experienced his own sonship through both his mother's reassuring, steady presence, and the way his father ushered him into manhood with challenge and

---

[17] Terruwe, A., & Baars, C. 2016. *Psychic wholeness and healing.* Eugene, Oregon: Wipf and Stock Publishers, p. 116.

[18] Baars, S. M. 2013. *The role of affectivity in forming the man of communion: Receiving the priestly identities,* in *Seminary Theology III: Seminary Formation and Psychology.* Omaha, Nebraska: IPF Publications, p. 17.

[19] Terruwe, A. A. Unpublished talk, *Affectivity in religious life.*

encouragement. He has observed what healthy fatherliness and motherliness are throughout this same process. Both aspects of the masculine, sonship and fatherhood, are crucial for his own identity formation, first through receiving his identity as son, then later knowing what it is to be a father. He has been sharpened by these familial relationships into being a man of communion: "as iron sharpens iron, so one man sharpens another" (Proverbs 27:17). In fact, one might say that he has been endowed with identity through the affirming nature of these very relationships.

Familial relationships thus are crucial to the development of the man of communion, as they can nurture or inhibit the capacity for identity and therefore relationships. Pope Benedict XVI says, "The family is the privileged setting where every person learns to give and receive love."[20] He also states, "the family is…a school which enables men and women to grow to the full measure of their humanity. The experience of being loved by their parents helps children to become aware of their dignity as children."[21]

Parents who know how to be open, receptive, and attentive, and who have made time for each other and their children are in effect educating them in the school of love, the basis of a Christian and fully human life. They themselves realize the value of this way of living. They are not consumed by providing *for* the family to the exclusion of being *with* the family. Even the activities of the children, although good in themselves, do not override the focus of family unity. All this serves as an example for how the man lives in his adulthood. Even more importantly, the foundation for his own humanity has been laid within him, and has fostered the capacity and desire for sacrificial love.

Authentic affirmation requires that parents spend time with their children so that they are aware of the child's emotional and intellectual growth and can aid him to learn how to manage any difficulties that may arise. Moreover, it is the affirming presence of parents that enables the child to *feel* his own worth, to have self-confidence and a feeling of security, and so have the inner strength to be himself and act in the world. In this way, an affirming presence engenders the boy's identity, through his parents' reflection of their *felt* sense of the child's goodness and intrinsic worth. The boy who is affirmed is strengthened as he grows to manhood: he feels capable of facing things and can navigate difficulties. It is in this way that parents' *feelings of love* strengthen their children and engender identity. While discipline and education are without question important to the formation of children, their

---

[20] Pope Benedict XVI, Vigil of the 5th World Meeting of Families, Valencia, Spain. 2006.

[21] Pope Emeritus Benedict XVI, Vigil of the 5th World Meeting of Families. 2006. http://www.vatican.va/holy_father/benedict_xvi/speeches/2006/july/documetns/hf_ben-xvi_spe_20060708_incontro-festivo_en.html.

feelings of love are the foundation of identity, security, self-confidence and the growing capacity for unselfish, self-restraining love. It is in and through this lived human formation that the future priest becomes affectively mature.

All this affects the man studying for priesthood; if he grew up in a family that did not make time for him or for fostering the community of family life through time together, he likely lacks the experience of others being truly present to him. Some families, although their focus is on instilling the *gift of faith*, emphasize knowing religious principles and developing the spiritual life to the virtual exclusion of the simple joys of being together. This in effect stifles the emotional life, and leaves its stamp on the child. As Terruwe and Baars note, this premature growth of reason or spiritual truths comes at a cost. Often the child represses his emotions due to either incorrect teaching or example, or he has a skewed understanding of what it means to lead a Christian life. In either case, the man coming from such a family does not bear the stamp of healthy human formation, despite perhaps knowing his faith well intellectually. Despite knowledge of spiritual truths and religious practices, this man may lack the emotional development that would enable him to live spontaneously, effortlessly, and joyfully.

Effects of the Lack of Affirming Love in the Family

When there has been insufficient affirming love and personal presence while growing up, the man's affectivity and level of emotional maturity is of course influenced one way or another, to a greater or lesser extent, depending on the level of severity of lack of affirmation. If he has an innately asthenic temperament, he may develop a syndrome in adulthood of emotional deprivation, the less severe unaffirmed state, or an affective disorder. The symptoms of this syndrome include deep feelings of inferiority, inadequacy, insecurity and uncertainty, and an inability to establish rapport with other adults. Internally some persons may even feel younger than their chronological age, making it difficult to develop age-appropriate friendships. This leaves these persons lonely and alone, and vulnerable to being manipulated by others, as they want to be accepted and loved.

On the other hand, if the unaffirmed person has a stronger personality and temperament, insufficient affirming love may spur him to find his worth through being noticed for his performance, by gaining power or notoriety, by putting others down so that he can feel more important, by indiscriminate sexual liaisons, or by amassing money or having many material possessions. Of course, none of these can fill the void that can only be satisfied by the authentic, unconditional love of another person.

The significance of emotional deprivation cannot be underestimated, particularly in the case of men called to the priesthood. Persons deprived of unconditional love either remain narcissistic and selfish or feel weak and inadequate to the task of confronting difficulties, let alone the complexity of the evils of our times. However, healing from these wounds is possible. These difficulties can be overcome through psychological counseling and also through healing prayer. Many have found the imaginative prayer which St. Ignatius proposes in the Spiritual Exercise helpful for healing these deeper wounds which have come from a lack of affirmation.

The healing of these wounds is particularly important in the man who struggles with transitory same sex attraction. Deep-seated same sex attraction is an exclusive attraction with regard to persons of the same sex, a rejection of the Church's teachings on same sex attraction and may include advocacy of the gay lifestyle. Transitory same sex attraction may be understood as an attraction which the man desires to overcome and with which he is dissatisfied. In a man who seeks a means to recover his own masculinity by healing the wounds which arose from an absent, distant or rejecting father, there is hope for resolution. His willingness to enter into this struggle is the beginning of a relationship with himself in a new way - itself a masculine endeavor. Some men may also have negatively internalized other past events such as bullying or rejection by peers as compounding factors. In any case, once the man can be helped to see that the attraction to another man actually manifests the very traits he feels are lacking in himself, he is empowered to begin to repair the wounds to his masculinity. According to Joseph Nicolosi, same sex attraction in itself is an unconscious attempt to repair wounds to masculinity, which he terms

'the reparative drive.' This reparative attempt at mastery is made through the effort to conquer and gain the love of a feared object, the unavailable man (usually the father), and thus to repair a felt deficit of masculine affirmation through an input of virility, power and confidence.[22]

Once the man realizes this, he may become more hopeful in being able to fulfill properly the masculine needs he has, as this does not depend on acting out with another man - something morally repugnant to the man with transitory same sex attraction.

In any case, the environment in which the man grew up affects the man's affective maturity positively or negatively. If it has been positive for the development of affective

---

[22] Nicolosi, J. J. 2016. *Shame and Attachment Loss: The practical work of reparative therapy.* Liberal Mind Publishers, p. 78.

maturity, the man's emotional life has been developed so that the man is free to cultivate his desire for what is good both on the natural and spiritual levels. This enables freedom to live out of motives of desire to love God rather than from motives of obligation. The man's emotions have been educated to follow his faith-informed reason and actually support his will as he chooses what is good. This is Aquinas' conception of the life of virtue: "A passion of the soul increases the goodness of an action."[23] The Catechism of the Catholic Church says, "The human person is ordered to beatitude by his deliberate acts: the passions or feelings he experiences can dispose him to it and contribute to it."[24] Hence, developing the capacity to experience and respond to feelings and emotions is necessary for human integration, as the emotions participate in and can support the development of virtuous habits.[25] Just as it is easier to do difficult things if one so desires, so too does virtue become more and more a natural habit, if the desires for such things have been cultivated over time. Then the will is not the only faculty engaged in doing good – it is supported by the emotions of love, desire and joy. The opposites of these emotions, hate or dislike, aversion and sadness, also help the man to hate evil in all its forms, and his hope, anger and courage will help him to fight it, whether in physical, spiritual or moral manifestations.

Affective Maturity and Celibacy

Affective maturity is a requirement for chaste celibacy. This means on the one hand there is not simply a holding back, a repression of one's sexual feelings, nor on the other a license to act as one pleases. Affective maturity and chastity lie in the mean between these extremes, affective maturity being the proper integration of reason and will with the emotions and chastity being "the successful integration of sexuality within the person" (CCC 2337). Chastity requires the capacity for loving self-restraint for the sake of another, based on affective maturity. When the man is affectively mature, he is free to give himself completely, either in marriage or in chaste celibacy.

Christ's own chaste celibacy showed that He was fully human (affectively mature) and completely and willingly obedient to the Father's will, without compromise of His own identity. To say that Jesus Christ was perfect is inadequate for us to understand His human

---

[23] Glenn, Paul J. 1960. *A Tour of the Summa,* referencing S.T. Ia, IIae, q. 24, art. 3. St. Louis, MO: B. Herder Book Co.

[24] *The Catechism of the Catholic Church*, 1762.

[25] Baars, S. M. 2015. *St. Thomas Aquinas and Affective Maturity.* In *The Priest as Beloved Son.* Omaha, Nebraska: IPF Publications, p. 32.

nature and the implications of His coming to earth as a man and growing up within a human family with a mother and father. Christ's human formation in his relationships with the Blessed Virgin Mary and St. Joseph in the ordinariness of Nazareth speaks to the significance of a man's own human formation.

The Program For Priestly Formation 74 says, "The foundation and center of all human formation is Jesus Christ, the Word made flesh. In His fully developed humanity, He was truly free and with complete freedom gave himself totally for the salvation of the world."[26] In fact, it could be said that Christ's identity as the Father's Son was fulfilled in and through His affective maturity. He was able to be Himself and freely remain docile to the will of the Father's Spirit, giving Himself for the redemption of the world.

Assessing the Seminarian's Level of Affective Maturity

How can formators help the man who feels called to priesthood but who struggles with self-mastery, who is not affectively mature, and who therefore may not yet be capable of chaste celibacy? Learning what affective maturity looks like is only a preliminary step, as this can remain an intellectual exercise and out of reach for the man. However, the seminary community itself can provide clues as to the man's level of maturity, and what kinds of things may be helpful to move him towards affective maturity and developing the capacities for affectivity to mature.

The most powerful assessment will lie in how the man manages and responds to the relationships within the seminary community itself. How he relates to his peers, whether he can be vulnerable with them, and has at least a few deep friendships, will be key. Is he able to be helpful to other men, but does not identify his own weaknesses, or share his own vulnerabilities? Can he do this with his formators? Does he know his own weaknesses, or does he lack self-knowledge in this regard? The man who is able to discuss these things with his formators is at least on the way to becoming more mature in his affectivity. The man who lacks this insight will also struggle in his relationships.

Does the man stay overly busy, and perhaps lack the *capacity* for authentic leisure? This may indicate someone who is running from himself, from marriage, or who does not know there is a better, more open way of living. If he does not have hobbies or other interests, this may also indicate that he has not yet developed the ability to love persons and things for their own sake, but only for what they can offer him. He may be living a utilitarian life without much love for the life. Introducing him to the affirming life may help him to

---

[26] Quoted in Cozzens, A. (n.d.). Human Formation Benchmarks for the Diocesan Seminarian.

become aware of his own thoughts, feelings and desires. At least, formators may observe how he handles not being busy all the time. It is also important to ask and observe if he knows the value of solitude where loneliness can be transformed by the Spirit into silent communion? Does he intentionally practice living within intentional times for solitude and interior communion where he can experience Christ's desires for him to be *friend*?

Is the man overly rigid in his beliefs and attitudes? Such inflexibility may be more of a defense against the possibility of being open and having to consider other things. It may be a comfortable way of living, versus having the ability to be confidently open to how others think and feel.

How does the man manage conflict? Can he rise to defend himself without difficulty? Is he conflict-avoidant, on the other hand?

Does the man chronically struggle with pornography? Does he consider that it is a problem and desires to overcome it, or does he excuse himself, with a suspension between his beliefs and how he lives? What is his attitude towards masturbation?

All these areas reveal whether the man's affectivity has been developed or not because they illustrate the way he lives life. If affectivity is clearly integrated into his life, the man will at least be aware of the importance of how he interacts with others, and their effect on him. If this is not the case, it is likely that the man will lack insight into himself, how he affects others and how others affect him. Things in his life will be more perfunctory and utilitarian. Effectivity will be out of balance and evident as a striving to get things done, rather than practicing life-affirming activities that cultivate an interior savor and enjoyment of the goodness and beauty of being human. Good friendships will not be cultivated or enjoyed.

If the man's human formation is successful in aiding him to develop a healthy affectivity, the man will be best able to live his priesthood happily. "The priest is called to have within himself the same feelings and attitudes that Christ has towards the Church, loved tenderly through the exercise of the ministry. Thus, he is required to "be capable of loving people with a heart which is new, generous and pure - with genuine self-detachment, with full, constant and faithful dedication and at the same time with a kind of 'divine jealousy' (cf. 2 Cor 11:2) and even with a kind of maternal tenderness."[27] Such formation is oriented not merely to the attainment of ordination, but to the happy fulfillment of the priestly vocation.

---

[27] Ratio fundamentalis Institutionis Sacerdotalis, III. 39.

Conclusion

Those in seminary formation do well to attend to a man's human formation, particularly his affective maturity. The anthropology of St. Thomas Aquinas is helpful to seeing into the interior life of the man called to priesthood, in order to assess his readiness, willingness and abilities in the process towards ordination. In particular, examining the man's capacity for affectivity sheds light on his ability to know himself and form relationships. This is crucial for a man called to communion with others, and may reveal to formators a way to ascertain whether the man has received his own identity. How the man lives his affectivity out in relationships in the seminary community can be a helpful way to assess his level of affective maturity. Can he laugh at himself, or is he caught up in self concern? Does he take himself too seriously? Can he suffer rejection with Christ without falling into prolonged self-pity and being self-absorbed? Can he rejoice with Christ amid failures at the cross?

In this way, the Church recognizes that human formation must be healthy, so that grace can perfect the man more readily, enabling him to conform himself more and more to Jesus Christ the Good Shepherd. Humor and joy are especially important indicators that a man is maturing affectively. G.K. Chesterton talked about *mirth as one's ability to laugh at oneself.* And, Pope Francis in his Apostolic Exhortation "Rejoice and Be Glad" encourages us; "Christian joy is usually accompanied by a sense of humour. We see this clearly, for example, in St. Thomas More, St. Vincent de Paul, and St. Philip Neri. Ill humour is no sign of holiness. 'Remove vexation from your mind' (Eccl. 11:10). We receive so much from the Lord "for our enjoyment" (1 Tim. 6:17), that sadness can be a sign of ingratitude. We can get so caught up in ourselves that we are unable to recognize God's gifts" (#126).

Human formation within seminary can aid the man towards a more integrated life: a full affective maturity, necessary for becoming a spiritual father in his priesthood. May our heart's affectivity be imbued with the passions at work in Christ's own Heart as His Spirit is laboring in love for us. And, may we taste the joy that flows from following Him daily as His friends.

Prayer of St. Claude La Colombiere, S.J.

"O God, what will you do to conquer the fearful hardness of our hearts? Lord, you must give us new hearts, tender hearts, sensitive hearts, to replace the hearts that are made of marble and bronze. You must give us your own Heart, Jesus. Come loveable Heart of

Jesus. Place your Heart deep at the center of our hearts and enkindle in each heart a flame of love as strong, as great, as the sum of all the reasons that I have for loving you, my God. O Holy Heart of Jesus, dwell hidden in my heart, so that I may live only in you and only for you, so that in the end, I may live with you eternally in heaven. Amen.

Practicum Reflection Questions for Formators

1. Does the man have real friends? Is he capable of real friendship? Does he have relationships that are deep, or are they more superficial? Is he a people-pleaser? What needs to develop to strengthen his capacities for friendship? How does the man relate to the other men in seminary? Is he at ease, able to share personally with them? Is he characteristically withdrawn, avoidant, anxious?

2. Can he share about himself in spiritual direction and formation advising? Does he have real self-knowledge regarding his own weaknesses as well as his strengths? Is he learning to love his own existential weakness, his poverty of spirit?

3. Is he able to live chastely? Does he have an ongoing struggle with pornography? Does he see it as a problem?

4. Is the man capable of loving persons and things for their own sake, or does he appear to be more utilitarian in his pursuits and interests?

5. Does his continence in chaste celibacy also reflect real spousal and paternal characteristics? How aware is he of his capacities to serve as a good spiritual husband and spiritual father of a future parish family? Is he experiencing spousal love in the spiritual gift of chaste celibacy and can he articulate that as in parish adult education classes? How does he practice virtues that reveal his abilities to serve as a good spiritual husband and spiritual father?

6. Is the man capable of real leisure time? Is he overly busy and does not seem to enjoy people and things?

7. How does the man react to encouragement to grow within the community?

8. How does he handle his own vulnerability? Is he defensive or overwhelmed? Does he withdraw? Can he face the challenge of questions about his inner life?

9. Can he laugh at himself? What are some examples of his ability to not take himself overly seriously, able to serve as a joy-filled and docile instrument in the Spirit?

10. Can the man face difficulties with courage? Alternatively, does he avoid difficult tasks?

Suggested Resources

1. Baars, C. W. (2008). *I Will Give Them a New Heart: Reflections on the Priesthood and the Renewal of the Church.* Staten Island: Society of St. Paul.

2. Baars, S. M. (2015). *St. Thomas Aquinas and Affective Maturity.* In *The Priest as Beloved Son.* Omaha, Nebraska: IPF Publications.

3. Nicolosi, J. J. (2016). *Shame and Attachment Loss: The Practical Work of Reparative Therapy.* Liberal Mind Publishers.

4. Terruwe, A. A., & Baars, C. W. (2002). *Healing the Unaffirmed.* Staten Island, NY: Society of St. Paul.

5. Terruwe, A. A., & Baars, C. W. (2016). *Psychic Wholeness and Healing: Using All the Powers of the Human Psyche.* Eugene, OR: Wipf and Stock Publishers.

6. Van Den Aardweg, Gerard J.M. (1997). *The Battle for Normalcy: A Guide for Self Therapy for Homosexuality.* San Francisco: Ignatius Press.

Chapter Twelve

A TESTIMONIAL AND SOME PASTORAL WISDOM

Mr. Daniel Almeter, M.A.

Dan Almeter is a long time leader of the Alleluia Community, an ecumenical community in Augusta, Georgia. He moderates the Alleluia Catholic Fellowship within the Diocese of Savannah which has been gifted by the Holy Spirit producing about 15 priests and several religious. Dan is a licensed professional counselor and spiritual director. His background includes 6 years of seminary formation. For 40 years, he has overseen his community's formation. He has also been involved as a counselor with priests and seminarians for a number of years. Dan teaches and travels nationally and internationally, speaking to both clergy and laity primarily on 3 topics: growing in deeper prayer, ecumenism, and dealing with the truth about same sex attraction. His book, "Unity: on Earth as in Heaven," has just been translated into Polish. Dan is married to Marie for 39 years, has 6 children and 17 grandchildren.

When I was approached about contributing to this book it came as a bit of a surprise. First of all, I am a layman, married with six children and 16 grandchildren. I don't pretend to have the theological expertise of my collaborators in this book. But, as I prayed about the request to give a testimonial, along with providing some wisdom from my practice of counseling, I realized that I could make a valuable contribution. My own personal journey from transitory same-sex attraction to a secure masculine identity as a husband and father, as well as my accompaniment of others making a similar journey, provides what I believe to be a helpful "nuts and bolts" approach that can foster understanding and hope for vocation directors, seminary formators and bishops. It can also afford hope and some practical understanding for those men who have transitory same-sex attraction and desire someday to seek admission to seminary. I would like to start with a very brief summary of my life experience to help put into context all that I will be sharing.

I grew up in a very traditional Catholic family and I was one of ten children. My dad was a dairy farmer and my entire existence evolved around farm life, with a strong sacramental and devotional life. In 1970, at the age of 16, our entire family experienced Baptism in the Holy Spirit through participating in the emerging Catholic Charismatic Renewal. My life was radically changed and I felt an immediate call to enter the seminary. I was accepted right out of high school. The problem was that my affective maturity did not match my cognitive maturity. My identity and personhood were affected by what Dr. Suzanne Baars calls "emotional deprivation disorder." I had not been adequately affirmed as a child and as a result my emotional development was thwarted. Because the affective deprivation was most keenly experienced at the hand of my father, there was an element of rejection by myself of "the masculine," which ultimately came to be experienced as a certain level of transitory same-sex attraction. I became aware of this in my later teen years. Needless to say, I speak of this now very objectively, but at the time, this was experienced only on a semi-conscious level. I only knew that, interiorly, my life was an emotional roller coaster. I was experiencing both heterosexual and same-sex attraction, and rather than feeling like a man, I felt like a needy little boy inside who was fearful of my masculinity.

I sailed through seminary with all of this internal conflict, but spoke very little to anyone about it. I focused on spirituality and my academics. My personal relationship with God was real and it is what got me through in day-to-day life with relative peace. But, I was broken inside. What added to the inner confusion and turmoil was the number of times I was "hit on" by priests and seminarians while in seminary formation. I began to ask myself, "Maybe I am a homosexual?" Outwardly, I was the model seminarian. I was even voted president of my class in first year of theology. Because my conscience was formed deeply by my Catholic faith, I never acted out sexually. But, the temptations to act out were present in day-to-day life.

What happened next was my assignment in the summer between my second and third years of theology. As part of my Clinical Pastoral Education training, I was assigned 900 miles away from familiar relationships for the summer. I served as a student chaplain in a psychiatric hospital. The location of this hospital was in a city where a vibrant intentional Christian covenant community existed. It was made up mostly of lay people. I lived in this community for the summer of my chaplaincy, and there for the first time, found a place of unconditional love and support. I could begin to receive healing for my "issues." I returned to seminary to begin my third year of theology, but after only one month, it became very clear that my call was to leave seminary and join this Christian community. My spiritual director encouraged me to leave everything behind, and to follow this sense of call to Christian community life. I did so and immersed myself in this community life. Over the next few years a healing transpired that fundamentally completed my overcoming transitory same-sex attraction and any affective deprivation left over from my childhood. To be honest, I often shudder to think what would have become of me if I had stayed in seminary, and was ordained without experiencing this healing. I would have been ordained carrying immense emotional baggage. Could I have maintained chaste celibacy? Could I have ever received the healing of insecurities that would have hindered my ministry to be an effective priest? Could I have focused on others, without suffering from a narcissism that kept me focused on myself? Could I have ever achieved mature masculinity? The quality of mature masculinity, that I eventually discovered, was very necessary to be effective in leading others, especially in leading other men. In this healing journey I would eventually become able to teach others how to allow ourselves to participate in Christ's own mature manhood (Eph 4:11-16).

I came to understand that it is not possible to live out the integrated human formation that is essential to being a well-balanced and fully effective priest, without aggressively dealing with one's transitory same-sex attraction. One may have good intellectual, spiritual and pastoral formation as the "Ratio" rightly calls for in seminary formation. But, in human formation there is a special deep need for healing if a man is carrying transitory same-sex attraction. Paragraph 94 of the "Ratio" says it well: "Human formation, being the foundation of all priestly formation, promotes the integral growth of the person and allows the integration of all its dimensions." All too often bishops, vocation directors and formators commonly proceed in a manner guided by this simple attitude: "What is the big issue as long as a man can maintain continence in celibacy?" This type of thinking perpetuates a cycle of ordaining men with transitory same-sex attraction, and this attitude can open the door for deep-seated homosexuality being deemed acceptable for Holy Orders. The "Ratio" and overall Church tradition does not support this attitude. A thorough overview of the Church's desires and teaching is provided in Fr. Earl Fernandes' fine book, "Seminary Formation and Homosexuality."

Same-sex attraction affects the human person in profound ways. It is important to note that sexual acting out is the external behavior that points to internal conflicts that cry out for attention and compassionate resolution. The "Ratio" in Paragraph 199 clearly calls for those with "deep-seated homosexual tendencies" not to be admitted to seminary. In Paragraph 200 it distinguishes between "deep-seated homosexuality" and "homosexual tendencies that were only the expression of a transitory problem - for example, that of an adolescence not yet superseded." I would like to refer to Fr. Brett Brannen's book, "To Save A Thousand Souls," for basic distinctions between deep-seated homosexual attractions and transitory homosexual attractions. This book is very popular among diocesan vocation directors. It has been successful in promoting vocations to diocesan priesthood. On pages 242 - 243 of this compelling book, Fr. Brannen relies on Dr. Richard Fitzgibbons' overview that is a result of reflecting upon his clinical experience as a psychiatrist.

Deep-seated homosexual tendencies include the following:

- Identify himself as homosexual
- Under severe stress may experience strong physical and sexual attractions to adult males and to adolescents of the same sex
- Engage in homosexual behaviors
- Harbor excessive anger toward the Church because of the teachings on sexual morality
- Refuse to defend the sacrament of marriage
- Have strong narcissistic conflicts
- Refuse to try to understand their emotional conflicts which lead to same-sex attraction
- Defend the use of homosexual pornography
- Demonstrate excessive anger toward those who are faithful and loyal to the Church's teaching on sexual morality

In contrast, a person with transitory same-sex attraction would:

- Not identify himself as homosexual
- Be motivated to understand and to overcome emotional conflicts
- Seek psychotherapy and spiritual direction
- Desire to live and teach the fullness of the Church's teaching on sexual morality
- Not support the homosexual culture, but see it as antithetical to the universal call to holiness
- Support the sacrament of marriage and the right of a child to a father and a mother

Before providing more of my personal story, along with what I have learned as a counselor by accompaniment with other men seeking a greater affective maturity to be secure husbands and fathers, it is important to mention the wider perspective regarding numbers in the population who describe themselves as homosexual. Most estimates state that 2%-4% of the general population identifies as either exclusively homosexual or bisexual. And, evidence suggests that there are 1% more male homosexuals than female homosexuals. In the 2013 survey done by the C.D.C. (Center for Disease Control), the first large scale government survey measuring sexual orientation in the U.S., it was found that 96.6% of the population identify themselves as heterosexual. It was also found that 2.3% identify as homosexual or bisexual. Only 0.6% identified as transgender, and another 1.1% declined to answer. This is especially significant since the percentage of men with same-sex attraction who desire ordination and entrance into seminary is much higher than 2.3%. The recent study done by Fr. Paul Sullins, sponsored by the Ruth Institute at Catholic University of America, is a gold mine of wisdom and knowledge. The title of the study is "Is Catholic Clergy Sex Abuse Related To Homosexual Priests." This research is very credible and it illuminates the harm that comes to the wider Church community when men who do not have the capacity for spousal and paternal chaste celibacy are advanced to Holy Orders.

It is very understandable that men with transitory same-sex attraction would seek security and affirmation within the seminary as a safe structure in the desire to remain continent in their call to chaste celibacy. But, in my estimation the seminary is not the place for this security to be cultivated while at the same time there is the expectation that a man is being evaluated for advancement towards Holy Orders. The Church is called to offer many ministries and parish outreach programs where men with same-sex attraction can receive healthy affection, compassion and hospitality. COURAGE and other ministries in the Church offer this type of welcome and ongoing support.

There are probably a significant number of men today who desire to apply to seminary who have bisexual desires. They have both heterosexual and homosexual attractions transpiring within their hearts. This is the category that I placed myself in while in seminary. One way of stating this would be that the affective emotional deprivation I experienced as a child, and what was associated with a rejection of my masculinity due to my "father wound," was not as severe as those who have exclusive deep-seated homosexual orientation. I would also suggest that this group of men who experience bisexual attractions carry something closer to what is referred to as transitory same-sex attraction.

For someone who has bisexual attractions the requirements to overcome the same-sex attraction will need to include the following: a very high motivation, a commitment to cultivating a personal life of prayer, integration work within personal counseling, opportunities for male bonding, and regular spiritual direction, and inner healing prayer. The counselor and the spiritual director need to be guides who embrace the Church's teachings regarding human sexuality. For someone who has a deep-seated homosexual orientation, the change (if it occurs) would normally take several years based upon my reading and clinical experience. Fr. John Harvey's book, "The Truth About Homosexuality," provides a fine introduction and overview of very valuable research in this area.

It is "doing the work" that I will be speaking of for the remainder of this article while interweaving quotes from the "Ratio." It is "doing the work" that determines whether one will remain in transitory same-sex attraction or emerge into emotional freedom and mature masculine identity. "Doing the work" is another way of saying that pure determination along with the development of a deep prayer life are the two most critical factors for progress in overcoming transitory same-sex attraction. As the "Ratio" says in paragraph #43, "This means humbly and ceaselessly working on oneself."

There is one area of discussion that is critical to mention, before moving on to the practical nuts and bolts of describing how to help a man who desires to apply to seminary who struggles with transitory same-sex attraction. This has to do with the definition of same-sex attraction. Here, I am not focused on the variety of interior factors that create transitory same-sex attraction. My major concern is to describe how affectivity is experienced for the man with transitory same-sex attraction. What is the essence of transitory same-sex attraction? This personal definition is based on my own previous reality as well as what I see at work while counseling dozens of adult men and teens. I sum it up in this manner: transitory same-sex attraction for adult men and teens can be defined as *a lack of an internal sense of masculinity.* This is critical for bishops, formators and vocation directors to understand. Men who struggle with transitory same-sex attraction suffer a lack of feeling masculine, identifying with being masculine. This is something that is taken for granted in the normal development of most boys.

I could spend the rest of this article discussing many of the developmental reasons for this affective sense of having a masculine deficit. Some of those developmental reasons include; a defensive detachment to men due to an emotionally distant father, having experienced harshness from a father who was difficult to please, growing up with an overprotective and controlling mother, suffering a lack of male peer bonding, etc. Suffice it to say, the primary issue with transitory same-sex attraction is this lack of an internal sense of identification with being masculine. A secondary definition, very closely related to the first definition, is that transitory same-sex attraction is an **over-emotional dependence on another man, looking for male love and acceptance.** This practical definition helps us understand how men are prone to act out sexually in an unhealthy reliance upon another man. According to these definitions we can imagine how it is possible for a seminary applicant to white knuckle chaste celibacy, while remaining deeply out of balance emotionally. The seminary applicant could well be hurting inside, feeling a deep sense of masculine shame and inferiority. He could be looking for "Mr. Right" who he imagines will magically meet his emotional needs. Such a man, without undergoing what is necessary to overcome transitory same-sex attraction, is not a good candidate for priestly ordination, nor would he be a good candidate for marriage.

As I move forward with describing the "solutions" to helping a man overcome transitory same-sex attractions, I will be talking about typical issues that most of these men struggle with in day-to-day life. I won't say that these solutions and struggles are universally true because each man has his own story and unique personality. But, I can say that what I will be describing provides a basic template that serves to strengthen our pastoral understanding. Almost all the men I have treated could identify with most of what I will be describing. I will be interspersing this section with personal anecdotes of how I overcame transitory same-sex attraction. I am not particularly fond of self-revelation, but I think real examples will be most helpful. This is not just a "pray-it-away" issue. It takes a great deal of "doing the work." Many men with transitory same-sex attraction would simply rather not deal with doing the interior work that is necessary to appropriate the healing that strengthens their masculine identity. Unless a man is able and willing to do the interior work he will be a poor candidate for seminary formation. Doing the work requires a willingness to remain vulnerably receptive to the grace of following Jesus' presence as a companion. Real fortitude flows from first receiving in our weakness as St. Paul teaches, that with Christ, "it is when I am weak that I am strong (2 Cor 12:10).

The first issue that must be addressed is the issue of pornography. This is the one area I never struggled with personally, perhaps due to my well-formed conscience in Catholic catechesis. What is more likely however is that I did not grow up with easy access to male pornography. We did not have internet four decades ago.

This is "the" one area almost every man I counsel is struggling with in his life. The reason this must be faced directly is because the same chemicals released to give intense pleasure when a man is engaged in genital sexual activity, are also released simply by looking at pornographic sexual images. This chemical release and the accompanying pleasure can be very addictive. This is true for both homosexual and heterosexual pornographic images. Neuron pathways are being built within a man's brain that cannot be erased. These neuron pathways can be stimulated instantly as pornography is viewed. Until a man with transitory same-sex attraction is on the road to overcoming his male pornography addiction, he will be blocked from developing mature masculinity. Again, in a similar fashion this is true of heterosexual pornography addiction as well.

Mature masculinity seeks to protect others and not view other people as objects for their pleasure. An addiction to homosexual pornography helps to keep a man locked into the emotional aspects of transitory same-sex attraction which are innately unhealthy to the essential quality of feeling masculine within, something the seminary applicant needs to have in place in a foundational way, in order to serve well later as a priest.

After almost 20 years of professional counseling I am familiar with clergy who "play at" giving up heterosexual or homosexual pornography but never seriously root it out of their ordinary patterns of behavior. If one is unable to stop using homosexual pornography, it is then essential for him to get the help of an addiction counselor and/or become part of a program or support group. Group work helps overcome shame that binds us and enslaves us within, and group work assists in supplying healthy interdependent male relationships that offer greatly needed support.

There are also very good resources that are available on the internet. Many of these specifically help men overcome both heterosexual and homosexual addictions to pornography. This can require some financial investment. But, to ordain someone who has not made serious headway in this area of addiction to pornography would be sad and tragic. The "Ratio" states in Paragraph #43, "…the priest will learn how to interpret and understand his own motivations, his gifts, his needs and his frailties, so as to 'free himself for all disordered affections'…".

In Paragraph 28 of Lumen Gentium, it is said that the priest is "consecrated in the image of Christ" and "acts in the person of Christ." This truth has very important consequences for the candidate for priesthood. That means that masculinity, as essential to Christ's identity is not peripheral, as contemporary culture would try to force us to accept and believe. Similarly, since the priest is also "in persona Christi capitis," he not only has the image of Christ within, as do all Christians through baptism, but the priest is also commissioned and ordained by the Church to represent Christ as the spiritual father, as head of the ecclesial (parish) family. One can't say that a priest's secure affectivity in knowing and trusting in the goodness of his masculine identity is incidental. To represent Christ in a mature manhood is to represent a confident, healthy masculine identity as bridegroom for the Church. The priest is also representing Christ's paternity as spiritual father, shepherding the ecclesial (parish) family.

Our sexuality penetrates and permeates our being to its very depths. Again, to quote the "Ratio" Paragraph #93 says, "…the seminarian is called upon to develop his personality, having Christ, the perfect man, as his model and source." And, herein lies a very serious issue in ordaining men who have transitory same-sex attraction. Though he has a male body the man with transitory same-sex attraction has a personal/affective sense of masculine identity that is weak and considerably undeveloped. His male personhood is affectively limited, not able to serve affectionately in the spousal and paternal capacities that the people of God need.

If seminary formators and bishops promote men with transitory same-sex attraction towards ordination, they promote men who have many affective handicaps. These men are not able to affectionately relate to people with a level of security and maturity that is free enough to provide for the people the spousal and paternal loving that strengthens their own identities in Christ, who is bridegroom and head of the Church (Eph 4:7-16). The man with transitory same-sex attraction will not be able to give away the masculinity of Christ within himself that is being experienced in faith as spousal and paternal. This gift of himself is meant to fill the Church with a certain quality and certain characteristics of human loving. In sacramental marriage, when a man makes love to his wife he is giving a total gift of himself, his masculinity. He knows and believes that as a gift to his wife he compliments and completes the truth of their one flesh union in Christ. So it is with the Church in the beautiful mystery of the priest's life as a living sacrifice of praise at the altar each day. He pours himself out for his bride the Church (Eph 5:21-33). Chaste celibate priesthood is a participation in Christ's own marriage to the Church as his body.

This may come as a surprise to some, but often men who struggle with same-sex attraction and are in the married state, cannot truly give themselves in affective maturity to their wife, even as they give them their bodies away in marital intimacy. What frequently transpires is that the man with same-sex attraction psychologically assumes the identity of another very masculine man in his imagination, as he attempts to freely give himself to his wife. The truth is that his imagination is not connected with reality. He is not really free to give of himself. Instead the man with same-sex attraction is hindered to give himself away as a gift to his wife because he does not experience himself as being masculine within his own being. This type of situation illuminates the struggle to freely renew and enjoy his marital covenant through regular sexual intercourse. Internally in affective immaturity he cannot give of himself without having to assume another man's identity in his imagination. In my opinion this is actually a form of dissociative disorder that can be mild or strong. I am aware of several situations where an annulment was granted because it was proven that sacramental marriage did not actually transpire even through the vows were spoken. The annulment cases revealed a lack of interior freedom. The human capacity to freely enter into marriage as a husband and father had not been realized.

All of this by analogy has a great deal to do with priestly formation. If a candidate for priesthood is lacking, in the true sense of experiencing masculine identity because of transitory same-sex attraction, this will color and fashion his life. In many areas of his life he will be unable to be a true gift of his masculine self. This weak sense of masculine identity means the seminary candidate could end up struggling greatly to make friendships with married men. And, these married men will need him to serve as a peer "to provide for" and "protect" their own affective needs, so that they may be strengthened to serve their wives and children as good husbands and fathers.

As a seminarian, I was able to make friends with my brother seminarians and priests, but I always kept a distance from the more athletic ones. I felt very inferior and ashamed. I was afraid of being rejected by them. Rather than reach out to the athletes, I built up an inner defense that did not allow me to receive from them in friendship. As a child I was not athletic though I played sports from time to time. An important incident occurred when I was thirteen years old, and this cemented my interior defenses that prevented me from associating with men who played sports.

Along with my close friend and cousin I rode my bike to a local recreation department to play a friendly game of baseball. My close friend and cousin was a girl one year younger than myself. Captains were picked. And, then one by one the teams were chosen. My younger female cousin was chosen right away. I was chosen last. The humiliation registered very deeply in my heart and the pain of rejection at that moment was indescribable. Inside myself I made a conscious vow never to get involved in sports again. I wanted to prevent that kind of humiliation and those painful feelings of rejection from ever happening again. Why do I tell this story? I retell it because it represents a major dimension of the fear many men with transitory same-sex attraction have with regard to sports and relating to strong masculine men.

One of the greatest desires of men with transitory same-sex attraction is to have close friendships and to enjoy a vibrant sense of brotherhood. The fear of being rejected by masculine men is one of the major issues that leads to the phenomena of inner shame, creating a type of inner wall, behind which hides a great deal of compounded pain. For men with transitory same-sex attraction common symptoms that point to the need for this fear of rejection to be healed are frequent depression, loneliness and deep anxiety. This is a reality that is more true for men with transitory same-sex attraction than is experienced in the general population.

If a man has been accepted into seminary formation with transitory same-sex attraction, something the "Ratio" permits, but something that I respectfully do not recommend, seminary formators need to be especially attentive to affective markers for growth in maturation as a man. In working with men who have transitory same-sex attraction three years prior to diaconate, men who are attempting to "do the work" need to overcome this affective immaturity. And, they need to be aware of the dynamics associated with a consistent sense of male inadequacy and its serious consequences. Straightforward gentle conversations need to be normalized between the seminarian and seminary formators with regard to the decrease or increase of affective desires that are associated with gaining the self-knowledge that one can indeed serve well as a spiritual husband and father for the parish family. These desires are not sufficient though they are an important starting point. There needs to be encouragement and emerging evidence of the actual "readiness," "ability," and "willingness" to serve the people in the parish with spousal and paternal love. Virtuous behaviors need to be evident that speak of one's willingness and abilities to provide for and protect others.

How could such a person be helped? Men with transitory same-sex attraction have to work hard at developing a sense of mutuality with other strong men. Because the majority of men with transitory same-sex attraction struggle with feeling like "little boys" inside, boys that never grew up, there is a strong tendency to make idols of other men who exhibit characteristics of strong masculinity. Men who are affectively immature and who carry transitory same-sex attraction are often looking for the another man that can meet their emotional needs. It truly becomes a form of spiritual idolatry. These men struggle to not fall into relationships of emotional dependency which is a form of disordered affections that can become rightly ordered through a consistent receptivity to tasting the love that Jesus reveals, and the unconditional love of the Father who is strong, tender, compassionate and full of mercy (Psalm 103).

Building strong brotherly and healthy emotional relationships with other men, relationships that are interdependent and mutually enriching, is something that the seminary formator needs to mentor. The seminary formator is a type of coach. The formator would need to enter into the mystery of the man with transitory same-sex attraction. This man with transitory same-sex attraction would need to identify inner lies that promote a certain insecurity and inadequacy, lies that hinder him from experiencing the goodness of his own masculinity. The man with transitory same-sex attraction sees in other men what he seems to lack.

Through encouragement and real life pastoral assessment a variety of virtues can be learned that reveal to the seminarian the reality and goodness of his own masculinity. This need not come solely through participation in sports, though our culture greatly emphasizes athletics. And, participating in sports can be very healing as I will later testify to in my own story. A maturing sense of the man's masculinity can come through promoting the masculine characteristics of being able "to protect" and "provide for" in daily life. These characteristics can be gradually discovered through consistently participating in some of the following activities: working with one's hands in manual labors such as farming or carpentry, fishing, hunting, using skills for others in a generative fashion, skills in computer technology, skills in music and singing, etc. In Italian culture serving as a cook and waiter are revered jobs for men who need to support their families. One could learn how cooking is a masculine activity if mentored properly.

What is essential in seminary formation is the need to be mentored out of self-concern, and to overcome fears that I am not masculine enough, to give of myself to the Church as my spouse. The man needs to know that he can benefit others, that he has what it takes to be a good husband and father. And, there is the essential need to for the man to be served by a coach who promotes the seminarian's increasing enjoyment and confidence in the goodness of himself as a man, a man who has something worthwhile to give as a gift.

I want to return to the strong and frequent tendency among men with transitory same-sex attraction to make idols of other men. These men are looking to other men for emotional needs and this often leads to unhealthy and emotionally exclusive relationships in seminary. In my pastoral experience I see that this often explodes when the mutual unhealthy dependency gets to the point where one breaks off the relationship. And, this is sometimes due to experiencing some sort of sexual advance.

Working at male friendships that are not overly intense, and where interdependence and enriching mutuality in friendship is developed gradually, is a major goal for men with transitory same-sex attraction. This is true in the general population as well, but it is important to remember that these men carry a particular affective insecurity in the goodness of their maleness. The desire and human need for male intimacy in friendships and close brotherhood is a normal and very healthy drive that is universal for men. These are holy desires built into us by Jesus as the Creator (Gen 1:26-31). The problem is that men with transitory same-sex attraction experience an affective deficit. It is often related to having suffered a deficit in affectionate bonding with one's father. This can be true with a "mother wound" as well, but I often see the men that I work with needing to forgive their earthly fathers and begin to receive humanly and spiritually from other men in healthy friendships. These men can also begin to receive affection, in and around wounds of rejection, from entering into a deep relationship with their Heavenly Father. As we cry out in faith "Abba, Father" from within the memories of rejections, we can begin to receive real affection and a regenerating taste of God's glory amid what has been suffered (Rom 8:14-17).

For the man with transitory same-sex attraction, when his maleness was not affirmed in childhood, the need for a fuller acceptance and affection is often met in adolescence or adulthood in unhealthy ways. As sexual hormones mature physically during puberty, the overall affective deficits that cry out for acceptance and affirmation of maleness, can cause immense emotional pain wherever emotional immaturity remains.

When I left seminary and joined the Christian community, a community that I am now still a part of, my spiritual mentor recognized that I was overly dependent (emotionally) on one particular man. My mentor urged me to spread out and to broaden my relationships in the community. He encouraged me to intentionally build friendships with a couple other strong masculine men who were about my age. Following my mentor's advice was scary. The fear of rejection and my experience of shame about my masculinity were strong. Nonetheless I followed his advice obediently. I began reaching out to the men that I normally wouldn't spend time with in my regular routine. Eventually it paid off. Instead of feeling inferior to these other men, I saw both their strengths and weaknesses. I no longer put them on a pedestal. A true mutuality was the result. Feeling "mutuality" and real acceptance from other strong masculine men, is a major factor in restoring one's sense of masculine identity. Experiencing this "mutuality" and "foundational acceptance" by strong men, with their own clay feet so-to-speak, also decreased my transitory same-sex attraction over time. Being in these healthy relationships gradually set me free to know myself as a good man capable of giving myself as a gift to women, and eventually to my future my wife and family. When one feels more and more masculine within, one receives more and more of the attraction and desire to be married to a woman and to father children in family life.

I want to say again that sports are not the end all of fostering masculine identity. At the same time, in a sports crazed culture like ours, it is especially important and a major way that men relate to each other. In my experience this cannot be underestimated. When I was in seminary, I was able to avoid the athletic type of brothers in many opportunities for competitive action. I was so uncomfortable around my athletic brothers that I would not even sit down and watch a sports event on TV with them. I didn't know much about game rules in popular sports, and I didn't want to put myself in a place to be rejected. My old memory of rejection as a child was in need of healing.

Once I left seminary, I had some really hard choices to make. Would I re-engage the sports world? The Christian community that I joined had a weekly softball intramural team. I made a decision to join. Because of my inability to even throw a ball well, I took a chance and asked a male friend to come out to the ball field with me for about an hour each week. We would practice throwing and hitting the ball before each game. I slowly improved in my abilities to participate. My inner confidence gradually grew. After three years of practicing and playing softball, I was eventually made coach of one of the teams. We even went on to win the regional championship that year! You can only imagine what a boost this was for an interior sense of the goodness of my masculinity.

At the same time all this was happening, my spiritual mentor asked me to join a weekly men's group of pastoral leaders. I was happy to join thinking this would be a spiritual growth group with some strong men. We did enter into a bit of spiritual conversation, but the group's main activity was watching Monday night football every week. The men valued leisure time together. As pastoral leaders they desired each other's company just to relax together and get recharged.

Now this was really challenging. I never played football growing up and knew none of the rules or any of the team names. I was scared witless inside when I went to participate in the first few weeks of Monday night football together. I hardly said a word. I am sure the other guys thought there was something wrong with me. And, in a sense there was something wrong. My emotional pain regarding a deep sense of masculine inferiority was being faced. I had a hard decision to make. I could either quit the group or learn about football. I believed God was offering me an opportunity for healing through learning to participate in being together with these men in some real sense of mutuality. I ended up going secretly to the library to get a book on football rules, and I started memorizing the names of the teams and the Sunday scores in the Monday morning newspaper. Eventually, I found myself able to relax and enjoy drinking beer and chatting about football, teams, plays, scores, etc., with the rest of the men.

The acceptance by my strong male peers was huge in promoting the healing that I needed. Paragraph #63 in the "Ratio" says, "…it is useful to have recourse to physical exercise and sports, along with preparation for a well-balanced lifestyle." In my estimation this cannot be overestimated in its value for a candidate for seminary formation who needs to overcome transitory same-sex attraction. That quote also mentions physical exercise, as does paragraph #94 of the "Ratio." How important this is for men who have transitory same-sex attraction to experience! The majority of these men tend to avoid physicality. Yet, appreciating physical strength is an essential part of masculine identity. Getting men with transitory same-sex attraction engaged in a routine of running, lifting weights, working with their hands and doing manual labor, are all good activities that help engender inner confidence and self-acceptance in the goodness of being male.

One seminary candidate that I counseled was able to get into a weight lifting routine with several other men at the local fitness center. Reluctant at first, because he knew nothing about weight lifting, he started going three mornings a week. This man became very proficient at lifting weights and was soon mentoring other guys. This growth in real abilities to engage in such physicality helped increase his sense of masculinity. This routine increased his real sense of physical strength, and it placed him regularly on a mutual playing field with other masculine men. It is my firm belief that in our age of computer technology and social media there is a special need for men to engage in and learn from the dignity of manual labor. Participation in farming, carpentry, the rigor of vocal training, painting, cooking, restoring homes for the poor, and many other physical activities need to be a regular part of life. The physicality associated with the masculine characteristics of "providing for" and "supplying protection for" good human needs must be exercised and integrated into regular patterns of how we spend our time.

I am taking the time to give real life and personal examples because the practical and seemingly mundane activities are so important. It is so easy to hide behind intellectual abilities in seminary formation and avoid what is practically and critically needed by men who struggle with transitory same-sex attraction. I loved theology. I loved academics. I excelled in them. But, I went unchallenged in seminary formation, in my human formation especially, in the areas that I needed the most help with in order to be strengthened as a man who could later serve a parish family as their spiritual husband and father. Again, though the "Ratio" allows for men with transitory same-sex attraction to be in seminary up until three years prior to diaconate, my experience tells me that it is far better to give this hard work of human formation integration a primary focus prior to seminary formation. It is my experience that the academic pressures and goals for advancement towards ordination that are ever present in seminary are counterproductive. These pressures pull away from being able to integrate a secure masculine identity for the man who needs to overcome transitory same-sex attraction.

Another extremely common trait of men who struggle with transitory same-sex attraction is to hang out socially with women when provided the opportunity. If you put one of these men into a social situation that is mixed half with women and half with men, you can usually pick out the man who has transitory same-sex attraction issues. He is usually much more comfortable relating to the women. At least that was me, and I see these patterns of behavior in the guys I have counseled. This is what often happens in a parish with men who get ordained and have transitory same-sex attraction issues. They tend to relate mostly to the women of the parish and avoid relating with strong men who desire to share in parish leadership. Most men with transitory same-sex attraction have developed characteristic feminine attributes, and there is an affinity to relating easily with women. On the other hand, I have learned that a few men with transitory same-sex attraction will treat women as second class citizens. This dimension of unintegrated internal conflict has the man with transitory same-sex attraction showing special emotional dependency needs, and so he is only interested in relating to masculine men. He tends to exclude women or he treats them with a certain dismissiveness. But, my overall experience in counseling is that since seminary candidates with transitory same-sex attraction have not developed a secure sense of their masculinity, they tend to feel very insecure and uncomfortable around strong masculine men.

Needless to say, if a man is going to be a priest, he has to be able to relate well with women while being comfortable relating to other strong men. He needs to be able to collaborate creatively with both men and women as he orders and orchestrates leadership responsibilities. The "Ratio" speaks to this in paragraph #94 when it mentions, "...his ability to establish mature and well balanced interpersonal relationships." For a man to serve the people well in the parish he needs to possess a certain interior confidence in the Father's affection and the Holy Spirit's desire to work through him (Rom 5:5, Rom 8:14-27). He needs to know deep within himself that the Father is pleased with him and favors him as a son in the Son (Matt 3:13-17).

It has been said, and it is true, that the healthy candidate for celibate priesthood will also make for a healthy spouse should he decide that marriage is his vocation. That is because this type of candidate exhibits the same masculine virtues and traits. To name a few of these virtues and traits a good candidate for Holy Orders and/or Matrimony is a man who exercises courage, protects his wife and children in ordinary ways through daily self-sacrifice in joy, through patience and long suffering. He is gentle and self-giving in his attentiveness to others needs. He is generative in affectionate self-donation.

For a man to get ordained, it is so important to have a healthy development of many masculine traits and virtues that every man needs to cultivate. These are traits and virtues that ordinary healthy woman are looking for in a man. How can I best sum up these masculine traits and virtues from my own experience of being healed of transitory same-sex attraction and from my experience in counseling? I believe that these traits and virtues can be summed up in three major words or phrases. Some have already been mentioned. At the heart of mature masculinity are the following: a sense of "benevolent responsibility to lead", the abilities "to provide for" and "to protect" the family, the community, etc. There is an excellent book written by Baptist theologian Dr. John Piper that discusses these traits and virtues in detail. It is entitled, "What's The Difference?," and it is worth reading. These qualities are either present or they are lacking in a man's internal abilities, sense of identity and patterns of behavior. Their presence is indication of an affectivity that speaks of mature masculinity. One can be heterosexual and sexually active with his spouse, but if these qualities are lacking, the man is immature in his masculinity.

Why am I discussing these three qualities with regard to men who struggle with transitory same-sex attraction? It is because these three qualities are especially under-developed in men with transitory same-sex attraction. And, people in the pews can sense when these traits are not operative in a priest. People need to be able to trust their parish leadership. We need to be able to entrust our children to parish leaders who know how to cultivate secure masculinity and femininity in family life by the way they shepherd us and by what they teach us. We also need to be challenged to develop our own identities and gifts in the Church as the Body of Christ (Eph 1:22, 1 Cor 12:4-26).

Let's start with talking about the trait "to lead". Of course women lead as well; but, there is a certain kind of leadership which men need to have to display a mature masculine personhood. The "Ratio" in Paragraph #119 mentions that "the seminarian will begin to see himself as a group leader." Quite a number of men who struggle with transitory same-sex attraction have a hard time with leadership for several reasons. There is a prevailing self-consciousness, a consuming self-concern that the man with transitory same-sex attraction lives with in the everyday. It is a form of narcissism that keeps him self-focused. This makes it especially difficult to tune into the needs of others. Much of this is due to a deep sense of shame that pervades his consciousness. He is almost always concerned about what others are thinking of him. He typically is quietly desperate to be accepted by others. And, because of experiencing a lack of affirmation and validation of his feelings as a child, he develops a "people pleaser" personality trait. He has learned that most feelings of anger and sadness were not safe or affirmed and validated as a child. To express such normal human emotions just got him in trouble. The serious "people pleaser" defense mechanism developed so that he could get along with his parents and family of origin relationships. Often these candidates are not aware of the fact that they have stuffed their feelings of anger and sadness and taken on the persona of being a "nice little boy" who lives to please others. This may serve as a great defense mechanism as a child, but it does not work in mature adult manhood.

In men with transitory same-sex attraction there is a real inner reluctance to lead, because in leading there is the real need to express one's opinion and take initiative. In an underdeveloped masculinity the man fears stating his opinion or taking action until he is sure that his opinion and action is compliant with what everyone else in thinking and doing. In a conversation or discussion, the man with transitory same sex attraction is likely to be the last one to express an opinion, not out of humility, but to be sure that his opinion fits in with all the others. Being liked by everyone is more important than having his own authentic personal opinion.

Sometimes, as I counsel men with transitory same-sex attraction, I hear the men say, "I don't know who I really am." This is because they often really don't know. They have lived most of their lives not knowing what they think and feel. They often spend their energy trying to please others. These are all "nice guys" and would be described as such. "Niceness" in this context is almost always a fear-filled cover for a poor self-image. And, this inner affective immaturity can very much compromise the man with transitory same-sex attraction in the future as a priest when hard choices and unpopular decisions need to be made in the parish. As the "Ratio" mentions in Paragraph #33, future priests should be educated to not "yield to the temptation of modelling their lives on the search for popular consensus."

One of the ways to help a man combat this insecurity is to encourage him to assume leadership positions when these opportunities are possible. As counselors and seminary formators we need to encourage him to be one of the first to express his opinions and his feelings instead of waiting to be one of the last. He needs to take risks and believe in the value of his feelings and opinions. True authenticity, transparency and a strong sense of self-identity, all critical for strong leadership, need to be developed. Basically, one of the goals is to teach/mentor the man with transitory same-sex attraction to learn healthy self-assertion. Because many of these men have stuffed legitimate anger for much of their lives, it is not uncommon to deal with occasional bursts of anger flowing from these men, outbursts that are out of proportion to the situation at hand. Mentoring/coaching the man in how to assert himself without emotionally overreacting in a given situation is a normal part of mentoring/coaching these men in the art of overcoming the affective immaturity that is part and parcel to transitory same-sex attraction.

Another critical aspect of learning how to lead in a masculine way is to mentor the man in how to deal with authority. If expressing thoughts and feelings is difficult in groups, the man with transitory same-sex attraction is especially challenged to express his true thoughts and feelings with authority figures. Again, this is most likely related to fears as a child of expressing himself with authority figures, especially his father. Paragraph #44 of the "Ratio" suggests the following: "In the process of formation, it is necessary that the seminarian should know himself and let himself be known, relating to the formators with sincerity and transparency." The temptation for the man with transitory same-sex attraction is to avoid confrontation with authority figures at all costs. The result is often witnessed in an "unmanly" condition being lived out. Often a regular habit of gossiping with others about authority figures behind their backs has become a way of being and living. This signals a large deficit of masculine courage that can negatively affect his priesthood if not remedied in seminary formation. When a man is prone to gossip and complaining to others, instead of confronting conflicts and misunderstandings, especially with authority figures, seminary formators need to address the root internal causes and motivations. The mentor/coach formator has a privileged position as he assists the man in overcoming the internal fears and anxieties that have been allowed to govern his habitual behaviors. Helping a man acquire self-confidence by teaching healthy conflict resolution can be immensely encouraging and healing. Teaching the man how to confront and resolve misunderstandings is an ordinary skill that he must learn if he is going to be an effective pastor.

Along with knowing how to "lead," the importance of a man knowing how "to provide for" and "protect" are also an essential traits and virtues that need to shine out from mature masculinity. This necessitates a certain kind of assertiveness, a willingness to suffer lovingly for the other. It is a masculinity that tastes and enjoys serving with a mature compassion as the man lives in an awareness of the needs of others. The enjoyment of this compassionate self-donation flows from the man's willingness and ability to put the needs of others above his own needs for immediate comfort. The opposite trait is not engaging in relationships through anxious or self-centered passivity.

In marriage, if we ask ordinary healthy wives, they will report that an anxious passive husband is no fun. This causes unnecessary marital anguish. Part of the husband's protective role is to ensure that the wife's physical, emotional and spiritual needs are being met. The man with transitory same-sex attraction is very often beset by personal inertia. To do those things that are difficult, either physically or emotionally, to care for or protect others, is something he needs to learn to enjoy. Active ways of learning to "be for" the other carries a promise of interior satisfaction and joy. These activities need to be intentionally cultivated if they are to engender positive masculine traits.

This is hard to quantify or describe, but it is real and qualitatively known in relationships. I will use as an example, a personal revelation of how I came to understand this in my own life. When I left seminary at the age of 24, I moved into a Christian household that consisted of a married couple with two children. They had a boy age 14 and a girl age 10, and there were 2 other single women in the household. It was somewhat like an extended family. I had duties and chores. Overall life was good. One day one of the single women approached me and said she did not feel very protected by me. She said, "I feel more protected by the 14-year-old boy in our household than I do you." That was a blow to my male ego! And, all that I could think was, "What does she mean by that?" I am 10 years older than the boy in the house. I had been through 6 years of seminary formation, held down a full time job, etc. I spent many days afterwards discussing this incident with my pastoral mentor. We conversed at length about what it meant to be a "protector" of women. He urged me to intentionally observe the other mature, masculine men in the community and notice how they related to women. As I came later to discover, I was giving off a kind of insecurity, a certain unattractive weak passivity. I had an indifference towards others simple needs, and an unwillingness to put myself out to help others in ordinary ways. Even simple cultural norms like opening a car door or pulling out a chair, or ordering at a restaurant, were lacking in my manner of living. If the car needed repair, it wasn't me that initiated to take care of the repair. If the pipe was leaking, I made no move to fix it. Simple "masculine" tasks were something I didn't do. In essence, I was stuck in that inner feeling like I was still a nice little boy being provided for rather than initiating care and protection for others. In order to face what I was lacking, and develop positive male traits, I ultimately chose to take a crash course in human formation. It was a course that dealt with ways of breaking out of this un-masculine persona.

I speak of all this because most of the men I have counseled with transitory same-sex attraction struggle with this feeling of being "a little boy" inside. They don't feel secure, confident, or assertive enough to really be the kind of man it takes to lead effectively. One man who I had been counseling for three years summed up this idea very well. He said that in his prayer time he had received a word from the Lord. He said, "The Lord told me that I was not aware of the fact that I always wanted someone to care for me in my needs." This word of knowledge from the Lord in prayer was related to the call to cultivate a mature masculinity that focuses on a healthy caring for oneself while meeting other people's needs, instead of first seeking to find someone to care for one's own personal needs.

One of the reasons why men who struggle with transitory same-sex attraction don't consider marriage is that they are afraid, and they feel an inability to adequately "provide for", "protect" and "lead" in a committed relationship with a woman. They may also fear dealing with a woman's emotions. A seminarian who has not overcome these aspects, often associated with transitory same-sex attraction, could get ordained and negatively relate to women in an immature way. In my opinion this is another important aspect that the "Ratio" talks about in Paragraph #94 when it says that the seminarian should display his ability "to establish mature and well balanced interpersonal relationships."

It is a well-documented reality that men who struggle with same-sex attraction have a higher incidence of depression and anxiety. The current culture would have us believe that this is due to a lack of affirmation of homosexual activity as normal and good. And, the current non-biblical worldly way of thinking would have us also believe that if we would just be more accepting, these higher rates of depression and anxiety would disappear. There is no scientific evidence that this is the case. I can say with complete honesty, that I have not ever counseled someone with same-sex attraction that does not have some level of high anxiety, often mixed with depressive feelings. The origins of the anxiety, depression and often other disorders, are undoubtedly often related to developmental trauma, and a lack of treatment for the interior affective causes of the same-sex attraction.

As I mentioned earlier in this article, living with transitory same-sex attraction as I did for years, can feel like being on an emotional roller coaster in day-to-day life. These emotions can easily trigger addictive behaviors that are attempts to bring about temporary relief. Thus, alcohol, the use of a variety of drugs, compulsive masturbation and compulsively viewing pornography are ways that are often part and parcel to dealing with emotional conflicts. These are all destructive addictions. A man with transitory same-sex attraction may experience basic stability in seminary, due to the very supportive environment, dealing somewhat constructively with emotional conflicts. But, when put to the test to cultivate an important prayerful solitude in parish life, where he will face difficult pastoral situations, and where loneliness needs to be transformed regularly into a generative communion with the Lord, the balance needed to remain free from significant attachments and addictions is often not realized.

Any candidate for seminary who has transitory same-sex attraction needs to get help in uncovering and dealing constructively with these emotional conflicts. Often it takes professional counseling. Part of growth counseling with men who desire to grow out of an affective immaturity that engenders high anxiety, and an unhealthy focusing on their self-centered needs, means teaching them how to recognize and deal immediately with interior triggers that promote the anxiety and depressed feelings.

A high level of shame is the universal inner posture these men suffer. It is essential to help them break out of the sense of shame and self-hatred that inwardly binds them to unhealthy patterns of thinking, feeling and desiring. These patterns of shame if left unchecked will prevent a healthy self-acceptance, and this is most essential. Integrating counseling with helping the man cultivate an interior life of prayer, where he daily encounters the unconditional love of his Father through Jesus' presence, is necessary for true interior freedom from shame and self-hatred. The affectionate favor of the Father as revealed through Jesus needs to take root in his heart. It is especially helpful to have access to a strong male authority figure who can serve him (counselor, vocation director, spiritual director, seminary formator). This strong male authority figure is someone the candidate for seminary can open up to in an ordinary ongoing experience of male friendship. This relationship is an analogy to Abba's unconditional love and acceptance.

Listening to "the man's story" with full acceptance and without judgement is crucial. It is a necessary dimension of accompaniment that fosters the affective healing. As a counselor, I try to help the man know that his human needs are normal by simply explaining that their need for feeling loved and accepted by other men is a universal truth that all men have at work in their hearts. The need for male acceptance and affection need not be bound to a disordered desire for same-sex genital activity. This need for male acceptance and affection need not be associated with unhealthy emotional dependency where other men are idolized for what I believe is deficient in my masculinity. What irrational fear has taught me to believe about myself can be unlearned and healed.

This universal healthy need for male affection and affirmation, a need that was not met adequately growing up in the man with transitory same-sex attraction, can now be received in healthy ways that promote affective maturity. These men need to learn to find healthy new ways for these inner needs for male affection and affirmation to be met.

The men who have the greatest chance of overcoming transitory same-sex attraction are those who, along with strong determination, have developed and experienced a deep intimacy with the Trinity in prayer. And, a particular relationship with the Father's fierce affection is especially important. Healing "father wounds" is usually critical. "Mother wounds" sometimes come into play within the growth counseling, but my experience is that most often "father wounds" cry out for attention and healing. Often deep inner-healing through an experienced team familiar with this type of prayer can be very helpful.

The man with transitory same-sex attraction needs to learn how to participate in forgiveness in and through Jesus' cry to the Father; "Forgive them they do not know what they do" (Luke 23:34). If he learns to identify inwardly with Jesus' forgiving love while suffering rejections, he will receive an experience (hopefully ongoing) of the freedom that flows from forgiveness. The man with transitory same-sex attraction can learn how to forgive those who may have contributed to the affective immaturity. He can also learn to repent of any lack of trust that he has held on to instead of entrusting his fears, angers and anxieties to the Lord of all consolation and mercy. He can take ownership for how he has believed lies that have flowed from shame and fear. Entering into ongoing forgiveness, by exercising the gift of faith, is an essential reality in the process of growth in overcoming transitory same-sex attraction. Without the experience of the Father's unconditional love and mercy, it will be very difficult for any man to extend real compassion to others. In growth counseling it becomes clear that any self-judgement or self-condemnation, only lead the man to extending harsh judgement and some form of rejection toward others.

I have some summary thoughts. The important thing for counselors and seminary personnel to see in the candidate with transitory same-sex attraction is clear and substantial progress in freedom from affective insecurities that negatively affect his readiness, willingness and ability to "lead," "provide for" and "to protect" the ecclesial family. The man needs to have overcome transitory same-sex attraction by clearly, behaviorally living in a virtuous manner that is a joyful witness to his capacities for spousal and paternal love. His seminary formation will be dedicated to strengthening his abilities to serve the parish family.

If the man with transitory same-sex attraction was accepted into seminary then I think two options are advisable. It would be beneficial to both the man and the sponsoring diocese for the man to be given a conditional 2-3 year leave of absence to work specifically on the internal issues that are at the root of the affective immaturity. A second option is to embark upon intensive interior work while remaining in seminary three years prior to diaconate. This second option, as previously stated, seems to me to be less optimal because of all the academic pressures that seminarians have to focus on while in formation. There is also great pressure in the culture of seminary life to comply with expectations placed upon the seminarian so that he is approved for advancement towards ordination.

In my eyes those men that are willing to "do the work" to overcome transitory same-sex attraction are heroic. They exhibit a form of manly courage. I have the deepest compassion for these men and I have devoted much of my life to assisting them find freedom, self-acceptance and the unconditional love of Jesus, revealing the Father's tender affection.

I believe that ordaining men who struggle with transitory same-sex attraction, as a form of male affective immaturity, is not God's desire and the "Ratio" affirms this. It is the Father's desire to further complete our joy in parish family life by strengthening our abilities day by day to enjoy living in and through Jesus' presence. This learning to remain with Jesus promises life to the full. I believe that to ordain men with transitory same-sex attraction is an exercise in false compassion. If a future bride said she willingly wanted to marry someone who is same-sex attracted, knowing he did nothing to overcome it, we would say she was foolish or naïve at best. Why would the Church, the bride of Christ, want to ordain someone in a similar situation? Again, we could add the adjectives foolish, risky, imprudent, naïve, etc. I thank God for the "Ratio" that promotes a healthy, happy and affectively mature priesthood. When we live in obedient love, according to the Holy Spirit speaking through the ordinary magisterium of the Church expressed in the "Ratio," we are promised shepherds who live with a manly confidence in the goodness and vitality of their call to serve as spiritual husbands and fathers for the Church as an ecclesial family. May it be so...well into the future.

Prayer

Lord Jesus, please give me the wisdom and discernment to know how to approach (name)_____with my concerns for his growth in his masculine identity. Let me be compassionate, clear and full of your love. Give me the courage to be straightforward. At the same time protect (name)_____ from experiencing shame or rejection. May he hear affirmation in my straightforward approach. May he know unconditional love through me in and real hope in your Gospel which brings freedom from all fears that bind us. I pray this through the intercession of Mary and St. Joseph, model of fatherhood.

Practicum Reflection Questions for Formators

1. If you are mentoring a man with transitory same sex attraction do you see evidence of the necessary motivation needed to "do the work" that promotes interior healing of male insecurities?

2. Do you see an interior ambivalence about marriage with the men that you are mentoring? What has caused any ambivalence? How can I foster a more whole hearted desire to taste to the goodness of marriage as the foundation for priestly chaste celibacy? Do my men believe that they have what it takes to serve well as future spiritual husbands and fathers for parish families?

3. How can I encourage masculine virtues in my mentoring? What ways can I mentor/teach my men how to increasingly enjoy their abilities to "lead," "protect" and "provide for" others?

4. Are my men experiencing a daily encounter with Jesus' risen presence, revealing the fierce and tender affection of the Father's Heart? How can I coach my men to taste and see this daily encounter?

Suggested Resources

1. "Growth Into Manhood," by Allan Medinger (caveat - his view of masturbation is not in line with Catholic moral teaching but the book provides much wisdom)
2. "What's The Difference?" by John Piper
3. "The Truth About Homosexuality," by Fr. John F. Harvey, O.S.F.S.
4. "Shame and Attachment Loss: The Practical work of Reparative Therapy," by Dr. Joseph Nicolosi

Chapter Thirteen

Integrity, Identity And Fidelity

I will raise up for myself a faithful priest,
who shall do according to what is in my heart and in my mind.
(1 Samuel 2:35a)

Dr. Eileen M. Raffaniello Barbella, Ph.D.

Dr. Eileen M. Raffaniello Barbella is a licensed psychologist with formation as a spiritual director in the Ignatian tradition. After earning a Ph.D. in Educational Psychology from the University of Texas in Austin, she developed a graduate course in family interventions at the University of Cincinnati. She also began to integrate her study and practice of Ignatian Spirituality with her work as a psychologist. She did this as a pastoral associate/campus minister, as a co-director of a diocesan training program for spiritual directors in Austin, as an adjunct professor at St. Edward's University, Regis in Denver, and the University of St. Thomas School of Theology at St. Mary's Seminary in Houston, as a systems consultant to churches (Catholic, Episcopal, Presbyterian, Methodist and Baptist) and religious congregations (Benedictine, Carmelite, Dominican, Norbertine, Redemptorist, Jesuit, Incarnate Word and Divine Providence), and as a retreat and workshop leader. She also presented workshops at Assumption Seminary in San Antonio and St. Vincent de Paul Seminary in Florida.

In January 2015, Dr. Barbella moved to West Texas. While taking a six month sabbatical, she focused on deepening her understanding of the connections between spirituality and psychology for her work as both a coach and a consultant. From July 2015 - January 2017 she served as Shalom Center's only full time psychologist and as Clinical Director for the Shalom Center. Now living in San Angelo, Dr. Barbella was hired by Shannon Health as the first full time psychologist at Shannon Clinic.

As we began the 21st century it was clear that the two sacraments at the service of communion, Holy Orders and Matrimony, were in crisis. In Chinese, the word crisis consists of two pictograms – "danger" and "opportunity." There was and is plenty of danger, but there is also a great opportunity to form strong male leaders who will serve as strong husbands and fathers, married men leading families and priests leading parishes.

Marriage has become one more plastic word. The nuptial meaning of the body is undermined by a secular redefining of marriage as no longer limited to a man and a woman. Even the sacrament of marriage is being threatened as some suggest accommodations that do not honor the indissolubility, exclusivity and unconditionality of the spousal union. It is a union that is a sign of God's redeeming love for us in Christ and of the inner life of the communion of Love that is the Trinity.

Almost a quarter into the 21st century, there are still reverberations from the sexual abuse scandal. Not only is childhood sexual abuse by pedophile priests being addressed but also the abuse of vulnerable seminarians and young priests by older homosexual priests with a corrupt misuse of power and authority. As a psychologist, I am very aware that mental health professionals did not always help bishops and others in authority deal with this sexual abuse effectively and transparently. Psychiatric treatment centers may have convinced bishops that sexual offenders could be treated and rehabilitated with unrealistic diagnostics. In my training, in dealing with adult survivors of childhood sexual abuse and sexual offenders in the late 1980s, I was taught that one could only be sure that an offender would not re-offend "a minute after their heart stopped". In this same era the American Psychiatric Association made changes to the DSM (Diagnostic and Standard Manual) "normalizing" homosexuality based on political correctness, not scientific evidence.

The "Triumph" and the Failure of the Therapeutic

My doctoral training in Educational and Community Psychology focused on learning and development as well as systems thinking. When I worked in Campus Ministry and consulted with religious and church groups, I was surprised at how much their thinking was informed by psychoanalytic theories.

Book titles in of themselves can capture a dimension of reality. Sociologist and social critic Philip Reiff in his book, *The Triumph of the Therapeutic: Uses of Faith after Freud* (1966), points out that even those who would never go into therapy accepted the untested assumptions of human nature based on Freudian theory. Later, came the book, *We've Had a Hundred Years of Psychotherapy – And the World's Getting Worse* (James Hillman and Michael Ventura, 1993).

Fr. Benedict Groeschel, C.F.R., writing in *First Things* (June/July 2007, p. 13-14.) on the life and death of religious life, points out that "many shaky theories of psychology, most of them now gone over the waterfall of time, were substituted for the gospel and sacred teaching." And, he also reminds us that contemporary positive psychology has rejected the general intellectual and emotional bankruptcy of the Freudian position. Specifically, Groeschel noted that one founder of positive psychology, Aaron Beck, pointed out that there was an almost complete lack of common sense in psychotherapy from the 1940s to the 1980s.

If we do accept that grace builds on nature, it is necessary to find a theory of human behavior that is scientific in its approach. To date, the only theory that I believe does this in a comprehensive way is Bowen Theory. This natural systems theory moves beyond polarization and blame, and deals with what it takes to be mature persons in spite of how our emotions tend to sabotage us.

Psychological theories are just that – theories to be tested. They are to be tested in the light of the "facts of life." A rigorous science, by study and observation of the natural physical world, can inform us about the facts of life and offer theories about human nature.

Bowen Theory "is for anyone, but not for everyone"

"What is needed is no less than a unified concept of man, a frame of reference that will enable us to understand the necessary connections between cell and psyche and perhaps between psyche and the entity we know as the soul." (Murray Bowen, "A Family Concept of Schizophrenia")

To my way of thinking, the best way to be a good father is to be a good spouse. And, the best way to be a good spouse is to be the "best version of yourself." In other words, to be a good father and a good spouse, one needs to live fully one's baptismal call to holiness and evangelization. This is true for both physical and spiritual fathers. This is also about living and leading with integrity.

What does it mean to live with integrity? The synonyms for the Latin *integritas* include wholeness, entirety, completeness, chastity and purity. The dictionary definition gives two senses of living with integrity: 1) the quality of being honest and having strong moral principles, and 2) the state of being whole and undivided. In the first sense "ethics" is synonymous with "integrity." The second is about the integration of an entity as a whole. And, both senses of integrity are critical to being the "best version of one's self."

Most theories of leadership agree that all leadership begins with self-leadership. All too often the focus is on techniques and quick fixes, not on substance. And, despite frequent reference to "thinking outside the box," few approaches address how to really accomplish the prerequisite change in the order of our consciousness that is necessary for leadership in the 21st century.

Leading with integrity is leadership that focuses on the integrity of our very self; (1) in our way of being, (2) in our way of thinking and (3) in our way of doing. Leading with integrity is for those individuals who have the courage to be contemplative, requiring the consciousness necessary for clarity of mind, and the character to be compassionately conscientious. Leading with integrity is also a sign of an individual's affective maturity.

To achieve this kind of integrity requires a different way of thinking about the human. Much of 20th century psychology, torn between two equally unhelpful poles – the semi-mystical mythologizing of Freud and Jung, and the sterile behaviorism of John Watson and B.F. Skinner – did not offer much help in meeting the mental and emotional demands of our contemporary world. Conrad Baars and Murray Bowen are two preeminent 20th century psychiatrists who took different paths away from traditional psychiatric models. Murray Bowen turned to the natural sciences, and Conrad Baars to Thomistic philosophy. Bowen developed a family systems theory, while Baars focused on affirmation as one of the four basic human needs.

Bowen wanted to develop a "science of the human", a scientific theory of human behavior rooted in the facts of life. I was introduced to this theory in October 1990 in a workshop entitled *Leadership through Self-Differentiation: A Healing Model for Family and Religious Life*. The presenter was Rabbi Edwin Friedman. He had been a pulpit rabbi for thirty years before deciding to learn more about the family as a system. By the time I first heard him, his seminal book, *Generation to Generation – Family Process in Church and Synagogue* (1985) was required reading in some seminaries and on the shelves of many clergy. This theory is not for everyone, but it is for anyone who wants to learn about leadership through differentiation of one's self, about the kind of maturity required to lead with integrity in all that we do.

Science, of course, is not enough. A rigorous science, by study and observation of the natural physical world, can inform us about the facts of life and offer theories about human nature. Wisdom traditions, through study and contemplation, can instruct us about truth and insights that go beyond the natural world. This wisdom is written in nature, in Sacred Scripture, and in spiritual teachings that constitute the living tradition of the Church, something we as Catholics rest in and enjoy. The living tradition of the Doctors of the Church and other saints provide pathways for us to become relationally absorbed into the

Trinity's beauty, goodness and truth.

The physical and social sciences can teach us much about the world and about ourselves. A scientific view of the human such as Bowen Theory can teach us how to recognize "how" and "when" our emotions *sabotage* rather than *serve* our principles. But, it cannot teach us the living principles and beliefs.

Integrity of Being

Integrity in our way of being is about our capacity to be not only self-defining but also self-regulating. In this age of ever-increasing demands and expectations, it is increasingly harder for any of us to be a non-anxious presence. Many of us are successful at appearing non-anxious, but often at the cost of really being present. Self-regulation is about how well we manage to be both less anxious and more present. Before we can think clearly, we need integrity in our way of being. Wisdom traditions as well as contemporary sciences recognize the need for disciplines that reduce our anxiety and increase our capacity to be living in the "now," to be conscious and aware of who we are and what we are in the present moment. This kind of contemplative mindfulness requires choosing and practicing daily disciplines for self-awareness and receptivity to the Holy Spirit.

Bowen Theory offers a new way of thinking about anxiety and its ways of sabotaging of our ability to be ourselves. Chronic anxiety is the anxiety that is embedded in the very fabric of our physical being, our protoplasm. Chronic anxiety, unlike acute anxiety, is about imagined threats. A fact of life is that mature humans are not really independent autonomous selves but are radically interdependent "selves-in-relation". The human is only a self in and through relationships. Chronic anxiety is about the imagined and real threats to our ability to be both our own selves, and to stay connected to important others, to manage the competing biological forces for individuality and for togetherness.

Integrity of Thinking

Integrity in our way of thinking is not about how smart we are. It is about the *order of consciousness* (Cf. Robert Kegan's *In Over Our Heads – The Mental Demands of Modern Life*) in which we exercise our smartness or our lack of it. Today's world requires that we be able to not only think logically but "think systems." It is most challenging to "think systems" about ourselves, and the emotional systems in which we live and love and work.

As we "grow a self" and become better able to be non-anxious and present, our capacity for thinking increases. Natural systems thinking suggests that this "growing a self" is an evolutionary process of increasing one's ability to differentiate between the two human guidance systems – the emotional guidance system of our instincts and feelings and the intellectual guidance systems of our thinking and principles. This requires a shift from the individualistic focus on feelings to a systemic awareness of relationships. With greater maturity and more integrity, principle-centered choices more consistently replace automatic anxious reactivity.

Integrity of Doing

Integrity in our way of doing is about an increased capacity to not only act on, but to also persevere and follow through, on principle-centered choices. All too often in human systems, the least mature and/or most "schizophrenic" member in the system of relationships tends to run the show. It is as Ed Friedman pointed out, a "failure of nerve in an age of quick fix." Leading with integrity is about being conscientious about being one's best self. Leading with integrity is committing to what it takes to increase a solid self. Leading with integrity is working daily, and over the long haul, to increase one's level of differentiation or, in the language used by formators, one's "affective maturity".

Sabotage is the word Ed Friedman used to describe the kind of resistance to growth that is an inevitable part of all human systems and a key to a *natural systems* view of leadership. Any individual's capacity to be more self-defining and self-regulating, to maintain their own integrity while being connected to others is both *maturity* and *leadership*. Sabotage or "sin" (the word for sin in both Hebrew and Greek is "to miss the mark") is how, in the face of crisis or challenge, we can be tempted to reactively regress and *grow down, or* consciously choose to act responsibly and *grow up*. At higher levels of maturity and self-leadership (i.e. differentiation of self), an individual is both able to recognize and distinguish, or differentiate, their emotions and feelings from their principles and beliefs. An individual is able to consciously choose between the two guidance systems.

Sanity is about the health and integrity of our intellect. It is *seeing what is really there*. *Sanctity* or wholeness is about the health and integrity of our will. It is loving *what is good and right and true*. Both are important goals for each of us. Prudence requires that we *discern* the true good and *choose* the right means of acting. Discipline and detachment are prerequisites not only for our emotional well-being but also for the kind of discernment needed to act with integrity.

Chastity as Integrity of the Person

"Love is the fundamental and innate vocation of every human being" (CCC 2392).

The vocation to chastity is beautifully and accurately described in the *Catechism of the Catholic Church* (2337- 2350). In particular it describes the chaste person as one who "maintains the *integrity* of the powers of life and love placed in him" (2338). For over thirty years I have addressed the issue of sex, sexuality and sexual expression as a Catholic campus minister, as therapist and retreat leader working with married couples in therapy, as a teacher and workshop leader with seminarians and priests, and as a psychologist and spiritual director for priests and religious in a residential treatment program. A constant has been the confusion about the differences between sex, sexuality and sexual expression. And, there has also been, especially among older priests, a negative focus on the requirement of celibacy rather than a positive focus on the gift of celibate chastity.

Ronald Rolheiser, in his book *The Holy Longing,* writes clearly about chastity. It is to reverence and respect the *integrity* of all that is in reality. To be chaste is to experience people, things, places, entertainment, the phases of one's life, life's opportunities and challenges, our own incarnation and that of all persons, in a way that does not violate our own or their moral, psychological, sexual or aesthetic boundaries. To be chaste is to not let irreverence, impatience or narcissistic selfishness ruin what is gift. "Chastity is respect and reverence and patience. Its fruits are *integration*, gratitude and joy. Lack of chastity is irreverence and impatience. Its fruits are disintegration, bitterness and cynicism" (Rolheiser, 202).

Sex (Gender), Sexuality and Sexual Expression

Sex refers to whether we are male or female (cf. behavioral ecologist Bobbi Low's book *Why Sex Matters*). If to be sexual is to be "sexed," to be either a man or a woman, then our sexuality is the way we relate to everyone and everything as a man or as a woman. Our sexuality and our spirituality reflects that we are embodied spirits, enfleshed souls. Concurrent with the erotic crisis of the 20th century (i.e. the reduction of eros to romantic-genital connection between two persons) "sex" no longer refers to whether we are male or female. Instead, *gender* is used as a grammatical fluid term, instead of the given state of being male or female according to what we are as human bodies.

Sexuality is well described by Ronald Rolheiser in his book *The Holy Longing.* He writes that it "is an all-encompassing energy inside of us. In one sense, it is identifiable with the principle of life itself. It is the drive for love, communion, community, friendship, family, affection, wholeness, consummation, creativity, self-perpetuation, immortality, joy, delight, humor and self –transcendence" (Rolheiser, 194). *Genitality*, or what is now referred to as "having sex," is only one aspect of that larger reality of sexuality.

In 1983, Sam Keen opened his book *The Passionate Life* by naming as the "erotic crisis" the reduction of *eros* to romantic-genital connection between two persons.

"The root word *eros* means simply to 'love or desire ardently.' Greek philosophers considered eros the prime mover the motivating principle in all things human and nonhuman. It was the impulse that made all things yearn and strive for fulfillment. The acorn was erotically moved by its destiny to become an oak, just as human beings were motivated by eros to become reasonable and to form political order, as just and as harmonious as nature. Eros was inseparable from the potentiality or promise (the potency or power) that slept in the substance of all things.

Thus, in the original vision that gave birth to the word, erotic potency was not confined to sexual power but included the moving force that propelled every life-form from a state of mere potentiality to actuality" (p. 5).

Antidotes to the Erotic Crisis: living and loving as fully erotic and spiritual

In a secular answer to the erotic crisis Keen asserted that love, sexuality, and power can only be healed by returning to the original meaning of eros; by seeing the pleasures of the flesh within the context of a vision of human promise, as it unfolds over the course of a lifetime within the ambience of the *community* and the *cosmos*. Even the non-religious Keen understood that our erotic ethics cannot be narrowly selfish and cut off.

In Christian terms, the true function of eros is to propel us not toward sex or beauty for its sake alone, but always toward the holy. Again Rolheiser, in his book *The Holy Longing,* reminds us that "Spirituality concerns what we do with this desire. It takes root in the eros inside us and it is all about how we shape and discipline that eros" (Rolheiser, 7).

Identity and Fidelity

Faith is about how we see and lean into life. Beliefs are about what we are willing to live and to die for in the everyday. As individuals, each of us must freely and consciously choose our core beliefs and key life-directing principles. This is the developmental task of *identity* vs. *identity diffusion* (conformity, rebellion or confusion) that leads to the virtue of fidelity. This ability to take responsibility for and to define a self is essential to leading with integrity.

According to developmental psychologist Erik Erikson (*The Life Cycle Completed,* pp. 32-33), the maturing individual is faced with challenges and crises at each stage that could strengthen or weaken the person's social and personality development. His vision of a mature individual is one who underwent the *crises of the life cycle* and achieved the *virtues.* The virtue of wisdom comes with the mature resolution of the final psychosocial crisis of adulthood, *integrity* vs. despair. There life is proven to be meaningful and there is self - acceptance.

The task of adolescence is that of identity vs. identity diffusion. This requires one to be able to be, in Bowen's terms, both self-regulating and self-defining. The virtue of *fidelity* is achieved when an individual, overcoming conformity/rebellion/confusion, can answer the question "Who are you" with clarity and full conviction. The individual then has the capacity to be oneself and to share being.

The task of young adulthood is that of intimacy and solidarity vs. isolation. When the virtue of love is achieved the individual has the "capacity for intimacy without fear of a loss or compromise of the self." This is especially true in occasions of conflict. The individual is able to lose and to find oneself in another.

Years ago, it became clear to me, in working with persons who had sexual affairs, that the issue was not a symptom of a problem with intimacy, but a symptom of a problem with identity. Polonius' advice to his children, in Shakespeare's *Hamlet*, drives home the importance of a mature identity:

"This above all, - to thine own self be true;
And it must follow, as the night the day,
Thou canst not then be false to any man." (Act 1, Scene III)

A more contemporary example is in the movie *Moonstruck*. Rose Castorini, the long suffering wife played by Olympia Dukakis knows that her husband Cosmo is unfaithful. And, as usual, she has gone to dinner at a restaurant by herself. Rose watches an altercation between an NYU professor (Perry) and his much younger date who leaves after throwing a glass of wine at him. Rose invites Perry to join her for dinner. After dinner, he walks Rose to her home and asks if he may come in, attempting to seduce her. She says, "No." He speculates that it is because someone is there. She retorts, "No, because *I know who I am!*" It is that kind of clarity about her identity that ensures her fidelity to her marriage promises.

Identity precedes intimacy. And the virtue of fidelity requires that one knows who one is and where one is going. It requires that one first answer the identity question of "Where am I going" before asking the intimacy question of "With whom."

Making A Difference - Ignatian Spirituality and Bowen Theory

In general, human formation happens in a three-fold process of self-knowledge, self-acceptance, and self-gift. (PPF 80)

My way of thinking about human growth and development is rooted in *The Spiritual Exercises* of St. Ignatius of Loyola and shaped by Murray Bowen's Family Systems Theory (BFST). For my own self, and in my work with others as a psychologist and spiritual director, these frameworks guide my daily practice and thinking. Both help to develop greater interior freedom which is the foundational benchmark of affective maturity.

Identity, Integrity, and Affective Maturity

In his book, *Always Discerning,* Joseph A. Tetlow, points out that "The human person works with head and heart and hands. That work is charged, energized by grace, by our baptismal call" (p.21). We use head, heart and hands as we live out the common vocation of our baptismal call to "holiness and evangelization" (*CCC* 1533), our particular sacramental vocation to Holy Orders or to Marriage (*CCC* 1534), as well as our "personal vocation." Our "personal vocation" as defined by Herbert Alphonso in *Discovering Your Personal Vocation,* is "the deepest secret of unity and integration at the heart of life precisely because it is the unique God-given meaning in life; and again, it is the unique God-given meaning in life precisely because it is for each of us our personal Jesus. For the Father there is just no meaning outside Christ Jesus" (p.25).

The distinction between *approval* and *acceptance* is not made in Bowen Theory. This distinction comes from the wisdom of *The Spiritual Exercises* of St. Ignatius Loyola. If we are to deal with our *experience*, it is necessary to become *conscious* of it and then it is necessary to *accept* it for what it is in reality. That kind of acceptance is not easy. All too often we think that consciousness of our experience automatically involves acceptance. As Herbert Alphonso points out in the first appendix of *Discovering Your Personal Vocation* (p.60), "the fact is that we have a kind of spontaneous inner dynamic of *nonacceptance* operative within each one of us." It is far too easy for us to justify, blame, excuse or deny, rather than truly accept our experience for what it is in reality. He makes a clear distinction between *approval* and *acceptance.*

Approval or disapproval is a *judgment.* Acceptance is an *attitude.* God accepts each of us unconditionally without approving of all that we do. And, what God does for me I need to do for myself. If I do so, then my being will be gracious, my understanding will be clear, and my acting will be loving towards all. I will live enacting the virtues of faith, hope and love.

The awareness of our common, particular and personal vocation helps us to clarify our identity. It requires the kind of self-knowledge and self-acceptance that leads to self-gift. Healthy resolution of the psychosocial crisis of identity calls for the ordering of our desires and the freedom to not have to conform, rebel or get stuck in confusion. As self- knowledge and self- acceptance lead to self-gift we have the freedom to be "true to ourselves and to the Father's hopes in us." And, we have the freedom to move into healthy intimacy with others, rather than isolating or enmeshing, for a "covenant living that transposes all identity questions into vocational questions" (Fowler, *Becoming Adult, Becoming Christian,* p.93). We move away from the question "Who am I" to the question "*Whose* am I." And, our identity and our vocation is the integrated response that we make with our full selves to God's call to co-labor with Him in the world.

Sin, Affective Conversion and Self-Regulation

Sin in both Greek and Hebrew has to do with "missing the mark." As Kathleen Norris recounts in her book *Dakota,* she learned from the fourth-century monks to see that looking at sin is not about a load of needless guilt, but a useful tool for confronting the negative side of human behavior. Sin is the failure to be conscious and aware of who we are, what we are and what we are doing; or "any thought or act that interferes with our ability to love God and neighbor (p.97-98). Both *The Spiritual Exercises* and Bowen Theory offer ways of becoming more conscious and aware of ourselves.

The spiritual exercise, the one designated as most important in everyday life by St. Ignatius, is the one we often neglect in our desire to seek after and find God's presence caring for us and guiding us in daily life. That daily exercise is the Examen Prayer. One of the most reprinted articles from the *Review for Religious* was George Aschenbrenner's "The Consciousness Examen: Becoming God's Heart for the World." It was included in *Ignatian*

Exercises: Contemporary Annotations (p.113-123). His foundational article the "Consciousness Examen" is provided for our appropriation later on in this book. Aschenbrenner showed how a daily examination of consciousness facilitates a transforming experience of one's own heart into becoming more and more conformed to the beloved of one's heart, the Sacred Heart of God in Jesus. Beginning with an invocation of the Holy Spirit in gratitude and aware of how much we are loved, we are taught to look at how we missed or did not miss the mark in our being, thinking, feeling and doing in daily living. We come to recognize how we did or did not place the most important living principles first, those living principles that are personally flowing from Jesus' Heart. We also come to taste inwardly how we did or did not choose to abide with those interior movements that are Jesus' Spirit indwelling. Once we have basically learned the art of this interior listening, being present to the present moment and tasting God's communication indwelling, we can see *who we allowed ourselves to be with*, and if we allowed ourselves to remember, *where it is that we are going*. After receiving the grace of consoling sorrow for often missing the mark, we receive regenerating mercy and love. Even in not missing the mark there is a consoling sorrow because of our smallness in the face of such magnanimous love. This sorrow is a natural grace for us as creatures standing before and receiving our Creator's lavish love and mercy.

The Examen Prayer (15 minutes a day) concludes with a sense of hope-filled resolution for future choices in faith, choices to remain with and abide with the one whose love and mercy "makes all things new" (Rev. 21: 5). In this hope we gradually become more like the one whom we contemplate.

A few years ago, I thought I had an original idea. I had begun thinking that the practice of virtue might be a way, not only to be holier, but to be more mature and better differentiated. I soon learned that I was not the only psychologist thinking about and advocating the practice of virtue. Martin Seligman and other positive psychologists use the practice of virtue to help with depression and anxiety. For me, in "thinking emotional systems," it was important to help increase the reliance on living principles, and their intellectual guidance systems, rather than relying upon the emotional guidance system. And, it was the daily Examen Prayer that shaped my focus on a healthy practice of virtue. The reality is that we can simply hold a value without practicing it. But, the Examen Prayer draws us to taste the goodness of responding to God's indwelling presence providing us with personal living principles, and it engenders a consolation of communion in the practice of virtue. The Examen Prayer also saves us from being in a self-made aloneness, as we can tend to engage in self-improvement resolutions in practicing virtue, resolutions that can often be self-motivated and self-centered, rather a response to our goodness in God's sight.

In one of his early encounters with Dominican Inquisitors, St. Ignatius of Loyola told them that he praised virtue. Recently (2010) the Jesuit Gerald Fagin wrote his book *Putting on the Heart of Christ- -How the Spiritual Exercise Invite us to a Virtuous Life.* He offers two definitions for virtues: 1) The permanent dispositions of your heart which you enact daily; and 2) The enactment of a habit of your heart which is the same as the habit of heart that Jesus enacted – a habit you learned in imitation of Christ when contemplating the life of Jesus of Nazareth.

Practicing the Examen Prayer, praying honestly, assures ongoing conversion. In *Review of Ignatian Spirituality* (XXXIV, i / 2003 / No. 102), Joseph Tetlow gave an overview of Donald L. Gelpi's work on *A Foundational Christology,* and Gelpi's identification of five forms of conversion: affective, intellectual, personal moral, socio-political, and religious. In each form of conversion there is the turn (*Tesuvah*) from irresponsible to responsible behavior in some realm of experience. Although Gelpi did not indicate a particular order, it is my thinking that affective conversion – "a decision to take responsibility for the health of one's emotional and imaginative life" – may be necessary for intellectual, as well as personal and socio-political moral conversion. Pope Benedict XVI in the first volume of *Jesus of Nazareth* states that the affective dimension of the soul first apprehends the presence of God and that this affective apprehension gives the will and the intellect their direction (pp. 92-93). When I reflect on my own experience I see the truth of what Pope Benedict is teaching us. I also believe that religious, Christian conversion – "a decision to take responsibility for one's response to the eschatological and normative revelation of God in Jesus and in the mission of His Spirit" transcends the other forms of conversion.

Affective Conversion and Differentiation of Self

"The Church as a communio must be understood as a differentiated totality, as a body of an organism in which the various organs cooperate in varied manners for the good of the whole." (Lumen Gentium, 16)

Psychology assists formators in dealing with understanding human development. Tools from Cognitive Behavioral Therapy (e.g. David Burns' *Daily Mood Log*) and Dialectical Behavioral Therapy/Mindfulness can be used to help individuals to regulate their emotions and achieve greater affective conversion. Bowen Family Systems Theory does not provide "tools," but it does provide a way of thinking about the self that leads to greater self-knowledge and self-acceptance. The life-long effort to be better differentiated includes the capacity to self-regulate one's emotions, contributing to affective conversion, as well as to better define a self (identity) while being able to stay connected to important others (intimacy). All of which is necessary for what seminary formators call "affective maturity".

Differentiation of self is the central metaphor of Murray Bowen's *Natural Family Systems* theory of the families as *emotional systems* (a non-dichotomized biological model of emotional *interdependence*). It is the life-long *process* of striving to keep one's being in balance through the reciprocal external and internal processes of *self-regulation* and *self-definition.* It requires knowing *where one's own self ends and another person begins.* It is the capacity to be one's own integrated "aggregate-of-cells person" while still belonging to and being able to relate to a larger "colony-of-cells." It is the individual's ability to maintain their own truth *and* stay connected; to stand in one's own truth (not fused/enmeshed) without cutting off from one's tradition. It is the ability to regulate one's own reactivity, and to not react to other's reactivity. It means taking maximum responsibility for one's own emotional being and destiny rather than blaming either others or the context. Psalm 84 is lived out in such differentiation of self - "The Lord withholds no good to those who walk without blame…O Lord of hosts, happy are those who trust in you."

Applying Bowen's theory to daily life means recognizing and being a *self* as category of **integrity** and maturity, not an instance of narcissism. Differentiation of self is not to be equated with similar sounding ideas such as individuation, autonomy or independence. Ed Friedman most famously referred to differentiation of self as the capacity to be a "non-anxious presence." The reality is that we cannot ever be non-anxious, but by working on differentiation of self we can be less anxious and more present to what we are thinking, feeling and desiring in the present moment.

Bowen's theory assumes that there are two basic biological forces – the force for togetherness and the force for individuality or differentiation of self. Conflict between these two forces is the source of chronic anxiety or emotional reactivity. Bowen's theory also assumes that we have two guidance systems, an emotional and an intellectual one. One of Bowen's observations was that all too often psychological theories focused on our intellectual guidance system and our neocortex and neglected to see the impact of the emotional guidance system with its tendency towards "reptilian regression" in the face of threat, to not only our physical selves, but to our sense of self and of connection. "Thinking systems" requires unlearning conventional concepts, to *not* apply linear cause and effect thinking to human emotional processes, and, to *not* ask "why" questions or look for "why" explanations that blame and justify. Thinking systems requires the capacity to wonder and to see the non-linear interdependence of emotional processes; to ask "what", "where", "when", and "how" questions; to wonder at and be curious about life.

I cannot here provide an exhaustive explanation of the eight concepts of Bowen Family Systems Theory. I was told when I began my study of theory that it would take a minimum of six years of study to gain an independent working knowledge of the theory – but only if that study included using the theory in my own life. What I hope to provide is a sufficient introduction to this new way of thinking about the human to show that it has the potential to make significant contributions to the quality of community life in the Church. My own initial experience of using the theory to manage my reactivity was both calming and fruitful. And, it continues to be so, whenever I use what I have learned.

Triangles, the Triune Brain and the Trinity

One of the major benefits of "thinking emotional systems" is that it offers an "antidote" to polarization and blame. Bowen studied the work of Jack Calhoun at National Institute of Health (NIH) on scapegoating in rats, and like Rene Girard he saw how scapegoating serves to "bind anxiety." Thinking emotional systems also provides a new basic hypothesis about the nature of mental illness; –i.e. mental illness is seen as a dysfunction of that part of the human that is shared with lower life. Using the research of Paul Mc Lean on the triune brain Bowen Theory redefines the concept *emotional* as synonymous with the instinctive life force that governs automatic behavior in all living things. It does not see a dichotomy between thinking and feeling, but sees that our feelings can either fuel or flood our thinking. Our emotions can either serve or sabotage our principles.

Most psychological theories tend to focus on the individual and what goes on inside of the individual. One of the key concepts in Bowen Theory is that of the *triangle*. It looks at individuals not in terms of individual psychodynamics and types of psychopathology, but in terms of the nuclear family emotional system and levels of differentiation. Though there is nothing within the Bowen theory that contradicts a Catholic anthropology, many of those who use the theory are materialists. I however made an immediate, analogous connection between "thinking triangles' and the Trinity.

Triangles are ubiquitous not only in life but also in theory. The theory states that the triangle, a three-person emotional configuration, is the molecule or basic building block of any emotional system, whether it is in the family or any other group. The triangle is the smallest stable relationship system. A two-person system may be stable as long as it is calm, but when anxiety increases, it immediately involves the most vulnerable other person to become a triangle. When tension in the triangle is too great for the threesome, it involves others to become a series of interlocking triangles. Gossip, rumor- mongering and making insinuations are among the numerous well-known moves in which outsiders in triangles seek to form togetherness. In the original triangle of two parents and a child, symptoms can show up in either of the spouses, in the marriage or in one of the children. In intense triangulation, one needs to work towards becoming emotionally calmer, and to get into the observing mode, so as to be able to think a little more objectively. These same patterns can occur in any human system, though with less intensity than in the nuclear family.

Anxiety can be defined as the response of an organism to threat, real or imagined. *Acute anxiety* generally occurs in response to real threats and is experienced as time-limited (fear of *what is* present.) *Basic anxiety* is my term for an anxiety that is deeper than the psychological. Fulton Sheen writes in *Peace of Soul* (p.16-18) that this type of deep anxiety is rooted in the nature of the human being and the "double law of gravitation, one pulling him to earth, where he has his time of trial, and the other pulling him to God, where he has his happiness. The anxiety underlying all modern anxieties arises from someone trying to be himself without God, or from trying to get beyond himself without God." This is a fear of *what we are,* dependent creatures, not the Creator. *Chronic anxiety* generally occurs in response to imagined threats and is not experienced as time-limited. This anxiety is relational, a fear that I cannot be both my own self and be connected to important others. This is a fear of *what might be* or of *can I be myself.*

Emotional reactivity and *anxiety* are processes that are not easily distinguished from each other and so the terms are used interchangeably in Bowen Theory. The distinction between "activity" and "reactivity" is important. Many seemingly inactive, low response people are called "non-reactive" when, in fact, their inactivity is a way of managing a high level of reactivity.

"Differentiation of self is one of two principal variables or processes defined by family systems theory to explain level of functioning. The other variable is *chronic anxiety.* The lower a person's level of differentiation, the less his adaptiveness to stress. The higher the level of chronic anxiety in a relationship system, the greater the strain on people's adaptive capabilities." (Michael Kerr, *Family Evaluation,* p. 112)

We can "bind" or cover over our anxiety rather than naming and facing the anxiety with both individual mechanisms or with relationship patterns within emotional systems. The individual mechanisms include a long list including of ways of relating to people and to things and to ourselves. Some examples include idealization and romanticism of people, places and activities; hoarding or overspending money; overeating and undereating;

preoccupation with physical health and physical symptoms; sexual acting-out such as the increased use of pornography; undervaluing self or others; "beliefs" & "principles" when they are part of pseudo-self and used as an anxiety binder; and the most common mechanism - scapegoating (justify/blame).

Bowen described five mechanisms or relationship patterns within an emotional system that can be used to "bind" anxiety: Distance; Conflict (blaming and posturing); Triangulation (dysfunctional child); Reciprocal Functioning (adapting to preserve relationship harmony; dysfunctional spouse); Cut-off. In her book, *Extraordinary Relationships,* Roberta Gilbert points out that these relationship patterns are the immature or anxious ways that we manage the tension/anxiety of balancing the biological forces of "togetherness" and "differentiation". "Since trying to make a self out of a relationship cannot work, the attempt itself creates a certain amount of anxiety. In order to manage that anxiety, partners begin to posture themselves in recognizable ways, and certain well-known relationship patterns form. These patterns form to 'solve' the problem of relationship anxiety. The basic problem, emotional immaturity, does not get addressed" (p. 41).

In his Apostolic Exhortation, *Familiaris Consortio,* St. John Paul II wrote, "The relationships between members of the family community are inspired and guided by the law of 'free-giving.' By respecting and fostering personal dignity in each and every one as the only basis for value, this free giving takes the form of *heartfelt acceptance, encounter and dialogue, disinterested acceptance, generous service and deep solidarity.*" These virtues or principles seem to me to be ways to face our relational anxiety and replace the automatic relational mechanisms that simply bind anxiety. Encounter and dialogue need to be a way of living. We need to learn how not to distance ourselves from each other. Heartfelt acceptance can replace conflict and blame. Disinterested availability rather than triangulation can be fostered. And, generous service can be cultivated instead of reciprocal functioning. These can become a way of living in faith. A deep solidarity instead of cut-off will promote relational hope. This is self-gift that follows from self-knowledge and self-acceptance. This also is a reflection of the Three in One Love that is the Trinity.

Going a Different Way

"Focus on self, an awareness of the emotional processes in the family, and the ability to not be governed by anxiety and emotional reactivity are all components of a long-term effort to increase one's level of differentiation." *Family Evaluation,* Michael E. Kerr and Murray Bowen, 1988. (p. 79)

Bowen Theory – or natural family systems theory- is based neither on prescribing techniques nor providing tools, but on helping the therapist think systems and promote that same thinking in the client. At the end of that 1990 seminar on Bowen Theory in Austin, I approached Rabbi Friedman about studying in his training program. I wanted to learn more about how to go this different way of thinking about the human. There was a problem. The Center for Family Emotional Process was only for ordained clergy. Friedman did agree to offer a postgraduate seminar in Austin beginning in January 1992. For the next four years I was able to participate in that program that was not limited to clergy, though I was the only psychologist who participated. Current postgraduate programs in Bowen Theory, also attract more clergy than psychologists. Bowen theory can be used not only by mental health professionals, but also any interested seminary formator. And, it is important to note that Friedman wrote his first book's *Generation to Generation: Family Process in Church and Synagogue* for clergy.

"Going a different way" was how Friedman talked about thinking family emotional systems or Bowen Family Systems theory. Some of the shifts in moving from more traditional relationship psychology to thinking Bowen theory include a focus on strength not pathology; focus on responsibilities not rights; a focus on relationship patterns rooted in family emotional processes. It is more a science than a social science; and, it is a "systems thinking" that is rooted in biology, not mathematics. In my work as a Bowen Family Systems *coach*, I work collaboratively adult to adult; and, know that the real work will not happen in the session but in everyday life. The key shift I experienced as a Bowen coach was keeping my focus on managing my own reactivity and anxiety rather than focusing on the anxiety of clients or directees. My essential "continuing education" is that of working on my own differentiation of self, my ability to be less anxious and more present in each and every moment.

Roberta Gilbert now has a postgraduate program for clergy at the Center for the Study of Human Systems. She has written a series of books to go with each year of the program. The books are a great introduction to thinking family emotional processes. It is good to begin with the basics: *The Eight Concepts of Bowen Theory*. Thinking through the eight inter-linking concepts (Differentiation of Self; Triangles; Nuclear Family Emotional Process; Family Projection Process; Transmission over Multiple Generations; Emotional Cut-off; Sibling Position; and, Emotional Process in Society) is Gilbert's "go to" for how to "think systems."

I learned from Bowen's successor as director of the Georgetown Center, Dr. Michael Kerr, to always look for the reciprocal functioning: This is about seeing relational processes as interactively achieved - not my fault, not your fault but what we both contribute to the "dance". I find this to be key in avoiding polarization and blame. And, find a parallel in the concluding verses of Psalm 84 that proclaim that "God cannot refuse any good to those who walk without blame."

To be a spiritual husband and spiritual father, a man has to have a clear sense of his identity so that he can be faithful. To have achieved that clarity from the perspective of Bowen Theory would be to work on differentiation of self, on one's capacity to be both self-regulating and self-defining, to be affectively mature. The "emotional neutrality" achieved by this effort is not unlike Ignatian "active indifference" or what St. Ignatius Loyola calls "The Principle and Foundation" for each human being. Both help an individual to know but not be defined by feelings and desires. A young man who has transitory same sex attraction or a young priest who "falls in love" both need help to not let those feelings be how they identify themselves, or to dictate choices based on emotions and instead of choices grounded first in living principles.

Seen from a family systems perspective, same sex attraction - like any other emotional, physical or social symptom - would be seen as reflecting the multigenerational transmission of anxiety and immaturity. A systems coach would not focus on why, or etiology, but on what the person is thinking and how they think about themselves. And, the coach would see the symptom not as explanatory but as simply phenomenological. How, what, when, with whom, where are the questions asked so as to observe and be curious about in Bowen coaching/mentoring. Beginning with differentiation of self, a systems coach would want to hear how the person defines themselves, what triangles are in play and where the individual is in the triangles. Using a family diagram (See Appendix II, p. 473), a systems coach would invite the individual to look at the nuclear family emotional processes as well as the family projection process. Identifying emotional cut-offs and exploring sibling position through the generations helps to get a broader focus. And, today I want to note that transitory same sex attraction and our understanding of it is greatly influenced by emotional processes in society.

St. Francis de Sales wrote that "we must not concern ourselves with what we feel or do not feel, since the greater part of our feelings and satisfactions are only the movements of self-love" (*The Art of Loving God,* p.22). Similarly, a systems coach would help a young man see and accept that his feelings are real, but they are not the facts of his life. As I say regularly, "Feelings are like little children, we need to pay attention to them but not put them in charge." Bowen Theory says that we want to make sure that it is our intellectual guidance system (our principles) not our emotional guidance systems (our feelings and emotions) that is leading us.

In his book, *Putting on the Heart of Christ – How the Spiritual Exercises Invite Us to A Virtuous Life*, Gerald Fagin, builds on the insights of *virtue ethics;* "that the real question of ethics is not "What should I do?" but rather "Who should I become?" (p. xvi). And though we begin by observing what we feel and what we should do, we want to be able to and help others to answer the three key questions of virtue ethics as articulated by Alasdair MacIntyre and quoted by Fagin (p. 9) - "Who am I? ; Who ought I become?; and, How am I to get there?

St. John Paul II's "Theology of the Body makes clear that men with a strong masculine identity want to be both "a provider and a protector." In the Epilogue that Bowen wrote for *Family Evaluation,* his description of a family leader is a good template for answering the question of "Whom do I want to be?"

> Operationally, ideal family treatment begins when one can find a family leader with the courage to define self, who is as invested in the welfare of the family as in self, who is neither angry nor dogmatic, whose energy goes to changing self rather than telling others what they should do, who can know and respect the multiple opinions of others, who can modify self in response to the strengths of the group, and who is not influenced by the irresponsible opinions of others. When one family member moves toward "differentiation," the family symptoms disappear. A family leader is beyond the popular notion of *power.* A responsible family leader automatically generates mature leadership qualities in other family members who are to follow (p. 342-343).

When Bowen was hospitalized towards the end of his life, he was given a copy of the famous Prayer of St. Francis of Assisi:

> Lord make me an instrument of your peace.
> Where there is hatred, let me sow love.
> Where there is injury, pardon.
> Where there is doubt, faith.
> Where there is despair, hope.
> Where there is darkness, light.
> Where there is sadness, joy.
> O Divine Master,
> grant that I may not so much seek to be consoled as to console;

to be understood as to understand;

to be loved as to love.

For it is in giving that we receive;

it is in pardoning that we are pardoned;

and it is in dying that we are born to eternal life.

Bowen remarked that he thought it was a good summary of working on differentiation of self. The goal of differentiation of self is to continue to develop the capacity to be the person one wants to be, regardless of sabotage by self or others.

"If you have hope, this will make you cheerful. Do not give up if trials come; keep on praying." (Romans 12:12, Jerusalem Bible)

In the face of the present crisis there is a real danger of becoming discouraged, disillusioned, disappointed and even to despair. "Desolation is now living Dissed," a title of one of the chapter's in Tetlow's *Always Discerning,* identifies a reality that we are living with in the present moment. In the face of this dangerous sign of our times, it is imperative that we have hope, that we do not give up and we keep praying. This present crisis is also an opportunity to exercise faith and to participate in tasting and receiving in the Father's sovereign providential care as Lord of history. The Church needs strong, mature male leaders who have both clarity of mind and emotional generosity. The Church needs men who can serve as mature spiritual husbands and fathers as they lead parish families.

St. Augustine of Hippo names the Trinity as the Lover, the Beloved and the Love (as relational ways of being between them). Michael Downey, in writing about Catherine La Cugna's *grammar* of the Trinity, names a grammar of gift that speaks of God as Giver, Given, Gift/ing. Giving is relational. The grammar of the Trinity names God and all reality as personal, as *being toward* another, and *for* the other, in relation.

Again, we remember that love is the fundamental and innate vocation of every human being. Made in the image of God that is a Trinity - a communion of love - human beings are created with the capacity and responsibility to live in "love and communion." Our God is Holy and we must be holy as well. Our lives are lived in relationship with others and our vocations call us to live with each other in good and holy relationships. Our daily experience tells us that it is no easy task. Recognizing that "grace builds on and perfects nature," it is my hope that the deeply Trinitarian wisdom found in the Examen Prayer through Ignatian Spirituality, and the clarity about human relationship patterns explicated in Family Systems

Theory (Bowen Theory) can help all of us to grow in our capacity to live in "love and communion."

Prayer

This, then, is what I pray, kneeling before the Father, from whom every family, whether spiritual or natural, takes its name:

Out of God's infinite glory, may God give you the power through the Holy Spirit for your hidden self to grow strong, so that Christ may live in your heart through faith, and then, planted in love and built on love, you will with all the saints have strength to grasp the breadth and the length, the height and the depth, until, knowing the love of Christ, which is beyond all knowledge, you are filled with the utter fullness of God.

Glory be to God whose power, working in us can do infinitely more than we can ask or imagine; glory be to God from generation to generation in the Church and in Christ Jesus for ever and ever. Amen.

- Ephesians 3: 14 – 21 (The Jerusalem Bible)

Practicum Reflection Questions for Formators

1. What living principles from the teachings and tradition of the Church are most important to you in your sense of identity?

2. In your interior life of reflection and prayer what *helps* and what *hinders* your awareness of when your feelings are flooding your thinking? what *helps or hinders* knowing when your emotions are serving and not sabotaging the major living principles that you desire to live?

3. How do you experience anxiety – acute (fear of what is); basic (fear of what we are, our radical dependence); and, chronic (fear that I cannot be both my own self and be connected to important others)? As you look back at the individual and relational ways of "binding anxiety", can you identify your own ways of not dealing with, but covering over, your chronic anxiety/emotional reactivity?

4. In your interior life of reflection and prayer how do you stay mindful of "where you are going" before you start thinking of "with whom"?

5. What is your experience of God's love like in the daily practice of the Examen Prayer? Do you have the courage to accept His loving acceptance of your being? Can you distinguish between that loving acceptance, and approval or disapproval of your behaviors?

Suggested Resources

1. The work of **Rabbi Edwin Friedman** is a primary resource for understanding his concept of "leadership through differentiation of self. He did not get to finish *A Failure of Nerve: Leadership in the Age of the Quick Fix* but it was published posthumously. However, the DVD "Reinventing Leadership" (DVD) that his editors at Guilford Press asked him to do in 1997 is an excellent overview of his leadership concept. The only caveat is that he made no mention of Bowen Theory. Unfortunate, since the differentiation of self is the cornerstone concept of Bowen Theory. And to understand Friedman's leadership concept, one needs a basic understanding of Bowen Family Systems Theory. His 1990 book, *Friedman's Fables,* makes explicit links to Bowen Theory. It also comes with a discussion guide that gives the moral for each fable and ten discussion questions.

2. *Generation to Generation.* New York: The Guilford Press, 1985.

3. "Reinventing Leadership" (DVD). New York: The Guilford Press, 1997.

4. Roberta Gilbert, MD, was a psychoanalytically trained psychiatrist who turned to Bowen Theory. She is currently offering training for clergy in Bowen Theory through the Center for the Study of Human Systems, www.hsystems.org. For that program she has written a series of books, *The Eight Concepts of Bowen Theory* (Leading Systems, 2004, 2006); *Extraordinary Leadership* (2006), and *The Cornerstone Concept – In Leadership, In Life* (2008).

5. **Herbert Alphonso, SJ** identifies the "personal vocation" which is a very significant contribution to understanding vocation. Beyond that seminal contribution, the appendix of *Discovering your personal vocation: The search for meaning through the Spiritual Exercises* (Paulist Press, 2001) makes a clear and crucial distinction between "approval" (an unconditional attitude towards the being of a person) and "approval" (a judgment about the behavior of a person). I have found this to be extraordinarily helpful for myself and for those I work with in counseling. The book is based on the use of the Examen Prayer, and it assists greatly in opening the

human heart to receiving a particular personal name by listening interiorly to Trinitarian love.

References

Alphonso, H. *Discovering your personal vocation: The search for meaning through the Spiritual Exercises.* Paulist Press, 2001.

Bowen, M. *Family Therapy in Clinical Practice.* New York: Jason Aronson, 1985, 1983, 1978.

Downey, M., *Altogether Gift: A Trinitarian Spirituality.* Orbis Books, 2000.

Erickson, E. *The Life Cycle Completed.* New York: W.W. Norton, 1982.

De Sales F. *The Art of Loving God: Simple Virtues for the Christian Life,* 2004.

Fagin, G., *Putting on the Heart of Christ,* Loyola Press (2010).

Fowler, J. *Becoming Adult, Becoming Christian.*

Friedman, E.H. *A Failure of Nerve: Leadership in the Age of the Quick Fix.* The Edwin H. Friedman Estate/Trust, 1999.

—————. *Friedman's Fables.* New York: The Guilford Press, 1990.

—————. *Generation to Generation.* New York: The Guilford Press, 1985.

—————. "Reinventing Leadership" (DVD). New York: The Guilford Press, 1997.

Gilbert, R. *The Eight Concepts of Bowen Theory.* 2004, 2006.

————. *Extraordinary Leadership.* Leading Systems Press, 2006.

————. Center for the Study of Human Systems, www.hsystems.org

Hillman, J., and Ventura, M. *We've Had a Hundred Years of Psychotherapy – And the World's Getting Worse.* Harper Collins, 1993.

John Paul II, Apostolic Exhortation *Familiaras Consortio.* (November 22, 1981)

Keen, S. *The Passionate Life.* San Francisco: Harper & Row. 1983.

Kegan, R. *In Over our Heads – The Mental Demands of Modern Life.* Harvard University Press, 1994.

Kerr, M., and M. Bowen. *Family Evaluation.* New York: W.W. Norton, 1988.

Low, B. *Why Sex Matters,* Princeton, NJ: Princeton University Press, 2000.

Norris, K. *Dakota: A spiritual geography.* New York: Houghton Mifflin, 1993.

Ratzinger, J. (Pope Benedict XVI). *Jesus of Nazareth.* Volume 1. New York: Doubleday, 2007.

Reiff, P. *The Triumph of the Therapeutic: Uses of Faith after Freud.* Chicago: The University of Chicago Press, 1966.

Rolheiser, R. *The Holy Longing.* New York: Doubleday, 1999.

Sheen, F.J. *Peace of Soul*. Ligouri, MS: Triumph Books, 1996. (1949)

Tetlow, J.A., *Always Discerning*. Chicago, Loyola Press, 2016.

A Foundational Christology. Review of Ignatian Spirituality XXXIV, i/2003/No. 102 *Choosing Christ in the World: Directing the Spiritual Exercises of St. Ignatius Loyola According to Annotations Eighteen and Nineteen*. St. Louis, MO: Institute of Jesuit Sources,1989.

Chapter Fourteen

STRIVING FOR AFFECTIVE MATURITY AND AUTHENTIC PEACE OF SOUL: THE ROLE OF DEEP FORGIVENESS AND SECURE ATTACHMENT

Dr. Peter Martin, Psy.D.

Dr. Peter Martin, a licensed psychologist, is the Internship Director of Integrated Training and Formation at Catholic Social Services (CSS) of Southern Nebraska, an APA-accredited site where he is responsible for the psychological and faith-integrated formation of pre-doctoral psychology interns and other mental health professionals. In 2008, through CSS, he started and currently heads a clinical outreach site at the Newman Center at the University of Nebraska-Lincoln where he provides therapy to university students and consultation services to the priests, FOCUS missionaries and other staff. He provided growth counseling services from 2012-2013 to seminarians at the Institute for Priestly Formation summer program in Omaha, Nebraska. He served on the Executive Board of the Catholic Psychotherapy Association from 2013 to 2016. He has served on the Board of Witness to Love: Marriage Preparation Renewal Ministry since 2015. His areas of interest include supervising therapists in faith-integrated treatments of psychological disorders, in practicing trauma-informed therapy, Forgiveness Therapy, treating "implicit God image" problems and psychological obstacles to authentic spiritual encounters with God and giving and receiving love, in studying the psychology of belief and unbelief, and in the social scientific understanding of religious conversion. He developed an assessment procedure called the Holy Trinity and Mary Projective (HTMP) drawings, which is currently being used at his site in conjunction with other attachment-focused instruments to evaluate both the psychological and spiritual functioning of current and future diocesan and religious seminarians.

The great principle of the interior life is the peace of the soul, and it must be preserved with such care that the moment it is attacked all else must be put aside and every effort made to try and regain this holy peace, just as, in an outbreak of fire, everything else is neglected to hasten to extinguish the flames."[1]

---

[1] Jean Pierre de Caussade, *Abandonment to Divine Providence: With Letters of Father de Caussade on the Practice of Self-Abandonment*, Third English Edition (San Francisco: Ignatius Press,

Fully integrated spiritual husbands and fathers are veritable men of peace. A deep spiritual interiority and intimacy with God help to soothe and calm elevated agitation in their hearts. Through curious and compassionate psychological introspection of their mental and emotional[2] life, they deepen and broaden authentic self-knowledge as secure and affectively mature men. They wisely protect the grace-filled inner harmony of seasoned spiritual and psychological serenity and go to great lengths to maintain it. This inner stillness ideally manifests in their behavioral choices and is observable by others who are likely drawn to these men of peace as trustworthy fathers who foster imitation and Christian discipleship. Indeed, their priestly example of this serenity, flowing interiorly from God and through them to others beautifully demonstrates their witness of Christ, the Prince of Peace.

On the contrary, a persistently compromised internal peace greatly impairs living out the mission of these spiritual husbands and fathers. It places extra and undue burdens, heavy loads on many of the genuinely unshakable, inherent crosses endemic to their vocation. The priest can experience this internal disquiet as rather debilitating. It makes the development of husbandly and fatherly character strengths exceedingly challenging. To revisit de Caussade:

> One of the principal reasons why certain souls do not advance is because the devil continually throws them into a state of uneasiness, perplexity and anxiety, which makes them *incapable* of applying themselves seriously, quietly and with constancy to the practice of virtue.[3]

Indeed, a man can carry a great weight (i.e., disquiet) over a short distance, but over the span of a lengthy service—a lifetime devoted to living out his call to serve the Lord and his people—a lighter, wieldier cross is undoubtedly a more welcome "companion" on the road to a virtuous priesthood (see Matt 11: 25-30).

With peace of soul as a solid foundation for priestly efforts and as a focal point of this

---

2011), Letter XIII.

[2] "Most theories of emotion share some common themes. One is that emotion involves complex layers of processes that are in constant interaction with the environment. At a minimum, these interactions involve cognitive processes (such as appraisal or evaluation of meaning) and physical changes (such as endocrine, autonomic, and cardiovascular changes), which may reveal some repeated patterns over time." Daniel J. Siegel, *The Developing Mind: How Relationships and the Brain Interact to Shape Who We Are* (New York: The Guilford Press, 2012), 148.

[3] de Caussade, *Abandonment to Divine* Providence, Letter XIII, Emphasis added.

chapter, a discussion will ensue with respect to two major ways of maintaining a sustained internal peace: Attachment security in close relationships and interpersonal forgiveness. First, the following sections will detail struggles with connecting in close relationships, including secure and insecure patterns of attachment in adulthood and how emotional security is critical for authentic serenity in human formation. Then after a brief consideration of various problems associated with cultivated anger, this study will discuss some of the anger-reducing and life-giving benefits of forgiveness, including relevant research outcomes and common interventions found in therapy research promoting forgiveness. Subsequently, there is a section devoted to empirical research on associations between attachment patterns (secure and insecure) and therapy interventions promoting forgiveness research. Finally, a few considerations will be made on relevant transitory same sex attraction issues. Overall, attachment security and forgiveness are conceptualized as critical means to assisting the priest, in his peaceful instrumental service, in transforming and generating a refreshing newness of all things in Christ.

Continuum of Connectedness

Close, 2-person (dyadic) interpersonal relationships present a particularly complex set of challenges on the journey toward enduring peace. Styles of relating to the other valued individual vary widely, and some persons are emotionally and implicitly (i.e., nonconsciously) postured toward closeness whereas others prefer much more distance. To explain, rather than being understood as having no overlap, patterns of extreme interpersonal *independence* and *dependence* can be understood as insecure opposites on a continuum. On one end is the pseudo-secure, yet excessively and habitually independent individual who resists leaning on others for emotional support. In his mind, he is an island unto himself, and all humans should have and stay mostly on their respective islands as well. Overlapping with this style of relating in natural, horizontal human relationships, such persons are more likely to keep God and other spiritual persons "at arm's distance" as well.

At the opposite pole is the individual who implicitly and insecurely leans toward excessive dependence on others and questions his own ability to handle even basic life challenges without the advice and emotional reassurance of another. For this man, his spiritual relationships can also take on a "clingy" flavor, relentlessly petitioning the Lord in a demanding way. Whereas one type of insecure individual finds solace in utter autonomy and considers interdependence as too intimate or encroaching, the extremely dependent person cannot fathom such an approach to relationships. Independence feels foreign and scary—even interdependence seems too distant and untenable. His often deeply felt insecurity instead has convinced him that what others call healthy autonomy is in fact a veiled form of isolation and seclusion.

Neither the extremely independent nor extremely dependent individual has learned to strike the emotional balance that instinctively places one foot firmly on the side of autonomy and plants the other foot equally firm on the side of interpersonal connectedness.[4] Unfortunately, the man of independence emphasizes autonomy to the exclusion of connectedness—a stark contrast to the man of dependence who emphasizes connection to the exclusion of autonomy. Both may intellectually think and emotionally trust their style of relating to be the best approach to interpersonal relationships, and if so, both—from a Christian theological and psychological standpoint—are unfortunately mistaken. Neither has struck the critical, golden mean of secure intimacy to the detriment of their human formation and a corresponding abiding personal and interpersonal peace.

Patterns of Attaching

Secure Attachment

To further explain, a well-researched way of understanding a person's experiences in close, dyadic relationships is through a model known as attachment theory. The founder of attachment theory, John Bowlby, viewed humans, in particular when experiencing distress or significant need (which activates the "attachment system"), as naturally inclined to seek out and strive for proximity those individuals who were comforting and soothing.[5] The term "attachment" communicates that human persons form strong emotional bonds with others who provide "protection, comfort, and support."[6] The attachment system itself is a

---

[4] George Lockwood and Poul Perris, "A New Look at Core Emotional Needs," in *The Wiley-Blackwell Handbook of Schema Therapy: Theory, Research, and Practice*, Ed. Michiel van Vreeswijk, Jenny Broersen, and Marjon Nadort (Oxford: John Wiley & Sons, Ltd, 2012), 61. The authors indicate that connection and autonomy are two broad categories commonly found in large research-based analytic models considering core human emotional needs. Both connection and autonomy thus seem to be necessary in discussions considering authentic human formation of priests.

[5] Mario Mikulincer and Phillip R. Shaver, "Boosting Attachment Security to Promote Mental Health, Prosocial Values, and Inter-Group Tolerance." *Psychological Inquiry* 18, no. 3 (2007), 140.

[6] Mario Mikulincer, Phillip R. Shaver, Yael Sapir-Lavid, and Neta Avihou-Kanza, "What's Inside the Minds of Securely and Insecurely Attached People? The Secure-Base Script and its Associations with Attachment-Style Dimensions." *Journal of Personality and Social Psychology* 97, no. 4 (2009),

mechanism of emotional regulation[7] with a set goal of establishing sustained care and protection to bring about felt safety and security.[8] This is the primary attachment strategy selected by securely attached individuals, in contrast to the 2 primary insecure patterns of attaching, described later.[9] Once the distress is sufficiently remedied, the soothed and secure individual ends proximity-seeking behaviors and can calmly pursue other non-attachment activity.[10] Interpersonal efforts can now be more focused on others, i.e., more love-based. Successful efforts to gain proximity to an attachment figure and attain "felt security"—not merely thinking that one is secure—are important for the maintenance and promotion of mental health, psychological growth and healthy relationships.[11] These experiences of, ideally, initial experienced distress and subsequent dyadic relational soothing start to "soak in" and shape the way the developing person implicitly (i.e., unconsciously) perceives self and others.

The developing mind makes generalized internal representations from these repeated, close relationship experiences with attachment figures and encodes them in the brain, forming the foundation of "mental models" which are the basic components of implicit memory.[12] These mental models assist in interpreting present situations and anticipating future experiences more readily and rapidly, and if activated, the individual subjectively experiences them, even if distorted, as simply the present reality.[13] Influencing more than a

---

615.

[7] Mario Mikulincer and Phillip R. Shaver. *Attachment in Adulthood: Structure, Dynamics, and Change.* 2nd ed. (New York: The Guilford Press, 2016), 188.

[8] Mario Mikulincer and Phillip R. Shaver, "Adult Attachment Orientations and Relationship Processes." *Journal of Family Theory & Review* 4, no. 4 (2012), 260. Intellectual security or merely thinking one is secure is likely insufficient for soothing.

[9] A fourth classification of attachment (which will not be discussed in this chapter), known as Disorganized or Unresolved, often has elements of both avoidant and anxious attachment. Frequently, this category includes individuals who have unresolved trauma histories. Psychotherapy with a specialist trained in working with trauma, dissociation, and/or attachment insecurity is generally recommended for these individuals who commonly have fearful emotional reactions to their attachment figures.

[10] Mikulincer and Shaver, "Boosting Attachment Security," 140.

[11] Mikulincer and Shaver, "Boosting Attachment Security," 140.

[12] Daniel J. Siegel, *The Developing Mind: How Relationships and the Brain Interact to Shape Who We Are.* 2nd ed. (New York: The Guilford Press, 2012), 52.

[13] Siegel, *The Developing Mind*, 55.

few situations, the mental models result in a style or orientation of attaching to others,[14] a context-dependent and learned or developed[15] habitual type of coping or responding to a real or perceived threat. Even explicit memories of the past are filtered through these more implicit mental models, which, for good or ill, cast their "shadows" on one's recollections of earlier relationship experiences.[16] As will be shown later, even if undesired by a younger or older priest, an unprocessed and activated insecure mental model can elevate worries, exacerbate unhealthy coping, and influence the man to make decisions based more on fear rather than love.

Strongly influenced by implicit mental models of close relationships, the attachment-oriented method to achieving emotional security (i.e., regularly seeking soothing from another) is a strategy used throughout the lifespan: Distressed children seek their mothers, fathers and/or caregivers; distressed adults do likewise, though they also may search for a mentor, romantic partner or spiritual attachment figure such as a saint, an angel, or a divine Person of the Trinity. In contrast to childhood, in adulthood the main strategy to attain felt security does not always include physical nearness-seeking behaviors. Individuals can regulate personal distress by simply imagining comforting persons who reliably cared for them, though, if this effort fails to downregulate one's discomfort, even secure adults will often seek physical proximity to an attachment figure for consolation.[17]

Those who are securely attached generally benefit greatly from this patterned approach to remedying distress. When encountering difficulty, the secure person can effectively engage in problem planning and solving, place experiences of desolation in perspective and in context, rally support from others to assist in problem solving or reducing stressful outcomes, develop self-soothing skills, and focus on helpful alternatives.[18]

On a related note, secure priests can more effectively and with less effort authentically live out the internal and external demands of their vocation. They can experience, own, and

---

[14] Mikulincer and Shaver, "Adult Attachment Orientations," 261.

[15] Davis, E. B., Granqvist, P., & Sharp, C., "Theistic Relational Spirituality: Development, Dynamics, Health, and Transformation." *Psychology of Religion and Spirituality* (2018), 7.

[16] Siegel, *The Developing Mind*, 67.

[17] Mikulincer and Shaver, "Boosting Attachment Security," 141.

[18] Mikulincer and Shaver, *Attachment in Adulthood*, 188-189. Secure individuals "can also reappraise situations, construe events in relatively benign terms, symbolically transform threats into challenges, maintain an optimistic sense of self-efficacy, and attribute undesirable events to controllable, temporary, or context-dependent causes." Mikulincer and Shaver, *Attachment in Adulthood*, 189.

communicate emotional experience without getting overwhelmed and with few distortions and can calm themselves autonomously, yet are able to seek support as needed.[19] Secure priests are not only better at maintaining general internal peace, but are more adept at utilizing attachment figures as safe havens (for soothing and comfort) and secure bases (to assist in exploring the external world and internal experiences) and have greater access to a richer "secure-base script"[20] that is something like the following: "If I encounter an obstacle and/or become distressed, I can approach a significant other for help; he or she is likely to be available and supportive; I will experience relief and comfort as a result of proximity to this person; I can then return to other activities."[21] The notion of the utterly independent, yet authentically peaceful priest is thus greatly called into question. This "script" highlights the great need to develop secure mentor relationships and support especially young priests to handle the particularly challenging first few years of their presbyterate as well as later transitional periods.

Insecure Attachment

However, for the insecure many, these attachment-related bids for soothing through a supportive other are generally unsuccessful, thus compromising their overall level of internal peace. As a result, the effects of ongoing dyadic attachment insecurity grab them, begin to strengthen and eventually take on a firm and habitual internal disposition. For a future spiritual husband and father, this developed insecure pattern presents major obstructions to obtaining a critical mass of affective maturity in adulthood and to, as we will see, deep forgiveness. Though rooted in one's particular attachment history, this struggle fashions a considerable obstacle to securing sustained psychological and spiritual tranquility.

When attachment figures are unreliable for protection and comfort, one's sense of security is compromised. Consequently, instead of seeking emotional regulation (i.e., ways to manage and calm emotional experience) via proximity to these attachment figures the developing person copes by enlisting insecure *secondary attachment strategies* that include the 2 primary dimensions of attachment-related anxiety and avoidance.[22] In brief, at one extreme are the preoccupied (anxious) attachments, which include excessive anxiety and

---

[19] Mikulincer and Shaver, *Attachment in Adulthood*, 224.

[20] Mikulincer et al. "What's Inside the Minds," 630.

[21] Mikulincer and Shaver, *Attachment in Adulthood*, 189.

[22] Mikulincer and Shaver, "Boosting Attachment Security," 141.

even chaotic intrusions of past memories into current experiences; and at the other extreme are the dismissing (avoidant) attachments, which restrict emotional experience.[23] Both attachment strategies have cognitive and emotional biases that engender excessive dependence (anxious) or excessive autonomy (avoidant), and influence the style of conflict resolution, patterns of interpersonal communication, and thoughts, feelings, and behaviors in close relationships.[24] The avoidant and anxious patterns of attachment will each be addressed in turn.

The *avoidantly attached* individual defensively inhibits emotions such as fear, anxiety, sadness and shame because they can be perceived as emotional examples of weakness or vulnerability that contradict this person's self-image as being strong and independent.[25] An unconscious mental script triggers the individual's need to block or stuff these emotions or disconnect them from the painful emotional consequences on their experiences and behaviors.[26] Thus, avoidants "downplay threats and vulnerabilities, deny negative emotions, and suppress or repress negative memories."[27] Interpersonally, he is less likely than a secure individual to reflect on his own experiences and those of others, he may not be cognizant of how disconnected he is to others, and he is likely to engage in emotionally detached, analytic thinking.[28] Practically speaking, rather than seeing pastoral sensitivity and doctrinal firmness as a "package deal", the avoidant priest may instinctively devalue a particular parishioner's need to receive orthodox Catholic teaching in a warm and supportive way. Instead, this priest may harshly emphasize "truth over love" and unwittingly be ineffective in communicating Christ's message of agapic love in a manner that transforms this member of his flock.

Avoidants habitually downplay relationships, can struggle to recall detailed childhood interpersonal experiences, are less likely to notice the physiological changes associated with emotional experiences (e.g., desolation and consolation), have difficulty experiencing intimacy in close relationships, and their inner world "seems to function with independence as its banner."[29] They also work to "maintain behavioral independence and emotional

---

[23] Daniel J. Siegel, *The Developing Mind: How Relationships and the Brain Interact to Shape Who We Are*. 2nd ed. (New York: The Guilford Press, 2012), 145.

[24] Mikulincer and Shaver, "Adult Attachment Orientations," 262.

[25] Mikulincer and Shaver, *Attachment in Adulthood*, 190.

[26] Mikulincer and Shaver, *Attachment in Adulthood*, 190.

[27] Mikulincer and Shaver, *Attachment in Adulthood*, 225.

[28] Siegel, *The Developing Mind*, 120-121.

[29] Siegel, *The Developing Mind*, 143.

distance from partners."[30] It is no wonder that, from a psychotherapy standpoint, a primary treatment objective is to help avoidants on their journey away from isolation and toward the much more fulfilling goal of genuine intimacy.[31]

On the other end of the attachment insecurity spectrum are *anxiously attached* individuals who, like avoidants, also experience significantly less comfort in close dyadic relationships than those who are securely attached. Yet contrary to the avoidantly attached, anxious persons deeply desire closeness and are often preoccupied with it. Attachment anxiety indicates the individual's level of worry about a partner's consistency and availability to comfort during a time of distress.[32] While avoidants almost always struggle to rely on others, the anxiously attached struggle to believe they sometimes can rely *on themselves*.[33] Rather than self-identifying as strong and independent, anxious persons view themselves as helpless and incompetent and often amplify their distress to attachment support figures even though they doubt the latter's consistent availability and fear rejection.[34] Indeed, an outward display of "conspicuous insecurity has become the most reliable means for gaining the attention of unreliable others."[35] Nonetheless, this "heightening" (in contrast to the avoidant's "suppressing")[36] style of managing one's distress has its own set of problems.

The anxiously attached's conflicted, internal push-and-pull bond with the attachment figure may paradoxically lead to a preoccupation of the attachment figure, maximizing the anxious person's focus on the inconsistent relationship.[37] Consequently, they may be ambivalent about seeking support, exacerbating an internal wrestling match that leads them to *indirectly* express their needs for protection (e.g., magnified nonverbal communication of sadness without actually verbally asking for help) in order to decrease the probability of rejection.[38] For example, the anxiously attached priest may hint at his struggles to superiors who do not pick up on the magnitude of the real underlying, latent issues, which may

---

[30] Mikulincer & Shaver, "Boosting Attachment Security," p. 141.

[31] David J. Wallin, *Attachment in Psychotherapy* (New York: The Guilford Press, 2007), 211.

[32] Mikulincer et al. "What's Inside the Minds of Securely and Insecurely Attached People?" 616.

[33] Wallin, *Attachment in Psychotherapy*, 224.

[34] Mikulincer and Shaver, *Attachment in Adulthood*, 191.

[35] Wallin, *Attachment in Psychotherapy*, 225.

[36] Peter C. Costello, *Attachment-Based Psychotherapy. Helping Patients Develop Adaptive Capacities* (Washington, DC: American Psychological Association, 2013), p. 151.

[37] Siegel, *The Developing Mind*, 101.

[38] Mikulincer and Shaver, *Attachment in Adulthood*, 191.

include feeling unsafe, helpless, or abandoned. Thus his heightened distress lingers, remaining unresolved, and he stays emotionally dysregulated. The anxiety perpetuates in part because of his indirect style of expressing the deeper issues, which if communicated consistently could bring about real interpersonal soothing and authentic internal calm.

In contrast to avoidants, anxiously attached persons are more likely to focus attention on internal signals of insecurity and distress, serving to intensify and perpetuate the cycle of experienced distress and related negative rumination even after the threat passes.[39] Though personally contributing to this painful cycle, they often feel they are trapped in it or victims of it, and helpless to effectively break out of it.[40] They may struggle to emotionally self-soothe at all. Anxiously attached individuals catastrophize their assessments of events, instinctively and unconsciously magnify threating details of even minor challenges, sustain overly negative beliefs about their own capacity to cope with struggles, and ascribe threatening events to their own personal inadequacies and causes that are out of their own personal control.[41] They generally experience powerful emotions and desires to be loved and comforted, but if their intense fears of rejection are actualized through a breakup or loss, they are prone to overreact and deeply doubt their ability to recover.[42] One can imagine how painful the rejection experience might be for a priest with a general anxious attachment style after a snubbing by the parish council or multiple fruitless efforts to acquire needed assistance from a bishop or other respected priest.

In sharp contrast to avoidants who wall off and communicate few memories of their interpersonal past, the anxious individual has "leaky boundaries between past and present"[43] and the past can obfuscate and distort present experiences, most especially when in a state of distress. Indeed, their current thoughts and feelings can be dominated by intrusive affective worries of personal lovability and fears of another's availability to comfort and soothe,[44] often rooted in childhood experiences of limited emotional support from caregivers. As will be discussed later, this dynamic will greatly challenge the anxiously attached individual's ability to forgive. The painful rumination of the past injustice and memories of the offender frequently leak into their present awareness, plaguing their mental life and leaving precious little room for them to let go of the past and move on. Indeed,

---

[39] Mikulincer and Shaver, *Attachment in Adulthood*, 192.

[40] Mikulincer and Shaver, *Attachment in Adulthood*, 192.

[41] Mikulincer and Shaver, *Attachment in Adulthood*, 191.

[42] Mikulincer and Shaver, *Attachment in Adulthood*, 225.

[43] Siegel, *The Developing Mind*, 131.

[44] Siegel, *The Developing Mind*, 130-131.

these painfully charged, intrusive experiences of the anxiously attached might thwart even their initial steps on the forgiveness journey.

In summary, felt attachment security is an essential component of internal psychological peace. Attachment theory makes no claims that an individual—even one who is securely attached—can entirely avoid distress. Nor does it indicate that if a person is in a state of desolation, he can always transcend it independently. Instead, critical to human security is the implicit trust that the following if-then propositions will be met during a time of difficulty: "If I encounter an obstacle and/or become distressed, I can approach a significant other for help; he or she is likely to be available and supportive; I will experience relief and comfort as a result of proximity to this person; I can then return to other activities."[45] The corresponding spiritual implications of God as the ultimate attachment figure are profound. King David can bravely "walk through the valley of the shadow of death" without paralyzing fear of evil, because the Lord, as the exemplar attachment figure, accompanies and comforts him along the way (see Ps 23:4).[46] King David's likely implicit and secure trust in the divine Shepherd, a faith that rested deep in his heart, enabled him to tolerate distressing situations in which insecurely attached individuals would generally struggle. If one has developed a secure internal working model of close relationships and experiences this soothing outcome generally consistently throughout life, interpersonal relationships feel more reliable and less threatening than if one is avoidantly or anxiously attached: The world is mostly safe, support figures will comfort when invoked, and one can have rewarding relationships with others.[47]

Furthermore, the secure individual can more effectively explore the internal (i.e., intrapsychic and spiritually interior) and external world with a curious and compassionate stance that rests on a firm foundation of authentic internal peace and self-confidence. As we will see later, whereas insecurely (i.e., avoidant and anxious) attached persons may not view genuine and deep forgiveness as a sufficiently safe, reasonable and viable option, secure persons are more likely to take a different position. Indeed, secures are "experts" in seeking out others to provide felt safety and security,[48] and thus much better equipped to select the sometimes challenging and risky, yet life-giving path of letting go of resentments toward a perpetrator. Rather than stewing in anger or entertaining glorified revenge rituals for months or even years or decades, secure persons seem to have a greater capacity to

---

[45] Mikulincer and Shaver, "Boosting Attachment Security," 142.

[46] *The Holy Bible: Revised Standard Version* (New York: Collins, 1973).

[47] Mikulincer and Shaver, "Boosting Attachment Security," 142.

[48] Mikulincer et al. "What's Inside the Minds" 630.

steadfastly follow the path of deep forgiveness—one of the healthiest of all long-term methods of personally addressing an injustice—and effectively "move on" with life.

Anger: A Major Obstacle to Internal Peace

A key obstacle to moving on with life and to an enduring internal peace is toxic and sustained anger, most especially if it is deliberately cultivated. Satan commonly tempts us to cling to anger, to rule with and by it, as if it is a close friend or ally, or even perhaps a formidable weapon necessary for survival. Yet if resentment is not properly and sufficiently abandoned, in truth we soon begin to be ruled by it. It becomes our master and we its slaves. It soaks in, and eventually we "become" anger. The enticing voice of the Enemy fools us into trusting that anger makes us stronger and more competent to cope with unhealed wounds originating from earlier experiences of interpersonal injustice.[49]

Anger, from a conventional psychology standpoint, is a "hard" and secondary emotion. On the surface, its role is to protect us from re-experiencing the more "soft" and vulnerable, primary emotions like fear, helplessness, toxic shame, or the depths of loneliness. We may even trust that anger helps prevent us from re-wounding ourselves. Yet when the veil of anger is deliberately removed to see the wound beneath, one can see it as paradoxically a wolf in sheep's clothing on the journey of healing. Even with the best and most noble of intentions, anger generally perpetuates the pain, propagates more wounds, and unfortunately generalizes or trickles into numerous important areas in the priestly vocation such as one's parish life, family, and spiritual life.

Along with this unwelcome laundry list of problems is a very real and damaging set of responses to the pain and insecurity: maladaptive moral and behavioral coping. Not entirely unlike an addiction, anger distorts our view of self and other. We simply cannot think clearly when we experience cultivated anger. Consequently, through and with our anger, the Enemy can easily deceive us. He can convince us that our anger—even if prolonged, cultivated and intense—is thoroughly righteous and our corresponding sinful and unhealthy behavior is thoroughly justified. Unfortunately, righteous anger all too easily lapses into self-righteous anger. Anger that has turned into hatred, says St. Francis de Sales,

---

[49] There most certainly is a proper place for righteous anger. This includes even the extended and intense levels of it needed to survive, e.g., during the profound and horrific injustices experienced by Jews and other groups oppressed by Nazi Germany. There is definite value in this type of prolonged anger for strength to manage this and other gruesome contexts. This chapter is *not* about this kind of anger.

"is nourished by a thousand false pretexts; there never was an angry man who thought his anger unjust."[50] This is likely one reason why scripture prescribes resolving anger sooner than later: "Be angry but do not sin; do not let the sun set on your anger, and do not leave room for the devil" (Eph 4:26).

Forgiveness: A Life-Giving Remedy for Anger

The Strength and Wisdom of Forgiveness

A critical and thoroughly Christian way to resolve interpersonal anger is through forgiveness of the perpetrator. Forgiveness is central to Christ's mission of redemption. It is not a choice of the weak, but displays elements of the unwavering strength of the omnipotent and Fatherly Lord. As the *Catechism* puts it: "God is the *Father* Almighty . . . God reveals his fatherly omnipotence by the way he takes care of our needs; by the filial adoption that he gives us . . . finally by his infinite mercy, for he displays his power at its height by freely forgiving sins"[51] In forgiving sins, the Father's omnipotence, at its strongest, is on full display. In addition, genuine forgiveness is not a senseless option selected by the ignorant or the foolhardy, but instead reflects the infinite wisdom of the eternally omniscient God. The rationale for forgiveness includes a paradoxical prudence found in the divine algorithm that concludes it is better to forgive others who have or will sin against you than to harbor anger and resentment. Rather than settling for the much lower, more primal and antiquated path of survival-based, angry fight-or-flight reactivity, authentic forgiveness focuses on much more laudable goals: the high road to integral human formation, to intentional Christian discipleship and, ultimately, to beatific intimacy with God in His heavenly residence.

Truly, spiritual fathers and husbands are summoned to prepare a pathway for the Lord, not unlike Saint John the Baptist (cf. Matt 3:1ff.), and the natural obstacles to receiving and transmitting God's grace and love do not entirely begin in one's own lifetime. The human obstructions extend back to previous generations, even to the Original Sin of our first prehistorical, biological father, Adam. Similar to Christ's salvific forgiving act that repaired the rupture between God and man, so too can a priest's free choice to forgive his neighbor

---

[50] Francis de Sales, *Introduction to the Devout Life,* Third Part of Introduction, 8, trans. John K. Ryan (New York: Image Books, 1972), 136.

[51] *Catechism of the Catholic Church*, 2nd ed. (Washington, DC: United States Catholic Conference, 2000), 270.

in Christ—and ideally forge the virtuously firm and steady disposition of "forgivingness"[52] through Christ's grace—assist in repairing a rupture between him and his spiritual children.

Deep forgiveness is not an eye-for-an-eye strategy, or a survival-based fight-flight-freeze-faint reaction, or a defense mechanism (e.g., denial), or a maladaptive coping strategy (e.g., avoidance) chosen by an insecure human. It is a deliberate, security-focused and benevolent act of a right-minded person that embodies and communicates the powerful *agapic* love of the Divine. Indeed, from an attachment theory perspective, only when a person attains a certain degree of felt safety and security can most individuals trust others to be not only sources of support and comfort but also individuals who deserve support and comfort,[53] Similarly, it is likely that a "critical mass" of emotional safety and security is necessary to give an authentic gift of self through forgiveness. As articulated in the *Catechism of the Catholic Church*, sin (both Original Sin and all subsequent sin) is tied to a type of insecure relationship with God, a lack of trust in Him and/or His goodness.[54] In addition, one's capacity for authentic self-giving, genuine charity can decrease by a lack of faith and hope.[55] Limited trust in God and limited faith and hope combined may lead one to distrust God that forgiveness is a good to pursue.

Clarifying Forgiveness and Reconciliation

Further complicating the giving of the gift of forgiveness, there is a general confusion surrounding what forgiveness is and is not, likely obstructing genuine efforts to choose it as a viable option. A precise definition is needed. To borrow from Enright and Fitzgibbons, forgiving is defined as follows:

> People, on rationally determining that they have been unfairly treated, forgive when they willfully abandon resentment and related responses (to which they have a right) and endeavor to respond to the wrongdoer based on the moral principle of beneficence, which may include compassion, unconditional worth, generosity, and moral love (to

---

[52] Robert D. Enright, *The Forgiving Life: A Pathway to Overcoming Resentment and Creating a Legacy of Love* (Washington, D.C.: American Psychological Association, 2012), 349-350.

[53] Mikulincer and Shaver, "Boosting Attachment Security," 147.

[54] *CCC*, 397.

[55] Jacques Philippe, *Interior Freedom*, trans. Helena Scott. (New York: Sceptor Publishers, Inc., 2007), 21.

which the wrongdoer, by nature of the hurtful act or acts, has no right).[56]

Note the definition's important emphasis on the forgiver's rational conclusion that a real injustice has occurred. Also note the associated, essential volitional choice to "abandon resentment and related responses," and instead opt to respond with beneficence and possibly other life giving options like compassion, generosity, etc. In a word, forgiveness is a moral choice to generously respond to a *real* perpetrator who committed a *real* injustice against a *real* person (i.e., the victim).

Further clarifying some of the confusion surrounding forgiveness, Enright and Fitzgibbons also list helpful distinctions of what forgiveness is not. Forgiveness is **not**: pardon, legal mercy, or leniency; absolving; condoning; tolerating; accepting the other's apology; reconciliation; conciliation; justification; forgetting; becoming less disappointed; balancing the scales; self-centering; letting time heal the wound; a quick fix, etc.[57] These clarifications allow the victim of injustice to at least intellectually grasp that forgiveness is a real good that is personally good for him to pursue.

However, before considering research outcomes on forgiveness interventions, a word on attachment and reconciliation seems important. Though the development of secure attachment necessitates repeated and consistent connections between a child and an attachment figure, there will always be times of disconnection in need of repair and reconnection.[58] The repair of a relationship rupture with their children is a primary focus for parents, and a primary role of the priest as spiritual father is to assist in the repair of his flock's relationship with God. Even if reconciliation with a perpetrator is contraindicated, a bad idea, rugged and deliberate persistence in unforgiveness continually ruptures one's relationship with God. Also, for those with insecure attachments there are significant obstacles to relationship connection and repair. Avoidants only infrequently reconnect, and it is not soothing even if they do. Thus they experience no relationship repair. Anxiously attached persons connect in unpredictable ways that are sometimes intrusive and

---

[56] Robert D. Enright and Richard P. Fitzgibbons, *Forgiveness Therapy: An Empirical Guide for Resolving Anger and Restoring Hope* (Washington, D.C.: American Psychological Association, 2015), 26-27.

[57] Enright and Fitzgibbons, *Forgiveness Therapy*, 39-56. The authors make helpful philosophical distinctions, consider accurate yet incomplete views, and address common colloquialisms regarding forgiveness that skew its meaning.

[58] Siegel, *The Developing Mind*, 141.

overwhelming,[59] consequently blocking reconciliation with valued other persons.

Since the Christian understanding of forgiveness in the Sacrament of Reconciliation leads to a deepened spiritual intimacy or reconnection of the believer with God, this too can be intimidating and painful depending on one's attachment history. For a spiritual father or husband who is insecurely (i.e., either anxiously or avoidantly) attached to God, it is probable that a deepened connection with Him is not an entirely comfortable or comforting experience. As with close human relationships, insecure individuals' efforts to deepen a spiritual and affective bond with even an objectively loving and merciful divine Father can range from mildly unnerving to scary. If it feels unsafe to connect, his prayer life may include emotionally detached recitation of rote prayers rather than more intimate versions of meditation and contemplation. Using a well-known parable to highlight, despite the magnanimous efforts of the merciful father to warmly welcome and abundantly celebrate his prodigal son's return (Lk 15:11-32), one wonders about the likely battle waged inside the prodigal during the process of reconnection. Indeed, activated insecure internal mental models could have painfully skewed the entire experience in anticipation of, during, and subsequent to his reconnection with his father.

Research on Therapy Promoting Forgiveness

There is substantial evidence on the efficacy of forgiveness, with a large number of studies indicating positive outcomes on a wide range of variables. This section will review research on trait and state forgiveness (toward others), self-forgiveness,[60] core components used in psychological-based forgiveness treatment, and attachment styles and forgiveness. Reviews of individual studies as well as meta-analytic research (i.e., "study of studies" in which the researchers combine results from a number of studies to find common effects) are also discussed below.

---

[59] Siegel, *The Developing Mind*, 141.

[60] There are legitimate concerns about the concept of self-forgiveness, itself. See Paul C. Vitz and Jennifer M. Meade, "Self-Forgiveness in Psychology and Psychotherapy: A Critique." *Journal of Religion and Health* 50 (2011), 248. Vitz and Meade prefer the term "self-acceptance" over self-forgiveness. One could also posit "self-compassion" as a useful alternative label to self-forgiveness. However, despite my shared leanings away from endorsing the construct of self-forgiveness, part of this section reviews some of the research on self-forgiveness rather than the conceptual problems with the construct itself. The focus here is to, among other things, merely highlight the evidentiary differences between forgiveness and self-forgiveness.

Forgiveness is not merely a means for preparing a better afterlife; it produces noteworthy positive psychological and physiological changes in the here and now. A large body of research in the social sciences indicates forgiveness is a healthy remedy for a wide range of personal afflictions. Indeed, the lack of forgiveness toward an offender one is close to can result in physiological tension that may lead to elevations in unease, physical symptoms, loneliness and stress.[61] In contrast, numerous studies have shown the many benefits of the choice to forgive.

Forgiveness has been shown to result in significantly reduced depression and anxiety as well as increases in hope and esteem for a group of incest survivors (average age was 36), half of whom indicated abuse from their biological fathers.[62] These results maintained at a follow-up 14 months later.

Forgiveness therapy was also used with individuals in a substance abuse residential facility for a total of twelve 1-hour sessions.[63] Though the control group received training in the effects of drug use, stress avoidance, and social support, the forgiveness therapy group had greater decreases in depression, anxiety, anger, vulnerability to drug use and had the added benefit of increases in forgiveness and self-esteem. The results maintained a third of a year later at follow-up.

Men with coronary artery disease used a forgiveness intervention resulting in significantly positive outcomes.[64] As compared with a control group that was trained in proper exercise, diet and stress management, the group receiving a forgiveness intervention for ten 1-hour weekly meetings increased forgiveness and had less restriction of myocardial blood flow when thinking about an earlier experience of being a victim of injustice." The results also maintained a third of a year later at follow-up.

Another forgiveness-focused intervention was used with ten men (including 3 agnostics) who received treatment to address anger associated with the abortion decision of

---

[61] Kathleen A. Lawler-Row, Laura Hyatt-Edwards, Karl L. Wuensch, and Johan C. Karremans, "Forgiveness and Health: The Role of Attachment." *Personal Relationships* 18, no. 2 (2011), 170.

[62] Suzanne R. Freedman and Robert D. Enright. "Forgiveness as an Intervention Goal With Incest Survivors." *Journal of Consulting and Clinical Psychology* 64, no. 5 (1996), 983.

[63] Wei-Fen Lin, David Mack, Robert D. Enright, Dean Krahn, and Thomas W. Baskin, "Effects of Forgiveness Therapy on Anger, Mood, and Vulnerability to Substance Use Among Inpatient Substance-Dependent Clients." *Journal of Consulting Clinical Psychology* 72, no. 6 (2004), 1114.

[64] Martina A. Waltman, Douglas C. Russell, Catherine T. Coyle , Robert D. Enright, Anthony C. Holter, and Christopher M. Swoboda, "The Effects of a Forgiveness Intervention on Patients With Coronary Artery Disease." *Psychology & Health* 24, no. 1 (2009), 11.

a partner.[65] They experienced a significant decrease in state anxiety, anger, and grief as well as an increase in forgiveness.

There is also substantial meta-analytic evidence supporting forgiveness as an efficacious approach for increasing various types of functioning. A 2008 meta-analysis by Lundahl et al.[66] indicated a variety of studies showed that persons who received interventions of forgiveness were more likely to forgive, had an increase in positive emotion and self-esteem, and had a decrease in negative emotions. These improvements mostly endured at follow-up. Of note, forgiveness interventions delivered to individuals were shown to have better outcomes compared to interventions delivered to groups.

Wade et al.'s 2014 meta-analysis on forgiveness-promoting psychotherapy interventions[67] also indicated a variety of positive outcomes. As compared with the research subgroups that received no treatment, forgiveness treatments yielded greater positive changes in depression, anxiety and hope. Longer interventions and individually delivered (as compared with group delivered) programs were more successful at bringing about forgiveness change.[68] An important finding for persons who have been a victim of an extreme injustice, the severity of offense was associated with increased forgiveness as an outcome when comparing forgiveness versus alternative (i.e., not forgiveness-focused) treatments, suggesting that, from a forgiveness standpoint, there is more room for change for such individuals.[69] In general, the significant improvements maintained at follow-up.

"Common Core" Forgiveness Interventions

Though there are a variety of forgiveness interventions, some more effective than others, there are a "common core" or set of interventions used in the research on various

---

[65] Catherine T. Coyle and Robert D. Enright, "Forgiveness Intervention With Postabortion Men." *Journal of Consulting and Clinical Psychology* 65, no. 6 (1997), 1042.

[66] Brad W. Lundahl, Mary Jane Taylor, Ryan Stevenson, and K. Daniel Roberts, "Processed-Based Forgiveness Interventions: A Meta-Analytic Review." *Research on Social Work Practice* 18, no. 5 (2008), 465.

[67] Nathaniel G. Wade, William T. Hoyt, Julia E. M. Kidwell, and Everett L. Worthington, Jr., "Efficacy of Psychotherapeutic Interventions to Promote Forgiveness: A Meta-Analysis." *Journal of Consulting and Clinical Psychology* 82, no. 1 (2014), 154.

[68] Wade et al., "Efficacy of Psychotherapy Interventions to Promote Forgiveness," 154.

[69] Wade et al., "Efficacy of Psychotherapy Interventions to Promote Forgiveness," 165.

treatments to promote forgiveness.[70] These may assist in the formation of priests who not only help others to forgive, but also are striving for a deep personal transformation themselves to become forgiving and merciful, Christ-like figures.

In 2005, Wade and Worthington summarized common interventions used in evidence-based efforts focused on increasing forgiveness, though they acknowledge that "consensus does not necessarily indicate efficacy."[71] However, with an eye to the previously reviewed positive research outcomes on forgiveness treatments, the following "common core" interventions may be useful to consider when forming men for priestly service. Then they can better accompany another on the focused forgiveness journey toward enhanced hope and freedom:

1. *Defining Forgiveness* – As mentioned earlier, misconceptions about what forgiveness is and is not are common and, if the actual definition of forgiveness is not clearly laid out the misunderstandings can be obstacles to choosing to deeply forgive.

2. *Recalling the Hurt* – This intervention can bring about a cathartic, emotional release of pent up anger or tension and reduce some of the consequent pain from the offense.

3. *Building Empathy for the Perpetrator* – Assisting the victim to "walk in the shoes" of the perpetrator helps the victim to understand the experiences of the offender before, during or after the offense that may have been difficult for him or her.

4. *Acknowledging One's Own Offenses* – The victim takes an inventory of his own personally committed injustices, which assists in developing humility, a key element needed to forgive.

5. *Committing to Forgiveness* – Since deep forgiveness of a painful injustice is less a quick sprint and more of a lengthy journey, the volitional choice to commit to working through the internal conflicts and other difficulties endemic to the journey assists in successfully following through with deep forgiveness.

---

[70] Nathaniel G. Wade and Everett L. Worthington, Jr., "In Search of a Common Core: A Content Analysis of Interventions to Promote Forgiveness." *Psychotherapy: Theory, Research, Practice, Training* 42, no. 2 (2005), 160.

[71] Wade and Worthington, "In Search of a Common Core," 175.

6. *Overcoming Unforgiveness* – Though not directly aimed at forgiveness, a number of forgiveness-focused studies made efforts to control anger, resentment and/or rumination in ways not included in the aforementioned interventions.[72]

Attachment and Forgiveness Research

The activation of internal mental models of attachment is more implicit and reactive, generally known more through emotional and visceral experiences than through conscious awareness. Forgiveness, in contrast, is more explicit and proactive. It can effectively address some of the most sensitive and agonizing of wounds: attachment wounds and ruptures. Forgiveness is a deliberate choice to let go of the anger that paradoxically binds the victim to the perpetrator.

The anger that the victim perceived would give him more power over and more space from the perpetrator instead inundates his mind and heart with images from the painful past. The wounded party's life becomes saturated with the very person he intensely desires to be done with, to escape. Anger makes him more, not less, preoccupied[73] with the transgressor who triggered the anger in the first place. Thus no escape from the offender occurs. The victim feels more hopelessly trapped in the oppressive and sticky web of anger and pain.

Anger toward another—especially extreme levels for extended periods of time toward a key attachment figure—makes it impossible to think clearly and balanced about that individual. It thus shrinks one's capacity to love the transgressor properly. It becomes a psychological obstacle to living spiritually in the present moment and being a consistent and intentionally loving disciple of the Lord. Whereas attachment *in*security and anger stifle authentic masculine maturation and a consistently compassionate disposition, attachment security and deep forgiveness foster genuine human maturity toward merciful, priestly spiritual husbands and fathers.

The main types of forgiveness researched include the following: *Trait forgivingness* considers the degree that an individual generally tends to forgive across variables of time, situations and different relationships; *state forgiveness* describes the extent that a person forgives a particular offense; and *self-forgiveness* refers to the degree one forgives oneself for committed offenses.[74] Of note, meta-analytic research indicates that relationships having

---

[72] Wade and Worthington, "In Search of a Common Core," 164-172.

[73] Cf. Philippe, *Interior Freedom*, 66.

[74] Don E. Davis, Everett L. Worthington, Jr., Joshua N. Hook, and Peter C. Hill, "Research on

more positive views of the sacred are associated more with trait forgiveness than state forgiveness, and they have a greater likelihood of self-forgiveness.[75]

Forgiveness research has also considered correlations with patterns of attachment. As mentioned previously, there are 3 primary patterns of attaching to another in a close relationship: Secure, insecure-avoidant, and insecure-anxious. Each includes implicit, internal working models of relationships that, when activated, contribute to either overcoming or constructing obstacles to intimacy. Regarding the state / trait forgiveness research: "The working model of attachment seems more predictive of the personality measure [i.e., trait] of forgiveness, while current relationship commitment and intrusiveness were more associated with state forgiveness."[76]

Patterns of attachment influence levels of health, with insecurely attached persons demonstrating less forgiveness and more health problems.[77] Though secure attachment to God is associated with higher levels of optimism and self-esteem, and secures who feel forgiven by God also experience greater personal wellness, the same study showed that avoidants seem to feel greater self-reported "wellness" by decreasing their interest in forgiveness from God.[78] The comfort with diminished interest is similar to the avoidant style of attaching in general. Both patterns of insecure attachment are less inclined to exhibit trait forgiveness, with the anxiously attached less likely to forgive due to *excessive rumination* and the avoidantly attached less likely to forgive due to *lack of empathy*.[79]

A study on attachment theory and forgiveness of a partner showed that individuals with either anxious or avoidant attachment were less likely to attribute benign reasons for a partner's transgressions.[80] As level of avoidant attachment increased, the less empathy

---

Religion/Spirituality and Forgiveness: A Meta-Analytic Review." *Psychology of Religion and Spirituality* 5, no. 4 (2013), 233.

[75] Davis et al., "Research on Religion/Spirituality and Forgiveness," 238.

[76] Kathleen A. Lawler-Row, Laura Hyatt-Edwards, Karl L. Wuensch, and Johan C. Karremans, "Forgiveness and Health: The Role of Attachment." *Personal Relationships* 18, no. 2 (2011), 179.

[77] Lawler-Row et al., "Forgiveness and Health," 179.

[78] Blake Victor Kent, Matt Bradshaw, and Jeremy E. Euker, "Forgiveness, Attachment to God, and Mental Health Outcomes in Older U.S. Adults: A Longitudinal Study." *Research on Aging* 40, no. 5 (2018), 456.

[79] Jeni L. Burnette, Don E. Davis, Jeffrey D. Green, Everett L. Worthington, Jr., and Erin Bradfield, "Insecure Attachment and Depressive Symptoms: The Mediating Role of Rumination, Empathy, and Forgiveness." *Personality & Individual Differences* 46, no. 3 (2009), 278.

[80] Jonathan G. Kimmes and Jared A. Durtschi, "Forgiveness in Romantic Relationships: The Roles of Attachment, Empathy, and Attributions." *Journal of Marital and Family Therapy* 42, no. 4

individuals had for a romantically-associated offender; and as level of anxious attachment increased, the more likely the person would pessimistically perceive the unjust behaviors of their partner as intentional.[81] The authors recommend that if assisting anxiously attached individuals to forgive, the outcomes may improve by focusing on attributions rather than empathy since such individuals tend to have elevated levels of negative rumination. The authors also suggest helping more with developing empathy than reframing attributions when assisting avoidants, who are disposed to emotional distance, for improved outcomes in the forgiveness process.

Research on self-forgiveness has also demonstrated positive psychological outcomes, though differently than outcomes on forgiving others. In a study of over 400 college students, though forgiving others significantly reduced anger, self-forgiveness was more likely to reduce depression, anxiety and anger.[82] Of note, at higher levels of self-forgiveness, neither anxious attachment nor avoidant attachment were associated with depression, suggesting self-forgiveness may be more effective at decreasing the association between attachment insecurity (both avoidant and anxious) and depressive symptoms.[83]

Attachment and Forgiveness Considerations
for Transitory Same Sex Attraction

Attachment theory also provides possible insights into transitory same sex attraction (SSA). Even a SSA that is transitory can present considerable challenges to a man's vocation as spiritual father and husband. Jane Guenther's and Fr. John Horn's perspective on parental contributing factors in the development of same sex attracted men apply here.[84] They state that "Father wounds occur when a father is perceived by a child as distant, critical, selfish, angry or alcoholic." Similarly, Nicolosi describes the significant adverse influence of fathers on their sons who eventually develop same sex attraction: The sons often see their fathers as emotionally and/or physically distant or critical,[85] which over time leads to a shame wound. Nicolosi also describes the general profile of their mothers who,

---

(2016), 653.

[81] Kimmes and Durtschi, "Forgiveness in Romantic Relationships," 653.

[82] Kelly Yu-Hsin Liao and Meifen Wei, "Insecure Attachment and Depressive Symptoms: Forgiveness of Self and Others as Moderators." *Personal Relationships* 22, no. 2 (2015), 224.

[83] Liao and Wei, "Insecure Attachment and Depressive Symptoms," 224.

[84] See Chapter 18 in Segment 3 of this book.

[85] Nicolosi, *Shame and Attachment Loss*, 28-29.

due in part to personal insecurities, lead their sons to develop a negative view of men and masculinity, which in the future can seem mysterious and "other-than-me."[86] Throughout the lifespan, these sons can maintain anxiously attached, even dependent, relationships with their mothers.[87] It is recommended here that such individuals who are searching for enduring peace in their vocations to the priesthood seek out deeper security through forgiveness of either or both parents. If the situation allows for it and it is prudent, it is also suggested that they pursue any needed reconciliation with both parents.

From an attachment perspective, an insecure attachment to one's father or mother, or both, can lead—through activated internal mental models of relationships—a person to struggle deeply with authentic intimacy in close relationships, and compromise introspection and self-knowledge. An insecure relationship with parents can engender an unstable self-identity that develops through and in filial relationships, and consequently a person may question aspects of his sexuality and sexual desires. These experiences are less likely to plague a man who is more securely attached. Indeed rather than downgrading masculinity and seeing it as "not me" and/or overcompensating and putting it on an unattainable pedestal, a securely attached man is more likely to value masculinity and see his own masculinity as a part of his identity.

Shame is generally a key struggle for individuals with SSA, and both gay-affirmative and other therapists consider it to be a primary therapeutic issue, though for different reasons.[88] Also, if the male with transitory SSA is generally anxiously attached, fears of abandonment or instability in relationships will be paramount, and a desire for approval from others may be amplified, because approval in many ways is an experiential opposite to abandonment and rejection. The man with transitory SSA who is anxiously (or even avoidantly) attached should never journey alone the path of forgiveness of and/or reconciliation with his parents. Indeed, a great task that a man is more prone to fail if pursued alone, he is more likely to successfully accomplish when buttressed by the support of others.

To elaborate, if a man feels afraid or unsafe, he needs a protector figure; if he feels abandoned or ashamed, he needs a nurturing figure; if he feels confused or struggles with choosing the better path in life, he needs a wisdom figure;[89] and if he struggles with motivation to change or developing the momentum to grow, he needs an encourager.

---

[86] Nicolosi, *Shame and Attachment Loss*, 27.

[87] Nicolosi, *Shame and Attachment Loss*, 63.

[88] Nicolosi, *Shame and Attachment Loss*, 18.

[89] cf. Laurel Parnell, *Attachment-Focused EMDR: Healing Relational Trauma*. (New York: W. W. Norton & Company, Inc., 2013), 45-72.

Establishing a deep and heartfelt connection to any or all the Persons of the Trinity, the Blessed Mother or other saint, who provide felt protection or nurturing, or wisdom or encouragement can be a saving grace during the sometimes scary, lonely, confusing, depressing journey to change. Also, connecting with a human mentor who compassionately understands the man and his struggles can be immensely helpful to provide counsel and encouragement to forgive and/or reconcile if his family and life context allows.

A focus for a man with transitory SSA, not unlike persons with opposite-sex attraction, is to successfully relinquish his anger and to understand his same-sex attractions and desires as not being a part of his fundamental identity. Indeed his true identity as being an *imago Dei* is categorically more than his sexual desires and greater than all of his insecurities or associated maladaptive compulsions combined. Truly, being made in God's image is a banner on the heart that is nobler than the aggregate of natural virtues he will develop or acquire throughout the duration of his life. Though not denying its presence or hating himself for it, it is important for him to "unblend" from the side or part of him that experiences transitory SSA in order to get to know and understand it. This needed space away from being engulfed in SSA experiences allows a clarity of mind to acknowledge and reasonably understand such experiences rather than become intellectually clouded and emotionally confused by them. A deeper, curiously compassionate awareness of this current yet transitory part of his personality, supported by a trusted and affectively mature mentor, and complemented by an acknowledgement that it is not his true identity in God, will allow the Lord to strengthen his masculinity through an emotionally regulated and more secure, peaceful self.

Toward Reconciliation and Relationship Enhancement

The man with transitory SSA likely needs to mend his relationship with his father and/or mother, at minimum "from afar" through forgiveness (since one can forgive without reconnecting). However, ideally and if at all possible and prudent, the mending can occur "from up close" through reconciliation. But reconciling with his father may be a great challenge due to not fully identifying with and possibly even fearing authentic masculinity and corresponding desires and interests.

Securely attached son-to-father dyads demonstrate the "stronger, wiser other" component of the father as an attachment figure. In such relationships, the father compassionately and steadily—through warmth, without aggression, and at the right times—pursues the son even if intermittently resisted by the son, and he is comforted by and reconnected to his father. This is most importantly the case when the son feels unlovable. Yet to make the move toward mature masculinity and perhaps more importantly the merciful fatherhood so necessary in the priestly vocation, the son himself may actually need to proactively pursue the mending of the rupture with his father since the father has not effectively achieved it. With an eye to God's style of pursuing like the "Hound of Heaven", the son becomes more God-like in his pursuit of healing his attachment experiences with his father or mother through forgiveness and/or reconciliation efforts.

These efforts are best processed with a trusted attachment figure, like a mentor or spiritual director, perhaps a therapist, who can accompany the man during the courageous effort to reconnect with his parent. Generally, it would be best to reconnect more slowly on more peripheral issues such as news, weather, and sports. When in doubt, in reconciliation efforts he should err on the side of slower, to prevent hasty reunions and circumvent amplifying fear in the process. Though efforts to connect on surface issues may initially seem unhelpful, they actually assist in the young man's efforts to develop felt security and psychological momentum toward attaining a helpful level of connection to the degree that his parent is sufficiently ready and open to the reconnection (e.g., the father has converted to being less critical, more emotionally available, etc.). Efforts to emotionally connect with consistently implemented boundaries, even on more surface things, may be a worthwhile pursuit. This structured approach has the potential to counteract emotional detachment from his father or residual anger or ambivalence toward his mother. Active reconciliation is critical, because developed attachment security and trust is not nurtured by merely passively waiting for connection, but more by the son actively choosing to either pursue or at minimum be actively open and receptive to being pursued in a healthy and prudent way by one's father or mother.

Summary and Conclusion

The priestly vocation to generate a newness of life in the Spirit rests on the priest's capacity to be a peace-filled instrument of grace to others. Insecure attachment-related struggles in close relationships, cultivated anger and unforgiveness have been described as significant obstacles to a calling to become a spiritual husband and father. Striving for felt (not merely intellectual) implicit attachment security, possibly through deep forgiveness of an offender of a past injustice, can bring about life-transforming experiences that fortify a priest in his efforts to fully reconcile his spiritual children in and with God. Empirical evidence displayed the significant, enduring positive outcomes of a focused effort on forgiveness as well as its associations with different patterns of secure and insecure attachment. Then a discussion of relevant forgiveness and attachment pattern considerations were applied to the subject of transitory same sex attraction, especially any necessary work needed to address attachment insecurities and wounds associated with one's parents.

It is hoped that the Lord may breathe abundant life into all his priests as they pursue a mature, spiritually and psychologically integrated life—with the support of mentors and other attachment figures—transformed through deep forgiveness and/or reconciliation and an established attachment security. May this security penetrate the fibers of their being, take root and allow the Lord to reign deep within their hearts. Transformed by grace and with our triune God as their trusted interior companion, may they intimately bond with supportive and comforting others, to Our Lady the most blessed of all mothers, and most importantly to God the Father, Son, and Holy Spirit—the ultimate secure attachment figures. It is through the grace and support of these relationships that a priest can truly "do all things" in Christ who strengthens him (Phil 4:13).

Prayers

> *O blessed Jesus, give me stillness of soul in You. Let your mighty calmness reign in me. Rule me, O King of Gentleness, King of Peace.*
> —Saint John of the Cross

Practicum Reflection Questions for Formators

1. In what ways have my own human (especially emotional and/or attachment) insecurities been obstacles to authentically forgiving others and/or to the conversion of others? Do I view connection and autonomy as incompatible, polar opposites, or do I experience and express them in my life as complementary strengths that build on each other? Do I tend toward too much independence or too much dependence in close relationships, and how does my relational style influence how I serve others? Who can I emulate that is a good role model of balanced, healthy and seasoned autonomy and connectedness?

2. Who are the key people toward whom I harbor anger and need to forgive? Have they truly committed an injustice against me? Is my anger justifiable? If so, have I clung to it for too long, let "the sun set" on it (Eph 4:26) and allowed it to devolve

into self-righteous or unjustifiable anger? Who do I trust as a supportive and genuine instrument of God's love to help me make sense of my anger and move on?

3. In what ways has my example of unforgiveness been an obstacle to my conversion and/or others' conversions and authentic discipleship? How can I nurture forgiveness in my life to be an instrument of grace and conversion for others? Is reconciliation at all possible and prudent?

4. Have I sinned in choosing to cultivate self-anger or self-hatred rather than self-acceptance or self-compassion? How has my self-anger been an obstacle to another's growth in Christ? What can I do to genuinely love myself more like the way the Lord loves me, so I can love others more like the way the Lord loves me?

Suggested Resources

1. *Forgiveness is a Choice: A Step-by-Step Process for Resolving Anger and Restoring Hope,* by Robert D. Enright, APA LifeTools, Washington, D.C., 2001.

2. *The Forgiving Life: A Pathway to Overcoming Resentment and Creating a Legacy of Love,* by Robert D. Enright, American Psychological Association, Washington, D.C., 2012.

3. On Divine Mercy (*Dives in misericordia*), Encyclical by John Paul II, 30 November 1980.

4. *The Return of the Prodigal Son: A Story of Homecoming,* by Henri J. M. Nouwen, Doubleday, New York, 1992.

5. *Searching for and Maintaining Peace: A Small Treatise on Peace of Heart,* by Fr. Jacques Philippe, trans. George and Jannic Driscoll, Society of St. Paul, Staten Island, NY, 2002.

Bibliography

Anderson-Mooney, A. J., Webb, M., Charbonneau, A. M., & Mvududu, N. (2015). Dispositional forgiveness and meaning-making: The relative contributions of forgiveness and adult attachment style to struggling or enduring with God. *Journal of Spirituality in Mental Health, 17* (2), 91-109.

Burnette, Jeni L., Don E. Davis, Jeffrey D. Green, Everett L. Worthington, Jr., and Erin Bradfield. "Insecure Attachment and Depressive Symptoms: The Mediating Role of Rumination, Empathy, and Forgiveness." *Personality & Individual Differences* 46, no. 3

(2009): 276-280.

Catechism of the Catholic Church. 2nd ed. Washington, DC: United States Catholic Conference, 2000.

de Caussade, Jean Pierre. *Abandonment to Divine Providence: With Letters of Father De Caussade on the Practice of Self-Abandonment,* Third English Edition. San Francisco: Ignatius Press, 2011.

Costello, Peter C. *Attachment-Based Psychotherapy. Helping Patients Develop Adaptive Capacities.* Washington, DC: American Psychological Association, 2013.

Coyle, Catherine T., and Robert D. Enright. Forgiveness Intervention With Postabortion Men. *Journal of Consulting and Clinical Psychology* 65, no. 6 (1997), 1042-1046.

Davis, Don E., Everett L. Worthington, Jr., Joshua N. Hook, and Peter C. Hill. "Research on Religion/Spirituality and Forgiveness: A Meta-Analytic Review. *Psychology of Religion and Spirituality* 5, no. 4 (2013): 233-241.

Davis, E. B., Granqvist, P., & Sharp, C. (2018). Theistic relational spirituality: Development, dynamics, health, and transformation. *Psychology of Religion and Spirituality.*

Enright, Robert D. *The Forgiving Life: A Pathway to Overcoming Resentment and Creating a Legacy of Love.* Washington, D.C.: American Psychological Association, 2012.

Enright, Robert D., and Richard P. Fitzgibbons. *Forgiveness Therapy: An Empirical Guide for Resolving Anger and Restoring Hope.* Washington, D.C.: American Psychological Association, 2015.

Freedman, Suzanne R., and Robert D. Enright. Forgiveness as an Intervention Goal With Incest Survivors." *Journal of Consulting and Clinical Psychology* 64, no. 5 (1996): 983-992.

The Holy Bible: Revised Standard Version. New York: Collins, 1973.

Kent, Blake Victor, Matt Bradshaw, Jeremy E. Euker. "Forgiveness, Attachment to God, and Mental Health Outcomes in Older U.S. Adults: A Longitudinal Study." *Research on Aging* 40, no. 5 (2018): 456-479.

Kimmes, Jonathan G., and Jared A. Durtschi. "Forgiveness in Romantic Relationships: The Roles of Attachment, Empathy, and Attributions." *Journal of Marital and Family Therapy* 42, no. 4 (2016): 645-658.

Lawler-Row, Kathleen A., Laura Hyatt-Edwards, Karl L. Wuensch, and Johan C. Karremans. "Forgiveness and Health: The Role of Attachment." *Personal Relationships* 18, no. 2 (2011): 170-183.

Liao, Kelly Yu-Hsin, and Meifen Wei. "Insecure Attachment and Depressive Symptoms: Forgiveness of Self and Others as Moderators." *Personal Relationships* 22, no. 2 (2015):

216-229.

Lin, Wei-Fen, David Mack, Robert D. Enright, Dean Krahn, and Thomas W. Baskin. "Effects of Forgiveness Therapy on Anger, Mood, and Vulnerability to Substance Use Among Inpatient Substance-Dependent Clients." *Journal of Consulting Clinical Psychology* 72, no. 6 (2004): 1114-1121.

Lockwood, George, and Poul Perris. "A New Look at Core Emotional Needs," in *The Wiley-Blackwell Handbook of Schema Therapy: Theory, Research, and Practice*, Ed. Michiel van Vreeswijk, Jenny Broersen, and Marjon Nadort. Oxford: John Wiley & Sons, Ltd, 2012.

Lundahl, Brad. W., Mary Jane Taylor, Ryan Stevenson, and K. Daniel Roberts. "Processed-Based Forgiveness Interventions: A Meta-Analytic Review." *Research on Social Work Practice* 18, no. 5 (2008): 465-478.

Mikulincer, Mario, and Phillip R. Shaver. "Adult Attachment Orientations and Relationship Processes." *Journal of Family Theory & Review* 4, no. 4 (2012): 259-274.

Mikulincer, Mario, and Phillip R. Shaver. Boosting Attachment Security to Promote Mental Health, Prosocial Values, and Inter-Group Tolerance." *Psychological Inquiry* 18, no. 3 (2007): 139-156.

Mikulincer, Mario, and Phillip R. Shaver. *Attachment in Adulthood: Structure, Dynamics, and Change.* 2nd ed. New York: The Guilford Press, 2016.

Mikulincer, Mario, Phillip R. Shaver, Yael Sapir-Lavid, and Neta Avihou-Kanza. "What's Inside the Minds of Securely and Insecurely Attached People? The Secure-Base Script and its Associations with Attachment-Style Dimensions." *Journal of Personality and Social Psychology* 97, no. 4 (2009): 615-633.

Nicolosi, Joseph J. *Shame and Attachment Loss: The Practical Work of Reparative Therapy* (rev.). Liberal Mind Publishers, 2016.

Numata, M., Konno, H. (2014). The relationship between forgiveness and adult attachment style. *Japanese Journal of Personality, 23*(2), 113-115.

Parnell, Laurel. *Attachment-Focused EMDR: Healing Relational Trauma.* New York: W. W. Norton & Company, Inc., 2013.

Philippe, Jacques. *Interior Freedom*, trans. Helena Scott. New York: Sceptor Publishers, Inc., 2007.

Ross, Scott R., Matthew J. Hertenstein, and Thomas A. Wrobel. "Maladaptive Correlates of the Failure to Forgive Self and Others: Further Evidence for a Two-Component Model of Forgiveness." *Journal of Personality Assessment* 88, no. 2 (2007): 158-167.

de Sales, Francis. *Introduction to the Devout Life.* Third Part of Introduction, 8. Trans. John K. Ryan. New York: Image Books, 1972.

Siegel, Daniel J. *The Developing Mind: How Relationships and the Brain Interact to Shape Who We Are.* 2nd ed. New York: The Guilford Press, 2012.

Vitz, Paul C., and Jennifer M. Meade. "Self-Forgiveness in Psychology and Psychotherapy: A Critique." *Journal of Religion and Health* 50 (2011): 248-263.

Wade, Nathaniel. G., and Everett L. Worthington, Jr. "In Search of a Common Core: A Content Analysis of Interventions to Promote Forgiveness." *Psychotherapy: Theory, Research, Practice, Training* 42, no. 2 (2005): 160-177.

Wade, Nathaniel G., William T. Hoyt, Julia E. M. Kidwell, and Everett L. Worthington, Jr. "Efficacy of Psychotherapeutic Interventions to Promote Forgiveness: A Meta-Analysis." *Journal of Consulting and Clinical Psychology* 82, no. 1 (2014): 154-170.

Wallin, David J. *Attachment in Psychotherapy.* New York: The Guilford Press, 2007.

Waltman, Martina A., Douglas C. Russell, Catherine T. Coyle , Robert D. Enright, Anthony C. Holter, and Christopher M. Swoboda. "The Effects of a Forgiveness Intervention on Patients With Coronary Artery Disease." *Psychology & Health* 24, no. 1 (2009): 11-27.

Yarnoz Yaben, Sagrario. "Forgiveness, Attachment, and Divorce." *Journal of Divorce & Remarriage* 50, no. 4 (2009): 282-294.

Chapter Fifteen

Guideposts for the Seminary Formator in Understanding and Assessing Levels of Preoccupation with Use of Internet Pornography and a Formative Process for Moving from Vice to Virtue[1]

Sr. Marysia Weber, R.S.M., M.A., D.O.

Sister Marysia Weber, R.S.M., M.A., D.O. is a physician, board certified in psychiatry with a fellowship in consultation-liaison psychiatry, who trained at the Mayo Clinic in Rochester, MN. She also holds a Master's degree in Theology from Notre Dame, South Bend, Indiana. She practiced psychiatry at her religious institute's multidisciplinary medical clinic, Sacred Heart Mercy Health Care Center in Alma, MI from 1988-2014. She became the Director of the Office of Consecrated Life for the Archdiocese of Saint Louis in 2014. She currently serves as a member of the Saint Louis Archdiocesan Review Board, the Child Safety Committee, is a facilitator for Project Rachel, is chair of the board of directors of MyCatholicDoctor, an executive board member of the Saint Louis Guild Catholic Medical Association and the Institute for Theological Encounter with Science and Technology. She also serves as Adjunct Clinical Instructor in the Department of Psychiatry at Washington University School of Medicine in Saint Louis, Missouri.

Sister Marysia offers workshops on a variety of topics including human attachment, boundaries and character development, depression and anxiety, dialogue and conflict resolution, as well as on social media and its effects on the brain for clergy, seminarians, women's and men's religious communities, parents, teachers and students. She is a formator within her own religious community. She presents on Internet pornography addiction—a Catholic approach to treatment to bishops, clergy, seminarians, religious communities, and laity throughout the United States and Europe She

---

[1] Portions of this chapter have been published in Seminary Journal, Vol 18 no 2 Fall, 2012, pp. 107-116.

presented to the U.S. Bishops in Dallas TX in 1992 on "Pedophilia and Other Addictions". She was a member of the USCCB Ad Hoc Committee on Sexual Abuse in 1994-1995. Sister Marysia has presented to the Curia, Vatican City State on "Sexual Abuse of Minors by Clergy in North America" in 2002. She has served as a psychological expert consultant for the Secretariat of Clergy, Consecrated Life and Vocations, USCCB.

Sister Marysia's publications include "Medical Aspects of Addiction"; "The Roman Catholic Church and the Sexual Abuse of Minors by Priests and Religious in the United States and Canada: What Have We Learned? Where Are We Going?"; "Pornography, Electronic Media and Priestly Formation"; Her publications in *Seminary Journal* include: "Significant Markers of Human Maturation Applied to the Selection and Formation of Seminarians"; "The Discernment of a Priestly Vocation and the Expertise of Psychiatry and Psychology"; and "Internet Pornography and Priestly Formation: Medium and Content Collide With the Human Brain". She has published two books: *The Art of Accompaniment: Practical Steps for the Seminary Formator* (En Route Books and Media, 2018) and *Screen Addiction: Why You Can't Put that Phone Down* (En Route Books and Media, 2019). Her chapter "Guideposts for the Seminary Formator in Understanding and Assessing Levels of Preoccupation with Use of Internet Pornography and a Formative Process for Moving from Vice to Virtue" in Spiritual Husband-Spiritual Fathers: Priestly Formation for the 21st Century is pending publication. She also has a short video on "Screen Addiction" located at www.cathmed.org/videos.

"For we do not have a high priest who is unable to sympathize with our weakness, but one who was tempted in every way that we are, yet never sinned." (Hebrews 4:15)

Introduction

Not all who view Internet pornography are chronic users. Not all are unable to resist viewing Internet pornography to the detriment of other activities. As with alcohol, part of the difficulty in measuring the harm of Internet pornography is that it does not affect all individuals in the same way. In some cases, a casual sporadic user may be harmed by his pornography habit, more than a chronic daily user. We might also discover that some people are more disposed toward heavy pornography consumption than are others. These are areas of research that need to be further explored. Nonetheless, pornography does evoke, in some users, behaviors that scientific literature calls "addictions", just as in cases of addiction to alcohol, nicotine and other substances.

Over the last two decades, mental health professionals have reported a dramatic increase in the number of people who present for therapy, seeking to address their growing urges to view Internet pornography. Accurate statistics regarding the use of Internet pornography are difficult to locate; however, available research demonstrates prolific numbers of pornographic Internet sites. According to available data, "sex" is the number one search topic on the Internet.[2]

There are 60 million daily pornographic search engine requests, 40 million adults in the US regularly access Internet pornography and 10% admit to an addiction to Internet pornography. Porn hub is a video sharing site which received 2.4 million visitors per hour in 2015 alone. That is 46 million viewers per day. This number rose to 80 million daily users in 2017. It is estimated that 64% of college men and 18% of college women spend time on line for Internet sex every week. Also, 56% of divorce cases involved one party having an obsessive interest in pornographic websites.[3]

Recent surveys report that 90% of teenage boys view online pornography while doing homework.[4] Additionally, young, sexually inexperienced persons, especially males, find it easier to engage in sexual behavior accessing Internet pornography than to risk rejection in the context of a face-to-face encounter with a real person.

The expansive reach of Internet pornography has also touched a very young demographic. Notably, the average age of children who are first exposed to Internet pornography is eleven years old.[5] Exposure to Internet pornography in children four to five years old is also being reported. In addition 28% of boys and 18% of girls have viewed bestiality online and 39% of boys and 23% of girls have seen sexual bondage online.[6] Pornographers use character names such as *Pokémon* and *Action Man* to appeal to children who unknowingly may be accessing a pornography site.

Researchers now predict that millions of Americans are addicted to Internet pornography. In fact, sources assert that the number of users of Internet pornography has sky-rocketed, making Internet pornography one of the foremost addictions in the world.[7]

Narrowing the focus, Internet pornography also has a substantial impact on men who,

---

[2] https://www.quora.com/Whats-the-most-searched-thing-on-the-Internet [accessed Dec. 22, 2018].

[3] http://www.familysafe.com/pornography-statistics/ [accessed Dec. 4, 2018].

[4] http://www.ministryoftruth.me.uk/wp-content/uploads/2014/03/IFR2013.pdf [accessed Dec. 4, 2018].

[5] Ibid.

[6] https://www.covenanteyes.com/ [accessed Dec. 4, 2018].

[7] Kimberly S. Young, Xiao Dong Yue and Li Ying, "Prevalence Estimates and Etiologic Models of Internet Addiction", in *Internet Addiction: A Handbook and Guide to Evaluation and Treatment* (John Wiley and Sons, Inc., 2011), pp. 3-6.

coming from our highly sexualized culture, enter seminaries. Internet pornography can be a menacing presence for men who seek priestly formation, especially in light of a lifestyle of chastity and the discipline of celibacy. To address this challenge to priestly formation, increased awareness of the effects of Internet pornography is essential for bishops, vocations directors and seminary personnel.

This chapter will lead formators into an increased awareness of the effects of Internet pornography. At the onset, a connection between addictive behavior and pornography is established. Second, contributing factors to the sky-rocketing prevalence of Internet pornography use is considered. Third, the neurological effects of Internet pornography which prompt many users to seek more intense erotic images in order to achieve heightened experiences of sexual arousal is addressed. Fourth, treatment protocols that can promote affective maturity and reverse the changes in the brain created by viewing Internet pornography are suggested. Templates for formators to assess the level of preoccupation with the use of Internet pornography and means of redirecting urges to view Internet pornography toward virtuous living are also presented.

Criteria for Internet pornography addiction

Originally, mental health care providers connected the term "addiction" to the use of chemicals such as alcohol, drugs, and nicotine. Psychiatrically, addiction refers to levels of tolerance and withdrawal that hinder affective or psychosocial functioning. These are physiologically mediated symptoms.[8] Tolerance is present when the same amount of a substance elicits less response. For example, a person who drinks two glasses of wine is affected by the alcohol. With continued use, the same person will need more than two glasses of wine to produce physiologic reactions. In this way, a person has developed a tolerance for the effects of alcohol. On the other hand, withdrawal refers to the physiologic reaction elicited when the amount of a substance is less present or absent in the body. Withdrawal symptoms include tremors, anxiety, elevated blood pressure, and increased rate of pulse and respirations. Affective or emotional disturbances may also be present and include depression, irritability, impulsivity, impaired concentration, disrupted sleep, or aggressive behavior. These symptoms are observable when an individual is experiencing withdrawal from alcohol or street drugs.

Following a similar pattern of tolerance and withdrawal, experts in addiction disorders

---

[8] *Diagnostic and Statistical Manual of Mental Disorders,* Fourth Edition (Washington, D.C.: American Psychiatric Association, 1994) pp. 176-9.

describe five successive and interdependent stages through which people pass on the way to an addiction to Internet pornography, including experimentation, intermittent use, habituation, compulsivity and addiction. Progression through these stages may be gradual or may occur rapidly after discovering pornographic websites.[9] Once a person stumbles onto a pornographic website, opening the door for further exploration and by the anonymity of electronic transactions, users secretly experiment with sexual material online without getting caught. This can lead to a growing curiosity and intermittent desire to view pornographic images. With repeated exposure—similar to building a tolerance to alcohol—users develop a habit of sexual fantasies and access pornographic material to increase arousal levels. As users become desensitized to online sex, heightened sexual intensity is necessary to achieve desired levels of arousal. Over time, the habit of accessing Internet pornography becomes a compulsion and is associated with tension reduction, relieving feelings of guilt, anxiety, or depression. Compulsive Internet pornographic behavior is driven largely by tension and agitation, much like an alcoholic is driven to drink at moments of excessive stress. At this stage, men and women jeopardize careers and relationships in order to satisfy their compulsive urges. Despite potential risks, men and women deceive family members and friends to conceal the extent of their involvement with Internet pornography, which is no longer a voluntary activity. Restlessness and irritability emerge when attempting to abstain from this behavior. At the addiction stage, users of pornography are unable to find the will power necessary to stop and they feel hopeless against persistent and dominant urges to view sexual images online.

Reasons for the addictive nature of Internet pornography

Over the last 40 years, several factors have created a solid platform for the introduction and acceptance of Internet pornography into American society. Principally, the introduction of the birth control pill to the public in the 1960's intensified the heat of the

---

[9] Kimberly S. Young, Ph.D., *Tangled in the Web: Understanding Cybersex from Fantasy to Addiction* (1ˢᵗ Books Library, 2001), pp. 40-44; Bruce Hannemann et al, *Rescuing Our Youth from the Porn Trap-A Parent Primer* (Elizabeth Ministry International – RECLAIM Sexual Health Division, 2014), pp. 19-20; Mark R. Laaser, *Healing the Wounds of Sexual Addiction* (Zondervan, 2004), pp. 59-70; Matt Fradd, *Delivered – True Stories of Men and Women Who Turned From Porn to Purity* (Catholic Answers Press, 2013), pp. 50-52; Peter Kleponis, *The Pornography Epidemic, A Catholic Approach* (Simon Peter Press, 2012), pp. 55-58; Familius, *Fortify: The Fighter's Guide to Overcoming Pornography Addiction* (Fight the New Drug, 2015), pp.10-12.

smoldering sexual revolution, as American society separated sexual intimacy from its core purposes of unity and procreation. Artificial contraception reduced sexual intimacy to pleasure-seeking recreation while limiting the possibility of conception. The advent of the World Wide Web made immediate the availability of adult entertainment and amplified the perceived recreational purpose of sexuality. Following this trend, today more teenagers are becoming sexually active at a time when they are emotionally vulnerable, uncertain about their moral beliefs, and confused about the purpose of sexuality.

Three primary features have added to the appeal of Internet pornography. They are: accessibility, affordability and anonymity which is sometimes referred to as the "Triple A Engine"[10] First, the omnipresence of computers, cell phones, or other electronic devices allows men and women immediate access to the Internet, which makes Internet pornography readily accessible. Most households today have at least one computer and most workers have access to a computer at their jobsites. Approximately 20% of men and 17% of women admit to accessing Internet pornography at work placing pornography as the second most frequent diversion and misuse of the Internet in the workplace, after accessing personal email.[11]   Second, since many pornographic websites offer free access, they are affordable to viewers of every age and social status. Studies indicate that 80-90% of persons who use online pornography pay nothing and 10-20% of users pay an average of $60.00 per month.[12] Pornographic preferences generally vary by gender. For example, male viewers seek photographs, videos, and live-camera feeds for sexual gratification while women are twice as likely as men to enter chat rooms,[13] seeking friendly conversations that lead to sexually explicit exchanges.

Third, enabling users to pretend to be anyone or no one when accessing pornographic websites, the anonymous quality of Internet pornography contributes to the false belief that no untoward repercussions will occur from accessing pornographic sites. The cybersex "relationship" feels more intimate than actual relationships while remaining "safely" anonymous. Fostering dishonesty, fear, self-focus, de-sensitization, and self-deceit, men and

---

[10] Al Cooper and Eric Griffen-Shelley, "The Internet: The Next Sexual Revolution," in *Sex and the Internet: A Guidebook for Clinicians* (Brunner-Routledge, 2002), pp. 5-6.

[11] Al Cooper, Irene McLaughlin, Pauline Reich, Jay Kent-Ferraro, "Virtual Sexuality in the Workplace: A Wake-up Call for Clinicians, Employers, and Employees," in *Sex and the Internet*, 2002, pp.111-112.

[12] K. Doran, "Industry Size, Measurement, and Social Costs", in *The Social Cost of Pornography: A Collection of Papers* (Witherspoon Institute, 2010), p. 185.

[13] https://www.covenanteyes.com/pornstats/ [accessed Nov. 10, 2018].

women addicted to Internet pornography value their anonymity and enhanced sexual stimulation, resulting in increased incidences of compulsive masturbation and more deviant sexual activities, sometimes leading to overt illegal behavior.[14] Accessibility, affordability, and anonymity, blending with the change of sexual mores in the use of Internet, contribute to the highly addictive quality of Internet pornography.[15] Not surprisingly, this "Triple A Engine" presents challenges to one's spiritual life. Accessibility counters custody of the eyes and celibate chastity, affordability counters poverty of time and possibly money and anonymity counters accountability and obedience.

Neurological implications of Internet pornography

Scientific research indicates that alterations in the human nervous system can also result from Internet pornography use. The human nervous system[16] has the capacity to build new nerve[17] connections, strengthening and increasing some connections while weakening and decreasing others. This change ultimately alters the functioning of the nervous system, modifying the process the brain employs to arrange information. To

---

[14] Stephen Arterburn, *Addicted to "Love", Understanding Dependencies of the Heart: Romance, Relationships, and Sex* (Regal Books, 2003), pp. 117-121.

[15] Al Cooper and Eric Griffen-Shelley, "The Internet: The Next Sexual Revolution," in *Sex and the Internet: A Guidebook for Clinicians* (Brunner-Routledge, 2002), pp. 5-6.

[16] The human nervous system is made up of the central nervous system (brain and spinal cord) and the peripheral nervous system (nerves in the body that carry messages from the brain and spinal cord to the rest of the body, such as muscles, organs and glands).

[17] The central and peripheral nervous systems are comprised of neurons or nerves. A neuron or nerve has three parts. The portion of the neuron that receives input from other neurons is called the dendrite and is shaped like tree branches. The dendrites lead into the cell body which contains DNA and the other elements necessary to keep the neuron alive. The axon is the cable of the nerve and is of varying length depending on its location and function. The nerves in the leg, for example can be several feet long depending on the height of the person. The neurons in the brain are microscopic in length. These axons are similar to electric cables and carry electric signals toward the dendrites of the neighboring neurons. Axons, or cables of the nerves, do not touch the neighboring dendrites. They are separated by a microscopic space called a synapse. Once an electric signal gets to the end of the axon, it triggers the release of a chemical messenger, called a neurotransmitter into the synapse. The neurotransmitter floats over the dendrite of the adjacent neuron, exciting or inhibiting it. If a neuron receives enough excitatory signals from other neurons, it will fire off a signal. When it receives enough inhibitory signals, it will not fire.

illustrate, when a child first learns to ride a bike, he initially teeters back and forth on the wheels of his bike until he falls. By repeatedly riding the bike, the child's central nervous system (brain and spinal cord) and peripheral nervous system (nerves in the body carrying messages from the brain and spinal cord to the rest of the body) communicate more effectively so that motor skills necessary to ride the bicycle become more precise and efficient. In this way, the youngster develops skills necessary to balance himself on the bicycle and propel himself forward with a pedaling motion. The brain's capacity to adapt the operation of the nervous system to various stimuli is a normal lifetime phenomenon.

In the same way, studies show that intense and repetitious sexual images initiate modifications at the synapse (the space between nerves through which nerve cells communicate with one another), which changes information processing in the human nervous system.[18] Two primary factors are responsible for this modulation: 1) the volume of pornography viewed and the rate at which it is viewed, and 2) the neurochemical impact on the brain.

Marshall McLuhan, a pioneer in the study of the effects of television on the human brain, was the first to describe the first factor. He described the medium of the message as playing a more significant role in altering the neural tracts of the central nervous system than the content of the message.[19] In other words, McLuhan's research demonstrates that seeing images that are "alive" on television impacts the brain more significantly than comparable "static" images as in the case of a photograph. Television as a "moving film" naturally provides a higher rate of stimuli to the brain. Now, with respect to pornography, it is the volume and rate (medium) at which the Internet pornography images are delivered that alter the brain's response to the stimuli more than static pornography images (the content) themselves. As such, the effects on the human nervous system from electronic media are increased exponentially with the emergence of high speed Internet. Handheld devices such as cell phones and iPads can alter how the human nervous system processes information because of the speed and volume of electronic stimuli they produce.

Second, the neurochemicals produced in the brain as a response to viewing pornography also impact the intensity of the addiction equation. Consider the following scenario: Upon viewing pornography, pleasure centers are triggered in the brain of the

---

[18] M.J. Koepp, R.N. Gunn, A.D. Lawrence, V.J. Cunningham, A. Dagher, T. Jones, D. J. Brooks, C.J. Bench, and P. M. Grasby, *Nature,* 1998, vol 393, no. 6682, pp 266-268; Doidge, Norman, *The Brain That Changes Itself* (Penguin Books, 2007), p. 309.

[19] W.T. Gordon, ed. *Understanding Media: The Extensions of Man, Critical Edition* (Ginkgo Press, 1994), p. 19.

viewer. Initially, the appetitive or excitatory pleasure system releases dopamine, which the body experiences with enjoyable activities, such as laughing, eating a good meal, running, or being sexually aroused. Acetylcholine[20] is also discharged into the brain, which plays an important role both in learning and memory and helps the brain focus and form sharp recall of pleasurable experiences. Acetylcholine stores these pleasurable images in the brain and makes them readily available for recall. Secondarily, the consummatory pleasure system, which produces sensations of calm and satisfaction after recreational experiences, secretes oxytocin and serotonin, bringing feelings of serenity and bonding. Endorphins are also released heightening euphoria.

Beyond viewing pornography in magazines or film strips, viewing pornography over high speed Internet, with its capacity for delivering rapid bursts of endless images, hyper-activates the appetitive pleasure center, powering a surge of dopamine through the pleasure center and forcing the attentional and motivational mechanisms of acetylcholine to focus most intensely on what is triggering the dopamine surge.[21]   With repeated excessive stimulation, the brain adapts to the stimuli dampening the pleasure system's ability to respond, not only to the same sexual stimuli, but to all ordinary pleasures. Under-stimulated, the addict needs more and more novel Internet pornography to experience pleasure. Introducing new pornographic images, such as scenarios of sex with violence or humiliation, sparks the release of more dopamine, as well as adrenaline and generates more arousal. At this stage, persons keep watching because they like the "pleasure rush" of dopamine release, dismissing the significance of how the changes in the pleasure centers of their brain have altered what sexually arouses them.

Acetylcholine, which both stores pleasurable images in the brain and makes them readily available for recall, along with oxytocin, a neurochemical that contributes to bonding, combine to create an associative quality to Internet pornography use.   To illustrate, a pianist who becomes sexually aroused when viewing Internet pornography while playing classical music can associate classical music with sexual stimulation.

---

[20] Acetylcholine plays a central role in the health of the brain. It is stored in the nerve and can be released into the synapse once the nerve is activated. Acetylcholine has several functions. For example, the parts of the brain involved in memory, learning and mood use acetylcholine extensively. It is also responsible for sending messages from the brain to certain muscles causing them to move, helps maintain optimum muscle tone, ensures that mucous membranes are always lubricated and moist and help to schedule REM or dream sleep necessary for restful sleep.

[21] The same is true of screen addiction in general. See a five-minute video by this author at https://enroutebooksandmedia.com/screenaddiction/.

Additionally, typing on a computer keyboard can remind him of playing the piano, which also triggers sexual arousal. At this juncture, the addict can "play the keyboard" of his computer to become sexually aroused.

Addictions often begin with voluntary choices to engage repeatedly in a particular behavior, like the choice to consume alcoholic beverages, smoke cigarettes, or use drugs. Over time, the body builds a tolerance to the stimuli and thresholds of consumption increase. In the same way, Internet pornography use may begin with occasional choices to view sexual images. However, high speed Internet and the release of neurotransmitters, like dopamine and acetylcholine, blend to create a powerful force that temporarily pleases while creating a malfunction in the pleasure centers. The addict's neurons, assaulted by abnormally high levels of dopamine, respond defensively by reducing the number of receptors to which dopamine can bind. The addict experiences a dopamine deficit. While Internet pornography addicts begin using Internet pornography for pleasure, they end up viewing pornography to alleviate feelings of depression and irritability. Reclaiming power and control over the pleasure centers of the brain will require concerted effort.

A Catholic Approach to Treating Internet Pornography

The addictive quality and deleterious effects of Internet pornography require a dedicated plan to temper and convert the urges to view Internet pornography. Simply suppressing the sexual appetite is insufficient.

Saint John Paul II stated the redeemed man is one who loves others rather than uses them.[22] As Catholics, we understand that simply suppressing the sexual appetite will not do. It needs to be converted to not treat persons as objects; to live by reason and not by urges. Converting our appetites requires the habitual moderation of the very desires that lead to sexual behavior. This is the goal of chastity. The values of chastity must be internalized. True, this is not easy for someone addicted to Internet pornography, but people do change, and they change dramatically. If it took two or three years to embrace the benefits of chastity three or four times a day, which would require maybe five minutes a day, would it be worth it? Absolutely!

Pope Emeritus Benedict says that our world has made love a feeling. It is not a noun, a thing. Love is a verb, to love, it is something we do, an action we take. It is the sacrifice we make in giving ourselves to another. Benedict stated that love, though tarnished, must be taken up again, brought back to its original splendor so that it may illumine our life and

---

[22] Karol Wojtyla, *Love and Responsibility* (Farrar, Straus and Giraux, 1982).

bring it back on the right path.[23]

Saint John Paul II said the real problem is not eros, but lust, which distorts and cheapens eros by reducing the other person to an object. In a sense, Saint John Paul is saying that sexual desire that is mere lust is not erotic enough. It is a counterfeit of true eros. It fails to recognize the true dignity and preciousness of the human person revealed through the body. It sees only the surface and regards the body as a mere object for one's gratification.[24]

What is key to overcoming the addiction to Internet pornography is the mindset of achieving the virtue of chastity through the arduous work of remapping the brain and converting the appetite toward viewing the human body in its true dignity and preciousness that yearns for union with the Beloved. We have learned many lessons from those who have succeeded in overcoming an addiction. The greatest lesson is that it requires motivation. If there is not motivation, the first step is to find a reason to get motivated. Once motivated, the next step is to find additional reasons to stay motivated. Hope that a problem can be solved is also a crucial ingredient to motivation because hope creates a mind-set that the problem can be solved. It is also crucial to learn from mistakes and keep striving to overcome this addiction.

It will be necessary to block stimuli that contribute to hyper-stimulation of the pleasure center and renew or create healthy stimulation tracks for the pleasure centers. The following metaphor provides a helpful perspective. When navigating a mountain slope covered with a fresh layer of snow, a skier creates a track that is determined by the contour of the slope and the movement of the skier. On the skier's second run down the mountain, the track will be very similar to the first set of tracks, based on minimal amount of change to the contour of the slope, the movement of the skis, and the texture of the snow. After navigating this mountain slope for the remainder of the day, the skier will create a reliable track that will be preferable to unchartered areas of the slope.

A similar phenomenon occurs in the human nervous system. With repeated exposure to stimuli, the brain slowly changes itself neurologically[25] to create mental tracks or neural pathways, which can lead to either good habits or bad habits. In other words, through repeated exposure to helpful stimuli, good habits become embedded in thought processes

[23] Pope Emeritus Benedict XVI, *Deus Caritas Est,* Encyclical Letter, 2005.

[24] Saint John Paul II, *Man and Woman He Created Him: The Theology of the Body* (Pauline Books and Media, 2006), pp. 314-320.

[25] J.M.Schwartz and S.Begley, *The Mind and the Brain: Neuroplasticity and the Power of Mental Force* (ReganBooks/HarperCollins, New York, 2002).

and provide reliable and useful skills. In the same way, through repeated exposure to harmful stimuli, bad habits are embedded in thought processes, limiting capacity for healthy and effective functioning.

It is important to work to identify the weaknesses or shortcomings which give an opening to lustful temptations. These include the symptoms of the acronym blasted—bored, lonely, angry/apathetic/afraid, stressed and tired. In order to better understand what is driving a habit, when beginning to fantasize, consider asking: What does this fantasy mean? What am I feeling? Am I sad, lonely or frustrated, for example?

How to change a habit

What drives a habit, especially one that is challenging to change is not always obvious. When working to change a habit, it is very important to write down the routine of the behavior you want to change. Doing so forces you to become aware of what you are thinking and feeling when you experience the cue and engage in your routine. This helps to identify distorted or inaccurate thoughts you might have about yourself and how these trigger feelings of anxiety, hopelessness, sorrow, etc. This also helps to assess if the reward for your current routine is truly the reward you are striving for. Recall that motivation and hope are key to this process. Motivation has to do with sufficient willpower to strive toward a goal. Hope has to do with believing that a new habit is possible (i.e., stop viewing pornography). And active faith—even the size of a mustard seed (cf. Mt)—opens the doors of the soul to allow the grace of the sacraments to flourish into good habits.

Changing routines requires willpower, that is, what motivates why I do what I do. Willpower is important in developing the ability to delay short-term gratification to reach long-term goals. Next let's consider some basics of how a habit is developed and then look at how to change a habit. We understand that habits are choices that are repeatedly continued without having to make a conscious decision to engage the behavior associated with the choices. In other words, a habit is formed when routines develop for behaviors that are triggered by cues that bring a reward.[26] Saint Thomas Aquinas states that just as a man can increase the strength of a habit by acting in accordance with it, so conversely, he can lessen its strength and eventually lose it either by acting contrary to it or by ceasing to use it.[27]

---

[26] Charles Duhigg, *The Power of Habit: Why We Do What We Do in Life and Business* (Random House Publishing Group, 2012).

[27] Saint Thomas Aquinas, *Summa Theologica*, I-II, q. 53-54 (Christian Classics, 1981).

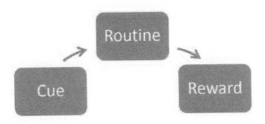

Charles Duhigg[28] states that the stronger the link between the cue and the routine, the stronger the habit. A cue kicks a routine into gear, without needing to think. Scientists estimate that roughly 40% of what persons do happens on "autopilot". Consider the Cue: You feel the buzz of your phone in your pocket. This triggers the urge to know, "Who is contacting me? I want to find out?" The Routine: stop what I am doing and check my phone. Reward: pleasure from momentary distraction from a text, email or Tweet.

The key to changing a habit is identifying the stimuli which is difficult to resist that has been triggered by a cue and build a specific plan *beforehand* for how to work it through. Persons striving to become free of the urges to view Internet pornography need to ask themselves these questions: What is the major stumbling block I can predict to changing my habit of viewing Internet pornography? What is the specific routine I can use to get through this stumbling block? In addition, researchers demonstrate that the ability to delay gratification and strengthen the willpower "muscle" has a rippling effect in other areas of one's life.[29] Therefore, strengthening the capacity for self-regulation in one area of life will

---

[28] Charles Duhigg, *The Power of Habit: Why We Do What We Do in Life and Business* (Random House Publishing Group, 2012).

[29] 1) Research has repeatedly demonstrated that will power is critical to personal success and that willpower is less like a skill and more like a muscle. Walter Mischel, PhD psychologist at Columbia University is famous for his Marshmallow Test. He studied willpower in four year old children. The children were placed in a room and presented with a marshmallow on a plate. Each child was told, "You can eat this marshmallow right away or you can wait a few minutes and I will give you two marshmallows." The adult then left the room and watched what each child did. Most children (70%) twisted and squirmed before snatching the marshmallow and eating it joyfully while 30% of the children suppressed their urges and gained the longer term reward of two marshmallows. Decades later, researchers tracked these children's performance in high school. The minority of individuals who could delay gratification ended up with better grades and SAT scores and had better social skills than those individuals that exhibited more immediate gratification behaviors. (Walter Mischel, *The Marshmallow Test: Mastering Self-Control* (Little Brown and Company, 2014). 2) Angela Duckworth and Martin Seligman of Pennsylvania did a similar test of self-control on eighth graders. They gave the children the option of receiving $1 immediately or waiting a week and

positively affect self-regulation in other areas of daily living such as refraining from viewing Internet pornography.

It is also important to seek out a spiritual director, confessor, formator or trained coaches for constructive and guiding advice when tempted to view pornography and who is willing to assist in constructively addressing old behaviors.[30] Essential to this process is honest transparency. For some, the urges to access Internet pornography are so strong that professional help is necessary.

Consider the following scenario:

Raymond is a 24 year old seminarian who sought psychiatric evaluation and treatment. He was referred by his spiritual director who was concerned that Raymond exhibited symptoms of depression and anxiety.

During his psychological evaluation, Raymond disclosed that he first looked at Internet pornography at age eleven "out of curiosity." He was aroused by the images and began to masturbate. Desiring a more intensely pleasurable experience, Raymond began to search for more stimulation by exploring various pornography sites. He added that he had disclosed this to his spiritual director before discerning a call to the priesthood and entering the seminary.

His spiritual director at the time instructed Raymond to pray and to stop viewing pornography; however, he was not given specific direction on how to address the problem nor did his spiritual director ask him more questions about his reported concerns.

Now in seminary, Raymond was still experiencing urges to view Internet pornography.

---

receiving $2. These researchers found that students who ranked high on self-discipline had better grades, better school attendance and higher standardized test scores. Self-discipline, the researchers concluded was more important than IQ for predicting academic success. Their hypothesis was that being able to resist short term temptations had a rippling effect in nearly all areas of life. These patterns held even after the researchers controlled for the children's socioeconomic status, home lives and general intelligence. These results have also been replicated across dozens of experiments. (A. Duckworth & M Seligman, "Self-Discipline Outdoes IQ in Predicting Academic Performance in Adolescents", *Psychological Science*, 16(12):939-44 January 2006).

[30]   Consider the Catholic online program Reclaim Sexual Health located online at (https://reclaimsexualhealth.com/) which provides individuals the privacy to receive coaching 24/7 on brain science of change, action plans on how to address setbacks, emotional triggers, healthy outlets and more. Other resources include STRIVE, Integrity Restored and Covenant Eyes.

Raymond feared his formators would dismiss him from the seminary and this fear kept him from bringing this problem into the external forum with his seminary formator. Soon, he withdrew from other seminarians and faculty. Believing that he was helpless to address his problem, Raymond despaired of being free of these urges.

Lust can lead to despair of becoming free of the urges to view Internet pornography because it directs a person's attention largely to sensory pleasures that encourage intemperance. The strong desire for bodily pleasure drives out the affection for the spiritual good. Saint Thomas Aquinas also notes that sloth is a cause of despair, because a person afflicted with sloth is sorrowful, which encourages despair when confronted with the difficulties of cultivating a spiritual life.[31]

At the beginning of treatment, Raymond admitted "All of my adult life I have used pornography to deal with frustrations and loneliness". He was ashamed of the behaviors that resulted in his fantasizing about women he had viewed on the Internet. We spoke of the fact that strategies for healing from the strong urges to view Internet pornography were not complicated. Most important, however, was whether the person was willing to commit to the process of learning new ways to address unwanted urges, do the work of facing the hurts, shame, guilt and anger of his past and to be open to the graces of God.

Over the next several weeks of intensive therapy, we reviewed in detail his patterns of Internet pornography use and his early childhood history. Raymond was asked to write down the cues and each step of his routine that led to the behaviors he wanted to change. He named his triggers, emotions, images, thoughts and physiologic reactions as well as beliefs he held about his behaviors. He wrote down vulnerable moments to help him identify the specific images, feelings and thoughts that contributed to his relapses. He worked on preparing alternative thoughts to his previously telling himself he deserved a break when feeling overwhelmed, frustrated, lonely or unappreciated. When one of his triggers for seeking pornographic images presented themselves, he planned an alternative routine such as calling his accountability partner, contacting his spiritual director, praying for God's assistance, doing some physical work and reminding himself how he felt after viewing pornography.

Through this process of detailing his cues and routines, Raymond gained insights into the power that he had given to pornographic images. There is no quick or easy way to erase from the memory pornographic images associated with cybersex activities. Spiritual, mental, emotional and physical discipline are necessary to be free from these images and

---

[31] ST, II-II, qu. 35.

behaviors.[32] Raymond began to realize that pornography is not something that is simply overcome through exerting strong willpower. Rather, he had to prepare *beforehand* what alternative routine he would engage in when he had the urge to view Internet pornography. He was also reminded that overcoming these urges was a process and not an event.

Next, he committed to reviewing his routine each time a cue triggered a response in order to assess the effectiveness of his new routine. This process contributed to a new found capacity to become freer of the urges to view pornography. The third component of the healing process came when Raymond began to explore the power he had given his distorted or negative beliefs. Throughout the years, he had formed negative or distorted beliefs about himself which evolved from childhood experiences. These beliefs fueled his relapses. Some of his core beliefs were:

- ○ I am inferior, inadequate, unlovable
- ○ I am alone
- ○ Nobody understands how hard I am trying, but I cannot stop
- ○ I have repeatedly told myself that I would not relapse again but I keep going back to it
- ○ I deserve some pleasure that does not hurt anyone else
- ○ I am a bad person
- ○ Nobody would like me if they knew who I really was
- ○ I cannot meet the expectations of becoming a priest

These beliefs kept Raymond trapped in what he referred to as "my black box." He had not realized this until he wrote down these negative or distorted beliefs and saw how these thoughts were hopelessly guiding his daily living. This process of examining the impact of his negative thoughts broadened his self-understanding. We worked together to have him challenge each negative belief about himself and worked at bringing reality to bear on these self-limiting thoughts.

It is important to challenge unhealthy beliefs. Many persons never question whether their beliefs are accurate or inaccurate. Change occurs when thoughts or beliefs that guide behaviors are reframed. This step takes time and almost always creates a new perspective. In Raymond's case, challenging his unhealthy beliefs was a turning point in his creating new routines for healthier habits.

By challenging his unhealthy beliefs, Raymond began the process of identifying his

---

[32] See additional suggestions in Intra-Chapter Appendix 2.

personal, interpersonal, and work values and developing an action plan to engage these values in order to avoid derailment by urges to access Internet pornography. As Catholics, we know these values as living a life of Christian virtue.

Value-based Routines as Means of Moving from Vice to Virtue

Values guide and motivate our lives, adding richness and fulfillment. They are compasses that direct the way we interact with God, individuals and the community. Above all, values form foundations for our convictions, behaviors, personal vision, and the strengths and qualities we want to develop. In other words, moving from vice to virtue entails outlining specific practical means of values-based living[33]. It is these practical means that comprise alternate routines which, if well planned, become the means of remapping the neurocircuitry of the brain away from the vice of urges to view Internet pornography to the virtue of chastity. There are three primary areas of value-based living: personal, interpersonal and apostolic/work. For example, persons choosing to live by the value of personal health might focus on the spiritual, physical and emotional areas of their lives. Interpersonal values include relationships within the seminary community, as well as family and friends. Work values might include specific aspects of vocational ministry. Raymond began by outlining *beforehand* specific routines that help him develop the qualities he was striving toward.[34]

By virtue of the primacy of values in daily life, value-based living informs and directs a person's decisions and behaviors as well as his or her long-range plans. Values alone are insufficient, however, to treat the urges to view Internet pornography. While value-congruent goals *direct* choices and behaviors, a healthy routine of committed actions is required for *success*. In other words, a person struggling with urges to view Internet pornography can safely stare at the compass of his or her values; embracing a healthy routine of committed actions, the person struggling with temptations to view Internet pornography will apply the means to live by core values to overcome the influence of pornographic images, even in the face of pain and discomfort. In the end, value or virtue based living and congruent committed routines are necessary for affective maturity, which contribute to a freedom for chastity.

Raymond identified growth in holiness, emotional balance, and physical well-being as

---

[33] S.C. Hayes, S. Smith, *Get Out of Your Mind and Into Your Life: The New Acceptance and Commitment Therapy* (New Harbinger Publications, Oakland, CA, 2005).

[34] See chart *Striving to Become a Gift For Others*, Intra-Chapter Appendix 1.

specific and desired values for his personal health. To live these values, creating SMART goal routines was necessary for Raymond. There are various versions of the acronym for SMART. One descriptive acronym is specific, measurable, attainable, relevant and trackable.

For example, Raymond developed a SMART goal routine for growth in holiness. Before going to bed, Raymond gets on his knees, calls on Our Lady to be with him, begs her for purity and says three *Hail Mary's* like he really means it. Once in bed, he next prays the *Saint Michael* prayer. He then has the routine of holding onto the crucifix of his rosary with both hands and recalls Jesus' love for him and then focuses his imagination on the mysteries of the rosary praying for a specific intention with each bead. Raymond also posts Scripture passages and holy images in key places (e.g. computer, monitor, bedroom, bathroom, office). He plays or sings spiritual songs at home to help protect him and help him focus on God. He tunes his radio and TV to Christian stations or turns them off. He listens to tapes and CDs and reads books that encourage his efforts at purity. He invests in wholesome videos and DVDs. This can be a challenge but planning a routine *beforehand* is very helpful in his gradually purifying his mind of pornographic images. He also re-committed to more attentively praying the Liturgy of the Hours, 15 minutes of daily reading from Sacred Scripture, a daily five-minute examination of conscience and frequenting the Sacrament of Reconciliation along with daily Mass.[35]

Realizing that he was most vulnerable to relapse when he concealed his urge to view Internet pornography, felt isolated, and ignored emotional issues, Raymond created SMART goal routines for emotional balance that reflect his value of personal well-being. These routines include calling his accountability partner daily, turning off his computer every evening by 5:00 pm, discontinuing Internet service for his cell phone and participating in a weekly seminarian's support group.[36] He also engages a sensory awareness exercise to help shift attention away from his sexual temptations and onto a healthier focus and activity. This involves intently focusing, for two seconds, on five things he sees, then five things he feels and lastly five things he hears in his immediate surroundings and completing the phrase for each item, "Now I am aware of..." For example, "Now I am aware of seeing a halo around Our Lady in this picture on the wall." He continues this exercise looking carefully for two seconds at the next item he chooses to focus on completing the phrase, "Now I am aware of..." He then engages his sense of hearing by listening to five different sounds he is aware of (a car going by outside, the ticking of a clock in the room, another person's voice, etc.). Third, he engages his sense of

---

[35] Ibid.

[36] Ibid.

touch noting five things he is aware of feeling (his shoe on the floor, his glasses on the bridge of his nose, etc.). If present, he also notes a smell (like the aroma of coffee brewing or something cooking in the refectory, for example). This sensory awareness exercise is a very powerful tool to aid in purifying the imagination. We cannot concentrate intently on two different things at once. It is helpful to make a habit of engaging this exercise with domestic activities such as when brushing one's teeth or going for a walk. Becoming more aware of the here and now, the duty of the moment, helps to sensually focus on the present environment and distance one's imagination from the fantasy world of pornography. It is not possible to ignore all distractions, but it is possible to redirect one's attention to healthier images.

In addition, Raymond developed SMART goal routines for his interpersonal values, which he identified as connecting, caring and contributing [37] to other seminarians, faculty, family, friends and parishioners in keeping with his vocation. This was a new found opportunity for him to grow in performing acts of the little virtues. Raymond named evangelization through preaching, teaching and witnessing to Christ for his work or ministerial value. His SMART goal routines for this value focused on mentoring the Bible study participants, RCIA students and religious education students he was given responsibility for at his parish assignment. These values and goals were not new for Raymond; what was new was his commitment to engage these values and SMART goal routines as roadblocks to accessing Internet pornography through competitive alternative action. In so doing, Raymond was creating neural pathways that lead him to a life of virtue and away from the vice of lust. He still, however, was struggling with urges to view Internet pornography.

Defusion[38]

Raymond acknowledged the conflict between his use of pornography and his promise to live chastely. The process of defusion is an effective strategy that diminishes the influence of painful and unpleasant thoughts through acknowledging their presence while refocusing on values and SMART goal routines pertinent to the present moment. Defusing from negative ruminations and choosing value-based routines gradually refashioned the neural pathways in Raymond's brain, making them more congruent with healthy activation of the

---

[37] Ibid.

[38] S.C. Hayes, K.D. Strosahl and K.G. Wilson, *Acceptance and Commitment Therapy: An Experiential Approach to Behavior Change* (Guilford Press, New York, 1999).

pleasure centers. For example, his "good for nothing" story was triggered by the news that one of the eighth grade kids at the parish school he was assigned to was being bullied online by another eighth grader. Rather than allowing his overwhelmed thoughts and feelings about this presenting problem to lead to accessing Internet pornography, Raymond refocused on the present moment and contacted the parish priest and school principal to plan an intervention, which had several positive results. One, the intervention addressed the present bullying problem and provided an occasion to educate parish staff, children and parents about bullying. Two, through parent teacher meetings and a staff workshop on how to address bullying, they developed an educational anti-bullying program for each grade level in the parish school. This approach of connecting, caring, and contributing to his parish school relationships was hopeful and inspiring for him. Most significantly, no longer thinking about Internet pornography, Raymond succeeded in blazing healthier routines when feeling stressed or overwhelmed.

The chief element in the process of defusion is the observing-self. Responsible for focus, attention, and awareness, the observing-self is an internal viewpoint from which a person gains awareness of self and awareness of the external environment. With the observing-self, men and women connect more fully with experiences in the present moment, enabling them to fulfill committed actions that are consistent with their personal values and intended SMART goal routines. Alternatively, without the observing-self, a person does not gain self-awareness nor engage in value-based routines. For example, when feeling lonely and unappreciated, Raymond acknowledged that his "good for nothing" story was playing. He refocused his attention, engaged his observing-self to defuse from this story line and employed one of his value-based SMART goal routines. He could choose to call his accountability partner, exercise, request a meeting with his spiritual director or formator, call a family member, call a friend to go for a jog, wash his car, do a kind act for another, or pray. He discovered that there were numerous value-based routines he could engage, regardless of what he was thinking, feeling, or imagining. With time, his committed action routines, congruent with his values, diminished both the intensity and frequency of pornographic imagery.

Today, Raymond continues to take radical steps in order to avoid both the remote and the approximate occasions of sin. He makes daily a heartfelt decision to break free of Internet pornography and then acts on that decision. He has purged his computer of all pornographic images, moved his computer to an open location, uses Internet minimally, installed a multi-layered Internet filtering system, has an accountability partner whom he calls every day as well as when he is tempted to view pornography. He has recommitted to daily praying the Liturgy of the Hours, meditation, Mass, reading Sacred Scripture, spiritual reading and regular confession. He strives to make acts of faith, hope, and charity and to grow in the little virtues. An essential factor to his continued human growth and development is that his struggle is out in the open now and he is working, one day at a time, to continue to resist the urge to view pornographic images, seeking not only to be prudent and vigilant in guarding his gift of celibate chastity, but also relating his deepest desires, including sexual desires, to God in prayer.[39]

When persons begin to heal, their behaviors begin focusing on things they value. Persons feel freer when they allow their deep convictions and values to guide their behaviors. Remember that change is a process not an event. The suggested resources and the steps outlined need to be reviewed and repeated several times before temptations subside. It requires persistence and resolve to stop giving into lustful thoughts. When we repeatedly exercise our spiritual and affective "muscles", we grow stronger in using our free will making it easier to resist the next temptations we face. Do not give up after setbacks. If you fall, get up and keep striving.[40]

Assessing the Level of Preoccupation With the Use of Internet Pornography

An important formation question to begin this section might be, is it appropriate for a formator to discuss sexual impulses and drives with a seminarian as part of gaining a deeper understanding of a man's level of affective maturity and where he has room to grow? In other words, can growth in maturity be evaluated in the external forum? I propose that the answer is yes. To further clarify, this is not a suggestion to question the validity of the distinctions between the internal and external forum, nor to violate the internal forum. Consider the area of celibate chastity. The *Program for Priestly Formation* #93 states:

Certain habits or skills are necessary instruments on the path to effective and healthy celibate chastity, and these are to be encouraged in seminary programs. Among these habits and skills are appropriate self- disclosure, a cultivated capacity for self-reflection, an ability to enter into peaceful solitude, ascetical practices that foster vigilance and self-mastery over one's impulses and drives, and a habit of modesty. An especially important practice is holding all persons in the mystery of

---

[39] Saint John Paul II, *Pastores Dabo Vobis* (Post-Synodal Apostolic Exhortation, 1992), no. 44.

[40] See Intra-Chapter Appendix 2 for additional means of purifying the memory and imagination of pornographic images.

God, whether they are encountered in the course of formal ministry or ordinary life.

As well, the *PPF* #86 states: "Candidates should give evidence of having interiorized their seminary formation." In other words, the *PPF* indicates that the evidence of effective and healthy celibate chastity includes not only internal motivations and commitments but external observable behaviors as well. A seminarian must be able to speak about his relationship with God and promote an encounter with God in other persons. If not, a wonder needs to arise as to whether such a man can be recommended for ordination. It is in this sense that what is in the internal forum also moves and shows itself in the external forum.

The chapter on Markers of Human Maturation in Seminary Formation—Becoming a Gift for Others[41] provides questions that a seminarian might be asked by his formator. The assessment tool assists the human formation advisor in assessing whether or not a seminarian is interiorizing his formation experience. It is an instrument of the external forum. The goal of this instrument to is help assess, with respect to his human growth, whether a seminarian is bearing fruit from his formation and where he has room to grow. This helps identify if a seminarian's vocation is being authored by God and if so, what are the means and ways to continue to grow in his priestly identity.

For example, if a seminarian has viewed Internet pornography, where is he with respect to self-awareness regarding celibate chastity? Is he moving toward self-knowledge and self-direction regarding this aspect of priestly identity?

Assessing preoccupation with the use of Internet pornography is most accurately described on a continuum rather than describing someone as addicted or not addicted. For example, someone may view Internet pornography for days or weeks and then not again for months. Someone else might view Internet pornography only on weekends. We do not have clear answers as to why there is such variability in persons' viewing of Internet pornography. Likely, contributing fluctuations are reflective of stress, changes in relationship, family or work circumstances and emotional well-being.

Assessment tools help individuals determine their level of involvement in pornography so that they can receive specific guidance on the frequency and effects of viewing Internet pornography. Such tools have been helpful for screening purposes used by counselors, bishops, clergy and family members who want to help individuals who are addicted to pornography. There are several online versions which offer personalized feedback and

---

[41] See Segment 2, Chapter 1.

graphs based on the answers provided by the respondent. A screening instrument is never diagnostic by itself, however. If there is a concern about the use of Internet pornography, assessment by a trained professional should be sought.

To follow are some key features describing increasing levels of pornography use[42] with a narrowed focus on seminary formation considerations:

Experimental:

- View pornography one or two times a year or can count the number of times on both hands
- Viewing pornography is a random act and not a focus of thoughts and everyday actions

Intermittent:

- Desire to view pornography does not dominate thoughts
- Fantasies are minimal
- There is a growing curiosity and desire to view pornographic images
- Efforts to refrain from viewing pornography are generally successful
- Seminarian is appropriately addressing this unchastity with his spiritual director and formator. For example:
  - Where is the seminarian with respect to self-awareness regarding celibate chastity? Is he moving toward self-knowledge and self-direction regarding this aspect of priestly identity? Or, is celibate chastity something he is accepting as an external discipline, a deprivation?
  - Is he on the way to integrating celibate chastity as part of his evolving priestly identity? If so, what experiences is he having that contribute to this deepening process? For example, is he experiencing celibate chastity as a means to better enable him to be a gift to others? How is he handling successes and failures in his strivings? Can he speak joyfully of remaining celibate for love of Christ and the Church that others might be made holy?

---

[42] Skinner, Kevin B., *Treating Pornography Addiction: The Essential Tools for Recovery* (GrowthClimate, Inc., 2005); Kimberly S. Young, Ph.D., *Tangled in the Web: Understanding Cybersex from Fantasy to Addiction* (1st Books Library, 2001); Al Cooper and Eric Griffen-Shelley, "The Internet: The Next Sexual Revolution," in *Sex and the Internet: A Guidebook for Clinicians* (Brunner-Routledge, 2002). J. Brian Bransfield, *Overcoming Pornography Addiction: A Spiritual Solution* (Paulist Press, 2013).

      o What is a plan for more deeply developing this aspect of priestly identity?

Habitual:

- Extra effort is needed to fight off thoughts and desires to view pornography
- It is difficult to refrain from viewing pornography for more than one month
- There may be periods of binging for one or two days before attempting to quit viewing pornography
- Generally more erotic forms of pornography are being accessed
- Withdrawal symptoms may emerge with a strong urge to view
- Counseling with a therapist trained in addictions is necessary at this level
- The formation team needs to closely accompany such a seminarian and discern if formation can continue watching for affective growth from vice to virtue

Compulsion:

- Viewing pornography escalates to weekly or every other week accompanied by strong and challenging desires to give in to viewing pornography
- At this level, there is an increase in fantasies about pornography
- It is quite an effort to fight off urges to view pornography
- Persons become more isolative in order to give in to viewing pornography
- Persons are more involved with pornography than they want to be
- If persons can acknowledge that there is a problem, they can ward off more deeply seated compulsive behaviors
- Assessment by a professional counselor trained in addictions is essential at this level
- Formation team needs to prayerfully discern if affective growth is evolving or if leave of absence from seminary is in order to address the compulsive viewing of pornography and thorough reassessment if seminarian requests to return for seminary formation

Addiction:

- At this level, pornography is impacting day to day living
- Individuals spend significantly more time thinking about sex and looking at pornography
- Viewing pornography has increased to three to five times per week
- More hard-core pornography is being viewed

- Symptoms of withdrawal are quite evident at this level (irritability, restlessness, insomnia, for example)
- Thinking about pornography impacts prayer, school work and social relationships
- Persons are on the brink of giving up trying to "fight off" the urge to view pornography
- Feelings of hopelessness leads persons back to viewing more pornography
- Assessment by a professional counselor trained in addictions is essential at this level
- Removal from the seminary may best serve such an individual so as to address the more deeply entrenched neurobiopsychosocial effects of Internet pornography addiction.

Closing Recommendations:

The *Program of Priestly Formation* states, "Care should be taken to ensure that issues of human formation that properly belong to the external forum are not limited to the spiritual direction relationship for their resolution."[43] One of the goals of seminary formation is to help the seminarian articulate an honest understanding of himself, with his complex make-up, weaknesses, and potentialities toward a priestly identity. The Program for Priestly Formation continues, "Just as the seminary recognizes that the positive qualities of a seminarian's prior formation can both indicate a vocation and provide a solid foundation for further growth, it should also address possible deficiencies in the candidate's earlier formation and find means to address them."[44]

The external formator and spiritual director have obligations to facilitate interiorizing and strengthening of the seminarian's commitment to the priestly vocation. Recall Raymond did not begin to break free of his compulsion to view Internet pornography until his routine was no longer a secret and appropriate persons were guiding and supporting his process of vocational growth and development.

At the same time, respecting a seminarian's right of privacy is necessary, and careful management of confidential materials must be observed. "This is especially true in the case of sharing confidential information with a team of formators, while at the same time ensuring that those charged with the candidate's growth and integration have clear and specific information so they can help the candidate achieve the growth necessary to become

---

[43] *Program of Priestly Formation*, 5th ed. (Washington, DC: United States Conference of Catholic Bishops, September, 2006), n. 131.

[44] Ibid., n. 88.

a 'man of communion.'"[45]

Consider the following actions be taken where possible:

- Develop a consent form for seminarians who engage in counseling during seminary years of formation which gives formators permission to receive from/share with the counselor/therapist pertinent vocational information

    o Indicate that the sole purpose for granting permission to receive/share this information is to aide in the process of a seminarian's vocational discernment and personal growth
    o Specify the persons who may receive such information (e.g. seminary formation faculty, vocation director, bishop)

- Establish similar protocols for records kept by formators
- Determine a period of retention of records, and establish a process of destruction of these records by the dioceses, religious communities, and seminaries.

The seminarian's relationship with his formation team and his continued cooperation with the work of divine grace are necessary to unfold the uniqueness of each seminarian in his developing priestly identity.

Conclusion

With inexhaustible abilities, the Internet can be a powerful tool for learning and communicating. In his address on the occasion of the 2002 World Day of Communications, Saint John Paul II wrote:

The Internet causes billions of images to appear on millions of computer monitors around the planet. From this galaxy of sight and sound will the face of Christ emerge and the voice of Christ be heard? For it is only when his face is seen and his voice heard that the world will know the glad tidings of our redemption. This is the purpose of evangelization. And this is what will make the Internet a genuinely human space, for if

---

[45] Mark L. Bartchak, "Canonical Issues Concerning Confidentiality, Privacy Rights, Access to Data, and Record Keeping", *Seminary Journal*, 14, n.1 (Spring 2008): 7.

there is no room for Christ, there is not room for man. Therefore…I dare to summon the whole Church bravely to cross this new threshold, to put out into the deep of the Net, so that now as in the past the great engagement of the Gospel and culture may show to the world 'the glory of God on the face of Christ' (2 Cor 4:6). May the Lord bless all those who work for this aim.[46]

The new frontier of the second millennium, cyberspace, is replete with interplay of danger and promise. Providing a flood of information, the Internet offers facts but does not teach values. In this light, formators must instruct seminarians to employ committed routines as they engage with the Internet, as a means of fashioning and refashioning neural pathways toward virtue-based living. Armed with the vision of our transcendent dignity as persons, each one of us is summoned to the great adventure of using the Internet's potential to proclaim the Gospel of Christ.

Striving to Become a Gift for Others*

(*see chapter section *Value-based Routines as Means of Moving from Vice to Virtue*)

Areas of Well-Being	Value (Quality to be developed)	SMART Goal Routine (Specific, Measurable, Attainable, Relevant, Trackable) Committed Actions (planned beforehand)
	Spiritual **(Growth in Holiness)**	Before getting into bed: Pray the Saint Michael prayer then pray to Our Lady for purity. Get into bed, holding onto the crucifix of my rosary with both hands and recall Jesus' love for me, then focus my imagination on the mysteries of the rosary praying for a specific intention with each bead. Post Scripture passages and holy images in key places, re-commit to more

[46] John Paul II, *Internet: A New Forum for Proclaiming the Gospel*, #6, World Communications Day, 2002.

Personal:		attentiveness during liturgical prayer. Engage more deeply in formation meetings.
	Emotional Balance	Call accountability partner daily, turn off computer by 5 pm, discontinue Internet on cell phones, and participate in weekly seminarian support group. Engage daily in sensory awareness exercises-while brushing teeth, walking outside.
	Physical Health (food, sleep, exercise)	Eat healthy snacks, take appropriate portions of food at each meal. Get up as soon as alarm goes off in the morning, lights out by 11 pm. Exercise in weight room Mondays/Thursdays; go jogging for 20 minutes Tuesday, Wednesday, Friday afternoons.
Relationships:	**Care, Connect, Contribute**	Look for opportunity to do one daily act of kindness, weekly choose a different person to write a note to, call or speak to expressing gratitude for something they have done or said. In an ongoing fashion, strive to make acts of faith, hope and charity and grow in the little virtues.
Apostolic/work:	**Bring Jesus to others**	Prayerfully prepare for Bible study, RCIA classes given responsibility for and pray for participants. Pray to be attentive and take opportunity to speak about the faith when situations present themselves.

Self-Awareness → Self-Knowledge → Self-Direction → Self-Control → Self-Discipline → Self-Governance → Virtue → Leads to True Freedom

Intra-Chapter Appendix 1

Striving to Become a Gift for Others

Areas of Well-Being	Value (Quality to be developed)	SMART Goal Routine (Specific, Measurable, Attainable, Relevant, Trackable) Committed Actions (planned beforehand)
Personal:	Spiritual (Growth in Holiness)	
	Emotional Balance	
	Physical Health (food, sleep, exercise)	
Relationships:	Care, Connect, Contribute	
Apostolic/work:	Bring Jesus to others	

Self-Awareness → Self-Knowledge → Self-Direction → Self-Control → Self-Discipline → Self-Governance → Virtue → Leads to True Freedom

<u>Intra-Chapter Appendix 2</u>

Means of purifying the mind of pornographic images:

- In order to avoid both the remote and proximate occasions of temptation, *destroy all pornographic material*. Also, *pray for persons*, most often, women *who provide the images and videos for Internet pornography*.

- *Install accountability software* on all computers, cell phones and other Internet capable electronics. Realize that no filtering system is fool-proof. A layered filtering system is necessary. Today's electronic environment requires a filtering system for the network hub or wireless router. As well, filtering and accountability services need to be installed on each individual device.[47]

- *Involve a spiritual director, formator, counselor, trusted friend or pastor* who is equally committed to helping with the goal of filtering out undesirable material.

- If you must go online for legitimate purposes, *before logging onto the Internet, prepare a list of specific tasks that need to be accomplished online*. Stick to that list as you use the Internet.

- *Seek a Catholic accountability person or group* which offers a safe anonymous place for persons struggling with Internet pornography to receive support and appropriate guidance.[48]

- As Catholics, we have a wealth of resources. *The Sacrament of Reconciliation*--the divine medicine cannot heal the disease in the soul if it is not confessed. This sacrament brings us into communion not only with God, but with people as a church. *Holy Eucharist*--Holy Communion augments our union with Christ, separates us from sin, strengthens our charity and helps preserve us from future mortal sins. Another means of helping to diminish pornographic images is taking time to read and memorize *Scripture* every day. Saint Thomas More once said,

---

[47] OpenDNS, CleanBrowing.org, Mobicip, Circle Go, Qustodio, Covenant Eyes for example.

[48] Consider the Catholic online program Reclaim Sexual Health located online at (https://reclaimsexualhealth.com/) which provides individuals the privacy to receive coaching 24/7 on brain science of change, action plans on how to address setbacks, emotional triggers, healthy outlets and more. Other resources include STRIVE, Integrity Restored and Covenant Eyes.

"Occupy your mind with good thoughts or the enemy will fill them with bad ones. Unoccupied, they cannot be."[49] Recite Scripture passages during quiet times of the day or during temptations. Be aware that when a person begins the process toward healing, the struggle for purity will appear to get worse before getting better.

Additional means of purifying the imagination include:

- *Custody of the external senses.* What do we choose to see, hear, touch and taste? It is necessary to control the external senses, especially the sense of sight, because it most often provides the images the imagination retains and reproduces, thus arousing the passions and weakening the will to consent to lower level desires and temptations.
- *Prudent selection of reading material.* Some reading material can fill the imagination with useless images. Light reading can be a good source of relaxation, but it is necessary to provide holy and profitable material so that the imagination will be directed positively toward the good. Thus, spiritual reading can contribute a great deal to the proper use of the imagination.
- *Attention to the duty of the moment.* The habit of attending to the duty of the moment has the double advantage of concentrating our intellectual powers and of disciplining the imagination, by preventing it from being distracted to other objects which can dissipate and tempt.
- *Healthy Lifestyle.* Get sufficient hours of sleep. Electronic devices should go to bed before you do and you get up before the device does. Use an alarm clock, not your cell phone. Silence your phone except for phone calls that may signal an emergency. Tell friends, co-workers, family, those who need to know that at night, if there is an emergency, to call on the phone. Let others know not to text or email at night as you will not have these functions on. Beware of excessive fatigue. Defenses and coping skills decline with too little sleep and high levels of chronic stress. Eat properly. Get sufficient exercise. Consider a retreat day for spiritual renewal to refocus on God.
- *Learn how to establish healthy boundaries and develop healthy relationships.* Develop friendships that strive for a mutual growth in Christian virtue. Avoid

---

[49] W. Jos Walter, *Sir Thomas More: Selections From His Works* (Barrington and Haswell Printers, 1841), p. 312.

friendships based on sensuality or that negatively influence behavior. Exhibit genuine modesty in matters of dress and behavior.

- *Key to affective maturity is self-knowledge.* We cannot come to self-knowledge without self-awareness and most often we need others to help us become aware. Once we have some self-awareness, we can build on this toward self-control and self-direction, then toward self-discipline, and further toward self-governance and living according to the virtues.

Additional means of purifying the memory include:

- *Forge forward from past sins or offenses against others.* Once one has repented and been forgiven of sins or offenses against others, the vivid remembrance of a sin or offense can be a means of new temptation, and therefore, the soul must reject immediately any remembrance of this kind. True repentance for sin leads to conversion, and gratitude for forgiveness of sin yields to joy, peace, and mercy.[50]
- *Cease thinking of past injuries.* This principle is indispensable to a soul which seeks to sanctify itself. The vivid remembrance of a past injury will disturb the peace of conscience. It is better to truly "let go" and forget the disagreeable episode, and realize that our offenses against God are much greater, and that He demands that we pardon others in order to receive pardon. The soul that nourishes resentment or bitterness, however justifiable it may seem (and it is never so in the "eyes" of God), will be prevented from attaining sanctity.[51]
- *Remember the benefits you have received from God.* This pertains to the positive purification of the memory and is an effective means for directing the memory to God. The recollection of the immense benefits we have received from God, of the times He has pardoned our faults, of the dangers from which he has preserved us, of the loving care He has exercised over us, is an excellent means of arousing our gratitude toward God and the desire of cooperating more faithfully with His graces.
- *Consideration of the hope for our own salvation.* This is an unmerited gift from God through the life, passion, death and resurrection of Jesus. The remembrance of an

---

[50] Saint John Paul II, *Dives in Misericordia*, Encyclical, 1980; Wilfrid Stinissen, *Into Your Hands, Father: Abandoning Ourselves to the God Who Loves Us* (Ignatius Press, 2011), pp. 37-40; Saint Thomas Aquinas, *Summa Theologica*, II, II q. 28-30.

[51] Wilfrid Stinissen, *Into Your Hands, Father: Abandoning Ourselves to the God Who Loves Us* (Ignatius Press, 2011), pp. 40-44.

eternity of happiness, which is the central object of Christian hope can be a powerful tool in helping us to disdain the corruptible things of earth and raise our spirits to God.

- *Exercise ascetical principles.* Fasting and abstinence is another aide for sexual temptations. Saint Thomas Aquinas wrote that fasting helps to bridle the lusts of the flesh. Fasting is the guardian of chastity and is useful in atoning for and helping to prevent sin.[52] Saint Augustine wrote that "Fasting cleanses the soul, raises the mind to higher things, scatters the clouds of concupiscence, quenches the fires of lust and enkindles chastity.[53]

- *Pray for help and protection.* Long prayers will often not move us away from temptation. A brief and trusting call to "Jesus!" for help or making the sign of the cross or saying a prayer to Saint Michael the Archangel have all conquered temptation, sin and Satan. Beg Our Lord for purity. If tempted when getting into bed, get out of bed, ask Our Lady to be at your side, get on your knees and pray three *Hail Mary's* like you really mean it.

- *Ask friends to pray for you.* Also ask a contemplative religious community to pray for you daily in their intentions. Remarkable answers to prayer have resulted through such intercessory requests.

Prayer

"For I know the plans I have for you," declares the Lord, "plans to prosper you and not to harm you, plans to give you hope and a future. Then you will call on me and come and pray to me, and I will listen to you. You will seek me and find me when you seek me with all your heart." (Jeremiah 29:11-13)

Practicum Reflection Questions for Formators

"Christ loved the Church and gave himself up for her, that he might sanctify her." (Eph 5:25-26).

1. How are you meeting Christ in your call to celibacy?
2. Where are there sorrows and where are there joys in your call to celibacy?
3. How do you experience Mary's role in your call to celibacy?

---

[52] Saint Thomas Aquinas, *Summa Theologica,* II-II, q. 147, art. 1.

[53] Ibid.

4. How have you "given up yourself" for Holy Mother Church? How are you sacrificing yourself that others might be made holy?

5. How do you receive the love of others as gift?

Suggested Resources

1. Skinner, Kevin B. *Treating Pornography Addiction: The Essential Tools for Recovery.* (GrowthClimate, Inc., 2005).

2. Charles Duhigg, *The Power of Habit: Why We Do What We Do in Life and Business* (Random House Publishing Group, 2012).

3. Matt Fradd, *The Porn Myth: Exposing the Reality Behind the Fantasy of Pornography* (Ignatius Press, 2017).

4. J. Brian Bransfield, *Overcoming Pornography Addiction: A Spiritual Solution* (Paulist Press, 2013).

SEGMENT 3

Affective Maturity: Spiritual Tools for the Interior Life

Chapter Sixteen

A Paradigm for the Interior Life Necessary for Evangelization

Fr. Peter Williams, STL

Fr. Peter Williams is currently serving as Pastor of Saint Ambrose of Woodbury Catholic Community in the Archdiocese of Saint Paul and Minneapolis. He was ordained a priest in 2004 and received his STL in the New Evangelization from Sacred Heart Seminary in Detroit in 2018. In addition to serving previously as a Pastor for eight years, he has served in various capacities of seminary and priestly formation, including Director of Vocations, Director for Ongoing Clergy Formation, Vice Rector of the St. Paul Seminary, formator at St. John Vianney College Seminary, and Minister to Clergy. Having served as an adjunct faculty member in the Spiritual Direction Program of the Institute for Priestly Formation, he is privileged to accompany brother-priests in spiritual direction on a monthly basis.

There has been a seismic shift over the past fifty years in how the Catholic Church conceives of her identity. This renewed understanding has involved a fundamental turning of the Church to evangelization. Pope Paul VI articulated the foundational truth on which this renewal revolves: "Evangelizing is in fact the grace and vocation proper to Church, her deepest identity. She exists in order to evangelize."[1] Standing within this conviction and with a keen attentiveness to the signs of the times, Pope John Paul II heralded a "new evangelization" as "the primary service which the Church can render to every individual and to all of humanity in the modern world…which seems to have lost its sense of ultimate realities and of existence itself."[2] It could be argued that summoning the Church to an evangelization that is "new in its ardor, methods, and expressions,"[3] served as the constant

---

[1] Paul VI, *Evangelii Nuntiandi*,(Boston: Pauline Books and Media, 1975), n. 14.

[2] John Paul II, *Redemptoris Missio* (Boston: Pauline Books and Media, 1990), n. 2.

[3] John Paul II, *Compendium on the New Evangelization* (Washington D.C.: Libreria Editrice Vaticana,2015), n. 125.

reference point and unifying thread of his lengthy and influential pontificate. The implications of this focus continue to unfold under the leadership of Pope Francis, who reaffirmed "that missionary outreach is paradigmatic for all the Church's activity."[4]

Concurrent with this call for a new evangelization has been a call for all the baptized to live integral lives of holiness. Indeed, "the universal call to holiness is closely linked to the universal call to mission."[5] It would be a mistake to conflate evangelization with updating pastoral techniques or better coordinating ecclesial resources. What is needed rather is a new ardor for holiness among missionaries. What is needed is contemplatives in action. "Unless the missionary is a contemplative he cannot proclaim Christ in a credible way. He is a witness to the experience of God, and must be able to say with the apostles: 'that which we have looked upon…concerning the word of life,…we proclaim also to you' (1 Jn 1:1-3)."[6] This paper will attempt to respond to this conviction by proposing a paradigm for the interior life necessary for evangelization.

Towards the conclusion of the Great Jubilee of the Year 2000, Cardinal Joseph Ratzinger gave a catechesis in Rome to catechists entitled *The Way to True Happiness.*" In his reflections, he put forth a compelling synthesis of what it means to evangelize, its essential contents and structure, and the vital interior life necessary for its fruitfulness. At its most elementary, evangelization is the activity of revealing the path to true happiness by teaching the art of complete living in Christ.[7] As such, it must consider thoughtfully and respond pertinently to the full range of questions experienced and asked by unique human beings. It is essentially an art that can ultimately be communicated only by Christ through credible witnesses.

In looking for new ways of bringing the Gospel to all, the correct method of evangelization will derive from its essential structure. Moreover, discerning new ways to convey the message of salvation, of making the voice of the Lord accessible and comprehensible in the contemporary situation, will be intimately bound up with the essential contents of the new evangelization. Ratzinger identifies four basic features that must shape the Church's proclamation of the kerygma, namely, conversion, the living God as the decisive reality, Jesus as Savior, and eternal life. He then proposes three interior

---

[4] Pope Francis, *Evangelii Gaudium* (Washington D.C.: Libreria Editrice Vaticana, 2013), n. 14

[5] John Paul II, *Redemptoris Missio* (Boston: Pauline Books and Media, 1990), n. 90.

[6] Ibid., n. 91.

[7] Cardinal Joseph Ratzinger, *"The Way to True Happiness,"* located online at http://www.piercedhearts.org/benedict_xvi/Cardinal%20Ratzinger/true_happiness_12_10_2000.htm (accessed July 31, 2017), 1.

dispositions that must be cultivated in the missionary disciple: poverty, suffering, and silence. We will briefly examine each of these in turn and their import for evangelization.

Jesus' inaugural sermon in Luke 4:18-19 offers a succinct window into his understanding of his mission. He has been made the Messiah by the Father through the anointing with the Holy Spirit. And the purpose of this anointing is to "evangelize the poor." Jesus is essentially saying, "I have come to respond to the fundamental question of your existence. I am here to show you the path of life, the path to holiness. I am, in fact, that path."[8] This means that his preaching is good news *because* the very message is performative. The message bears the promise of his presence, which conveys power to transform. And the privileged recipients of this power of new life with him and in him are the poor. How might we understand the nature of being poor?

Ratzinger will assert that the deepest consideration of poverty is "not material poverty, but spiritual poverty: the inability to be joyful, the conviction that life is absurd and contradictory...[which] leads to the inability to love."[9] Indeed, "when the art of living remains unknown, nothing else functions rightly."[10] The poor that Jesus comes to evangelize are precisely those who are languishing without a sense of ultimate realities and of existence itself. As the central goal of evangelization is to make contemporary and present the call of Jesus himself, the Good News of God and the very first evangelizer,[11] the Church must understand the existential implications of this condition of being poor into which Jesus evangelizes, from which she herself is constantly re-evangelized, and as the condition to which she must reverently attend in her evangelizing activity.

Monsignor Luigi Giussani developed an effective method of evangelization based upon his keen insights into existential poverty. He intuitively observed the widespread inability of Catholics to conceive of the relationship between the faith that they identified themselves with and openly professed and "their way of looking at the world, their way of making judgments about circumstances and events, their way of evaluating (i.e. assessing the real value) of the situations they had to deal with in life."[12] It was as if "the doctrine that was transmitted in an orthodox way no longer penetrated life; it did not become experience."[13]

---

[8] Ibid., 1.

[9] Ibid., 1.

[10] Ibid., 1.

[11] Paul VI, *Evangelii Nuntiandi*,(Boston: Pauline Books and Media, 1975), n. 7.

[12] John Janaro, "Man in the Presence of Mystery: An Introduction to the Theological Anthropology of Luigi Giussani," *Faith and Reason* 23 no. 3-4 (1998), 274.

[13] Julian Carron, *Disarming Beauty* (Notre Dame: University of Notre Dame Press, 2017), 37.

Giussani traced this disconnect, and the consequent inconsistencies introduced into daily living, to a "weakness of awareness."[14] This reduction in the capacity to behold the whole of reality in accord with one's elementary experience is like losing the thread of one's heart. "Not only is a constantly alive religious sense needed for Christianity to be acknowledged and experienced for what it is…but also, it is precisely in the encounter with the Christian event that the religious sense is revealed in all its original importance, reaches ultimate clarity, is educated, and is saved. Christ came to educate us to the religious sense. A lively religious sense therefore means a verification of faith."[15]

The heart of Giussani's proposal is that "we are made for truth, and truth is the *correspondence* between reality and consciousness…finding the ultimate truth is like discovering something beautiful along one's path."[16] The religious sense is "reason's capacity to express its own profound nature in the ultimate question."[17] "And reason, being coherent, will not give in until it has found an exhaustive answer."[18] This is a crucial understanding in Giussani's approach, which will give him a certain confidence in engaging people influenced by various worldviews or ideologies. And yet, there is an inherent disproportion in this dynamic: ultimate questions that we must ask if we are to be honestly human, and answers that always seem inadequate. What we discover does not satisfy. There is a disproportion before the total answer, which points to a structural disproportion in man himself. Man either remains true to being a tireless searcher in a posture of great openness before the ultimate, which always lies beyond him, or he settles for a certain conception of life that is predetermined and imposed. Besides imprisoning man in his circumstances in a way that suffocates and leaves him a stranger to himself,[19] this settling can leave him subject to the powers of worldly influence. "The common mentality, created by mass media and the whole network of instruments held by power – which it strengthens constantly…atrophies the religious sense, atrophies the heart, or better, totally anesthetizes it."[20]

Insofar as we remain true to the existential disproportion of our human condition, choosing the examined life, a life lived with awareness, then we can expect a corresponding sadness. This acute sadness is essentially the desire for an absent good. It is here where

---

[14] Ibid., 38.

[15] Ibid., 73.

[16] Luigi Giussani, *The Religious Sense* (Montreal: McGill-Queen's University Press, 1997), 34.

[17] Ibid., 47.

[18] Ibid., 47.

[19] Julian Carron, *Disarming Beauty* (Notre Dame: University of Notre Dame Press, 2017), 75.

[20] Ibid., 89.

Giussani's analysis brings us to an important place for evangelizing modern men and women in their experience of poverty. How are we to bear this sadness, this suffering want? Is it haunting or sacred? Where does it lead? One choice is the frenetic grasping after pleasure, the attempt to fill this sadness. As the pleasures are not infinite, however, they invariably end in disgust. Or there is a kind of distraction tendency, which ultimately leads to indifference or boredom. Or there is hope – letting the awareness of such sadness tutor us, that we may become more conscious of the greatness of life and learn to intuit life's destiny. Giussani's since/therefore dialectic highlights the value the poverty as the privileged grounds for receptivity to the Gospel:

> Expectation is the very structure of our nature, it is the essence of our soul. It is not something calculated: it is given. For the promise is at the origin, from the very origin of our creation. He who has made man has also made him as 'promise.' Structurally man waits; structurally he is a beggar; structurally life is a promise.[21]

> Only the hypothesis of God, only the affirmation of the mystery as a reality existing beyond our capacity to fathom entirely, only this hypothesis corresponds to the human person's original structure...which is mendicity, insatiable begging, and what corresponds to him is neither he himself nor something he gives to himself, measures, or possesses.[22]

Being attentive to "the structural disproportion that constitutes our 'I',"[23] and the corresponding experience of sadness (or the manifestations of the denial of this sadness), is imperative to fruitfully evangelize others. The proclamation of the Gospel cannot give answers, even right answers, that are not shaped by the questions that arise from this existential experience of poverty. "The more a person takes their own humanity seriously, the more they will realize the nature of their own needs and feel all the incapacity – their own and everyone else's to answer them."[24] It is here that man is most acutely waiting for and open to the gift of Jesus. And evangelization is essentially "one beggar telling another beggar where to find bread."[25]

---

[21] Luigi Giussani, *The Religious Sense* (Montreal: McGill-Queen's University Press, 1997), 54.

[22] Ibid., 57.

[23] Julian Carron, *Disarming Beauty* (Notre Dame: University of Notre Dame Press, 2017), 94.

[24] Ibid., 97.

[25] J.T. Niles, http://quotationsbook.com/quote/12792/, 1.

Ratzinger identifies the law of expropriation as another "fundamental condition of the true commitment for the Gospel" in the context of proposing that the "new evangelization must surrender to the mystery of the grain of mustard seed."[26] The morale of this parable (Mk 4:30-32) for evangelization means simultaneously never being content with our efforts to find new ways of bringing the Gospel to all while at the same time not giving into the temptation of impatience or of pretentiously expecting success according to secular criteria. We must not only leave up to God the time and manner in which the Kingdom will grow (Mk 4:26-29), but we must, like Christ, surrender to the expropriation of one's person for the salvation of others. Jesus came in the Father's name (cf. Jn 5:43), he preached by day and prayed by night, and his entire life was a path toward the cross. "Jesus did not redeem the world with beautiful words but with his suffering and death…[which] is the inexhaustible source of life for the world."[27] He is the grain of mustard seed that falls into the earth and dies, bearing much fruit (cf. Jn 12:24). This law of expropriation, which is valid until the end of time, is demonstrated in the history of Christianity, especially in the life of St. Paul, "whose fruitfulness was tied to suffering, to communion with the passion with Christ (cf. 1 Cor 2:1-5; 2 Cor 11:30; Gal 4:12-4)."[28] This losing one's life for the sake of the Gospel is directly, albeit mysteriously, related to giving room in the world for the Lord's voice to be accessible and comprehensible.

It is not insignificant that the very first time Pope John Paul II used the expression "new evangelization" in Poland on June 9, 1979, he related it directly to the cross.[29] The cross is the sign par excellence of the Gospel being proclaimed. That the Cross of Christ never be emptied is "the cry of the new evangelization."[30] It is a cry that extends the "sitio" of Jesus on the Cross.[31] The theme of suffering as a precious instrument of evangelization is integral to John Paul II's vision: "It is necessary to be aware that evangelization draws unimagined and inexhaustible energy from the cooperation of the suffering."[32] The evangelist must

---

[26]   Cardinal Joseph Ratzinger, "*The Way to True Happiness*," located online at http://www.piercedhearts.org/benedict_xvi/Cardinal%20Ratzinger/true_happiness_12_10_2000.htm (accessed July 31, 2017), 3.

[27] Ibid., 4.

[28] Ibid., 4.

[29] John Paul II, *Compendium on the New Evangelization* (Washington D.C.: Libreria Editrice Vaticana,2015), n. 184.

[30] Ibid., n. 772.

[31] Ibid., n. 456.

[32] Ibid., n. 671.

therefore "value suffering in its many forms, uniting that suffering to the sacrifice of Christ for evangelization: that is, for the redemption of those who still do not know Christ."[33]

The life of Father Walter Ciszek serves as a remarkable testimony to the law of expropriation. His reflections on the long years of isolation and suffering he experienced in Russia highlight the profundity and fruitfulness of communion with Christ in his passion.[34] Suffering breaks through our routines of self-reliance and the habit of settling into this world and looking to it for our support.[35] Suffering purifies our initial enthusiasm in following the Lord's call.[36] Suffering helps to purify our prayer of petition from merely asking for relief to offering up pains experienced for others.[37] Suffering can be the impetus to cross important thresholds of surrender in our relationship with God and fidelity to his will.[38] Suffering is worked out through the medium of the flesh.[39] And suffering is the fuel for priestly fruitfulness.[40]

In Chapter 12 of *He Leadeth Me*, Ciszek details his discovery of "pain and suffering in the larger context of the apostolate."[41] "From a purely human standpoint, my sojourn in the Soviet Union could have been considered the most senseless action of my life. But I saw these hardships, this drab reality, as an integral part of my apostolate."[42] The keynote of every Christian vocation is Christ's faithfulness to the Father's will through sacrifice, pain and suffering.[43] This real participation in Christ's obedience to the Father's will allows for seemingly unimportant efforts to be "somehow redemptive," "the source of grace for all."[44] It was the recollection of this truth that not only sustained Ciszek, but gave him joy and hope:

"Day by day, I learned to experience in some measure the power of God as manifested

---

[33] Ibid., n. 200.

[34] Walter Ciszek with Daniel Flaherty, *He Leadeth Me* (Garden City: Doubleday and Company, Inc, 1973), 13.

[35] Ibid., 21.

[36] Ibid., 38.

[37] Ibid., 60.

[38] Ibid., 85.

[39] Ibid., 105.

[40] Ibid., 121.

[41] Ibid., 126.

[42] Ibid., 128.

[43] Ibid., 127.

[44] Ibid., 127.

in the mystery of the passion. Pain and suffering comprised the sacrifice needed in the passion for saving souls…For the actual conversion of people required much prayer, much persevering trust in God, many trials and sacrifices…It seemed to me that I could see arising out of the devastated and blighted lives around me, a whole new Church to come…a Church formed out of a generation of persecution and frustration, tried as gold in the furnace.[45]

The first two interior dispositions, accepting our poverty as a place to encounter the God who comes to save us, and suffering in union with Christ for the salvation of souls, give rise to the third interior attitude – silence. Ratzinger refers to this need for silence in his catechesis as a "practical aspect" of the proclamation of the living God which naturally follows from a serious consideration of God as man's one necessity.[46] "To proclaim God is to introduce to the relation with God: to teach how to pray. Prayer is faith in action. And only by experiencing God does the evidence of his existence appear."[47] This posture of silent openness before the mystery of the living God is exemplified in the desire of John the Baptist: "He must increase, but I must decrease" (Jn 3:30). Because of the frenetic pace, the proliferation of technological distractions, and the sheer noise that is characteristic of contemporary world, "schools of prayer, communities of prayer, are so important."[48]

This aspect of the very condition for a mature interior life, necessary for evangelization, was not lost on John Paul II. In his seminal document on the pastoral strategy for the new evangelization, *Novo Millennio Ineunte*, he proposes starting afresh from contemplating the face of Christ in silence. "Our witness would be hopelessly inadequate"[49] without coming to know and fall in love with the Person of Jesus. He calls for a Christian life that is "distinguished above all in the art of prayer…[that progresses] as a genuine dialogue of love, to the point of rendering the person wholly possessed by the divine Beloved, vibrating at the Spirit's touch, resting filially with the Father's heart."[50] To this end, Christian communities "must become genuine 'schools' of prayer, where the meeting with Christ is expressed not

---

[45] Ibid., 130-132.

[46] Cardinal Joseph Ratzinger, "*The Way to True Happiness*," located online at http://www.piercedhearts.org/benedict_xvi/Cardinal%20Ratzinger/true_happiness_12_10_2000.htm (accessed July 31, 2017), 6.

[47] Ibid., 7.

[48] Ibid., 6.

[49] John Paul II, *Novo Millennio Ineunte* (Boston: Pauline Books and Media, 2000), n. 16.

[50] Ibid., 32-33.

just in imploring help, but also in thanksgiving, praise, adoration, contemplation, listening, and ardent devotion until the heart truly 'falls in love."[51]

In his magnificent book, *The Power of Silence*, Cardinal Robert Sarah lays the theological foundation for the imperative of silence in the life of a disciple. He contrasts "the racket of contemporary life" and its "insidious danger for the soul" with the silence that "is the assurance of meeting God."[52] While acknowledging the "difficult confrontation" that silence initially entails, it is nonetheless only through suffering silence that we "become accustomed to being with God."[53] We must not surrender to the "diabolical situation" of getting "drunk on all sorts of noises,"[54] which only serves to numb the heart. Rather, even as "the difficulties encountered today in finding silence are more formidable than ever,"[55] we must be committed to the silent search for God. "Today the Church has one central mission. It consists of offering silence to the priests and the faithful."[56]

There in an interdependence of poverty, suffering and silence in the interior life. Each requires the other to develop. Without the regular discipline of silence, we cannot accept our poverty as a place of encounter with Christ and live our sufferings in communion with Christ, nor can we effectively evangelize. Indeed, these three characteristics are necessary for the new evangelization and correspond directly to the missionary spirituality envisioned by John Paul II. We must receive "intimate communion with Christ" in our poverty, we must burn with "the charity of Christ" and with his zeal for souls to the point of suffering, and we must learn "complete docility to the Holy Spirit" by being "molded from within by the Spirit" in silent prayer.[57]

Prayer

Invitation to pray Psalm 143 (RSV) from the place of deepest seeing and need upon reading this article.

---

[51] Ibid., 33.

[52] Cardinal Robert Sarah, *The Power of Silence* (San Francisco: Ignatius Press, 2017), 230.

[53] Ibid., 230.

[54] Ibid., 230.

[55] Ibid., 230.

[56] Ibid., 231.

[57] John Paul II, *Redemptoris Missio* (Boston: Pauline Books and Media, 1990), n. 87-89.

Practicum Reflection Questions for Formators

1. How do you personally experience the call to holiness and the call to mission in your formation in seminary?

2. Identify an experience of being spiritually poor in your life and describe how you experienced Christ's Presence ministering to you in this place of need and dependence. How do you hear the cry of the poor in the apostolate?

3. How do you understand remaining "true to the existential disproportion of our human condition"? What is you experience of sadness? What are your typical patterns of responding to sadness?

4. What might it look and feel like to understand oneself as a beggar, as a mendicant?

5. How does the importance of the law of expropriation in the task of evangelization make you feel? Can you concretely name your share in the Cross of Jesus for the sake of others?

6. What is your experience of silence in day-to-day life, when you are in company with others, and when you are alone? Does silence ever feel oppressive, or full? Describe.

Suggested Resources

1. Giussani, Luigi. *Is it Possible to Live This Way: Faith.*
2. Cisek, Walter. *He Leadeth Me.*
3. Sarah, Robert Cardinal. *The Power of Silence: Against the Dictatorship of Noise.*

Bibliography

Caron, Julian. *Disarming Beauty: Essays on Faith, Truth and Freedom.* Notre Dame, Indiana: University of Notre Dame Press, 2017.

Cisek, Walter. *He Leadeth Me.* Garden City, NY: Doubleday and Company, Inc. 1973.

Giussani, Luigi. *The Religious Sense.* Montreal and Kingston: McGill-Queen's University Press, 1997.

Janaro, John. *"Man in the Presence of Mystery: An Introduction to the Theological Anthropology of Luigi Giussani."* Faith and Reason 23 no. 3-4, 1998.

John Paul II. *Redemptoris Missio.* Boston: Pauline Books and Media, 1990.

John Paul II. Novo *Millennio Ineunte.* Boston: Pauline Books and Media, 2001.

Paul VI. *Evangelii Nuntiandi*. Boston: Pauline Books and Media, 1975.

Pontifical Council for the Promotion of the New Evangelization. *Compendium on the New Evangelization*. Washington D.C.: Libreria Editrice Vaticana, 2015.

Pope Francis. *Evangelii Gaudium*. Washington D.C.: Libreria Editrice Vaticana, 2013.

Ratzinger, Joseph Cardinal. *"The Way to True Happiness: Jubilee for Catechists."* Dec. 2000. http://www.ewtn.com/new_evangelization/Ratzinger.htm.

Sarah, Robert Cardinal. *The Power of Silence: Against the Dictatorship of Noise*. San Francisco: Ignatius Press, 2017.

Chapter Seventeen

Christian Masculine Affective Maturity in the Way of the Spiritual Exercises of St. Ignatius Loyola

Fr. John Horn, S.J., D. Min.

Fr. John Horn, S.J., D. Min. is a priest of the Maryland Province of the Society of Jesus and was ordained in 1985. He is a Co-Founder of The Institute for Priestly Formation at Creighton University in Omaha, Nebraska and is currently serving as a spiritual director and professor in Spiritual Theology at St. Vincent de Paul Regional Seminary in Florida. In his early years of priesthood, he served in the Jesuit Refugee Service and Jesuit Secondary Education. For over twenty-five years a call within a call to serve diocesan seminarians and priests has been his apostolic mission in the ministry of The Spiritual Exercises of St. Ignatius Loyola. He is Co-Founder of the Seminary Formation Council and previously served as President-Rector of Kenrick-Glennon Seminary St. Louis. He also serves in prison ministry. Fr. Horn has written several books including "Heart Speaks to Heart – A Review of Life And Healing Prayer," Editor for "Eyewitnesses – Biblical Foundations in Christian Spirituality," and authored "Healing Prayer –Practical Mysticism and St. Ignatius Loyola's Spiritual Exercises." In Priest Magazine (1994) he published an article, "Spiritual Fecundity and Virginal Love - A Christian Anthropology of the Heart."

Mrs. Jane Guenther, M.Div.

Jane Guenther M.Div., is currently the Director of the Catholic Renewal Center of the Archdiocese of St. Louis. She acquired her Masters in Divinity in 2005 from Aquinas Institute of Theology. For 16 years she has been offering weekly healing prayer at Kenrick Glennon Seminary and facilitating a weekly prayer meeting. She has taught an elective course on Spiritual Warfare, Deliverance and Exorcism at Kenrick and frequently is a guest at the Confession Practicum classes for the Deacon classes. Jane has written numerous articles for Pentecost Today Magazine and pamphlets on the Isaiahian Gifts, The Charism of Miracles and Tapping in to the Fire of Your Baptism. She co-authored a Spiritual Gifts Inventory that she uses with the Second Year Theologians as a workshop experience at Kenrick. She has spoken at conferences on the topics of discernment and spiritual warfare, recently at N.C.D.V.D. on "Spiritual Warfare in Vocation Work." She also serves as a Practicum Mentor, Presenter and Spiritual Director in the Spiritual Formation Council's Certificate in Seminary Formation for Missionary Discipleship, a continuing education program for seminary personnel.

This article explores the ways in which Christian men grow in affective maturity as they grasp their core identity as sons of the Father, brothers of the Son, and temples of the Holy Spirit. As conversion allows us to recognize our participation in the life of the Blessed Trinity, we affectively experience God's love in poverty of spirit and thus learn to take joy in God's glory at work in our lives. As this takes place, the Holy Spirit's presence reorients our affective disorders—interior attachments that vary from the truth revealed in God's creation. After discussing this theological foundation, we then apply these spiritual principles to the specific question of candidates for priesthood who struggle with transitory same-sex attractions. We propose a concrete way to approach priestly formation and spiritual accompaniment that both affirms the Church's magisterial teachings and applies the instructions of the 2016 *Ratio fundamentalis* (*The Gift of the Priestly Vocation*) on this subject.

As is well known, the Magisterium teaches that homosexual acts are "intrinsically disordered" because they "do not proceed from a genuine affective and sexual complementarity." (*CCC* 2357) The Church distinguishes between homosexual actions and persons who experience homosexual tendencies, saying about the latter:

This inclination, which is objectively disordered, constitutes for most of them a trial. They must be accepted with respect, compassion, and sensitivity. Every sign of unjust discrimination in their regard should be avoided. These persons are called to fulfill God's will in their lives and, if they are Christians, to unite to the sacrifice of the Lord's Cross the difficulties they may encounter from their condition. (*CCC* 2358)

Moreover, the Church insists that those who struggle with same-sex attraction are called to chastity as are all the baptized:

Homosexual persons are called to chastity. By the virtues of self-mastery that teach them inner freedom, at times by the support of disinterested friendship, by prayer and sacramental grace, they can and should gradually and resolutely approach Christian perfection. (*CCC* 2359)

We will explore how this gradual and resolute progress in Christian perfection occurs through God's healing work.

Contents Guide for this Article

Foundations in Trinitarian Spirituality

Affective Maturity through Participation in the Trinity's Affectivity

St. Augustine spoke well about the pathway to a man's affective maturity:

> Late have I loved you, O Beauty ever ancient ever new, late have I loved you! You were within me, but I was outside, and it was there that I searched for you. In my unloveliness I plunged into the lovely things which you created. You were with me, but I was not with you. Created things kept me from you; yet if they had not been in you they would not have been at all. You called, you shouted, and broke through my deafness. You flashed, you shone, and you dispelled my blindness. You breathed your

fragrance on me: I drew in breath and now I pant for you. I have tasted you, now I hunger and thirst for more. You touched me, and I burned for your peace (Excerpt from the *Confessions* in *Liturgy of the Hours*, Vol. IV, p. 1357).

In a similar vein, Michael Ivens, S.J., remarks on how the Holy Spirit touches our affections:

In the Spiritual Exercises of St. Ignatius Loyola the language of "affection" and "affectivity" refer to many variants of love and desire, together with their antithesis, hate and fear. The affections operate on many levels, from that of quite transient feelings to the level where they affect a person's way of perceiving reality, making judgments, choosing and acting. The Spiritual Exercises have to do with conversion of affectivity, with letting the Holy Spirit enter into our affectivity, change it and act through it. Only when this is clear is it possible to understand St. Ignatius' insistence on freedom from disordered affections — our affectivity in so far as it moves us in the directions not ordered or conducive to the transcendent end of the human person (*Understanding the Spiritual Exercises*, p. 2).

Indeed, affective maturity for the Christian man depends upon learning how to "taste" and "savor" the glorious mystery of the Trinitarian relationships alive in our hearts. We hunger for this knowledge with insatiable human desire. And it is precisely through these desires that God draws us to himself. We find God and are found in these interior affective relationships with the Father, Son and Holy Spirit. They draw us into being more and more satisfied by divine love. These relationships are our Baptismal inheritance. Through these interior relationships with the Father, Son and Holy Spirit a Christian man's identity is revealed and understood, and his affective maturity for mission flows from accepting this same identity. The Christian man comes to know himself to be another image of Jesus through the blessed mercy of adoption in the Holy Spirit. The Father's tenderness, all-powerful gentleness and mercy are being communicated in our hearts to strengthen us at every turn in ordinary life. The Trinity's desires are laboring in love for us. God made us for himself to be his delight (Is. 62:4)! He desired to give himself a gift! Ever since our baptism, the Trinity has dwelt within us, even if we have been oblivious to this divine presence. We each hunger and thirst for divine love. As the ancient hymn from the *Didache* states, "Father we thank thee who has planted thy holy Name within our hearts." We can remain, as St. Augustine did for a time, on the outside of the human heart's interior life, attempting with futility to be satisfied by feeding our interior hungers with creature comforts instead of feeding on the presence of the Creator and Comforter within us. The Spirit desires to daily carry us into the arms of the Father of all mercy and consolation, as we abandon ourselves moment by moment to the Father's providential care (John 14:26).

After initial conversion, the Christian man embarks on an ongoing radical reorientation of his entire personality, discovering his true identity in and with Jesus. The Christian man, maturing in humble receptivity to receive the Father's Spirit, comes to a point in his affective conversion when he is not able to know himself apart from Christ. He begins to echo St. Paul's words, "it is no longer I who live but Christ within me" (Galatians 2:20). Our masculine affective maturation transpires each day in faith as we become more willing to admit our need for the Father's loving care and entrust ourselves to him as beloved sons in and with Jesus as Son. This affective maturation takes time and depends on a dedicated prayerful listening for the Father's Spirit in everyday life. The man matures by generously responding to the Father's love seeking to "abide in him" (John 15:5) by living in daily docility to the Holy Spirit (note the importance of the daily Consciousness Examen prayer).

Indeed, amid our desires to be secure in the fundamental goodness of our humanity, each man's heart cries out for a secure masculine identity hoping to taste and savor the knowledge that he is pleasing to the Father (Gen. 1:26-28, Matt. 3:17). We desire to live in the kingdom that the Father is pleased to give us (Lk.12:32). When we begin to daily discover the fresh interior knowledge that we are desirable, chosen as the Father's delight, and that judgments have been removed against us, we become more and more capable of providing for and leading families in faith as confident spiritual husbands and fathers (Is. 62:3-4, Zeph. 3:14-27).Priests live this call to spiritual fatherhood in different ways: It may mean guiding individual families in a traditional parish family. It may mean walking with and serving families through an ecclesial movement. It may mean leading others as a priest-formator in the seminary. Regardless of a priest's assignment, he is called to live out his masculine identity by embracing spiritual fatherhood.

We can remain spectators to this interior life of grace or we can participate with our whole hearts. Masculine affective maturity corresponds to the depth of our participation. We can participate with lukewarm desires, marked by contempt for our poverty of spirit, where Jesus abides and reveals himself (Matt. 5:3). And we can even refuse to seek after Jesus' indwelling presence: "The evil one uses this ambivalence for deceptive purposes" (*The Devil You Don't Know*, Cameli, p. 19). Life without prayerful listening and generous responsiveness easily becomes a life of quiet misery and loneliness. Everyday burdens become oppressive. We distract ourselves from pursuing the interior life, and we thus gradually separate ourselves from being alive in God's love and mercy. We can even refuse to seek Jesus' indwelling presence. This interior disposition of not needing to seek and find God creates a self-made aloneness. We can easily remain in this isolation and avoid accompaniment with Mary, Our Blessed Mother, who teaches us that the most fruitful human activity is to receive God daily in faith (Fr. Jean Corbon, O.P., *Wellspring of Worship*, p. 21). What a hellish way to live!

In contrast, we learn in and with Jesus that without him we can do nothing, while remaining and abiding in him makes life fruitful (Jn. 15:1-9). We learn as disciples and living images of Jesus that we need to rely on what we see the Father doing at every turn as he pours the Holy Spirit into our hearts (Rom. 5:5). We come to recognize the necessity of worshipping God alone. Our first priority—the principle and foundation of our lives—is to praise, reverence and serve the Father in ordinary life, for he is Lord of heaven and earth. Through our commitment to child-like faith, the Father reveals hidden mysteries to us as Jesus draws us to into tasting the sweetness of new life at the cross, because he always eases the yoke of life and makes our burdens light (Matt. 11:25-30). The Father, in Jesus' Name, sends the Holy Spirit into our hearts, as the Advocate who teaches us everything and reminds us in peace of all that Jesus has taught us (Jn. 14:26-27).

New life and new birth are ordinary everyday interior events for the Christian man to experience as our affections mature in faith (Lamentations 3:20). But we must choose to exercise the gift of faith and enter the encounter with Jesus' death that is at work in us, as well as his resurrecting love (2 Cor. 4: 7-15). We can rely upon the interior helps of the Holy Spirit that are available through the gift of courage and the accessibility to taste and savor wisdom, understanding and knowledge, indeed all the gifts of the Spirit. We must humbly respond daily in faith to receive love, mercy and regenerating glory. This daily infilling of God's grace orders our disordered affectivity (Eph. 1: 23).

Over time, we come to enjoy the fruits of serving the Father through participating in Jesus' own life through the power of the Spirit. We learn how to serve as spiritual husbands and fathers by savoring the Father's affectionate faithfulness. The Spirit transforms our fear of inadequacy into a daily confidence in his power, at the service of the Father's providential care. We taste patience, self-control, peace, love, generosity, faithfulness, gentleness, long-suffering and joy (Gal 5:22-23). In fact as we mature affectively in our masculinity by tasting the goodness of the Father's love and mercy, we recognize joy not just as a fruit of the Holy Spirit but as the sure sign of God's presence in our hearts. The Father's Spirit is Joy! By surrendering to receiving the Father's affectionate care, we become filled with his joy.

Affective Experiences of God's Glory

Two major Hebrew meanings for "glory" (*kabod*) help us understand the Spirit's power at work for each of us as we journey in faith, affectively maturing in Christ. In the Scriptures Glory often means light, radiance, and luminescence. But glory also carries another important meaning. It means fame in God's sight, his affective appreciation and pleasure, his favor (Ps. 8: 4-6; Ez. 43:1-9). C.S. Lewis wrote about this meaning of glory, describing it in his moving essay, "The Weight of Glory": "When I began to consider this matter I was shocked to find such different Christians as Milton, Johnson, and Thomas Aquinas taking heavenly glory quite frankly in the sense of fame with God, approval or (I might say) 'appreciation' by God." Fame here does not mean worldly vainglory and self-concern. It is not a worldly fame that measures our value according to material wealth. This Biblical meaning of glory (*kabod*) refers to the Father's delight in us. It refers to the weight of his appreciation for each of us and the immeasurable blessings that he desires as our Father to bestow upon us. It speaks of his desire to lavish us with more glory, more heartfelt appreciation. God offers us his love at work in every moment of everyday. The Father's love teaches us that everything is a gift. We live in his glory when we receive this gift (Eph. 1: 11-14).

Also relevant to this discussion of glory is the Hebrew verbal root *halal*. This which is often translated praise, refers to glory as being the power of God at the service of his love. This is the light of the Holy Spirit's presence that is forever invading our hearts as a jealous lover. It is a regenerating power that can frighten us at first because it exposes our nakedness and poverty of spirit, but only to heal and strengthen the image of Jesus at the center of our personalities ("Glory," *Dictionary of Biblical Theology*, p. 203 by Xavier Leon-Dufour). St. William of Thierry writes, "When in your life of faith, you are confronted with the deeper mysteries it is natural to become a little frightened. When this happens, take heart, faithful Christian. Do not raise objections, but ask with loving submission, 'How can these things be?' Let your question be a prayer, an expression of love and self-surrender to God" (*Liturgy of the Hours*, Vol. III, p. 1764). St. William encourages us around our initial fright and assures us that this is a normal experience as we encounter the Holy Spirit's activity as glory invading our hearts. St. William wants us to approach the throne of grace with increasing confidence (Heb. 10: 19).

Glory as the power of God at the service of his love invades us to regenerate our memories. It is the Holy Spirit as glory in-filling us to make all things new, to make something better happen where I had sinned than if I had not sinned! It is what St.

Augustine is stating in faith in that prayer that gives testimony to Jesus' reparation transpiring at the center of our hearts. Fr. Wilfrid Stinissen in his marvelous book *Into Your Hands, Father* instructs us about this truth:

> As soon as you show him your wounds and expose yourself to his healing power, the healing process begins, one that is not like ordinary healing. It is not a question of something old that has caused you much pain and finally ceases to torment you the healing goes back into time and transforms the very moment when you were hurt into a moment of grace. The very wound that was the cause of so much suffering is transformed into a blessing, and all the bitterness it caused is changed into meaningful and fruitful suffering (p. 41).

To receive the Holy Spirit's regenerating glory helps us understand the Biblical truth that "the one who is forgiven the most is the one who loves the most" (Lk. 7:47). We often miss this truth in the confessional. We repent of our sins believing that they are cancelled and taken away by the Father's forgiving love and mercy. This transpires through Jesus' praying and interceding at the center of the Church, his mystical body, as the priest prays the words of absolution. But we tend to forget or miss the reality of the Holy Spirit *regenerating* our hearts as glory at the service of God's love. Through the words of absolution, the Holy Spirit as glory is also actively *regenerating our memories* in the Sacrament of Penance.

Interior Desires in Faith

Faith teaches us that our interior desires for transcendent love were planted in us by God and that he draws us to himself through them (Acts 17:22-32). Attentiveness to the interior life provides access to "tasting" God's presence and "savoring" his tenderness. This interior attentiveness is necessary for a man to affectively mature. As St. John Paul II stated, "Christ reveals man to himself" (Encyclical *Redemptor hominis*, 4 March 1979, I, 9).

The words from St. John's Gospel speak of Jesus' desire to quench our thirst for divine love: "If you knew the gift of God and who is saying to you, 'Give me a drink,' you would have asked him and he would give you living water" (Jn. 4:10). Jesus is thirsting to pour the life-giving water of the Holy Spirit into our hearts every moment of everyday (Jn. 19:28). In relation to this gospel truth, I remember some beautiful wisdom learned from the late Cardinal Francis George while he was serving as Chair of the Institute for Priestly Formation Bishops' Advisory Council. A meeting of that advisory council followed the promulgation of the 2005 "Instruction Concerning the Criteria for the Discernment of Vocations with Regard to Persons with Homosexual Tendencies in View of Their Admission for Seminary and to Holy Orders." At this meeting to discuss the nuances of IPF's affirmative response to this document, Cardinal George opened by sharing a pastoral story. With real love and grief for his priests, he told us that he had frequently spoken with priests who struggled with homosexual desires. He asked them *the* question in faith: "Do you believe and relate to Jesus Christ as your core identity while struggling with homosexual desires, or do you relate to Jesus Christ from the belief and identity that you are a homosexual man?" What did the man believe to be his core identity? The simple precision of Cardinal George's question about one's *disposition in faith* makes all the difference when we contemplate the power of the Living Word and receive Jesus' Eucharistic risen body. Because each of us is the object of the full affection of the Holy Spirit, any affective disorder at work in us becomes more and more fashioned by the power of God if we are vulnerably receptive in daily faith. The Spirit's active love is glorifying us whenever we turn to him, acknowledging Jesus Christ as our core identity and allowing him to love us.

One could say in answering Cardinal George's question, "I am a beloved son of the Father in Jesus Christ, who is my core identity, and I relate to my affective homosexual desires within this mystery of being an image of Jesus, beloved by my Father. I walk day by day, allowing the Holy Spirit to penetrate my affectivity. This is the only way I know how to become more chaste, fruitful and happy. I believe this to be my core identity because for me Jesus is my way, my truth and my life" (Jn. 14:6). That sort of *disposition in faith* and that sort of response humbly participates in the eschatological mystery of the Trinity's indwelling, laboring love. It allows for disordered affections to be tamed and transformed over time until we taste one day the fullness of the heavenly wedding banquet where "the former heaven and the former earth have passed away," where a new Jerusalem comes "down out of heaven from God, prepared as a bride for her husband"… and where we will hear a loud voice saying "Behold I make all things new." (Rev. 21:1-5).

We already see this promise of the new Jerusalem in ordinary glimpses of God's glory. We live today in the reign of God. "The more concentrated we are in being present to the present moment, and the Father's providence at work, and the more we live from moment to moment, the more space opens up to us and we feel we are living in a kind of boundlessness. The present moment is the incarnation of God's eternity. Those who live in the present moment drink unceasingly of eternity" (Stinissen, *Into Your Hands, Father*, p. 61).

In the present moment, as we learn to live in the kingdom of God with a wide variety of affective disorders at work in our hearts, we can experience that interior tears are being wiped away, for death is dying as mourning gives way to joy. The transitory is passing away. "We do not lose heart because our inner being is renewed each day even though our body is being destroyed at the same time. The present burden of our trial is light enough and earns for us an eternal weight of glory beyond all comparison. We do not fix our gaze on what is seen but on what is unseen. What is seen is transitory; what is unseen lasts forever" (2 Cor. 4:16-18). God is all in all. Disordered affections of any type are being ordered gradually by the faithfulness of the Father's providential care. What matters in faith is our *disposition*, that is, our *readiness* and *willingness* to receive the Holy Spirit whose desires to possess us and penetrate our hearts with the affectivity of the Father's Heart is reality (see *The Heart*, by Dietrich von Hildebrand). The Father's tender mercy and the Spirit's regenerating glory are being bestowed upon us as beloved sons in Jesus as Son.

Healing Affective Disorders

Each day all disordered affections in human hearts are presently being fashioned by Jesus' risen Heart. As Creator and Redeemer Jesus is pouring the Holy Spirit into us as he intercedes at the right hand of the Father, drawing us into the Father's rejoicing and joy as the Lord of history. This is the living mystery of the Ascension. Jesus still dwells in each of our hearts although outside of time, risen from the dead. He is at the Father's right hand, interceding for each of us and affectionately drawing us to savor the Father's joy. Through obedience to "savoring" his presence as a way of participating in interior worship, giving thanks and praise, we allow ourselves to receive from the Trinitarian relationships that are governing history. And we allow ourselves to receive "the more" that is always accessible, because it is always the Father's desire to further complete our joy (1 Jn. 1:1-4). We need only be disciples humbly willing to learn how to participate and access our heavenly inheritance (Eph. 1: 3-23). Humbly receiving a taste of the Father's tender mercy and regenerating glory in everyday faith helps each of us come to know that we are greater than our disorders, that Jesus Christ is our core identity, and that participating in the reign of the Father's affection and delight frees us more and more to accept ourselves as "I am" in union with Him.

Each man's human affectivity was created by Jesus' Spirit and is called through the mystery of the Incarnation to be transformed, to be ordered by the Father's righteousness (2 Cor. 5:17-21). His righteousness is love, tender mercy and regenerating glory. Fr. Jean d'Elbee, in his beautiful book *I Believe in Love*, wrote these inspiring words taken from St.

Theresa the Little Flower:

> A beautiful prayer to pour forth from your heart throughout the day is 'Jesus, repair what I have done badly; supply for what I have left undone.' Or, an even more beautiful way to pray is 'Jesus, I know that you make reparation in me, that you supply for me; I know that you will draw the good from the bad that I do, and even, as St. Augustine said, 'a greater good than if there had been no evil in it.' Is this not worthy of adoration? I have a Jesus who does all of that in me and for me! (p. 29).

We need to learn how to subjectively receive what is objectively present in the Father's forgiveness. The Holy Spirit is being poured into our hearts as we receive absolution. The Holy Spirit as glory is simultaneously exposing our nakedness and poverty of spirit as images of Jesus, while definitively deleting our interior structures (patterns of thoughts, feelings and desires) of unbelief, unforgiveness and all sin. The creature dies, and we are given new life in and with Jesus. And the Holy Spirit as glory brings about something better for us and the world, at the precise interior place where we had participated in unbelief, unforgiveness and sin (Rom. 8:16-17). St. Augustine's life makes this clear. He writes his *Confessions* from those interior places where he had sinned. He testifies to God's mercy and glory at work in those same interior places where sin had been exposed amid disordered affections. For centuries, readers of the *Confessions* have plunged into new depths of faith, hope and love. God makes something better happen right where St. Augustine had sinned! The goodness of God shines forth!

Each of us needs to acknowledge that we are alive in Jesus Christ. We need to live in the truth that we are not our own. We are his possession (Eph. 1: 14). He comes to us amid our disordered affections and attachments, as we cling to what is transitory. He comes to us in the middle of our worldly interior attitudes that are often based upon fearing our powerlessness. But this powerlessness is precisely the poverty of spirit where the Spirit conforms us into Jesus' image. Jesus' poverty and death meet us in our powerlessness (Matt. 5:3). As baptized Christian men, we are an image of Jesus, bound in the Holy Spirit to the Father's delight and providential care. The Holy Spirit as the glue of love desires to penetrate our affectivity daily in faith, engendering ever more freedom from disordered affectivity. By willingly sharing in Jesus' poverty and death rather than running from our powerlessness, we can relish eternal riches in the everyday. New life and happiness flow for us beyond what we can imagine in relationship with Jesus, who is our poverty of spirit (Eph. 3:20-21).

If we do not recognize our core identity as beloved sons of the Father, we lack a proper *disposition in faith*. Romano Guardini offers an excellent definition of this disposition:

> Faith means getting into communication with God's reality as it appears in the Revelation handed down to us; it means hanging on to this truth, this reality, and living by it. This involves risk, effort, rearrangement and transformation of one's being toward this reality and what stems from it. This reality comes from "on high." It means a constant recurring struggle for faith, combat, mastery and perseverance with increasing certitude and confidence in God's providential care (*Meditations on the Christ Model of Holiness*, pp. 57-58).

If we live this disposition in faith, we will not live by way of self-assertion or by clinging to affective disorders. Indeed, these disordered affections need to be informed by the *Father's affectivity*. Our need for ongoing conversion and affective maturation in the Holy Spirit becomes evident when we remember the truth that only more freedom, love and happiness await us when we entrust all our thoughts, feelings and desires to Jesus' presence.

Faith can easily be misconstrued if we think that holiness depends upon our attempts to be good and do good. Doing good deeds often falls into pride as we attempt to affirm ourselves through doing, as though we needed to earn the Father's love. The truth is that he loves us as much when we are doing good deeds as when we are doing bad deeds. His love is unconditional, and our friendship and sonship is all about who we are as we surrender to *being with him*.

If faith is misconstrued or if we lack a disposition to receive God's affection, we can come to believe that we are a perfectionist, lazy, angry, lustful, etc. Instead of surrendering these disordered affections to the Father's delight and the Spirit's regenerating power each day, we can try to convince ourselves that we are good and avoid being with Jesus' poverty and death at the center of our baptized personality. We often chase the Father's blessing when we already have it (Lk. 15:31). We thus forget that we are beloved sons of the Father in the power of the Holy Spirit, men who struggle, like everybody else, with affective disorders. But these disorders are not our core identity.

Affective Maturity and Transitory Same-Sex Attraction

As the Church teaches, same-sex attractions are a specific disordered affection. We can thus apply what we have discussed above in relating them to the mystery of divine love. The

Church believes, because of our fundamental identity in Jesus Christ and because of his mercy and regenerating glory, that chaste celibacy can be learned and lived in continence with joy for all who struggle with same-sex attractions.

One of the Church's major concerns in the *Ratio* is that her priests live chaste celibacy, serving within a chaste celibacy that is not only continent, but explicitly spousal and paternal. It is good to note the continuity with which the 2005 document from the Congregation for Catholic Education "Instruction Concerning the Criteria for the Discernment of Vocations with regard to Persons with Homosexual Tendencies in View of their Admission to the Seminary and to Holy Orders" has been elevated and quoted verbatim in Pope Francis' approval of the *Ratio*:

> Consistent with her own Magisterium, "the Church, while profoundly respecting the persons in question, cannot admit to the seminary or to holy orders those who practice homosexuality, present deep-seated homosexual tendencies or support the so-called 'gay culture.' Such persons, in fact, find themselves in a situation that gravely hinders them from relating correctly to men and women. One must in no way overlook the negative consequences that can derive from the ordination of persons with deep-seated homosexual tendencies." (*Ratio fundamentalis* #199)

In issuing these overarching guidelines for seminary formation the Congregation for the Clergy reminds us that "the desire alone to become a priest is not sufficient and there does not exist a right to receive sacred ordination" (*Ratio fundamentalis* #201).

The Church also recognizes that homosexual tendencies can be a transitory problem. The *Ratio* states regarding homosexual tendencies that "the expression of a transitory problem – for example, that of an adolescence not yet superseded" can be identified and possibly be overcome. "It is necessary that these tendencies be clearly overcome at least three years before ordination to the diaconate" (*Ratio fundamentalis* #200).[1]

In the Church we believe that those who experience same-sex attractions can grow in freedom by receiving the Father's compassionate love. The Trinity's love is laboring in each person's core identity. Transitory homosexual tendencies occur often in men who are affectively immature, and they can overcome these transitory tendencies. Many men with transitory affective immaturities can mature by cultivating and strengthening their capacities to serve as fruitful husbands and fathers.

---

[1] For more on the distinctions between deep-seated and transitory homosexuality, see Dan Almeter's article, "A Testimonial and Pastoral Wisdom," in chapter 12 of the present volume.

Because of the regenerating power of the Holy Spirit's presence as glory, any transitory affective disorder can be winnowed away gradually if we accept ourselves to be images of Jesus relating to the Father's delight and favor. Affective disorders of any type need to be faced and accepted as the so-called "location" for humble and vulnerable receptivity in faith. We need to admit that we are powerless over having affective disorders: perfectionism, tendencies to be consumed by anger, gluttony for comfort, paralysis by fears of abandonment, suffering scrupulosity, and so on. These can be understood on a spectrum ranging from very deep-seated to very transitory, with some tendencies that are somewhat deep-seated or somewhat transitory. In Christian relationships, the mystery of the human heart and a man's personal history call out to be reverenced at every turn. Regular regenerating grace that is accessible in Confession, inner healing prayer, and Christian growth counseling need to be understood as normal in the everyday life of the Church as a field hospital. Jesus the Divine Physician always heals. We need only discern how his love, mercy and regenerating glory are working this healing. Gradual healing brings us to fuller stature to live in Jesus Christ as our true identity (Eph. 4:12-13). Some healing occurs this side of physical death. Some healing transpires the other side of death through purgation in the compassionate fire of divine love.

Anyone who struggles with same-sex attractions is an image of Jesus at the core of his heart, where the ability to savor the glory of the Father's delight is real. The same is true of our ongoing regeneration. In faith, the human heart is being glorified day by day. The eschatological reality of the heavenly wedding banquet, which we all await, will not disappoint. Jesus as the bridegroom has wed himself to the Church, and the universal call to holiness is the bride's longing for her groom. We need only to be faithful disciples turning to him to receive more spousal love each day. Mary taught the apostles how to receive and abide in the Holy Spirit. She desires to teach us as men too.

Interior Listening and Responding in Faith

Each day our personal *interior disposition in faith* makes all the difference. St. Ignatius and his close friend St. Peter Favre encourage us to notice what we are thinking and feeling as we wake up in the morning. As we learn in simplicity to notice the interior movements that are flowing in our hearts as we awake, we can learn to turn to Jesus and relate these thoughts, feelings and desires to him. We can also turn in on ourselves and just try to live our day without inwardly tasting Jesus' love by remaining in and with him. But if we choose to turn to and be in companionship with Jesus, we will either accept those waking thoughts, feelings and desires as being in harmony with his love and grace, or we will exercise faith by rejecting them if they are not in harmony with his love, going against them to live in increasing freedom (*The Spiritual Writings of Pierre Favre*, Murphy and Padberg, S.J., p. 304). This way of waking and exercising faith makes an immense difference in relation to whether we will embrace our identity as beloved son or instead live in unnecessary misery.

The Two Standards Contemplation

If we relate our waking thoughts, feelings and desires to Jesus in faith, we will be learning to live under that Standard of Jesus Christ. Jesus reveals to us our human identity. He is a warrior whose combat for us has won the victory over disordered affections. There is no need to live under the Standard of Satan, the enemy of true human nature. Jesus has reconciled everything to the Father (Eph. 1,2: 1-10). "The accuser of the brothers has been cast out"(Rev. 12:10). We thus need to walk humbly with God (Micah 6:8), tasting our goodness as an intimate friend of Jesus, recognizing him as our true self. Each day we need to be receptive to his Living Word, allowing him to invade our affectivity with his Holy Spirit. Human fears will be tamed, and demonic fears will depart. Self-hatred will be transformed as we learn to affectionately remain with Jesus in the blessings that flow from accepting our powerlessness and poverty of spirit at the cross (Matt. 5:3). We are called to remain in and with Jesus unceasingly. He has made his home in each of us, and we need to mature by living life apart from the lie that we are alone (Jn. 15:1-9). There is no need to live with the burden and pains that accompany self-reliance and other forms of pride. Life is easier with Jesus. Life apart from him becomes miserable and burdensome. He is Life! (Matt. 11: 25-30, Jn. 14:16).

The taming of fears and hatred brings about freedom and love to accept ourselves as we are. Interior accusations and lies lose their teeth to bite with *disappointments* and *doubts*. Learning to abide with Jesus' presence in a prayerful way of living dissipates any fear of suffering. And fear of death also dissipates in small and large ways.

What is my starting point in faith? Is my identity being received first and last by interior relationships with the Father, Jesus and the Holy Spirit? Do I allow myself to be accompanied by the comforting presence of Mary in daily life? My affective disorders are part of a larger composite of affective tendencies that can gradually taste freedom and love instead of hate and fear when I relate to myself living under the Standard of Jesus Christ. I can live in peace and joy under the Standard of Jesus, or I will live in isolation and fear of my inadequacy under the Standard of Satan.

The Two Standards contemplation from The Spiritual Exercises of St. Ignatius Loyola is foundational in understanding how we assess where and how we are living our lives. We are always living under one or the other Standard; there is no neutral. We are either living in a humble *disposition in faith* that is vulnerably receptive to Jesus' love and mercy, or we are not living in such a receptive disposition.

St. Ignatius believed that indeed there is a battle between good and evil going on in the world and more importantly in our hearts. It is necessary that we discern how we dwell in this battle. What is our *disposition in faith*? How do we exercise faith? The Ignatian contemplation on The Two Standards leads us to imagine the armies of Jesus Christ and Satan in a large field. Each group has a standard or flag, which helps everyone know his position on the battlefield. Pope Francis in his Ignatian formation remains true to the Two Standards when he indicates; "The thing the church needs most today is the ability to heal wounds and to warm the hearts of the faithful, it needs nearness, proximity. I see the church as a field hospital after the battle." ("A Big Heart Open to God," *America*, Sept. 19, 2013.)

First, St. Ignatius asks us to focus on Satan as the enemy of our human nature. He describes a fearful image of Satan sitting on his throne of fire and smoke and instructing his followers to go out into the world and ensnare our hearts so that we are not open to God's will. To trap us, he uses wealth, possessions, honors, and pride. Satan starts by luring us to fixate on our possessions. Satan wants our wealth and possessions to become the focus of our lives and worldly success to be the goal of our lives. These fixations become structures of thoughts, feelings and desires in the interior life of the human heart, and they become the seedbed for our affective attachments and disorders. These fixations are rooted in deeper interior structures of unbelief and unforgiveness towards ourselves and others.

Satan also whispers to us that we need the praise and acceptance of others, and he also tells us that we deserve honors because of our successes. Finally, Satan tries to convince us that we accomplished our successes by ourselves. He tells us to be proud of what we have accomplished. He wants us to adopt the attitude of "Look at me and what I have done."

On the other hand, St. Ignatius asks us to consider Jesus as he stands on the great field in a lowly place. We are to listen as Jesus instructs his followers to go out into the world and lead everyone to freedom. Living under Jesus Christ's Standard, we see spiritual poverty, insults, and humility. These lead in faith to knowing, tasting and savoring increasing love and true freedom.

Spiritual poverty means we recognize and accept that all that we have is a gift from God. Possessions are not something to be worshipped or even valued. Regarding insults, St. Ignatius tells us that we are to let God's love lead us through the illusion of self-satisfaction and the approval of others to a life of serving others. We are called to a life of selflessness, and such a life will put us at odds with the world's values. In the world we will endure insults and rejection with Jesus and share in consolations at being insulted and rejected for the sake of his Name. Finally, Jesus calls us to a life of humility, a life of unconditional love and service for God and others.

The purpose of this contemplation is to help us understand the personal value systems of Jesus Christ and Satan, thus seeing which personal value system we are embracing in the way we live daily life. Periodically, we need to look at our lives to see where we are standing in relation to the Standards of Jesus Christ and Satan. If we find that we have drifted a little, close to Satan's standard, we can strive to live a life of spiritual poverty by serving others through humble love and compassion. Remembering that we are called to live in this world while still participating in the reign of God keeps us vigilant, and we can learn to abide in the interior freedom that flows from tasting and savoring Jesus' love. Let us remember the beauty of Psalm 95:7-8, "If today you hear his voice harden not your hearts." May we respond with generosity by following Jesus' voice as our Good Shepherd (Jn. 10: 14-17).

Clinging to Christ's Heart: The 2 C's and 4 H's

The Standard of Jesus can be understood as the 2 C's and 4 H's. This is easy to remember if we think of the "CH" as abbreviating "Christ's Heart!" The 2 C's are *courage* and *community* and the 4 H's are *held*, *hope*, *humility* and *happiness*. *Courage* is defending what is right and facing all disaster without cringing as we choose to abide always in Jesus' presence. When we have a fear of displeasing God, we will not let fear of man affect us (1 Samuel 11:7; Proverbs 29:25). *Community* is the natural place for us to abide and live, we who are made in the image and likeness of God which is the *community* of the Father, Son, and Holy Spirit. We long for union with one another. It can be said that by analogy, the tripersonal God is imaged in the human community. The New Testament emphasizes the ultimate self-disclosure of God, the Trinity. Examples can be cited from the Baptism of Jesus and the Trinitarian formulas found in Paul and especially in the Great Mandate of Mt. 29:19: "Go therefore and make disciples of all nations, baptizing them in the name of the Father and of the Son and of the Holy Spirit." This formula, a reflection of the authentic mind of Jesus lived by the early Christians, is a summary of our faith, and reminds us that it is into the tripersonal God that all are to be baptized (see also Jn. 17). We note also the passage in which Philip asks Jesus to show his disciples the Father, "and that will be enough." Jesus' response makes the point clear: "Whoever has seen me has seen the Father"

(Jn 14:8-9).

The 4 H's are progressive by nature as Jesus offers us himself as "the Lamb of God" whom we are invited to "behold" (John 1:29). We *behold* him in the Eucharist, and then Jesus offers us to become what we partake in, his own self. We become the One we contemplate. We *behold* Jesus risen and are *beheld* in the Eucharist. The picture by Thomas Blackshear, called *Forgiven*, depicts Jesus *holding* a man who was ready to crucify him and, perfectly captures so much about who we are and who he is for us: our weakness his strength, our wretchedness and his glory, our hopelessness and is faithfulness; our sin and his love.

Not only this, but Jesus *holds* him and sustains him. On his own, this man who represents us all as *Forgiven* would be lost, his life in ruins. But when he can stand no more, Jesus stands for him. When he is close to falling, Jesus *holds* him up. Jesus is so strong, and we are so weak.

This reality leads us in the Spirit to more fully live in *hope*, as it says in 1 Peter 3:15: "But in your hearts revere Christ as Lord. Always be prepared to give an answer to everyone who asks you to give the reason for the *hope* that you have. But do this with gentleness and respect." We are a people of *hope*. St. Thomas Aquinas defined hope as the stretching forth of our desire toward a future good, even if that good is difficult to attain (*Summa Theologia* II, q. 17, obj.3). In other words, *hope* means choosing to act in ways that lead me closer to what is good and loving, even though the future is often unknown and beyond my control. We also *hope* because God is with us, right now, encouraging us to love wherever we are standing in the present moment. *Hope* is an action for today, stretching into tomorrow. The ability to abandon ourselves in *hope* leads us toward greater *humility*.

St. Ignatius' third point in contemplating the Two Standards about spiritual poverty and *humility* is addressed in Adolphe Tanquerey's work *The Spiritual Life*. He poses the three degrees of humility:

The first degree consists in perfect submission to the law of God, so that we should be ready to refuse the empires of the whole world, or even to sacrifice our lives, rather than transgress any precept which obliges us under pain of mortal sin. The second degree of humility is more perfect. It consists in the indifference of the soul towards riches or poverty, honor or shame, health or sickness, provided the glory of God and the salvation of souls are equally secured. And, the third degree of humility is the love of the Cross and the love of humiliation in union with Christ and out of love for Him (pp. 534-535).

Christ's presence at work within our hearts leads us to greater *hope* and an understanding of the power of true *humility*. True *humility* with Jesus Christ makes everyday life a journey into tasting more happiness and glory as the affection of the Father's Spirit regenerates our disordered affections. Following the Father's will is the truest *happiness* that we can experience. To live in union with Christ under his Standard is to recognize that Jesus' docility to the Father's will is our call as sons of the Father. The understanding of our identities, through participating in these Trinitarian relationships gives way to *hope*. Each of us as beloved sons through baptism is being *beheld* by God. *Humility* gives us the desire to be *evermore disposed and generous* in seeking the Father's will in all things. This disposition and acting in faith will lead to a greater interior relishing of His glory alive, and our *happiness* will be multiplied. We can live each day walking in faith from glory into glory. Our disordered affections need to be offered to the Father's loving gaze as he *beholds* us. If we humbly receive the Father's gaze of love, mercy and glory with Jesus at the cross in the power of the Spirit, the Father will gradually heal us of the disordered affections that hold us captive.

The Colloquy with the Trinity and Mary

As a means of cultivating what we have just described as the 2 C's and 4 H's, St. Ignatius Loyola suggests in his Spiritual Exercises praying a colloquy to the Trinity and Mary. The colloquy is an intimate conversation that St. Ignatius recommends at the end of each meditation and contemplation. The colloquy is to be done with a transparent heart, without fear of showing affection as a friend speaking to another friend. The colloquy is a two-way conversation that one enters into with Jesus, the Father, the Holy Spirit and Mary at the end of every prayer exercise or as one feels moved to at any point in the prayer exercises in the Spiritual Exercises. Through the colloquy, the Trinity may reveal previously unknown things to us that have affected our lives, and so free us to live more fully integrated lives. The colloquy can be a major instrument of discovery and freedom as one talks out one's experiences and pours out one's thoughts. Affectivity becomes gradually ordered by Trinitarian and Marian loving.

The triple colloquy of St. Ignatius is somewhat famous for it leads us into Trinitarian intimacy at the Cross:

First with Mary, then with Jesus, then with the Father – in which we beg to be chosen to walk with Jesus Christ in poverty and rejection, I ask "that I may be received under

Jesus Christ's Standard, first in the most perfect spiritual poverty and if God should choose me for it, to no less a degree of actual poverty and second, in bearing reproaches and insults, that through them I might imitate him more" (*Spiritual Exercises* #147). Praying this famous triple colloquy helps break down our resistance to being with Jesus in poverty and rejection. Its deeper motivation, however, is love (*The Call to Discernment in Troubled Times New Perspectives on the Transformative Wisdom of Ignatius of Loyola*, Dean Brackley, S.J., p. 85).

We want to note that Christians have had a long tradition of going to Mary in sorrowful recognition of the fact that we are sinners. *Lumen Gentium* #65 states, "The faithful still desire to conquer sin and grow in holiness. And so, they turn their eyes to Mary who shines out to the whole community of the elect as the model of virtues." Mary, who was a human like us and was called to live her life totally free from sin, shines for us as the one who intercedes for us before her Son. She is very approachable because of her gentleness, and she provides us with great strength and comfort.

Second, in praying the triple colloquy we enter into conversation with Jesus, who was seen in the first meditation on sin in the Spiritual Exercises. He is nailed to the Cross for our own sins. He is the ultimate reason that we can attain the graces we request in prayer. So we go to Jesus as our Redeemer and ask for a true knowledge and disgust for our sins as well as their affective sources, in order to become free from them.

Third, in praying the triple colloquy we turn to the Father, the One we have offended more than any other by our sins. It is the Father who sent His Son to Earth to re-unite us with Himself. We seek the Father in praying the triple colloquy. It is the Father who desires this reunion more than anything else, and we ask again to understand how we came to be separated from Him, and how we were influenced to make those choices. We beg for this interior knowledge in order that we may never be separated from Him again.

The "ID" of Satan: The 2 I's and 4 D's

Of course, the Evil One is all too happy to separate us from God. *Happiness* is thwarted by the enemy of our human nature; as much as God has a plan for us, Satan does too. St. Ignatius states it clearly:

The chief of all the enemy summons innumerable demons and scatters them. Some to one city and some to another throughout the whole world, so that no province, no place, no state of life, no individual is overlooked. He goes around to lay snares for men to seek to chain them. First, they are to tempt them to covet riches, as Satan himself is accustomed to do in most cases, that they more easily obtain the empty honors of this world and then come to overweening pride. The first step then, will be riches, the second; honor, the third; pride, from these three steps the one leads to all other vices (Meditation/Contemplation on the Two Standards, Point #3, The Spiritual Exercises).

Understanding the identity of Satan will help us resist the way we can easily fall prey to his tactics. If we learn from prayer where we are most vulnerable to attack, we can receive in humility new depths of freedom to be in love with Christ and live in intimate friendship with Him at the cross. We can also receive new wisdom to protect us from the evil one's tactics.

The ID of Satan as a tactic of attacking our humanity can occur through 2 "I's" and 4 "D's." Satan wants us not to receive faith in trusting the beauty of our poverty of spirit in and with Jesus. The "ID" of Satan is easy to remember if we think of the "ID" as representing the "Identification" of Satan as the enemy of human nature, the father of lies, the accuser.

The 2 I's are *isolation* and *inadequacy*. The 4 D's are *disappointment, discouragement, doubt and despair*. There can be natural psychological and spiritual occurrences of these 4 D's. Because Satan cannot read our minds but can react from our responses, he has acquired useful tactics to use against us. We need to be aware of these tactics and be vigilant in discernment.

If the natural is ruled out, then it is important to resist becoming *isolated* as a reaction to fears of rejection or even challenges by others to become all that we are called to be. The same would be true of the tactic of *inadequacy*. It is necessary to carefully discern if a reaction to spiritual, intellectual or physical growth results in *inadequacy*. We should also ask if Satan is trying to exaggerate our feelings and frustrations resulting in false *inadequacy*. Seminarians frequently fall prey to these tactics and contemplate abandoning their vocation because of this spiritual warfare. How often we have heard the words, "I'm not good enough," "I'm not worthy," and "I feel all alone." We know that loneliness leads to many sexual sins, so recognizing the tactic of the enemy can help us arrest these temptations more readily. We can acquire healthy habits that overcome these temptations, rendering newfound confidence in the power of the Spirit amid human weakness.

The 4 "D's" are more precisely understood as a progression. All of life carries *disappointments*. Because this is a common occurrence for all of us, Satan knew this would be a place of vulnerability for all humans. Taking each *disappointment* that comes our way and exacerbating the *disappointment* to the level of *discouragement* is movement toward paralyzing the individual. This *discouragement* ratchets up to *doubt*, and then as *doubt* gains strength it leads to *despair*. When the progression is rapid and irrational in nature, it is more recognizable as Satan's work. Concretely, if a seminarian finds himself habitually drawn to pornography, his *disappointment* in himself can lead to *discouragement* and a belief in the lie that he can never be free from this. Then he can easily *doubt* his vocation due to this struggle. Soon the seminarian falls into *despair* and withdraws into himself. He then begins to withdraw from his brothers and can eventually withdraw from the seminary system itself.

If we recognize that discernment and holy interrupters in spiritual combat—aided by attentiveness to one's thoughts and one's intellect—can slow the progression of the 4 D's, we can see how personal vigilance and self-knowledge will allow the seminarian to see the provocation readily, and learn that the progressive series of temptations are from the evil one.

Renewing the Sacrament of Penance through Discernment

We are called to persevere in the struggles and make progress towards freedom from sin. The wise counsel from Fr. Jacques Philippe's book, "Searching for and Maintaining Peace" states,

"One of the most common strategies of the devil in his efforts to distance us from God and to slow our spiritual progress is to attempt to cause the loss of interior peace. Here is what Don Lorenzo Scupoli one of the great spiritual masters of the 16th century, who was highly esteemed by St. Francis de Sales, said: 'The devil does his utmost to banish peace form one's heart, because he knows that God abides in peace and it is in peace that he accomplishes great things.' It would be well to keep this in mind because quite often in the daily unfolding of our Christian life, it happens that we fight the wrong battle, if one may put it that way, because we orient our efforts in the wrong direction. We fight on a terrain where the devil subtly drags us and can vanquish us, instead of fighting on the real battlefield, where on the contrary, by the grace of God, we are always certain of victory. In other words, do not stir up trouble; rather, keep calm, do God's will, persevere in the trial. If trouble or difficulties show themselves as recognizable by the evil spirit you will, cope accordingly if you exercise faith: "That which is in you is greater than that which in the world"(1 John 4: 4).

We are called daily, at every step of the way in spiritual combat, to fight against the interior lies that spring from and accompany spiritual desolation. The evil one uses spiritual desolation to make us feel separated from God's love when in fact he is near. Pope Francis makes this point in *Gaudete et Exultate*:

> The gift of discernment has become all the more necessary today, since contemporary life offers immense possibilities for action and distraction, and the world presents all of them as valid and good. All of us, but especially the young, are immersed in a culture of zapping. We can navigate simultaneously on two or more screens and interact at the same time with two or three virtual scenarios. Without the wisdom of discernment, we can easily become prey to every passing trend (#167).

The Church's living tradition speaks of the Seven Deadly Sins. Remedies to these are the Seven Heavenly Virtues. At the root of the deadly sins can be lies that we have believed, which often cover over even deeper fears in our hearts. Some of the common lies and fears that often operate within us when we are not exercising the gift of faith can be prayed through by reading Appendix I, which is dedicated to contributing to renewing the Sacrament of Penance-Confession.

Imagine if a man struggling with the affective disorder of prideful self-criticism and harsh self-judgment becomes aware in discernment of the particular lies and fears that are binding him to certain patterns of thoughts, feelings and desires, and imagine also that he becomes aware of deeper fears that are grounded in areas of unbelief and unforgiveness. Participating in the Sacrament of Penance becomes especially fruitful and freeing for the penitent. The objective truth of the redeeming affectivity of Jesus and the Father, whose judgement is always mercy and consolation, becomes able to be received subjectively in the penitent's heart. The regenerating glory of the Holy Spirit can begin to be tasted and savored, engendering freedom and hope in his struggles with the affective disorders of prideful self-criticism and harsh self-judgment. He could say in Confession; "In the Name of Jesus, I renounce the lies and fears that -I am alone' and that 'I need always to look out for myself.' These lies and fears have led me to the pride of self-criticism and harsh self-judgment. Father, I trust that you are always with me and that you desire to care for me." Such a man struggling with these particular faces of pride learns to renounce the particular lies and fears in the Name of Jesus by the authority given him in Baptism, while asking the

Father for the corresponding heavenly virtue, which is *humility*.

In this sort of Confession based on a deeper listening for affective movements or "spirits" in ordinary discernment, the Father is allowed to be the object of the man's needs for love and affection. At the same time the man as a penitent matures deeply by exercising faith as he allows himself to be who he really is as the object of the Father's affection in merciful forgiveness. Maturity transpires as the man finds himself in the embrace of the Father's love and mercy, being *held* by mercy. The man as penitent finds *happiness* and *hope* by returning home to himself alive because of God's love. The penitent also receives regenerating glory as a man who exercises *courage* to abide in a *receptive disposition*. The Holy Spirit can then be received to restore the joy of his salvation in his battle with this affective disorder of self-criticism and harsh self-judgment that can be so debilitating and harmful (see Ps. 51:14).

Applications to Transitory Same-Sex Attraction

We have now looked at the Trinitarian foundations of Ignatian spirituality, discussed the Church's teaching of same-sex attraction as a disordered affection, and explored ways in which the Spiritual Exercises teach us how to discern interior movements of the heart. We are thus now ready to apply these tools of discernment to help seminarians address transitory same-sex attraction in a manner consistent with the norms of the 2016 *Ratio fundamentalis*.

The work of the evil spirit, the enemy of our human nature, can exacerbate what can be some of the primary reasons for transitory same-sex attraction. In healing-prayer ministry, we often deal with those affected by father wounds, mother wounds and adolescent wounds which result in presenting transitory same-sex attraction.

Application #1

Father wounds occur when a father is perceived by a child as distant, critical, selfish, angry or alcoholic. This produces, amid ordinary human conflicts related to affectively maturing, yet another combination of crucial conflicts in the development of a boy's masculine identity. "As children and adolescents, these men yearned for acceptance, praise and physical affection from their fathers, but their needs were never met," states Dr. Rick Fitzgibbons (Culture of Life Foundation website, "The Origin and Therapy of SSAD," Nov. 21, 2005). In exercising the pastoral ministry of counseling and inner healing prayer, a seminarian came for healing prayer. His father had been distant most of his life. The seminarian struggled much with transitory same-sex attraction. As we prayed for healing of memories, we discovered that what supported his belief of his father's rejection was believing an inner lie from childhood. The seminarian took on this lie when his father, who was a minister, had to leave suddenly on the seminarian's birthday to go to a congregant family who was suffering from a tragedy. The seminarian's interior belief was that others were more important than he was to his dad. The seminarian had come to believe this so much that as he was growing up he sought to find others for affection and affirmation, especially male friends. These male friends made him their priority. When Jesus' presence was invited into the little boy's birthday memory, during the inner healing prayer session, Jesus' Spirit spoke truth into the lie of the rejection. The seminarian found himself able to recognize all the ways in which he in turn had rejected his father's desire to be in relation with him and spend time with him over the years. The seminarian recognized how deceived he was by some men who had pursued him in very seductive ways. He was able to accept forgiveness from Jesus' Spirit, offer forgiveness to his father, and to those who pursued him. What transpired over time was an inner transformation as the seminarian felt the tendency towards same-sex attraction and need for affection in that disordered fashion to cease. The seminarian's interior need for male affection was being ordered through forgiveness to receive from the Father who Jesus revealed him to be and Jesus does the same for us in any disordered affection. With follow-up spiritual direction and good counsel, the seminarian found himself over time to be able to engage in healthy relationships with other males. He recognized the way the initial *disappointment* in his earthly father had been moved to a *doubt* and how this *doubt* moved into *despairing* when he was in college. This then led to the transitory same-sex attraction and disordered affections that he had acted out in relationships that needed to be ordered by the Father's love, mercy and regenerating glory.

Application #2

The mother wound is another area that can result in transitory same-sex attraction. A mother wound is an internalized set of limiting beliefs and patterns of trust originating from the relationship with one's mother. Self-blaming and very low self-esteem that manifests itself as a core system of beliefs from a mother wound often leads into transitory adolescent same-sex attractions. The core belief is frequently stated this way: "There is something wrong with me." It is a system of interior believing that is minimizing oneself so that the person is always seen to be likable and accepted. The inability to speak up authentically and express one's emotions fully and the tendency to practice behaviors that are often the result of unprocessed anger (that lies below the surface) can be the result of a boy's wounded relationship with his mother. These are some of the ways that the mother wound can lead toward disordered affections. Of course, there are other windows of interior belief systems that can thwart participating in affections being ordered by awakening to indwelling Trinitarian relationships.

One young man who came for healing prayer was suffering from a mother wound that produced much unprocessed anger. Always being angry at women led him to seek male companionship because he did not like himself for being angry at women. The young man was *isolating* himself. And, in that *isolation* a belief system of certain thoughts, feelings and desires were interiorized, and the evil one let him believe the lie that he was not attracted to women. This was coupled with the lie that women were not attracted to him. So, the young man's desire for love could only come through other men because of this interior belief system. The young man shared that his mom had been very domineering, and it made him angry that she never let his father, whom she eventually divorced, have any say in family situations, especially those of disciplining himself and his two brothers. At a very young age, this young man, being the middle child, always wanted to be the peacemaker. And so he did not acknowledge his anger. This led to finding himself rejecting teachers and even classmates who were female. During the times spent praying for a healing of memories this young man began to allow his inner child to embrace the anger from his childhood. He gave it to Jesus who then opened up his sensitivity to women. The young man began to taste and see inwardly a capacity for compassion that had not been realized. He began to taste inwardly the potential he had for compassion. He worked in counseling and spiritual direction for over a year. He came to understand that he did not desire men as he had once believed. He was truly able to overcome the disordered affections and went on in his studies in seminary. This young man is a very compassionate priest today.

Application #3

In the third scenario we look at the way in which an adolescent, whose wound was incurred through subjectively absorbing the conflicts between his mother and father, took on an underdeveloped and pained affectivity. This scenario points to how an interior perception took on a system of inner beliefs that resulted in a transitory same-sex attraction. The interior belief system was that "power struggles are best avoided." When the issue became one of control over the adolescent's life, over choices like friends or school achievement or future direction, the parents imposed their will against the teenager's inner way of desiring and proceeding.

Now what mattered most to the dad, for example, was asserting his authority, proving that he was in charge. It was a way of relating to his son that taught that dad always knows best. It was a way of dominating at all cost. The father always gets his way in the relationship with his adolescent son. Harsh tactics like intimidation, humiliation and even punishing through physical force can be employed to show a son that the dad is still the boss. At the same time the mother may convey this attitude towards her son, "You're correct. It is not my job to make you do what you refuse to do. As an adolescent son you must manage your own decisions. I respect your right to make your own decisions. And I am interested in hearing everything you have to say about your right to manage your decisions." The mother basically takes on the attitude and way of life that states, "My job is not to control your decisions. … It is my job to inform them." (Psychology Today Parental Put Downs and Power Strengthening Adolescence, Carl E. Pickhardt, PhD Feb 6, 2012 Internet Post).

These ways of being dealt with by adults can bring about in the adolescent a real interior confusion. The young man can wonder; "How am I to proceed in my life?" His confusions result in affective disorders in ways of proceeding in relationships. This inner confusion and the resulting pain can then equate to a confusion in personal identity. Identity confusion then brings about the need to know myself. And, as the individual sometimes seeks answers he begins exploring gender identity. We have seen young men seeking relationships, men who do not have proper sexual boundaries, try to resolve or determine their sexual identity. The amount of shame and guilt that accompanies these decisions to experiment in a variety of sexual relationships results in fostering deep self-condemnation. This then impedes the young man's ability to mature.

Helping to determine the source of the interior condemnation, humiliation and self-deception is key for fruitful healing prayer, regular spiritual direction and pastoral counseling. The interior habits of allowing these sources of self-condemnation and humiliation especially influence sexual attractions serve to perpetuate the lies that accompany the inner condemnations. Usually, there are complex psychological influences at work in the man's heart, however it is important to root out where the condemnation, humiliation and self-deception are coming from so that the person can seek to heal these wounds. Again, good spiritual direction and counseling that embraces the truth and beauty of the Church's teachings in human sexuality will help the man. Clarity about what the root causes are to experiencing tendencies towards transitory same-sex attraction can be discovered.

Pastorally, we knew of a young man who had grown up with these confusions. In his own life he began to sexually act out during college with other men. He came to understand his true feelings. As the humiliation that he had experienced as an adolescent came to the surface of his memories, humiliations that were suffered at his own father's hands due to his desire to stop playing football in high school, healing began to transpire. Deep pain was being brought into the light. Whereas the young man had been *isolated* and alone in pain, he was now able to become relational with Jesus' healing presence. Once a series of these type of humiliations were acknowledged, his relationship with his father began to experience increasing healing love from Jesus' presence. In the process of several sessions of healing of memories prayer the process brought about a new clarity of his identity. He started to recognize his own guilt and the roots of his shame. He could then develop self-worth and identity, which resulted in turning away from his previous sexual choices. After two years of interior work, the young man was able to receive forgiveness and recognize God's call in his own life.

Summary and Conclusion

As we have tried to articulate some wisdom through focusing upon receptivity in prayer within St. Ignatius' Spiritual Exercises and in particular his meditation/contemplation called "The Two Standards," the reality is that affective maturity is realized and lived best when fully informed of the forces working against us and the virtues needed to persevere. St. John Paul II rightly stated in *Pastores dabo vobis*, "affective maturity, which is the result of an education in true and responsible love, is a significant and decisive factor in the formation of candidates for the priesthood" (#43).

The gift of the Spiritual Exercises vivifies and makes the human heart radiant because of tasting and savoring the Father's affectionate delight in the regenerating power of the Holy Spirit's mercy and glory. Affective maturity is engendered through the vital ministry of the Spiritual Exercises as affective disorders meet the risen Jesus and are drawn into Trinitarian love. This love is laboring in all creation and for each of us to make all things new (Rev. 21:5). Fr. Wilfred Stinissen offers a beautiful reflection on the power of this healing love:

We not only have the ability to form and shape our present and future, we also have power over our past. When we see our past in the light of the Holy Spirit, with the eyes of God, it is created anew. What we pray for in the Psalms comes true: "Make us glad as many days as you have afflicted us, and as many years as we have seen evil." (Ps. 90:15)

We receive a completely new past. The best moment for this transformation of our past is, of course, at the Eucharist. Do we really mean it when we say: "Say but the word and I shall be healed?" He comes to us to heal our wounds, to transform all sorrow into joy. Do we give him the opportunity to heal us? Do we show him our wounds? We pray: "Into your wounds hide me." "By his wounds you have been healed", we read in the first letter of Peter (1 Pet. 2:24). The more we come in contact with these wounds, the more all of our wounds heal. In the Eucharist, the Lord comes to us wounded and sacrificed. (*Into Your Hands, Father*, pp. 40–41)

This article has been a small humble attempt to speak about how the Lord desires to make seminarians who struggle with transitory same-sex attractions "new." We have thus provided an overview of how the spirituality of the Spiritual Exercises, and in particular the meditation/contemplation on The Two Standards, contributes to engendering affective maturity. The Spiritual Exercises focuses us on unleashing the power of the Holy Spirit that is being poured into our hearts (Rom. 5:5). Part of the mystery of affectivity being ordered by the Trinity's love can be understood in what we have referred to as "healing of memories prayer." When a person enters into prayer during the Spiritual Exercises, the identification with the mysteries of the life of Christ becomes intimately known and tasted. In the human capacity to remember life experience and events we can notice affective patterns of thoughts, feelings and desires. These affective patterns are carried both in the memory and imagination. In reality, the human capacities of memory and imagination are elevated by the gift of faith to taste and see the Trinity's sovereign love laboring in all times and places. When human memory is healed the glory of God is seen and affections are ordered by love. We hope that our contribution may open the doors to the Trinity's healing work.

Prayer: Anima Christi

Soul of Christ, sanctify me.
Body of Christ, save me.
Blood of Christ, inebriate me.
Water from the side of Christ, wash me.
Passion of Christ, strengthen me.
O good Jesus, hear me;
within your wounds hide me
Let me never be separated from you.

From the malicious enemy defend me.
In the hour of my death call me
and bid me come unto you
that I may praise you with your saints
and with your angels,
forever and ever.
Amen.

Practicum Reflection Questions for Formators

1. What do I need to learn so that I can taste and savor in daily prayer the presence of the Indwelling Trinity addressing my spiritual senses? When I reflect on St. Augustine's inspiring words at the beginning of this article what is my own experience in faith of knowing the Lord's presence communicating and loving me through my spiritual senses?

2. How am I listening for and receiving a deepening confidence in my identity as a beloved child of God? What is life like when I walk in this confidence? What is the contrast like when I forget to walk with Jesus' presence to live under His standard, seeking first to live in His kingdom?

3. Am I willing to repent daily of holding on to disappointments, discouragements and doubts, entrusting myself to the Father's providential care at the cross, believing in His desire to further complete my joy? What is my experience of practicing this daily interior surrender of my personality in and with Jesus' dependence on the Father in the power of the Holy Spirit?

4. In the face of the fears that accompany feeling inadequate and alone how have I turned to receive and experience the desire of Jesus' risen Heart to give me courage and confidence in the community of believers? What has been my experience whenever I choose interiorily to abide with Jesus' presence in humility and happiness amid daily trials?

Suggested Resources

1. *Understanding The Spiritual Exercises*, by Fr. Michael Ivens, S.J. Gracewing, Gloucester, England, 2016.

2. *Healing: Bringing God's Gift of Mercy to the World*, by Mary Healy, OSV, Huntington, Indiana, 2015.

3. *Scripture, Mercy and Homosexuality*, by Mary Healy, Catholic Answers, San Diego, 2016.

4. *Discernment - Acquiring The Heart Of God*, by Marko Ivan Rupnik, S.J., Pauline Books and Media, Boston, 2006.

5. *Abba's Heart - Finding Our Way Back to the Father's Delight*, by Neal and Matt Lozano, Chosen Minneapolis, 2015.

6. *Into Your Hands, Father*, by Wilfrid Stinissen, Ignatius Press, San Francisco, 2011.

7. *The Soul of Shame*, by Curt Thompson, M.D., InterVarsity Press, Westmont, IL, 2015.

Chapter Eighteen

CONSCIOUSNESS EXAMEN

Fr. George Aschenbrenner, S.J., STL

Several decades ago, following Vatican II and the call to recover original charisms in religious life, Fr. George Aschenbrenner emerged as an international leader in the search to recapture the original spirit and practice of The Spiritual Exercises of St. Ignatius Loyola. His groundbreaking research and writing on the "Consciousness Examen" breathed new life into the practice of the daily Examen Prayer which had been a major component in the formation of religious women and men, lay leadership and diocesan clergy during the lifetime of St. Ignatius and his first companions in the Society of Jesus. Fr. Aschenbrenner is currently retired after having served as Director of the Jesuit Retreat Center for Spiritual Growth in Wernersville, PA, as the Director of Spiritual Formation at the Pontifical North American College in Rome, and as Director of Novices for the Maryland Province of the Society of Jesus. He is a Co-Founder of the Institute for Priestly Formation in Omaha, NE that is dedicated to serving diocesan seminarians and priests in spiritual formation through teaching Ignatian contemplative prayer. He specializes in diocesan priestly spirituality and the discernment of spirits. Fr. Aschenbrenner is the author of "Quickening The Fire In Our Midst – The Challenge of Diocesan Priestly Spirituality" as well as "Stretched for Greater Glory - What To Expect From The Spiritual Exercises." Recently, a collection of his major essays and articles in spiritual formation were published entitled "The Hidden Self Grown Strong."

Examen is a practice without much significance for many people in their spiritual lives. This is true for a variety of reasons, but all the reasons amount to the admission (rarely explicit) that it is not of immediate practical value in a busy day. All these reasons and their false conclusion spring from a basic misunderstanding of this spiritual practice. Examen must be seen in relationship to discernment of spirits. It is a daily intensive exercise of discernment in a person's life.

Examen of Consciousness

For many people today, life is spontaneity. If spontaneity is crushed or aborted, then life itself is stillborn. In this view, examen is living life backwards and once removed from the vibrant spontaneity and immediacy of the experience itself. These people today disagree with Socrates' claim that the unexamined life is not worth living. For these people, the Spirit is in the spontaneous, so anything that militates against spontaneity is not of the Spirit.

This view overlooks the fact that welling up in the consciousness and experience of each of us are two spontaneities, one good and for God, another evil and not for God. These two types of spontaneous urges and movements happen to all of us. So often, the quick-witted, loose-tongued person who can be so entertaining and the center of attention and who is always characterized as being so spontaneous is certainly not being moved by or giving expression to the good spontaneity. For people eager to love God with their whole being, the challenge is not simply to let the spontaneous happen but rather, to be able to sift through these various spontaneous urges and give full existential ratification to those spontaneous feelings that are from and for God. We do this by allowing the truly Spirited spontaneity to happen in our daily lives. But we must learn the feel of this true Spirited spontaneity. Examen has a central role in this learning.

When examen is related to discernment, it becomes examen of *consciousness* rather than of conscience. Examen of conscience has narrow moralistic overtones. Its prime concern is with the good or bad actions we have done each day. In discernment, the prime concern is with the way God is affecting and moving us (often quite spontaneously!) deep in our own affective consciousness. What is happening in our consciousness is prior to, and more important than, our actions, which can be delineated as juridically good or evil. How we are experiencing the "drawing" of God (Jn 6:44) in our own existential consciousness and how our sinful nature is quietly tempting us and luring us away from intimacy with God in the subtle dispositions of our consciousness—this is what the daily examen is concerned with prior to a concern for our response in our *actions*. Hence, it is examen of consciousness that we are concerned with here, so that we can cooperate with and let happen that beautiful spontaneity in our hearts that is the touch of God and the urging of the Spirit.

Examen and Spiritual Identity

The examen we are talking about here is not a Ben Franklin-like striving for self-perfection. We are talking about an experience in faith of growing sensitivity to the unique, intimately special ways that God's Spirit has of approaching and calling us. Obviously, it takes time for this growth. But in this sense, examen is a daily renewal of and growth in our spiritual identity as unique flesh-spirit persons loved and called by God in the inner intimacy of our affective world. It is not possible for us to make an examen without confronting our own unique identity in imitation of Christ before God.

And yet, so often, our daily examen becomes so general and vague that our unique spiritual identity does not seem to make any difference. Examen assumes real value when it becomes a daily experience of confrontation and renewal of our unique spiritual identity and an experience of how God is subtly inviting us to deepen and develop this identity. We should make our examen each time with as precise a grasp as we have now on our spiritual identity. We do not make it as just any Christian but as this specific Christian person with a unique vocation and grace in faith.

Examen and Prayer

The examen is a time of prayer. The dangers of an empty self-reflection or an unhealthy self-centered introspection are very real. On the other hand, a lack of effort at examen and the approach of living according to what comes naturally keep us quite superficial and insensitive to the subtle and profound ways of God deep in our hearts. The prayerful quality and effectiveness of the examen itself depend upon its relationship to our continuing contemplative prayer. Without this relationship, examen slips to the level of self-reflection for self-perfection, if it perdures at all.

In daily contemplative prayer, God carefully reveals to us the order of the mystery of all reality in Christ—as Paul says to the Colossians: "But now it has been manifested to his holy ones, to whom God chose to make known the riches of the glory of this mystery among the Gentiles" (Col 1:27). The contemplator experiences in many subtle, chiefly nonverbal ways this revelation of God in Christ. The presence of the Spirit of the risen Jesus in the heart of the believer makes it possible to sense and "hear" this challenge to order ourselves to this revelation. Contemplation is empty without this "ordering" response.

This kind of reverent, docile (the "obedience of faith" Paul speaks of in Romans 16:26), and nonmoralistic ordering is the work of the daily examen—to sense and recognize those interior invitations of God that guide and deepen this ordering from day to day and not to cooperate with those subtle insinuations opposed to that ordering. Without that contemplative contact with God's revelation of reality in Christ, both in formal prayer and in informal prayerfulness, the daily practice of examen becomes empty; it shrivels up and dies. Without this "listening" to the revelation of God's ways, which are so different from our own,[1] examen again becomes that shaping up of ourselves that is human and natural self-perfection, or, even worse, it can corrupt into a selfish ordering of ourselves to our own ways.

Examen without regular contemplation is futile. A failure at regular contemplation emaciates the beautifully rich experience of responsible ordering to which the contemplative is continually invited by God. It is true, on the other hand, that contemplation without regular examen becomes compartmentalized, superficial, and stunted in our lives. The time of formal prayer can become a very sacrosanct period in our day but so isolated from the rest of our life that we are not prayerful (finding God in all things) at that level where we really live. The examen gives our daily contemplative experience of God real bite into all our daily living; it is an important means to finding God in everything and not just in the time of formal prayer.

A Discerning Vision of Heart

When we first learn and practice the examen, it seems stylized and artificial. This problem is not in the examen-prayer but in ourselves; we are beginners and have not yet worked out that integration in ourselves of a process of personal discernment to be expressed in daily examens. This should not put us off.

Examen will always be fundamentally misunderstood if the goal of this exercise is not grasped. The specific exercise of examen is ultimately aimed at developing a heart with a discerning vision to be active, not only for one or two quarter-hour periods in a day, but continually. This is a gift from God—a most important one, as Solomon realized.[2] So we must constantly pray for this gift, but we must also be receptive to its development within our hearts. A daily practice of examen is essential to this development.

Hence, the five steps of this exercise of examen as presented in the *Spiritual Exercises* of St. Ignatius Loyola (#43) are to be seen, and gradually experienced in faith, as dimensions of the Christian consciousness, formed by God's work in the heart as it confronts and grows within this world and all of reality. If we allow God gradually to transform our minds and

---

[1] See Isaiah 55:8-9: "For my thoughts are not your thoughts, nor are your ways my ways—oracle of the LORD. For as the heavens are higher than the earth, so are my ways higher than your ways, my thoughts higher than your thoughts."

[2] See 1 Kings 3:9-12.

hearts into that of Jesus, so that we become truly Christian through our living experience in this world, then the examen, with its separate elements now seen as integrated dimensions of our own consciousness looking out on the world, is much more organic to our outlook and will seem much less contrived. There is no ideal length of time arbitrarily set for each of the five elements of the examen when it is practiced. Rather, the examen is a daily organic expression of the spiritual mood of our hearts. At one time, we are drawn to one element longer than the others and at another time, to another element over the others.

The mature Ignatius, near the end of his life, was always examining every movement and inclination of his heart, which means he was *discerning* the congruence of everything with his true Christ-centered self. This was the overflow of those regular intensive prayer-exercises of examen every day. As beginners or "old-timers," we must understand both the point of the one or two quarter-hour exercises of examen each day—namely, a continually discerning heart—and the point of the necessary gradual adaptation of our practice of examen to our stage of development and to the situation in the world in which we now find ourselves. And yet, we are all aware of the subtle rationalization of giving up formal examen each day because we have "arrived at" that continually discerning heart. This kind of rationalization prevents further growth in faith sensitivity to the ways of the Holy Spirit in our daily lives.

Let us now take a look at the format of the examen as presented by St. Ignatius in the *Spiritual Exercises*, #43, but in light of these previous comments on examen as discerning consciousness within the world.

Prayer for Enlightenment

In the *Exercises*, Ignatius has an act of thanksgiving as the first part of the examen. The first two parts could be interchanged without too much difference. In fact, I would suggest the prayer for enlightenment as a fitting introduction to the examen.

The examen is not simply a matter of the natural power of our memory and analysis to go back over a part of the day. It is a matter of Spirit-guided insight into our lives and courageously responsive sensitivity to God's call in our hearts. What we are seeking here is that gradually growing appreciative insight into the mystery that "I am." Without God's revealing grace, this kind of insight is not possible. We must be careful not to get locked into the world of our own human natural powers. Our technological world poses a special danger in this regard. Founded on a deep appreciation of the interpersonal, the Christian in faith transcends the boundaries of the here-and-now with its limited natural causality and discovers a God who loves and who works in, through, and beyond all. For this reason, we begin the examen with an explicit petition for that enlightenment that will occur in and through our own powers but that our own natural powers could never accomplish all by themselves: that the Spirit may help us to see ourselves a bit more as Gods sees us!

Reflective Thanksgiving

Our stance as Christians in the world is that of poor persons possessing nothing, not even ourselves, and yet being gifted at every instant in and through everything. When we become too affluently involved with ourselves and deny our inherent poverty, then we lose the gifts and either begin to make demands for what we think we deserve (often leading to angry frustration) or blandly take for granted *all* that comes our way. Only the truly poor person can appreciate the slightest gift and feel genuine gratitude. The more deeply we live in faith, the more we become aware of how poor we are and how gifted; life itself becomes humble, joyful thanksgiving. This should gradually become an element of our abiding consciousness.

After the introductory prayer for enlightenment, our hearts should rest in genuine faith-filled gratitude to God for the personal gifts of this most recent part of our day. Perhaps in the spontaneity of the happening, we were not aware of the gift and now, in this exercise of reflective prayer, we see the events from a very different perspective. Our sudden gratitude—now the act of a humble, selfless pauper—helps make us ready to discover the gift more clearly in a future spontaneity. Our gratitude should center on the concrete, uniquely personal gifts that each of us is blessed with, whether large and obviously important or tiny and apparently insignificant. There is much in our lives that we take for granted; gradually, God will lead us to a deep realization that *all is gift*. It is only right to give praise and thanks!

Practical Survey of Actions

In this third element of the examen, ordinarily we rush to review, in some specific detail, our actions of that part of the day just finished so we can catalog them as good or bad. Just what we should not do! Our prime concern here in faith is with what has been happening to and in us since the last examen. The operative questions are: What has been happening in us? How has God been working in us? What is being asked of us? Only secondarily are our own actions to be considered. This part of the examen presumes that we have become sensitive to our interior feelings, moods, and slightest urgings and that we are not frightened by them but have learned to take them very seriously. It is here in the depths of our affectivity, at times so spontaneous and strong, and at other times so shadowy, that God moves us and deals with us most intimately. These interior moods, feelings, urges, and movements are the "spirits" that must be sifted through, discerned, so we can recognize God's call to us at this intimate core of our being. The examen is a chief means to this discerning of our interior consciousness.

Discernment presumes a real faith approach to life—that life is first listening, then acting in response. The fundamental attitude of the believer is one who listens. It is to the Lord's utterances that he gives ear. In as many different ways and on as many varied levels as the listener can discern the word and will of the Lord manifested to him, he must respond with all the Pauline "obedience of faith." It is the attitude of receptivity, passivity, and poverty of one who is always in need, radically dependent, conscious of his creaturehood.[3] Hence, there is a great need for interior quiet, peace, and passionate receptivity that attunes us to listening to God's word at every instant and in every situation and *then* to responding in our own activity. Again, in a world that is founded more on activity (becoming activism), productivity, and efficiency (whereas efficacy is a norm for the kingdom of God), this faith view is implicitly, if not explicitly, challenged at every turn in the road.

Our first concern here is with these subtle, intimate, affective ways in which God has been dealing with us during these past few hours. Perhaps we did not recognize God's calling in that past moment, but now, our vision is clear and direct. Secondarily, our concern is with our actions insofar as they are *responses* to the calling of the Holy Spirit. So often our activity becomes primary to us, and all sense of response in our activity is lost. We become self-moved and self-motivated rather than moved and motivated by the Spirit.[4] This is a subtle lack of faith and a failure to live as a son or daughter of God. In the light of faith, it is the *quality* of responsiveness of the activity, more than the activity itself, that makes the difference for the Kingdom of God.

In this general review, there is no strain to reproduce every second since the last examen; rather, our concern is with specific details and incidents as they reveal patterns and bring some clarity and insight. This brings us to a consideration of what Ignatius calls the particular examen.

This element of the examen, perhaps more than any other, has been misunderstood. It

---

[3] David Asselin, S.J., "Christian Maturity and Spiritual Discernment," *Review for Religious*, 27 (1968): 594.

[4] See Romans 8:14: "For those who are led by the Spirit of God are children of God."

has often become an effort to divide and conquer by moving down the list of vices or up the list of virtues in a mechanically planned approach to self-perfection. A certain amount of time is spent on one vice or virtue, and then we move on to the next one on the list. Rather than a practical, programmed approach to perfection, the particular examen is meant to be a reverently honest, personal meeting with the Holy Spirit of God in our own hearts.

When we become sensitive and serious enough about loving God, we begin to realize that some changes must be made. We are deficient in so many areas, and so many defects must be done away with. But God does not want all of them to be handled at once. Usually, there is one area of our hearts where God is especially calling for conversion, which is always the beginning of new life. God is interiorly nudging us in one area and reminding us that if we are really serious about life in the Spirit, this one aspect of ourselves must be changed. This is often precisely the one area we want to forget and (maybe) work on later. We do not want to let God's word condemn us in this one area, and so we try to forget it and distract ourselves by working on some other, safer area that *does* require conversion but not with the same urgent sting of consciousness that is true of the former area. It is in this first area of our hearts, if we are honest and open with God, that we very personally experience the fire of the Holy Spirit confronting us here and now. So often, we fail to recognize this guilt for what it really is, or we try to blunt it by working hard on something else that we may want to correct, whereas God wants something else here and now. It takes time for beginners to become interiorly sensitive to God before they gradually come to recognize the Spirit's call to conversion (maybe involving a very painful struggle) in some area of their lives. It is better for beginners to take this time to learn what God wants their particular examen now to be, rather than just to take some assigned imperfection and get started on it.

And so, the particular examen is very personal, honest, and—at times—a very subtle experience of the Spirit calling in our hearts for deeper conversion. The matter of the conversion may remain the same for a long period of time, but the important thing is our sense of this personal challenge to us. Often, this experience of God's calling for conversion in one small part of our hearts takes the expression of good, healthy guilt that should be carefully interpreted and responded to if there is to be progress in holiness. When the particular examen is seen as this personal experience of God's love for us, then we can understand why St. Ignatius suggests that we turn our whole consciousness to this experience of the Holy Spirit (whatever it may be in all practicality, for example, more subtle humility, or readiness to get involved with people on their terms, and so on) at those two very important moments in our day—when we begin our day and when we close it, besides the formal examen times.

In this third dimension of the formal examen, the growing faith sense of our sinfulness is central. This is more of a spiritual faith reality as revealed by God in our experience than a heavily moralistic and guilt-laden reality. A deep sense of sinfulness depends on our growth in faith and is a dynamic realization that always ends in thanksgiving—the song of a "saved sinner."

Contrition and Sorrow

The Christian heart is always a heart in song—a song of deep joy and gratitude. But the Alleluia can be quite superficial and without body and depth unless it is genuinely touched with sorrow. This is our song as sinners constantly aware of being prey to our sinful tendencies and yet, being converted into the newness that is guaranteed in the victory of Jesus Christ. Hence, we never grow out of a sense of wonderful sorrow in the presence of our Savior.

This basic dimension of our heart's vision, which God desires to deepen in us as we are converted from sin, is here applied to the specifics of our actions since the last examen, especially insofar as they were selfishly inadequate *responses* to God's work in our hearts. This sorrow especially springs from the lack of honesty and courage in responding to God's call in the particular examen. This contrition and sorrow is neither a shame nor a depression at our weakness but a faith experience as we grow in our realization of our dear God's awesome desire that we love with every ounce of our being.

After this description, the value of pausing each day in formal examen and giving concrete expression to this abiding sense of sorrow in our hearts should be quite obvious and should flow naturally from the third element of practical survey of our actions.

Hopeful Resolution for the Future

This final element of the formal daily examen grows naturally out of the previous elements. The organic development leads us to face the future, which is now rising to encounter us and become integrated into our lives. In the light of our present discernment of the immediate past, how do we look to the future? Are we discouraged or despondent or fearful about the future? If this is the atmosphere of our hearts now, we must wonder why and try to interpret this atmosphere; we must be honest in acknowledging our feelings for the future and not repress them by hoping they will go away.

The precise expression of this final element will be determined by the organic flow of this precise examen now. Accordingly, this element of resolution for the immediate future will never happen the same way each time. If it did happen in the same expression each time, it would be a sure sign that we were not really entering into the previous four elements of the examen.

At this point in the examen, there should be a great desire to face the future with renewed vision and sensitivity as we pray both to recognize even more the subtle ways in which God greets us and to recognize the Spirit calling us in the existential situation of the future—and then to respond to that call with more faith, humility, and courage. This should be especially true of that intimate, abiding experience of the particular examen. Great hope should be the atmosphere of our hearts at this point—hope not founded on our own deserts or our own powers for the future but rather, much more fully in our God, whose glorious victory in Jesus Christ we share through the life of the Spirit in our hearts. The more we trust and allow God to lead in our lives, the more we will experience true supernatural hope in God in and through, but quite beyond, our own weak powers—an experience at times frightening and emptying but ultimately joyfully exhilarating. St. Paul, in a whole passage from the letter to the Philippians (3:7-14), expresses well the spirit of this conclusion of the formal examen: "Brothers, I for my part do not consider myself to have taken possession. Just one thing: forgetting what lies behind but straining forward to what lies ahead" (3:13).

Examen and Discernment

When examen is practiced each day, it becomes an exercise that so focuses and renews our specific faith identity that we should be even more reluctant to omit our examen than our formal contemplative prayer each day. This seems to have been St. Ignatius's view of the practice of the examen. He never talks of omitting it, though he does talk of adapting and abbreviating the daily meditation for various reasons. For him, it seems the examen was central and quite inviolate. This strikes us as strange until we revamp our understanding of the examen. Then, perhaps, we begin to see the examen as so intimately connected to our growing identity and so important to our finding God in all things at all times that it becomes our central daily experience of prayer.

For Ignatius, finding God in all things is what life is all about. Near the end of his life, he said that "whenever he wished, at whatever hour, he could find God."[5] This is the mature Ignatius, who had so fully allowed God to possess every ounce of his being through a clear,

---

[5] Ignatius Autobiography, #99.

abandoning "Yes" that radiated from the very core of his being that he could be conscious at any moment he wanted of the deep peace, joy, and contentment (consolation) that was the experience of God at the center of his heart.[6] Ignatius's identity, at this point in his life, was quite fully and clearly "in Christ," as Paul says: "For his sake I have accepted the loss of all things and I consider them so much rubbish, that I may gain Christ and be found in him, not having any righteousness of my own based on the law but that which comes through faith in Christ." (Phil 3:8-9). Ignatius knew and was his true self in Christ.

Being able to find God whenever he wanted, Ignatius was now able to find that God of love in all things through a test for congruence of any interior impulse, mood, or feeling with his true self. Whenever he found interior consonance (which registers as peace, joy, contentment) from the immediate interior movement and felt himself being his true, congruent self, then he knew he had heard God's Word to him at that instant. And he responded with that fullness of humble courage so typical of Ignatius. If he discovered interior dissonance, agitation, and disturbance "at the bottom of the heart" (to be carefully distinguished from repugnance "at the top of the head"[7]) and could not find his true congruent self in Christ, then he recognized the interior impulse as an "evil spirit" and he experienced God by "going against" the desolate impulse.[8] In this way, he was able to find God in all things by carefully discerning all his interior experiences ("spirits"). Thus, discernment of spirits became a daily, very practical living of the art of loving God with his whole heart, whole body, and whole strength. Every moment of life was loving (finding) God in the existential situation in a deep, quiet peace and joy.

For Ignatius, this finding God in the present interior movement, feeling, or option was almost instantaneous in his mature years because the central "feel" or "bent" of his being had so been grasped by God. For the beginner, what was almost instantaneous for the mature Ignatius may require the effort of a prayerful process of a few hours or days, depending on the importance of the movement—impulse to be discerned. In some of his writing, Ignatius uses *examen* to refer to this almost instantaneous test for congruence with his true self—something he could do a number of times every hour of the day. But he also speaks of examen in the formal restricted sense of two quarter-hour exercises of prayer a day.

The intimate and essential relationship between these two senses of examen has been the point of this whole essay.

---

[6] Spiritual Exercises, #316.

[7] John Carroll Futrell, S.J., *Ignatian Discernment* (St. Louis: Institute of Jesuit Sources, 1970), 64.

[8] See the Spiritual Exercises, # 319.

"Consciousness Examen" is from *Quickening the Fire in Our Midst: The Challenge of Diocesan Priestly Spirituality* (Loyola Press, 2002). It was originally published in *Review for Religious* and is reprinted with the permission of the U.S. Central and Southern Province, Society of Jesus.

Prayer

Come Holy Spirit,... enfold my heart in your wisdom and love. I praise and thank you for actively drawing me this day into a greater participation in your life. Lead and guide me to taste and see your goodness and beauty at work in all creation, and help me to trust the Father's providence in all of the events of my day...Amen.

Practicum Reflection Questions for Formators

1. What helps me to listen for and attend to the interior movements of the Holy Spirit in my heart, rather than turning the Examen Prayer into a self-evaluation of 'how I did today?" What needs to happen for me to move away from a self-evaluative disposition in my prayer?
2. When during the day am I finding it most beneficial to practice the Examen Prayer? Please describe.
3. What have been some of the fruits in everyday life of practicing the Examen Prayer? What difference does practicing this prayer make in my daily life?
4. As I taste and see the Holy Spirit laboring in all things to love me, what helps me to live with daily events as a "we" in communion with a sense of the Holy Spirit's presence? What attitudes draw me away from the Holy Spirit's presence into living an "I" in isolation and self-determination? Please describe.

Suggested Resources

1. "The Examen Prayer," by Fr. Timothy Gallagher, O.M.V., Crossroads Publications.
2. "The Prayer that Changes Everything," by Jim Manning, Loyola Press, 2011.
3. Fr. James Kubicki, S. J. https://archive.org/details/Fr.JamesKubicki_S. J.EveningReviewwithFr.Kubick

Chapter Nineteen

FORGIVENESS

Fr. George Aschenbrenner, S.J., STL

Several decades ago, following Vatican II and the call to recover original charisms in religious life, Fr. George Aschenbrenner emerged as an international leader in the search to recapture the original spirit and practice of The Spiritual Exercises of St. Ignatius Loyola. His groundbreaking research and writing on the "Consciousness Examen" breathed new life into the practice of the daily Examen Prayer which had been a major component in the formation of religious women and men, lay leadership and diocesan clergy during the lifetime of St. Ignatius and his first companions in the Society of Jesus. Fr. Aschenbrenner is currently retired after having served as Director of the Jesuit Retreat Center for Spiritual Growth in Wernersville, PA, as the Director of Spiritual Formation at the Pontifical North American College in Rome, and as Director of Novices for the Maryland Province. He is a Co-Founder of the Institute for Priestly Formation in Omaha, NE that is dedicated to serving diocesan seminarians and priests in spiritual formation through teaching Ignatian contemplative prayer. He specializes in diocesan priestly spirituality and the discernment of spirits. Fr. Aschenbrenner is the author of "Quickening The Fire In Our Midst – The Challenge of Diocesan Priestly Spirituality" as well as "Stretched for Greater Glory - What To Expect From The Spiritual Exercises." Recently, a collection of his major essays and articles in spiritual formation were published entitled "The Hidden Self Grown Strong."

All our lives, we are in search of our true selves. Many people's search for self-value and self-worth reaches a frenetic pitch. Our culture has provided some new and exciting avenues for the search though they are known already to be dead-ends. Saint Augustine would remind us that true knowledge of self is impossible without the intimate knowledge of Our Father and Creator. If it is His creative loving gaze on us that breathes life into us from moment to moment, then really to know Him is to discover ourselves.

We receive ourselves as gifts from others, but most especially from Another, Our Father and Creator. And so, our true worth so clearly is in being loved and in loving. But this discovery of our genuine dignity essentially involves the experience of being forgiven. Jesus' words to the woman at Simon's dinner express it well: "So I tell you, her many sins have been forgiven; hence, she has shown great love. But the one to whom little is forgiven, loves little" (Lk 7:47). The experience of forgiveness reveals and integrates all our energies for living and loving in all situations as sons and daughters of a loving Father.

There is often a great anxiety at the prospect of facing one's self. However, the ultimate sadness is to live life in darkness—without the enlightenment of *knowing* the mystery of ourselves mirrored in God's great hopes and dreams for each one of us. Any humiliation and worry and fear is worth that ultimate discovery!

Our Need To Be Helped

The journey to self-identity commences with the realization of our need to be helped. Our real self-worth and identity is given only in forgiveness; it is never self-fabricated. The first real step toward self-identity is allowing God to reveal our sinfulness. This is never easy, especially not today. Many people are anguishing over questions such as these: Is there such a thing as sin? Does not the old notion of sin lead to neurotic guilt complexes and self-hatred? And what does all this imply about a loving God? In a world so filled with evil who, if anybody, is to be blamed for the sin?

The Church is experiencing the inevitable confusion of a transitional growth in her understanding of the mystery of sinfulness, which obviously is affecting many other things, such as the use of the Sacrament of Penance. However, this confusion is most urgent in its effect on our deepest Christian self-identity through forgiveness. One can see much evidence today of this basic identity confusion in the Church and in the world.

Our sinfulness is not something we can become aware of all by ourselves if we put our mind to recalling past failures. Too often, this is where we look for our own sense of sin. God, however, must *reveal* to us our sinfulness. There is no other way to come to it. In the light of His love for us, our sinfulness is revealed. Many times, when we pray carefully about our Father's uniquely personal love for us, a kind of uneasiness begins to stir in our hearts. This can be the beginning of the revelation of sinfulness. The more intimately and personally aware we become of His love for us, the more our sense of sinfulness is revealed. Since the mystery of sinfulness must be revealed by God, we should pray for it if we truly desire to know ourselves.

In this sense, we can speak of the *grace* of sinfulness. To be more and more aware of the mystery of sinfulness in our hearts is a grace given only by God. Such an awareness is not received through an introspective moralistic examination of conscience. We need to be more reverently and humbly aware of the intimacy and depth of detail of His love for us rather than to stir up our own guilt-laden anxiety over past failures. If we really could know how much God loves us, we would be intensely aware in sorrow of our sinfulness! To stand openly in the light of His love will touch off in our hearts the shame, embarrassment, and sorrow of a sinner.

There is an unhealthy guilt and anxiety that is not relational; it does not draw us beyond ourselves. It simmers in our hearts and corrodes our peace. The grace of sinfulness is quite otherwise. We can make one another feel guilty but not sinful. Only a relation beyond ourselves to God's goodness and holiness reveals our sinfulness. A deficient sense of sin usually speaks of a deficient or immature relationship with God.

For some people, sin is a juridical matter—serious in itself and consciously posited in a voluntary action. Within this minimal conception of sin, it is difficult for many to experience the Spirit of God accusing them of sin as in 1 John 1:10: "If we say, 'We have not sinned,' we make him a liar, and his word is not in us." A growth in faith experience brings us to a more refined sense of sinfulness beyond the juridical concept of actions posited.

Paul says in Romans 14:23, "Whatever is not from faith is sin." Here, we have a much more mature sense of sinfulness recognized in direct proportion to the extent and depth of our faith experience. To be juridical and childishly automatic about faith is to maintain a minimal sense of sinfulness. To have the blindness of our unbelief pierced by the light of faith brings concomitantly a sense of our sinful past. This sense of sinfulness is not as much dependent on consciously posited actions as on the objective fact—*then* not consciously recognized but now enlightened in faith—of a past life of ignorance of and blindness to the reality of God. A grown person *now* intimately aware of his loving Father can be deeply sorrowful for repeated rebellious refusals in his teens to worship the Father who was *then* so loving and gracious to him. No wonder the saints who love so deeply in joyful and grateful faith know themselves to be so deeply sinful. This same vision of the relationship between sinfulness and faith can face the confessor with the danger of interpreting what he hears in the light of his own weak faith and erroneously trying to inform the deeply gifted penitent that what was confessed is not really a sin. A live sense of sinfulness and an intimate awareness of a loving Father gifting us in all are inseparable!

A passing and temporary trial of slight scrupulosity often accompanies this growing refinement of a sense of sinfulness. We must be careful to interpret this interior movement as a good healthy sign. We are not, here, talking of a pathological emotional disorder. A person's conscience is simply catching up with his faith! This happened in the conversion of

Saint Ignatius Loyola and of many other saints.

A Dynamic Reality

Our awareness of sinfulness grows gradually. What might first register as guilt will soon grow to shame and sorrow as sin is situated within the context of a personal love relationship with our loving Father gifting us in everything. To appreciate sin from God's viewpoint is to bring shame, embarrassment, and confusion into our heart. This is neither a nice nor pleasant experience but a deeply Christian one and it verges on the discovery of gratitude in forgiveness. It is a consolation and a grace. Because it is a true experience of God, it is, therefore, compatible with a deep peace and even a quiet joy.

Self-hatred is something very different from awareness of sinfulness and can be a real interference to the genuine grace of sinfulness manifesting itself in shame, embarrassment, and confusion in the awareness given us of our sinfulness by a Father who continues *right now* to love and gift us. To face our sinfulness and ingratitude outside of the presence of our loving Father is always destructive and not renewing. It is precisely the tangible evidence of His continuing love *here and now* that brings the shame and embarrassment and confusion. His mercy has always been there; in fact, our sin stands out precisely in that contrast. There can be a subtle temptation, however, to avoid the shame and sorrow of our sins by concentrating too simply, and yet superficially, on God's love for us. To give real body and depth of our song of gratitude in forgiveness, we must see the mystery of *what* is forgiven. Only in appreciating the costliness of the forgiveness can we avoid too superficial a sense of our dignity as sons and daughters sharing God's life and Spirit.

It is not enough to see sin as harming ourselves or other people. We need to have revealed to us the disappointment that sin is to God. We need to see our own ungrateful and insensitive response in terms of our gracious Father, so disappointed, puzzling over the mystery of the "sour grapes" in Isaiah 5:4, "What more could be done for my vineyard that I did not do? Why, when I waited for the crop of grapes, did it yield rotten grapes?" This can be a powerful moment in the dynamic of the grace of sinfulness; a moment, too, that makes possible a deeper experience of the absolute gratuity of God's forgiveness.

Unless we come, in grace, to see that our sinfulness in its blindness, insensitivity, and rebellion (however polite or civilized!) does not deserve forgiveness, we superficialize our Father's loving forgiveness of us. Without the frightening awareness that our sins really deserve to be punished and even to have us rubbed out of existence, we take very much for granted our Father's forgiveness and turn it into a cheap commodity. We lose the sense of the precious, and our life is deprived of deep reverence. "If you, Lord, keep account of sins, Lord, who can stand? But with you is forgiveness and so you are revered" (Ps 130:3-4). This realization of our sin's relationship to our loving Father is a grace. This realization brings the basic experience of being ashamed and embarrassed in the presence of God, which does not prevent the full joy, surprise, and gratitude of knowing the gratuitousness of His forgiveness of us. It is, rather, the awareness of living on "borrowed time," as that is lovingly given by a Father whose fidelity is beyond question. But it is *borrowed* time! Borrowed time, nevertheless, that in this victoriously given Father's love becomes *our* time, in the raising of His crucified Christ.

Another moment in the dynamic that is the grace of sinfulness leading to forgiveness can be one of real fright. It is what Paul speaks of in Romans 7:24: "Miserable one that I am! Who will deliver me from this mortal body?" This can be a moment of sobering realization of how trapped we are. To fixate on this moment is to despair. The grace of this moment, which may last quite a while, is to call forth in deep, joyful gratitude the realization in faith of the Father's forgiveness, Who is Jesus on the Cross. It brings the intimate love-experience of Jesus, which is salvation and which reorients a person's whole life. "Thanks be to God through Jesus Christ our Lord" (Rom 7:25).

As the moments of shame, embarrassment, and confusion pass through a frightening fear and grow to deep sorrow in the presence of our Father whose love is constant, in the very depths of our sense of sinfulness, there comes the strong and joyful gratitude of a helplessly trapped sinner suddenly and freely forgiven—for no reason but the mystery of a Father's love expressed in forgiveness. The joy, peace, and gratitude of forgiveness do not replace the sinfulness; rather, they complement and transform it. One has seen his selfish sinfulness too deeply ever to forget that aspect of self-knowledge. So that even in the joy and gratitude, there is always and easily an element of sorrow. In this life, we never step beyond the awareness of our sinfulness.

Renewal Through Humiliation

In tracing the development of the various moments in the grace of our sinfulness as that happens in us, we are demonstrating that forgiveness itself is a process in us. It is the process of conversion into and discovery of our true selves. Far from happening instantaneously, this is a lifetime growth process, though there usually are periods of greater intensity. In all of us, there are areas of our heart that need to experience the Father's forgiveness Who is Jesus. In these areas of our heart, we are still not truly free; we are not truly ourselves because Jesus is not Lord for us there yet.

In these unredeemed parts of our heart, we have not humbly acknowledged sin. Our proud independence often prevents the humiliation inevitable for new life in forgiveness. Roustang says in *Growth in the Spirit*, "If in the least particle of ourselves we think we are just through our own efforts, into this tiny particle Christ cannot bring the gratuitousness of his salvation."[1] Forgiveness can take effect only through the humiliating acknowledgement of sinfulness. It is the hopeful cry for help in our need that calls forth our Father's forgiveness. "A bruised reed he will not break, and a dimly burning wick he will not quench" (Is 42:3). It is much easier to talk about humility than to feel the hurting sting and shame of humiliation before our loving Father. However, to avoid or rationalize away or go light on this shameful humiliation is to lighten the experience of new life through His forgiveness. Forgiveness can happen in no other way. And yet, our sinful selves will always squirm before this searing humiliation. Forgiveness is always a Paschal experience—something must die in shame if new life is to be given in love.

Often in an ordinary use of the Sacrament of Penance, the humiliation can be as simple and yet elusive as the admission that I have not yet allowed myself to be cleansed of those same small acts of ingratitude to God. It humiliates us to admit that honestly before our Father in the presence of a human minister of the Church. To avoid this personal shame before our Father is to avoid the very depths of our understanding of sin and until we come to appreciate the humiliation involved in forgiveness, we will not appreciate the new view of the Sacrament of Penance as not just for removing serious sins but much more—for continuing spiritual progress in God's forgiveness.

Life As Thanksgiving

Realized forgiveness turns life itself into thanksgiving and wonder. The dynamic of the grace of sinfulness always concludes in gratitude. Our Father is with us daily to convert us from sinfulness to free and joyful gratitude through the mysterious power of His forgiveness in our humiliated powerlessness. Gratitude is the truest identity of the Christian believer. But only scars of shame and humiliation can remind us reverently of its precious quality. Often, fear of the pain of confronting the revelation of our humiliating sinfulness impedes a more invigorating experience of forgiveness and, thus, keeps us only on the surface of thanksgiving. We do not find our real selves in peace and in joy and in Christ who is the Father's forgiveness.

---

[1] Francois Roustang, *Growth in the Spirit* (London: Burns and Oates, Ltd., 1966).

The gratitude in our forgiveness motivates our every action. To be a grateful person in everything is the clearest sign of a believer. "And be thankful. . . . And whatever you do, in word or in deed, do everything in the name of the Lord Jesus, giving thanks to God the Father through him" (Col 3:15,17).

This thanksgiving will daily take expression joyously in humble, loving service without any pretense or delusion of selfish grandeur and power. The sorrow, now turned into joy, has not been completely forgotten. Gentleness and reverence are close at hand because the grateful person finds the forgiving hand of the Father in everything. "Your kindness should be known to all. The Lord is near" (Phil 4:5). The grateful heart is constantly growing in wonder and awe, giving sight to eyes to see what and who really is present in all.

Ministry of Reconciliation Among Men

We live today in a world so much in need of forgiveness. Hearts shamed and embarrassed in the uneasy need for forgiveness and healing often cover up with a thin politeness or a facade of smug self-sufficiency. They cry out, however, for the experience of gratitude. In religious life, as we are led into a new age, one of our greatest needs is to forgive one another. The daily newspaper reveals on all levels of our society and on the international scene the painful evidence of the need for forgiveness and for healing. The ministry of reconciliation is so much in demand today. How much the embarrassed smugness and the frightened sadness want to smile in healed thanksgiving! But we must appreciate the depth of this demand on us all. Without a gratitude daily deepening in our experience of our Father's free forgiveness of us, our own involvement in a ministry of reconciliation cannot succeed. He is always the initiative and the example of how true forgiveness happens. "Be merciful just as [also] your Father is merciful. 'Stop judging and you will not be judged. Stop condemning and you will not be condemned. Forgive and you will be forgiven'" (Lk. 6:36-37). The joyous good news of a Father's gracious forgiveness can only be known as it is lived and shared by His sons and daughters in our world. Saint Paul is beautiful and clear in 2 Cor. 5:17-12:

So whoever is in Christ is a new creation: the old things have passed away; behold, new things have come. And all this is from God, who has reconciled us to himself through Christ and given us the ministry of reconciliation, namely, God was reconciling the world to himself in Christ, not counting their trespasses against them and entrusting to us the message of reconciliation. So we are ambassadors for Christ, as if God were appealing through us. We implore you on behalf of Christ, be reconciled to God. For our sake he made him to be sin who did not know sin, so that we might become the righteousness of God in him.

Reconciliation among men requires far more than a grasp of the dynamics of interpersonal relationships and the demands of justice and the protocol of equity.

True self-worth and identity is never found through the power and force of self-assertion. It is never self-fabricated! It must be gratefully received in the experience of a Father's forgiveness. "So I tell you, her many sins have been forgiven; hence, she has shown great love. But the one to whom little is forgiven, loves little" (Lk 7:47).

This article was published in *The Hidden Self Grown Strong: The Collected Essays of Father George Aschenbrenner, S.J.* (Omaha: IPF Publications, 2018) and is published here with the permission of the publisher and author.

Prayer

Dear Jesus, Grant me the grace to know my sinfulness and to taste your tender forgiveness. May my capacities increase to receive your love and mercy. Help me and to give that same love and mercy away freely to everyone in your holy Name. Amen.

Practicum Reflection Questions for Formators

1. Since "it is the experience of being forgiven that reveals and integrates all of our energies for living and loving in all situations," what would I want to say as a testimony about Jesus' mercy to an R.C.I.A. class in the local parish about my own experience of being forgiven by Him?

2. Please explain the distinction between healthy guilt and shame and unhealthy guilt and shame in the process of receiving God's forgiveness.

3. In his book "Growth in the Spirit," Roustang says, "If in the least particle of ourselves we think we are just through our own efforts, into this tiny particle Christ cannot bring the gratuitousness of his salvation." How I am learning this truth that he is teaching?

4. "Realized forgiveness turns life itself into thanksgiving and wonder." Provide a testimony to the beauty of this truth. How has my thanksgiving and wonder increased as a result of forgiveness?

Suggested Resources

1. "Becoming Human," by Jean Vanier, Paulist Press, 1998.
2. "Confession," by Adrienne von Speyr, Ignatius Press, 1985.
3. "The Church of Mercy," By Pope Francis, Loyola Press, 2014.

Chapter Twenty

UNILATERAL FORGIVENESS

Rev. Larry Christenson

Rev. Larry Christenson was a former San Pedro, CA pastor of Trinity Lutheran Church (1960-1982). He was a pioneer in the Charismatic Renewal and was active in national and international ecumenical gatherings of mainline Protestant and Roman Catholic leaders. Rev. Larry Christenson was an acclaimed speaker, writer and ecumenical leader fostering receptivity to the Gifts of the Holy Spirit. He died in 2017 at the age of 89.He had graduated magna cum laude from St. Olaf College in 1952 and was a member of Phi Beta Kappa. He graduated from Luther Theological Seminary in St. Paul, MN in 1959.Christenson authored several books, the best known being "The Christian Family." Other titles included "Speaking In Tongues," "The Renewed Mind," "Back To Square One," "Welcome The Holy Spirit," and "Ride The River." He is survived by his wife of 66 years, three sons, a daughter, 18 grandchildren and 5 great-grandchildren. His famous presentation "Unilateral Forgiveness" features his study of Dietrich Bonhoeffer and "empathetic repentance." It has been especially instrumental in fostering fruitfulness in inner healing ministry.

For our talk this morning, let's just look once again at the Epistle for the Day, in the third chapter of First Peter, the eighth and ninth verse. "Finally, all of you have unity of spirit, sympathy, love of the brethren, a tender heart and a humble mind. Do not return evil for evil or reviling for reviling, but on the contrary, bless. For to this you have been called, that you may obtain a blessing."

When I received the invitation to come out here to Bethany for the conference, it was asked that I speak and share on this theme of family life. It's interesting that this text, the Epistle for the Day, comes right following the verse in First Peter that deals with a particular aspect of the relationship between husbands and wives. It's a sort of fitting conclusion to certain comments upon family life. And in another sense, it's a beginning of any real consideration of family life.

Some of you may remember the lovely song from "The Sound of Music," where the governess for the children says, "Let's start at the very beginning, a very good place to start. In writing you begin with A, B, C. In singing, it starts with do, re mi." If we could paraphrase that, we would say, "Let's start at the very beginning. It's a very good place to start. In writing, you begin with A, B, C. In discipleship, you begin with, "Lord, forgive me."

Forgiveness is the very basis of our life in Christ, and forgiveness, in a unique sense, is the basis of a Christ-centered family live. In our congregation, we have sort of made a part of the marriage liturgy a sermon that was written by Dietrich Bonhoeffer while he was a prisoner in a Nazi cell – written for the wedding of a niece of his. It was read at her wedding since he was in prison and could only pass out the manuscript. In it, he says a number of very wise things to a young couple about to be married, and one of the things he said is this: "Live together in the forgiveness of your sins."

This morning as we begin, I'd like to share with you just some thoughts about living together in the forgiveness of your sins, some practical ways in which this finds expression in our life so that our life becomes a forgiven and a forgiving life. For do this, we've been called to bless one another with this greatest single blessing of the Gospel – the beginning of the Gospel of Christ – to repent and be forgiven.

I was once speaking to a woman, a dear friend of ours, who shared with us an experience she'd had with a daughter who had caused her great grief. The daughter had run off and gotten married to a man somewhat older than herself, whom the parents did not altogether approve of, with a different religion, that is, a different denomination than they were. In any case, the daughter had not even had the good grace to tell the parents that she was going to be married. She just ran off and got married. This grieved the mother. This embittered the mother.

She finally went down and was going to see the daughter with her new husband, but as she went, her heart was so choked up with bitterness, that she didn't know how she could even present herself at the door. She came into the town where the daughter was now living. She went to a priest of her church, and she was a woman of prayer. She went to this priest and said, "You've got to help me find God. I can't get through any longer." He talked to her and counseled her for a while and then suggested that she go into the Sanctuary and just be there in the silence. It was a darkened Sanctuary. She could see the stained-glass window up there at the altar with the picture of Jesus. She knelt there and prayed, and then she said she suddenly had an overwhelming sense of the presence of God and a vision, as it were, of the power of the blood of Christ to cleanse away all sin.

It was like a mammoth vacuum cleaner came in and just sucked all of that bitterness out of her, and she was utterly at peace. Then, in the wake of that experience, the Lord brought to her a Word of Wisdom. In her thoughts came this very clear word: "You do not lose your peace over someone else's sin, but only over your own." In other words, the daughter's sin, which was sin enough, of having dealt thoughtlessly with the parents who had loved her and cared for her and brought her up – the sin of the daughter was not what robbed the mother of her peace. This she saw clearly in the wake of her own forgiveness. She saw that it was her own bitterness that had robbed her of her peace, for you do not lose your peace over someone else's sin, but only over your own.

This is what Peter is getting at in this text when he said, "Bless, don't revile." This is what you've been called to do, to extend blessing and not allow bitterness to clog you up, because this is the way that you, yourself, obtain a blessing.

Now, we want to be as practical as we can about this and move sort of in two steps or phases of thinking this morning and consider how this forgiven life of Christ is going to become a power by which we can live the victorious life that we are gathered here to consider.

The text that we have here from Peter deals with our relationships with other people, and isn't it true that it's at that point that our Christianity rises or falls? Now, to bring it down to even a more intimate context of families, isn't it true that the reality of our Christian life is going to rise and fall with the validity of the testimony that we live in our families and among those who know us best. That was brought out so wonderfully in the opening message this morning – that what the world needs today are people who will live up to the truth that they have learned and come to know.

So here we are in our relationships within our own family, here we are in our relationships within our congregations. We say, "How can I live this life?" You don't live in an intimate relationship very long before you rub shoulders with somebody that rubs you the wrong way, and that's where the test comes. Now comes the grinding process, and how am I going to relate to this person who rubs me the wrong way, in whom I see things that are not as they ought to be.

I believe the key lies in a deeper appropriation of this whole life of forgiveness.

The first thing I want to suggest to you is that as we live together in our intimate relationships and see things in the lives of other people…a husband, a wife, a child, a pastor, an elder, a fellow member of the congregation…whatever it might be. We see things as they ought not to be. There is sort of a two-step process that we can enter into…not in a mechanical way, but in a very living and practical way.

The first step I would call "Empathetic Repentance." I'll give you two fairly long words today. If you write them down and dwell upon them, maybe in time they'll come to have kind of an appeal with you.

Empathy is the ability to enter into the experience of another person and feel and live with him. When I see something in another person that I know not to be according to God's will, the first step I can take is to enter into a living and feeling with that person with what I could call Empathetic Repentance. What do I mean by that? Let me illustrate it by a story out of my own life.

I was visiting the Evangelical Sisterhood of Mary in Darmstadt, Germany back in 1964. Some of you may have been there. Some of their books may have been published by Bethany. A marvelous work of God that began in the late 1940s.

As I came there, I was greeted by the Sisters, and one of them took me up to the room that had been reserved for me. As I came into the room, I found there a basket of fruit, and there was a Scripture pasted up on the wall. I just sort of glanced at it. The Sister left, and then the thought came to me, "I'm going to have a prayer right now," so before I started the private retreat that I was just on for a few days, I knelt down by the bed and began to pray, and the prayer welled up sort of spontaneously from within me. I didn't reflect much upon it. I just began to pray spontaneously, and I prayed something like this. I said, "Lord, may You have joy in these days." This was not the normal way I would have prayed. I would have said, "Lord, give me a blessing." That's what we usually pray, you know. We want to get blessed. Like one person said, "We've rewritten the 103rd Psalm. We say, 'Bless thou my soul, O Lord' instead of 'Bless the Lord, oh my soul.'"

We're looking for blessings. Well, that's very typical, and God doesn't shame us for that, but, nevertheless, on this particular instance, I just prayed that the Lord might have joy in these days. Then I looked up and read the Bible verse that was there. It was from the fifth chapter of James. In English, it's something like this: "The prayer of a righteous man has great power in its effects." "The fervent effectual prayer of a righteous man...." in King James.

In German, it comes off a little differently. If I were to translate it back from German, it would be something like this: "The prayer of a righteous man has great power in its effects, if you really mean it." In other words, if you really take seriously the prayer you prayed. So it was like the Lord was saying, "Do you really mean that prayer you prayed today?"

I went over to the basket of fruit, and there I saw a little envelope. It had a Bible word written on it. They give each guest as they come a special word that they have drawn out of a group of Bible Scriptures, which they believe is God's particular word for the guest. So I read that Bible verse, and it started right out with the theme of my prayer. It says, "There is more joy in Heaven over one sinner who repents." Well, that was sort of a glum iceberg. That wasn't exactly the kind of joy I had in mind.

I charged that off to coincidence and went down to lunch. They asked one of the Sisters to come in and be my hostess there in the little private dining room, so she sat down, and she asked the blessing at the table, and she said, "Oh, Lord, who sat at the table with sinners, sit at the table with us." I was beginning to feel uncomfortable.

That evening, the Sister who was supposed to have met with me was taken up with something else, so another Sister came and talked with me. She wasn't very much prepared, but she was going to share something of their life, and what did she do? For about an hour, she talked to me about the joy that she had found in repentance. This was beginning to sort of get to me.

Then the next day, which was Sunday, the pastor from the local area came in to preach, and what did he preach on? Repentance. Well, I'm sort of like the person who said, "I don't need to be hit by a ten-ton truck, Lord." Just to make sure I didn't miss the message, when I went back to my room, I noticed what I had not noticed the first time I went in. It had a name on there, which, in English, means "The Plum Orchard." That's a funny name for a room. As it turned out, it was the chapter title from one of their books, so I read the chapter. There I began to get the clue of what God was trying to say to me through this almost comical series of events.

This was the story of a woman who owned a plum orchard in the neighborhood of the Sisterhood's property. They had asked the woman if she would like to sell the land because they wanted to expand and build a printing plant. No, she didn't want to sell the land, because she had received it as an inheritance, and she didn't want to sell it. They went back and offered to trade it and went back many times to see if she had changed her mind, but she was absolutely immovable. Their whole program of expansion was sort of stymied, because that piece of property went right through the middle of two pieces of property they had, so they were sort of like a separated country there, with a channel down the middle that they couldn't build upon.

One day, one of the Sisters went over there again after some time to see if perhaps the woman might have changed her mind, and a little five-year-old boy met her at the door. It turned out to be the grand-nephew of this woman. She wasn't home, but he invited her in and asked if she would like to see the house. She said all right since she hadn't been in before and had always talked on the outside. So she went into the house, and the little boy began to show her around. Finally, he came and showed her the aunt's bedroom. He opened the door, and the Sister took one look at the aunt's bedroom, and she said in an instant, it fell into place, and she knew what they were up against.

The room was crowded with enough furniture to furnish three houses, that one little bedroom. Over on the bed, there were about 13 mattresses stacked on top of the bed and a step-ladder so that she could climb up the ladder to get on the top mattress and sleep there. Why? Well, you see, she had received all of these pieces of furniture from relatives who had died, and she had it in her mind that it was a thoughtless and loveless thing to do ever to part with anything you received by inheritance – you had to use it all. Well, she had gotten 13 mattresses as an inheritance, you see, so she had to use them all. She slept on top of the 13th one.

She realized then what they were facing. It was not simply that she did not want to part with the property, but she was she was bound by the things of this earth in a terrible way. So she went back and reported this to the Sisterhood.

Then, there was given into that group of young women, you see, with their two mothers as their leaders, an insight into this thing that we call Empathetic Repentance.

Now there are three ways I suppose they could have dealt with this. They could have gone to the woman and preached her a sermon about the evils of bondage to the things of this earth and turned her off completely, or they could have been a little more subtle. They could have prayed about it and said, "God, change that hard heart that is bound by the things of the world. Lord, change that woman's heart," and prayed against her.

Yet, there was a third way that the Lord revealed to them – the way of Empathetic Repentance, by which they went into a time of prayer and fasting in which they invited God to judge in their lives the very thing they saw in the life of this woman. You get the picture? Empathetic Repentance. In other words, instead of standing against the woman and judging her, they entered into the lists with her, and they said, "Lord, let us see in our life any hint of, any trace of, any evidence of the very thing that we see in her life."

Any psychiatrist would tell you that we have a great human tendency to project upon other people the very things that are really latent within ourselves and maybe hidden and piously covered over, and yet they're there, and so they're glaringly evident in the lives of others.

They went into a time of fasting and prayer, and one by one, God began to touch the heart of these Sisters. Maybe it was a little thing like a postcard or something, for they had to give up everything as they came into the Sisterhood as part of the discipline. Some little thing that they had clung to, and in their heart they had said, "Lord, don't take that away."

This was the cross to them – to have to give up some little thing that nobody else would ever know about, but God, who reads the heart, knew that there was a bondage there, and He touched these things one by one, and there came genuine repentance in that very area of their life that they saw was a problem for this woman.

The interesting upshot of it was that the next time that Sister went back to speak with that woman, the woman began the conversation, before ever a question was raised, and said, "Well, you know, I really wouldn't mind parting with the plum orchard, if I could still have the plums when they come into harvest." So they were able to draw up a contract by which the yearly produce of the plum trees, which wouldn't be affected by the building, would go to the woman year by year.

You see, God entered into that situation and changed her heart with never a word having been spoken, simply because He found people who were willing to identify with her and bless her, instead of judge her and condemn her. Their own repentance became an avenue for them to extend forgiveness to her. I can't explain altogether how this works. It's a spiritual phenomenon, but I have seen it work.

I remember when I came back from Germany that very time, there was a particular family in our congregation that was having real marital problems, and I thought for some time that I must speak to the wife and talk with her about the situation. I had already spoken with the husband. The husband had come to me and had some deep concerns about the spiritual welfare of his wife. I shared with him this idea of Empathetic Repentance. I said, "Suppose you and I, for ten days, put ourselves under the gun and say, "God, judge in us the very thing that we see in your wife. Anything in our own life in that very area that's out of order, Lord, you bring it under conviction and deal with it. Let it be forgiven and cleansed."

After ten days, I drove up there to see the wife one afternoon. I didn't know what was going to happen and didn't know what I was going to say, but I went up there, and for two hours, we were able to share in the deepest possible way the things of God and the things that God wanted to do in that family. She was a housewife with some small children, and when two hours had passed, she said, "I don't know what's happening to that youngest one of mine. It's like he was drugged. He's never slept this long on a nap. He'd be up." Well, you know what it's like to carry on a conversation if children are demanding attention and need attention. But it was as though God carved out two hours of time where His word could have primary emphasis in that situation.

Now, that's the first thing I thought to share is just the possibility we see in our family situations, in our spiritual family, in the congregations, in our community. We can see certain things, and God does not expect us to wink at them and pretend that they really aren't so bad. See, a lot of people say, "Well, I'm not supposed to judge, and therefore I'll just be accepting of everything, so you accept sin and corruption and everything else and never have any kind of moral discrimination. No. God doesn't expect us to lay aside our moral discrimination, but He says, "I don't want you to be the judge. There's a better thing that you can do. You can enter into the whole dynamic process of forgiveness. You can be an agent of mine for forgiveness."

The second step that I want to share with you is the possibility that God opens up to us to actually convey forgiveness to other people. Did you ever realize that Jesus never had a person come up and ask him for forgiveness. That shocked me when I first discovered it in Scripture. So far as I know in the Scripture, there is never a case of a person coming up and saying, "Lord, forgive my sin," and yet Jesus forgave sin. How did He do it? He did it unilaterally. You know what a unilateral agreement is? It's one that stems from one side only.

The paralytic came up, and Jesus said, "Be of good cheer. Your sins are forgiven." The man hadn't asked for forgiveness. He hadn't come for forgiveness. He'd come for healing, but Jesus unilaterally declared forgiveness to him.

A woman came and washed His feet. He said, "Thy sins be forgiven thee." She didn't ask for it. The Scripture records no word of her asking for forgiveness.

The most dramatic of all, as He hung on the Cross, He said, "Father, forgive them, for they know not what they do." Now, those Roman soldiers didn't have any more sense of a need for forgiveness than the man in the moon. They didn't think they needed to be forgiven, but Jesus knew it, and He declared it unto them unilaterally. He came to His disciples after the Resurrection, and He said, "Whose soever sins you forgive, they are forgiven." He committed to His Church, the authority to declare forgiveness – not simply waiting for when people come and repent – but to declare it unilaterally the way He did.

When I first began to get this thought, it seemed to me almost shocking – the awesome authority and power that Jesus had commissioned his Church to exercise. Yet, I've seen it change lives.

In 1968, I was in Leipzig meeting with a group of Lutheran pastors. One of the pastors there told how he has suddenly been rousted out of his home in the middle of the night by the Communist authorities, taken to prison, incarcerated, held there for 13 months and treated brutally. One guard in particular was apparently out to do everything he could to make this man's life miserable – physical beatings and interrogations at all hours of the night and all of that. This man prayed and said, "Lord, what shall I do, especially about this man?"

The Lord said, "Bless him. Forgive him."

"Forgive him?! Lord, he doesn't have any more repentance than a mustard seed."

"Forgive him."

"All right."

He knew the Lord was speaking to him, so silently (he never said a word to the man) in the spirit began to forgive that man. He'd hear the steps come down the walk – the man's heavy tread – toward his cell. And he began to bless him. "Lord, forgive him for his blasphemy. Forgive him for his cruelty. Forgive him for all of that, Lord." This went on for three days.

They were coming back from an interrogation, and the pastor said to this guard, "You know, I was taken out of my home in the middle of the night with no warning, and my mother, who was quite ill, was with us at time. She may even have died in the interim. Would it be possible to just put in a telephone call and find out how my mother is?" And this hard and cruel guard said, "We'll see." He came back and said, "I'm going to be alone tonight. We'll go up to the office and put in a telephone call. Now, mind you, you can't say a word, but I'll ask the question for you." They went up to the office and put in a telephone call. The guard said, "Now, remember, you can't say a word."

The moment the phone was lifted on the other side, he took it from his own ear and shoved it over to the pastor. The pastor was startled and said, "Hello." The voice on the other end said, "Papa, is that you?" It was his little daughter. "Where's Mama?" "She's not home now." So the father spoke briefly with the daughter and hung up. The man said, "Well, we'll wait and call later when your wife is home."

So they sat there and talked. He said in the hour they were sitting there in the office, that man was completely open. He said, "I talked to him about Jesus and communicated to him anything I wanted to, with no objection. Whether that ever found root, I never found out, but he heard the Gospel. Then they called again. Five times they called, and finally the wife came home. All the time, the guard was saying, "Now remember, when she answers, you can't say anything. I'll ask the questions." The moment the wife answered on the other side – the fifth time they called – he shoved the phone over to the man, and he talked with his wife. He found out that his mother was all right at that time.

Then he went down, and the guard said, "How's the food?" The pastor said, "Well, honestly, it's not very good." The guard said, "We'll see." He came back a little later with his own dinner and gave it to the pastor. He said, "Would you like to have a bath?" He'd been there a couple of weeks now and was feeling pretty crummy because he hadn't had a chance to wash. He said, "Tomorrow I'm going to be alone again, and I'll take you to the washroom, and I'll lock the door from the outside so nobody will see you. All the hot water you want – you can have a shower."

This is the power that was released, you see, to break the shell of that man, because this one man was willing, you see, instead of judging and condemning, to forgive. "Whose soever sins you forgive, they are forgiven." You see, sin is not only a problem of guilt – God comes and deals with an individual at the question of guilt – but sin is also a power that binds, and we have always taken the approach, you see, that if you repent now and ask for forgiveness, then we'll give it to you. It's like a dog jumping for a wiener. "Here's the wiener. Now, you jump high enough and ask forgiveness, and then you get the wiener." That's forgiveness, you see – not realizing some people are so bound up, they can't jump two inches. They're so bound by the power of sin that until someone in the priestly power of God comes and declares unto them forgiveness – not going up and telling them – this is in the Spirit – saying "God, in the Name of Jesus Christ, I declare forgiveness to him, and I bless him. Do not condemn him. I forgive him in your Name – unilaterally – the way Jesus did." Then you watch that shell begin to break.

This is spiritual warfare. Paul says we're fighting a war, but we're not fighting it with the weapons of carnality – not the weapons of this world. We're fighting it with spiritual weapons, and these weapons are mighty to bring down strongholds.

The most powerful weapon that has been given into the hand of the Church of God is the power of forgiveness. That's the power that brings down strongholds, and we are given the privilege, you see, of beaming this out to people. And if we give the world – the tired and hurt and bleeding world – less than that, we're giving them less than God has made available.

I remember when we had a dear lady, Olivia Henry, visiting in our home one day. She's an ordained minister in the African Methodist Episcopal Church. She has a little church in the inner city of Philadelphia. At one point in her ministry there, she felt this leading of God, together with four other ministers in that area, to have no part of any demonstrations or any maneuvers which would attempt to bring pressure on the social and political institutions but, rather, to simply live out their life of the Gospel there in that situation. You can imagine in the climate today, this was not too well received, especially among some of her own people.

She said, "As we began to experience some persecution because of our refusal to become identified with this or that cause or demonstration or march, the Lord showed me something beautiful in the Scripture. I was reading the Scripture one day, and it suddenly fell into place that my Lord Jesus was born in poverty and lived in poverty and died in poverty, and never once did He gather together a boat load of poverty-stricken Jews and take them to Rome to camp on Caesar's doorstep.

That was right at the time of the Resurrection City incident in Washington, but you see He gave them a power greater than the power of demonstration. He gave them the power of healing through the Gospel, and out of that little center in Philadelphia has gone forth a tremendous power.

You see, it is not that some of these things one might otherwise do are bad. It's simply that they're not the best, and the enemy of the best is always something that's good. It isn't enough to do something good, if God has given us something better. And in the power of forgiveness, God has given us the best. He's given us the power to beam out forgiveness. You see, this is unlimited in its scope. This isn't just somebody that has hurt you. That man on the stretcher hadn't offended Jesus. He just needed forgiveness.

I love the story that David du Plessis tells us of sitting down between two ladies on an airplane. He was very tired and said, "Lord, just let me sleep and have some rest, and please keep me away from the smokers, because I can't sleep with smoke blowing in my face." So he was walking down the aisle, and he saw a middle seat, and there were two ladies – an elderly lady and a young lady – and he thought there was a pretty good chance he'd be free from second-hand smoke, so he sat down. He said no sooner did the warning light go off, than their lights went on, and they started to smoke.

He said, "Lord, why did you do this to me?"

He said the Lord spoke and said, "Forgive them, David."

"Forgive them?"

"Yes, bless them."

"All right. I don't know why. I've never wanted to bless anybody smoking before, but I'll do it. Lord, I forgive them, and if they get some enjoyment in it, I'll bless them in it."

He said, "I dropped off to sleep. I had the most wonderful sleep, and they didn't smoke again the rest of the trip."

Well, that's just almost a humorous illustration of what happens – and you'll find this happening in your life – you're going to see people change, and they won't know what hit them. They won't know that somebody has interceded before the throne of God to convey to them forgiveness. And what does that do? It opens their heart. Then God can begin to deal with them.

Karl Barth says, "Sin never really burns until it comes under the white, hot light of forgiveness." See, we thought we can't come to someone with forgiveness until they're all broken out in repentance. No, "While we were yet sinners, Christ came and died for us" and declared forgiveness to us, and in the wake of that, we enter into this forgiven life.

This is the way Jesus forgave – unilaterally – because He saw in other people the need to be forgiven. And this is a wonderful thing. In my own congregation, we have a deep chancel, and I walk up to the chancel for part of the service and then out to the congregation for other parts of the service. As I come out to the congregation after the confessional service or right after the opening hymn before the confessional service, I find it just wonderful thinking, "Lord, I don't know what these people have been up to this week. I can keep track of them all, and some of them may have fallen into sin, but, Lord, right now I'm just a big parabolic reflector for you, and I'm beaming forgiveness out to this whole congregation right now – that the power of it may be broken and that your forgiveness might enter in and deal with each life according to your abundant mercy."

You wake up in the morning, and you think of things in your own family, and before you ever speak a word of correction, before you ever try to lead and direct and guide your family, you beam out to them forgiveness. The children do something that irritates the life out of you, the first thing you do is say, "Lord, in the Name of Jesus Christ, I beam forgiveness to that child." Then can come well enough a word of correction, but it comes now not in a judging spirit, not in a condemning spirit, but in a blessing and in a helping and correcting spirit – to build up and not to tear down.

This morning as we conclude, I want you to put this into practice. I want you to invite you to think of one person. If it can be a person in your own family, so much the better – in whom you see a need for forgiveness. Not because you're some great judge, but because God has given you the Scripture, you know what's contrary to God's word, and you see this person and know that there's an area of their life where they need to be forgiven. They need to be cleansed. They need to have a fresh beginning.

As I pray, I'm going to invite you to think and name that one person in your heart before God, and beam out to that person the forgiveness of Jesus Christ – the cleansing of Calvary, and that person's life is going to be changed.

Father in heaven, right now, we come before your throne. We recall your previous promise that whosoever sins we forgive, they are forgiven. Give us the readiness, Lord, always to stand under judgment by you whenever we have sinned and fallen short of our light. Lord, right now, we hold up before you this one person who may have rejected your word, who may have spoken thoughtlessly or cruelly, who may have sinned against you in one way or another. We hold this person up to you, Lord, and in love, we present them before you, and we bathe them in the light of forgiveness right now. We beam out to them the powerful forgiveness of Calvary. We see it penetrate into their innermost being. We see it break loose the shackles of sin. We see it destroy the deceptions of the devil. We see them set free. We see the chains begin to fall away. We see a new light come upon their face as the forgiving and reconciling work of Calvary breaks in upon them at the level of their spirit and begins to work up into their thoughts, into their actions, into their whole fabric of life, and we believe, Lord, that in this very moment, we have done a transaction that will last for all eternity, because your word will not return void. Amen.

This article was published with the permission of the author.

Prayer for Reparation and Forgiveness

Dear Jesus, I believe that you are the Lord of History, and that the Father's providence is sovereign over all evil, even bringing good out of evil through the regenerating power of the Holy Spirit. With confidence in your love and mercy I repent of withholding my heart in any way. I am sorry for holding on to any sorrow, anger, anxiety, doubt or fear in the face of the spiritual and moral failures committed by any bishop, priest or seminary formation personnel. I desire to receive your consolation and strength at the cross and to allow you to love me into new life.

In your holy Name, Lord Jesus, I bless and forgive each member of the episcopacy, or any Church leader, that has advanced men to Holy Orders who are not affectively mature, men who are unable to renounce sacramental marriage in joy for the sake of the kingdom. I entrust these leaders to your just and merciful care.

I thank you Lord Jesus for all of the victims of sexual abuse and for all those who have exercised the gift of courage to bring this unacceptable violence into the light. Grant all victims who have been betrayed, and all of us, an increase of faith to receive the power of your healing presence. Grant a new inner strength to receive your Spirit of forgiveness for any perpetrator. I pray also for the perpetrators. May each of them awaken to your compassion and mercy.

Send the Holy Spirit, Lord Jesus, to fill your Church anew with a Pentecost that captivates and strengthens us to proclaim the Gospel. Restore the integrity and gift of the priesthood throughout the world. Create in your Church new structures of accountability to the Biblical understanding of human sexuality. Form spiritual husbands and spiritual father to shepherd your Church. I desire to rest always on your risen Sacred Heart. I entrust these intentions to you through Mary, Star of the New Evangelization as I pray... Hail Mary, full of grace...

Practicum Reflection Questions for Formators

1. What is my understanding of practicing "empathetic repentance" as the first vital step in entering into practicing unilateral forgiveness. Please give an example.

2. As I look back over my life where do I especially need to enter into "unilateral forgiveness?"

3. Have I seen any changes in the atmosphere of my workplace or home as a fruit of practicing "unilateral forgiveness?" Please describe.

4. Do I understand "forgiveness to be the very basis of our life in Christ, and forgiveness, in a unique sense, as the basis of a Christ' centered family life?" Please describe.

Suggested Resources

1. "The Name Of God Is Mercy," by Pope Francis, Random House, 2016.

2. "Helping Clients Forgive – An Empirical Guide for Resolving Anger and Restoring Hope,' by Robert D. Enright and Richard P. Fitzgibbons, by American Psychological Association, 2000.

3. "Real Mercy," by Fr. Jacques Philippe, Scepter Publishers, 2016.

Chapter Twenty-One

THE SEMINARY AS NAZARETH: FORMATION IN A SCHOOL OF PRAYER

Deacon James Keating, Ph.D.

Deacon James Keating, PhD is Director of Theological Formation in The Institute for Priestly Formation at Creighton University, Omaha, NE. Previous to his appointment at IPF he was Professor of Moral and Spiritual Theology at the Pontifical College Josephinum, Columbus, Ohio. Deacon Keating serves as well as the Director for Deacon Formation in the Archdiocese of Omaha. He also serves in the ministry of spiritual direction and has been a presenter on topics related to seminary formation at a wide variety of national and international conferences. He has published numerous books and articles in Spiritual and Moral Theology. These include: "Resting On The Heart Of Christ - The Vocation and Spirituality of the Seminary Theologian," "Listening for Truth - Praying Our Way To Virtue," "The Priest As Beloved Son" (editor), and his latest book, "Remain in Me: Holy Orders, Prayer and Ministry" (Paulist Press, 2019).

Pastoral study and action direct one to *an inner source, which the work of [priestly] formation will take care to guard and make good use of: This is the ever-deeper communion with the pastoral charity of Jesus,* which…constitutes the principle and driving force of priestly ministry. It is a question of a type of formation meant not only to ensure scientific, pastoral competence and practical skill, but also and especially *a way of being in communion with the very sentiments and behavior of Christ.*[1]

How does the seminary guard this inner source? How does formation lead a seminarian to be in communion with the very sentiments and behavior of Christ? In this essay I will explore one way that such a communion may be established and guarded. It is a way of prayer and meditation that invites the seminarian to enter Nazareth and live there with the

---

[1] Pope John Paul II, Pastores *Dabo Vobis*, 57 (1992).

Holy Family. This way of being and praying is expressed well by Pope Paul VI.

> "Oh, how I would like to become a child once again and start my studies over in this humble and sublime school of Nazareth. How I would like with Mary, to receive once again the true knowledge of life and the superior wisdom of divine truths."[2]

Here the Pope reveals his deepest heart, his desire to live with the Holy Family. Such a desire can be satiated as time and space do not deny its fulfillment. At its core such a desire expresses a man's longing to live with God, to live where holiness defines all of reality .Incipiently many seminarians come to the seminary looking to have the same desire fulfilled: I want to live where Christ lives. Vocation Directors usually use John 1: 38 to attract the attention of young men who are weary of aspects of our current culture and want to seek the "more." In this part of the Gospel of John we hear a question asked by any sincere seminarian, "Master, where do you live?"(v.38) Jesus says in return, 'Come and See." In John 1:43ff there is another version of this conversation that is more relevant to our present meditation on Nazareth, however. In this version Nathaniel asks if "anything good can come from Nazareth?" and Philip responds, "Come and See." What did Philip want Nathaniel to see, the town of Nazareth? No. He wanted Philip to see the kind of man that is formed in Nazareth, a formation that is taken up into the love between Mary and Joseph and their reception of the love of God the Father. Here the "come and see" invites the disciple to behold the kind of man *formed* in Nazareth, a man who can see very deeply, who gazes with love on the full truth of a man. He *sees* Nathaniel, *knows* him and then in response to Nathaniel's astonishment over this knowledge reveals even more: the source of this knowledge, which is Jesus' communion with all things divine. "You will see heaven open up." In other words, you will see what I see.

As the seminarian gets closer to the mystery of Christ's own identity and his communion with Mary, Joseph and the love of the Father he gains a sure footing for entering priestly ministry. The kind of man Nazareth forms is one who ministers to others needs from out of his own communion with the mystery of Divine and human love. The seminarian is called to let Christ tutor him in this mystery of ministry: the mission of priesthood can only be sustained throughout the life of a priest if he *receives* love and *stays in communion* with that love. Here is the core curriculum of the seminary; here is its "content":

---

[2] Paul VI, Visit to the Basilica of the Annunciation in Nazareth (January 5, 1964).

The first task of intellectual formation [in the seminary] is to acquire a personal knowledge of the Lord Jesus Christ, who is the fullness and completion of God's revelation and the one Teacher. This saving knowledge is acquired not only once, but it is continuously appropriated and deepened... Intellectual formation has a... missionary purpose and finality.[3]

There may be a number of seminarians who respond to the call to priesthood only to recognize that their "personal knowledge of the Lord Jesus Christ" remains undeveloped. If such ignorance lingers while he is still in seminary his future priesthood may become burdensome because he does not know how to receive love and stay in love. His priesthood is secured and continues toward holiness when it flows from communion with Christ and all who He is. This reception of Christ's love as 'personal knowledge' reaches its apex in mission, for communion founds mission. Christ, Himself, did not remain in Nazareth but was sent forth from his family; even still He continues to spiritually receive their love and affection. Nazareth has not vanished; it is the love between Mary, Joseph and Christ in the presence of the Trinity. Not only can good come from Nazareth it is the very home of goodness and holiness.

A Spousal Love

The seminary, then, is foremost a transfiguring encounter with Trinitarian love, a love made known in and through a "personal knowledge of the Lord Jesus Christ." If the priesthood Christ wishes to share with the seminarian is to be effectively received and *personally internalized then he must allow Christ to become intimate with him.* To enter communion with the Trinity is a gift of grace, a grace each seminarian has been appropriating since his baptism. This spiritual sonship, given to each man by the Father through Christ and in the Spirit, founds the fullness of his vocation as one who lives to give himself away in love.[4] As a man's priestly vocation becomes clear and he enters seminary *a new configuration of this grace of baptism was waiting*: the grace of spousal love. This grace is activated and internalized when a seminarian acknowledges that his vocation is *a way of spousal self-donation.*

---

[3] United States Conference of Catholic Bishops, *Program of Priestly Formation* (5th edition, 2006), n. 137.

[4] Documents of Vatican II, Gaudium et Spes, n.24; "....man, who is the only creature on earth which God willed for itself, cannot fully find himself except through a sincere gift of himself."

All spousal love has its origins in God ("Therefore, behold, I will allure her, and bring her into the wilderness, and speak tenderly to her" ,Hos 2:14)[5] who wishes to be close to His Bride (humanity, church) through the ministry of Christ the Bridegroom who then, in turn, shares His own mission with priests. The Incarnation, therefore, is the gracious overflow of God's spousal love for creation; a love that culminates in the self-donation of the Bridegroom on the cross (Mt.9:15; Eph.5:25). Christ himself was formed by the spousal love of Mary and Joseph (Lk. 2:51-52), a love reflecting God's own for His creation. Mary *received Jesus into her own love for Joseph and God the Father;* Jesus in turn received their love and gave himself to them (Luke 2:51), and eventually His own spouse, the Church.

The seminarian is invited to enter the grace of familial-nuptial love in the same way Christ knew such love on earth: through the reality of Nazareth, through the reality of Mary and Joseph's love for God, for one another, and for the Son, Jesus. In our current time when the spousal relationship is undergoing profound cultural attacks, and when married couples and priests alike struggle to be true to their vows we need to receive Nazareth in grace and invite it to *enter the seminary as refining fire.* Seminarians are called to be formed in a prophetic way as men espoused to the Church. That which is now being *rejected*, marriage, Nazareth ("can anything good come from married love?" Jn. 1:46), will in the end purify, elevate and rectify the priesthood. By virtue of his prophetic character the priest is summoned to participate in the communion of love[6] that is Mary, Joseph and Jesus. "[The priest] proclaims the word in his capacity as "minister," as a sharer in the prophetic

---

[5] "And in that day, says the Lord, you will call me, 'my husband', and no longer will you call me, 'my Baal'.... And I will betroth you to me forever; I will betroth you to me in righteousness and in justice, in steadfast love, and in mercy. I will betroth you to me in faithfulness, and you shall know the Lord" (Hos 2:16, 19-20). "Yet I will remember my covenant with you in the days of your youth, and I will establish with you an everlasting covenant" (Ez 16:60). "For your Maker is your husband.... For a brief moment I forsook you, but with great compassion I will gather you. In overflowing wrath for a moment I hid my face from you, but with everlasting love I will have compassion on you, says the Lord, your Redeemer" (Is 54:5, 7-8). "You shall be called My delight is in her, and your land Married; for the Lord delights in you, and your land shall be married. For as a young man marries a virgin, your Builder shall marry you; and as the bridegroom rejoices over the bride, so shall your God rejoice over you" (Is 62:4-5).

[6] 'In the words of the Council, the communion of persons is, in a certain sense, deduced from the mystery of the Trinitarian 'We', and therefore "conjugal communion' also refers to this mystery. Marc Cardinal Ouellet, *Divine Likeness : Toward a Trinitarian Anthropology of the Family* (Mich: Eerdmans, 2006), p.34.

authority of Christ and the Church."[7] In his chaste spousal love the seminarian gives witness to the *singular attention* Christ gave to His own Bride, the Church.

Time and Grace

One rationale for the existence of a seminary is to form the seminarian to cherish time. This cherishing is not for its own sake. Time is cherished as sacred because of what the Spirit is doing to and for the seminarians. He is advancing them in age, wisdom and grace (Lk. 2:52). This is how it was in Nazareth. This focus on time and relationships is ordered toward the completion of a masculine identity that was given to the seminarian at birth. His manhood was then related to the mystery of salvation at baptism. Under the loving discipline of his parents he further appropriates his identity as a *son* and *brother and* now, in seminary, moves toward *espousing* the church and this vocation's inevitable *paternal* fulfillment.[8] The seminary, then, is primarily a relational process of formation in a *priestly identity that can only be established upon a solid process of human and spiritual maturation.*[9]

In order for this identity to be maturely appropriated by a priest he needs to receive and enter into the communion of love that is Mary, Joseph and Jesus. The reception of such love defines the formation of one who is to share in the original priesthood of Christ, a priesthood that had a significant portion of its character established by way of this same

---

[7] Pope John Paul II, *Pastores Dabo Vobis*, n. 26.

[8] See, Pope John Paul II, *Man and Woman He Created Them: A Theology of the Body* (Boston: Pauline, 2006) 78:5.

[9] In the *Institute for Priestly Formation* we have come to see the priestly identity as encompassing four realities: good shepherd, spiritual father, chaste spouse, spiritual physician. See John Paul II, *Pastores Dabo Vobis* (1992) where these identities are noted, especially n. 3 (shepherd and spouse) 60 (spiritual physician), and for spiritual father we go to scripture, particularly in Paul, "I write not these things to shame you, but as my beloved sons I warn you. For though you have ten thousand instructors in Christ, you do not have many fathers: for in Christ Jesus I have begotten you through the Gospel." [I Cor 4:14-15]

See also PDV where John Paul II refers to the priest having spousal qualities: "The gift of self, which is the source and synthesis of pastoral charity, is directed toward the Church. This was true of Christ who 'loved the Church and gave himself up for her' (Eph. 5:25), and the same must be true for the priest. With pastoral charity, which distinguishes the exercise of the priestly ministry as an *amoris officium*,....[W]ith this concrete spirituality he becomes capable of loving the universal Church and that part of it entrusted to him with *the deep love of a husband for his wife.*" (*Pastores Dabo Vobis* n. 23).

familial-nuptial love. The Holy House of Nazareth, then, is to be *transported* to each seminary. To have the seminary become the house of Nazareth is to acknowledge that *Christ carried Nazareth within Him during his ministry.* He was the *"product"* of the silence, the work, the prayer, and the mystery of masculine-feminine love that He received. When the disciples met Christ, they met Nazareth. Those 30 years of *full silence are* carried in Christ's Heart, carried there to be forever shared with His priests in their own *amoris officium*[10]. Nazareth is still germane to the formation of priests because Nazareth *has never ended*; Christ remains in unceasing unity with the Father, Mary and Joseph.

Trinitarian Love

This domestic fellowship becomes the seminarian's *entry way* to deeper participation in Trinitarian love. It was the *Incarnation itself* that revealed the Trinity to man so that humanity might be purified and elevated to know and participate in God's love. As a result of his coming in the flesh we become capable of entering divine love and dwelling there with Him and his saints forever. "The basic principle of priestly spiritual formation is …to live in intimate and unceasing union with God the Father through his Son, Jesus Christ, in the Holy Spirit" (PPF 107).To be drawn to the Trinity in and through the holiness of Joseph and Mary's marital love is the way of purification and renewal *for all spouses*, particularly for those who share in Christ's own chaste spousal love. By seeking communion with the first "domestic church", which is Nazareth, the seminarian remains in fellowship with Mary, Joseph and Jesus thus glimpsing the origin of nuptial love itself: the Trinity. [11]

By remaining in such fellowship Christ gives to His sons what was given to Him by Mary, Joseph and The Father. Christ assures the future priest; "I will not leave you orphan, I will come to you" (John 14:18). Some translations express the word orphan as "desolate." In the intimacy of Nazareth the seminarian will find the truth of his spiritual life: desolation is *not his inheritance.* Seminary spiritual formation is ordered toward moving men out of desolation and toward the consolation that Christ carries for them within His own receptive Heart. Desolation ends when one receives *the content of Christ's own heart,* a heart defined by communion with the Father and bound in love (the Spirit) to Mary and Joseph. To live in such communion gives rise to priestly mission and a lifetime of self-donation for the welfare of the Church.

---

[10] See *Program of Priestly Formation* 5th edition, *n. 25.*

[11] *Program of Priestly Formation* 5th edition, n. 15. See Also, Angelo Cardinal Scolo, *The Nuptial Mystery* (Grand Rapids: Eerdmans, 2005), 335-336.

Nazareth in Practice

Succeeding the story of Nathaniel, as mentioned above, St. John moves us to *the beginning* of the wedding feast of the Lamb (Rev. 19:7ff and John 2:1-12) where all things are made new (Rev.21:5) because the Bridegroom *has emerged from His formation* (Jn.2:1ff). This formation of Christ's *was nuptial-familial.* It was a formation received through a marriage sourced in heaven, announced by an angel and sustained by mystical dreams (Mt 1:20). From such communion Jesus emerged to reveal His ultimate identity as the One who *constantly beholds the loving gaze of His Father.*

Nazareth, as formational reality, protects interiority by promoting and esteeming the *communion* that is the Holy Family and introducing the seminarian to participate in this communion. The seminarian participates in Nazareth by living where the Holy Family lives, in truth and love. He has to remain with the Holy Family in such humility so they can relate to him, reach him and "see" him. The seminarian progressively learns that he has to inhabit *the same reality* as the Holy Family, to dwell in a freely offered "Yes" to the will of the Father. If he does so the Holy Family will heal him, instruct him and send him.

Christ said yes and embraced Nazareth (Lk 2:51), Mary said yes to the approach of God (Lk.1:38), and Joseph said yes to both God and Mary (Mt. 1:20). Joseph had to suffer *a new idea about marriage*, one not of his choosing but of God's. Hence Joseph had to trust and depend upon God and Mary in a radical way, since *the newness came to him through her. The seminarian must do the same and stand before the Holy Family in all truth and humility. "Here are my wounds, my poverty; may I meet you in the place where our mutual poverty and dependency lead us to depend upon God?"[12]*

The Gift of Nazareth

What should seminarians, who have received the grace of Nazareth, concentrate upon during their four years of formation? In answering this question recall that the *Program of Priestly Formation* saw spiritual formation as the heart and core of seminary.[13] Hence, I would invite seminarians to follow the example of Pope Paul VI and cry out in prayer *for a*

---

[12] The formation staff seeks to teach seminarians what to do with their pain, their wounds, and their "poverty." Such poverty is to be related to the love held for them in the Holy Family. Pain cannot be run from or hidden it must be shared and entrusted to those who trust God, and have entrusted themselves to Him.

[13] *Program of Priestly Formation* 5th edition, n. 115.

new spiritual childhood. "Oh, how I would like to become a child once again and start my studies over in…the school of Nazareth. " Formators can assist the seminarians to become spiritual children by encouraging them to live in *trust, surrender and complete honesty.* Paradoxically spiritual childhood is THE way to affective and spiritual *maturity. The more seminarians make their interior lives available to God the Father, and the communion of love that is the Holy Family,* the more they will be on the way to full manhood *in Christ* (Eph 4:13). Such growth in maturity is made possible because Nazareth is safe; it is held in love by He who is Truth, and by the One who measures growth in priestly formation not simply by academic years but by an eager receptivity to divine love. [14]

The fruit of having communion with the "residents" of Nazareth is not simply spiritual and affective maturity alone, it *is also mission.* Certainly, Nazareth, as the core (PPF 115) of seminary life, deepens a life of *interiority for mission.* Christ did not stay "hidden" for thirty years *for himself;* he stayed in a bond of love with the Father, Mary and Joseph for the sake of his mission. The very nature of seminary invites seminary formators to intentionally order the contents of class, spiritual direction, human and pastoral formation toward interiority for mission. Out of such formation a priest will be able to lead the laity, those who transform culture, to the very source of their mission: the indwelling Spirit of Christ. Without a love of interiority a priest may not have the capacity to assist the laity in internalizing and securing their own mission. The more he appropriates his own call to *holiness* as <u>the gift</u> *he gives to the laity* the more the evangelical mission which marks the laity will be secured by them, as holiness diffuses itself. [15]

---

[14] See Karen Dwyer and Edward Hogan, "Assessment of Spiritual Formation for Diocesan Seminarians" *Seminary Journal* (Winter 2008) 37-41, for a method and discussion about measuring objective spiritual growth.

[15] See Father John Cihak, "St. John Vianney's Pastoral Plan" www.ignatiusinsight.com/features2009/jcihak_cureofarshpr2_june09.asp, for an insightful essay on the relationship between holiness and lay conversion and mission.

Also we note this from John Paul II: "An essential characteristic of missionary spirituality is intimate communion with Christ. ….The universal call to holiness is closely linked to the universal call to mission. …The missionary must be a contemplative in action…the future of mission depends …on contemplation. The missionary is a witness to the experience of God" (*Redemptoris Missio,* n. 91).

John Paul II again, "…it would be wrong to think that ordinary Christians can be content with a shallow prayer that is unable to fill their whole life. Especially in the face of the many trials to which today's world subjects faith, *they would be not only mediocre Christians but "Christians at risk".* They would run the insidious risk of seeing their faith progressively undermined, and

What draws a seminarian to Nazareth?

In prayer the seminarian draws close to the nuptial love of Joseph and Mary learning from them what loving the Church means. Entering this love a seminarian comes "home", he is taken up into the love between mother and father. Emotional safety is crucial for growth in affective maturity. As we direct a seminarian to enter the love between Joseph and Mary in his prayer we are entrusting him to the foundational love of all Christian marriages. We are beckoning him to surrender himself and learn from Joseph how to love the "woman" (Jn.2:4; 19:26-7). Since this tutorial is accomplished *in the imagination of the seminarian at prayer* the fullness of his own life in relation to Mary and Joseph is opened to him in the Spirit, the source and giver of life. The Spirit protects the imagination from becoming fantasy and therefore disconnected from doctrinal and spiritual truth. At the heart of *nuptial love* is life, fecundity. Formators should be directing the seminarian to this heart as if the seminarian were a thirsty man needing water. [16] What should the seminarian pay attention to when he is in the heart of such prayer? He is to imagine *the life* at the core of Mary and Joseph's *love*!

Jesus is formed for mission out of this maternal-paternal love. He is ready for mission because He is formed in humility. This humility flows throughout the love between Jesus, Mary and Joseph. We see it in Christ doing the Father's will, the *Fiat* of Mary and the 'Yes' of Joseph to care for Mary as his spouse. Priestly formation is time immersed in the Holy Family's love. During this time the seminarian experiences spiritual sonship in a new way. He shares his deepest affections with the Holy Family and the grace he receives from this love prepares him to become an emotionally and spiritually mature spouse and father. It is impossible for man to receive fatherhood as a vocation unless he has experienced being loved as a son. This love founds his capacity to make himself one who endures sacrifice for the love of his children. In the priest who bypasses spiritual childhood, spiritual and affective deformation occurs.[17] Tragically, this kind of man takes power and remains

---

would perhaps end up succumbing to the allure of "substitutes", accepting alternative religious proposals and even indulging in far-fetched superstitions. It is therefore essential that *education in prayer* should become in some way a key-point of all pastoral planning." (*Novo Millennio ineunte,* n. 34).

[16] Cardinal Marc Ouellet, *Divine Likeness,* p. 35.

[17] "Spiritual childhood…means that we acknowledge our nothingness; that we expect everything from the good Lord, as a child expects everything from its father; it means to worry about nothing…it means that we must not be discouraged by our faults, for children fall frequently." St.

isolated and unrelated to the joy *that is known in being loved*. In this case one becomes authoritarian rather than fatherly, or he becomes a "taker" filled with delusions of entitlement.

The seminary is a place of personal vulnerability to the healing love of the primordial Christian family. In this way all facets of formation; academic,[18] human, pastoral and spiritual ought to invite the seminarian to "stay" within the loving relations of the Holy Family. Each person of the Holy Family will bring a particular facet of the mystery of his vocation to the seminarian. In reality the persons and the relationships between the persons in the Holy Family become crucial "content" in the process of formation.

Jesus, Joseph and Mary

We do not need to linger here on how the person of Christ relates to the seminarian since this relationship is covered so thoroughly in priestly documents and theology.[19] We can make one point here about Christ, however. There is no guarantee of or right to ordination once a man enters the seminary, but if he enters formation fully, there is *a hope* that he will meet Christ. Christ will then communicate to him a sense of self that is healthy

---

Therese of Lisieux as quoted in F. Jamart, *The Complete Spiritual Doctrine of St. Therese of Lisieux* (NY: Alba House, 2001), 15-16.

[18] The seminarian's theological imagination is not to be defined by *academics*, a course of studies to be completed in four years. His spiritual-theological imagination is ordered by his communion with Christ and the saints. The seminary is to promote and *protect this imagination* as its staff and structures of daily living (*horarium*) facilitate the knowledge necessary to receive love from the living God and His saints. Academics only deepen a man's love of such communion with the Trinity. Since a seminarian's identity is not exclusively "student" all studies are to be sublated into his emerging identity as a priest. No seminary reduces a seminarian's identity to "student" *as a policy*, this reduction happens as a result of a disproportionate weight given to academics in the minds of some students and faculty. Giving academics such weight is, as it were, a default mode of existence for most American seminarians. To study the mysteries of Christ on the way to possessing an intellectual competency in theology is a necessity of the highest order, but the mysteries themselves open the seminarian to **want more** than competency, they summon him to wisdom---the eventual triumph of love being integrated with knowing the truth. See, James Keating, *Resting on the Heart of Christ: The Vocation and Spirituality of the Seminary Theologian* (Omaha: IPF Publications, 2009).

[19] For example see especially chapters 1-4 in *Pastores Dabo Vobis;* Cardinal Avery Dulles, *The Priestly Office* (Mahwah, NJ: Paulist, 1997); Jean Galot, *Theology of the Priesthood* (San Francisco: Ignatius, 2005).

and spiritually mature, *since it was born in the interchange between the seminarian's own receptivity to host the truth and Christ's own desire to be that truth for him.* Here the seminarian must come to awareness that Christ is his gift and that all facets of formation conspire to show him Christ. In academic, pastoral and human formation seminary formators want each seminarian to host the truth about self, doctrine, or charity, but more so they want the seminarian to know that it is Christ himself who is the Truth. All seminary formation ends in the sharing of Christ's own priestly heart, a heart formed out of love for truth, His Father's will, and the love between Mary and Joseph. Let me close then with a meditation on a reality that is not as well trod as a seminarian's relationship with Christ: a seminarian's relationship with Joseph and Mary

How can the seminarian approach Joseph?

In a March 2009 homily, Pope Benedict XVI said:

Joseph agreed to be part of the great events God was beginning to bring about in the womb of his spouse. He took Mary into his home. He welcomed the mystery that was in Mary and the mystery that was Mary herself.... Joseph teaches us that it is possible to love without possessing.

In contemplating Joseph, [we] come to experience healing from emotional wounds, if only [we] embrace the plan that God has begun to bring about in those close to [us], just as Joseph entered into the work of redemption through Mary and as a result of what God had already done in her....

He then defined what this healing means later in the homily:

... Joseph was caught up at every moment by the mystery of the Incarnation. Not only physically, but in his heart as well, Joseph reveals to us the secret of a humanity which dwells in the presence of mystery and is open to that mystery at every moment of everyday life. In Joseph, faith is not separated from action. His faith had a decisive effect on his actions. Paradoxically, it was by acting, by carrying out his responsibilities, that he stepped aside and left God free to act, placing no obstacles in his way.[20]

---

[20] Homily of Pope Benedict XVI ; First Vespers of the Solemnity of St Joseph, Basilica of Marie Reine Des Apotres Yaounde (MARCH 2009).

If the seminarian can learn to "dwell" in the presence of Mystery and relate all that he is thinking, feeling and desiring to that loving mystery of God he will be healed of that which drags at his soul, and fetters his hope of holiness. Joseph stands close to the seminarian as one who knows the intimate call to spousal chastity in service to the mystery of Christ's own vocation. He intercedes for the future priest to trust in Mary, to let her guide him to all that is good about nuptial self-donation. Joseph is ready to ask Christ to gift the seminarian with the graces and virtues of Christ's own priesthood. Joseph will also counsel the seminarian on his participation in the renewal of creation, his vocation as an eschatological sign. The seminarian should invite Joseph to pray for him to welcome within his own body the coming of the "new age", the age that orders all love through the lens of God's spousal love for his people. Joseph wants to tutor the seminarian in this truth, "God wants to renew everything from within the family." [21] As patriarch Joseph passes on to the seminarian a love of authority, an authority that flows from and is sustained by, his love of Mary and God.[22] Joseph is for the seminarian an advocate for true fatherhood, a paternity that flows from his own love of his spouse. This paternal love is always fruitful as it shares in God's own love for all those He has created.

Here is what Joseph teaches the seminarian:

- welcome the mystery that is Mary
- love your bride without possessing
- live in the presence of mystery and be open to this mystery at every moment. Seek to be docile to the truths inherent in the mystery of your own vocation
- Do not separate faith from everyday life. Place no obstacles in God's way, so God can act through your ministry.

These characteristics of Joseph, alone, are sufficient to ponder as content for seminary formation. But, of course there is more.

What is the gift that Mary brings?

Every aspect of priestly formation can be referred to Mary, the human being who has responded better than any other to God's call. Mary became both the servant and the disciple of the Word to the point of conceiving, in her heart and in her flesh, the Word

---

[21] Marie Dominique-Philippe, OP, *The Mystery of Joseph* (Bethesda: Zaccheus Press, 2009), 80.

[22] Ibid, 81.

made man, so as to give him to mankind. Mary was called to educate the one eternal priest, who became docile and subject to her motherly authority.[23]

And, Pope John Paul II adds,

It is [the priest's] task to proclaim Christ her Son. And who can better communicate to you the truth about him than his mother? It is your task to nourish men's hearts with Christ. And who can make you more aware of what you are doing than she who nourished Him? [24]

Mary communicates to the seminarian the truth about her Son. The most absolute truth she speaks is: "Do whatever He tells you" (Jn. 2:5). She knew Him so well that it was at her word that the public ministry began, "They have no more wine" (Jn. 2:3). She did not ask for wine she simply informed Him of the truth: the human race is depleted and they need the joy and the healing of the Spirit. The seminarian seeks out Mary to converse about his own mission, his own appropriation of the truth of Jesus' identity and mission. Here her mystery looms large in the academic study and teaching of theology. She is the one who internalizes the Word, and then lets the intimacy the Word's presence compel her to mission (Lk 1:39).

The seminarian also approaches her to receive the mystery of woman, to have her tutor him like she tutored Joseph in the ways of a startling and surprising nuptial life: spousal self-donation to the church as a sign of Christ's *own* gift. As then Joseph Ratzinger noted, "Mary's motherhood becomes theologically significant as the ultimate personal concretization of Church… She is the church in person and as a person. She is the personal concretization of the Church."[25] If this is so then the seminarian needs to receive from her the satisfaction of his deepest desire to be "for woman." She will instruct him to know, like Joseph, that God's Spirit is ready to console and elevate the affections and intellect in a way that "indicates another kind of closeness in marriage. The spiritual closeness arising from marital union and the interpersonal contact between man and woman have their definitive origin in the Spirit, the Giver of Life (cf. John 6:63). Joseph, in obedience to the Spirit, *found in the Spirit the source of love, the conjugal love that he experienced as a man. "*[26] Joseph grew

---

[23] *PDV*, 82.

[24] Pope John Paul II, *Holy Thursday Letter to Priests* (1979), n. 11.

[25] Hans urs Von Balthasar and Joseph Ratzinger, *Mary: The Church at the Source* (San Francisco: Ignatius 2005), 30.

[26] John Paul II, *Redemptoris Custos* (1989), n. 19.

in his reception of his deepest identity: spouse of Mary, the New Eve, and the Church. Friendship with him, in contemplative prayer, will result in similar growth in the seminarian. Joseph consented to a life lived in virtuous continence but he "had to do so in dependence upon Mary."[27] In contemplative prayer the seminarian will learn *from Joseph* to depend upon "the woman" to teach him how to embrace her (Mary, the Church) *in loving service* rather than *physical intercourse.* This is analogous to a husband *learning from his wife* how best to love her within the patterns of marriage defined by natural family planning. In loving Mary in accord with God's will Joseph "found *in the Spirit* the source of love, the conjugal love that he experienced as a man." Can this truth about Joseph become the centerpiece of all priestly formation on chaste spousal love?

Here is what Mary teaches the seminarian:

- Mary educates the seminarian in the processes of internalizing the Word.
- Mary communicates to the seminarian the truth of who her Son is.
- Mary gifts the seminarian with the truth about woman, and his own spousal gift of self-donation to the Church.

Conclusion

The love of God, of Mary and Joseph is real. Their love is affecting the seminarian even now. The saints are living. We all note these statements as true discursively, but in the rush of pragmatism and productivity that is the hallmark of western culture we can forget that *Mary, Joseph and Jesus' love for one another is still pulsating dynamically between them.* Christ wants *to gather his priests within this source* of formation to prepare them for a life of hosting the truth about man and God, the mystery of mankind approached through the mystery of Christ. Such a host, such a victim priest needs to be communing with those who have this mystery at the heart of their being: The Holy Family. If the seminarian is courageous enough he can be drawn into their love for another and know this mystery himself. Receiving this nuptial- familial love he will be sent, like the Beloved Son, to change water into wine and wine into the very life of Christ. 'Oh, how I would like to become a child once again and start my studies over in this humble and sublime school of Nazareth.'

---

[27] Marc Ouellet, *Divine Likeness* (Grand Rapids: Eerdmans, 2006), 118.

This article was originally published in *Homiletic & Pastoral Review* (http://www.hprweb.com, 2011). It is republished here with the permission of the author, who has additionally provided the following prayer, practicum reflection questions, and suggested resources.

Prayer

'Oh, how I would like to become a child once again and start my studies over in this humble and sublime school of Nazareth. How I would like with Mary, to receive once again the true knowledge of life and the superior wisdom of divine truths." Lord bring me to Nazareth and refashion my heart into one of a vulnerable child, one who receives in wonder both your love and all that you share with me about how to live a wonderful life of grace in the ordinary days of my life. Amen.

Practicum Reflection Questions for Formators

1. The truth of Mary looms large in the academic study and teaching of theology. She is the one who internalizes the Word, and then lets intimacy with the Word compel her to mission (Lk 1:39). What is the Marian dimension of your study of theology? How do you allow the truths of theology, doctrine become internalized in your heart?

2. Joseph wants to tutor the seminarian in this truth, "God wants to renew everything from within the family." Joseph is for the seminarian an advocate for true fatherhood, a paternity that flows from his own love of his spouse. In what ways can you imagine your parish putting the meaning of family in the forefront of its spiritual initiatives?

3. Christ assures the future priest; "I will not leave you orphan, I will come to you" (John 14:18). Some translations express the word orphan as "desolate." Desolation is not your inheritance. Seminary spiritual formation is ordered toward moving men out of desolation and toward the consolation that Christ carries for them within His own receptive Heart. In what ways can you enter a better, more generous relationship with your spiritual director?

4. Here is the core curriculum of the seminary; here is its "content":

    The first task of intellectual formation [in the seminary] is to acquire a personal knowledge of the Lord Jesus Christ, who is the fullness and completion of God's revelation and the one Teacher. This saving knowledge is acquired not only once, but it is continuously appropriated and deepened... Intellectual formation has a... missionary purpose and finality.[28]

How can you receive and stay in communion with the Father even as you study?

Suggested Resources

1. James Keating, *Remain in Me: Holy Orders, Prayer and Ministry* (Paulist Press, 2019).
2. Jacques Philippe, *Time for God* (Scepter, 2008).
3. Pope Emeritus Benedict XVI , *Called to Holiness* (Catholic University Press, 2017).

---

[28] United States Conference of Catholic Bishops, *Program of Priestly Formation* (5th edition, 2006), n. 137.

Chapter Twenty-Two

NAZARETH, A MODEL

From an address by Saint Paul VI, Pope
(Nazareth, January 5, 1964)

Nazareth is a kind of school where we may begin to discover what Christ's life was like and even to understand his Gospel. Here we can observe and ponder the simple appeal of the way God's Son came to be known, profound yet full of hidden meaning. And gradually we may even learn to imitate him.

Here we can learn to realize who Christ really is. And here we can sense and take account of the conditions and circumstances that surrounded and affected his life on earth: the places, the tenor of the times, the culture, the language, religious customs, in brief, everything which Jesus used to make himself known to the world. Here everything speaks to us, everything has meaning. Here we can learn the importance of spiritual discipline for all who wish to follow Christ and to live by the teachings of his Gospel.

How I would like to return to my childhood and attend the simple yet profound school that is Nazareth! How wonderful to be close to Mary, learning again the lesson of the true meaning of life, learning again God's truths. But here we are only on pilgrimage. Time presses and I must set aside my desire to stay and carry on my education in the Gospel, for that education is never finished. But I cannot leave without recalling, briefly and in passing, some thoughts I take with me from Nazareth.

First, we learn from its silence. If only we could once again appreciate its great value. We need this wonderful state of mind, beset as we are by the cacophony of strident protests and conflicting claims so characteristic of these turbulent times. The silence of Nazareth should teach us how to meditate in peace and quiet, to reflect on the deeply spiritual, and to be open to the voice of God's inner wisdom and the counsel of his true teachers. Nazareth can teach us the value of study and preparation, of meditation, of a well-ordered personal spiritual life, and of silent prayer that is known only to God.

Second, we learn about family life. May Nazareth serve as a model of what the family should be. May it show us the family's holy and enduring character and exemplify its basic function in society: a community of love and sharing, beautiful for the problems it poses and the rewards it brings, in sum, the perfect setting for rearing children—and for this there is no substitute.

Finally, in Nazareth, the home of a craftsman's son, we learn about work and the discipline it entails. I would especially like to recognize its value—demanding yet redeeming—and to give it proper respect. I would remind everyone that work has its own dignity. On the other hand, it is not an end in itself. Its value and free character, however, derive not only from its place in the economic system, as they say, but rather from the purpose it serves.

In closing, may I express my deep regard for people everywhere who work for a living. To them I would point out their great model, Christ their brother, our Lord and God, who is their prophet in every cause that promotes their well-being.

Prayer

Dear Jesus... please increase my capacities to receive and exercise the gift of child-like faith. Help me to see you in the ordinary events and circumstances of my Nazareth. And, in seeing you, draw me into generous service so that others may taste and see the beauty of your redeeming love... Amen.

Practicum Reflection Questions for Formators

1. How am I seeking and discovering Jesus' presence alive in the ordinary events and context of my Nazareth, my ordinary life?
2. When I accept living with child-like faith what is it like to experience Mary's closeness? What occurs between us in this closeness?
3. Am I permitting myself the enjoyment of engaging regularly in the dignity of manual work like Jesus did with Joseph as a craftsman's son? Do I recognize this as

a necessity of tasting the dignity of manual labor in regular life? Please describe. What sort of manual work do I want to maintain in this age of computer technology so that I may learn to receive a harmonious balance between mental labors and physical labors?

4. How am I cultivating the value of silence in day to day life? What have the benefits been like in my life of faith? How can I better intentionally cultivate silence in the future?

Suggested Resources

1. "Praying The Psalms As Jesus Did," by Fr. Lawrence Kriegshauser, O.S.B.
2. "Jesus Of Nazareth," Volumes I, II, III, by Pope Benedict XVI
3. "Searching for and Maintaining Peace," by Fr. Jacques Philippe, St. Paul's Publishers, 2002.

APPENDIX I

Confession and Receiving God's Mercy
A Guide for Penitents and Priests

"When someone realizes that he is a sinner and is saved by Jesus, he admits the truth to himself and discovers the hidden pearl, the buried treasure. He discovers how great life is; that there is someone who loves him so deeply that He gave his life for him."

— Pope Francis

Through the Holy Spirit and the grace of baptism, we are **beloved sons and daughters** of the Father in Jesus. But our sins have affected this relationship and we often live separated from God. God is **always seeking us**. He even sent His Son Jesus, not to condemn the world, but to give His life to redeem it *(Jn 3:16)*. May we allow Jesus to find us, and may we **receive His mercy!**

Confession is our invitation to reject the isolation of sin and receive God's perfect love, which casts out all fear *(1 Jn 4:19)*. **Choose now** to accept the Father's merciful embrace and live in communion with Jesus, who makes all things new *(Rev. 21:5)*.

Isolation: Bad Fruit   **Communion:** Good Fruit

To be in **isolation from Christ** means that a person is living according to **the lie that "I am alone."** When we live in isolation, we rely on ourselves rather than on God. When we are in isolation, we are **not disposed to receiving God's love and forgiveness.** To live in isolation is to live in a place of darkness, heaviness, emptiness, insecurity, and unbelief.

Jesus gives a strong warning to those who are living in isolation: "If a man does not abide in me, **he is cast forth as a branch and withers,** and the branches are gathered, thrown into the fire and burned" *(Jn. 15:6).* This isolation is the root of so many of our sins. Living in isolation leads to **"bad fruit"** — "immorality, impurity, ... idolatry, sorcery, hatreds,

Christ invites his followers into a **deep communion with the Father.** To be in communion with Jesus means to live in **close friendship** with Him. He says, "I am the vine, you are the branches. Whoever remains in me and I in him will **bear much fruit,** because without me you can do nothing." *(Jn. 15:5).*

When we are in communion with Jesus, we live by faith and **rely on Him** in everything we do. To be in communion with Jesus means to experience His **forgiveness, constantly receive His love** for us, and allow that love to flow outward to others. When we are living in communion with Christ, the good **"fruit of the Spirit"** is borne in our midst, namely "love, joy, peace, patience, kindness,

rivalry, jealousy, outbursts of fury, acts of selfishness, dissensions, factions, occasions of envy, … and the like" *(Gal. 5:19-21)*.

generosity, faithfulness, gentleness, self-control" *(Gal. 5:22-23)*.

"One of the deepest forms of poverty a person can experience is isolation … Poverty is often produced by a rejection of God's love, by man's basic and tragic tendency to close in on himself, thinking himself to be self-sufficient. … It is not by isolation that man establishes his worth, but by placing himself in relation with others and with God."

— *Pope Benedict XVI*

"If in our heart there is no mercy, no joy of forgiveness, we are not in communion with God, even if we observe all of his precepts, for it is love that saves, not the practice of precepts alone. ... This is the love of God, his joy: Forgiveness. He waits for us always! Maybe someone has some heaviness in his heart: 'But, I did this, I did that … .' He expects you! He is your father: He waits for you always!"

— *Pope Francis*

Preparing for Confession

The Church's living tradition speaks of the **Seven Deadly Sins**. Opposed to these are the **Heavenly Virtues**. At the root of the deadly sins can be **lies we've believed**, which often cover over even **deeper fears in our hearts**. Below, in the left column, are some **common lies and fears** that can operate within us if we don't exercise the gift of faith. In the right column are some Scriptures that can help us grow in communion with Christ, from which the life of **virtue and holiness flourishes**. Prayerfully **ask the Holy Spirit** to reveal any **lies and fears** that have led you to sin. As you become aware of these lies and fears, renounce them **in the name of Jesus** by the authority given to you in baptism, and ask the Father for the opposing **Heavenly Virtue**. For example, *"In the Name of Jesus, I renounce the lie and fear that I am alone, which has led me to the pride of self-reliance. Father, I trust that You are always with me."* Or, *"In the Name of Jesus, I renounce the lie that I am abandoned. Believing this lie has led me into a fear of loneliness and the sin of lust. Father, I trust You will never reject me."*

SEVEN DEADLY SINS		HEAVENLY VIRTUES
that lead us to *isolation* from Christ		**that lead us to *communion* with Christ**

Pride

Vanity · Arrogance · Self-Reliance

"I am alone. I need to look out for myself."

"I determine what is right or wrong."

Humility / Loving Obedience

Lk. 1:38 "Here I am the handmaid of the Lord, let it be done to me according to your word."

Envy

Comparison · Jealousy · Criticism

"I must be perfect. I am inadequate."

"Nothing good ever happens to me."

Kindness / Admiration

Lk. 15:31 "My son, you are here with me always; and everything that I have is yours."

Greed

Selfishness · Love of Money · Covetousness

"It should be mine." · "My time is my own."

"God is not enough for me."

Charity / Generosity

Phil. 2:3–4 "In humility, count others better than yourselves. Let each of you look not only to his own interests, but also to the interests of others."

Gluttony

Worthlessness · Self-Pity · Instant Gratification

"I can't say no to myself or to others."

"It doesn't matter anyway."

Temperance / Self-Control

Ps. 23:1–2 "The Lord is my shepherd; there is nothing I shall want. Fresh and green are the pastures where he gives me repose."

Lust

Loneliness · Insecurity · Escaping to Impurity

"I am not desirable and will be abandoned."

"Others exist for my sexual pleasure."

Chastity / Purity

Ps. 51:12, 14 "Create in me a clean heart, O God; put a steadfast spirit within me. ... Restore to me the joy of your salvation, and sustain in me a willing spirit."

Anger

Resentment · Self-Hatred · Revenge

"I am never going to forgive _____."

"I am not up to what's being asked of me."

Patience / Forgiveness

Lk 23:34 "Father forgive them, for they know not what they do."

Sloth

Doubt & Slow to Trust · Apathy · Despair

"I have to earn God's love."

"God has no plan for my life."

Diligence / Zeal

Jer. 29:11 "For surely I know the plans I have for you, says the Lord, plans for your welfare and not for harm, to give you a future full of hope."

Celebrating the Sacrament

1. PREPARE AND BEGIN

Recall the words of Jesus: "**Come to me** all you who are weary and find life burdensome, and **I will refresh you**" *(Mt. 11:28)*. **Ask the Holy Spirit** to help you examine your conscience (using the guide to the left), then **present yourself** to the priest with a readiness to name and confess your sins. Make the **sign of the cross** to formally begin.

2. HEAR THE WORD

The priest will **welcome you** and may provide a Biblical passage or image that encourages you to **trust** in the Father's goodness and to **be open and receptive** to His healing mercy. For example:

Lk. 15:11–32 The image of the Father **running towards you** with great tenderness and joy to embrace you and welcome you home.

Jn. 10:10–16 Being **carried home** by Jesus, the Good Shepherd, who says, "I have come so that you may have life and have it in abundance."

Lk. 2:7,16–20 Being **held by Mary**, the Blessed Mother, as Jesus was in the Nativity.

Lk. 7:40–48 The truth that the one who is forgiven more is **able to love more**.

Lk. 19:9–10 Jesus saying to Zacchaeus,

"Today, **salvation has come to your house** … for the Son of Man has come to seek and to save the lost."

Jn. 13:1–10 Jesus washing the disciples' feet —*your* feet as a **believer.**

3. CONFESS YOUR SINS

At this time, tell the priest an estimate of **how long it has been** since your last confession. Then **name and confess your sins.** You may also name the lies and fears that have led you to sin. By confessing your sins, you declare that they are not welcome in your heart, and you give God permission to **break their power** over you.

4. MAKE AN ACT OF CONTRITION

The priest will then invite you to pray an **Act of Contrition**. You may use the one on the back of this brochure, another Act of Contrition from the Church's tradition, or a brief prayer from your heart that expresses **sincere sorrow**. For example: *"Jesus Son of the living God, have mercy on me a sinner."*

5. RECEIVE GOD'S MERCY

The priest will then pray the **prayer of absolution, forgiving your sins** in and through the Father's mercy, the Son's presence as reconciling love, and in the healing power of the Holy Spirit. The priest prays with the **unique authority** of his ordination, forgiving **in the person of Jesus** *(Jn. 20:22–23)*, and reconciling **on behalf of the entire Church**. Listen to the words of absolute forgiveness and **receive the beautiful gift** of God's mercy.

6. GIVE THANKS AND GO IN PEACE

After praying the absolution the priest may say: "**Give thanks to the Lord** for He is good." You respond: "**For His mercy endures forever**." The priest concludes the sacrament by saying: "The Lord has **freed you** from your sins. Go in peace." This is your invitation to receive the **peace of Jesus**, the peace the world cannot give *(Jn. 14:27)*.

7. DO YOUR PENANCE

After you depart, **do the penance** that the priest prescribed as soon as time permits. The penance could be a prayer or act of charity that will act as a **spiritual medicine** and assist you in receiving the forgiving love of Jesus. Recall an image that disposes you to living in communion with God. Give thanks again for the Father's mercy, asking to walk humbly and confidently with Jesus as **friend and companion**.

An Act of Contrition

Lord Jesus, to know You is eternal life.

I believe You are the Messiah, the Son of the living God. I love You and I place my trust in You. **I am sorry** for all of my sins and for withholding myself from You in any way. Please forgive me and heal any pain I have caused others. I forgive anyone who has hurt me, and I ask You to bless them. In Your Name, Jesus, I renounce anything in my life that is not of You that I have welcomed into my mind or heart. Wash me in mercy and fill me with Your Precious Blood and the Holy Spirit.

Father, all of my need for love and affection is found in Your embrace. May I never leave my home in Your heart again. By Your grace, I resolve to remain in Your shelter and abide in Your shade, where You restore to me the joy of Your salvation *(Ps. 91, Ps. 51)*. Amen.

"God never tires of forgiving us; we are the ones who tire of seeking his mercy. ... With a tenderness which never disappoints, but is always capable of restoring our joy, he makes it possible for us to lift up our heads and to start anew."

— Pope Francis

Nihil Obstat:
Rev. George Welzbacher, Censor librorum

Imprimatur:
+ Most Rev. Bernard A. Hebda
Archbishop of St. Paul and Minneapolis, April 2017

Reproduced with permission. For brochure style copies, email:
guideforconfession@gmail.com
© Institute for Ongoing Clergy Formation

Heart Speaks to Heart[1]

A Review of Life and Healing Prayer
The Inner Heart of My Faith Journal

---

[1] Most Rev. George J. Lucas provided the imprimatur for the original printing of this section of the book as a pamphlet. Fr. Matthew J. Gutowski, JCL, provided the nihil obstat. Originally published by Fr. John Horn, S.J., and The Institute for Priestly Formation in 2010, with second edition in 2015.

Wisdom from Pope Francis and Pope Benedict XVI

"This love, this fidelity of the Lord manifests the humility of His heart. Jesus did not come to conquer men as the kings and powerful of this world, but He came to offer love with meekness and humility. This is how He described Himself: 'learn from me; for I am gentle and lowly in heart' (Matthew 11:29). And the meaning of the feast of the Sacred Heart of Jesus ... is that of discovering increasingly and of letting ourselves be enveloped by the humble fidelity and meekness of the love of Christ, revelation of the Father's mercy." – Pope Francis, Homily at Holy Mass on the Solemnity of the Most Sacred Heart of Jesus, Rome, Italy (June 27, 2014)

"This search of man's heart ends when one discovers God's Heart."– Pope Benedict XVI, Preparation for Consecration of Youth to the Sacred Heart, Madrid, Spain (July 16, 2011)

Endorsements for Heart Speaks to Heart

"Every summer seminarians from across the country come together at the Institute for Priestly Formation, sent by their bishops, to deepen their prayer life and grow in communion with Christ. In Fr. John Horn's new workbook *Heart Speaks to Heart* a similar experience within a review of life, coupled with the blessing of healing prayer, can touch the heart of every pastor and every parishioner concerned about growing in intimacy with Christ and tasting God the Father's love." **Archbishop Robert Carlson, St. Louis, MO**

"Today as in the times of Jesus, the faithful ask of priests, "… teach us to pray." This book is an answer to people's desire to pray. Those who prayerfully use it, clergy and laity, will grow in their love for Scripture and grow in a deeper intimacy with the Father, Jesus and the Holy Spirit. They will learn how to speak "heart to heart" with the living God." **Archbishop Samuel Aquila, Denver, CO**

"This beautiful book developed a method to lead the reader deeper, in a living way, into relationship with Jesus Christ. Its strength lies both in its simplicity and in its prayerful discernment of the "how" which directs the reader towards the "Who" for whom we all long. This practical guide identifies a clear path into the mystery of communion with God." **Suzanne Baars, MA, Catholic Psychotherapist, Director of In His Image Christian Counseling Service, Irving, TX**

"Anyone who seeks to serve the Lord in sincerity and truth will benefit from this prayerful review of their life before the Lord. *Heart Speaks to Heart* offers new strength for service through a courageous remembering of one's life before the healing image of Jesus' risen, pierced Heart. This workbook-journal offers a valuable service when used in the formation of priestly hearts, providing a formation in personal prayer that is transformative and life-giving. If offered in seminaries, the potential value of *Heart Speaks to Heart* for the spiritual formation of the faithful cannot be overestimated." **Bishop Joseph Hanefeldt, Grand Island, NE**

"The college students I encounter every day have a profound need to experience the truth and power of Jesus' healing love for them. To say 'Jesus is Lord of history' is one thing. To have a lived experience of the truth that Jesus is Lord of every moment of my personal history is quite another. *Heart Speaks to Heart* offers the reader wisdom, encouragement and concrete tools to taste and see the healing love of Jesus available and victorious in each moment of their life." **Very Rev. Scott Traynor, Rector, St. John Vianney Theological Seminary, Denver, CO**

"'Come to me...for I am meek and humble of heart; and you will find rest for yourselves' (Mt 11:28-29). *Heart Speaks to Heart* guides seminarians and others in responding to Christ's invitation to 'come' to Him, behold His Sacred Heart, and receive His healing love. It is an insightful and practical instrument for spiritual and human formation that illumines the path to greater self-knowledge, affective maturity, genuine freedom, enriched prayer, and deeper conversion to Christ." **Fr. Brian McMaster, Pastor, St. Helen Catholic Church, Georgetown, TX**

"If we are to win hearts for Christ, we cannot meet their depths with our shallows. This book provides a way to bring the deep cry of human hearts into conversation and contact with the infinite depth of Christ's healing love. Let all who are thirsty come to the water! When hearts are drawn into conversation and relationship with Jesus, healing always happens. But how can we draw people into that conversation and into that relationship? Here's your 'how to' guide! Thanks be to God!" **Dr. Ed Hogan, Director, Pontifical Paul VI Institute of Catechetical and Pastoral Studies, Associate Professor, Kenrick-Glennon Seminary, Archdiocese of St. Louis, MO**

"It brings the reader into the very heart of God. This fine, grace-filled workbook is a thoughtful and beautifully designed tool that allows the Holy Spirit to have his way with each reader. It's the only way to live!" **Dr. Ron and Adrienne Novotny, Co-Directors of the Cenacle of Our Lady of Divine Providence Retreat Center, Clearwater, FL**

A Review of Life and Healing Prayer
The Inner Heart of My Faith Journal

Overview

The Inner Heart of My Faith journal provides a simple format for narrative reflection uniting human formation and spiritual formation in a highly personal manner. It also emphasizes the need to increasingly awaken the human heart in exercising the gift of faith. The exercising of faith provides windows into seeing, assessing and discerning the human heart's desires, abilities, willingness and readiness to surrender to receiving and abiding in God's love, in Jesus' risen, pierced Heart.[2]

Uses

Awakening: The first purpose of this personal reflection instrument is to assist in awakening the human heart to the healing love that is readily accessible within Jesus' risen, pierced Heart.

When a person's living memories are allowed to be placed in relationship with Jesus' risen, pierced Heart, through exercising the gift of faith, healing always transpires. The type of healing simply needs to be discerned. God cannot but love us in His faithfulness (1 Cor 1:4-9). Any contact with Jesus' Heart heals and strengthens us (Eph 3:14-19; 4:11-24).

Living memories are accompanied by a variety of thoughts, feelings, and desires. Exercising Christian faith occurs whenever a person prays in childlike trust by acknowledging and relating thoughts, feelings and desires to Jesus' presence. Christian faith also transmits the

---

[2] St. John Eudes, *Liturgy of the Hours,* Vol. IV, 1331-1332.

heart of Jesus' own thoughts, feelings, and desires as we receive the mind of Christ through the activity of the Holy Spirit indwelling by way of baptism (1 Cor 2:10-16).[3]

The Holy Spirit's presence communicates love continually in our hearts, and this engenders new life that can only be received (Acts 17:22-25). The human heart cannot manufacture new life in the Spirit. A maturing faith understands this, in a growing humility, as the affective dimension of the human heart learns that real prayer is "pure receptivity" to God's love, and that it is God's plan to unite all things in himself—things in heaven and things on earth (Eph 1:3-10).[4]

This receiving requires an ongoing response if we are to grow in our call to holiness. The Christian understanding of healing love carries us into a joyful sharing in the suffering of Jesus' Heart so that His glory and love radiate through us for the sake of all that we meet (1 Pt 4:12-14).

When used well, this reflection instrument not only assists in the awakening of the human heart to the healing love of Jesus, but it also promotes Christian maturation in living the Gospel. As inner structures of unbelief and unforgiveness in the human heart receive deepening faith and Jesus' healing love; the call of the new evangelization can be realized, for the external structures of a culture of life and a civilization of love depend upon individuals who know how to interiorly receive and abide in Trinitarian love (2 Cor 4:13-18, 5:1-5; 1 Tim 4:1-10; Jas 4:1-10; Col 3:12-17).

Interior Data: The second purpose of *The Inner Heart of My Faith* journal is to establish a baseline ability to qualitatively measure affective maturation in living humbly, in the power of the Holy Spirit. It provides windows into "the affective dimension of the soul which gives the intellect and will their direction."[5] This baseline of affective data is what church leadership in human and spiritual formation needs in order to develop a variety of "spiritual readiness indicators" that serve all of the calls to holiness. The journal provides the affective, the human spirit's interior data, which is necessary for fruitful qualitative assessments that encourage Christian conversion and maturation (Col 1:27-29; Eph 4:11-16). When linked with assessments that focus on behavioral habits and the living out of Christian virtue,[6] this instrument provides a special encouragement for bishops, seminary rectors, vocation directors, priests, and lay leaders serving in Christian human and spiritual formation. The interior windows that help us see the human heart's desires, abilities and willingness to

---

[3] Ibid.

[4] Pope Benedict XVI, World Youth Day Homily (Randwick, July 20, 2008).

[5] Pope Benedict XVI, Jesus of Nazareth (Doubleday Publishing, 2007) 92-93.

[6] St. Columban, *Liturgy of the Hours,* Vol. IV, 1581-1582.

exercise the gift of faith by acknowledging, relating, receiving and responding with Jesus' indwelling Spirit are invaluable. These windows serve formators in the Christian life by helping them see relational reference points for maturing conversation for teaching and pastoral guidance.

Diagnostic Tool: The third purpose of *The Inner Heart of My Faith* journal is to provide a pastoral diagnostic tool that can serve spiritual directors, pastoral counselors and spiritual formation personnel in their ministries of healing. The healing of memories and particular relationships can be brought into the light of Jesus' desires. A particular relational focus can be identified (e.g., a particular sorrow or fear) so that the person completing the journal review can more readily receive the Holy Spirit's in-filling, healing love.

A Review of Life

How to Begin

This review of life invites you to remember people, events and relationships that shaped my attitudes about life. The reflection instrument used for your remembering is called *The Inner Heart of My Faith*. By participating in this way of reflecting upon your personal history, you are invited to ask for new faith in the risen Jesus' desire to heal your heart of anything that prevents you from receiving and giving love. You are invited into a way of praying that promises new life in the everyday as you learn to listen for and receive the words of love that Jesus' Heart speaks to your heart.

How to Proceed

1. Read "The Image: Jesus' Risen, Pierced Heart." This provides the foundation and overall context for your life review and entrance into healing prayer. All your personal memories will be placed in relationship with the living truth that this image communicates.

2. Review "Journal Reflection: *The Inner Heart of My Faith.*" This explains the purpose of the journal and how it is an instrument for reflection. It will be encouraging and provide a description of how to pray in a very personal way.

3. Look over the "Journal Reflection: *Instructions for The Inner Heart of My Faith.*" This will inform you about the process of entering into remembering major experiences of gratitude and thanksgiving, sorrow, anxiety and fear, love and joy, images of self and images of God, as well as remembering what you learned throughout life's ups

and downs. It will provide you with a sense of the timeline that is needed to complete the journaling. A prayer also is provided; you are invited to pray it frequently as you look back over your personal history.

4. Begin the process of working with and completing this review of life journal by making a commitment to take time to remember and reflect. It usually takes two to three weeks. The review and prayer is not so much a task to be done as a mystery to be remembered and savored, providing a narrative of your life.

The Image: Jesus' Risen, Pierced Heart

The living image of Jesus' risen and pierced Heart serves us as sovereign love. God as love abides in this living image. In faith, the image is not a metaphor; rather, by analogy, the reality of the living image communicates to our imaginations at prayer. We actually receive the living God as love by learning how to pray more relationally, thus living as contemplatives even in action. We are invited through this living image to learn to live a life of communion in the power of the Holy Spirit.

Images speak as they communicate to our hearts' desire to feel, hear, see, smell, touch, and taste love. The Holy Spirit can use images to actively draw us into reality, into being who we really are in relationship with God as love.

We all desire to know a love that is always desiring us. We want to be received in the depths of our hearts, by someone who wants to make a home with us (Jn 14:23; 19:25-27). Jesus' promise can kindle our desire to seek Him. He tells us, "Whoever loves me will keep my word, and my Father will love him, and we will come to him and make our dwelling with him" (Jn 14:23).

In prayer, if we truly seek Him, our heart can begin to receive from Jesus' risen and pierced Heart. Jesus' own sentiments and attitudes, His mind and Heart,[7] are within us (Rom 12:1-2). As Cardinal Newman says, the Christian's life of faith and prayer is where we taste and experience the truth that "heart speaks to heart" (*Cor ad cor loquitur*).

In the *Anima Christi* prayer, we pray "Jesus suffer me not to be separated from You" and "Jesus hide me in Your wounds." These beautiful phrases contain all of reality and all of history! Jesus' suffering love at the Calvary event now is risen, and from His pierced Heart flows the Holy Spirit, a fountain of refreshing love, a living water that saves, redeems, heals, and regenerates each of us to be who we really are in Christ (Col 3:1-4). From Jesus' risen,

---

[7] St. John Eudes, *Liturgy of the Hours*, Vol. IV, 1331-1332.

pierced Heart we are re-created, as is all of creation. All things are made new (Rom 8:18-30; Rev 21:5).

Anyone who learns how to really pray with this particular living image can count on receiving Jesus' healing love. This truth is acclaimed by St. Paul in Romans 8:31-39:

If God is for us, who can be against us? He who did not spare his own Son but handed him over for us all, how will he not also give us everything else along with him? Who will bring a charge against God's chosen ones? It is God who acquits us. Who will condemn? It is Christ [Jesus] who died, rather, was raised, who also is at the right hand of God, who indeed intercedes for us. What will separate us from the love of Christ? Will anguish, or distress, or persecution, or famine, or nakedness, or peril, or the sword? As it is written: / "For your sake we are being slain all the day; / we are looked upon as sheep to be slaughtered." / No, in all these things we conquer overwhelmingly through him who loved us. For I am convinced that neither death, nor life, nor angels, nor principalities, nor present things, nor future things, nor powers, nor height, nor depth, nor any other creature will be able to separate us from the love of God in Christ Jesus our Lord.

Indeed, whenever, in our littleness, we hide our hearts in Jesus' risen wounds, His pierced Heart, we can actively participate in the loving mystery, "as Christ's sufferings overflow to us, so through Christ does our encouragement also overflow" (2 Cor 1:5). Nothing can separate us from Jesus' love. We can learn to live in a prayerful communion with the Holy Spirit's desire to comfort and console us, especially at the Calvaries in our lives (2 Cor 1:3-7). We can become extensions or living images of Jesus' risen, pierced Heart. We can taste and see, in faith, the everyday triumph of love in Jesus' Heart.

Whenever we encounter suffering apart from the love of Christ, we can learn to surrender daily to being filled with the refulgent love of the Holy Spirit that flows for each of us from Jesus' risen, pierced Heart. This prayerful way of living in faith requires a daily, humble acknowledgement of what we humanly need and desire. It requires a childlike abandonment in trust to the Father's providence at work in all things (Rom 8:28-29) and the truth that He has already given us everything that is in His Heart, all that we need (Lk 15:31-32).

Learning each day to receive from the living image of Jesus' risen, pierced Heart calls us to an ongoing repentance for those times when we have listened to fears at work within our hearts, and not trusted that the Father desires to do everything for us. In Jesus' Heart, the truth is revealed in suffering beauty that the Father is caring and desires to lighten all of our burdens (Eph1:3-14; Mt 11:25-30).

When we pray in a relational manner with this living image, we are invited to hide in Jesus' risen, pierced Heart. There we can receive the confidence in faith that assures us in the Holy Spirit that love "bears all things, believes all things, hopes all things, endures all things. Love never fails" (1 Cor 13:7-8).

As we receive a new awareness of our personal history in *The Inner Heart of My Faith* prayer journal, the desire in Jesus' risen, pierced Heart is to pour the healing love of the Holy Spirit into our heart anew (Rom 5:5). Through this living image, all of the wounds within our heart can receive healing and become a glorified risen and pierced heart, in Jesus' Heart.

Mercy flows as we learn in humility and faith to unite our hearts to His Heart. We can trust that He is especially attracted to relieving our miseries, so much does Jesus' Heart burn with love for us (Heb 12:28-29). And we can trust that He desires to transform these miseries into new life because of the greatness of His love. Any rejection, any hurt, can be resurrected and transformed by Jesus' love. Any suffering was and is already contained in Jesus' risen, pierced Heart. He is the Lord of all history.

As we reflect, journal, and pray, may we run to Him in childlike trust as we revisit the events and relationships that fashioned our lives, our personal history. May we receive new life and the transforming power of His love (Jn 16:20-24; 1 Jn 1:1-4).

Journal Reflection:
The Inner Heart of My Faith

The purpose of this journal reflection and prayer is to further awaken the gift of faith in the hearts of all who give themselves over to the intentional remembering and healing prayer that is central to these spiritual exercises.

The Inner Heart of My Faith engages the affective dimension of our soul where the Holy Spirit's desire to communicate love can be sensed in everyday faith. Knowing and tasting the presence of the Holy Spirit as Consoler and Comforter invites us to fall more deeply in love with Jesus' Heart abiding within our hearts.[8] And we are invited through these exercises to learn how to abide in Jesus' loving Heart, through an ongoing, and surrendering to the Holy Spirit's presence so that we can enjoy fruitful living (Jn 15: 1-11).

Our hearts are made to belong to God, to the Trinity, to Love. We are His children. But often we have not experienced, in faith, the Holy Spirit' loving us amid all of the

---

[8] Ibid.

transitions, trials, and sufferings of life. This journal invites us to prayerfully read Hosea 11:1-4, and listen to what the Holy Spirit speaks to us: *When Israel was a child I loved him, / out of Egypt I called my son. / The more I called them, / the farther they went from me, / Sacrificing to the Baals / and burning incense to idols. / Yet it was I who taught Ephraim to walk, / who took them in my arms; / I drew them with human cords, / with bands of love; / I fostered them like one / who raises an infant to his cheeks; / Yet, though I stooped to feed my child, / they did not know that I was their healer.*

By contemplating the beauty and truth of these inspired words, we can recognize and sense, in faith, the wonderful truth that the Holy Spirit was with us in every moment of life. We can also begin to notice our desire to taste such a love, a love that heals and strengthens the inner self to live within Jesus' risen, pierced Heart (Eph 3:14-19).

The great paradox about Christian maturation is that it depends upon growing in childlike trust (Ps 131; Mt 19:13-14). This is how we come to mature and grow in stature within Jesus' Heart (Eph 3:14-19). As you reflect and remember, by journaling with *The Inner Heart of My Faith,* ask regularly for a renewal of faith and childlike trust in God's love. And ask the Holy Spirit to reveal how He was carrying you in His arms when you did not know it was Him. Pray by acknowledging and relating everything that is in your heart—all thoughts, feelings, and desires—to Jesus' risen, pierced Heart. Surely, in this personal heart to heart conversation you will receive an entirely new tasting and seeing of Jesus' love and desire to serve you (2 Cor 1:3-7; 1 Jn 1:1-4). You will need to respond to this reality in faith. Be encouraged! Pray as boldly and honestly, as much as is possible, trusting that Jesus' Heart is burning in love for you and all of your desires and needs (Heb 12:28-29).

Journal Instructions:
The Inner Heart of My Faith

Take a moment to look over the journal on page 12. The explanations below refer to the areas of reflection on the top of the journal pages. To fill out the journal, on each page in each section, use a word, phrase, or brief sentence which expresses your memory. Then name any thoughts, feelings, or desires that accompanied it. It is not necessary to fill out the section in great detail. If you are unable to complete certain segments, just leave them blank. Blank segments carry a value, too. Remember you are doing the exercise for yourself and to facilitate a spiritual conversation, a heart to heart conversation with the risen Jesus. It will be especially helpful to review your journal reflections and experiences in prayer with a spiritual friend or a spiritual director who can listen well and pray with you.

Chronology: Start on the first page of the journal and continue your reflection in three-year intervals from the year of your birth to the present year. Note that pages can be copied if more years are needed.

Basic Philosophy of Life and Key Relationships: In a phrase, provide a basic description of how you looked at your life experience. Key relationships include any relationship that you feel had a significant impact on your life at the time. The people mentioned need not be living now, and you need not have known them personally. In other words, key relationships could be people who influenced you through reading or hearing about them.

Major Experiences of Gratitude and Thanksgiving: What living memories of people, objects, institutions, and events recall experiences of real gratitude and thanksgiving? Describe simply these heartfelt experiences by naming the thoughts, feelings, and desires that accompanied them.

Major Experiences of Sorrow: What living memories of people, objects, institutions, and events recall experiences of real sorrow? Describe simply these heartfelt experiences by naming the thoughts, feelings and desires that accompanied them.

Major Experiences of Anxiety and Fear: What living memories of people, objects, institution, and events recall experiences of real anxiety and fear? Describe simply these heartfelt experiences by naming the thoughts, feelings, and desires that accompanied them.

Major Experiences of Anxiety and Fear: What living memories of people, objects, institution, and events recall experiences of real anxiety and fear? Describe simply these heartfelt experiences by naming the thoughts, feelings, and desires that accompanied them.

Major Experiences of Love and Joy: What living memories of people, objects, institutions, and events recall experiences of real love and joy? Describe simply these heartfelt experiences by naming the thoughts, feelings, and desires that accompanied them.

Image of Self: Here you can record how you thought and felt about yourself in the environments in which you lived, played, and worked. It may be helpful to describe how you spent your time, and/or name an image that portrays how you experienced life. It can also be helpful to remember and name what you were wanting or hoping for in life.

Icon of God: This is an invitation for you to record in a phrase or two what your thoughts about or images of God were (positive or negative) at different times in your life. If you had no image of God or cannot remember one, answer accordingly.

Heartfelt Revelations, Healings, and Teachings: Mention any pertinent learning that dawned for you and which significantly affected your growth in faith. Healings should be understood as any experience that significantly enlarged your heart's capacity to receive and to give love.

Timeline

The timeline for working with and completing this reflection instrument is general. The timeline is fashioned by what is possible given your life circumstances and age. A suggested timeline is two to three weeks. This reflection instrument is best approached by carving out a daily time of prayerful reflection and intentional remembering in faith. This is not so much a task to be done as it is entering into a personal mystery, a personal narrative that unveils and invites you to revisit your life story while believing in God's desire to pour healing love into your heart.

A Prayer to Pray

You are encouraged to pray the following words in your own manner as you spend time looking back over your life. May new faith be received. May the healing love in Jesus' risen, pierced Heart bless you and strengthen you in real hope.

Dear Jesus, I ask for a new depth of the gift of faith so that I can receive Your healing love for me. Take all of my thoughts, feelings, and desires—in every event and every relationship of my life—and unite them to Your burning Heart of love. I repent of any way in which I held on to them and did not trust that you were with me in them. Redeem and regenerate my heart with the thoughts, feelings, and desires that are abiding in Your loving Heart. And, help me to see, taste, touch, smell, and hear Your Holy Spirit's presence, because I believe that You desire to guide me and love others through me each day. Amen.

Upon Completion

After you have finished your work with the journal, spend some time thinking about your life as a whole. Try to feel its movement and its flow, its continuities and discontinuities, its desolations and consolations. As you look at the journal, let yourself imagine your life as a drama or a play. Where would the segments in it naturally fall? If you were to divide it into chapters or episodes, what would these be titled? When you have a sense of how your life might be divided into chapters, jot down the titles on the inside back cover of the journal.[9]

Reflection on this experience helps a person become aware of how Jesus' Spirit is active in his or her life. In the coming days or months, you may want to return to *The Inner Heart of My Faith* for deepening reflection and add things that may come up for you later. Some people find that this spiritual exercise is a good beginning for keeping a regular spiritual journal or diary. If you come back to this exercise after some time has passed, you may find that the chapters and titles in your life of faith will be different as you look at them in the light of new experiences.

---

[9] With permission, Fr. John Horn, S.J., of the Institute of Priestly Formation, adapted Dr. James Fowler's pastoral counseling reflection instrument called "The Unfolding Tapestry of Life." This adaptation focused reflection on human affectivity. This adaptation provides foundations for personal applications of St. Ignatius Loyola's Rules for the Discernment of Spirits. In Christian spirituality, the human heart's deepest affective movements are "spirits" to be discerned.

Journal Worksheet: *The Inner Heart of My Faith*

Chronology	Basic Philosophy of Life and Key Relationships	Major Experiences of Gratitude and Thanksgiving	Major Experiences of Sorrow	Major Experiences of Anxiety and Fear
0 – 3				
4 – 7				
8 – 11				
12 – 15				

Major Experiences of Love and Joy	Image of Self	Icon of God	Heartfelt Revelations, Healings, Teachings

Journal Worksheet: *The Inner Heart of My Faith*

Chronology	Basic Philosophy of Life and Key Relationships	Major Experiences of Gratitude and Thanksgiving	Major Experiences of Sorrow	Major Experiences of Anxiety and Fear
16 – 18				
19 – 21				
22 – 25				
26 – 29				

Major Experiences of Love and Joy	Image of Self	Icon of God	Heartfelt Revelations, Healings, Teachings

Journal Worksheet: *The Inner Heart of My Faith*

Chronology	Basic Philosophy of Life and Key Relationships	Major Experiences of Gratitude and Thanksgiving	Major Experiences of Sorrow	Major Experiences of Anxiety and Fear
30 – 33				
34 – 37				
38 – 41				
42 – 45				

Major Experiences of Love and Joy	Image of Self	Icon of God	Heartfelt Revelations, Healings, Teachings

Journal Worksheet: *The Inner Heart of My Faith*

Chronology	Basic Philosophy of Life and Key Relationships	Major Experiences of Gratitude and Thanksgiving	Major Experiences of Sorrow	Major Experiences of Anxiety and Fear

Major Experiences of Love and Joy	Image of Self	Icon of God	Heartfelt Revelations, Healings, Teachings

Preparing for Healing Prayer

How to Proceed

1. After completing the Journal Worksheet, reread your personal reflections alongside "A Journal Commentary: To Prepare for Healing Prayer."

2. Use the "Healing Prayer Journal Worksheet" on page 24-25 to list memories and accompanying thoughts and feelings that may be important areas to receive Jesus' healing love. In the space provided, describe the fuller stories surrounding the memories you desire to have healed.

A Journal Commentary:
To Prepare for Healing Prayer

Key Relationships: The invitation in faith is to trust that every key relationship in your life, from conception until the present moment, can be experienced and understood as a gift when placed in relationship within the light of Jesus' loving Heart. In and with Jesus all things work for the good (Rom 8:26-28).

Gratitude and Thanksgiving: Gratitude is a highway into Jesus' risen, pierced Heart. The more you actively thank and praise Jesus for having been present—in all of the circumstances and relationships of your life—especially when you did not feel like thanking Him—the more you will be able to abide in God's love. Often, sufferings closed you in on yourself, perhaps unknowingly. Perhaps you withdrew and isolated yourself, trying to fix the pain or acted in fear and shame rather than receive the love that was and is present for you in Jesus' risen, pierced Heart. You can now act in faith and open your heart to receive the healing and redeeming love of Jesus' Spirit. He will love you into new life (2 Cor 1:3; Phil 4:4-7).

Sorrow: Sorrow can be frightening because it reveals your real poverty-of-spirit. Christian sorrow shares the griefs that are alive in Jesus' Heart. Christian sorrow is accompanied by consolation because you can know, in faith, that you are not alone; you are with Jesus, sharing in His life, His rejections, His insults. The beautiful truth of the beatitude, "Blessed are they who mourn, / for they will be comforted," can be tasted in childlike trust (Mt 5:4).

Sorrow also can be rooted in pride. It can reveal where your heart's inner structures are not believing in the beauty and goodness of your littleness and God's powerful love at work in and through your smallness. If you do not let yourself receive a childlike faith, and act in childlike trust, you will be sad that you are not big and important according to the ways of the world. This type of sadness is not Christian. It reveals where fear and pride are gripping your heart, where a conversion in faith and more humility needs to replace self-centeredness. It can reveal ingratitude where you are not thankful for sharing in and with Jesus' suffering love (Gal 5:13-25).

Anxiety and Fear: In faith, you are invited to cast all anxiety and fear onto the loving heart of Jesus. Contact with love casts out fear (2 Tim 1:7; 1 Jn 4:15-19). There is nothing wrong with feeling anxiety and fear, but Christian faith calls you to receive God's love whenever you turn to Jesus' risen, pierced Heart to acknowledge, relate, and receive from Him. Your response of trust is a daily choice that does not re-open doors and windows of doubt or unbelief within your heart. Knowing what the patterns of anxiety and fear say in your heart is helpful so that you can act in faith by rejecting any interior thoughts, feelings, or desires that are opposed to Jesus' love within you (Eph 5:1-20).

Love and Joy: Where real love and joy have been tasted, you are called to recognize the presence of Jesus' Spirit. Perhaps you have not known in faith how Jesus' Spirit was personally present for you in love and joy throughout your life. Jesus' Spirit has always been pursuing you, desiring to reveal the totality of His love for you (Jn 10:14-18).

In faith, the question arises: "How much love and joy will you permit yourself to receive from Jesus' risen, pierced Heart?" The invitation is to see patterns where you have been deceived into thinking and believing that you can control God's desire to give Himself completely and lavishly to you in love. You also are invited to begin to see where and how you set the terms or limits of how much love you will permit yourself to receive before you take control of the relationship again. You are invited to pray and to ask Jesus' risen, pierced Heart to consume you in love. You are invited to identify with St. Thomas in John 20:24-28 and notice Jesus walking through the locked doors of your heart, so that all of your wounds from any self-made aloneness can now be placed into Jesus' risen, pierced Heart to receive healing love. Jesus tells you: "I will not leave you orphans; I will come to you" (Jn 14:18). Now is the time to receive awe and joy. Your redeemer lives! His love is alive and dwelling in your heart.

Image of Self: Is the image you have of yourself coming from seen through Jesus' eyes of love, or is it based upon interior judgments and conclusions that have fashioned your understanding apart from living in real faith? Praying within the truth of biblical images alive with love for you is important. Can you hear the Father's voice in the Holy Spirit saying to you, with love, what He said to Jesus at His baptism: "This is my beloved Son [daughter], with whom I am well pleased" (Mt 3:17)? Can you soak in the truth of your baptism in Jesus Christ by hearing and really receiving and trusting the words of Isaiah 43:4: "You are precious in my eyes"? True self images can emerge once you place your heart's thoughts, feelings, and desires in relationship with God's living Word in Scripture "I am a living image of God alive. I am the glory of God alive" (Gn 1:26-28; Col 3:3-4).[1] Jesus desires to complete your joy, carrying you into a new fullness of the Father's love (Jn 15:9-17; 16:29-33). You must surrender in trust to the truth of God's Word.

Icon of God: Whenever you have enjoyed relating to and receiving from a biblical image of God's love, you are invited in faith to discover how Jesus' Spirit desires to make these truths fresh and new each day. The invitation is to receive new depths of communion and strength within Jesus' risen, pierced Heart.

Perhaps your fear of the Father, who Jesus revealed, as someone who will punish you. Jesus' judgment and the Father's judgment are mercy. Jesus is attracted to your miseries to consume them within His loving Heart.[2] Perhaps fear arises in your heart, fear that the Father's authority will rival your deepest desires, and that He will deprive you of what you really want and need most. Praying with biblical images that are alive with the truth and beauty of the Father's tenderness and gentleness is helpful. The Father's Heart revealed in Jesus is always actively waiting for you to come home to live in Him. Whenever you turn toward Him to seek Him, the Father can be seen in faith, running toward you to kiss you. He celebrates with you, no matter how far you have allowed yourself to drift from living at home in His love. He also pleads with you to recognize that "everything I have is yours" (Lk 15:11-32). This can cut through your interior patterns of unbelief where you have been deceived into thinking that you need to earn the Father's love. Turn to the Father in prayer, and ask Him for new faith to receive the truth and beauty of His love for you, revealed in Jesus' loving Heart.

Revelation, Healings, Teachings: The invitation in faith is to savor and receive more from the loving activity of the indwelling Trinity: Abba, Jesus, and the Holy Spirit are at work in your heart. By intentionally savoring God's presence, you can learn and enjoy obedience in faith. There is always more love for you to receive in Jesus' risen, pierced Heart. His love is infinite. As you pray and come to realize the overarching truth of Hosea 11:1-4, tasting and seeing how God was present and active throughout your life, a desire to have others come to know Jesus' love, will dawn. Ask Him to heal and redeem every moment of your life and to strengthen His life within your heart (Eph 3:14-21).

May the emerging desire to have others come to know the love of Jesus' Heart become a thirst within you. May you humbly learn how to continually pour yourself out in love, for love, to become love. As Jesus said:

---

[1] St. Irenaeus, *Liturgy of the Hours*, Vol. IV, 1499.

[2] Fr. Jean C.J. d'Elbée, *I Believe in Love,* 2nd ed. (Manchester, N.H.: Sophia Institute Press, 2001), 29.

I give praise to you, Father, Lord of heaven and earth, for although you have hidden these things from the wise and the learned you have revealed them to the childlike. Yes, Father, such has been your gracious will. All things have been handed over to me by my Father. No one knows the Son except the Father, and no one knows the Father except the Son and anyone to whom the Son wishes to reveal him. Come to me, all you who labor and are burdened, and I will give you rest. Take my yoke upon you and learn from me, for I am meek and humble of heart; and you will find rest for yourselves. For my yoke is easy, and my burden light. (Mt 11:25-30)

Guidelines: To Prepare
For Healing Prayer

Within the human heart are two sets of inner structures, two inner ways of thinking, feeling, and desiring. One set of these inner patterns or structures thinks, feels, and desires with Jesus' Spirit. This pattern is created by living in childlike trust in the Father's providence at work in all things. This inner way of being unites you to Jesus' Heart.

The second set of inner patterns at work in your heart are thoughts, feelings, and desires that create a hellish, self-made aloneness. These patterns are evil because they maintain or promote self-centeredness and self-reliance rather than dependence upon God. These inner structures prevent you from receiving the Holy Spirit's desire to comfort you in all suffering (2 Cor 1:3-7).

The first set of the heart's inner structures breed new life in and with Jesus' risen, pierced Heart. These are structures of faith that readily forgive, in and with Jesus' Heart. The second set of the human heart's inner structures are structures of isolation and self-absorption. They breed evil and death. These are structures of unbelief where despair, shame, fear, and doubt prevent you from entering into real, loving relationships. Interior structures of unforgivingness can compel you to harshly judge yourself and others while managing pain instead of entrusting it to the loving Father, who only desires to make all things new (Rev 21:1-7).

As you pray through your reflections within *The Inner Heart of My Faith* journal, taste and see how the goodness of God has been at work every day, in your personal history. Re-read and pray with the text of Hosea 11:1-4. Allow the Holy Spirit write history through you in the days ahead, as your heart's interior structures of faith and love are strengthened through receiving love from God in prayer. Surely, interior structures of unbelief and unforgivingness will be brought to light for healing within Jesus' risen, pierced Heart.

As the consoling patterns of Jesus' Spirit become more recognizable within you, may you fall more deeply in love with Jesus' risen, pierced Heart (Jn 14:18-28). May you praise, reverence, and serve this Heart always!

But before re-reading and entering into several days and weeks of healing prayer, receive the encouragement offered in these inspiring words of St. John Eudes:

All that is his is yours: breath, heart, body, soul and all his faculties. All of these you must use as if they belonged to you, so that in serving him you may give him praise, love and glory. You belong to him as a member belongs to the head. This is why he earnestly desires to serve and glorify the Father by using all your faculties as if they were his. He belongs to you, but more than that, he longs to be in you, living and ruling in you, as the head lives and rules in the body. He desires that whatever is in him may live and rule in you: his breath in your breath, his heart in your heart, all the faculties of his soul in the faculties of your soul, so that these words may be fulfilled in you: "Glorify God and bear him in your body, that the life of Jesus may be made manifest in you."

You belong to the Son of God, but more than that, you ought to be in him as members are in the head ... Apart from him you will find only death and destruction. Let him be the only source of your movements, of the actions and the strength of your life ...

Finally, you are one with Jesus as the body is one with the head. You must, then, have one breath with him, one soul, one life, one will, one mind, one heart. And he must be your breath, heart, love, life, your all. These great gifts in the follower of Christ originate from baptism ... Through the Holy Eucharist they are brought to perfection.[3]

---

[3] St. John Eudes, *Liturgy of The Hours*, Volume IV, From a Treatise on the Admirable Heart of Jesus, 1331-1332.

Journal Worksheet: *The Inner Heart of My Faith*

Chronology	Basic Philosophy of Life and Key Relationships	Major Experiences of Gratitude and Thanksgiving	Major Experiences of Sorrow	Major Experiences of Anxiety and Fear

Major Experiences of Love and Joy	Image of Self	Icon of God	Heartfelt Revelations, Healings, Teachings

Healing Prayer in an At-Home Retreat

How to Proceed

1. Begin by reading "How to Pray with My Journal Reflections."

2. Look over the section "Praying Healing Prayer: Hide Me in Your Wounds." This invites you into understanding the operating definition of your experience of prayer. It also provides the Scripture passages that serve you in this encounter with the living truth of Jesus' risen, pierced Heart, speaking new words of healing love to your heart.

3. Pray using the segments set aside to Acknowledge, Relate, Receive, and Respond. These pages can be copied and used for personal journaling as much as is needed as I review my life and pray to receive more of Jesus' healing love.

How to Pray with My Journal Reflections

The Inner Heart of My Faith is a resource you can use to enjoy a retreat that promises healing in the midst of your busy life. People go on retreats all the time and for many different reasons. Some retreats are at monasteries, others are at retreat centers, and still others are at churches. Regardless of how or where, a retreat is essentially a time where a person commits to being present to God: to pray, to listen, to receive, and to respond to God's love.

But you are busy and getting away is difficult, right? This at-home retreat is just for you as you learn to pray in a more personal way and exercise your desire to receive healing love from the living image of Jesus' risen, pierced Heart. A few helpful hints will assist you as you begin.

Getting Started

The first thing you need is commitment. In John 15:16, Jesus says, "It was not you who chose me, but I who chose you." Jesus has called you to reflect upon and pray through your life history. He desires you to know how loved you were and are at every moment of life. He also wants to write history through you as you allow His love to flow through your heart to others. So, when you commit to praying every day, you commit to a person, Jesus, who is committed to being with you as you pray. His Holy Spirit is dwelling in your heart. His Heart is already speaking in your heart. Prayer is all about learning to listen for the Holy Spirit, the Consoler, and humbly receiving love in everyday faith.

Find a place—a room, a church, a park, wherever. Find a place where you can focus on God without distractions. Find a place where you can relax, be still and listen to what is happening in your heart.

Make time. Ask Jesus to show you how to find the time. You are busy, and perhaps finding 20-30 minutes each day will require you to sacrifice doing some of your favorite things.

Hosea 11:1-4 is the overarching theme of this at-home retreat. Ask regularly for a renewal of faith and childlike trust in God's love for you as you enter into praying with *The Inner Heart of My Faith* journal.

Praying with ARRR (Acknowledge, Relate, Receive, Respond)

As you sit with God's Word in Hosea 11:1-4 in light of all of your reflections in *The Inner Heart of My Faith* journal, let yourself feel what God is saying to you. *Acknowledge* what stirs within you. Pay attention to your thoughts, feelings, and desires. These are really important.

Once you have *acknowledged* what is going on inside your heart, *relate* that to God, to Jesus' risen, pierced Heart. Do not just think about what is being stirred in your heart. Do not just think about God. Do not just think about how Jesus might react. *Relate* to God, to Jesus' Heart. Tell Him how you feel. Tell Him what you think. Tell Him what you want. Share all your thoughts, feelings, and desires with God. Share everything with Jesus' risen, pierced Heart.

Once you have shared everything with God, pay attention and learn to *receive*. Listen to what He is telling you. It could be a subtle voice you hear. It could be a memory that is highlighted. Maybe Jesus invites you to re-read the Scripture passage. Perhaps you feel something in your body. Perhaps He invites you into a still, restful silence. Trust that God is listening to you and *receive* what He wants to share with you. Notice any change in the thoughts, feelings, and desires you initially related to Christ. The presence of God is often experienced through a simple transformation of these movements. He speaks in any heartfelt increase in faith, hope, or love.

Now *respond* however you want. It could be more conversation; it could be a resolve to abide with His presence; it could be tears or laughter. In some way you are encouraged to say your "yes" to Jesus' risen presence. *Respond* to what you are receiving.

In your own words ask for the courage to *receive* more of the love for you that abides in Jesus' risen, pierced Heart.

If you feel blocked in an inability to pray, simply ask for a deepening faith and desire to be with Jesus' love. Check to see if there is some unbelief that is being challenged or some unforgiveness in your heart toward yourself or another. Ongoing forgiveness in Jesus' name keeps the doors in your heart's many rooms open to receive Jesus' healing and redeeming love (Jn 14:1-7).[1]

Praying Healing Prayer

"Hide Me in Your Wounds"...
Believing in Faith, Repenting, and Forgiving

Christian prayer is not something you do. Prayer is permitting the Trinitarian God to love you as you learn in childlike trust to acknowledge, relate, receive, and respond (ARRR) within your heart to the Holy Spirit's presence, love pursuing you and desiring to communicate with you (Ps 131 and Rom 8:26-28).

Whenever Christian prayer is real it involves each of these dimensions of personal communication. And real prayer always strengthens and heals the human heart. God as love can only heal. Jesus promises not to leave us desolate because of His love (Jn 14:18-24). The Living Word of God proclaims and actualizes Jesus' teaching, "I came so that they might have life and have it more abundantly" (Jn 10:10).

Pope Benedict XVI gives you a beautiful description of Christian prayer that you can apply to your heart. You are invited here to see the activities of Trinitarian healing love at work in your heart. Pope Benedict XVI writes:

Yet this power, the grace of the Spirit, is not something we can merit or achieve, but only receive as pure gift. God's love can only unleash its power when it is allowed to change us from within. We have to let it break through the hard crust of our indifference, our spiritual weariness, our blind conformity to the spirit of this age. Only then can we let it ignite our imagination and shape our deepest desires. That is why prayer is so important: daily prayer, private prayer in the quiet of our hearts before the Blessed Sacrament, and liturgical prayer in the heart of the Church. Prayer is pure receptivity to God's grace, love in action, communion with the Spirit who dwells within us, leading us, through Jesus, in the Church, to our heavenly Father. In the power of his Spirit, Jesus is always

---

[1] Fr. Mark Toups, *"Theotokos"* (Adore Resources, 2008) 3. Used with permission, this segment is a series of quotes and adaptations of Fr. Mark Toups' writing in *"Theotokos,"* an Advent Retreat.

present in our hearts, quietly waiting for us to be still with him, to hear his voice, to abide in his love and to receive power from on high, enabling us to be salt and light for our world.[2]

As you remember particular aspects of your review of life, and if you pause and pray with Isaiah 53:1-5 and John 20:24-28 while asking God for a new childlike faith, you can make many particular applications of ARRR within the truth and beauty of Pope Benedict's words. Truly you are being healed by His stripes, His wounds, as you identify with St. Thomas the Apostle from St. John's Gospel and place your wounds within the risen, pierced Heart of Jesus.

(Is 53:1-5) *Who would believe what we have heard? / To whom has the arm of the* LORD *been revealed? / He grew up like a sapling before him, / like a shoot from the parched earth; /There was in him no stately bearing to make us look at him, / nor appearance that would attract us to him. / He was spurned and avoided by men, / a man of suffering, accustomed to infirmity, / One of those from whom men hide their faces, / spurned, and we held him in no esteem.*

Yet it was our infirmities that he bore, / our sufferings that he endured, / While we thought of him as stricken, / as one smitten by God and afflicted. / But he was pierced for our offenses, / crushed for our sins, / Upon him was the chastisement that makes us whole, / by his stripes we were healed.

(Jn 20:24-28) *Thomas, called Didymus, one of the Twelve, was not with them when Jesus came. So the other disciples said to him, "We have seen the Lord." But he said to them, "Unless I see the mark of the nails in his hands and put my finger into the nailmarks and put my hand into his side, I will not believe." Now a week later his disciples were again inside and Thomas was with them. Jesus came, although the doors were locked, and stood in their midst and said, "Peace be with you." Then he said to Thomas, "Put your finger here and see my hands, and bring your hand and put it into my side, and do not be unbelieving, but believe." Thomas answered and said to him, "My Lord and my God!"*

---

[2] Pope Benedict XVI, World Youth Day Homily (Randwick, July 20, 2008).

Journal: ARRR (Acknowledge, Relate, Receive, Respond)

Acknowledge: Permit yourself to be attentive and aware of all of your thoughts, feelings, and desires as you prayerfully re-read these passages from Scripture. It is important that you not edit out or omit any thoughts, feelings, or desires that you judge to be wrong to be experiencing. Thoughts, feelings, and desires are amoral, not right or wrong. What you do with them in faith is what relationally matters in Christian moral living. Do you relate all of your thoughts, feelings, and desires to Jesus' risen, pierced Heart, or do you simply sit in your awareness of them? This can be an easy way to get stuck in a self-centered awareness. If you just think about your thoughts, feelings, and desires or just think about God, you have not truly prayed. You must *relate* and *receive* in relationship with Jesus' loving, risen, pierced Heart.

What are the thoughts, feelings, and desires present in your heart as you prayerfully re-read Isaiah 53:1-5 and John 20:24-28 in light of any particular aspect of your review of life journaling?

My Thoughts:_____

_____

_____

_____

My Feelings:_____

_____

_____

_____

My Desires:_____

_____

_____

_____

Relate: You can now place all of your thoughts, feelings, and desires in the risen, pierced Heart of Jesus, hiding them in a real sense within Jesus' loving wounds. You can let go in a variety of ways. You can invite Jesus' presence into everything you have *acknowledged*. In your own way you can present your personal needs. But it is vital that you do not just talk about your needs, speaking in the third person as if Jesus were distant. You are invited to speak to Jesus directly in the first person. Jesus' loving heart is not distant, rather He is immediately present, dwelling within your heart. You must speak to Jesus not *about* your thoughts, feelings, and desires but *from* them. You must permit yourself to be vulnerable in a real, trust-filled relationship.

There is a need, a call by Jesus to relate believing in His divine love, that He alone is Lord. There is a call to believe that Jesus desires to heal my heart. In this friendship, there is a need to repent of any way that I did not entrust my pain to Jesus' Heart during any suffering that I endured throughout my life.

Wherever I sinned mysteriously by turning in on myself, holding on to anger, sorrow, fear, anxiety, or resentment of any kind is a place in my heart where I need to actively repent and turn to Jesus in this new depth of relationship. I need to actively forgive anyone who injured or hurt me. I also need to actively repent of the ways I turned anger, sorrow, fear, anxiety, and resentment against myself. My humanity is Jesus' humanity. I am a temple of His Holy Spirit. Whenever I have rejected the goodness and beauty of my own humanity in Christ, I reject Him. Jesus is my human poverty-of-spirit, my weakness, my littleness. When I dislike or disdain my poverty-of-spirit, my human weakness and littleness, I am divided against my true self in Christ Jesus. He is indwelling through my Baptism. He lives in my heart.

After repentance, I need to forgive and bless in, with, and through the all-powerful Name of Jesus. I call to mind and remember who it was who injured or hurt me; and as they come to mind, I pray forgiveness for each of them in the Name of Jesus. Then, I bless them in the Name of Jesus. This healing prayer creates a new unity between my heart and Jesus' Heart. It also serves the one(s) who offended me by sending real blessings to them in Jesus' Spirit.

Following this spiritual exercising, I am called to make a commitment in faith to remain in emptiness with Jesus' poverty-of-spirit living within me. I am called to choose to remain with Jesus, abiding in His disposition of depending on the Father's providential care at all times. In abiding with Jesus in this poverty-of-spirit, I permit myself to receive the Holy Spirit's power in my daily life.

Journal and express your thoughts, feelings, and desires to Jesus' loving Heart in light of any particular aspect of your review of life.

My Thoughts:_____

_____

_____

_____

My Feelings:_____

_____

_____

My Desires:_____

_____

_____

Receive: Once you have *related* to Jesus' loving Heart anything and everything present in your heart, you are invited to exercise the gift of faith and wait in childlike trust to *receive* communication from Jesus' Spirit indwelling. He is mercy and forgiveness. Remaining vulnerably receptive to God as love is utterly important. Let waiting on the Lord be your strength (Ps 18:2 and Ex 14:14, 15:2), exercising courage rather than listening to inner fears that would have you either withdraw from trusting in God or become self–assertive and overactive, trying to control the relationship with God. If you trust that God is faithful and full of love for you (1 Cor 1:4-9), you will *receive* more than you can ask for or imagine (Eph 3:20-21). Jesus' risen, pierced Heart is yearning to heal, forgive, repair, and enlighten your heart (Jn 14:12-27).

Describe your experience and what transpired as you *related* and entrusted all of your thoughts, feelings, and desires to Jesus' risen and pierced Heart. A particular aspect of your review of life can be highlighted here.

My Thoughts:_____

_____

_____

My Feelings:_____

_____

_____

My Desires:_____

_____

_____

Respond: What is your *response* to God's presence in faith? You may sense Jesus' Spirit consoling your heart. You may need to exercise faith by further entrusting a struggle or standing against the lies that a desolation is speaking to your heart. Again, be honest, vulnerable and humble in *responding* to what you have *received*. Trinitarian relationships are real. These develop and unfold and mature in time as you learn to open you heart to Jesus' loving Heart. Discovering an inner resistance to your relationship with Jesus' risen, pierced Heart can be a very positive sign. The resistance signifies activity in the relationship. An inner threshold of something new is most likely ready to in-break within your relationship with God. More believing, repenting, forgiving, and new blessing will transpire as you mature in being with and adhering to Jesus' Spirit. If there were no active resistances, no activity, something in your heart would be dead. There is no neutral in a relationship with God. You are either growing closer in love each day or more distant in a self-made deadening aloneness.

Discovering an inner refusal to *acknowledge, relate,* and *receive* reveals a real problem. An inner refusal is turning a deaf ear to God's desire to communicate with you. Such refusal is a step away from being willing to seek after, listen for, and follow Jesus as the Way, the Truth, and the Life (Jn 14:6-7). This can only lead to personal destruction.[3]

Humbly saying yes to Jesus Spirit's ongoing communications will yield new life (Rom 8:14). You will receive victory over the fear of death if you respond in self-emptying humility by thanking the Father for His presence in any suffering and by releasing any and all pain that accompanies life's sufferings. Jesus' own cries within you, when *acknowledged* and *related,* will open your heart to *receive* the Father's faithful, resurrecting, and consoling love (Rom 8:14, 37-39; 2 Cor 1:3-10, 1 Peter 3:3-9).

Honestly describe your inner heart's *response* in faith to Jesus' risen, pierced Heart.

My Thoughts:_____

_____

_____

_____

My Feelings:_____

_____

_____

_____

---

[3] St. John Eudes, *Liturgy of the Hours*, Volume IV, 1331-1332.

My Desires:_____

_____

_____

_____

Surely, as you mature in humility, by *receiving* the healing light and love of the Holy Spirit, your formal prayer and prayerful living will carry you into becoming who you contemplate. All of your heart's wounds can become a living image of Jesus' risen, pierced Heart. This revolution of healing love can begin to be enjoyed today, and into eternity. [4]

The Sacrament of Penance: Confession

For Catholic Christians, the Sacrament of Penance or "Confession" offers an inestimable gift of healing forgiveness. The fullness of the affection and mercy of Jesus' Risen Heart is bestowed upon the heart of the believer as the priest prays the Church's absolution. In receiving this in-filling of Jesus' Spirit, the believer's heart is not only consoled but regenerated by mercy, so much so that a greater good now transpires for the forgiven sinner than if he or she had not sinned.

Following this review of life, it is most beneficial to enter into the Sacrament of Penance, Confession, which can be done by making an appointment to see a priest. You may want to opt for an anonymous confession instead. It offers a unique sense of security and safety. The private appointment for face-to-face conversational celebration of the Sacrament is a way of assuring adequate time to make a "general confession." This type of confession is a review of life in which the content for the confession consists of naming omissions and commissions in light of the Ten Commandments and the Beatitudes. A general confession can also be brief and simple. I can receive a new past and a hope-filled future when Jesus' Spirit is poured into my heart in the present moment in and around a pattern of fear in my life that is brought to light, acknowledged, and confessed. The priest's absolution in the name of Jesus as head of the Church heals me in the present moment which contains the past in my memory. The present moment in time is Jesus' vehicle for making me a new creation. After all, He is Lord of all time, governing history.

Fruitful confessions consist in naming fears, angers, sorrows, anxieties, and resentments that I have not surrendered or entrusted to Jesus' Heart, through my life.

---

[4] Joseph Cardinal Ratzinger, *Behold the Pierced One* (Fort Collins, Colo.: Ignatius Press, 1986), 69.

Confessions may contain an identification of lies or inner vows, attitudes of my heart, where I have not believed the truth and beauty of Jesus' love for me. I may want to confess my unbelief of who I am in His sight.

Lies and matters of unbelief or unforgiveness often stem from believing the thoughts, feelings, and desires that accompany the inner pain of shame and fear. I can often take on a false identity that does not flow from Jesus' love and regenerating mercy. The Aids to Foster Belief, Repentance, and Forgiveness section below provides several tools that will assist you to prayerfully prepare for this manner of celebrating Jesus' healing forgiveness in the Sacrament of Penance, Confession.

Following a "general confession" that is based upon a review of life, frequent ordinary confession is encouraged. This will serve to strengthen my true identity in Jesus' Spirit. Regular ordinary confession can be brief and simple as I permit myself to receive forgiving love and mercy from Jesus' Heart. In the Sacrament of Penance, the truth is that my particular heart becomes the focal point for receiving Jesus' love and mercy. When the priest prays the absolution blessing, a sending of the in-filling presence of the Holy Spirit, places of unbelief and sinfulness are regenerated by God's mercy. I begin to taste that He died personally for me. I begin to experience in faith all that is His is mine. I learn again that Jesus delights in doing everything for me. Wherever I have pulled away from abiding in Jesus' poverty-of-spirit, a new confidence dawns because of His tireless mercy that lifts me up to begin anew.[5]

Pope Francis's inspired words offer us deep encouragement. He writes:

> "I invite all Christians, everywhere, at this very moment, to a renewed personal encounter with Jesus Christ, or at least an openness to letting him encounter them; I ask all of you to do this unfailingly each day. No one should think that this invitation is not meant for him or her, since 'no one is excluded from the joy brought by the Lord.' The Lord does not disappoint those who take this risk; whenever we take a step towards Jesus, we come to realize that he is already there, waiting for us with open arms. Now is the time to say to Jesus: 'Lord, I have let myself be deceived; in a thousand ways I have shunned your love, yet here I am once more, to renew my covenant with you. I need you. Save me once again, Lord, take me once more into your redeeming embrace.' How good it feels to come back to him whenever we are lost! Let me say this once more: God never tires of forgiving us; we are the ones who tire of

---

[5] The *Catechism of the Catholic Church* (sec. 2546) defines "poverty in spirit" as "voluntary humility."

seeking his mercy. Christ, who told us to forgive one another 'seventy times seven' (Mt 18:22) has given us his example: he has forgiven us seventy times seven. Time and time again he bears us on his shoulders. No one can strip us of the dignity bestowed upon us by this boundless and unfailing love. With a tenderness which never disappoints, but is always capable of restoring our joy, he makes it possible for us to lift up our heads and to start anew. Let us not flee from the resurrection of Jesus ..."[6]

Encouraging Truths from the Saints

"I appeal to you by the mercy of God. This appeal is made by Paul, or rather, it is made by God through Paul, because of God's desire to be loved rather than feared, to be a father rather than a Lord. God appeals to us in his mercy to avoid having to punish us in his severity.

Listen to the Lord's appeal: In me, I want you to see your own body, your members, your heart, your bones, your blood. You may fear what is divine, but why not love what is human? You may run away from me as the Lord, but why not run to me as your father? Perhaps you are filled with shame for causing my bitter passion. Do not be afraid. This cross inflicts a mortal injury, not on me, but on death. These nails no longer pain me, but only deepen your love for me. I do not cry out because of these wounds, but through them I draw you into my heart. My body was stretched on the cross as a symbol not of how much I suffered, but of my all-embracing love. I count it no loss to shed my blood: it is the price I have paid for your ransom. Come, then, return to me and learn to know me as your father, who repays good for evil, love for injury, and boundless charity for piercing wounds.

Listen now to what the Apostle urges us to do. I appeal to you, he says, to present your bodies as a living sacrifice." – **St. Peter Chrysologus**[7]

"May the Heart of Jesus Christ be our school! Let us make our abode there. Let us study its movements and attempt to conform ours to them. Yes, O Divine Jesus, I want to live there." – **St. Claude de la Colombiére, S.J.**

"My love reigns in suffering, it triumphs in humility and enjoys itself in unity." – **Jesus to St. Margaret Mary**

---

[6] Pope Francis, *Evangelii Gaudium* (2013), sec. 3.

[7] St. Peter Chrysologus, Liturgy of the Hours, Vol. II, 770-771.

"I need nothing but God, and to lose myself in the Heart of Jesus." – **St. Margaret Mary**

"Where can the weak find a place of firm security and peace, except in the wounds of the Savior? Indeed the more secure is my place there the more He can do to help me. The world rages, the flesh is heavy, and the devil lays his snares, but I do not fall, for my feet are planted on firm rock. I may have sinned gravely. My conscience would be distressed, but it would not be in turmoil, for I would recall the wounds of the Lord: He was wounded for our iniquities. What sin is there so deadly that it cannot be pardoned by the death of Christ? And so if I bear in mind this strong, effective remedy, I can never again be terrified by the malignancy of sin.

He was thinking thoughts of peace, and I did not know it: for who knows the mind of the Lord or who has been His counselor? But the piercing nail has become a key to unlock the door, that I may see the good will of the Lord. And what can I see as I look through the whole? Both the nail and the wound cry out that God was in Christ reconciling the world to Himself. The sword pierced His soul and came close to His Heart, so that He might be able to feel compassion for me in my weaknesses.

Through these sacred wounds we can see the secret of His Heart, the great mystery of love, the sincerity of His mercy with which He visited us from on high. Where have your love, your mercy, your compassion shone out more luminously than in your wounds, sweet, gentle Lord of mercy?" – **St. Bernard[8]**

"The loveliest masterpiece of the Heart of God is the heart of a mother." – **St. Thérèse of Lisieux**

"Without love, deeds, even the most brilliant, count as nothing." – **St. Thérèse of Lisieux**

"Let us love, since that is all our hearts were made for." – **St. Thérèse of Lisieux**

"In loving and serving, we prove that we have been created in the likeness of God, for God is Love and when we love we are like God." – **Saint Mother Teresa of Calcutta**

"Intense love does not measure ... it just gives." – **Saint Mother Teresa of Calcutta**

---

[8] St. Bernard, Liturgy of the Hours, Vol. III, 125-126.

"Yesterday is gone. Tomorrow has not yet come. We have only today. Let us begin."
– Saint Mother Teresa of Calcutta

"Moses wrote in the law: God made man in his image and likeness. Consider, I ask you, the dignity of these words. God is all-powerful. We cannot see or understand him, describe or assess him. Yet he fashioned man from clay and endowed him with the nobility of his own image. What has man in common with God? Or earth with spirit?—For God is a spirit. It is a glorious privilege that God should grant man his eternal image and the likeness of his character. Man's likeness to God, if he preserves it, imparts high dignity.

If man applies the virtues planted in his soul to the right purpose, he will be like God. God's commands have taught us to give him back the virtues he sowed in us in our first innocence. The first command is to love our Lord with our whole heart because he loved us first from the beginning, before our existence. Loving God renews his image in us. Anyone who loves God keeps his commandment, for he said: if you love me, keep my commandments. His command is that we love each other. In his own words: This is my command, that you love each other as I also have loved you.

True love is shown not merely in word, but in deed and in truth. So we must turn back our image undefiled and holy to our God and Father, for he is holy; in the words of Scripture: Be holy, for I am holy. We must restore his image with love, for he is love; in John's words: God is love. We must restore it with loyalty and truth, for he is loyal and truthful." **– St. Columban**[9]

"The priesthood is the Heart of Jesus." **– St. John Mary Vianney**

"Cordial love of the neighbor does not consist in feelings. This love flows not from a heart of flesh but from the heart of our will." **– St. Jane de Chantal**

"Since love grows within you, so beauty grows. For love is the beauty of the soul."
– St. Augustine

"The glory of God is the human person fully alive." **– St. Irenaeus**

---

[9] St. Columban, Liturgy of the Hours, Vol. IV, 1581-1582.

"I saw the abyss of my misery; whatever there is of good in me is Yours, O Lord. But because I am so small and wretched, I have a right to count on Your boundless mercy." – **St. Faustina Kowalska**

"Pure love … knows that only one thing is needed to please God: to do even the smallest things out of great love—love, and always love." – **St. Faustina Kowalska**

"May each one of us glorify the Lord with the soul of Mary and rejoice in God with the spirit of Mary." – **St. Ambrose**

"'Look, Daughter, and learn how to love' and He showed me His five open wounds."
– **St. Gemma Galgani**

"Perfect love of God means the complete union of our will with God's."
– **St. Alphonsus Ligouri**

"The things that we love tell us what we are." – **St. Thomas Aquinas**

Prayers

Take and Receive

Take, Lord, and receive all my liberty, my memory, my understanding and my entire will, all that I have and possess. You have given all to me. To you, O Lord, I return it. All is yours: dispose of it wholly according to your will. Give me your love and your grace, for this is enough for me. – **St. Ignatius Loyola**

Consecration to the Holy Spirit

O Holy Spirit, receive the perfect and complete consecration of my whole being. In all my actions, grant me the grace of being my Light, my Guide, and my Strength and the Love of my heart. I ask of you the grace to be faithful to your inspirations. Transform me through Mary, and in Mary, into a true image of Christ Jesus, for the glory of the Father and for the salvation of the world. Amen.

Act of Hope and Confidence in God

My God, I believe most firmly

that you watch over all who hope in you,

and that we can want for nothing

when we rely upon you in all things.

Therefore I am resolved for the future …

to cast all my cares upon you …

People may deprive me of worldly goods and status.

Sickness may take from me my strength

and the means of serving you.

I may even jeopardize our relationship by sin, but my trust shall never leave me.

I will preserve it to the last moment of my life, and the powers of hell shall seek in vain to grab it from me.

Let others seek happiness in their wealth and in their talents.

Let them trust in the purity of their lives,

the severity of their mortification,

in the number of their good works,

the enthusiasm of their prayers,

as for me, my Rock and my Refuge,

my confidence in you fills me with hope.

For you, my Divine Protector,

alone have settled me in hope.

This confidence can never be vain.

No one, who has hoped in God,

has ever been confounded.

I am assured, therefore, of my eternal happiness, for I firmly hope in it and all my hope is in you.

In you, O loving God, have I hoped:

let me never be confounded.

I know too well that I am weak and changeable.

I know the power of temptation against the strongest virtue.

I have seen stars fall and foundations of my world crack; these things do not alarm me. While I hope in you, I am sheltered from all misfortune, and I am sure that my trust shall endure, for I rely upon you to sustain this unfailing hope.

Finally, I know that my confidence
cannot exceed your generosity,
and that I shall never receive less
than I have hoped for from you.
Therefore I hope that you will sustain me against my evil inclinations, that you will
protect me against the deceitful attacks of the evil one, and that you will cause my
weakness to triumph over every hostile force. I hope that you will never cease to love
me and that I shall love you unceasingly.
In you, O loving God, have I hoped:
let me never be confounded.
– St. Claude de la Colombière, S.J.

Jesus I Know That You Make Reparation in Me

A beautiful prayer to pour forth from your heart throughout the day is "Jesus, repair what I
have done badly; supply for what I have left undone."
Or an even more beautiful way to pray is "Jesus, I know that You make reparation in me, that
You supply for me; I know that You will draw the good from the bad that I do, and even,
as St. Augustine said, 'a greater good than if there had been no evil in it.' Is this not
worthy of adoration? I have a Jesus who does all that in me and for me!" [10]

Anima Christi

Soul of Christ, sanctify me.
Body of Christ, save me.
Blood of Christ, inebriate me.
Water from the side of Christ, wash me.
Passion of Christ, strengthen me.
O good Jesus, hear me;
Within your wounds hide me;
Suffer me not to be separated from you;
From the malignant enemy defend me;

---

[10] Fr. Jean C.J. d'Elbeé, *I Believe in Love*, 2nd ed. (Manchester: Sophia Institute Press, 2001) 59-60.

In the hour of my death call to me,

And bid me come to you,

That with your saints I may praise you

Forever and ever, Amen.

– St. Ignatius Loyola

Center of Our Hearts

O God, what will you do to conquer

the fearful hardness of our hearts?

Lord, you must give us new hearts,

tender hearts, sensitive hearts,

to replace hearts that are made of marble and of bronze.

You must give us your own Heart, Jesus. Come, lovable Heart of Jesus.

Place your heart deep in the center of our hearts and enkindle in each heart a flame of love as strong, as great, as the sum of all the reasons that I have for loving you, my God.

O holy Heart of Jesus, dwell hidden in my heart, so that I may live only in you and only for you, so that, in the end, I may live with you eternally in heaven. Amen.

– St. Claude de la Colombiére, S.J.

Litany of the Sacred Heart of Jesus

Leader: *Let us meditate on the depths of the Sacred Heart of Jesus. Lord, have mercy on us.*

All: *Christ, have mercy.*

Leader: *Lord, have mercy on us. Christ, hear us.*

All: *Christ, graciously hear us.*

Leader: *God, the Father of heaven,*

All: *Have mercy on us (repeat this response after each invocation below).*

Leader: *God, the Son, Redeemer of the world …*

God, the Holy Spirit …

Holy Trinity, one God …

Heart of Jesus, Son of the eternal Father …

Heart of Jesus, formed by the Holy Spirit in the womb of the Virgin Mother …

Heart of Jesus, substantially united to the Word of God ...

Heart of Jesus, of infinite majesty ...

Heart of Jesus, sacred temple of God ...

Heart of Jesus, tabernacle of the Most High ...

Heart of Jesus, house of God and gate of heaven ...

Heart of Jesus, burning furnace of charity ...

Heart of Jesus, abode of justice and love ...

Heart of Jesus, full of goodness and love ...

Heart of Jesus, abyss of all virtues ...

Heart of Jesus, most worthy of all praise ...

Heart of Jesus, king and center of all hearts ...

Heart of Jesus, in whom are all treasures of wisdom and knowledge ...

Heart of Jesus, in whom dwells the fullness of divinity ...

Heart of Jesus, in whom the Father was well pleased ...

Heart of Jesus, of whose fullness we have all received ...

Heart of Jesus, desire of the everlasting hills ...

Heart of Jesus, patient and most merciful ...

Heart of Jesus, generous to all who turn to you ...

Heart of Jesus, fountain of life and holiness ...

Heart of Jesus, propitiation for our sins ...

Heart of Jesus, loaded down with opprobrium ...

Heart of Jesus, bruised for our offenses ...

Heart of Jesus, obedient to death ...

Heart of Jesus, pierced with a lance ...

Heart of Jesus, source of all consolation ...

Heart of Jesus, our life and resurrection ...

Heart of Jesus, our peace and our reconciliation ...

Heart of Jesus, victim for our sins ...

Heart of Jesus, salvation of those who trust in You ...

Heart of Jesus, hope of those who die in You ...

Heart of Jesus, delight of all saints ...

Leader: *Lamb of God, who takes away the sins of the world,*

All: *Spare us, O Lord.*

Leader: *Lamb of God, who takes away the sins of the world,*

All: *Have mercy on us, O Lord.*

Leader: *Jesus, meek and humble of heart,*

All: *Make our hearts like Yours.*

Leader: *Let us pray.*

All: *Almighty and eternal God, look upon the pierced Heart of Your most beloved Son and upon the praises and satisfaction which He offers You for the salvation of sinners. In Your great goodness, grant us forgiveness and the things we ask in the name of our Lord Jesus Christ, who lives and reigns with You forever and ever. Amen.*

Leader: *Let us go in the confidence and the peace of Jesus Christ.*

All: *Amen.*

Terms and Definitions

Faith

• "Faith is man's response to God, who reveals himself and gives himself to man, at the same time bringing man a superabundant light as he searches for the ultimate meaning of his life" (CCC 26).

• The Virgin Mary most perfectly embodies the obedience of faith. By faith Mary welcomes the tidings and promise brought by the angel Gabriel, believing that "with God nothing will be impossible" and so giving her assent: "Behold I am the handmaid of the Lord; let it be done to me according to your word" (Lk 1:37-38; cf. Gen 18:14). Elizabeth greeted her: "Blessed is she who believed that there would be a fulfillment of what was spoken to her from the Lord" (Lk 1:45). It is for this faith that all generations have called Mary blessed (cf. Lk 1:48) (CCC 148).

• When St. Peter confessed that Jesus is the Christ, the Son of the living God, Jesus declared to him that this revelation did not come "from flesh and blood," but from "my Father who is in heaven" (Mt 16:17; cf. Gal 1:15, Mt 11:25). *Faith is a gift of God, a supernatural virtue infused by him.* "Before this faith can be exercised, man must have the grace of God to move and assist him; he must have the interior helps of the Holy Spirit, who moves the heart and converts it to God, who opens the eyes of the mind and 'makes it easy for all to accept and believe the truth'" (*Dei Verbum* 5; cf. DS 377; 3010) (CCC 153).

• The desire for God is written in the human heart because man is created by God and for God; and God never ceases to draw man to himself. Only in God will he find the truth and happiness for which he never stops searching. The dignity of man rests above all on the fact that he is called to communion with God. This invitation to converse with God is addressed to man as soon as he comes into being. For if man exists it is because God has created him through love, and through love continues to hold him in existence. He cannot live fully according to truth unless he freely acknowledges that love and entrusts himself to his creator (CCC 27).

• Faith is first of all a personal adherence of man to God. At the same time, and inseparably, it is a free assent to the whole truth that God has revealed. As personal adherence to God and assent to his truth, Christian faith differs from our faith in any human person. It is right and just to entrust oneself wholly to God and to believe absolutely what he says. It would be futile and false to place such faith in a creature (CCC 150; cf. Jer 17:5-6; Ps 40:5; 146:3-4).

• Believing is possible only by grace and the interior helps of the Holy Spirit. But it is no less true that believing is an authentically human act. Trusting in God and cleaving to the truths he has revealed is contrary neither to human freedom nor to human reason. Even in human relations it is not contrary to our dignity to believe what other persons tell us about themselves and their intentions, or to trust their promises (for example, when a man and a woman marry) to share a communion of life with one another. If this is so, still less is it contrary to our dignity to "yield by faith the full submission of ... intellect and will to God who reveals," and to share in an interior communion with him (CCC 154).

• What moves us to believe is not the fact that revealed truths appear as true and intelligible in the light of our natural reason: we believe "because of the authority of God himself who reveals them, who can neither deceive nor be deceived." So "that the submission of our faith might nevertheless be in accordance with reason, God willed that external proofs of his Revelation should be joined to the internal helps of the Holy Spirit." Thus the miracles of Christ and the saints, prophecies, the Church's growth and holiness and her fruitfulness and stability "are the most certain signs of divine revelation, adapted to the intelligence of all"; they are "motives of credibility" (*motiva credibilitatis*), which show that the assent of faith is "by no means a blind impulse of the mind" (CCC 156).

• Faith is the theological virtue by which we believe in God and believe all that he has said and revealed to us, and that Holy Church proposes for our belief, because he is truth itself. By faith "man freely commits his entire self to God." For this reason the believer seeks to know and do God's will. "The righteous shall live by faith." Living faith "work[s] through charity" (CCC 1814).

• Our moral life has its source in faith in God who reveals his love to us. St. Paul speaks of the "obedience of faith" as our first obligation. He shows that "ignorance of God" is the principle and explanation of all moral deviations. Our duty toward God is to believe in him and to bear witness to him (CCC 2087).

• In faith, the human intellect and will cooperate with divine grace: "Believing is an act of the intellect assenting to the divine truth by command of the will moved by God through grace" (CCC 155).

Healing

• Christ's compassion toward the sick and his many healings of every kind of infirmity are a resplendent sign that "God has visited his people and that the Kingdom of God is close at hand. Jesus has the power not only to heal, but also to forgive sins; he has come to heal the whole man, soul and body; he is the physician the sick have need of. His compassion toward all who suffer goes so far that he identifies himself with them: 'I was sick and you visited me.'" His preferential love for the sick has not ceased through the centuries to draw the very special attention of Christians toward all those who suffer in body and soul. It is the source of tireless efforts to comfort them (CCC 1503).

• Moved by so much suffering Christ not only allows himself to be touched by the sick, but he makes their miseries his own: "He took our infirmities and bore our diseases." But he did not heal all the sick. His healings were signs of the coming of the Kingdom of God. They announced a more radical healing: the victory over sin and death through his Passover. On the cross Christ took upon himself the whole weight of evil and took away the "sin of the world," of which illness is only a consequence. By his passion and death on the cross Christ has given a new meaning to suffering: it can henceforth configure us to him and unite us with his redemptive Passion (CCC 1505).

• "Of this gospel I became a minister by the gift of God's grace that was granted me in accord with the exercise of his power. To me, the very least of all the holy ones, this grace was given, to preach to the Gentiles the inscrutable riches of Christ and to bring to light what is the plan of the mystery hidden from ages past in God who created all things, so that the manifold wisdom of God might now be made known through the church to the principalities and authorities in the heavens. This was according to the eternal purpose that he accomplished in Christ Jesus our Lord, in whom we have boldness of speech and confidence of access through faith in him. So I ask you not to lose heart over my afflictions for you; this is your glory. For this reason I kneel before the Father, from whom every family in heaven and on earth is named, that he may grant you in accord with the riches of his glory to be strengthened with power through his Spirit in the inner self, and that Christ may dwell in your hearts through faith; that you, rooted and grounded in love, may have strength to comprehend with all the holy ones what is the breadth and length and height and depth, and to know the love of Christ that surpasses knowledge, so that you may be filled with all the fullness of God" (Eph 3:7-19).

• Often Jesus asks the sick to believe. He makes use of signs to heal: spittle and the laying on of hands, mud and washing. The sick try to touch him, "for power came forth from him and healed them all." And so in the sacraments Christ continues to "touch" us in order to heal us (CCC 1504).

• Christ invites his disciples to follow him by taking up their cross in their turn. By following him they acquire a new outlook on illness and the sick. Jesus associates them with his own life of poverty and service. He makes them share in his ministry of compassion and healing: "So they went out and preached that men should repent. And they cast out many demons and anointed with oil many that were sick and healed them" (CCC 1506).

• The Holy Spirit gives to some a special charism of healing so as to make manifest the power of the grace of the risen Lord. But even the most intense prayers do not always obtain the healing of all illnesses. Thus St. Paul must learn from the Lord that "my grace is sufficient for you, for my power is made perfect in weakness," and that the sufferings to be endured can mean that "in my flesh I complete what is lacking in Christ's afflictions for the sake of his Body, that is, the Church" (CCC 1508).

• "Heal the sick!" The Church has received this charge from the Lord and strives to carry it out by taking care of the sick as well as by accompanying them with her prayer of intercession. She believes in the life-giving presence of Christ, the physician of souls and bodies. This presence is particularly active through the sacraments, and in an altogether special way through the Eucharist, the bread that gives eternal life and that St. Paul suggests is connected with bodily health (CCC 1509).

Heart

• Heart refers to the deepest place of relation and truth in persons, the seat of spiritual wisdom, understanding, knowledge and insight. The human heart is the place of grounding in faith where the Holy Spirit indwells.

• "The organ for seeing God is the heart. The intellect alone is not enough. In order for man to become capable of perceiving God, the energies of his existence have to work in harmony. His will must be pure and so too must the underlying affective dimension of his soul, which gives intelligence and will their direction. Speaking of the heart in this way means precisely that man's perceptive powers play in concert, which also requires the proper interplay of body and soul, since this is essential for the totality of the creature we call 'man.' Man's fundamental affective disposition actually depends on just this unity of body and soul and on man's acceptance of being both body and spirit. This means he places his body under the discipline of the spirit, yet does not isolate intellect or will. Rather, he accepts himself as coming from God, and thereby also acknowledges and lives out the bodiliness of his existence as enrichment for the spirit. The heart—the wholeness of man— must be pure, interiorly open and free, in order for man to be able to see God" (Pope Benedict XVI, *Jesus of Nazareth,* Doubleday Publishing, 2007, 92-93).

• "In terms of the encyclical *Haurietis Aquas,* spirituality of the senses is essentially a spirituality of the heart, since the heart is the hub of all the senses, the place where sense and spirit meet, interpenetrate and unite. Spirituality of the senses is spirituality in the sense of Cardinal Newman's motto: *Cor ad cor loquitur* (heart speaks to heart), which sums up, in perhaps the most beautiful way, what spirituality of the heart is, a spirituality focused on the heart of Jesus" (Joseph Cardinal Ratzinger, *Behold the Pierced One,* Fort Collins: Ignatius Press, 1986).

• Often it is necessary to go back beyond the psychological distinctions to the core of man's being, to the place where he enters into dialogue with himself (Gn 17:17 and Dt 7:17), accepts his responsibilities and opens himself or closes himself to God. In the concrete and global anthropology that we find in the Bible, man's heart is the very source of his conscious, intelligent and free personality, the place of his decisive choices, the place of the unwritten Law (Rom 2: 15) and of the mysterious action of God. In the Old Testament as in the New Testament, the heart is the place where man meets God, an encounter which becomes fully effective in the human heart of the Son of God.

God cannot be deceived as man can: "because man sees the appearance but the LORD looks into the heart" (1Sm 16:7). God "probe[s] the mind and test[s] the heart" (Jer 17:10 and Sir 42:18). He uncovers their lie and observes: "This people draws near with words only / and honors me with their lips alone, / though their hearts are far from me" (Is 29:13). Before God, man realizes he is called in question down to the depths of his being (Heb 4:12). To approach God is to risk one's heart (Jer 30:21).

Gradually, Israel learned that external religion is not enough. To find God, one must "search after him with your whole heart" (Dt 4:29). Israel learned that she must once and for all "wish with your whole heart to return to the LORD" (1 Sm 7:3) and "love the LORD your God, with all your heart" (Dt 6:5).

The fire of God is a fire of love that prevents him from allowing the destruction of his people. The mere thought of this overwhelms his heart (Hos 11:8). When he led his unfaithful spouse into the desert, it was to speak again to her heart (Hos 2:16). There will be an end to these trials and a new age will dawn, an age of inner renewal brought about by God himself. "The LORD, your God, will circumcise your hearts and the hearts of your descendants, that you may love the Lord, your God, with all your heart and all your soul, and so may live" (Dt 30:6). The Israelites will rebel no more, for God will establish with them a new covenant: "I will place my law within them, and write it upon their hearts" (Jer 31:33). Better still, God will give them a new heart (Jer 32:39), a heart with which to know him (Jer 24:7; cf, Dt 29:3). After the command, "Make for yourselves a new heart" (Ez. 18:31), God himself promises to achieve what he requires of them. "I will cleanse you. I will give you a new heart and place a new spirit within you, taking from your bodies your stony hearts and giving you natural hearts" (Ez 36:25-26). Thus is insured a lasting union of God and his people.

It is by Jesus Christ that this promise was fulfilled. Henceforth, it is faith in Christ, an acceptance in the heart, that brings about this interior renewal which is otherwise not achieved. Thus Paul announces, "If you … believe in your heart that God raised him from the dead, you will be saved. For one believes with the heart and so is justified" (Rom 10:9-10). By faith, the eyes of the heart are illumined (Eph 1:18), and Christ dwells in the heart (Eph 3:17). Into the hearts of believers a new spirit is sent, "the spirit of his Son into our hearts, crying out, 'Abba, Father!'" (Gal 4:6), and with the Spirit, "the love of God" is poured out (Rom 5:5). Thus "the peace of God that surpasses all understanding will guard your hearts" (Phil 4:7). This is the new covenant, one founded on the sacrifice of him whose heart was bruised with insults (Ps 69:21).

John speaks of the heart only to drive from it all trouble and fear. But he announces in other terms the fulfillment of the same promises. He speaks of knowledge (1 Jn 5: 20; cf Jer 24:7) and of communion (1 Jn1:3), of love and of eternal life. All these come to us through the crucified and glorified Jesus. Within Jesus (Jn 7:38; cf 19:34), there springs up a source of interior renewal for the believer (Jn 4:14). Jesus personally enters within his followers to give them life (Jn 6:56). According to John, it could even be said that Jesus is the heart of the new Israel, the heart that brings a close relation with the Father and establishes unity among all: "I in them and you in me, that they may be brought to perfection as one" (Jn 17:23; cf 11:52 and Acts 4:32); "that the love with which you loved me may be in them and I in them" (Jn 17:26). (Fr. Xavier Leon Dufour, adapted from *Dictionary of Biblical Theology*, Ijamsville, Md.: Word Among Us Press, 1995.)

Prayer

- "Prayer is permitting God to love me. Prayer is also responding to God's love at work in my heart." (Fr. Armand Nigro, S.J., *Praying with the Scriptures*, 1-2).

- "Yet this power, the grace of the Spirit, is not something we can merit or achieve, but only receive as pure gift. God's love can only unleash its power when it is allowed to change us from within. We have to let it break through the hard crust of our indifference, our spiritual weariness, our blind conformity to the spirit of this age. Only then can we let it ignite our imagination and shape our deepest desires. That is why prayer is so important: daily prayer, private prayer in the quiet of our hearts before the Blessed Sacrament, and liturgical prayer in the heart of the Church. Prayer is pure receptivity to God's grace, love in action, communion with the Spirit who dwells within us, leading us, through Jesus, in the Church, to our heavenly Father. In the power of his Spirit, Jesus is always present in our hearts, quietly waiting for us to be still with him, to hear his voice, to abide in his love, and to receive 'power from on high,' enabling us to be salt and light for our world" (Pope Benedict XVI, World Youth Day Homily, July 20, 2008).

- Contemplative prayer is *hearing* the Word of God. Far from being passive, such attentiveness is the obedience of faith, the unconditional acceptance of a servant, and the loving commitment of a child. It participates in the "Yes" of the Son become servant and the *Fiat* of God's lowly handmaid (CCC 2716).

- Meditation is a prayerful quest engaging thought, imagination, emotion, and desire. Its goal is to make our own in faith the subject considered, by confronting it with the reality of our own life (CCC 2723).

- Meditation engages thought, imagination, emotion, and desire. The mobilization of faculties is necessary in order to deepen our convictions of faith, prompt the conversion of our heart, and strengthen our will to follow Christ. Christian prayer tries above all to meditate on the mysteries of Christ, as in *lectio divina* or the rosary. This form of prayerful reflection is of great value, but Christian prayer should go further: to the knowledge of the love of the Lord Jesus, to union with him (CCC 2708).

- Contemplative prayer is the simple expression of the mystery of prayer. It is a gaze of faith fixed on Jesus, an attentiveness to the Word of God, a silent love. It achieves real union with the prayer of Christ to the extent that it makes us share in his mystery (CCC 2724).

• To meditate on what we read helps us to make it our own by confronting it with ourselves. Here, another book is opened: the book of life. We pass from thoughts to reality. To the extent that we are humble and faithful, we discover in meditation the movements that stir the heart and we are able to discern them. It is a question of acting truthfully in order to come into the light: "Lord, what do you want me to do?" (CCC 2706).

• Contemplative prayer is also the pre-eminently *intense time* of prayer. In it the Father strengthens our inner being with power through his Spirit "that Christ may dwell in [our] hearts through faith" and we may be "grounded in love" (CCC 2714, quoting Eph 3:16-17).

• Contemplation is a *gaze* of faith, fixed on Jesus. "I look at him and he looks at me": this is what a certain peasant of Ars in the time of his holy curé used to say while praying before the tabernacle. This focus on Jesus is a renunciation of self. His gaze purifies our heart; the light of the countenance of Jesus illumines the eyes of our heart and teaches us to see everything in the light of his truth and his compassion for all men. Contemplation also turns its gaze on the mysteries of the life of Christ. Thus it learns the "interior knowledge of our Lord," the more to love him and follow him (CCC 2715, citing St. Ignatius of Loyola, *Spiritual Exercises,* 104).

• Contemplative prayer is silence, the "symbol of the world to come" or "silent love." Words in this kind of prayer are not speeches; they are like kindling that feeds the fire of love. In this silence, unbearable to the "outer" man, the Father speaks to us his incarnate Word, who suffered, died and rose; in this silence the Spirit of adoption enables us to share in the prayer of Jesus (CCC 2717, citing St. Isaac of Ninevah, *Tract. Myst.* 66; St. John of the Cross, *Maxims and Counsels,* 53, in *The Collected Works of St. John of the Cross,* tr. K. Kavanaugh, OCD, and O. Rodriguez, OCD [Washington, DC: Institute of Carmelite Studies, 1979], 678).

Aids to Foster Belief, Repentance, and Forgiveness

Section A, Part 1: Understanding Sin and Sinfulness

"Without reference to God's original plan and its hope of restoration in Christ people tend to accept discord ... 'as just the way it is.' ... When we normalize our fallen state, it is akin to thinking it normal to driving with flat tires. We intuit that something is amiss, but when everyone drives around in the same state we lack a point of reference for anything different."[11] Most of us live with flat tires. We struggle; we cope; we just get by. We live with flat tires. Tired, yet hungry, we think our lives as we know them now are as good as it gets. We want more, but don't know how to break free of the chains that hold us bound. We want holiness, but don't know how to break free of the sins that we compulsively run to. The unrelated grief in our hearts traps us in our own prison.

However, there is good news. Healing, transformation, and freedom are indeed possible. Unfortunately, far too many of us doubt the power of God and His desire for our freedom. Pope Benedict XVI reminds us: "Healing is an essential dimension of the apostolic mission and of Christianity. When understood at a sufficiently deep level, this expresses the entire content of redemption."[12] The entire content of redemption—all of it—can be understood through God's desire for our communion, for our freedom.

To understand our call to freedom let us understand more personally our patterns of confusion. In his letter to the Romans, Saint Paul writes: "We know that the law is spiritual; but I am carnal, sold into slavery to sin. What I do, I do not understand. For I do not do what I want, but I do what I hate ... For I do not do the good I want, but I do the evil I do not want. Now if [I] do what I do not want, it is no longer I who do it, but sin that dwells in me ... Miserable one that I am! Who will deliver me from this mortal body?" (Rm 7: 14-15, 19-20, 24) Have you ever been there? Have you ever been confused with your desire for good, yet your tendency is to do what you do not want to do? If so, there is hope.

For insights into the supernatural world, we often may start with signs in the natural world. For example, let us look at apples and apple trees. Apples do not make apples grow. Apple trees make apples grow. Apples are best harvested in the summer. This summer you can harvest all the apples off the tree, picking the tree clean. However, assuming that the conditions are right, we can

---

[11] Christopher West, *Theology of the Body Explained: A Commentary on John Paul II's Man and Woman He Created Them*, rev. ed. (Boston: Pauline Books and Media, 2007), 60.

[12] Pope Benedict XVI, *Jesus of Nazareth: From the Baptism in the Jordan to the Transfiguration* (San Francisco: Ignatius Press, 2008), 176.

expect the apples to grow back. With the right weather, proper rain, and healthy conditions, all of us would assume more apples would grow next summer. If this is true with apples, in the natural world, why do we expect it to be different with sin, in the supernatural world? Apples do not make apples grow. Apple trees- a complex system of roots, trunk, and branches-produce apples. Likewise, sins do not simply pop up in our life in a mere response to temptation. Most of our repetitive sins are the product of our interior lives, with its own root system and so on.

At the risk of simplifying the great reverence of our spiritual experience, many of us have patterns of thinking that influence our patterns of sin. In other words, how I think influences what I do. Deep within many of our hearts are wounds: hurtful experiences in our past that have injured and pierced the heart. Wounds are often filled with pain, and pain is often insulated with fear. With great reverence we see, for instance, childhood experiences of divorce, father/mother rejections, or verbal, physical, or sexual abuse as examples of wounds filled with pain. When we are in pain and afraid, we often feel out of control. We instinctively seek something we can control. Thus, many of us, without knowing it, seek an answer for the pain. We think, "If I know why this happened, I'll know how to make it go away."

Unfortunately, many of the answers we get are not from the voice of truth. Thus, wrapped around pain are usually lies: lies we believe about ourselves, about others, or about God. These lies, while objectively false, are "true" to us. We believe them. We actually hold on to them, for often they are the only thing we have to hold on to insulating us from the pain and fear that accompanied being injured. Staying with the aforementioned examples of wounds, inner lies often borne within that pain may be thoughts like: "It's my fault"; "I'm alone"; "I'm dirty"; "God made it happen."

In response to the lies, many of us make inner vows. It is important to note the nature of vows. Think about wedding vows: they are before God; they are forever; they are binding. Inner vows are made in direct response to lies. For example, someone who believes the lie, "I am a failure" may make the inner vow, "I am never going to fail." Or, for example, someone who believes the lie, "I am unlovable" may make the inner vow, "I will do whatever it takes to get people to love me." Inner vows have an incredible influence over one's life.

Lies and inner vows together comprise interior structure of belief. They are the "roots" of the system. Like roots, they are hidden. Like roots, they feed the bad fruit (sin) we see. Lies and inner vows, these interior structures of belief, lead us into isolation from God. Isolation is the trunk of the tree, a posture of isolation that then branches out into patterns of our life eventually bearing fruit (sin). Thus, reverently, we see the distinction between my sinful actions and that structure of belief that feeds the sinful actions. No, apples do not make apples grow. Yes, there is more to sin than you see. Saint Paul says: "I don't know why I do what I do." St.

Paul knew something more was going on than just his sin. St. Paul's inner transformation, his learning to receive the Holy Spirit that was being poured into his heart (Rm 5:5) led him to teach redemptive and glorious truth. He discovered that living in and with Jesus as Lord, there is joy, for where sin abounds, grace is present all the more (Rm 5:20). May each of us discover this joy anew and live each day in the power of the Holy Spirit.

Section A, Part 2: Understanding Sin and Sinfulness

"What I do, I do not understand. For I do not do what I want, but I do what I hate. ... The willing is ready at hand, but doing the good is not. *For I do not do the good I want, but I do the evil I do not want. ...* So, then, I discover the principle that when I want to do right, evil is at hand. ... Miserable one that I am! Who will deliver me from this mortal body?" *Romans 7:15-24*

sin
The *fruit* of sinfulness.
Commission.
Omission.
Example #1
Obsessive materialism
Example #2
Promiscuity

sinfulness
This is the *source* of the action of sin.
Attitudes ... structures of belief ... the way we think ...
lies or vows we can't break
Example #1
"I don't have what it takes to be a man"
Example #2
"I'm abandoned"

pain
When we are wounded our hearts are pierced
This pain is the *root* of sinfulness
Example #1
Feeling as if your father rejected you
Example #2
Your parents divorced at an early age

Special thanks to Bob Schuchts, Ph.D. for his contribution and specialty. The Sinfulness Tree and all of Section A is reproduced with the permission of Fr. Mark Toups.

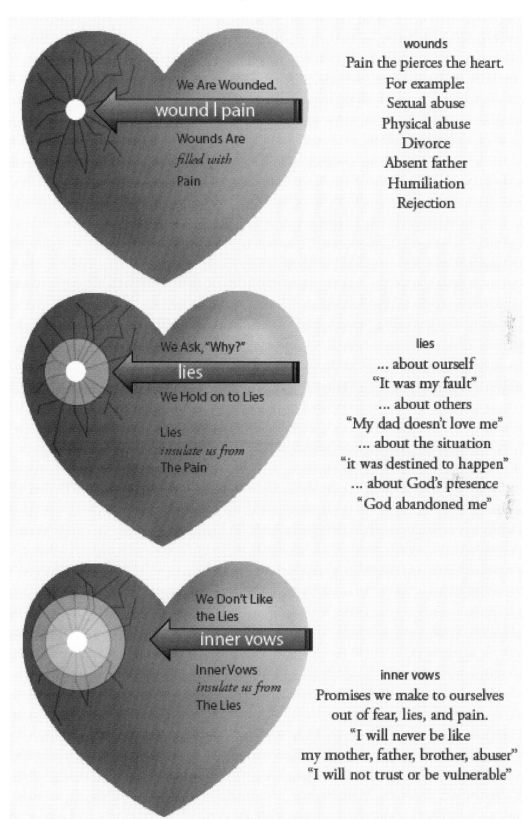

wounds
Pain the pierces the heart.
For example:
Sexual abuse
Physical abuse
Divorce
Absent father
Humiliation
Rejection

We Are Wounded.
wound I pain
Wounds Are
filled with
Pain

lies
... about ourself
"It was my fault"
... about others
"My dad doesn't love me"
... about the situation
"it was destined to happen"
... about God's presence
"God abandoned me"

We Ask, "Why?"
lies
We Hold on to Lies
Lies
insulate us from
The Pain

We Don't Like
the Lies
inner vows
InnerVows
insulate us from
The Lies

inner vows
Promises we make to ourselves
out of fear, lies, and pain.
"I will never be like
my mother, father, brother, abuser"
"I will not trust or be vulnerable"

What I Believe Influences What I Do

fruit—sins of flesh
Rage, revenge, retaliation,
murder, violence, malice,
verbal abuse, insults, slander

fruit—sins of flesh
Self-righteousness, judgement,
bitterness, resentment,
depression,
passive-aggressive behavior,
gossip, sarcasm

**isolation
from god**

lie
"I am not loved ...
no one wants or desires me ...
I am not good enough ...
I am not valued or important."

lie
"If I trust I'll be hurt ...
I need to protect myself or
something bad will happen."

vow
"I'll never trust ...
I'll do it on my own ...
I'll always be in control"

lie
"I feel helpless ...
I don't know what to do ...
everything is out of control"

Section B: The Five Keys and Lies to Renounce

The Five Keys information and the Lies to Renounce information is used with the permission of Neal Lozano and is adapted from UNBOUND Ministry's Web site,www.heartofthefather.com.

Part 1 – The Five Keys

Key #1 Repentance and Faith

- **Prayer of repentance:** *Lord, please forgive me for* _____.
- **Prayer of Surrender/Commitment to Christ:** *Lord, I am sorry for … Thank you for … I surrender …*

Key #2 Forgiveness

- **Prayer of forgiveness:** *In the name of Jesus, I forgive* _____ *for* _____. *(Be specific)*

Key #3 Renunciation

- **The spirit or the Lie:** *In the name of Jesus, I renounce* _____.
- **Occult involvement:** *In the name of Jesus, I renounce the spirit that operated in* _____ *(e.g., fortuneteller, etc.) and I take back the Authority (power) I gave to* _____ *(name). I break the power of the words they spoke when they said* _____.
- **Soul ties:** *I renounce every unholy tie with … or I renounce every physical and spiritual tie with* _____ *and I take back the authority I gave to him/her (what he/she took from me).*

Key #4 Authority

- **Word of Command:** In the name of Jesus, I break the power of every spirit that (he/she) has renounced and I command it to leave. (wait and ask what is coming to their mind)

- **Thanksgiving and declarations of faith:** related to their repentance, forgiveness, and renunciation. Thank you, Lord, that I have forgiven my dad.

Go back to the first four keys—only if necessary.

Key #5 The Father's Blessing

- **Words of blessing that come from the Father's heart over the person's identity and destiny.**

Part 2 – Lies to Renounce

The following gives you an idea of the range of lies that may be uncovered in a ministry session. The lies are as unique as the person's story. Reflecting on this list will help you pick up on lies as they are expressed.

Be aware that you can deal with the lies by renouncing the specific lie or renouncing the spirit. For example, the lie "I am a failure" may be dealt with by renouncing a spirit of failure. The lie "I am not a good mother/father" may be dealt with by renouncing self-rejection, self-criticism, self-accusation, and so on. The lie "No one needs me" may be dealt with by renouncing self-pity. It may be helpful to assist a person in naming the spirits behind the statements because you then can name related spirits that may be harassing them. On the other hand, it may be more effective to simply renounce the lie because the words of the lie precisely express their bondage. Your best guide is to listen to the heart of the person in front of you while being led by the Spirit.

Lies:

- I'm never where I'm supposed to be – I shouldn't be here – I should be dead – I don't belong – I am always in the wrong place
- I'll never amount to anything – I'll never be a success – I am a failure
- I am of no significance
- I have to do it all myself – No one will help me
- Nobody cares if I live or die
- I have to get it right – I have to be perfect/the best – I can't make a mistake (or something bad will happen)

- My mother/father/sister/brother/spouse's illness/death is my fault – I am responsible for their illness/death
- I do not have a voice – I am invisible
- It is always my fault
- Something's wrong with me
- I am ugly
- I am unworthy
- I am a terrible mom
- I'm nothing – I don't matter – I'm a mistake – I am worthless – I am not worthy
- God won't/can't help me – God doesn't want to help me – God doesn't care about me
- God can't be bothered with me
- God's mercy/blessing/favor is for everyone but me
- God is against me – God wants to punish/is punishing me – God is getting back at me
- God is not in control – I've destroyed God's plan for my life
- Someone/everyone is out to get me
- My life is cursed – My life is doomed – I've destroyed my life – Bad things always happen to me
- I am a victim – I can't do anything right – I'm not able to do anything
- God cannot forgive me
- I am in control – I can fix those I love
- What I want doesn't matter
- I am worthless – I am lazy – I am no good – I am garbage
- I am not normal
- I can't say no – Anyone can do whatever they want to me and I can't say no
- I should be punished
- Nothing good ever happens or will ever happen to me
- I can't do anything about it – I can't fight back – I'm too weak
- It's hopeless – I can never change
- Showing emotion means I'm weak
- If they knew the real me, no one would like me
- If I say/do the right thing, everyone will be happy
- God made a mistake when He made me a man/woman
- Their anger is my fault

- My father's/mother's/sister's/brother's/spouse's anger/abuse was my fault
- I have to earn God's love
- God has abandoned me – God has rejected me – God is not protecting me - God has forsaken me
- Nothing is ever good enough
- I deserve the abuse
- The enemy/Satan is stronger than God
- God wanted this to happen to me
- No one will ever believe me
- I'm stupid – I'm bad – I'm dirty – I'm shameful – I'm sick – I'm nasty
- I should have stopped them – I deserved it – I should have done something to stop it
- It's just a matter of time before it happens again
- If I let them into my life, they'll hurt me too
- Not even God can help me
- God could never want me because of what happened to me
- I am a burden
- No one needs me – I am unimportant
- God could never love me
- I'm never going to get any better
- I have no reason to live
- Heaven is not for me

Remember, whether a person renounces spirits, lies, or idols, the important thing is verbally breaking any internal agreement with the enemy's plan for their life. They are saying before witnesses, "I'm done with this." Renunciation is always done in the name of Jesus.

APPENDIX II

Two Exercises: Family Diagram and Prayer on My Dossier

Dr. Eileen Barbella

Family Diagram - Knowing our place in creation by observing multi-generational family emotional processes (not genealogy).

Prayer on My Dossier - Praying in gratitude for God's gifts (from the Preparation Days of the Spiritual Exercises of St. Ignatius)

First Exercise: Family Diagram (or Genogram – a psychological exercise)

Creating a family diagram involves three levels: 1) mapping the family structure, 2) recording family information, and 3) delineating family relationships.

1. Mapping the Family Structure

   This is a graphic depiction of how different family members are biologically and legally related to one another from one generation to the next.

   o Each family member is represented by a box (male) or circle (female).
   o Lines are doubled around the index person.
   o Birth and death dates are indicated to left and right. If dead, an X is placed inside the figure and the person's age at death is usually indicated within the figure.
   o Lines connect the figures representing family members.

      Male on the left, female on the right
      Marriage: lines that go down and across

Living together: dotted line down and across

Separation or Divorce: single or double diagonal line with date

Children: list in birth order beginning with oldest child on the left.

Pregnancy: triangle (not box or circle)

Stillbirth: box or circle with X, or triangle with X

Spontaneous abortion/ miscarriage: blackened small circle

Induced abortion: small X

Twins: indicate fraternal or identical

Foster placement or adoption: used dotted vertical line

2. Recording Family Information

   a) Demographic information - ages, dates of birth and death, locations, occupations, and educational level.

   b) Functional information - more or less objective data on the medical, emotional and behavioral functioning of different family members.

   c) Critical family events - important transitions, relationship shifts, migrations, losses and successes.

   d) Family chronology - listing in order of occurrence of important events in the family history; or special chronology for a critical time period.

3. Showing Family Relationships

This is the most inferential level. Since relationship patterns can be quite complex, and also fluctuate, it is often useful to represent them on separate family diagrams.

   a) very close or fused

   b) close

   c) fused and conflictual

   d) poor or conflictual

   e) estranged or cut-off

   f) distant

For greater details see McGoldrick, M., Gerson, R, and Petry, S. *Genograms – Assessment and Intervention, 3rd Edition.* New York: Norton, 2008.

Second Exercise: Prayer on My Dossier (a prayer exercise)

I jot down all the vital statistics of my life. As I note each piece of data, I raise my mind to God my Maker, and praise and thank the Creator for this detail in my life history and in my self. Note: God chose that I should come to be in a particular place and time, of particular parents and race, and all the rest. Am I content with God's choices for me?

So to begin, I write down my parent's full names, birthplaces, and birth dates. I note my own birthday, where I was born, and any significant medical details. I note my sex, race or ethnic group, hair and eye color, and my physical build. I also note my siblings - name, birthdays, significant details; and I note my extended family of uncles, aunts and cousins. I note the cities and addresses I lived at before I was seven. All this, God chose for me; for all this, I praise and thank God.

Then I note down a half dozen personal characteristics and qualities that were bred into me before I had a choice. Self-assurance or anxiety, intelligence, the language(s) I speak, activities I take pleasure in and so on. I note at the same time half a dozen characteristics and qualities that I have inherited from my parents or extended family, those I like and perhaps some that I would just as soon not have. All this, too, God chose for me within in the human family; for all this, I praise and thank God.

Next, I go on to note down five or six personal qualities in my self that I particularly like. I note down these qualities and acknowledge them as gifts from the One who makes me. For all this, too, God chose for me within the human family; for all this, I praise and thank God.

Finally, I note down five or six personal qualities in my self that I do not particularly like. I note down these qualities and acknowledge them as gifts form the One who makes me. For all this, too, God chose for me within the human family; for all this, I praise and thank God.

When my time of prayerful reflections is coming to an end, I recite Psalm 139. But I remember that God did not finish making me once, long ago, when I was conceived or born. I remember that God continues making me and has hopes for me and desires that I keep growing in love until I love as completely as God loves.

Tetlow, J. *Choosing Christ in the World: Directing the Spiritual Exercises of St. Ignatius Loyola According to Annotations Eighteen and Nineteen.* St. Louis, MO: Institute of Jesuit Sources, 1989. (p.119)

Healing of Memories for Oneself

Sometimes we experience a lack of freedom in ourselves, an inability to cope with something, an inability to forgive, a fear, a problem with uncontrollable anger, or something like that. No matter how we pray or what we do, nothing seems to help. The first step once again is discernment. We need to discover the root of the problem. Very often it helps to talk it over with a spiritual director.

Sometimes our weakness or unfreedom is a result of an inconsistent or inadequate prayer life. Sometimes it is a result of an unwillingness to face the truth, or to let go of something we want, or a lack of discipline in our lives. Sometimes it is because we are too busy or too tired. Sometimes it's because we have not forgiven another. In instances like these, what we need for healing is repentance not prayer. If we take time to discern and if we make use of spiritual direction, this sort of thing will come to light.

Sometimes, though, the problem or problems are rooted in the deep past, even in the time we were being carried in our mother's womb or in the process of birth. No matter how loving our home life has been, no matter how happy our childhood, it was not perfect, so we carry in ourselves the wounds of bad experiences, some of which we have not thought about in years…

There is a way of praying for the healing of past experiences. It is sometimes called "Healing of Memories", sometimes "Psychological Healing". It rests on the fact that Jesus is the Lord of all time, past, present, and future, that He can even change the past.

A year or so ago, one of the women in our community said to me in passing that I had a lot of bitterness in me. I was busy at the time and busy afterwards with a lot of things, so I did not do anything about it. From time to time her remarks reoccurred to me, and I did realize that occasionally a sharpness would develop in my tone of voice, a certain harshness would colour my relations with others. I would ask forgiveness when I could and move on. A few months ago I had an occasion … to use my prayer time to be healed of the effects of bad experiences in my past.

I began by settling quietly in God's presence, and after reminding myself of His perfect love and of His desire to heal me. I asked Him to bring to my mind the memories of the experiences which were at the root of this buried bitterness. The first memory came back almost at once. I saw myself on the stairway of my high school the first day of my freshman year. I was a fat little twelve-year-old between two much larger boys. It was a scene that I hadn't thought about in over 25 years. I saw their faces clearly and I even remembered their names. A priest walked by and I said, "Hello". I had served Mass for him many times. The other boys did not know the priests and began to ridicule me for trying to "get in" with them. I was both hurt and confused. I wanted very much to be friends with my classmates, but it looked as though I was getting off to a very bad start. I really couldn't understand why saying hello was so misunderstood.

At that point in my recollection I forgave each of them. Then in my imagination I walked back into that scene with Jesus by my side. I could imagine each of the boys becoming self-conscious and confused as they saw Jesus. I could see Jesus forgiving them and urging them to be more loving and understanding. Then he turned to the little boy (me) and He let me know that what I had done was all right, that the other boys were wrong in what they did and they were sorry. I really felt His love. I could see the little boy begin to smile, and then we walked out of the recollection. In the course of a week's prayer I had about fifty experiences like that, and I find that much of the bitterness and harshness has disappeared from my behavior. Praise God.

The elements of such prayer are simple:

1. Begin by resting in the presence of God.
2. Recall His love and power.
3. Ask Him to bring to your mind the memories of the bad experiences of the past which affect you now.
4. Be quiet and let them come to mind.
5. Walk back into those recollections with Jesus and imaginatively reconstruct what would happen.
6. Thank Jesus for His love and healing.

Sometimes this must be done more than once. You know when you are healed when the child or person in the memory is smiling and happy because of the presence and love of Jesus.

This segment is excerpted from *Freedom and Healing* by Joseph Lange and Anthony J. Cushing (Dove Publications, 1976, pp. 72-74) and has been republished with the permission of the Institute for Priestly Formation, Omaha.

An Outline of the Examen

Transition: *I become aware of the love with which God looks upon me as I begin this examen.*

Ignatius: I will pause "for the time I would take to pray an Our Father," and "with my understanding raised on high," consider "how God our Lord looks upon me" (*SpirEx*, 73)

Jesus looks upon *Nathaniel* and that look tells Nathaniel that he is deeply known and loved; it is a look that changes his life (Jn 1:48). Jesus sees *Levi* and his look gives fresh meaning to Levi's existence (Mk 2:14). Jesus sees a woman in tears and her tears are transformed into the joy of life restored (Lk 7:13).

A *man* approaches Jesus and the Gospel tells us that "Jesus, looking at him, loved him" (Mk 10:21).

Jesus sees a *woman* burdened for eighteen years with an illness; she is set free and sings God's praises (Lk 13:12-13).

Jesus looks upon *Peter* in his time of utter failure, a look that leads to tears and to renewal in a love that will never again be shaken (Lk 22:61).

John of the Cross: "the look of God is love and the pouring out of gifts."

Step One: Gratitude. *I note the gifts that God's love has given me this day and I give thanks to God for them.*

Unhurriedly, I look back over the hours of this day – my rising this morning, my different activities, my conversations with this or that person, my work this day, my times of prayer, the many thoughts and stirrings of my heart throughout this day to this point - calling concretely to mind *the large and small blessings received,* "pondering with much affection how much God our Lord has done for me, and how much he has given me of what he possesses and, consequently, how much, as far as he can, he desires to give himself to me" (*SpirEx*, 234).

I let the Lord tell me the concrete story of his love in the hours of this day.

Step Two: Petition. *I ask God for an insight and a strength that will make this examen a work of grace, fruitful beyond my human capacity alone.*

Jesus promises: "Ask, and it will be given you" (Mt 7:7); he says: "Whatever you ask in my name, I will do, so that the Father may be glorified in the Son" (Jn 14:13)

I ask for God's help in this examen, for the love and wisdom of the Spirit, who "searches everything, even the depths of God" (1Cor 2:10).

With faith, I repeat with Bartimaeus: "Jesus, Son of David, have mercy on me" (Mk 10:47), help me *to see* as I pray this examen. Silently, I lift my heart to the Spirit: "Come…."

Step Three: Review. *With my God, I review the day. I look for the stirrings in my heart and the thoughts which God has given me this day. I look also for those which have not been of God. I review my choices in response to both, and throughout the day in general.*

I look now at my day, "hour by hour, or from one period of time to another" *(SpirEx,* 43).

With the Lord, I look at how my day began: rising, preparing, times of prayer, conversations, a meal, beginning the day's occupations.. .. What were the spaces of the heart? The thoughts? What was the Lord offering? How did I respond?

I look concretely at my activity, my work, my prayer, my service, as the day unfolded, "hour by hour." Again, what was stirring in my heart? Spiritual consolation? Spiritual desolation? What can I recall of my thoughts? What was

God showing me in these events? What decisions did I make, in response to this person whom God placed in my life this day, in handling this task, in my life of prayer this day?

How aware of God's leading was I this day? How faithful to that leading was I? Where is God calling me to grow?

I review the experience of my day with the God whose unshakeable love I know….

Step Four: Forgiveness. I *ask for the healing touch of the forgiving God who, with love and respect for me, removes my heart's burdens.*

Now, with trust, I ask for healing forgiveness of the God who, as Ignatius writes, "loves me more than I love myself."

Jean Vanier: "We can only truly accept others as they are, and forgive them, when we discover that we are truly accepted by God as we are and forgiven by him. It is a deep experience, knowing that we are loved and held by God in all our brokenness and littleness."

"It is a deep experience, knowing that.. .." I open myself now to this experience, and, with confidence, I ask forgiveness of

God for any way in which I failed to notice and to respond to his call in the hours of this day.

"He ran to his son, embraced him and kissed him" (Lk 15:20): this is the God I encounter in step four of my examen prayer.

Step Five: Renewal. *I look to the next day and, with God, plan concretely how to live it in accord with God's loving desire for my life.*

Thomas Merton: "It is like a kind of awakening, a sort of intimation of all that may happen the day after tomorrow— what tremendous possibilities!" In the light of all that I have seen looking over my day, I now look to tomorrow and seek God's light on how he is calling me to grow spiritually in the specific circumstances of the day that awaits me.

Now my review of the past (this day) becomes spiritual clarity for the future (tomorrow): "A believer cannot sit still, as a man might sit with a pilgrim's staff in his hand; a believer journeys on." *(Soren Kierkegaard).*

Transition: Aware of God's faithful presence with me, I prayerfully conclude the examen with an Our Father, another

prayer I love, a phrase from Scripture, a prayer of praise, a moment of thanks....

This handout has been republished with the permission of Fr. Timothy Gallagher (IPF Publications) and the Institute for Priestly Formation, Omaha.

Five Movements of Examen

Prayer For Light

Begin by relaxing into God's Presence.

Ask for the Light to know myself as the Holy Spirit knows me.

Thanksgiving

Center on the concrete, uniquely personal gift.

I've been blessed with, whether obviously important or apparently insignificant with the deep realization that ALL IS GIFT

Practical Survey of Action

Look over the experiences of the day and the events that provoked these experiences: joy, pain, love, anger, anxiety, peace, etc.

Choose an experience that seems to be the most significant or dominant.

1. When or where has God especially touched my life?
2. When have I not allowed God in my life?
3. In what area of my heart is God especially calling for conversion?

Sorrow and Contrition

For not responding to what the Lord asks of me. This sorrow is hopeful, an awe-ful recognition of my inability to respond whole-heartedly to the Lord but, at the same time trusting in His faithful and personal love for me.

Responding in Practical Hope

To respond to what the Lord wants of me in the future. With a faith-filled vision and a discerning mind and heart, I stand before the Lord with a desire to see Him in all things. My hope for the immediate future will be expressed uniquely and in petition each time I pray the Examen.

This handout has been republished with the permission of the Institute for Priestly Formation, Omaha.

APPENDIX III

CONGREGATION FOR CATHOLIC EDUCATION
GUIDELINES FOR THE USE OF PSYCHOLOGY IN THE ADMISSION AND FORMATION OF CANDIDATES FOR THE PRIESTHOOD

Used with permission. Also available online at
http://www.vatican.va/roman_curia/congregations/ccatheduc/documents/rc_con_ccathedu
c_doc_20080628_orientamenti_en.html

I. *The Church and the Discernment of a Vocation*

1. "Each Christian vocation comes from God and is God's gift. However, it is never bestowed outside of or independently of the Church. Instead it always comes about in the Church and through the Church [...], a luminous and living reflection of the mystery of the Blessed Trinity." [1]

The Church, "begetter and formator of vocations",[2] has the duty of discerning a vocation and the suitability of candidates for the priestly ministry. In fact, "the interior call of the Spirit needs to be recognized as the authentic call of the bishop." [3]

In furthering this discernment, and throughout the entire process of formation for ministry, the Church is moved by two concerns: to safeguard the good of her own mission and, at the same time, the good of the candidates. In fact, like every Christian vocation, the vocation to the priesthood, along with a Christological dimension, has an essentially ecclesial dimension: "Not only does it derive `from' the Church and her mediation, not only does it come to be known and find fulfilment `in' the Church, but it also necessarily appears – in fundamental service to God – as a service `to' the Church. Christian vocation, whatever shape it takes, is a gift whose purpose is to build up the Church and to increase the kingdom of God in the world." [4]

Therefore, the good of the Church and that of the candidate are not in opposition, but rather converge. Those responsible for formation work at harmonizing these two goods, by always considering both simultaneously in their interdependent dynamic. This is an essential aspect of the great responsibility they bear in their service to the Church and to individuals.[5]

2. The priestly ministry, understood and lived as a conformation to Christ, Bridegroom and Good Shepherd, requires certain abilities as well as moral and theological virtues, which are supported by a human and psychic – and particularly affective – equilibrium, so as to allow the subject to be adequately predisposed for giving of himself in the celibate life, in a way that is truly free in his relations with the faithful.[6]

The Post-Synodal Apostolic Exhortation *Pastores dabo vobis* treats of the various dimensions of priestly formation: human, spiritual, intellectual and pastoral. Before the text deals with the spiritual dimension – "an extremely important element of a priest's education" [7] – it underlines that the human dimension is the foundation of all formation. The document lists a series of human virtues and relational abilities that are required of the priest, so that his personality * may be "a bridge and not an obstacle for others in their meeting with Jesus Christ the Redeemer of humanity." [8] These virtues and qualities range from the personality's general equilibrium to the ability to bear the weight of pastoral responsibilities, from a deep knowledge of the human spirit to a sense of justice and loyalty.[9]

  * *The specific understanding of "personality" in this document refers to affective maturity and absence of mental disorder.*

Some of these qualities merit particular attention: the positive and stable sense of one's masculine identity, and the capacity to form relations in a mature way with individuals and groups of people; a solid sense of belonging, which is the basis of future communion with the presbyterium and of a responsible collaboration in the ministry of the bishop; [10] the freedom to be enthused by great ideals and a coherence in realizing them in everyday action; the courage to take decisions and to stay faithful to them; a knowledge of oneself, of one's talents and limitations, so as to integrate them within a self-esteem before God; the capacity to correct oneself; the appreciation for beauty in the sense of "splendour of the truth" as well as the art of recognizing it; the trust that is born from an esteem of the other person and that leads to acceptance; the capacity of the candidate to integrate his sexuality in accordance with the Christian vision, including in consideration of the obligation of celibacy.[11]

Such interior dispositions must be moulded during the future priest's path of formation because, as a man of God and of the Church, he is called to build up the ecclesial community. Being in love with Him who is Eternal, the priest develops an authentic and integral appreciation of humanity. He also increasingly lives the richness of his own affectivity in the gift of himself to God, One and Three, and to his brethren, particularly those who are suffering.

Clearly, these are objectives that can only be reached by the candidate co-operating daily with the work of grace within him. They are objectives that are acquired with a gradual and lengthy path of formation, which is not always linear.[12]

A priestly vocation involves an extraordinary and demanding synergy of human and spiritual dynamics. The candidate, knowing this, can only draw advantage from an attentive and responsible vocational discernment, aimed at differentiating formation paths according to each individual's needs, as well as gradually overcoming his deficiencies on the spiritual and human levels. The Church has the duty of furnishing candidates with an effective integration of the human dimension, in light of the spiritual dimension into which it flows and in which it finds its completion.[13]

II. Preparation of Formators

3. Every formator should have a good knowledge of the human person: his rhythms of growth; his potentials and weaknesses; and his way of living his relationship with God. Thus, it is desirable that bishops – by making use of various experiences, programs and institutions of good reputation – provide a suitable preparation in vocational pedagogy for formators, according to the indications already published by the Congregation for Catholic Education.[14]

Formators need to be adequately prepared to carry out a discernment that, fully respecting the Church's doctrine on the priestly vocation, allows for a reasonably sure decision as to whether the candidate should be admitted to the seminary or house of formation of the religious clergy, or whether he should be dismissed from the seminary or house of formation for reasons of unsuitability. The discernment also must allow for the candidate to be accompanied on his path to acquiring those moral and theological virtues, which are necessary for living, in coherence and interior freedom, the total gift of his life, so as to be a "servant of the Church as communion".[15]

4. The document of this Congregation for Catholic Education, *A Guide to Formation in Priestly Celibacy*, recognizes that "errors in discerning vocations are not rare, and in all too many cases psychological defects, sometimes of a pathological kind, reveal themselves only after ordination to the priesthood. Detecting defects earlier would help avoid many tragic experiences." [16]

Hence, the need for every formator to possess, in due measure, the sensitivity and psychological preparation [17] that will allow him, insofar as possible, to perceive the candidate's true motivations, to discern the barriers that stop him integrating human and Christian maturity, and to pick up on any psychopathic disturbances present in the candidate. The formator must accurately and very prudently evaluate the candidate's history. Nevertheless, this history alone cannot constitute the decisive criterion which would be sufficient for judging whether to admit the candidate or dismiss him from formation. The formator must know how to evaluate the person in his totality, not forgetting the gradual nature of development. He must see the candidate's strong and weak points, as well as the level of awareness that the candidate has of his own problems. Lastly, the formator must discern the candidate's capacity for controlling his own behaviour in responsibility and freedom.

Thus, every formator must be prepared, including by means of specific courses, to understand profoundly the human person as well as the demands of his formation to the ordained ministry. To that end, much advantage can be derived from meeting experts in the psychological sciences, to compare notes and obtain clarification on some specific issues.

III. Contribution of Psychology to Vocational Discernment and Formation

5. Inasmuch as it is the fruit of a particular gift of God, the vocation to the priesthood and its discernment lie outside the strict competence of psychology. Nevertheless, in some cases, recourse to experts in the psychological sciences can be useful. It can allow a more sure evaluation of the candidate's psychic state; it can help evaluate his human dispositions for responding to the divine call; and it can provide some extra assistance for the candidate's human growth. These experts can offer formators an opinion regarding the diagnosis of – and, perhaps, therapy for – psychic disturbances. Moreover, by suggesting ways for favouring a vocational response that is more free, they can help support the development of the human (especially relational) qualities, which are required for the exercise of the ministry.[18]

Even formation for the priesthood must face up to the manifold symptoms of the imbalance rooted in the heart of man,[19] which is symptomized, in a particular way, in the contradictions between the ideal of self-giving to which the candidate consciously aspires, and the life he actually leads. Formation must also deal with the difficulties inherent in the gradual development of the moral virtues. The help of the spiritual director and confessor is fundamental and absolutely necessary for overcoming these difficulties with the grace of God. In some cases, however, the development of these moral qualities can be blocked by certain psychological wounds of the past that have not yet been resolved.

In fact, those who today ask admittance to the seminary reflect, in a more or less accentuated way, the unease of an emerging mentality characterized by consumerism, instability in family and social relationships, moral relativism, erroneous visions of sexuality, the precariousness of choices, and a systematic negation of values especially by the media.

Among the candidates can be found some who come from particular experiences – human, family, professional, intellectual or affective – which, in various ways, have left psychological wounds that are not yet healed and that cause disturbances. These wounds, unknown to the candidate in their real effects, are often erroneously attributed by him to causes outside himself, thus depriving him of the possibility of facing them adequately.[20]

It is clear that the above-mentioned issues can limit the candidate's capacity for making progress on the path of formation towards the priesthood.

"*Si casus ferat*" [21] – that is, in exceptional cases that present particular difficulties – recourse to experts in the psychological sciences, both before admission to the seminary and during the path of formation, can help the candidate overcome those psychological wounds, and interiorize, in an ever more stable and profound way, the type of life shown by Jesus the Good Shepherd, Head and Bridegroom of the Church.[22]

To arrive at a correct evaluation of the candidate's personality, the expert can have recourse to both interviews and tests. These must always be carried out with the previous, explicit, informed and free consent of the candidate.[23]

In consideration of their particularly sensitive nature, the use of specialist psychological or psychotherapeutic techniques must be avoided by the formators.

6. It is useful for the rector and other formators to be able to count on the co-operation of experts in the psychological sciences. Such experts, who cannot be part of the formation team, will have to have specific competence in the field of vocations, and unite the wisdom of the Spirit to their professional expertise.

In choosing which experts to approach for the psychological consultation, it is necessary to guarantee, as much as possible, an intervention that is coherent with the candidate's moral and spiritual formation. This is to avoid any harmful confusion or opposition. Therefore, it must be borne in mind that these experts, as well as being distinguished for their sound human and spiritual maturity, must be inspired by an anthropology that openly shares the Christian vision about the human person, sexuality, as well as vocation to the priesthood and to celibacy. In this way, their interventions may take into account the mystery of man in his personal dialogue with God, according to the vision of the Church.

Wherever such experts are not available, let steps be taken to specifically preparing them.[24]

The assistance offered by the psychological sciences must be integrated within the context of the candidate's entire formation. It must not obstruct, but rather ensure, in a particular way, that the irreplaceable value of spiritual accompaniment is guaranteed; for spiritual accompaniment has the duty of keeping the candidate facing the truth of the ordained ministry, according to the vision of the Church. The atmosphere of faith, prayer, meditation on the Word of God, the study of theology and community life – an atmosphere that is essential so that a generous response to the vocation received from God can mature – will allow the candidate to have a correct understanding of what the recourse to psychology means within his vocational journey, and will allow him to integrate it within that same journey.

7. In faithfulness and coherence to the principles and directives of this document, different countries will have to regulate the recourse to experts in the psychological sciences in their respective *Rationes institutionis sacerdotalis*. The competent Ordinaries or major superiors will have to do the same in the individual seminaries.

a) Initial Discernment

8. Right from the moment when the candidate presents himself for admission to the seminary, the formator needs to be able accurately to comprehend his personality; potentialities; dispositions; and the types of any psychological wounds, evaluating their nature and intensity.

Nor must it be forgotten that there is a possible tendency of some candidates to minimize or deny their own weaknesses. Such candidates do not speak to the formators about some of their serious difficulties, as they fear they will not be understood or accepted. Thus, they nurture barely realistic expectations with respect to their own future. On the other hand, there are candidates who tend to emphasize their own difficulties, considering them insurmountable obstacles on their vocational journey.

The timely discernment of possible problems that block the vocational journey can only be of great benefit for the person, for the vocational institutions and for the Church. Such problems include excessive affective dependency; disproportionate aggression; insufficient capacity for being faithful to obligations taken on; insufficient capacity for establishing serene relations of openness, trust and fraternal collaboration, as well as collaboration with authority; a sexuality identity that is confused or not yet well defined.

In the phase of initial discernment, the help of experts in the psychological sciences can be necessary principally on the specifically diagnostic level, whenever there is a suspicion that psychic disturbances may be present. If it should be ascertained that the candidate needs therapy, this therapy should be carried out before he is admitted to the seminary or house of formation.

The assistance of experts can be useful for formators, including when they are marking out a path of formation tailored to the candidate's specific needs.

When evaluating whether it is possible for the candidate to live the charism of celibacy in faithfulness and joy, as a total gift of his life in the image of Christ the Head and Shepherd of the Church, let it be remembered that it is not enough to be sure that he is capable of abstaining from genital activity. It is also necessary to evaluate his sexual orientation, according to the indications published by this Congregation.[25] Chastity for the Kingdom, in fact, is much more than the simple lack of sexual relationships.

In light of the objectives indicated above, a psychological consultation can, in some cases, be useful.

b) Subsequent Formation

9. During the period of formation, recourse to experts in the psychological sciences can respond to the needs born of any crises; but it can also be useful in supporting the candidate on his journey towards a more sure possession of the moral virtues. It can furnish the candidate with a deeper knowledge of his personality, and can contribute to overcoming, or rendering less rigid, his psychic resistances to what his formation is proposing.

The candidates can give themselves to God with due awareness and freedom, in responsibility towards themselves and the Church, when they have better mastered not only their weaknesses, but also their human and spiritual forces.[26]

A certain Christian and vocational maturity can be reached, including with the help of psychology, illumined and completed by the contribution of the anthropology of the Christian vocation and, therefore, of grace. Nevertheless, one cannot overlook the fact that such maturity will never be completely free of difficulties and tensions, which require interior discipline, a spirit of sacrifice, acceptance of struggle and of the Cross,[27] and the entrusting of oneself to the irreplaceable assistance of grace.[28]

10. It is possible that the candidate – notwithstanding his own commitment and the support of the psychologist, or psychotherapy – could continue to show himself unable to face realistically his areas of grave immaturity – even given the gradual nature of all human growth. Such areas of immaturity would include strong affective dependencies; notable lack of freedom in relations; excessive rigidity of character; lack of loyalty; uncertain sexual identity; deep-seated homosexual tendencies; etc. If this should be the case, the path of formation will have to be interrupted.

The same is also true if it becomes evident that the candidate has difficulty living chastity in celibacy: that is, if celibacy, for him, is lived as a burden so heavy that it compromises his affective and relational equilibrium.

IV. Request for Specialist Evaluations and Respect for the Candidate's Privacy

11. It belongs to the Church to choose persons whom she believes suitable for the pastoral ministry, and it is her right and duty to verify the presence of the qualities required in those whom she admits to the sacred ministry.[29]

Canon 1051, 1° of the Code of Canon Law foresees that, for the scrutiny of the qualities required in view of ordination, one should provide, *inter al.,* for an evaluation of the state of the candidate's physical and psychic health.[30]

Canon 1052 establishes that the bishop, in order to be able to proceed to ordaining the candidate, must have moral certainty that "positive arguments have proved" his suitability (§ 1) and that, in the case of motivated doubt, he must not proceed with the ordination (§ 3).

Hence, the Church has the right to verify the suitability of future priests, including by means of recourse to medical and psychological science. In fact, it belongs to the bishop or competent superior not only to examine the suitability of the candidate, but also to establish that he is suitable. A candidate for the priesthood cannot impose his own personal conditions, but must accept with humility and gratitude the norms and the conditions that the Church herself places, on the part of her responsibility.[31] Therefore, in cases of doubt concerning the candidate's suitability, admission to the seminary or house of formation will sometimes only be possible after a psychological evaluation of the candidate's personality.

12. The formational institution has the right and the duty to acquire the knowledge necessary for a prudentially certain judgement regarding the candidate's suitability. But this must not harm the candidate's right to a good reputation, which any person enjoys, nor the right to defend his own privacy, as prescribed in canon 220 of the Code of Canon Law. This means that the candidate's psychological consultation can only proceed with his previous, explicit, informed and free consent.

Let the formators guarantee an atmosphere of trust, so that the candidate can open up and participate with conviction in the work of discernment and accompaniment, offering "his own convinced and heartfelt co-operation".[32] The candidate is asked to be sincerely and trustingly open with his formators. Only by sincerely allowing them to know him can he be helped on that spiritual journey that he himself is seeking by entering the seminary.

Important, and often determinant in overcoming possible misunderstandings, will be both the educational atmosphere between students and formators – marked by openness and transparency – and the motivations and ways with which the formators will present their suggestion to the candidate that he should have a psychological consultation.

Let them avoid the impression that such a suggestion is the prelude to the candidate's inevitable dismissal from the seminary or house of formation.

The candidate will be able freely to approach an expert who is either chosen from among those indicated by the formators, or chosen by the candidate himself and accepted by the formators.

According to the possibilities, the candidates should be guaranteed a free choice from among various experts who possess the requisites indicated.[33]

If the candidate, faced with a motivated request by the formators, should refuse to undergo a psychological consultation, the formators will not force his will in any way. Instead, they will prudently proceed in the work of discernment with the knowledge they already have, bearing in mind the aforementioned canon 1052 § 1.

V. *The Relationship between those Responsible for Formation and the Expert*

a) Those Responsible in the External Forum

13. In a spirit of reciprocal trust and in co-operation with his own formation, the candidate can be invited freely to give his written consent so that the expert in the psychological sciences, who is bound by confidentiality, can communicate the results of the consultation to the formators indicated by the candidate himself. The formators will make use of any information thus acquired to sketch out a general picture of the candidate's personality, and to infer the appropriate indications for the candidate's further path of formation or for his admission to ordination.

In order to protect, in both the present and the future, the candidate's privacy and good reputation, let particular care be taken so that the professional opinions expressed by the expert be exclusively accessible to those responsible for formation, with the precise and binding proscription against using it in any way other than for the discernment of a vocation and for the candidate's formation.

b) Specific Character of Spiritual Direction

14. The spiritual director's task is not easy, neither in discerning the vocation nor in the area of conscience.

It is a firm principle that spiritual direction cannot, in any way, be interchanged with or substituted by forms of analysis or of psychological assistance. Moreover, the spiritual life, by itself, favours a growth in the human virtues, if there are no barriers of a psychological nature.[34] Bearing these two principles in mind, the spiritual director can find that, in order to clear up any doubts that are otherwise irresolvable and to proceed with greater certainty in the discernment and in spiritual accompaniment, he needs to suggest to the candidate that he undergo a psychological consultation – without, however, ever demanding it.[35]

Should the spiritual director request that the candidate undergo a psychological consultation, it is desirable that the candidate, as well as informing the spiritual director himself about the results of the consultation, will likewise inform the external-forum formator, especially if the spiritual director himself will have invited him to do this.

If the spiritual director should believe it useful that he himself directly acquire information from the consultant, let him proceed according to what has been indicated in n. 13 for the external-forum formators.

The spiritual director will infer from the results of the psychological consultation the appropriate indications for the discernment that is of his competence, as well as the advice he must give the candidate, including as to whether to proceed on the path of formation.

c) Help of the Expert to the Candidate and Formators

15. The expert – insofar as it is asked of him – will help the candidate reach a greater knowledge of himself, of his potentialities and vulnerabilities. He will also help him to compare the declared ideals of the vocation with his own personality, thus encouraging the candidate to develop a personal, free and conscious attachment to his own formation. It will be the task of the expert to furnish the candidate with the appropriate indications concerning the difficulties that he is experiencing, and their possible consequences for his life and future priestly ministry.

The expert, having carried out his evaluation, and also taking into account the indications offered him by the formators, will present them – but only with the candidate's previous written consent – with his contribution to understanding the subject's personality and the problems he is facing or must face.

In accordance with his evaluation and competence, he will also indicate the foreseeable possibilities as regards the growth of the candidate's personality. Moreover, he will suggest, if necessary, forms or pathways of psychological support.

VI. Persons Dismissed From, or Who Have Freely Left, Seminaries or Houses of Formation

16. It is contrary to the norms of the Church to admit to the seminary or to the house of formation persons who have already left or, *a fortiori*, have been dismissed from other seminaries or houses of formation, without first collecting the due information from their respective bishops or major superiors, especially concerning the causes of the dismissal or departure.[36]

The previous formators have the explicit duty of furnishing exact information to the new formators.

Let particular attention be paid to the fact that often candidates leave the educational institution spontaneously so as to avoid an enforced dismissal.

In the case of a transfer to another seminary or house of formation, the candidate must inform the new formators about any psychological consultation previously carried out.

Only with the candidate's free, written consent can the new formators have access to the communication of the expert who carried out the consultation.

In the case of a candidate who, after a previous dismissal, has undergone psychological treatment, if it is held that he can be accepted into the seminary, let first his psychic condition be accurately verified, insofar as possible. This includes collecting the necessary information from the expert who treated him, after having obtained the candidate's free, written consent.

In the case where a candidate, after having had recourse to an expert in psychology, asks to transfer to another seminary or house of formation and does not want to agree to the results being available to the new formators, let it be remembered that the suitability of the candidate must be proved with positive arguments, according to the norm of the aforementioned canon 1052, and, therefore, that all reasonable doubt must be excluded.

Conclusion

17. Let all those who, according to their different responsibilities, are involved in formation offer their convinced co-operation, in respecting the specific competencies of each, so that the discernment and vocational accompaniment of the candidates may be sufficient, thus "bringing to the priesthood only those who have been called, and to bring them adequately trained, namely, with a conscious and free response of adherence and involvement of their whole person with Jesus Christ, who calls them to intimacy of life with him and to share in his mission of salvation." [37]

The Supreme Pontiff Benedict XVI, during the Audience granted to the undersigned Cardinal Prefect on 13 June 2008, approved the present document and authorized its publication.

Rome, 29 June 2008, Solemnity of the Apostles SS. Peter and Paul.

Zenon Card. Grocholewski
Prefect
+ Jean-Louis Bruguès, o.p.
Archbishop-Bishop emeritus of Anger
Secretary

---

[1]John Paul II, Post-Synodal Apostolic Exhortation *Pastores dabo vobis* (25 March 1992), n. 35b-c: *AAS* 84 (1992), 714.

[2]*Ibid.*, n. 35d: *AAS* 84 (1992), 715.

[3]*Ibid.*, n. 65d: *AAS* 84 (1992), 771.

[4]*Ibid.*, n. 35e: *AAS* 84 (1992), 715.

[5]Cf. *ibid.*, nn. 66-67: *AAS* 84 (1992), 772-775.

[6]A very full description of these conditions is given in *Pastores dabo vobis*, nn. 43-44: *AAS* 84 (1992), 731-736; cf. C.I.C., canons 1029 and 1041, 1°.

[7]Inasmuch as "for every priest his spiritual formation is the core which unifies and gives life to his being a priest and his acting as a priest": *Pastores dabo vobis*, n. 45c: *AAS* 84 (1992), 737.

[8]*Pastores dabo vobis*, n. 43: *AAS* 84 (1992), 731-733.

[9]Cf. *ibid.;* cf. also Second Vatican Ecumenical Council, Decree of Priestly Formation *Optatam totius* (28 October 1965), n. 11: *AAS* 58 (1966), 720-721; Decree on the Ministry and Life of Priests *Presbyterorum ordinis* (7 December 1965), n. 3: *AAS* 58 (1966), 993-995; Congregation for Catholic Education, *Ratio fundamentalis institutionis sacerdotalis* (19 March 1985), n. 51.

[10]Cf. *Pastores dabo vobis*, n. 17: *AAS* 84 (1992), 682-684.

[11]Paul VI, in his Encyclical Letter *Sacerdotalis cælibatus*, deals explicitly of this necessary capacity of the candidate for the priesthood, in nn. 63-63: *AAS* 59 (1967), 682-683. In n. 64, he concludes: "The life of the celibate priest, which engages the whole man so totally and so delicately, excludes in fact those of insufficient physical, psychic and moral qualifications. Nor should anyone pretend that grace supplies for the defects of nature in such a man." Cf. also *Pastores dabo vobis*, n. 44: *AAS* 84 (1992), 733-736.

[12]In the developing formation process, affective maturity takes on a particular importance; this is an area of development that requires, today more than ever, particular attention. "In reality, we grow in affective maturity when our hearts adhere to God. Christ needs priests who are mature, virile, capable of cultivating an authentic spiritual paternity. For this to happen, priests need to be honest with themselves, open with their spiritual director and trusting in divine mercy" (Benedict XVI, Speech to priests and religious in the Cathedral of Warsaw [25 May 2006], in *L'Osservatore Romano* [26-27 May 2006], p. 7). Cf. Pontifical Work for Ecclesiastical Vocations, *New Vocations for a New Europe*, Final Document of the Congress on Vocations to the Priesthood and to the Consecrated Life in Europe, Rome, 5-10 May 1997, published by the Congregations for Catholic Education, for the Oriental Churches, for Institutes of Consecrated Life and Societies of Apostolic Life (6 January 1998), n. 37.

[13]Cf. *Pastores dabo vobis*, n. 45a: *AAS* 84 (1992), 736.

[14]Cf. Congregation for Catholic Education, *Directives concerning the Preparation of Seminary Formators* (4 November 1993), nn. 36 and 57-59; cf. especially *Optatam totius*, n. 5: *AAS* 58 (1966), 716-717.

[15]*Pastores dabo vobis*, n. 16e: *AAS* 84 (1992), 682.

[16]Sacred Congregation for Catholic Education, *A Guide to Formation in Priestly Celibacy* (11 April 1974), n. 38.

[17]Cf. *Pastores dabo vobis*, n. 66c: *AAS* 84 (1992), 773; *Directives concerning the Preparation of Seminary Formators*, nn. 57-59.

[18]Cf. *Optatam totius*, n. 11: *AAS* 58 (1966), 720-721.

[19]Cf. Second Vatican Ecumenical Council, Pastoral Constitution on the Church in the Modern World *Gaudium et spes* (7 December 1965), n. 10: *AAS* 58 (1966), 1032-1033.

[20]To understand these assertions better, it is opportune to refer to the following assertions of Pope John Paul II: "Humans, therefore, carry within themselves the seed of eternal life and the vocation to make transcendent values their own. They, however, remain internally vulnerable and dramatically exposed to the risk of failing in their own vocation. This is due to the resistance and difficulties which they encounter in their earthly existence. These may be found on the conscious level, where moral responsibility is involved, or on the subconscious level, and this may be either in ordinary psychic life or in that which is marked by slight or moderate psychic illnesses that do not impinge substantially on one's freedom to strive after transcendent ideals which have been responsibly chosen" (*Address to the Roman Rota* [25 January 1988]: *AAS* 80 [1988], 1181).

[21]Cf. *Ratio fundamentalis institutionis sacerdotalis*, n. 39; Congregation for bishops, Directory for the Pastoral Ministry of bishops *Apostolorum Successores* (22 February 2004), n. 88.

[22]Cf. *Pastores dabo vobis*, n. 29d: *AAS* 84 (1992), 704.

[23]Cf. Sacred Congregation for Religious and Secular Institutes, *Instruction on the Renewal of Formation for Religious Life* (6 January 1969), n. 11 § III: *AAS* 61 (1969), 113.

[24]Cf. John Paul II: "It will therefore be right to pay attention to the formation of expert psychologists, who, with good scientific qualifications, will also have a sound understanding of the Christian vision of life and of the vocation to the priesthood, so as to provide effective support for the necessary integration of the human and supernatural dimensions" (*Speech to the participants at the Plenary Session of the Congregation for Catholic Education* [4 February 2002]: *AAS* 94 [2002], 465).

[25]Cf. Congregation for Catholic Education, *Instruction concerning the Criteria for the Discernment of Vocations with regard to Persons with Homosexual Tendencies in View of their Admission to the Seminary and to Holy Orders* (4 November 2005): *AAS* 97 (2005), 1007-1013.

[26]Cf. *A Guide to Formation in Priestly Celibacy*, n. 38.

[27]Cf. *Pastores dabo vobis*, n. 48d: *AAS* 84 (1992), 744.

[28]Cf. 2 Cor 12, 7-10.

[29]Cf. C.I.C., canons 1025, 1051 and 1052; Congregation for Divine Worship and the Discipline of the Sacraments, Circular Letter to the Most Reverend Diocesan bishops and other Ordinaries with Canonical Faculties to Admit to Sacred Orders concerning: Scrutinies regarding the Suitability of Candidates for Orders" (10 November 1997): *Notitiæ* 33 (1997), pp. 507-518.

[30]Cf. C.I.C., canons 1029, 1031 § 1 and 1041, 1º; *Ratio fundamentalis institutionis sacerdotalis*, n. 39.

[31]Cf. *Pastores dabo vobis*, n. 35g: *AAS* 84 (1992), 715.

[32]*Ibid.*, n. 69b: *AAS* 84 (1992), 778.

[33]Cf. n. 6 of this document.

[34]Cf. note n. 20.

[35]Cf. *Pastores dabo vobis*, n. 40c: *AAS* 84 (1992), 725

Guidelines for the Use of Psychology in Seminary Admissions

Committee on Clergy, Consecrated Life and Vocations
United States Conference of Catholic Bishops
Washington, DC

"Psychological assessment serves in a supportive role to provide greater clarity about an applicant, so that those responsible for the admissions process have a fuller understanding of the applicant besides the many other components of the application process."

—Guidelines for the Use of Psychology in Seminary Admissions

Guidelines for the Use of Psychology in Seminary Admissions was developed and approved by the Committee on Clergy, Consecrated Life and Vocations, Bishop Michael F. Burbidge, Chairman. It was authorized for publication by the Administrative Committee at its March 2015 meeting. It has been directed for publication by the undersigned.

Msgr. Ronny Jenkins
General Secretary, USCCB

USCCB ISBN 978-1-60137-461-5
First Printing, April 2015

information storage and retrieval system, without permission in writing from the copyright holder.

Permission received from the USCCB for reproduction within the appendix of this book.

Table of Contents

Committee on Clergy, Consecrated Life and Vocations

Bishop Michael F. Burbidge, Chairman
Archbishop Samuel J. Aquila
Bishop Earl A. Boyea
Bishop William P. Callahan, OFM Conv.
Bishop Arturo Cepeda
Bishop Thomas A. Daly
Bishop Curtis J. Guillory, SVD
Bishop John G. Noonan
Bishop Daniel E. Thomas

To support the implementation of the directives contained in the *Guidelines for the Use of Psychology in the Admission and Formation of Candidates for the Priesthood*[1] (*Guidelines*) that were issued by the Congregation for Catholic Education in June 2008, and the pertinent

---

[1] Congregation for Catholic Education, *Guidelines for the Use of Psychology in the Admission and Formation of Candidates for the Priesthood* (*Guidelines*) (June 28, 2008), *www.vatican.va/roman_curia/congregations/ccatheduc/documents/rc_con_ccatheduc_doc_20080628_orientamenti_en.html*.

sections of the *Program of Priestly Formation*, 5th Edition (*PPF*),[2] the Committee on Clergy, Consecrated Life and Vocations of the United States Conference of Catholic Bishops provides the following guidelines for bishops, major superiors, and seminary rectors, when developing policies on the use of psychological evaluations in seminary admissions.

The Purposes of a Psychological Evaluation for Seminary Admissions

Psychological assessments help the diocesan or eparchial bishop, the major superior, and the seminary rector gain a greater understanding of developmental, psychological, and other personal factors at work in the life of an applicant and of how these may strengthen or hinder an authentic vocational discernment.

Psychological assessment by professional clinicians provides critical information that otherwise might not be obtained in the course of admissions interviews. Sometimes the psychological report is able to articulate important areas that need to be more fully screened, or it may identify features that warrant serious concern or further discernment by those making the final decisions about admission of the candidate. The process can also provide the applicant with knowledge of his own areas of strength and potential growth as well as some of the actual limits of his own freedom to hear clearly God's call. A thorough assessment can provide significant information for the applicant about his level of intellectual functioning, the presence of acute mental distress, and the characteristic ways he relates to himself and to others.

Psychological assessment serves in a supportive role to provide greater clarity about an applicant, so that those responsible for the admissions process have a fuller understanding of the applicant besides the many other components of the application process.[3]

Finally, psychological assessment can serve as confirmatory evidence in support of conclusions based on the entire admissions process, especially if there is a divergence of views during the screening process.

---

[2] United States Conference of Catholic Bishops, *Program of Priestly Formation, 5th Edition* (PPF) (Washington, DC: United States Conference of Catholic Bishops, 2006), especially nos. 42, 47, 51-57.

[3] *PPF*, no. 47.

Suggested Components of a Psychological Assessment and Report
for Admissions

Psychological assessment seeks to understand the intellectual, emotional, and psychological functioning of the applicant through the use of psychometric measures; it is the mental equivalent of a physical evaluation.

To assist those responsible for judging the suitability of the applicant for seminary formation, according to numbers 47 and 53-56 of the *PPF*, the following components of a psychological evaluation and written report would be especially instructive:

1. Clinical interview (a structured interview of the applicant that is focused specifically on his mental health history)

2. Psychosocial and Psychosexual Interview (an interview that generally covers "birth to the present" of the applicant)

3. Intelligence Assessment (the applicant's current cognitive functioning)

4. Psychological Testing (structured written, visual, or verbal measures administered to assess the cognitive and emotional functioning of the applicant)

5. Discussion Section (a written psychological assessment report that includes an overall summary, important areas of the applicant's past that continue to inform his present emotional and relational life, and identification of the applicant's strengths and areas for growth)

6. Recommendations (an assessment report that offers the applicant and admission personnel concrete suggestions to help him move toward his greatest potential)

7. Oral Feedback Session (a meeting of the psychologist with the applicant and some admission person to discuss the results of the psychological evaluation)

In presenting observations, it is helpful if the psychologist translates psychological vocabulary into language understandable to both the applicant and to the admissions personnel, as well as to the bishop or major superior. In addition, as prescribed by numbers 51 and 52 of the *PPF*, the reporting should demonstrate cultural sensitivity to Catholic anthropology, the ethnic background of the applicant, and the demands of eventual formation for the priesthood. In the end, the assessment will be most helpful if it identifies the positive traits the applicant possesses for a mature and healthy discernment of a calling to the priesthood.

Number 51 of the *PPF* encourages admission personnel to articulate for psychologists those human traits and qualities that contradict an authentic vocation to the priesthood. Without attempting an exhaustive list, the following contraindications are provided as a guide to psychologists as they write their report on the applicant's suitability:

1. Inability to be formed (blocks to growth and conversion); rigidity or inflexibility that precludes openness to guidance and influence

2. Psychopathology that cannot be managed easily with medication and that would disrupt or preclude healthy ministry

3. Areas of serious emotional vulnerability, given the demands of the priest's responsibilities, celibacy, and life as a public figure and man of communion

4. Personality traits and disorders inconsistent with or compromising healthy ministry

5. Pervasive developmental disorders that may lead to behaviors incompatible with the human formation traits and characteristics of healthy, priestly relationships and ministry

6. Relations with self or others that are so damaged or shame-based that the person cannot relate or assume healthy leadership

7. Significant troubles with addictive disorders or habits

8. Activity or inclination toward sexual activity with a minor or other traits that might indicate the person could be a harm to minors

9. Psycho-sexual disorders[4]

10. History of psychopathic deviance, criminality, and unethical, illegal, and unconscionable behavior

11. Multiple physical and medical concerns that significantly impair the ability of the candidate to function responsibly

12. Intellectual limitations that would hinder either higher academic studies or the navigation of the complexities of leadership in parish life

---

[4] *PPF*, nos. 55-56; Congregation for Catholic Education, "A Guide to Formation in Priestly Celibacy" (April 11, 1974), in *Norms for Priestly Formation*, vol. 1 (Washington, DC: National Conference of Catholic Bishops, 1994), 153-205; Congregation for Catholic Education, *Instruction Concerning the Criteria for Discernment of Vocations with Regard to Persons with Homosexual Tendencies in View of their Admission to the Seminary and to Holy Orders* (August 31, 2005), http://www.vatican.va/roman_curia/congregations/ccatheduc/documents/rc_con_ccatheduc_doc_20 051104_istruzione_en.html

13. Severe learning disorders and intellectual disability compounded with lack of intellectual curiosity

It may be discerned that an applicant is in need of some therapeutic services to address matters that are not entirely disqualifying for admission to the seminary. The timely discernment of and attention to such problems that would hinder the vocational journey can only be of great benefit to the applicant as well as to the Church.[5]

The report of the psychological assessment may recommend the postponement of admittance to the seminary, so that adequate therapy or counseling may take place. This is especially true when the applicant would require a significant duration (e.g., a year or more), frequency (e.g., multiple times per week), or intensity of therapy, which would limit the applicant's ability to engage fully in the seminary program.[6]

On the other hand, the report may recommend, for unresolved issues that do not require extensive therapy, the admission of the applicant while such therapy continues.

Desired Qualities of the Psychological Professional Who Conducts Evaluations for Seminary Admissions

Professionals in the field of psychology are educated in human behavior. They are taught to understand the unique emotional and relational components of human development in assessing applicants to the seminary. Their primary role is to provide information to the bishop or major superior, who along with the applicant is involved in the discernment process.

Number 51 of the PPF presumes that each seminary will develop its own guidelines for psychologists. It is especially important to engage professionals who are licensed and have the appropriate clinical experience and expertise to conduct the testing and evaluation process and to provide appropriate interpretation. Clinical experts are ethically bound to

---

[5] *Guidelines*, no. 8.

[6] Pope John Paul II, *Pastores Dabo Vobis* (*PDV*) (Washington, DC: United States Conference of Catholic Bishops, 1992), no. 61; *Guidelines* , no. 8; *PPF*, nos. 80-8. *PPF*, number 53, states, "If long-term therapeutic work is indicated, this is best accomplished before the decision is made concerning entrance into the seminary. At times, the gravity of family or personal issues is such that, if the candidate has not yet adequately dealt with these issues, entrance into the seminary program should be denied."

address only the areas in which they are properly educated, supervised, trained, experienced, and competent. They are to be outside consultants and not part of the formation team of a seminary.[7]

It is reasonable to expect that the professional chosen for the evaluation of an applicant would be able to demonstrate an understanding and knowledge of Catholic tradition and ecclesiastical culture; be familiar with the criteria for inclusion and exclusion to initial seminary formation; and evidence a respect for a vocation to the Catholic priesthood. It is critical, for example, that the psychological professional's evaluation of the applicant for the seminary adequately reflects the Catholic understanding of the human person as a

1. Transcendent being, created in the image of God
2. Who is a unity of body and soul, rational, real, and relational
3. Whose flourishing will be realized in a life of committed self-giving through the priesthood
4. Whose happiness cannot be reduced to the mere satisfaction of needs

Within this context, it is especially helpful were the professional to be familiar with the Catholic teaching on the nature of the priesthood and have a clear understanding of what chaste celibacy for the sake of the Kingdom means. Without these understandings, the clinician may limit the scope of the interviews and may not be able to provide relevant feedback or appropriate recommendations about the test data obtained.[8]

Psychological assessment is not a value-free endeavor. As was already intimated above, culture, ethnicity, and race influence the perception, thoughts, behavior, and beliefs of both the evaluator and the applicant. The professional must be able to interpret correctly the results of psychological testing in light of the cultural background of the applicant. In addition, most of the psychological measures currently available to the professional were developed and originally scaled based on the responses of Caucasian US citizens as the control group for the development of interpretive norms. Using the same tests on applicants from other cultures or countries can sometimes distort the results. Given the increasing number of foreign-born applicants, it is especially important that the psychologist be familiar with any cultural factors that may affect the reliability of the assessment findings.[9]

---

[7] *Guidelines*, no. 6. The necessary distinctions between the role of the psychological professional and the seminary formators are elaborated in *PPF*, no. 80.

[8] *Guidelines*, no. 6; *PPF*, no. 51.

[9] *PPF*, no. 52.

Privacy and Confidentiality

The natural right to safeguard one's privacy and the right to a good reputation[10] means that while a psychological evaluation may be necessary in assessing the applicant's suitability for admission to the seminary, no one can be forced or coerced into undergoing psychological evaluation that violates an individual's privacy. Therefore, as the *Guidelines* of the Congregation for Catholic Education make clear, before any attempt is made at undertaking a psychological evaluation, the applicant must give explicit, free, and informed consent.[11]

Admissions personnel would do well to have an articulated policy about how applicants are to be informed in advance of the nature of the process (what is involved in the interviews, standardized tests, etc.); who will be conducting the evaluation (the name and qualifications of the professionals involved); how the information will be used (to whom the report will be shown and its role in the admissions process); and how the information might be used in the future (in providing remedial assistance if the applicant is not immediately accepted or in assisting with the future formation of the seminarian who is accepted).[12]

While the applicant retains the right to privacy, the Church also has the right and responsibility to choose only suitable applicants for admission to the seminary. This would seem to require a determination not only of the absence of serious defects but also of the presence of positive indicators of the candidate's psychological health.[13]

The psychological evaluation that is part of the admissions process is such an inquiry,[14] And it is lawful, provided that the applicant's right to privacy is not illegitimately violated in the process.

A proper balance between the right and obligation of the Church to judge a man's suitability and his right to safeguard his privacy can be reached if the following additional principles are applied:[15]

---

[10] Cf. *CIC*, c. 220; *CCEO*, c. 23.

[11] *Guidelines*, no. 12.

[12] *PPF*, no. 57; *Guidelines*, no. 12.

[13] In the Latin Church, *CIC*, c. 1052 §1 explicitly indicates that the bishop may proceed to ordination only after an investigation has been conducted according to the norm of law and "positive arguments have proven the suitability of the candidate." See also *CIC*, c. 241 §1.

[14] *CIC*, c. 1051, 1º & 2º.

[15] These principles are found especially in *PDV*, nos. 44 & 69; *Guidelines* , no. 12; and *PPF*, no. 57.

1. The motivations for requiring the psychological evaluation and the ways in which that requirement is communicated to the applicant are done in a manner that engenders trust and cooperation rather than fear and apprehension.

2. The applicant is able to approach a psychological expert who is either chosen from among those indicated (when this is possible) by the vocation director or chosen by the applicant and accepted by the vocation director.

3. The vocation director observes a careful vigilance that protects the privacy and reputation of the applicants.

4. Clear policies are enunciated concerning who will have access to any of the admissions materials, under what conditions, and the degree of confidentiality to which those persons are bound regarding the information, including the civil obligation they may have as mandated reporters of child abuse or neglect.

5. There is a policy regarding retention of records, including after the non-admission of an applicant or the departure of the accepted applicant from the seminary.

Role of Psychological Information in Formation

The findings of the entire admissions process, if the applicant is accepted by the bishop or major superior, are to be shared with the rector and admission team of the seminary in a timely manner. [16] The rector may decide to share this material, including the psychological evaluation report, with the appropriate formation faculty. This report or an abbreviated version thereof may contain significant elements gleaned from the full psychological assessment but should avoid the most intimate details; it is appropriate that it include the assessor's recommendations for the applicant to succeed in the seminary formation program. [17] It is important for the seminary to articulate in its policy how this material is to be kept confidential and with whom it can be legitimately shared. In addition, this communication of the assessment findings may be made only when there is prior, explicit, free, and informed consent given by the applicant prior to the psychological evaluation.

Some ways in which the psychological assessment can be helpful to the formation team include the following:

1. To identify the presence of fundamental markers of human maturity

---

[16] *PPF*, no. 48.

[17] *PPF*, no. 57.

2. To highlight strengths and internal resources available for formation work and future pastoral ministry

3. To identify vulnerabilities that need to be addressed in the course of formation

4. To confront the seminarian with reliable information about himself that he may be tempted to resist

5. To note factors that will influence how formation staff can most effectively work with the seminarian and offer the support he needs

6. To help integrate the dimensions of seminary formation, especially in reference to human formation, such as the importance of affective maturity for intellectual, spiritual, and pastoral formation

Priestly formation requires the seminarian to face the difficulties inherent in the development of moral virtues and the contraindications between his conscious aspirations and the life he actually lives. The entire formation team is there to assist him in this process. Thus, the psychological report can be of great assistance to the seminarian and to those responsible for his formation.[18]

Obviously, the material above regarding privacy and confidentiality apply at the level of seminarian formation just as they do at the admissions level. Some additional principles may assist the seminary in this regard:

1. The seminarian is himself a necessary and irreplaceable agent responsible for his own formation.

2. The seminarian works to acquire the necessary affective maturity and training in freedom that is required of him in response to his vocation.

3. The formation atmosphere between the seminarian and the formators is marked by openness and transparency.

4. Formators guarantee an atmosphere of trust for the seminarian to provide appropriate self-disclosure and participate with conviction in the work of discernment and accompaniment, offering his own convinced and heartfelt cooperation.

---

[18] *Guidelines*, nos. 5 & 9.

Retention of Records

The retention of pre-admission psychological evaluation reports may become an issue especially with regard to the seminarian's early departure from the program of formation, due either to a voluntary withdrawal or involuntary dismissal. If a seminarian was dismissed from a program of priestly formation, his application to return to the same or another seminary may not be considered for at least two years following dismissal.[19] If a former seminarian wishes to reapply after a voluntary departure, sufficient time must be given for an evaluation of his prior background and his new application. The length of time is to be determined according to the circumstances of each individual.[20]

The departure of a seminarian suggests the necessity to retain the original report of the psychological evaluation and any other observations pertaining to its application during the seminarian's time in the formation program. The seminary rector is ultimately responsible for safeguarding these records. Generally speaking, no release of information is to be made without the consent of the seminarian, unless legitimately ordered by a court of competent jurisdiction. Since there may be applicable civil laws concerning the confidentiality of a psychological evaluation, whoever has responsibility for retaining the records would be advised to consult civil legal counsel before any information is released.[21]

---

[19] *PPF*, no. 62.

[20] Special attention should be given to The United States Conference of Catholic Bishop's *Norms Concerning Applications for Priestly Formation from Those Previously Enrolled in a Formation Program*, which are published as "Addendum A" in the PPF.

[21] Agreements with psychological experts may also govern the retention and further use of pre-admission psychological evaluations. Such would be the case where the psychological expert indicates that no further distribution of the evaluation may be made without prior consent. Experts may be concerned about the validity of a psychological evaluation that is several years old.

Confidentiality and Knowledge Requirements in Seminary Formation

Sister Joseph Marie Ruessmann, RSM, JD, JCD, MBA

The following by Sister Joseph Marie Ruessmann, RSM, is a comprehensive study of the historical development of the concept of internal and external fora. Her conclusion offers elements to be included in a statement of policy concerning confidentiality and inserted into seminary handbooks.

This article approaches the topic of confidentiality in seminary formation by applying the principles presented in the Church documents on priestly formation since those documents, besides the Code of Canon Law, are what would be considered the norms for seminaries to follow. The hierarchy of authority behind the documents is:

1) *The Code of Canon Law* (1983)

2) Documents of the Apostolic See

   a) Documents issued by the Congregation for Clergy (in January 2013, it became responsible for formation in seminaries), primarily:

   Ratio Fundamentalis Institutionis Sacerdotalis (issued on Dec.8, 2016) ("*Ratio*").

   b) Documents issued by the Congregation for Catholic Education before 2013, primarily:

   1. "Guidelines for the Use of Psychology in the Admission and Formation of Candidates for the Priesthood" (2008);

2.   Final Report on Apostolic Visitation of Seminaries in the United States (Dec.15, 2008);

3.   "Instruction Concerning the Criteria for the Discernment of Vocations with regard to Persons with Homosexual Tendencies in view of their Admission to the Seminary and to Holy Orders" (2005);

4.   "Instruction to the Episcopal Conferences on the Admission to Seminary of Candidates Coming from Other Seminaries or Religious Families" (1996);

5.   "Directives Concerning the Preparation of Seminary Educators" (1993) [*Origins* 23:22 (Jan. 27, 1994) 557-571; also published as "Directives on the Preparation of Formators in Seminaries," in *Enchiridion Vaticanum* 13 (1996) 3224-3253.

c) Documents issued by the Congregation for Divine Worship and the Discipline of the Sacraments, primarily:

"Circular Letter to the Most Reverend Diocesan Bishops and other Ordinaries with Canonical Faculties to Admit to Sacred Orders concerning: Scrutinies regarding the Suitability of Candidates for Orders" (1997).

d)   [for members of religious institutes]
Documents issued by the Congregation for Institutes of Consecrated Life and Societies of Apostolic Life, primarily:

Directives on Formation in Religious Institutes (1990).

3) United States Conference of Catholic Bishops, *Program for Priestly Formation*, 5th ed. (2005)(approved originally by the Congregation for Catholic Education, and approved in 2015 for another five years by the Congregation for Clergy)("*PPF*").

The *Ratio* promulgated by the Congregation for Clergy in December 2016 is similar to the previous *Ratio* (which was promulgated in 1985 by the Congregation for Catholic Education) in that it includes guidelines and norms regarding vocation promotion, minor and major seminaries, the four pillars of formation, the stages of formation, and roles of persons at the seminary; and calls for the conferences of bishops of the nations to submit their own *Ratio Nationalis* to the Congregation in conformity with the Congregation's *Ratio*. The new *Ratio* has a different tone than the previous *Ratio*. It emphasizes integrated and communitarian formation, the unity of formation, and personal accompaniment and community accompaniment of the seminarian, in an atmosphere of mutual trust.[1] The seminarian is to be formed to interior maturity and interior freedom, not just "demonstrating a 'veneer of virtuous habits,' a merely external and formalistic obedience to abstract principles."[2] The seminarian is to let himself be known, relating to his formators with transparency; and have frequent and regular conversations with his formators.[3]

The old *Ratio* spoke of "superiors."[4] The new *Ratio* instead speaks of "formators," which include at least the rector and the spiritual director,[5] and, depending on the size of the seminary, could include others, such as a coordinator of human formation.[6] The *Ratio* sometimes lists "formators" separately from "spiritual directors," applying the text to both groups equally.[7]

In this article, the term "formator" is used to mean only those whom are called "formation advisors/mentors and directors" in the *PPF*,[8] to distinguish this person from the spiritual director. (The *Ratio* includes both persons in its use of the term "formators," except where it refers separately to the spiritual director.)

Part A. Confidentiality requirements regarding the inner life of seminarians

Two canons of the Code of Canon Law are the bases of confidentiality requirements in seminary formation: c. 220 regarding the right (of everyone) to a good reputation and to protect one's privacy, and c. 240 §2 regarding the prohibition against asking a seminarian's spiritual director for his opinion as to whether the seminarian should be ordained.

---

[1] See nos. 3, 44-53, 90, 92.

[2] No. 41.

[3] Nos. 45, 46.

[4] Nos. 27-31.

[5] These two persons are the minimum formators required by the Code of Canon Law for a seminary. See *Ratio*, no. 133.

[6] No. 137.

[7] See section C4d2C below.

[8] No. 80.

1) Right to a good reputation and to protection of privacy

The seminarian has the right to his good reputation and to protect his privacy. Canon 220 states, "No one is permitted to harm illegitimately the good reputation which a person possesses nor to injure the right of any person to protect his or her own privacy."

One of the sources of canon 220 was the Second Vatican Council's pastoral constitution on the Church, *Gaudium et Spes*. *Gaudium et Spes* includes the rights to a good reputation and to protection of one's privacy as basic human rights, which originate in the natural law.[9] The document describes the forum of conscience as "man's most secret core, and his sanctuary, [where] he is alone with God whose voice echoes in his depths."[10]

The right to protect one's privacy is the right not to have to manifest one's conscience, with "conscience" understood as one's psychological or moral intimacy; the intimacy of one's interior.[11] Canon 220 is based on the dignity of the person, his right to guard his interior life, as a part of his person, from invasion or intrusion, as he might guard his property.[12]

According to an Instruction issued by the Vatican Secretary of State in 1976, the standard for the protection of a person's right to protect his privacy under c. 220 is that his consent be previous, explicit, informed, and free.[13] The Congregation for Clergy confirmed

---

[9] No. 26.

[10] No. 16.

[11] See Secretariat of State, *Instruction*, 6 Aug. 1976, issued to the pontifical representatives throughout the world to share with the bishops' conferences of their countries; and referred to in a 1998 decision of the Congregation for Clergy; as reported in Rev. Gregory Ingels, "Protecting the Right to Privacy when examining issues affecting the life and ministry of clerics and religious," in *Studia canonica* 34 (2000), pp. 439-466, p. 444.

Some canonists would interpret the canonical right to "privacy" more broadly. In his commentary on Code c.220, Fr. Daniel Cenalmor states, "...the right to one's own privacy also extends, within the Church, to everything that does not fall under the scope of the public nor commonly known..." *Exegetical Commentary on the Code of Canon Law*, University of Navarre (Midwest Theological Forum, Chicago, 2004), vol. II/1, pp. 126-132, p. 131.

[12] See Marcozzi, Vittorio, SJ, "Il diritto all propria intimità nel nuovo codice di diritto canonico," in La Civiltà Cattolica, Anno 134 (1983), vol. IV, pp. 573-580.

[13] The Instruction, which was issued to the pontifical representatives throughout the world, stated, "*It is illegal for anyone, even religious or diocesan superiors, to enter into the psychological or moral intimacy of a person without having obtained his previous, explicit, informed, and absolutely free consent...*"

the requirement of consent in a case of hierarchical recourse to the Congregation in 1998, agreeing with a priest that his bishop could not oblige him to undergo a psychological evaluation. The Congregation stated, "It is the consistent teaching of the Magisterium that investigation of the intimate psychological and moral status of the interior life of any member of the Christian faithful cannot be carried on except with the consent of the one to undergo such evaluation..."[14]

The "previous, explicit, informed, and free" requirement for consent seems to apply to psychological investigations (assessments, evaluations, consultations, and therapy), which have as their intent the probing of a person's interior life. The psychologist attempts to enter the person's "inner core," having him reveal his psyche, inducing disclosure, by various means, such as personality tests. This might be done, for example, on behalf of a seminary that is trying to determine if a person is suitable for entrance into the seminary.

It seems that the consent requirement does not apply to seminary spiritual directors and formators (or the Bishop or rectors) in their questioning of seminarians[15] because:

1. The Vatican Instruction and the Congregation for Clergy's decision, in presenting the consent requirement, spoke of it only in regard to obliging someone to undergo psychological testing or a psychological evaluation. They did not talk about the direct questioning of a subject by a superior.[16]

See my article "Internal Forum and External Forum in the Seminary Revisited—Part 2: The Role of the Rector and Formators," in *Seminary Journal*, Fall 2012, vol. 18, no. 2, pp. 95-102, pp. 95-96. See also Rev. Gregory Ingels, "Protecting the Right to Privacy...", pp. 443-444.

[14] See Ingels, "Protecting the Right to Privacy...", p.445.

[15] Nonetheless, since the seminarian's expectations might differ from those of the seminary, it seems advisable for the seminary to obtain from each new seminarian a signed agreement in regard to the seminary's policies. See below, the Conclusion.

[16] The Instruction to the pontifical representatives was accompanied by an article in 1976 by Vittorio Marcozzi, SJ, about the right to privacy: "Indagini psicologiche e diritti della persona," in La Civiltà Cattolica, Anno 127 (1976), vol. II, pp. 541-551. The article was about the violation of a person's right to privacy by obliging him to undergo psychological testing or evaluation, not about direct questioning by a superior.

In his commentary on Code c.220, Fr. Daniel Cenalmor states, "...no one can force another to let one's personal privacy be analyzed; one must first have explicit, informed and absolutely free permission." He cites Fr. Marcozzi's second article (see n. 12 above). *Exegetical Commentary on the Code of Canon Law*, University of Navarre (Midwest Theological Forum, Chicago, 2004), vol. II/1, pp. 126-132, p. 131.

2. In the Church documents on priestly formation since the Second Vatican Council, all of the references to the candidate's right to privacy relate to asking him to undergo psychological testing or evaluation, or to the results of psychological testing and other confidential materials.[17] None of the passages on privacy refer to questioning of seminarians by seminary staff persons or to seminarians' conversations with them.

3. The consent requirement does not seem practicable for conversations or dialogue with someone with whom one has an ongoing relationship, regular interaction, and with whom one lives in community; and

4. The consent requirement does not fit with the roles of the spiritual director and formator, who are to have frequent (regular) meetings with the seminarian for indepth conversations.[18]

Even if c. 220 would not prevent seminary spiritual directors or formators (or Bishop or rector) from asking a seminarian about his interior life ("inner core"), they may not require or insist upon a self-revelation. This can be deduced from the fact that seminary spiritual directors and formators may not oblige a seminarian to have a psychological consultation. The spiritual director can "suggest to the candidate that he undergo a psychological consultation – without, however, ever demanding it."[19] "If the candidate, faced with a motivated request by the formators, should refuse to undergo a psychological consultation, the formators will not force his will in any way. Instead, they will prudently proceed in the work of discernment with the knowledge they already have..."[20]

Requiring someone to undergo a psychological consultation would be to oblige someone indirectly to make a revelation of his "inner core." The fact that a spiritual director or formator cannot force a revelation of a seminarian's inner core through another implies that the spiritual director or formator cannot force it himself directly. He can ask for a self-revelation (a manifestation of "conscience") by a seminarian, but cannot insist on it. The c.

---

[17] See *The Gift of the Priestly Vocation: Ratio Fundamentalis Institutionis Sacerdotalis* ("*Ratio*"), L'Osservatore Romano, Vatican City 12/08/16, no. 194; "Apostolorum Successores," Directory for the Pastoral Ministry of Bishops, Feb. 22, 2004, no. 88; *Guidelines for the Use of Psychology in the Admission and Formation of Candidates for the Priesthood*, June 28, 2008, nos. 12, 13; USCCB's Program for Priestly Formation, 5th ed. (2005) ("*PPF*"), nos. 52, 57.

[18] See C4d below.

[19] Congregation for Catholic Education, *Guidelines for the Use of Psychology...*, no.14.

[20] *Guidelines*, no. 12.

220 right to privacy would allow a seminarian to refuse to discuss personal matters.[21] Code c. 246 §4 recognizes this when it says that each seminarian should have a spiritual director to whom he "can confidently open his conscience." The use of the word "can" instead of "ought to" or "must" indicates that the opening of one's conscience cannot be forced.

Similarly, the Code of Canon Law, in c. 630 §5 (which would apply to seminarians in religious institutes), forbids religious superiors from inducing a religious to make a manifestation of his conscience. This means that a religious superior may not insist on a manifestation, or put pressure on a member to make a manifestation. If a superior asks a member for a self-revelation and the member refuses, the superior must accept his refusal.[22]

2) Spiritual direction as a confidential relationship, "in the internal forum"

The USCCB's *Program for Priestly Formation* ("*PPF*") states, "Seminarians should confide their personal history, personal relationships, prayer experiences, the cultivation of virtues, their temptations, and other significant topics to their spiritual director...."[23] Spiritual direction is a confidential relationship, subject to the rules of moral theology regarding the extent of obligation of secrecy for the matter divulged.[24]

In the Code of Canon Law, the term "internal forum" signifies the exercise of the power of jurisdiction in the Church in a hidden way.[25] The Code does not use the term "internal forum" in relation to spiritual direction since the spiritual director does not exercise the power of jurisdiction. The Code does not say that the spiritual director is in the internal forum or that the spiritual director of a seminarian may never reveal to anyone that which he learned in spiritual direction. It only says that the opinion of the confessor and of the spiritual director may not be asked in regard to whether to admit a seminarian to Orders or to dismiss him from the seminary.[26]

The Congregation for Clergy, in its document on spiritual direction, does not say that

---

[21] His refusal to answer, though, could have consequences. The spiritual director would have the option to stop being his spiritual director, and the seminary could tell the seminarian that he may not continue at the seminary if he does not cooperate.

[22] See my article "Internal Forum and External Forum in the Seminary Revisited—Part 2: The Role of the Rector and Formators," in *Seminary Journal*, Fall 2012, vol. 18, no. 2, pp. 95-102, p. 97.

[23] Fifth edition, no. 128.

[24] See my article "Internal Forum and External Forum in the Seminary Revisited—Part 1: The Role of the Spiritual Director," in *Seminary Journal*, Fall 2012, vol. 18, no. 2, pp. 89-94, p. 91.

[25] See "Internal Forum and External Forum in the Seminary Revisited—Part 1, p. 89.

[26] C. 240 §2.

the spiritual director, even in the seminary, is in the internal forum. It says only that the "exercise of the power of jurisdiction in the Church should always respect the reserve and the silence of the spiritual director."[27] In its *Ratio*, the Congregation for Clergy states that the spiritual director is in the internal forum: the spiritual director has the "responsibility for the spiritual journey of the seminarians in the internal forum."[28]

The Congregation for Catholic Education, in its report on its visitation of seminaries in the United States, says, "There is confusion, in places, as to what the internal forum is (it covers only sacramental confession and spiritual direction..."[29] In another document, the Congregation says that the spiritual director, although he is bound to secrecy, represents the Church in the internal forum.[30]

The Congregation for Institutes of Consecrated Life and Societies of Apostolic Life ("CIVCSVA") [for members of religious institutes] also talks of the spiritual director being in the internal forum: "...religious should have a person available to them, who may be called a spiritual director or spiritual counselor, for the internal, even non-sacramental, forum."[31]

The *PPF* mentions four times that the spiritual director is in the internal forum.[32] For example, it states, "Disclosures that a seminarian makes in the course of spiritual direction belong to the internal forum. Consequently, the spiritual director is held to the strictest confidentiality concerning information received in spiritual direction. He may neither reveal it nor use it."[33] It also states, "Since spiritual direction takes place in the internal forum, the relationship of seminarians to their spiritual director is a privileged and confidential one. Spiritual directors may not participate in the evaluation of those they currently direct or whom they directed in the past."[34]

---

[27] *The Priest, Minister of Divine Mercy: An Aid for Confessors and Spiritual Directors* (Libreria Editrice Vaticana, 2011), no. 103.

[28] *Ratio*, no. 136.

[29] *Final Report on Apostolic Visitation of Seminaries in the United States*, Dec. 15, 2008, p. 14, no. 6.

[30] *Instruction concerning the Criteria for the Discernment of Vocations with regard to Persons with Homosexual Tendencies in view of their Admission to the Seminary and to Holy Orders*, Aug. 31, 2005, no. 3.

[31] *Directives on Formation in Religious Institutes*, Feb. 2, 1990, no. 63.

[32] Nos. 80, 134, 332, 333

[33] No. 134.

[34] No. 133.

Part B. Requirements for knowledge about the seminarian

The above principles of confidentiality restrict access to information about seminarians. On the other hand, Church documents indicate the need for limits on confidentiality in seminary formation for more fruitful formation of the candidates, for the sake of ordaining only suitable candidates, and for the early detection of problems in candidates.[35]

1) Openness as docility for formation

The seminarian needs to be open with his formators and spiritual director in order to be formed and directed spiritually to be suitable as a priest. Seminarians should be open and trusting not only with the spiritual director, but also with the formators. Trust and openness by the seminarian shows a mature appreciation of authority, and shows docility and obedience; an acceptance of God's will as manifested through one's superiors; and the desire for self-knowledge as a means to open oneself to conversion.[36]

2) Knowledge for determining suitability

The Code of Canon Law requires that the Bishop ensure that the candidate has the necessary qualities:

> "Only those are to be promoted to orders who, in the prudent judgment of their own bishop... all things considered, have integral faith, are moved by the right intention, have the requisite knowledge, possess a good reputation, and are endowed with integral morals and proven virtues and the other physical and psychic qualities in keeping with the order to be received." [37]

The Code requires that the suitability of the seminarian for ordination be positively proven:

---

[35] Federal and state laws protecting minors are a further reason for limits on confidentiality in the seminary. The viewing of child pornography, such as on the Internet, is a crime in many states. Also, statutes in many states require anyone who has information about the sexual abuse of a child to report it to the state.

[36] See section C3 below.

[37] C. 1029.

"For a bishop conferring ordination by his own right to proceed to the ordination, he must be sure…that, after the investigation has been conducted according to the norm of law, positive arguments have proven the suitability of the candidate." [38]

The Congregation for Clergy, in the *Ratio*, has elaborated that this suitability must be clearly demonstrated and reasons given or, in other words *"positive arguments give moral certainty of the suitability of the candidate,"* and not simply the absence of problematic situations…."[39]

The seminarian's rights to privacy and to protect his reputation are limited by the common good of the Church. Ecclesiastical authority is entitled to regulate, in view of the common good, the exercise of rights that are proper to Christ's faithful.[40] The ordaining of only suitable ministers is part of the common good of the Church. The suitability of a priest affects everyone—himself, his bishop, his fellow priests, the faithful he serves, and the public who see him as a representative of the Church. The priest is a public figure and should be a model, not a source of damage or scandal.

3) Timely detection of problems

The common good of the Church requires timely detection of problems in candidates to the priesthood. Detecting and addressing defects in candidates as early as possible is a way to help them and to avoid problems later. The Congregation for Catholic Education has stated, "The timely discernment of possible problems that block the vocational journey can only be of great benefit for the person, for the vocational institutions and for the Church"; and "…errors in discerning vocations are not rare, and in all too many cases, psychological defects, sometimes of a pathological kind, reveal themselves only after ordination to the priesthood. Detecting defects earlier would help avoid many tragic experiences."[41]

The Congregation for Divine Worship and the Discipline of the Sacraments, in 1997, wrote:

In the course of its examination and processing of the procedural acts relating to the dispensation from the obligations of the clerical state together with dismissal from the same

---

[38] C. 1052 §1.

[39] *Ratio* no. 206. See also *Guidelines for the Use of Psychology…*, no. 11.

[40] C. 223 §2.

[41] *Guidelines for the Use of Psychology…*, no. 8, no. 4, respectively.

state. It is often clear that among the reasons for the numerous defections of both priests and deacons is a certain haste in the analysis of the suitability of their promotion to Sacred Orders.

In these cases there have been departures from the requirement of ensuring, prior to Ordination, the absence of defects, impediments and irregularities in the candidate and the presence of the positive requirements dictated by prudence and prescribed by canonical norms, and an omission, too, of a serious evaluation of certain symptoms of unsuitability that have come to light during the years of formation.[42]

The *PPF* also recommends apprising seminarians of their progress and prospects as early as possible:

- "Each seminary must provide a procedure for the evaluation of the seminarians. As part of this procedure, each seminary should ensure…that the seminarians are apprised of their progress as early as possible in their formation, particularly if there are concerns…"[43]

- "Seminarians who lack the positive qualities for continuing in formation should not be advanced in the seminary program. They should be advised to leave the seminary. Seminarians not recommended for advancement should be notified as early as possible and in a constructive manner…."[44]

Part C. Resolution of potential tensions

Part A spoke of norms pertaining to restrictions on obtaining or revealing a revelation of a seminarian's interior life. Part B spoke of the need for openness by seminarians and the Church's need for indepth knowledge of candidates for the priesthood.

This Part C will present the norms that represent how the Church has resolved the potential tension or conflict between the two aspects. The resolution is by Church norms that:

---

[42] Cover Letter Nov. 28, 1997, to the Circular Letter, "Scrutinies regarding the Suitability of Candidates for Orders," Prot. 589/97, Nov. 10, 1997.

[43] No. 274.

[44] No. 287.

1. provide, in unusual cases, for action by the spiritual director;
2. provide, on a periodic basis, for information on a candidate through evaluations done by his fellow seminarians; and
3. (primarily) require self-revelation by the seminarian to his formators, including through a psychologist.

1) Actions of the spiritual director

The spiritual director is to act in regard to (important) problems of which he learns in spiritual direction.

1a) Refer seminarian to formator or a psychologist

If a seminarian indicates to his spiritual director personal problems that would affect his suitability as a priest, the spiritual director needs to act so that the issues be resolved. He should tell the seminarian to tell the formator about the problem, and/or refer the seminarian to a psychologist. As the *PPF* says, "Care should be taken to ensure that issues of human formation that properly belong to the external forum are not limited to the spiritual direction relationship for their resolution."[45]

According to the Congregation for Catholic Education, the spiritual director sometimes should ask the seminarian to have a psychological consultation:

…the spiritual director can find that, in order to clear up any doubts that are otherwise irresolvable and to proceed with greater certainty in the discernment and in spiritual accompaniment, he needs to suggest to the candidate that he undergo a psychological consultation–without, however, ever demanding it.

Should the spiritual director request that the candidate undergo a psychological consultation, it is desirable that the candidate, as well as informing the spiritual director himself about the results of the consultation, will likewise inform the external-forum formator, especially if the spiritual director himself will have invited him to do this.[46]

---

[45] No. 131.

[46] *Guidelines for the Use of Psychology…*, no. 14.

1b) Dissuade an unsuitable seminarian

If the seminarian is unsuitable, the spiritual director should dissuade him from proceeding towards ordination.

The Congregation for Catholic Education has spoken of the spiritual director's duty to dissuade an unsuitable candidate:

> In the discernment concerning the suitability for ordination, the spiritual director has an important task. Although he is bound to secrecy, he represents the Church in the internal forum....If a candidate practises homosexuality or presents deep-seated homosexual tendencies, his spiritual director as well as his confessor have the duty to dissuade him in conscience from proceeding towards ordination.[47]

The *PPF* speaks of the spiritual director's role of assessing the progress of the candidate against certain criteria, which implies the need for the spiritual director to act if the criteria are not met:

> ...the spiritual direction process must take into account the limited time of the program and preparation for ordination and that, therefore, one ought to have passed certain thresholds of spiritual development and commitment at different points in the seminary program (in contrast to the open-ended nature of non-seminary spiritual direction)...[48]

1c) Terminate spiritual direction

The *PPF* says, "The spiritual director should notify the rector if the director decides to discontinue spiritual direction with any student or if the student discontinues direction with him."[49] This implies that there might be occasions when a spiritual director would decide to stop being a seminarian's spiritual director. Such occasions might be:

---

[47] *Instruction concerning the Criteria for the Discernment of Vocations with regard to Persons with Homosexual Tendencies in view of their Admission to the Seminary and to Holy Orders*, Aug. 31, 2005, no. 3.

[48] No. 132.

[49] No. 135.

1. If the seminarian will not take the spiritual director's recommendation to take an important matter to his formator or to a psychologist, for example, the seminarian's viewing of Internet pornography;

2. If the seminarian is not open or honest with the spiritual director;[50] or

3. If the seminarian is obviously unsuitable for priesthood.[51]

If the spiritual director is also the confessor of the seminarian,[52] then it seems that the only reason for which he could terminate spiritual direction would be the seminarian's not being open with him.[53]

1d) Reveal a confidence, if an exception to the confidentiality of spiritual direction applies

If an exception to the confidentiality of spiritual direction applies, the spiritual director, unless he is also the confessor of the seminarian, may reveal the confidence.[54] The *PPF* states exceptions to the confidentiality of spiritual direction:

---

[50] *PPF* no. 132 states, "…a lack of readiness for spiritual direction itself ought to prompt a student to question his continuance in the seminary at this time and seriously to consider withdrawing from the program until he is ready."

[51] See 1b and 1d in this section.

[52] Since the *Ratio*, no. 107, says that it could be fitting, for integral formation, that the spiritual director also be the confessor; and since the *PPF*, no. 120, says that, ideally, the confessor is also the spiritual director, the seminarian will probably choose to have the spiritual director be his confessor also.

The Code of Canon Law does not make such a recommendation. It emphasizes the seminarian's choice of confessor, and adds that the opinion of the seminarian's spiritual director and confessors can never be sought (see c. 240).

[53] Otherwise, the spiritual director might violate the seal of Confession.

If the spiritual director was not also the confessor, then it seems that he could terminate the spiritual direction for the other reasons suggested above, besides the seminarian's lack of openness, and would not be violating confidentiality (by the termination's being an implicit warning to the rector), because: 1) the *PPF* allows a spiritual director to discontinue spiritual direction; 2) in those other cases besides lack of openness, the seminarian was not truly confiding in him but was being duplicitous; and 3) in those other cases, the moral theology exception to secrecy for matters that "conduce to the spiritual or corporal corruption of the community, or to some grave personal injury" (Summa II-II, Q. 70, A. 1) would apply.

[54] The reasons presented in n.53 would similarly apply to revealing a confidence.

...the spiritual director is held to the strictest confidentiality concerning information received in spiritual direction. He may neither reveal it nor use it. The only possible exception to this standard of confidentiality would be the case of grave, immediate, or mortal danger involving the directee or another person. If what is revealed in spiritual direction coincides with the celebration of the Sacrament of Penance... then the absolute strictures of the seal of confession hold, and no information may be revealed or used.[55]

The Congregation for Catholic Education's report on the visitation of U.S. seminaries[56] criticized seminaries for listing exceptions to the confidentiality of spiritual direction, saying "Other seminaries dilute the confidential nature of the internal forum: the spiritual directors and students are presented with a list of 'exceptions' to the confidentiality of spiritual direction (even if it is always emphasized that the seal of confession is inviolable)." Since the Congregation approved the *PPF*, it seems that the visitation report should have clarified whether it had considered in its criticism the exceptions in the *PPF*.[57]

If a seminarian indicated to his spiritual director that he was sexually attracted to children, by saying, for example, that he was accessing child pornography on the Internet; or that he had sexually abused a child, the *PPF* would not require the spiritual director to maintain the confidentiality, since the seminarian would pose a danger to children. *PPF* says, "Any credible evidence in the candidate of a sexual attraction to children necessitates an immediate dismissal from the seminary."[58]

2) Annual evaluations by peers

The rector is to obtain annual peer evaluations on each seminarian: "The opinion of the candidate's class companions, given in an absolutely secret and personal form, in which a positive or negative opinion concerning the suitability of the candidate is expressed clearly,

---

[55] No. 134.

[56] P. 14.

[57] The Congregation for Clergy approved the PPF in 2015, so the exceptions are still approved by the Apostolic See.

[58] No. 96.

together with reasons for that opinion." [59]

The *PPF* gives a description of the process of obtaining peer evaluations:

Peer evaluations are recommended as helpful in the evaluation process. Such evaluations should be conducted in a responsible and confidential manner. Seminarians completing peer evaluations should be exhorted to do so with honesty and in a spirit of charity. Positive or negative opinions concerning the suitability of a peer for advancement should be expressed clearly. [60]

3) The seminarian's openness, in an atmosphere of trust

The seminarian needs to be open and docile with his formators in order to be formed to be suitable to be a priest.

The *Ratio* indicates that the seminarian should be open and trusting with his formators:

1. "In the process of formation, it is necessary that the seminarian should know himself and let himself be known, relating to the formators with sincerity and transparency. Personal accompaniment, which has *docibilitas* to the Holy Spirit as its goal, is an indispensable means of formation." [61]

2. "In order for this training to be fruitful, it is important that every seminarian be aware of his own life history, and be ready to share it with his formators...." [62]

3. "The seminarian is required to be docile, to review his own life constantly and to be open to fraternal correction, so as to respond ever more fully to the workings of grace." [63]

---

[59] Congregation for Divine Worship and the Discipline of the Sacraments, Scrutinies, Enclosure II ("Documentation for the Scrutiny for each (Liturgical) Stage in the Candidate's Progress toward the Priesthood"), no. 7.

The "Scrutinies" are presented in a Circular Letter, with five "Enclosures," by the Congregation for Divine Worship and the Discipline of the Sacraments, "Scrutinies regarding the Suitability of Candidates for Orders" (Nov. 10, 1997) (Prot. n. 589/97). The Enclosures list the documentation, procedures, and guidelines for the preparation of reports necessary in order to ordain candidates to the priesthood.

[60] No. 277.

[61] No. 45.

[62] No. 94.

[63] No. 58.

4. "Conversations with formators should be regular and frequent. In this way the seminarian will be able gradually to conform himself to Christ, docile to the action of the Spirit...."[64]

It is similarly indicated in documents by the Congregation for Catholic Education:

1. "The success of the formational relationship depends in great part on these three capacities. On the one hand, there is the educator with his role of counseling and guiding, and on the other there is the student called to adopt an attitude of free initiative."[65]

2. "The candidate is asked to be sincerely and trustingly open with his formators. Only by sincerely allowing them to know him can he be helped on that spiritual journey that he himself is seeking by entering the seminary....Important, and often determinant in overcoming possible misunderstandings, will be both the educational atmosphere between students and formators – marked by openness and transparency..."[66]

3. The candidate:

> ...must offer himself trustingly to the discernment of the Church, of the Bishop who calls him to orders, to the rector of the seminary, of his spiritual director and of the other seminary educators to whom the Bishop or major superior has entrusted the task of forming future priests....the spirit of truth, loyalty, and openness that must characterize the personality of him who believes he is called to serve Christ and his Church in the ministerial priesthood.[67]

For religious seminarians, the Code of Canon Law says (c. 630 §5), "Members are to approach superiors with trust, to whom they can freely and on their own initiative open

---

[64] No. 46.

[65] "Directives concerning the Preparation of Seminary Educators" in *Origins*, Jan. 27, 1994, vol. 23, no. 32; #37; also published as "Directives on the Preparation of Formators in Seminaries," in *Enchiridion Vaticanum* 13 (1996) 3224-3253. The third "capacity" seems to be pedagogical sense on the part of the educator (formator).

[66] *Guidelines for the Use of Psychology...*, no. 12.

[67] *Instruction concerning the Criteria for the Discernment of Vocations with regard to Persons with Homosexual Tendencies...*, Aug. 31, 2005, no. 3.

their minds."

The formators should "guarantee an atmosphere of trust, so that the candidate can open up and participate with conviction in the work of discernment and accompaniment, offering 'his own convinced and heartfelt co-operation'."[68] The *Ratio* says in this regard:

> A necessary element in the process of accompaniment is mutual trust. The programme of formation should explore and outline the concrete ways in which this trust can be encouraged and safeguarded. Above all, those conditions should be sought and fostered, which can, in some way, create a peaceful climate of trust and mutual confidence: fraternity, empathy, understanding, the ability to listen and to share, and especially a coherent witness of life.[69]

The *Ratio* also says, "Certain formative instruments should be adopted for community formation and for a better knowledge of the individual seminarians, such as: sincere and open communication, exchange, review of life, fraternal correction, and community programmes."[70]

The *PPF* also expects seminarians to be open with their formators and rector, as it says, "Seminaries should expect of seminarians a spirit of joyful trust, open dialogue, and generous cooperation with those in authority...."[71] An example of this in the *PPF* is the annual self-evaluation done by the seminarian with his formator:

> A seminarian's self-evaluation can be a valuable instrument. Seminarians should prepare such evaluations with an honest and candid examination of themselves in the areas of human, spiritual, intellectual, and pastoral formation. They should recognize their strengths and weaknesses, and positive qualities as well as areas of needed growth. It is the responsibility of the seminarian to show positive qualities that recommend his advancement in formation. This self-evaluation is done best in consultation with a formation advisor/mentor.[72]

A seminarian could talk with his formator about intimate matters, even if he had told them

---

[68] *Guidelines for the Use of Psychology...*, no. 2 (quoting *Pastores dabo vobis*, n. 69b).

[69] No. 47.

[70] No. 90.

[71] No. 101.

[72] No. 276.

to his spiritual director, because:

1. The seminarian is not under an obligation of secrecy about the matters (his spiritual director is under the obligation of secrecy).
2. Seminarians are to be open and transparent with their formators and the rector.[73]
3. Church documents on priestly formation explicitly permit this:

    a) The *Ratio* states, "… in a relationship of sincere dialogue and mutual trust, the seminarian is obliged to reveal to his formators — to the Bishop, the Rector, the Spiritual Director and to other formators — doubts or difficulties he should have in this regard [homosexual tendencies]"[74]

    b) In *Guidelines for the Use of Psychology*, the Congregation for Catholic Education states:

    c) "Should the spiritual director request that the candidate undergo a psychological consultation, it is desirable that the candidate, as well as informing the spiritual director himself about the results of the consultation, will likewise inform the external-forum formator, especially if the spiritual director himself will have invited him to do this."[75] (Both the spiritual director and the formator would have the same confidential information revealed by the seminarian.)

    d) The *PPF* says, "Care should be taken that issues of human formation that properly belong to the external forum are not limited to the spiritual direction relationship for their resolution."[76] This indicates that the seminarian should talk with his formator or the rector about the same matter as he had talked about with his spiritual director.

4. There is an overlapping of roles of the formator and the spiritual director.[77]

---

[73] See above, and section C4d below.

[74] No. 200.

[75] No. 14.

[76] No. 131.

[77] See section C4d2C below.

4) Actions of the formator

The formator is to get to know the seminarian in various ways.

4a) Observe and ask about behavior

The formator's role of observing and asking questions about behavior, on a superficial level, could be described as monitoring. "Formation mentors/ advisors monitor seminarians assigned to them in all four areas of formation and they assist in the evaluation process."[78];

> [Regarding the annual written evaluations of a seminarian done by formators] "There should be accountability in the external forum for seminarians' participation in spiritual exercises of the seminary and their growth as men of faith. Within the parameters of the external forum, habits of prayer and personal piety are also areas of accountability.... — Fidelity to regular spiritual direction[79] and regular celebration of the Sacrament of Penance and a habit of spiritual reading…"[80]

Along with the monitoring role, the formator may ask the seminarian about his behavior or manifest troubles, such as the seminarian's looking troubled, or his being late for a scheduled activity, or a report that he was seen using the Internet late at night.

The formator's role of observing and asking questions about behavior is more than on a superficial level. The formator should systematically observe the behavior and habits of the seminarian, and offer him indepth feedback on them. The feedback is to be about seminarians' "general demeanor, their relational capacities and styles, their maturity, their capacity to assume the role of a public person and leader in a community, and their appropriation of the human virtues that make them 'men of communion.'"[81] The formator is to "single out which of his [the seminarian's] attitudes and inclinations are to be encouraged,

---

[78] *PPF*, no. 328.

[79] Seminaries require the seminarian to see his spiritual director on a regular basis (at least monthly). See *Ratio* no. 107; Congregation for Clergy, "The Priest, Minister of Divine Mercy: An Aid for Confessors and Spiritual Directors" (Libreria Editrice Vaticana, 2011) 68; *PPF*, nos. 110, 127.

[80] *PPF*, no. 280.

[81] *PPF*, no. 80.

which are to be corrected and the most significant traits of his personality."[82] The formator is to "offer encouragement, support, and challenge along the formational path."[83] This might include "personal mentoring or, at times, coaching."[84]

For this indepth role, the formator needs skill in perceiving and evaluating:

> ...the sensitivity and psychological preparation that will allow him, insofar as possible, to perceive the candidate's true motivations, to discern the barriers that stop him integrating human and Christian maturity, and to pick up on any psychopathic disturbances present in the candidate. The formator must accurately and very prudently evaluate the candidate's history. ...must see the candidate's strong and weak points, as well as the level of awareness that the candidate has of his own problems. Lastly, the formator must discern the candidate's capacity for controlling his own behavior in responsibility and freedom.[85]

4b) Use the psychologist's report

The information from a psychological evaluation or report on the seminarian is to be made available to formators,[86] and formators can and should use the psychological report in doing

---

[82] The Congregation for Catholic Education, *Directives concerning the Preparation of Seminary Educators [Formators]*, Origins, Jan. 27, 1994, vol. 23, no. 32, #57.

[83] *PPF*, no. 80

[84] *PPF*, no. 80

[85] *Guidelines for the Use of Psychology...*, no. 4.

The *PPF* (no. 92) states, "Formators should be attentive in discerning whether there is a merely formal and external respect given to the formation demands placed upon those entrusted to their care. Such an attitude would not help their integral growth but rather would make them accustomed, more or less unconsciously, to a purely servile and self-serving obedience."

[86] "In a spirit of reciprocal trust and in co-operation with his own formation, the candidate can be invited freely to give his written consent so that the expert in the psychological sciences... can communicate the results of the consultation to the formators indicated by the candidate himself." Congregation for Catholic Education, *Guidelines...*, no. 13.

The *Ratio* (no. 195) says, "...those authorised to have knowledge of the information provided by the expert are: the Bishop (of the Diocese of the candidate, and the Bishop responsible for the Seminary, if different), the Rector (of the Seminary in which formation occurs, and also of the diocesan Seminary, if different), and the Spiritual Director." One presumes, based on *Ratio* nos. 192 and 193 (quoted above), that the *Ratio* would agree that the rector, with the previous consent of the

formation and in vocational discernment.[87] The formators should use the information "to sketch out a general picture of the candidate's personality, and to infer the appropriate indications for the candidate's further path of formation or for his admission to ordination"[88]; and to learn ways to support the development of human, especially relational, qualities needed in the seminarian.[89]

The *PPF*, in the context of psychological records, says that the rector is to maintain "the traditional distinction between the internal and external forum."[90] There seems, however, to be no official "traditional distinction." The other Church documents on priestly formation

---

candidate, would share the psychologist's report with the formators.

The *PPF* states that the applicant should understand that the testing results will be shared with select seminary personnel in a way that permits a thorough review. *PPF*, no. 52.

[87] "…it is appropriate to obtain a psychological evaluation, both at the time of admission to the Seminary, and subsequently, when it seems useful to the formators." (*Ratio*, no. 193); "The contribution of the psychological sciences has generally been shown to be a considerable help to formators, as they are responsible for vocational discernment. This scientific contribution allows the character and personality of the candidates to be known better and it enables formation to be adapted more fittingly to the needs of the individual: *"It is useful for the Rector and other formators to be able to count on the co-operation of experts in the psychological sciences….* [quoting *Guidelines in the Use of Psychology…, no. 6*]" (*Ratio*, no. 192)

[88] *Guidelines…*, no.13.

[89] See *Guidelines…*, no. 5.

The formator is to use the information to help the candidate achieve the growth necessary to become a 'man of communion.'" *PPF*, no. 57.

[90] *PPF* no. 57. "Concerning the results of psychological testing and other confidential materials, the seminary must observe all legal requirements, inform the applicant in writing of his specific rights to privacy and confidentiality, and utilize appropriate release forms. Throughout the admission process and, if accepted, after entrance into the seminary, the candidate's right to privacy should be respected and the careful management of confidential materials is to be observed. This is especially true in the case of sharing confidential information with a team of formators, while at the same time ensuring that those charged with the candidate's growth and integration have the clear and specific information they need so that they can help the candidate achieve the growth necessary to become a 'man of communion.' The rector must observe a careful vigilance that protects the privacy and reputation of the seminarian in his relationship with the formation faculty. The traditional distinction between internal and external forum is to be maintained. Clear policies must be enunciated concerning who may have access to any of the admissions materials. Clear directives must be in place to determine any further use of psychological testing results or other admissions materials for formation or even counseling purposes."

do not use the term "external forum."[91] The *PPF* does not allude to any other Church document outside of itself in regard to the "traditional distinction."

This *PPF* sentence about maintaining the distinction between forums is also unnecessary, since that same paragraph (no. 57) elaborates on the steps to be taken to protect the candidate's right to privacy. The sentence also seems inconsistent, since:

1. The psychologist is not in the internal forum. The Church documents on priestly formation do not include the psychologist in the internal forum. As the Congregation for Education explicitly stated in its visitation report, "There is confusion, in places, as to what the internal forum is (it covers only sacramental confession and spiritual direction; psychological counseling may be confidential, but it is not internal forum)."[92]

2. The psychologist's report is not in the internal forum. The *PPF* allows the psychologist's report to be released (with the candidate's consent) to formators.

4c) Use the peer evaluations

It seems that seminary rectors, in practice, give to formators a copy of the evaluations of the seminarian by his peers, at least in summary form, for the purposes of formation and vocational discernment.

4d) Frequent and regular conversations with the seminarian

4d1) Help him to train his character and come to self-knowledge

The *Ratio* says that the formator is to have frequent and regular conversations with the seminarian, to help him become aware of his condition, talents, and frailties; to educate him in the truth of his being and to foster a sincere gift of self:

Conversations with formators should be regular and frequent. In this way the seminarian will be able gradually to conform himself to Christ, docile to the action of the Spirit. Such accompaniment must bring together all the aspects of the human person, training him in listening, in dialogue, in the true meaning of obedience and in

---

[91] See section C4d2C, n.139, below, regarding the one exception.

[92] No. 6, p.14.

interior freedom. It is the task of every formator, each according to his proper responsibilities, to assist the seminarian in becoming aware of his condition, of the talents that he has received, and of his frailties, so that he can become ever more receptive to the action of grace.[93]

....This process of [human] formation is intended to educate the person in the truth of his being, in freedom and in self-control. It is meant to overcome all kinds of individualism, and to foster the sincere gift of self, opening him to generous dedication to others.[94]

The *Ratio* says that the seminarian is to share his life with his formators:

In order for this training to be fruitful, it is important that every seminarian be aware of his own life history, and be ready to share it with his formators. This would include especially his experience of childhood and adolescence, the influence that his family and his relatives have exercised upon him, his ability to establish mature and well balanced interpersonal relationships, or his lack thereof, and his ability to handle positively moments of solitude. Such information will be helpful for choosing the most fitting pedagogical means, both for an assessment of the journey thus far and for a better understanding of any moments of regression or of difficulty.[95]

The Congregation for Catholic Education, in its *Directives concerning the Preparation of Seminary Educators*, states that the formator is to have frequent contacts and a real and profound communication with the seminarian, to help the seminarian to know himself in depth, and to measure his progress and orient his goals:

The success of the formational relationship depends in great part on these three capacities. On the one hand, there is the educator with his role of counseling and guiding, and on the other there is the student called to adopt an attitude of free initiative. In this relationship a great deal depends on psychologically well-chosen and well-spaced-out interventions of the educator. It is necessary to avoid behavior which is too passive and fails to promote dialogue, but also to avoid an excessive invasiveness which may block it. The capacity for

---

[93] No. 46.

[94] No. 63.

[95] No. 94.

real and profound communication succeeds in touching the center of the person of the student; it is not satisfied with an external perception, in essence dangerously deceptive, of the values which are communicated; it stirs up vital dynamisms of capacity for relationships that bring into play the most authentic and radical motivations of the person, who feels accepted, stimulated and appreciated. Such contacts should be frequent, to measure progress, to orient goals, adapting the formational assistance to the pace of each one and succeeding in this way in individualizing the level at which the true problems and difficulties of each person are grasped.[96]

...The educator should be sufficiently prepared as not to be deceived or to deceive regarding a presumed consistency and maturity of the student. ...An attentive and refined examination from a good knowledge of the human sciences is necessary in order to go beyond appearances and the superficial level of motivations and behavior, and to help the seminarian to know himself in depth, to accept himself with serenity and to correct himself and to mature, starting from real, not illusory, roots and from the "heart" of his person.[97]

This implies that the formator is to talk to the seminarian about his personal problems.

The Congregation for Catholic Education, in its *Guidelines for the Use of Psychology*, also indicates that the formator is to help the seminarian to train his character and foster the sincere gift of self:

Formators need to be adequately prepared to carry out a discernment that... must allow for the candidate to be accompanied on his path to acquiring those moral and theological virtues, which are necessary for living, in coherence and interior freedom, the total gift of his life, so as to be a "servant of the Church as communion."[98]

The CIVCSVA, in its *Directives on Formation in Religious Institutes* [for religious], states, "They [teachers] should also accompany religious along the paths of the Lord by means of direct and regular dialogue, always respecting the proper role of the confessor and spiritual director in the strict sense of the words."[99]

In regard to evaluations of a seminarian by his formator and others, the *PPF* states:

---

[96] No. 37.

[97] No. 57.

[98] No. 3 (quoting *Pastores dabo vobis*, n.16e).

[99] No. 30.

each seminary should ensure …that the seminarians are apprised of their progress as early as possible in their formation, particularly if there are concerns; that the formation advisor/mentor regularly communicates with the seminarian; …The process of evaluation should be conducted in an atmosphere of mutual trust and confidence. It should promote the continued growth of the seminarian in the four dimensions of formation.[100]

The formator talks with the seminarian periodically (in the United States, at least monthly) about evaluations of the seminarian, including his self-evaluation. The *PPF* says that the seminarian's self-evaluation "is done best in consultation with a formation advisor/ mentor."[101]

Based on the above quotes, the formator should not fear when a seminarian wants to open his heart to him (although not in Confession, so that the formator is not bound by the seal of Confession), and should not discourage a seminarian from doing so; should not tell him that such matter belongs only in spiritual direction.

While it seems that the formator can discuss with the seminarian any matter that the seminarian brings up, or any matter about which the formator learns from other than from the seminarian, it seems that the formator cannot ask the seminarian about matters of sin to learn (discover) his sins. The Congregation for Catholic Education, in its visitation report, criticized formation advisers for asking about matters of sin, saying: "There have also been cases of formation advisors invading the internal forum, asking about matters of sin"[102]; and "The internal forum needs to be better safeguarded…. In places, seminarians are being asked to reveal (in formation advising, in psychological counseling, in public confessions of faults, etc.) matters of sin, which belong instead to the internal forum."[103]

It seems that this prohibition against asking about matters of sin must be narrowly construed to mean that the formator cannot ask the seminarian to divulge his sins or whether he has done particular (named) sins. The reasons for this narrow interpretation are:

1. Part of the role of the formator is to help the seminarian to become aware of his

---

[100] No. 274.

[101] No. 276.

[102] P. 12, no. 5.

[103] P. 14, no. 6

frailties, to know himself in depth. As quoted above, "It is the task of every formator, each according to his proper responsibilities, to assist the seminarian in becoming aware of his condition, of the talents that he has received, and of his frailties, so that he can become ever more receptive to the action of grace."[104] "[The educator should] help the seminarian to know himself in depth, to accept himself with serenity and to correct himself and to mature, starting from real, not illusory, roots and from the 'heart' of his person."[105] He [the formator] must see the candidate's strong and weak points, as well as the level of awareness that the candidate has of his own problems.[106]

2. The *Ratio* recommends fraternal correction and other community formation programs: "Certain formative instruments should be adopted for community formation and for a better knowledge of the individual seminarians, such as: sincere and open communication, exchange, review of life, fraternal correction, and community programmes."[107]

3. Some sins are obvious and could not be considered as private matters. If a seminarian punched another seminarian, it probably would be a matter of sin, but it would not be confidential, since it would be evident to the victim and to anyone else who saw it. The formator could ask the seminarian about it.

4. The spiritual director might refer the seminarian to the formator for a resolution of a matter which is a matter of sin, such as viewing pornography.[108]

5. The rector and formators need to deal quickly with issues that make a seminarian unsuitable to be a priest.[109] For example, the *Ratio* states, "… in a relationship of sincere dialogue and mutual trust, the seminarian is obliged to reveal to his formators — to the Bishop, the Rector, the Spiritual Director and to other formators — doubts or difficulties he should have in this regard [homosexual tendencies]."[110] If a seminarian had some homosexual experiences in the past, the formator could ask him if there were any further episodes to ascertain whether he is suitable for the priesthood. The Congregation for Education, in its visitation report

---

[104] *Ratio*, no. 46.

[105] *Directives concerning the preparation of seminary educators* ("*Directives*"), no. 57

[106] *Guidelines for the Use of Psychology*, no. 4.

[107] No. 90.

[108] See section C1a above.

[109] See section B3 above.

[110] No. 200.

stated, "…here and there some case or other of immorality —again, usually homosexual behavior — continues to show up. However, in the main, the superiors now deal with these issues promptly and appropriately."[111]

It seems that formators and the rector can and should ask the seminarian about matters of sin that have been indicated to them.

4d2) Does not conflict with the role of the spiritual director

This role of the formator (in the previous subsection) does not conflict with the role of the spiritual director because:

1. There are important differences in their roles;
2. The confidential matters themselves are not in the internal forum; and
3. The Church documents on priestly formation indicate there is an overlap in their roles.

4d2A) Differences in the roles

There are importance differences between the role of the formator and the role of the spiritual director:

1. The formator is not to hear seminarians' confessions.[112]
2. The spiritual director may not reveal confidences or give his opinion about the seminarian.[113]
3. The spiritual director directs the seminarian's relationship with God and discernment of God's will, and he helps the seminarian to live in union with Christ. The Church documents on priestly formation indicate this role of the spiritual director:

---

[111] P. 11.

[112] See *PPF*, no. 120.

[113] See sections A2 and C1 above.

The *Ratio*:

"Spiritual formation is directed at nourishing and sustaining communion with God and with our brothers and sisters, in the friendship of Jesus the Good Shepherd, and with an attitude of docility to the Holy Spirit."[114]

"The heart of spiritual formation is personal union with Christ, which is born of, and nourished in, a particular way by prolonged and silent prayer."[115]

"The Spiritual Director…helps the seminarian to welcome the divine calling and to develop a free and generous response."[116]

The Congregation for Catholic Education, in its *Directives*:

"The role of the spiritual director or father is also very demanding. The responsibility for the spiritual journey of the seminarians in the internal forum falls upon him."[117]; and "The spiritual director, with his duty of offering to the community and to individuals, in the confidential relationship of spiritual direction, a sure guidance in the search for the will of God and in vocational discernment…The preparation of the spiritual director for his multiple duties and above all for that of care for the formation of the consciences of the students…the person who receives [spiritual] direction should live it as a means and stimulus for his own journey of faith and obedience to the will of God."[118]

The *PPF*: "Each seminarian is encouraged to have a regular confessor, who ideally is also his spiritual director…"[119]

---

[114] No. 101.

[115] No. 102.

[116] No. 136.

[117] No. 44 (The *Ratio*, no. 136, quotes this last sentence.)

[118] No. 61.

[119] No. 120.

In regard to members of religious institutes:

> Code c. 630,§1: "Superiors are to recognize the due freedom of their members regarding the sacrament of penance and direction of conscience…"; and CIVCSVA's *Directives on Formation in Religious Institutes* indicates the main responsibilities of the spiritual director are: "discernment of God's action; the accompaniment of the religious in the ways of God, the nourishing of life with solid doctrine and the practice of prayer…"[120]

4d2B) Confidential matters themselves not in the internal forum

The formator, in discussing personal matters of the seminarian with him, is not conflicting with the role of the spiritual director. The confidential matters themselves are not in the internal forum. It is the spiritual director who is in the internal forum.

The *PPF*, in two places (nos. 80 and 328, with the same language in both), says that formators "function exclusively in the external forum and are not to engage in matters that are reserved for the internal forum and the spiritual director." This leads to the question, "What is 'reserved for the internal forum and the spiritual director,' and by whom is it reserved?"

In regard to "the internal forum," Church documents on priestly formation since the Second Vatican Council say that the confessor and spiritual director are in the internal forum, and have not included anyone else.

Disclosures to the spiritual director are in the internal forum, i.e. the spiritual director may not reveal them. The *PPF* states, "…the spiritual director is held to the strictest confidentiality concerning information received in spiritual direction."[121]

Who determines what is "reserved for the internal forum"? It seems that it is the seminarian who determines this. The seminarian decides what is in the internal forum by what he chooses to confide to the spiritual director (and by what he confesses in Confession) and does not tell to others.

The seminarian's self-revelation to the spiritual director binds the spiritual director; no one else. It does not prevent the formator from asking about confidential issues. Since the matters confided to the spiritual director are secret, the formator would not know what they

---

[120] No. 63.

[121] No. 134.

are. The formator could ask the seminarian about anything (other than to ask his sins),[122] and it would be for the seminarian to decide whether or not to answer. The seminarian might choose not to answer because he wanted to speak about it only in spiritual direction. The seminarian might choose to answer, even if he had already spoken to the spiritual director about it, since it is the seminarian himself who determines what is "reserved for the spiritual director." (The seminarian is not bound to confidentiality.)

Some might argue that this interpretation of the statement in *PPF* 80 (and 328) (that formators "are not to engage in matters reserved for the spiritual director") renders the statement meaningless. It does not render the statement meaningless. The interpretation results in the same conclusion as one would reach in applying c. 220. The formator may ask about sensitive issues, but the seminarian can choose not to respond. If he chooses not to respond, then he has, in effect, reserved the matter to the spiritual director. In that case, the formator may not insist (persist), since the matter is reserved (by the seminarian). Canon 220 would lead to the same conclusion (the questioner may not insist on an answer).

This interpretation is supported by the fact that all confidential communications of a seminarian are not "reserved for the internal forum and the spiritual director," as indicated by the following:

(1) The spiritual director might advise a seminarian to reveal confidential matters to a psychologist or to a formator or the rector.[123]
(2) The self-evaluation that seminarians are to do with their formator could be considered to be confidential information.[124]
(3) Peer evaluations are to be done by the seminarians with honesty, and are confidential information.[125] In seminary practice, the formators receive a copy of them, at least in summary form.
(4) Confidential matters revealed by the seminarian to a psychologist are not in the internal forum.

If the seminarian or candidate to the seminary agrees to a release of psychological information to formators so that the formators can use it in formation, then the formators

---

[122] See section C4d1 above.

[123] See section C1a above.

[124] See section C3 above.

[125] See section C2 above.

also have the confidential information.[126]

Consequently, it seems that there are no particular areas (types of matters) that are in themselves "reserved for the internal forum and the spiritual director."

4d2C) Overlap in roles

The Church documents on priestly formation indicate there is an overlap in the roles of the formator and the spiritual director.

(1) Per the Congregation for Clergy in the *Ratio*

The Congregation for Clergy, in the *Ratio*, allows an overlapping of roles between the formators and the spiritual directors, as indicated by:

a) The Ratio does not repeat or cite the paragraph found in the Congregation for Catholic Education's *Directives* about the need for the spiritual director to guard his duties. The *Directives* say, "The spiritual director is therefore the first guardian of his own identity and of his own duties, which cannot be renounced or substituted for and which can neither be confused with those of the other educators nor improperly substituted for with other types of formational service."[127]

The *Ratio* cites the *Directives* fourteen times, including quoting from the document about the role of the spiritual director, but the *Ratio* does not cite this paragraph, and it would seem that the Congregation for Clergy would disagree with it, based on points (b)-(e) below:

b) The *Ratio* describes "formators" as including at least the rector (who is a person not in the internal forum) and the spiritual director, the two minimum formators required by the Code for a seminary.[128] The *Ratio*, in ten passages, speaks of "the spiritual director,"[129] and sometimes lists "formators" separately from "spiritual

---

[126] See section C4b above.

[127] No. 61.

[128] No. 133.

[129] Nos. 63, 65, 84, 88, 96, 107, 133, 134, 136, 200.

directors",[130] applying the text to both groups equally. For example, the seminarian must reveal to "his formators—to the Bishop, the Rector, the Spiritual Director and to other formators—" any doubts or difficulties he has in regard to homosexual tendencies.[131]

The *Ratio* indicates that the seminarian is to be open with his formators,[132] and the formator is to have frequent indepth conversations with the seminarian.[133] The *Ratio*, without distinguishing as to type of formator, says that the seminarian should be transparent with his formators and should converse frequently with them.[134] Every seminarian should be ready to share his life history with his formators.[135]

c) Every formator is to help the seminarian to become aware of his talents and frailties; to accompany the seminarian to help his human and spiritual growth.[136] Formation is to educate the person in the truth of his being.[137] The *Ratio* talks about conscience formation under human formation: Talking about human formation, the *Ratio* says, "In the moral sphere, it is connected to the requirement that the individual arrive gradually at a well formed conscience."[138]

d) An overlapping of roles is natural if formation is to be integral and not compartmentalized.

The *Ratio* states that the concept of integral formation is of the greatest importance:

> The concept of integral formation is of the greatest importance, since it is the whole person, with all that he is and all that he possesses, who will be at the Lord's service in the Christian community. The one called is an 'integral subject', namely someone who has been previously chosen to attain a sound interior life, without divisions or

---

[130] Nos. 63, 96, 134, 200.

[131] No. 200.

[132] See section C3 above.

[133] See section C4d above.

[134] Nos. 45, 46.

[135] No. 94.

[136] *Ratio*, nos. 46, 49, 63.

[137] *Ratio*, no. 63.

[138] *Ratio*, no. 94.

contradictions. It is necessary to adopt an integrated pedagogical model in order to reach this objective...[139]

The *Ratio* indicates that one reason for the importance of integral formation is that grace builds upon nature:

A correct and harmonious spirituality demands a well-structured humanity; indeed, as St. Thomas Aquinas reminds us, *"grace builds upon nature"* it does not supplant nature, but perfects it. Therefore, it is necessary to cultivate humility, courage, common sense, magnanimity, right judgement and discretion, tolerance and transparency, love of truth and honesty.[140]

Human formation, being the foundation of all priestly formation, promotes the integral growth of the person and allows the integration of all its dimensions....psychologically it focuses on the constitution of a stable personality, characterised by emotional balance, self-control and a well-integrated sexuality. In the moral sphere, it is connected to the requirement that the individual arrive gradually at a well formed conscience. This means that he will become a responsible person able to make the right decisions, gifted with right judgement and able to have an objective perception of persons and events....aware of his own talents and learning how to place them at the service of the People of God. ...aware of the social environment, and be helped to improve his capacity for social interaction, so that he can contribute to building up the community in which he lives....[141]

The use of the term "external forum," opposing it to the persons in the internal forum, seems to be contrary to communion in the seminary. It does not seem to promote an integral formation. The *Ratio* mentions the term "internal forum" only once, in no. 136 (see A2 above), and it does not mention "external forum" at all. The Congregation for Catholic Education's documents on priestly formation do not use the term "external forum."[142]

---

[139] No. 92.

[140] No. 93.

[141] No. 94.

[142] It seems that, of all the Church document on priestly formation since the Second Vatican Council, only one, besides the *PPF*, uses the term "external forum," the post-synodal apostolic exhortation *Pastores dabo vobis* by St. Pope John Paul II (1992). *Pastores dabo vobis*, no. 66, similar to

(e) The Congregation for Clergy does not want tension between the seminary spiritual directors and the formators regarding their respective roles, since the *Ratio* emphasizes the importance of communion in the seminary:

"The Seminary community is indeed a family, marked by an atmosphere that favours friendship and fraternity...."[143]; the priest is called to be a "man of communion"[144]; "...Community life in the Seminary is the most suitable context for preparing seminarians for true priestly fraternity. It is the environment in which the aforementioned dimensions come together and interact, and where they attain to mutual harmony and integration."[145]; "...he [the Bishop] should maintain frequent personal contact with those in charge of the seminary, placing his trust in them, so as to encourage them in their task and to foster among them a spirit of full harmony, communion and cooperation."[146]

(2) Per the Congregation for Catholic Education

The Congregation for Catholic Education indicates in its visitation report that there is an overlapping of roles between the formator and the spiritual director, as it says, "...the 'formation advisor,' who acts somewhat like a spiritual director but in the external forum. The advisor follows the candidate, including by means of frequent dialogues, helping him integrate the four dimensions (human, spiritual, intellectual, pastoral) of priestly formation ...."[147]

(3) Per the USCCB in the *PPF*

In the *PPF*, both the spiritual director and the formator have the roles:

5.   to assist the seminarian in vocational discernment,
6.   to assist the seminarian to prepare for the reception of ministries and orders, and

---

PPF no. 57 (see section 4b above), says that the priestly community of teachers are to safeguard "the distinctions between internal and external forum," without explaining the distinctions.

[143] No. 52.

[144] No. 52.

[145] No. 90.

[146] No. 128.

[147] P. 12, no. 5.

7.   formation for celibacy. [148]

PPF no. 79, which is in the section on "human formation," states, "Seminary formation in sexuality and celibacy must communicate to priesthood candidates and enable them to appropriate:…The requisite skills for living chastely: ascetical practice, prudent self-mastery, and paths of self-knowledge, such as a regular personal inventory and the examination of conscience…The spiritual path that transforms the experience of loneliness into a holy solitude based on a "strong, lively, and personal love for Jesus Christ…" The *PPF* indicates that the rector and formators have the role of educating the seminarians in understanding sexuality and living chastely,[149] and are to use encouragement, support, and challenge[150]; while "Spiritual formation in celibacy cultivates the evangelical motivations for embracing this commitment and way of life…"[151]

4e3) Application of canon 220

As mentioned above,[152] it would not fit with the role of the formator (described above) to require the formator to ask the seminarian for his consent each time the formator wanted to have a dialogue with him or ask him a personal question.[153] Canon 220 still has application, however. Canon 220 would restrict the formator in that:

1. To protect the seminarian's right to privacy, the formator may not oblige or insist upon the seminarian's answering his questions.[154]

It seems that formators might need training to establish a comfortable rapport with the seminarian so that he is open with the formator. Otherwise, the seminarian might resent questions and be closed. The *Ratio* states:

---

[148] See nos. 77-79, 90-92,103,110,132, 133.

[149] Nos. 77, 79.

[150] No. 80.

[151] No. 110.

[152] (In section A1)

[153] Nonetheless, since the seminarian's expectations might differ from those of the seminary, it seems advisable for the seminary to obtain from each new seminarian a signed agreement in regard to the seminary's policies. See below, the Conclusion.

[154] See section A1.

Each formator should be possessed of human, spiritual, pastoral and professional abilities and resources, so as to provide the right kind of accompaniment that is balanced and respectful of the freedom and the conscience of the other person, and that will help him in his human and spiritual growth. [155]

The more impersonal the questioning, such as if done in writing rather than in person, or if done to a group rather than to an individual, it seems the more likely that the questioning will meet with resistance and the seminarians might refuse to answer.

The Congregation for Catholic Education talks about the need for the formator to avoid excessive invasiveness that would block dialogue with the seminarian:

> It is necessary to avoid behavior which is too passive and fails to promote dialogue, but also to avoid an excessive invasiveness which may block it. The capacity for real and profound communication succeeds in touching the center of the person of the student…it stirs up vital dynamisms of capacity for relationships that bring into play the most authentic and radical motivations of the person, who feels accepted, stimulated and appreciated.[156]

2. To protect the seminarian's reputation, the formator may not divulge the personal information about the seminarian more than necessary (for formation and determining the suitability of the seminarian).

Conclusion

It is suggested that each seminary have a written policy regarding confidentiality at the seminary, and that each new seminarian be asked to sign a statement that he received a copy and agrees to it.[157] It is suggested that the seminary also put this policy in the seminary handbook.

The policy statement should:

---

[155] No. 49.

[156] "Directives concerning the Preparation of Seminary Educators" in *Origins*, Jan. 27, 1994, vol. 23, no. 32; #37. See n. 65 above.

[157] Informing the seminarian of the seminary policy is, in effect, obtaining his free consent to the requirement (of revealing his interior life). His consent would be free, since no one is requiring him to (continue to) be a candidate for the priesthood.

1. Say that the seal of Confession applies to anything said in Confession.

2. Say that everything that is said to the spiritual director outside of Confession may not to be revealed by him to anyone unless there is "grave, immediate, or mortal danger involving the directee or another person."[158]

3. Describe the role of the spiritual director.[159]

4. Say that everything that is said to other seminary staff, other than to the spiritual director (and confessor), can be used for the purpose of the seminarian's formation and for determining his suitability as a candidate for priesthood.

5. Say that the seminarian is to be open, trusting, and transparent with his formator, and to meet with him regularly.

6. Describe the role of the formator in helping the seminarian to train his character and come to self-knowledge.[160]

This suggested procedure would clarify matters for the seminarians and confirm their understanding and acceptance of the roles and extent of confidentiality at the seminary.

Sister Joseph Marie Ruessmann, R.S.M., J.D., J.C.D., M.B.A., was the Generalate Secretary of the Religious Sisters of Mercy of Alma, Michigan. She was a canonical consultant for her own and for other institutes, and taught canon law classes to other religious institutes.

---

[158] *PPF*, no. 134.

[159] See section C4d2.

[160] See section C4d.

About the Editors

Most Rev. Felipe J. Estévez, S.T.D.
Bishop of the Diocese of St. Augustine

The Most Rev. Felipe J. Estévez, S.T.D., was born Feb. 5, 1946, in Havana, Cuba, and arrived in the United States on an Operation Pedro Pan flight as a teenager. He was ordained in 1970 and has done extensive studies in spiritual theology, earning a doctorate from Gregorian University in Rome. He is fluent in English, Spanish, French and Italian. From 2001 to 2003, Bishop Estévez served as spiritual director of St. Vincent de Paul Regional Seminary in Boynton Beach, Fla. where he served as rector from 1980 to 1986. He was the pastor of St. Agatha Parish in Miami for 14 years, while also directing campus ministry at Florida International University. Appointed Auxiliary Bishop on Nov. 21, 2003, and ordained Jan. 7, 2004, he oversaw the archdiocese's Ministry of Pastoral Services including family life, youth, campus, prison and respect life ministries, as well as all church movements and new communities. In 2010, he was appointed Vicar General of the Archdiocese of Miami. On April 27, 2011, Pope Benedict XVI named Auxiliary Bishop Felipe J. Estévez the tenth Bishop of St. Augustine. He was installed on June 2, 2011, at St. Joseph Catholic Church in Jacksonville. Bishop Estévez is the second of three children (Carlos and Marty) of the late Adriano and Estrella Estévez.

Most Rev. Andrew H. Cozzens, S.T.D.
Auxiliary Bishop of the Archdiocese of St. Paul and Minneapolis

The Most Rev. Andrew Cozzens, S.T.D., is the Auxiliary Bishop of the Archdiocese of St. Paul and Minneapolis. He worked in seminary formation for 8 years as a formator in the external forum, professor, and interim rector. He currently serves as the President of the Seminary Formation Council, of which he is also a founding member, and the President of the Institute for Priestly Formation based in Omaha Nebraska. His doctoral dissertation,

Imago Vivens Iesu Christi Sponsi Ecclesiae: The Priest as a Living Image of Jesus Christ the Bridegroom of the Church through the Evangelical Counsels, focused on the relationship between the priesthood and the evangelical counsels based on the priest's call to live in imitation of Christ, the Bridegroom of the Church.

Made in the USA
Monee, IL
04 June 2020